MAKING THE MODERN SOUTH
David Goldfield, Editor

SOUTHERN MODERNIST

Arthur Raper from the New Deal to the Cold War

LOUIS MAZZARI

Louisiana State University Press
Baton Rouge

Published by Louisiana State University Press
Copyright © 2006 by Louisiana State University Press
All rights reserved
Manufactured in the United States of America
First Printing

Designer: Michelle A. Garrod
Typeface: Chaparral Pro, ITC Franklin Gothic
Typesetter: The Composing Room of Michigan, Inc.
Printer and binder: Edwards Brothers, Inc.

Library of Congress Cataloging-in-Publication Data
Mazzari, Louis.
    Southern modernist : Arthur Raper from the New Deal to the Cold War / Louis Mazzari.
      p.   cm. — (Making the modern South)
    Includes bibliographical references and index.
    ISBN-13: 978-0-8071-3189-3 (cloth : alk. paper)
    ISBN-10: 0-8071-3189-X (cloth : alk. paper)
    1. Raper, Arthur Franklin, 1899–   2. Social scientists—United States—Biography.
I. Title. II. Series.
H59.R237M39   2006
300.92—dc22

                                                                                           2006009307

The paper in this book meets the guidelines for permanence and durability of the Committee on Production Guidelines for Book Longevity of the Council on Library Resources. ∞

To my grandfather, Luigi Mazzari, who left Faro del Trebbia in the Po Valley south of Milan for the Lower East Side of Manhattan, where he worked washing dishes, before moving with Elena, his wife, to Massachusetts, where he became sous chef at the elegant Bancroft Hotel in Worcester. In the large, warm kitchen of the home he built for his family in 1920, he taught himself French reading recipe books and English reading H. G. Wells at midnight. He taught himself to drive, weaving down the Boston Turnpike in an old Model T filled with his friends toward another meeting of the Sacco and Vanzetti Defense Committee.

But mostly to my mother, Elizabeth Regina Kelahear Mazzari, who called herself Betty. A child of working-class Irish Catholic and French-Canadian parents born in the depth of the Depression, my mother left the dark, cold triple-deckers of Montreal's Hoshelaga Street and moved to sunny Miami in the rising affluence of the 1950s, where she met my father working the front desk in a beachside resort. Her own character made it easy to recognize in Arthur Raper's an ironic sense of humor and a balance of insight and compassion.

CONTENTS

Acknowledgments	ix
Introduction: "The Adventure of American Life To-day Is in the South"	1
1. Progress in Arcadia	15
2. Modernism, Chain Gangs, and Five-Cent Haircuts	33
3. The Strange Case of the Interracial Commission	51
4. *The Tragedy of Lynching*: "Let's Buy and Read"	77
5. *Preface to Peasantry*: Old South versus New Deal in the Black Belt of Georgia	106
New Deal Intermezzo: Brer Raper in the Briar Patch	141
6. "The Divine Right of the Common Good"	149
7. *An American Dilemma*: "'Human Nature' Is Changeable"	190
8. War and Change: "Is It Coming This Way Now?"	214
9. *Tenants of the Almighty*: "Uncle Sam Is My Shepherd"	238
10. "But What *Is* the American Way?"	263
11. Third World, Cold War: "I Wasn't Going to Play Cloak-and-Dagger"	287
12. Back to the Land	310
Notes	329
Bibliography	381
Index	389

ACKNOWLEDGMENTS

I want to thank my father, Dante Mazzari, for his lifelong support. Sincere thanks to members of the faculty at the University of New Hampshire for their advice and generosity, including Ellen Fitzpatrick, Lisa MacFarlane, Janet Polasky, Robert Mennel, and Jeffrey Bolster. Every step of the way, from the initial idea to the final editing, Bill Harris has been the guiding hand. Scholars in Chapel Hill—Jacqueline Dowd Hall, John Shelton Reed, Walter Beeker, Fitzhugh Brundage, David Perry, and Harry Watson—and elsewhere—Daniel Singal, John Inscoe, Jonathan Bryant, and Cliff Kuhn—were as helpful as they were kind, as were several members of the Raper family, Julius Jack Raper, Rebecca Raper Austin, and Gwynn Litchfield. I also want to thank the University of New Hampshire and the North Caroliniana Society for financial support. Thanks, too, to Laura Clark Brown and the staff of the Southern Historical Collection at Wilson Library, UNC, who cheerfully beat back a ceaseless barrage of request slips through the whole, hot summer of 2002.

SOUTHERN MODERNIST

INTRODUCTION

"The Adventure of American Life To-day Is in the South"

Entering the very depths of the Depression, at the start of the 1930s, Walter Lippmann waxed enthusiastic to an old, southern friend about his homeland. "The adventure of American life to-day," Lippmann wrote Howard Odum, "is in the South." It was a strange claim, especially to Odum, who knew better than most how few southerners considered their lots to be adventurous. Odum was a renowned figure during the 1920s and 1930s, because he led a group of sociologists centered at Chapel Hill who aimed to adapt their agrarian region to the modern world of the automobile, radio, factory floor, and airline terminal, and somehow, at the same time, to sustain its particular, and peculiarly American, character. To carry out such a grand scheme, many dragons needed slaying, and Odum was the Progressive South's St. George.[1]

In the minds of many of these men and women, the region was practically an economic colony of the northern United States, the world's first industrial empire. The debilitation of slavery continued to stain its people's lives in a thousand ways, from conversational etiquette to organized race terror, from limited economic and educational opportunities to degrading legal disfranchisement. So few of its black and poor white citizens could vote that "democracy" was not an accurate description of the South's forms of government. The agricultural system in which the South was rooted, and which bred its culture and mythology, had been strangling its economy for decades.

So when the nation tumbled in 1929 into the worst Depression in its history, at first, the South hardly noticed a change. A plague of boll weevils had already been visited upon the South, while blacks and whites in the greatest mass exodus in history left their farms in Milledgeville and Rosedale for the slums of Atlanta and Memphis, the slaughterhouses of Chicago, and the factories of Detroit. Facing the modern world of dynamos and electricity, of unions and financiers, the South was characteristically proud of being a land that looked backward. One might easily have thought the South to be beside the point in questions about America's future. In spite of all its defeat and lack of promise, Lippmann could see adventure in the South because it was the perfect testing ground for modern social science and Progressive improvement.

Where better but the most backward, least democratic region of America to apply the tools and skills of modernity? Where better than the least democratic region of America to work on behalf of equality of race and class? In fact, what most characterized the Chapel Hill sociologists, as a whole, was their fervor for applying modern social science where it was most needed— namely, to studies of race and the law and education, of social and environmental degradation, of chain gangs, poverty, and disease. As home to the innovative Institute for Research in the Social Sciences and the progressive University of North Carolina Press, Chapel Hill became the center of a high-profile effort to bring a new, scientific view to the racial, cultural, and economic issues of the 1920s and 1930s.

If Odum was the general of Chapel Hill sociology, Arthur Raper formed its *avant garde*. For it was Raper, most of all, who used those tools—not only of social science, but of the new mass media as well—to push the South from its exhausted, perhaps squandered, past toward accommodation with its technological future. He was convinced that wider recognition of the unconstitutionality of the southern legal system was the way to push it toward the fuller democracy it would need to keep it from falling farther behind an increasingly modern world. Raper also recognized the value of using the mass media in creating publicity to counter racial and social injustice. He not only studied the way the agrarian South was industrializing, but opened to public view the people who were free-falling into the modern era, the refugees pushed from their farms and pulled to the cities of the South and North.

The impact of television coverage in the 1960s of the marches on Selma and Birmingham had its roots in Raper's work in the 1930s. If it is an adventure to see the world through a sea change and take a large role in its transformation, then Raper's career well embodied Lippmann's insight.

Arthur Raper was a social scientist and a public intellectual, a white southerner who left his family's tobacco farm and took up the issues of race and class to advocate for change in a part of the world where adherence to the past was intransigent. He became a Progressive and controversial voice throughout the South from the 1920s through the 1940s in the farm communities and the cities of America as an activist intensively concerned with race relations and rural sociology, then through much of the Cold War engaged in agrarian democratization throughout Asia, the Middle East, and Africa. Raper's is the story of a political and social radical grown from archetypal conservative roots during the time of transition in America from agrarianism to modernity.

As though from some tall tale or myth of the American southland, Raper hailed from a North Carolina hamlet named Welcome, his family's farm situated near the crossing of Community and Enterprise county roads. It is a place where, even now, in the twenty-first century, people attend church picnics on warm Sunday evenings, and prim homes on treeless tracts of hillsides share winding roads with rotted tobacco barns smothered in kudzu. Raper's father, called "Mr. Frank" by everyone in the county, was a yeoman farmer of Scottish descent, who sacrificed his family farmland, acre by acre, to build a local church and school, and then to put each of his eight children through college. Raper's mother, Julia Crouse, was a Moravian, a member of a tightly organized communitarian religious sect, which emigrated as a body from central Germany to Pennsylvania and then south to Salem, North Carolina, in the late eighteenth century. Coming of age in the early twentieth century, Raper had learned to respect the duty-bound southern yeoman as well as the values and practicality of a cooperative-minded community.

Raper's later research and his lifelong political beliefs spring directly from this upbringing, and they were deeply influenced, too, by his family's part in the flowering of the Progressive movement. In the second decade of the twentieth century, the Methodists and Moravians of North Carolina were arguing less about religious doctrine than about expenditures for road building and teachers' salaries. Mr. Frank donated five of their most fertile acres to the county for a consolidated school, which taught his children that if their black neighbors could buy their own farms, they would be better neighbors and citizens, better able to help build the county.

Race became Raper's litmus test of modernity, a gauge for how realistic the South's approach to the twentieth century was. The region's race problem was feudal; perpetuation of its caste system was retrograde and antithetical to democracy and scientific advancement.

Right into the Depression, much of the rural South had continued to look and act like the "island communities" of the nineteenth century, in the phrase of historian Robert Wiebe. Isolated towns were cast widely across the southern countryside, substantially self-contained, with relatively limited communication outside their own townspeople and surrounding farmers. Throughout the 1930s, Raper's work focused on how race and class in the South played themselves out in the rural county courthouse and on the steps of small-town custom and public opinion. As a politically minded social scientist, Raper spent the Depression years traveling back into the last remnants of the Old South.[2]

In Raper's conception of southern culture and politics, race and economics were inextricable. It was the South's rigid race and class lines that created its economic feudalism and those elements that sapped democratic process—the one-party system, the white primary, and the poll tax. He was aware of the South's position as an economic colony, but he viewed the region's racial and social barriers as its primary limitation. Raper looked for race *and* class distinctions within the South's complex racial codes, in his studies and lectures, in the new slums of Nashville, and on the new streetcars of Atlanta.

As an outspoken advocate of civil rights, Raper spent all of the Depression working on the ground for social justice, voted the socialist ticket as a young man, and worked, beginning in 1927, for the Commission on Interracial Cooperation (CIC), the only white organization in the South concerned with ameliorating conditions for blacks. In 1933, he turned enthusiastically to the New Deal. Although he taught part-time at Agnes Scott College for a few years, he never held a permanent teaching position. He never held a job in private industry or in state government. The only organizations in the 1930s liberal enough to hire him were the CIC and Franklin Roosevelt's New Deal.

Raper's activism during the Depression helps focus the question of whether the New Deal was an adequate response to America's inequalities. Roosevelt himself rarely spoke to the country's appalling racial inequalities. It is common to hear claims that his commitment to helping black Americans was half-hearted at best, that the New Deal's programs only papered over the South's racial inequalities and did little to effect the systematic changes necessary to establish a more equitable society. Roosevelt was shrewder than to push black equality in the face of the white South that was responsible for keeping him in office. But in a very pragmatic way, he did much to foster sweeping change. He filled those New Deal programs with people like Raper, whose dedication to a realistic portrayal of the inequalities of American society was often so extreme as to run counter to the Democrats' political advantage. Roy Stryker's Farm Security Administration (FSA), for example, was a government agency that sought to document and publicize the problems of the American agricultural economy. Stryker even invited John Steinbeck to work with the FSA to research a novel that would dramatize the failure of American economic and agricultural policy. In *Twelve Million Black Voices*, a book that called for radical change, black Marxist Richard Wright employed photographs provided free of charge by the federal government. Raper provides an example of a dyed-in-the-wool white southerner who worked with the federal government on initiatives that were anathema to the southern political establishment on which Roosevelt relied for support.[3]

It was his belief in the activism of Progressive white southerners that allowed Roosevelt to avoid speaking directly to the inequalities of race and class in America. FDR depended on Odum and the Chapel Hill sociologists to plumb the fallacies beneath the myths of the South, and on other southern liberals, Will Alexander, for example, who headed the CIC and the FSA, and Aubrey Williams, who directed the National Youth Administration, to turn new knowledge into practical service. American socialist leader Norman Thomas remembered a meeting with the president, in which Roosevelt refused to back Thomas's call for strong union legislation. "I know the South," FDR told him, "and there is arising a new generation of leaders in the South and we've got to be patient."[4]

The prospect of government action during the 1930s galvanized the South's disparate activists. Raper's life and work, in particular, demonstrate the ways in which the New Deal provided a forum for social and civil rights activism. Raper became an integral part of Roosevelt's activist government, and he was also a participant in many civic organizations and liberal activities from the 1920s to the 1940s, ranging from the CIC to the Southern Conference on Human Welfare union organizing to Gunnar Myrdal's project, *An American Dilemma*. Because he lived in North Carolina and Georgia throughout the 1930s, Raper's engagement in local communities across the South proved integral to the way he pursued the study of sociology.

Rural sociology was for Raper a way to study the nation's past during an era absorbed in examining what it meant to be American. And because the South was undergoing such tremendous strain in the 1920s and 1930s, while change was happening so rapidly, it was a tremendous place to ask questions of modernity. How was the nation going to respond to a dramatic shift from a rural people to urban modernism? What would be the impact of new technologies on folk cultures and political ideologies? What roles would women play in the newly industrialized nation? Raper talked about these questions in cotton fields and on shop floors, in legislative hearings and in church groups, in newspapers and in magazines, over radio broadcasts, and in his own books. In so doing, Raper himself moved from the absolute periphery of modernity to its very point of incursion into the heart of the vanishing past.

Lawrence Levine points to the 1930s as the height of Americans' "yearning to combine the innocence and clarity of the past with the sophistication and technological complexity of the present." He points to Aaron Copland and George Gershwin, King Vidor and Frank Capra, Grant Wood and Thomas Hart Benton, as artists who "turned to the folk past and the small town in their search for the American Way."[5] In the rural South, though, the past was still alive, all the way through the Depression, although this particular past was neither innocent nor clear. And through social science and the mass media, Raper—with the CIC and, later, with the New Deal programs—added the sophistication and technological complexity of the present. This was industry and scientific modernism injected directly into the mainstream of a Victorian, agrarian society, and Raper's experience of the white South's response says it was at once both deeply entrenched and extraordinarily flexible.

All through the 1930s, while with Will Alexander at the CIC, Raper worked among the most notable figures shaping the direction of American race relations, from W. E. B. Du Bois to Charles S. Johnson, from Eleanor Roosevelt to H. L. Mitchell, from Margaret Mead to John Dollard. *Preface to Peasantry* bumped Faulkner from the cover of the *Herald Tribune*'s book review section. The *New York Times* said about *The Tragedy of Lynching*, "It would be difficult to praise too highly the careful manner in which the facts are marshaled, the impartiality of presentation, the value of the information assembled for those who would understand the causes of lynching. Here is a source book of genuine worth."[6]

Raper wrote books that were at once scientific and affectionate, radical and conciliatory, dispassionate and engaged. Throughout the South, he was able to play the roles of both insider and social scientist. He became a visiting scientist, a neighboring farmer, a criminal investigator, and a radical teacher. Raper looked at the anthropology of the ordinary in his studies of local communities, and he also knew southern folklife from the inside out. The introduction to his classic study, *Preface to Peasantry,* is a good example of his ability to speak from the perspectives of both detached social scientist and community member.

> I have spent considerable time securing data from the tax digests, court records, and other public documents on file in the courthouses and in the relief offices; I have interviewed all the Negro landowners at their homes, many white landowners, and scores upon scores of wage hands and tenants of both races; I have gone to church on Sunday, hung around the store at night, sat through the picture show and attended the carnival over the week end; now and then I have had the privilege of tramping after the hounds, or scrambling through the thickets along the Oconee and Flint rivers with farmers turned huntsmen and fishermen. Besides being a lot of fun, these various contacts have provided a basis for an understanding of attitudes and outlooks.[7]

Raper saw the instability of southern culture largely as the product of protracted frontier conditions.[8] Although the frontier had long been closed, the economics of the plantation system continued to retard civic organizations and institutions right through the Depression. Raper considered that economic reform was also advocacy of social and racial justice. He argued—along with Odum and Wilbur Cash—that the South's frontier ethos, prevalent in the region's most rural and least socialized areas, created its violence and lawlessness. In *Preface to Peasantry, Sharecroppers All,* and *Tenants of the Almighty,* he documented the different ways the plantation system and the white South's obsession with race perpetuated conditions for the farmers and working class of the hardscrabble lives of the frontier.

The values of the Moravian community that Raper grew up within are echoed in the southern regionalism he advocated in the 1930s. Regionalism was the southern liberal's response to the condition of the 1930s, using the modern tools of science and technology, but working to retain the folk culture of the preindustrial world. Regionalism, writes historian Robert Dorman, recognized that the nation was at the cusp of a great change—a "wilderness of transition," as Raper himself phrased it—from a rural, frontier, decentralized, producerist, farm and village society—the older America—into the modern commercialized, consumerist, and mechanized mass society of the metropolis. . . . Poets, folklorists, editors, historians, painters, and novelists were codiscoverers of the *region* with sociologists, conservationists, urban planners, and architects, who saw in the organicism embodied by the region—and its ethical and aesthetic implications as well—a sophisticated new tool for mitigating the effects of Progress.[9]

Regionalists were concerned with creating a sustainable, integrated society rooted in a sense of place. They tended away from the proprietary individualism of "many owners" and toward a full-fledged cooperatism and collectivism. Raper pushed this principle the furthest. He put regionalism into practice in his emphasis on local culture in the South, then later, after World War II, in rural districts across the Third World.[10]

Raper was among those modernists who spoke and wrote from the hinterlands, well-equipped to approach social questions from a scientific and secular mindset, rather than a religious or moralist's perspective. He joined C. Vann Woodward, Wilbur Cash, Eudora Welty, William Faulkner, and Lillian Smith, among others, in rejecting southern exceptionalism and writing about their society with an ironic, twentieth-century sensibility. The goal was to substitute clear-sightedness for the flourish and orotundity of southern rhetoric. Raper stressed the necessity of taking action, of choosing from among even poor options, while acknowledging human limitations and the constraints of historical circumstance.

"Wheels turning within wheels"

All his life, Raper used the phrase "wheels turning within wheels." He often had in mind the time he sat in Frank Porter Graham's class his freshman year at Chapel Hill and heard Graham talk about history as an "evolution of revolutions." He was fascinated by the idea of a rational world that was mechanical and deistic, "reasonable" in the sense of being both subject to the explanation of reason and open to discussion and resolution. To be reasonable was, in fact, Raper's passion. This wheel was on fire all his life, seeking a synchronicity within the innumerable other wheels he turned within and without.

He was a Jeffersonian in two ways: as an independent agrarian and as an heir to the Enlightenment. He did not, however, see the least government as the best. Raper instead viewed the machinery of government in the twentieth century as a way to distribute the fruits of the Enlightenment—its democratic institutions and humanistic values, its science and technology. A New Deal *philosophe,* Raper was optimistic about the possibility of political, social, and economic progress and about intellectual advancement. But he viewed neither in terms of Victorian spiritual or moral perfectibility. Democracy and science were entwined in a modern search for a large and accurate sense of reality.

In 1932, Virginius Dabney, editor of the *Richmond Times* and one of the South's foremost liberal voices, defined the goal of his generation's Progressives. "The individual wins reality for himself only as he takes part in this intense search of the modern age for more genuine and complete liberty."[11] The approach nicely defined Raper as well, who tried to square his homeland with modernity and a more genuine democracy, and in so doing confirm and deepen his own sense of reality.

Modernists in the 1930s were obsessed with discovering and defining America's particular reality, not only through the impulse to share the suffering of the Depression, but also because they were the first people in American history to have the technology to do so. They threw themselves into cultural self-definition like pioneers into new lands and gathered the real in true stories, with the faith of the naive. This impulse found expression in newsreels, on radio, through the Works Progress Administration's (WPA's) *American Guide* series, in *Life* and *Look,* in the Federal Theatre's documentary plays, called "Living Newspapers." It was at work throughout the whole culture, in the immediacy of radio broadcasts, photo magazines, and advertising. "Imagination is at a discount nowadays," complained Donald Davidson, the most conservative of the Fugitive writers and poets, who pined for a sweeter past. "People do not want any sort of myth, legend or poetry. They want something hard and scientific and real."[12]

For Raper, as for other modernists, realism was a counterpart to progress. Writing about the famous gathering of liberals at the Southern Conference on Human Welfare in 1938, he observed of civil rights activists that "it was their racial and class *realism* that attracted local opposition and more than a little outside attention" (emphasis added). His "realism" was bound up in recognition of what he called "the dynamic relations between man and land, between agriculture and industry, between economic status and political efficiency, between race theories and human relations, between actual deficiency and undeveloped resources—physical and human." By contrast, the South of Jim Crow and lynch law was a culture of stasis. To Raper, forestalling change was romantic and unrealistic.[13] Liberals like Raper saw themselves as the pragmatic realists of the modern South. Conservatives, on the other hand, were recalcitrants, who in a time of rapid change tried to stave off the inevitable collapse of obsolete racial customs, social conduct, and economic practices. They clung in a raging river to a branch about to break from the bank. His home, the South, obscured reality with its concocted past.

Through community-based democracy, assisted by social science, American society would advance toward greater fulfillment of the individual. This was what the "idealists" of the outmoded plantation and caste systems were retarding. To Raper, though, realism simultaneously sought both authenticity and progress, and was related to a sense of brotherhood and common humanity.[14]

Raper employed the new tools of modernity—radio, the public relations campaign, high-speed photography, social science, even the true-crime novel—in service to a Progressive sociology, written with an eye toward both strict accuracy and human detail, in support of racial and social egalitarianism. *Sharecroppers All* and *Tenants of the Almighty* combine text with photography to provide a greater immediacy, and *The Tragedy of Lynching*, with its lively sense of place, motivation, and detail, presents a sociological study as a series of detective stories. Through all, he delivers the facts of everyday life without either Old South ideals or a muckracker's zeal—but with an eye toward detail and a sense of narrative. Carolyn Ware articulated a similar approach to social science in defining the new field of cultural history in 1940, when she called for work that added the warm pulse of a story to statistically bound sociology.[15] Raper's own aesthetic type of sociology aimed to avoid both the idealism of moral exhortation and the positivism of social science.

During the 1930s, all the new mass media, most prominently radio, art, the documentary, and the movies, had in common an extraordinary sense of immediacy, of speed, of a sense of being there. Whether in stream-of-consciousness novels, or movie newsreels, or dance bands on the radio playing live from New York or Chicago, reality crept closer during the Depression and buttonholed the reader and listener at every turn. If there is a certain ahistorical aspect to the culture of the 1930s, it is because generating a sense of immediacy trumped the study of change over time. Immediacy felt more truly real, and the real was the highest aim. Raper, for his part, professed to love history, but pulled toward the immediate every time, which meant sociology. His books lack historical depth, while the clarity of their perspective of the present have made them, for today's readers, snapshots of Raper's own Depression South.

A Modernist Jeffersonian

A footnote near the end of *An American Dilemma* is a good place to begin asking questions about Arthur Raper. Along with W. E. B. Du Bois and Charles S. Johnson, he was chief contributor to Gunnar Myrdal's encyclopedic study of the effects of racism in America, concerned with how African Americans were treated by the police and the court systems. The footnote includes a rare, personal claim by Raper. "After several years' experience in rural Black Belt communities, the writer is thoroughly convinced that the local whites would be thrown into a panic if they knew the contents of the letters regularly going in and out of the Negro community." In the Depression South, Raper's access, as a white man, to the personal letters of black sharecroppers was remarkable.

Look, for contrast, at *Let Us Now Praise Famous Men,* where James Agee constantly fretted over the difficulty he and Walker Evans encountered trying to lessen the distance between themselves and the white tenant farmers with whom they briefly lived. How was Raper able to move between white social scientist and black sharecropper with the quality of a man speaking to his own people? How could a white southerner negotiate the racial caste system of the Depression South with enough finesse to gain the private thoughts of rural blacks, opaque to virtually all whites? Raper's crossing of race and class lines is filled with paradox. His books are politically and programmatically radical, but often gracious and conciliatory in tone and sentiment. How could he mix with so many while working on projects considered anathema to so much of the South?[16] And why is he now so nearly forgotten?

The problems and conditions of the South that Raper described and analyzed in such detail were made obsolete by the transformation of the South from an agrarian to an urbanized, industrialized consumer society. As Woodward observed from the early 1950s, the Depression seemed as though it had occurred way back beyond a great divide, from a different world. In many ways, of course, it had. The 1930s in America were the last vestige of the preindustrial world. At the start of the decade, nine out of ten farmhouses had no electricity. By World War II, nine in ten did. At the start of the decade, nine out of ten African Americans were Republicans. By the end of the war, nine out of ten were Democrats. In the 1930s, Alan Lomax recorded folk singers and musicians throughout the South—bricklayers, convicts in work camps, sometimes children on sidewalks and in schoolyards—who had never heard themselves singing. By the 1950s, the country watched itself each night on television, and the landscape of America, from tail fins to witch hunts, appeared in technicolor.

In fact, World War II neatly cleaves Raper's own career between his work on race in the South and his postwar work in the Third World. From the late 1940s through the early 1960s, while the issue of southern race relations roiled the United States, Raper was overseas, advising on community development and advocating democratic control by farmers of their lands in small agricultural communities. Right through the civil rights movement of the 1960s, Raper continued to work in the Third World.

In the 1930s, he had been saying that American cities would inevitably explode from unplanned growth and racial prejudice. By the late 1960s, when the ghettos of Detroit and Los Angeles were in flames, Raper and his wife Martha were retired on their farm of rolling hills outside Vienna, where the land begins to hint at the Virginia Piedmont, twenty miles west of Washington. The reasons Raper ended his involvement with the civil rights movement—a commitment for which he had, in the 1930s, placed his life on the line—are central to what makes that divide between the 1930s and the 1950s so wide.

The Jeffersonian farmer, for whom Raper had worked to promote racial and economic justice, evaporated with World War II and, along with that old life, the import of Raper's work in America. In 1940, Hollywood agents had approached him about a movie based on his recently published *Sharecroppers All* in hopes of drawing on the popularity of *The Grapes of Wrath*. Soon after, impressed with the changes the New Deal was making in Greene County, Georgia, *Life* magazine sent a camera crew to Raper and prepared a prominent layout, scheduled for mid-December 1941. Pearl Harbor pulled Raper's work from the pages of *Life,* and America lost interest in the family farm. By the 1950s, traditional America had quickly lost relevance. From the standpoint of the twenty-first century, Raper helps us see more clearly the distance between the Depression and Cold War worlds in terms of America's liberal politics and shifting race relations.

During the late 1940s and 1950s, Raper continued his work in rural sociology as an adviser to the reconstruction of postwar Japan, and then throughout Asia, the Middle East, and Africa, where he promoted the same mix of government planning and local control he had practiced in the New Deal South. He became a modernist Jeffersonian traveling in the Third World on behalf of Cold War America. Later in his career, Raper offered an unusual portrait, a 1950s Cold War official of the U.S. government overseas, guided by principles of social equality, without regard for fighting communism.

By the late 1960s, at the end of his career, Raper sometimes sounded like an advocate of the kind of top-down social engineering that was becoming discredited, not only by conservatives but also by African Americans and even Great Society liberals. In 1968, he wrote a new introduction for a reissue of *The Tragedy of Lynching,* originally published in 1933. He then noted, "Racial exploitation in many other forms continues to plague us," and he asked, "May not the overall situation improve as one segment after another of the problem is delineated, fully researched, and programmed for corrective action by appropriate leaders?"[17] Raper would spend his retirement working his farm and reflecting on the country's transformation from agrarian life to industrialization. He still saw a growing need for planning and oversight. He would clip articles from the *Washington Post* on Three Mile Island. He questioned the corporatization of agriculture and the influence of television. He and Martha had returned to the United States in time to witness the escalation in Vietnam and, while farming at Slope Oaks, he watched the drama of Watergate unfold day by day.

Raper had great trouble understanding what he came to see as seemingly purposeful irrationality. "I was late to come around on Vietnam," he recalled in a videotaped interview toward the end of his life. Looking pained and squinting into the camera, he asked, "How could all these well-qualified men with all the best data come out so wrong?" Raper was a 1930s liberal who never moved to the right throughout his long and effective career. His story throws into relief America's long shift in politics from the era of New Deal social engineering to the contemporary world of privatization and distrust of governmental initiatives.[18]

In retirement, from the late 1960s through the 1970s, Raper and his wife still grew their own food, recycled, worried about nuclear war, and hoped against a future yoked to the automobile. Even though he grew his white hair long and wore a full white beard in his later years, Raper had little feel for the counterculture of the late 1960s. Nonetheless, he may be the most direct link between the organicism of the southern regionalist movement and the cultural radicalism of the 1960s.

During the Depression, the South had been the most introspective region in the country at a time when cultural self-awareness had become a virtue throughout all of America.[19] An integral part of that examination, Raper spoke to and for liberals, and even moderates, who knew the South needed to change, but for whom the avenues of change were not clear. Even Lillian Smith, who had cleared several avenues of expression herself, relied on Raper's activism and his embodiment of the ideals of liberalism. As an old friend, she once wheedled him to come visit her in Asheville. "We have much to talk over with you, needing always your intelligence and fine fervor to fan the flame of our own energies. Whenever we say the words 'Arthur Raper' we feel a warm glow that there is such a man in the South and in the U.S.A. today."[20]

Arthur Raper connects the way New Deal policy was conceived and run with a close-up of the way people thought and lived day to day in the 1930s. He called the decade "a wilderness of transition," and the New Deal and the Great Depression are illuminated by Raper's life and work. In basement Rotary meetings, at parlor church groups, in college classrooms, and in union halls, he saw that in the teeth of their neighbors' fixation with the past, southerners all across the region were indeed ready for change. Raper shows us that across the white South, bigotry and intransigence were often countered by social concern. He drove across the broad South in his old Ford, invited to speak by everyone, he often said, wryly, except the Klan and the Daughters of the Confederacy. "There were always people who wanted to hear what I had to say in every small town, even though they may not have felt able, for whatever reason, to say it themselves."

Arthur Raper shows us now in sharp-focused, documentary detail the paradox of absurd racial inequality and a wealth of white southerners who acted on the belief that their black neighbors should be treated fairly. In fact, through the latter part of his career, after World War II, when he took his sense of Jeffersonian democracy to the Third World, he also shows us that the anticommunist ideology of Cold War America could prove an even more difficult adversary abroad than the poverty and racism of the Great Depression had been in the South.

1

PROGRESS IN ARCADIA

"The bottom is crowded, but there's always room at the top."

FRANK RAPER

"I was born at the tail-end of the last century," Arthur Raper liked to say—on November 8, 1899. He always liked to think of himself and the new century as clearing the same path into the future. At the tail-end of the last century, the township of Arcadia, Raper's home, was gently rolling farmland and scattered hamlets, two hundred farm families living a long, dusty, wagon ride south of Salem, in the heart of the Carolina Piedmont country. In Arcadia, said Raper, "reverence for tradition was near akin to religious fervor." At the turn of the century, Arcadia had no central village to serve as community center, no railway, electric line, or state highway. Few black farmers lived in Arcadia, and Raper remembered racial tension as having always been low. Yet, in spite of their isolation, the folks of Arcadia kept their own farms. Of its two hundred families, nine out of ten owned the land they farmed.[1]

Half a century later, Americans would look back wistfully through their televisions to a mythical Davidson County as the wellspring of traditional America, whose quiet and enduring values and small, good-natured follies were recalled by its favorite son, Andy Griffith, in a bucolic town called Mayberry. Even now, at the turn of another century, folks in Davidson value what they call "the common touch," a characteristic that Raper, in his time, leaned on heavily as a radical sociologist in the rural South.[2]

The farm family of William Franklin and Julia Crouse Raper, and their eight children, almost matched the myth. Near the crossing of Community and Enterprise roads, the Raper family farm—165 acres of rich, Carolina soil—raised corn and a small dairy herd, vegetables and fruit, chickens and hogs. The cash crop was tobacco, as it was for the region as a whole, but self-sufficiency was the family's strong suit. Like most of their neighbors, the

Rapers weren't rich, but they weren't altogether subject to the market, so cash in itself was less critical, all things considered, than a good growing season or the ability to put enough hands in the fields.[3]

"Mr. Frank," as his friends and neighbors called him, was the prototype yeoman farmer. The family traced its roots back to the fourteenth century along the Scottish border. Two Raper brothers had sailed from England to Charleston in the early eighteenth century. One moved north and raised a family on Abbot's Creek in the northeast corner of Davidson County. Two of his grandsons, Elisha and William Davis, acquired wooded tracts a few miles south of Salem in the 1820s and 1830s. Elisha served the Confederacy as a sergeant-major, was captured by Union soldiers, and, after Appomattox, walked home from captivity in Fort Monroe, Virginia, to take up his farm and family life. William Davis Raper raised a large family on a farm whose fields he had cleared himself, and he served as a Confederate, too. After the war, his children left home to make their ways in business and professions, all except for Frank, who, despite his interest in studying law, stayed to keep the farm going. Frank married Julia Crouse in 1894, started a family, and acquired his own land, across from the family homestead. Then, like his own father, he himself cleared the thick forest for cultivation.

Arthur Raper's childhood was filled with the labor and adventure of his father's pioneering. "I'll never forget the quaking thud of a giant oak as it hits the ground," he reminisced late in life, "the smell of green sawdust or the smoke from a burning brush-heap, and logs piled high that burned for days, the toughness of hickory roots and hard, hard work to plow new ground, the lush way everything grew amidst the stumps and roots, and in and through it all Dad's sweaty clothes when he came home at noon and at day's end."[4]

Raper's mother, on the other hand, was more of an oddity in late nineteenth-century America. Her family was Moravian. In a culture characterized by high-flown piety and free-wheeling, agrarian capitalism, the Moravians were practical communitarians. Even as the rhetoric and drama of the entrepreneur was hailed throughout America, the Moravians were a self-sufficient band of resolute quietists. A pietist sect organized in 1457 as the "unity of brethren," the Moravians were the spiritual heirs of John Hus, one of the earliest proto-Protestant leaders, who in 1415 had been burned at the stake. The Moravians eventually left their native Bohemia to settle near Bethlehem, Pennsylvania, in the early eighteenth century. They then bought a hundred thousand acres in the Carolina Piedmont in 1753, and in this Wachovia Tract established the villages of Bethabara and Bethania, Friedberg and Friedland, Hope and Salem. Moravian pioneering rested on a communal basis. "They brought their baker and candlestick maker and teacher and preacher and what not with them," Raper recalled. "It was a self-contained group. So I have this heritage of the typical American on the one side, who came over from North Europe, and after a while they formed a community, whereas my mother's people started off with a community. That made a tremendous difference in the way things were organized."[5]

Julia Crouse and Frank Raper each grew up in postwar Carolina on large family farms a few miles from each other. They did so at a time when Moravians, such as the Crouses, were coming to terms with the influx of many yeomen families such as the Rapers, most of them Methodist. Theirs was just the sort of marriage that led to the Moravians' decline from their preeminent position in the culture and politics of Davidson County. Still, all of Arthur Raper's work throughout the South and across the Third World carried the influence of Moravian life. For he learned early about an approach to community that would mesh well with the New Deal's future ideals.

As a boy, Raper wrote verse about "the City of the Equal Dead" at the Moravian churchyard. Moravian graveyards, meticulously tended and trimmed, are marked with equal-sized, flat stones, arranged not by prominence or wealth or family but by age and sex, as though the burial plots themselves form a record of their lives. "On the other side of the family picture was my father, Methodist," Raper later recalled, "but his people had been largely Baptist a couple of generations back. The graveyard at Mt. Olivet Methodist Church was built on land that my father's father donated for that purpose just off of our farm." Child poet of the equal dead, Raper crept through the wild brambles in Mt. Olivet's churchyard. "So here in the Methodist graveyard, my father's heritage, there were blackberries growing in the graveyard," he remembered. "My mother's graveyard had been very well kept, records, perfect from the beginning, still are."[6]

From the time they arrived in 1754, the Moravians kept track of the hunters who appeared one by one, drawn by the deer, bear, and wild turkey that filled the forests. These "wilderness dwellers" held various faiths, but against the monolithic Moravian culture, they gravitated to Methodism. All through the nineteenth century, the Moravians and Methodists remained separate in culture, as well as faith. The Moravians' tightly knit economic and cultural connections within their communities led to a highly developed social structure in Salem. At the end of the nineteenth century, a Ladies' Aid Society, and through it, the first Sunday school rooms were built. Later, the first electric lights were installed, and the first town clubs established. The Moravians continually initiated new methods or projects. They laid great stress upon carefully kept historical records, and they celebrated numerous festivals and created choirs and orchestras.

The Methodists, on the other hand, "looked upon such matters as dead formalism, of little use in the development of a deep spiritual life." Raper recalled that the Methodists developed a culture with fewer ties to Salem. They also tended to be more rural-minded and conservative. Methodists, Raper noted, formed a party that "generally scoffed at this 'new fangled stuff' with every innovation, only to incorporate the self-same practices in their own program after a short time."[7]

With population growth in the late nineteenth century, farmland became more scarce, and Moravians in search of acreage found more land available among the widely scattered farms of the Methodists. Transplanted Moravians who lived near Methodist churches began to attend the neighborhood services, rather than ride tired farm horses many miles to their own church. Reluctant to lose their congregations, Moravian leaders established neighborhood churches, and the Methodists responded in kind. Members of both denominations became jealous of their affiliations, and this extension of the two central churches into the countryside led to community disorganization. "Out of this condition grew many family rows—not serious enough to call feuds," said Raper, "but powerful enough to prevent any appreciable development of a broad community consciousness."[8]

From Raper's earliest memory, then, religion revealed itself as a source of social division as well as a locus of community life. He saw how the lives and savings of earnest churchmen, spent in service to the glory of God, could become wholly identified with the particular church in which they had invested themselves. Raper explained, "It is not surprising, therefore, that an attack upon one of these small churches was accepted by its promoters as an effort to destroy Christian civilization."[9] This recognition of the limits of religion would set him apart from earlier generations of reformers, whose work was driven by Christian enterprise.

Raper saw his own approach as secular and overarching, rather than parochial, and he would gravitate toward modern social science, with its emphasis on an objective understanding of community problems. While Raper remained interested in the community-building aspects of religious organization, he always rejected the doctrinal.[10]

Proposed improvements began to divide the town along political, rather than religious lines after 1910. Raper identified the churches, both Methodist and Moravian, as the locus of conservatism. Arcadia claimed dual communities, one made of Progressives and centered at the school house, while the other—the "non-Progressives"—was focused on the churches. As Raper put it, "The Progressives work together irrespective of denominationalism; the members of a church work in harmony irrespective of Progressivism."[11]

Sectarian controversies divided nineteenth-century Arcadia. Raper observed that such conflicts "occupied a great amount of attention, the local church groups often formed hostile camps and built up such barriers between them that it became difficult to unite in support of other community interests." With the rise of important political issues, early in the century, people redivided once again as Progressives and conservatives around issues such as whether they were for or against the consolidated school or the road bond. Such civic debate finally placed the church issues of the past into the background.[12] By 1915 the demand for good roads had become the most heated subject in Arcadia. In that year, the county issued $200,000 in bonds for road building, and thus provided a new topic for discussion "of far more practical interest than religious controversy." Finally, Raper wrote, the churches receded into the background.[13]

This shift to the secular was accelerated by the prosperity that followed American entry into World War I. Land that had been selling for $35 an acre was by 1918 earning a gross annual income of $350 per acre. Soon, ownership of a Model T became recognized as more than a mark of distinction. Transporting produce to Salem had taken a day's travel. Now farmers could make the trip in a morning. Raper noted the most important part in determining a family's status in the community was not church they belonged to, but the effort they had made in building the township's roads and the consolidated school house. The school bond narrowly passed and local farmers—Frank Raper prominent among them—helped to build it themselves. "In a real sense," Raper concluded, "the building belonged to the people for they had not merely fought for the right to build it, but had given freely of their time and strength in its construction." As in the road-building program, those who gave free labor were the Progressives.[14]

Even as a young man, then, Raper saw that cooperative projects in mutual aid overcame denominational jealousies and brought communities together. "Freed from the old religious conflict," he wrote, "the people have been able to build up a common community life around the school and its activities."[15] Arcadia's communitarian foundation deeply influenced Raper. It was a primer for Raper's work in the New Deal and all of his social activism. He remembered that "large crowds gathered for corn-huskings, tobacco barnraisings, and so on. If some highly respected man's house or barn burned, the people came together and replaced it partially or in full. In case of sickness the neighbors sowed the wheat of the sick man." The Enterprise Brass Band, popular through three counties, was employed at school commencements far and near. Members were principally Moravian, but included many Methodists. "The whole band—members and everybody—was proud of their gilt-lined blue serge uniforms." This was the setting of Raper's early life.[16]

"The stones were all created perfect"

Frank and Julia Raper would raise seven sons and a daughter. Arthur, the third son, joked that he was supposed to be the first daughter. For all the children, farm life was filled with shared and constant work. Raper's brother Luther kept a diary that well described the children's life. "Halled [sic] wood," it reads, on page after page. "Wednesday, September 30. Suckered tobacco, soed [sic] oats and clover in potato patch. Weather fair." "Monday, October 26. Halled manure and went to preaching. Weather rainy." "Thursday, November 26. Thanksgiving Day. Helped around the house and halled wood. Weather clear." "Wednesday, December 26. Cut wood and went playing Santa Claus." The years were rounds of killing hogs, hunting weasels, and snapping Kodaks, of spelling-school and Sunday church. "Monday, May 31. Took lame horse to Mr. George Miller's for treatment. Cultivated corn, pulled tobacco plants, and piddled. Weather fair." "Sunday, September 12. Went to Mt. Olivet Church. Uncle Jacob came down from Salem and ran about. He put fifty cents in the Sunday School class collection—people noted it and thought it a bit show-off-y."[17]

Arthur grew up enveloped by rituals shaped through the cycle of the seasons and belief in the values of Christianity. His days and weeks like wheels—themselves set within the wheels of his family—revolved within the rituals of church and work. Religion was the fragrance of warm pies at tent-meeting picnics. The thrill of his first crush shot up his spine when a laughing girl snatched his cap on the walk home from Sunday school. When, as a teenager, he thought about religion, it was from deep within. But the Methodist and Moravian traditions were each so strong in their own beliefs and practices that their differences pulled him outside to look at them both objectively. He became accustomed to puzzling over questions from within and without, simultaneously.

He saw the way his parents struggled to accommodate each other. At first, Frank had joined the Moravian church, in 1900, and their first four children were baptized into the faith. Julia felt it "strained" him, though, so the family later joined the local Methodist church, built on Frank's father's land. Throughout Arthur's childhood, the family went to both churches, and sometimes to a third, newer Moravian church as well. Raper remembered, "often twice or three times on a Sunday, we heard each church proving that it was *the* church, and had the great secret of salvation, exclusively. Now they knew all these people as friends and neighbors and school mates. How could they believe that either one was completely right and the other one wrong? So here was another reason to puzzle one's mind and heart about matters human."[18]

Where could he find common ground between the two? As a youth, in the first year of the Great War, suffused with the two traditions, Arthur was troubled by the questions of how to bridge the gap. One Monday night, he walked home from a revival meeting filled with the spirit of brotherhood. It was the opening evening of a week-long tent meeting, a still-typical event of the rural South. "I felt good as I went down by the tobacco barns and reached home still thinking of that fine sermon and the noble desires expressed by all the folks there. An entire community desiring the same thing," he marveled. "Well, surely a revival must come."

Arthur felt enlightened. "The preacher had prayed that we might see the true light, and turn, and live so God would have us live. It did me good. I never have said 'Amen,' in a service, but I did *feel* 'Amen' all over." The preacher explained that everyone was created for some service to God.

> He likened the Creator of men to a bricklayer laying a wall. The stones all looked good. The bricks appeared to be alike—and each brick was to aid in building the wall by occupying the connect space itself and by supporting the bricks above it. "God created each of us pure and innocent and fine and holy," the preacher exhorted. "The stones were all created perfect. But the stones are you and me. They may be good or faulty, and if a bad stone is in the wall, the wall is made weaker by this bad stone. How

can you wish to be a bad stone in the wall? How can you refuse to praise God? How can you refuse to help your fellow man? We should be bricks in God's temple. We have a place to fill. How will it be filled?"

The entire group stood up. Sinners and all. Everybody wanted to be a real man and woman and fill their place well. The people all went home really praying that they might be a good stone in the wall.[19]

On Tuesday, farmers and their wives worked their chores hard to get back to church by ten o'clock. The preacher began by telling them the story of Belshazzar, who had been weighed and found wanting. "Stand up!" bade the preacher. "All who really want to be weighed before God and found fit." Everybody stood. "I wanted to be weighed and found fit. I wanted everybody else to miss poor Belshazzar's fate. Most of all," thought young Arthur, "his condition, resulting from his situation"—not from any fate or flaw—"was to be evaded."[20]

Wednesday night, though, Arthur found himself bored as he flung himself into the mysteries of the Holy Ghost, the Holy Spirit, questions of worldly atonement, and the rewards to accrue "Up Yonder." The regular minister rose up on the platform and said he felt sure the Holy Ghost would come. Arthur looked around and saw his neighbors in tears. Old men trembled. Others slept, and young girls glanced at each other. "The preacher told of how Peter had raised the beggar to his feet. He then told how Peter had walked upon the sea. He was held up by the Holy Ghost. He couldn't sink. I was in a maze. I couldn't see at all. The sermon was very clear, I thought, and very impracticable." The revival preacher took the stage. "'This old world is a miserable place,'" he intoned to the crowd.

"I long to be free from this worldliness. I long to lie there. Let the wells go dry. Let everything happen to us except that we be snatched away from that which we desire most of all. Let us not think of worldly things. Let us think of spiritual things. Let us live as thou woulds't have us, then let us die and be safe on those streets of gold in the New Jerusalem, in Zion, in that City of Jasper Walk, in that city of pearly gates and mansions prepared for God's Children on earth. Let us live as long as thou woulds't have us live, then sever us from this world of trouble and tribulation and strife and pain and sin, and let us be with the angels on those shining crystal shores of eternity." He quit his prayer. I was glad. I felt miserable. I felt as though I didn't know what it was all about.[21]

The week went on, and the preachers grew less concerned with this world, and more worked up about the next. When the revival ended, Arthur thought the only days of real value were those that had stirred the folks to live together as bricks in a wall, before the spirit of the revival had swept them toward the pearly gates. It worried the young man. He felt sadly out of harmony with God's plan. Or else his neighbors were out of harmony. Or else there was more than one plan.

Arthur had fervently sought revival. "I had wanted to be a sound brick. I had wanted to be 'fit,' to be 'weighed' by God's scales. Maybe I am out of gear," he agonized. He had felt that a holy and decent life could be lived through the help of God. "But when the real revival—as they called it—came, I couldn't use it. It was not what I wanted, nor what I could enjoy when once I had gotten it. The real was unreal to me. The warming up period was real to me." The common ground between these two religious traditions was not found in any metaphysical precepts. Arthur was most moved by the social dimension the Moravians and Methodists shared. He felt more holy and more rooted by the thought of being a brick than an angel. The two sides split in terms of doctrine. What they shared was community concern. And the pragmatism appealed to young Arthur.[22]

In the way Arcadia worked, too, Arthur saw how sectarian rivalry could be a force for disunion. In all of his social activism, Raper would enlist ministerial support whenever he could. His own studies of racial inequality and most of his work with black sharecroppers were carried out on behalf of the Commission on Interracial Cooperation (CIC), organized and conducted by southern religious leaders. Will Alexander, founder and director of the commission, and Raper's boss, was himself a former minister. But Raper was also not surprised often to find white, southern clergymen among the last community voices to be raised toward equality. Raper often stressed the hypocrisy of belief in God without the practice of equality. As a child of two strong ecclesiastical traditions, whose metaphysics cancelled each other out, Raper was left believing that the virtues of religion lay in its ethics and its impact on community. Fellowship in religion appealed more to Raper than metaphysics. In the 1920s, he would be among the first white, southern reformers to approach questions of racial and social equality from a secular rather than a Christian viewpoint. He was not so concerned with Christian charity as he was with the development, progress, and spirit of participatory democracy.

"I went to Enterprise to prayer meeting one night in June 1914," he reminisced, looking back to his teenage years. "Nothing unusual about this, for I always went. The evening was one of these when the moon is visible through a thin skin of clouds. The fields and trees were green and living. The group of country people—God bless them every one—was called together by the keen, clear call from the small church bell in this small church building. I went as others went. I felt as others had felt and as others will feel."[23]

"We had plenty of talk"

The Raper household was aimed toward uplift and community concern, and it shared a good humor that transcended the differences between the Moravian and the yeoman. The Rapers took part in spelling bees, pie suppers, school plays, and church pageants. Bashful, Arthur walked girls home from church. He brought home a big, oak Victrola one Christmas, along with a collection of Red Seal records—Caruso, Fritz Kreisler, Paganini—and played "Silent Night" at the break of day. For a rural farm family, to be woken this way was a "glorious trick," both modern and spiritual.[24] Music was a staple, and Arthur and all his siblings, and later his children, took up an instrument. His son, Harrison, became a concert violinist.

"We had plenty of talk," remembered Raper, and much of it centered on politics, one topic that integrated all the others. "One of the things that was talked about the most as we were growing up was this matter of school bonds and road bonds," Raper recalled. "Two things Dad wanted. He wanted educated kids, and he wanted good roads." But Raper also saw that his father's push to educate his children had made him pull more out of his land than he had put into it. To make the county's roads less muddy, he donated topsoil, which left the farm slashed with gullies. His mother became evermore anxious about threats to the self-sufficiency of the family and developed a myriad of economies in response. Her son recalled that she "thought up ways for us to earn a little money by picking wild strawberries and blackberries and selling them, trapping rabbits for the table and selling the hides for a penny a piece." Typical of Julia Raper, she invested in a pair of mail-order scissors, so the family could cut each other's hair and learn a useful trade at the same time.[25]

Her children thought of Julia as a sympathetic person. She often told a story about a local farmer who attracted a great deal of local criticism because he did not work hard enough. He was slow to plow his fields, slow to cut wood for the winter, slow to do anything that required much effort. It seemed obvious that he was just lazy. When he died an autopsy showed he'd had heart trouble for many years and simply did not have the strength for exertion. He had kept his problem to himself, but his dignity had led to the unjust gossip of unknowing neighbors. Her children remembered—when someone was ill, or had made a mistake, or had done something wrong—Julia's frequently pronouncement, "I pitied him." Arthur learned early to take to heart the adage, "Judge not that ye be not judged."[26]

The differences between the Moravian and yeoman outlooks expressed themselves in many ways, but they often doubled back to become similarities. Raper's mother kept continuous contact with friends and church fellows in Salem, through her religious life and the household goods she prepared for sale. His father, from early adulthood, was involved in a web of local connections that included traveling south to pick up political news in Lexington, the county seat, and business trips north to Salem to sell wagonloads of melons and corn and to buy household goods and fertilizer. Frank sold his tobacco at auction in Winston, which had become Davidson's commercial center by the late nineteenth century. But even the explosion of the tobacco industry, following the introduction of machine-rolled cigarettes in the 1880s, did not push the family to rely exclusively on its cash crop. Both Moravian and yeoman outlooks contributed to the farm's self-sufficiency, as Raper described it. "A big family off to itself on a subsistence farm with parents like ours provided a dynamic learning situation. We did the farm work and shared the returns, most of which went for home consumption. What the family didn't eat, the cows, horses, pigs, dogs, cats, and chickens did—except for the tobacco, our cash crop. We learned early to live by the principle of share and share alike."[27] Such a farm was a small-scale laboratory in economic systems and social dynamics, and it offered a point of reference for Raper's studies throughout his career. His own early experience mirrored the way agrarian communities responded to the challenges of modernization.[28]

To Raper, the preeminent symbol and tool of modernity was the automobile, and all his life, Raper was fascinated by it. He viewed it as the machine that effected the most far-reaching social, economic, and environmental changes of the century. He talked wistfully about a teenager's struggle to crank a Model T, and the jolt that ended his first drive. In the 1920s, he would write a paper on "Lizzie's Contribution to Democracy." In the 1950s, he saw desire for the automobile spread across the globe to the poorest nations of the earth. Later, he tracked the rise of pollution as an environmental and political issue. He viewed the oil crisis of the 1970s as a day of reckoning. But in the first years of the twentieth century, with a country boy's excitement, he built totems to the auto's speed and power. "We wanted so much for an automobile to come by our house," he recalled, "that we went to a road where a car had passed, measured the distance between the tire tracks, tied a stick between two hoes, one for each tire track, and dragged them from there on down by our house, to make the dusty road look like an automobile had gone by."[29]

The kind of environmental and political issues raised by the car were already second nature to Arthur, whose father had steeped him in a tradition of community activism. "William Jennings Bryan! I remember going with him one time up above Winston-Salem—first time I ever rode on a train—up to the fairgrounds" Raper mused about his father. "And William Jennings was up there talking about the competitive armament. William Jennings Bryan says that—he boomed out this voice, you know, it was just tremendous—that it was like farmers living around a lake, and they all just got along together. They just got along very good. They're all neighborly. They all just had an idyllic community." But when one farmer begins to arm himself, warned the great orator, then competition, rather than cooperation, becomes the rule of the lake, and the result for everyone is a smaller share of the fruits of his labor and a dim chance for peace and prosperity. This kind of parable, where a local story revealed a universal message, where the specific illustrated the general, appealed to both generations, the populist Frank Raper, as well as the future New Dealer. Both agreed that those neighborly farmers around the lake couldn't be secure unless the larger community was as well.

All of the children were aware of the tension between the values of their parents. It was a tension between Moravian communitarianism and Methodist individualism. Julia's more traditional, family orientation ran against Frank's Progressive ideas about education. Raper explained, "My mother thought that what all of us boys and my sister ought to do was to go to school through about the seventh, eighth, or ninth grade or through high school, then we would get married and we would settle down and be at home with our families which would hopefully come along. To Dad, it didn't make any difference whether we stayed here. It doesn't make a difference whether the farm's free of debt. What makes a difference is, we get an education."[30] His mother wanted her children to be good farmers. She wanted, as he said, "the fields kept fertile and productive, the pigs fat, horses strong, cows contented, and in time her children to have families of their own and settle down and continue to maintain the local school, church, and cemetery, and a community in which mutual aid was writ large. Father shared these desires, but his top priorities were schools and road improvement, even if the farm was neglected, for he seemed to sense that most or all of us children would need to be prepared to make our way away from the home community."[31]

It was only after he had paid for six of his own children to attend boarding school that Frank Raper donated five acres, fifty pines, and two days of labor to build one of the first rural consolidated schools in North Carolina.[32] When the family first bought a telephone in 1910, they also built their share of the line, raising twenty-foot cedar poles to carry the wire. Two decades later, they did the same for electricity.[33] Raper grew up believing that his father's efforts were on a continuum of democratic action that would come to include an extensive network of state and federal public services. Influenced tremendously by his father's work in securing good schools and roads during the Progressive era, Raper himself would struggle to expand the reach of public services by combining the efforts of local, state, and federal agencies during the New Deal.

Despite her own judgment about the virtues of education, by the time the war had ended, Julia had finally told her husband, "Well, Frank, if you think that's what we ought to do, then we'll do it."[34] Julia managed the farm economy and Frank sold, piece by piece, his family land. Through the 1920s the Rapers sent all eight of their children to college, four to Chapel Hill, and others to North Carolina State, the State University at Greensboro, and Guildford College. Six went on to advanced degrees, three earning doctorates. Two entered the American Academy of Science. By the middle of the 1920s, Raper had seen the topsoil washed away from the land his father had cleared himself. Raw gullies appeared in the family's fields just at the time Mr. Frank's youngest son, John, received his Ph.D. in botany from Harvard.

"When we came home, it was a sight," said Raper. "Here we had grown up with parents—they were interested in things. We took a daily paper. We had a telephone. When radio came along we had a radio, but we didn't have one early, of course. But here we were, running into Milton and running into Darwin and running into higher criticism of the Bible, running into everything." The conversations around the kitchen table devoured contemporary issues long into the night. In 1925, "there were five of us then in college, and there was a discussion about this business of the 'monkey trial.'"

His father, who had sold his inheritance for his children's education, was reluctant to see education subvert religious faith. Hearing Arthur's defense of evolution, Frank brought up the subject of where the next child would go to college. "Now, look. Arthur, you went to the university." His father instructed, 'But Kenneth, now, he will go to a church school. We will not let him go to this atheistic university.'"

Raper argued for the state university:

> I said, "Now, Dad, I think you're wrong about this." I didn't say that ever to him but about twice. "You know Carl Wilson, and you know Frank Pearyman, and some of these boys that went over here to what you call this Christian College, Trinity," which later became Duke. "You know what? Those boys came over to Chapel Hill the other day, and they went to the honor boxes where you put in a nickel and take an apple or put in a nickel and take two lead pencils, and they just said, "Look, these things are free," and took them and put them in their pockets and didn't put any nickels in. Now, I don't think that's as good a Christianity as being at the state university and putting your nickels in." He didn't either.[35]

When push came to shove, the Progressive yeoman farmer put community before doctrine as a test of ethics. Kenneth ended up going to Chapel Hill, after all, and then received a fellowship from Harvard. He later became a prominent microbiologist.

Arthur remembered Kenneth going off to Cambridge in the mid-1930s with nothing in his trunk. "Six years later, he had a belt, and I looked at his belt and said, 'Wait a minute here, you're the same size you were six years ago, aren't you. It's the same holes you've been wearing that belt in all these years.' The point is, he had enough to eat and got his books and this, that, and the other, but he didn't have anything extra for anything. He was the kind of person who didn't need anything much extra because he was there to get an education, and that was what he was working for." The Raper children worked their various ways through college selling felt pennants and pillow cases, managing the student newspaper, cutting hair in the dormitories. As a freshman, Arthur paid tuition with no-interest loans from an older brother. Raper already looked for the balance point of a given social or economic system. As a case in point, he later pronounced genially that these family loans constituted an equitable policy, since "the farm became less productive as the farm labor pool dwindled and the fields eroded as the older boys left home."[36]

"They'd be better citizens"

When the Moravians and Methodists had started to coalesce into scattered villages, the community nearest the Rapers' farm began to be called Enterprise, as though its farmer families had taken the name of a patron saint or invoked the spirit of Jeffersonian agrarianism itself. The combination of rationalism and egalitarianism embodied by the two faiths led Raper's father to speak for equal economic opportunity as the key to racial justice. Frank Raper felt that if local black farmers had a chance to buy their own land, they could be counted on to pitch in with the community work he was so interested in. "These Negro tenants here ought to be owners," Raper remembers his father saying. "They'd be better farmers. They'd be better citizens."[37] Mr. Frank quietly helped some local black farmers to acquire land. "It wasn't land out on the main road, usually," Raper recalled. "It was land in back that could be bought more easily, more cheaply. They didn't have much money. But they became landowners." Then he drove home the lesson he had taken to heart. "So here wasn't any flaming sword or egalitarianism but a practical, sensible 'This we can do.' And it was done."[38]

Frank Raper's views on race, rooted in his egalitarian populism, would be critical to his son's later conception of social dynamics in the Depression South. Raper put it this way: "Now, really, what kind of life-determining ideas surface in a person's head, when in a given new situation, he is regularly and voluntarily treated as an equal? Why is it that we ever wondered why the blacks and poor whites have been so determined to own an automobile, even if it was to the exclusion of dental care, adequate clothing, and sometimes enough food for the family—that 'Man shall not live by bread alone' is a fact that we more readily recognize in ourselves than in others."[39]

Among the local farm folk in Arcadia, blacks comprised only 15 percent of the population, and racial tension was negligible. Nevertheless, Raper remembered the family's black neighbors as an integral part of the social fabric. There was Giles Glenn, for example, a Negro bachelor, who lived in a neat, small house, well-painted and shuttered, with trimmed shrubs and a fence, by the side of the road to Enterprise. Glenn helped the neighborhood women with housecleaning, and he traveled to farms around the county to cut children's hair. Some of the white boys around Arcadia made a sport of going to the county-wide black revivals, "to see and hear the Negroes 'get religion,'" said Raper. "Dad took the position that we were not to go unless we went for a religious purpose. I never did go."⁴⁰ In the Arcadia of that era, Raper had little sense of biological or racial determinism.

Julia Raper was less certain about her black neighbors. "We had a washerwoman who came to our place," Raper explained. "She'd bring her grandchildren sometimes. We played with them very, very well. I remember Mother saying to us one time, sort of halfway scolding us, 'It seems to be you get along better with colored children than you do with your own brothers and sister.' And then the children didn't come very much after that."⁴¹ What he called the "slight impatience" in his mother's voice hadn't been a prohibition, though, but left open a door that he would walk through time and again through the 1920s and 1930s. Martha Jarrell Raper noticed that Julia hadn't said, "'You ought not to play with those colored boys, you ought not to like them.' She left all that out. They weren't 'damn niggers,' but there was a little—." It wasn't quite resistance, but uncertainty about her feelings. Raper would grow up seeing his mother's uncertainty in the faces of folks all through the South. Folks who didn't embrace his sense of racial equality, but who didn't reject it out of hand, either, and were willing to listen to what he had to say, or at least to hold their tongues while he talked.

As an adult, Raper would use that hesitation among whites on race to push his advantage. Southerners, by and large, "didn't want to sink our boat," he said. Many were skeptical of his intentions, but many offered quiet support. "They wanted somebody to press up here and have some association with Negroes, treat them like people. *They* wanted it done. They didn't want to do it." Raper found a deep ambivalence in white southerners and his whole career in the South was predicated on working within the opportunities that ambivalence presented for change. Over the course of the next thirty or so years, Raper would come to depend on a web of sympathizers all across the South who were open to a shift in race relations. "My whole experience doesn't exist if that isn't true." Never was he in a southern city or town, no matter where, in which he could not find somebody who did not support his activism or concern for their black neighbors, where human decency did not somehow crop up.⁴²

Arcadia was a social laboratory for analyzing the many ways culture shaped personality and behavior. The conflict between Moravian and yeoman set the terms for the politics of rural Progressivism that played out around Raper, in Arcadia's farmlands and villages. He began in Arcadia to look at the ways in which people interpreted the world, and he began asking questions there about the significance of cultural patterns. The difference between a trimmed and ordered City of the Equal Dead and an overgrown and deserted Methodist graveyard were not important within themselves, Raper wrote. "But they represent human variances in terms of mental attitudes which not only have a tremendous force in fashioning the present, but also, to a marked degree, fix limits to the future beyond which human conscious direction seems unable to function."[43]

In Arcadia, too, Raper saw that American democracy did not run by consensus, but was worked out through conflict. His father addressed questions right at a time when his hometown's political landscape was shifting away from church matters toward municipal improvements. "The community," he concluded, was "no more united than it was in the old days when Moravians and Methodists struggled for supremacy. The scene of the conflict has merely shifted to other interests, and through the contention of opposing forces, advance in the direction of community improvement is made possible."[44] He saw Arcadia as a place that "after many years of conflict achieved sufficient solidarity to be known throughout the county as a well-knit community. . . . It is only the old resident who knows how superficial is this present appearance of unity and can appreciate the strength of the divided interests and various factions with their traditions and loyalties and power to disturb the present order when new controversial issues arise." Social progress, he learned, was made through the conflict of opposing forces.[45]

In Arcadia, social progress and technological achievement seemed joined. In 1918, while his oldest son was fighting in France, Mr. Frank bought an auto, although he soon found that he just couldn't bring himself to drive it. The family was still using its old wagon around the farm and to haul vegetables to market. Just before dawn on a chilly, fall morning, Arthur was trying to keep warm on the wagon's cold seat, driving a load of fruit to Salem. At eighteen, he was still home, a hand on the farm, done with school, though looking for a way to get to college. A wind from the north kicked up just at the sunrise, he recalled, years later. The wind carried a startling sound through the rustle of dry trees. For miles around, the sounds of bells and cannon being fired rang from Winston and Salem. When he reached town, Arthur joined the wagon, still heavy with harvest, to the long parade that wound the cheering streets, celebrating the end of war.[46]

A year later, he traveled to Chapel Hill with twenty-five dollars in his pocket. Wilsonianism had already become a bridge from the politics of Arcadia toward his New Deal liberalism, a Wilsonianism that could lead to practical solutions. As Raper developed his interests in politics and social science, he began to see in the history of the West, as Frederick Jackson Turner instructed, an ever-rising line of democracy. All his subsequent political viewpoints, from his rejection of capital punishment to his sense of the proper functions of government, relied on a fundamental question of judgment. Did the probable outcome of any given action move the country toward a future of equal opportunity?

Raper's intention that his sociological studies and political activism provide information and assistance to serve the end of democracy in work in the social realm, while not quite so quantifiable, seemed as rational and reasonable to him as an astronomer's charting the orbits of planets. He recognized Wilson's internationalism as democracy's future, because it expanded the long heritage of democratic cooperation. "We see this principle with the beginning of written history," he stressed. "It is the principle of giving up part of your personal liberty for the benefit of the whole." Jefferson had initiated hemispheric agreements. The Hague Conference had initiated an international community of nations. Now Wilson was pushing even further with his concept for a League of Nations.

As an undergraduate, Raper adopted a version of Wilsonianism based on a too literal and naive rationalism. "Since we have world-wide wars," he earnestly deduced, "it is only logical that we should have a world-wide peace." But at Chapel Hill, he developed an eye for the dynamism and interrelationships of different cultures and economic systems. In spite of its failings, the Versailles Conference, he wrote, "did recognize the effect upon all nations that the action of one nation produces. It did recognize that we could no longer exist an isolated confederation of states. It did recognize that the growth of this principle back of this international movement was an ever-increasing and ever-growing principle—this principle that will control the world of tomorrow even more than it had yesterday or does today." Raper had begun to make the principle of social and international unity his life's work.[47]

2

MODERNISM, CHAIN GANGS, AND FIVE-CENT HAIRCUTS

Before the harvest in the first fall after the Great War, Arthur Raper watched the still-green fields of Piedmont farmland unfurl past the window of his train like the succession of his nineteen years. The train's extended uproar broke the quiet concentration of cows who turned from their cud to peruse its passengers. Arthur looked across the aisle at his baggage and checked for his wallet again. He had twenty-five dollars in his pocket, from a summer of farming his own tobacco patch. He watched the rich fields and modest farmhouses pass by, so many like his own home, each a seeming dominion unto itself, but bound in alliance and sympathy with its neighbors. Arthur loved to reminisce about his childhood, his home, and the farm families with whom they shared their lives. In Chapel Hill, he would learn to develop and apply the lessons of Arcadia. He had walked to a one-room schoolhouse his father had built for the community on his own land. His teacher had graduated only from the seventh grade. There were no public high schools in the open country, so Arthur had attended an inexpensive boarding academy. Tobacco prices had risen with the war, so now Arthur could be spared from farm work to go to Chapel Hill.[1]

Over the next ten years—through the course of the 1920s—Raper would find mentors in two of the great figures of southern Progressivism. Howard Odum directed Raper's dissertation and oversaw his work in the Institute for Research in Social Science, then remained an adviser, an editor, and a liaison to the university press, which would publish most of Raper's books. Raper then moved on to work with Will Alexander, the founder and director of the Commission on Interracial Cooperation (CIC). Next to the Communist Party, the CIC would become, during the Depression, the white South's most racially progressive organization. Odum and Alexander became Raper's professional father figures during his twenties, but he in turn contributed to their legacies by practicing on the ground the kind of practical activism and modern social science that they sought for the future of the modern South. Odum taught Raper the methods of modern sociology, and Raper then pushed further than Odum the logic of his values and his regionalism. Along with Alexander and Eleazer, Raper would conduct a campaign to eradicate lynching, a highly visible, liberal initiative that made use of the recently developing mass media. Several years before the New Deal, Alexander's commission had begun to broadcast on radio and publish through the nationwide press services a vision of practical social change for the South. Using the tools of social science, the commission hoped to frame a cooperative response to the new world of modern, industrial America.

A Voice from the Future

When the University of North Carolina (UNC) was established in 1793, the first public university in the country, it was envisioned as entwining itself with the new town of Chapel Hill. Among the earliest civic buildings constructed by the community, the dormitories of Old East and Old West are the oldest public university buildings in America. After Raper arrived in town to attend UNC, he quickly became a prominent citizen of Old West. Once settled in the dormitory, Arthur had to find employment. Dismayed by the low wages for campus work, he scoured the town and found a used barber chair for twenty dollars in Chapel Hill's black section. He hung up a sign—"Haircuts—30 Old West"—and lived on his last five dollars until his friends and dorm mates began to stop in for haircuts. His entrepreneurial initiative paid him several times what he would have earned at a student job.[2]

Barbering also allowed him immediate access to the liberal currents running through Chapel Hill. "They were still talking evolution and talking birth control and talking about the international things," he recalled, "the Ludlow Amendment and this, that, and the other that was coming along about that time." And barbering provided invaluable practical training in sociological data gathering. He learned to interview people while cutting their hair. The barber's chair created a laboratory for studying how his peers thought and what they thought about. Raper observed, "They'd get their hair cut and talk—I knew what the students were thinking when they left. I knew pretty well what they would say yes to and what they would say no to, what they would fight about, what they would give their lives for, because of this continuous flow of them, and I was just sampling in on them live, all the time."[3]

In his junior year, Raper conducted a sort of barbershop case study that revealed his own orientation. A fellow student had told him one day, while sitting for a cut, "You know I don't believe anything, Raper." The dorm mate then launched into a litany of his disbeliefs. "I don't believe I have a soul. I don't believe there is a hell or a heaven. I don't believe in the Trinity. I don't believe in Baptism. I don't believe that Christ arose from the dead." His disbelief resonated with Raper, who was in the process of deciding that the "concept of God is man made; man made God in his own image." But as he trimmed the student's sideburns, he steered the conversation—as he generally did—away from metaphysics and toward the usefulness of religion in teaching ethical behavior. "The many questions in the Bible are good to argue over and fuss about," he concluded, "but the only thing in the Bible that we can live is the life of Christ—that is, approach it in our living."[4] Before long, Raper was able to put his new interviewing skills to use while interviewing members of a prison chain gang. He would eventually use them in Boise and Culver City, Afghanistan and Tehran.

Raper's first course at Chapel Hill was European history with Frank Porter Graham, whose discourse on the "evolution of revolutions," of cultural, geographic, legal, and economic "wheels turning within wheels," conveyed an organic conception of the movements and changes of society through history, developing toward a greater and greater exercise of individual liberty and cooperative endeavor. Howard Odum would later reinforce this fluid and manifold sense of social movements and structures. It was a set of ideas that would inform Raper's entire career. The trope of an individual's life, and of society and culture, as a set of fluid, concentric circles has a longstanding tradition in American intellectual history, appropriate to the optimism with which Raper approached modern social science. It reflected a line of thought that saw nature in the flux of history and claimed that life was change itself. "The bad act is partial," wrote John Dewey, "the good organic." Raper responded at Chapel Hill to the relativism and organicism emphasized by pragmatism. The correct action was that which most fully met the needs of a specific situation at a specific time, and expressed a sense of completeness.[5]

Ten years later, Graham would become president of UNC and lead it through the Depression and World War II as the most liberal academic institution in the South. "Dr. Frank's" personal charm and political savvy kept at bay the state's conservative politicians, some of whom, in historian Daniel Singal's words, "couldn't differentiate a sociologist from a socialist."[6] Raper remembered how Graham—"little, wiry thunderbolt that he [was]"—had ranged around the lecture hall on the first day of class, introducing himself to each of his students, and how Graham seemed to know something about everyone in the room. "He got down to me and I realized, he won't know a thing on earth about me. So he said, 'Arthur Raper. Kin to the Rapers at Lexington, North Carolina? Emery Raper? Any kin to Dr. Charles Lee Raper, who was on the faculty here until a little while ago?' so I just said, this man knows everything."[7] Graham's genealogical recall and his common touch would serve him well as a college president in handling touchy situations stirred up by modern sociologists poking into longstanding southern traditions, especially those concerning race.[8]

Raper's academic work focused on questions of democracy and progress. He explored "The Rise of Individualism," for example, arguing that in modern society individuals earned the most liberty by acting cooperatively. The tools of industrialism—the newspaper, cheap postage, new means of transportation and communications—had, he believed, lately augmented the political rise of individualism that followed the shift from feudalism to capitalism. The individualism of classic liberalism thus became "a degenerate, cut-throat, unprincipled competition—individualism ran riot." Subscribing to the doctrine of individualism in a society where blacks had no chance of equality was a cruel joke. Instead, a more evolved individualism would dictate that "the individual acknowledge his responsibility to the others; he demands that all have a chance."[9] Raper had seen how his father had helped the few black farmers in Arcadia purchase their own land, and Odum's influence at Chapel Hill led him to conduct studies involving African Americans in the South, from black folk life to unequal standards of education. At Chapel Hill, the study of race relations was encouraged for anyone wondering how the South would fare in facing the new questions of modernity.

Raper's academic work by itself did not satisfy him, though. "I'se des a livin'," he wrote in parody of his lack of drive. "To sit by the Victrola and hear Kreisler play Schubert's 'Serenade,' only accentuates my situation. . . . Just what I want I do not know. My whole being craves something. My nerves are ill at ease—At one time I think it's a girl; at another time I think it's conviction. . . . Maybe I just need something to be devoted to, need something to work for and with. Need some responsibility, perchance."[10]

Soon after he had arrived in Chapel Hill, Raper became involved with the South's preeminent institutions of social and racial activism, the YWCA and YMCA. He traveled around North Carolina under their auspices speaking to high school students on behalf of the university. In the cotton-mill towns, though, "we were kindly advised that we'd best leave off the 'let's go to the university' emphasis. The first time we hit this, I flinched; and after that the Deputation Team work seemed somewhat less meaningful."[11] Raper had flung himself into a number of organizations to get a sense of where he fit. He joined a contingent of pacifists from Chapel Hill to go to the Indianapolis Convention in 1925 and returned disillusioned about the inflexibility and doctrinaire attitude of what he called these "militant pacifists. I thought they were rather unattractive people. They couldn't talk; they could holler. They could tell you how it was, but they couldn't sit down and talk with you about it."[12] His own style was much different. Raper could talk with anyone, he claimed, and always felt the knack was important politically. He was voted "Best All Around Man" in his class, "but that was partly because they couldn't vote me for this, that and something else," he suggested, "and they needed to vote me something, so that was a catchall and they did it."[13]

Close to graduation, in 1924, he had decided to enter social work. He undoubtedly fulfilled the behavioral requirements. "I have a certain pride in my life—May I tell you?" he wrote to his mother with Victorian primness. "I'm not boasting: I have almost finished college without gratting a single class; I have not studied a bit on Sunday; I have not cheated on any quiz or examination; I made Phi Beta Kappa, and some other organizations; I have not had any relations with any girl that I would not be able to tell to my mother—I believe I have had very high esteem for girls."[14] All the while, back home during summers, growing his own acre-crop of tobacco to pay his tuition, Raper had become an anachronism in his youth, a Jeffersonian agrarian in the twentieth century, the last eighteenth-century republican. One July day in Arcadia, he was standing in a wagon, pitching out manure, when one of his brothers came "just a-running like he was going to tear himself to pieces and just screaming—I had a letter, I had a letter from Chapel Hill." He opened the letter and received word, while standing in a pile of dung, that he had won the university's Eben Alexander Prize in Greek.

In the early 1920s, the university boldly began to sponsor African American lecturers, as well as pacifists and leftists, including Sherwood Eddy and Kirby Page and Robert Spear. The first black speaker was Dr. R. R. Moton, president of Tuskegee Institute, Booker T. Washington's old college. Raper took notes following them all. "A big crowd looked at a big man and were impressed," he felt. Raper wasn't much swayed by Moton's philosophy of accommodation. "It was in the expected frame of reference," he remembered. But he was impressed by Moton's presence and reception. "But what I was interested in was, here was a black man talking to these Chapel Hillians, and they liked it. I was very much impressed. I had run into white people's response to a big black man, and they liked him. I thought, well, that's okay."[15]

By 1925, Raper himself had begun speaking on the "Negro question" in campus forums on the subject of "Race Co-operation for Town and County Advancement." The *Daily Tar Heel* carried an account of a speech in which Raper expressed hope that the black exodus from the farm to the city would result in the establishment of Negro social organizations, which would help blacks to gain political and economic power.[16] When he graduated, the university yearbook included a piece by Raper claiming, "Constructive cooperation between the whites and blacks in the Southern States will be realized. It is now being realized."[17]

But why did Raper focus so much energy on African Americans? He was asked about it throughout his life, and he always denied a particular conversion experience. "I was associated with [blacks] from the very beginning in this," he told Daniel Singal, "thought it was a good idea. You ask me why. I don't know. I just thought it was. I saw they were pretty much discounted by a lot of people. I thought they were real folks and had real feelings and deserved to be treated that way and I felt better when I treated them that way. And of course there's always this business of being better than—I may have felt I was a little better than the folks that looked down on them. I don't know how all these things equate, work out." When he went home to Arcadia now, Raper found that, during the talk around the kitchen table, "at these 11 o'clock sessions and all the rest, I could see some appreciation and understanding from all these folks that I knew best, in that here was something that had best be done."[18]

Raper had begun to believe that race played a critical role in the future of democracy. Without solving the fundamental discrepancy between America's foundational values and the contemporary caste system, the country would not be able to develop an egalitarian response to industrialization. "The world isn't so big as it used to be," he wrote in 1929. "With modern transportation and communication the world has shrunk—and it is still shrinking. . . . Colored peoples are becoming aware of the significance attached to color, and everywhere they are tending to evolve self-sufficient cultural units of their own. As a result, the spirit of nationalism, formerly found among the white peoples of the world, is sweeping the globe—the world is being made over. A new balance of power is appearing. Yellow men and brown men and red men and black men are tiring of the white domination."[19]

As an undergraduate, Raper claimed tremendous latitude of thought and action for the study of history. He followed the lead of Frederick Jackson Turner in looking at societies in ways that emphasized the interconnectedness of geography, industry, agriculture, and social developments, as well as through politics and economics, to study a region's culture.[20] Raper grew to feel at Chapel Hill as Turner had felt when he had claimed that "history is past literature; it is past politics; it is past religion; it is past economics. . . . all is society's endeavor to understand itself by understanding the past."[21] After graduating from Chapel Hill in 1924, Raper was uncertain about how to apply his convictions. He intended to teach history in high school until an uncle in Salem offered to lend him the tuition to pursue sociology at Vanderbilt.

Why, then, after majoring in history, did Raper move to sociology for his graduate work? Partly because he did not draw too fine a line between them. Graham's history courses, for example, were "just good social science."[22] He had also begun reading the work of Vanderbilt sociologists Gus Dyer and O. E. Brown and historian Walter Fleming, and he wanted to work with them. And Vanderbilt offered him a fellowship. He was drawn to use the sociological study of contemporary society as a practical tool for advancing democracy in modern America. He wanted to focus on places where progress was most needed and where the dislocation of modernity was most acute, among African Americans being driven by the thousands from southern farms to the new industrial workplaces and growing ghettos of the twentieth-century city.

In his later years, Raper felt the year might have been better spent otherwise. He found that, contrary to the course catalog, Dyer, Brown, and Fleming were all "off somewhere." Their classes were being taught by E. T. Krueger and Walter Reckless, who had just arrived from Chicago. He called theirs a "theoretical literary library approach. At Chapel Hill they were more geared to social welfare and more geared into people."[23] Raper became involved with black activists at Fisk University after interviewing blacks in Nashville and Memphis for a sociology project. He was active in YMCA and YWCA work. He taught Sunday school to white farm migrants, because he wanted to see what rural dislocation was doing to the growing urban neighborhoods. But he was never comfortable in Nashville, which he felt was deteriorating as fast as it was growing. Raper saw the way Nashville was urbanizing as a warning about the future of the South. He believed an unplanned exodus of the poor from the weevil-devastated, soil-exhausted farms of the South would make a ruin of the modern city and lead to greater and greater disparities of wealth, power, and opportunity.

His master's thesis at Vanderbilt looked at the various ways the South had coerced its black citizens into dependency over the decades since slavery had left them with no preparation for life in a capitalist system. He cited W. E. B. Du Bois and Chicago's Robert E. Park in tracing the social, legal, and economic dimensions of the "peonage" that followed emancipation and the massive migration that began in the second decade of the twentieth century. He traced the psychological impact as well. "The social attitudes toward the Negro in the South," he observed, "mean that he is not merely given menial work to do, but also that he is treated more like a domestic than a skilled worker." He examined in detail the economic and political policies that had granted to blacks only limited occupational opportunities and enmeshed them in a web of dependency that maintained their inferior position in southern and American society. He wrote, for example, about the way legal and social factors conspired against black political participation. "It is not surprising," he concluded, "that so few Negroes vote, but rather than so many exercise this privilege."[24]

Raper ran into members of the Fugitive group while in Nashville, who sought to refute the industrialization and standardization of modern America by reviving the values of the Old South. In Nashville, Raper's relations with them were, he remembered,

> nothing so pointed as I later had. . . . I just simply thought these boys were talking about something that didn't exist. Yes, it's nice to have poetry, it's nice to have the southern pastoral way of life—but you're going to have industry. You're going to have these big organizations and they aren't going to be rural, and—but I didn't have any run in with them. I wasn't big enough to have any run in with anybody. . . . I didn't think what they were talking about was very important, and insofar as they knew I existed they didn't think I was anything important.[25]

He left Nashville wondering what to do with his master's. "I was going to teach school, because I didn't know what else to do." Back home, an uncle from Winston-Salem approached him and asked what he would do with some money. Raper said he'd go back to Chapel Hill. "I took his money. He wouldn't take any interest. I paid him back. And I began graduate work with Odum, seriously."[26]

As an undergraduate, Raper had been fascinated with Odum's curiosity and drive. George B. Tindall makes the case that, through the first half of the twentieth century, Odum was the South's most perceptive observer. "He saw it whole," Tindall wrote, "the old and the new, the folk and the academic, the agrarian and the industrial."[27] Odum's holistic conception of southern culture attracted Raper, and it probably led to Odum's fall from prominence following World War II in a field that moved farther and farther toward rigorous specialization, quantification, and studies of thin slices of society. John Shelton Reed argues that Raper's dissertation for Odum, which became the blueprint for *Preface to Peasantry,* was a classic application of rural sociology that in later years would have been considered too broad a topic.[28] Odum's star later fell because, while he encouraged Raper and other students and colleagues, including Rupert Vance and Guy Johnson, to undertake groundbreaking and controversial work that pushed southern racial boundaries, Odum's own work was cautious and his writing obfuscatory and refractory, as though he was reluctant to speak his mind openly.[29]

Odum arrived in Chapel Hill in 1920, Raper's sophomore year, as a young star who had completed one doctorate under G. Stanley Hall at Clark University and another with Franklin Henry Giddings at Columbia. He was appointed dean of the School of Liberal Arts at Emory University following the end of the war, but quickly became disappointed when he realized he had not been hired to develop the Harvard or Columbia of the South. When his old friend and classmate Harry Woodburn Chase became president of UNC in 1919, he offered Odum a chance to begin a Department of Sociology. Immediately, Odum became a source of tremendous energy and new approaches. Within just a few years, Odum not only created UNC's Department of Sociology and brought it to nationwide attention, but also established the Institute for Research in Social Science and a School of Public Welfare, founded the journal *Social Forces* to explore questions of race and class in the contemporary South, and worked with and sometimes fought with director W. T. Couch, while Couch was making Chapel Hill's university press the South's preeminent academic and general-interest publisher. Raper saw Odum as an indefatigable questioner and catalyst. He was broadly and intensely animated by curiosity.

In class, his pedagogy was built on rapid-fire questions. "He's the only professor I've ever had, first of all, who can think of that many questions, and all relevant," Raper recalled. "They were right square on the nose." Odum juggled an incredible number of balls. He raised prize Jersey bulls in his spare time, apart from his research and sociological papers and books, his novel writing, and the administration of a research institute and a scholarly journal. But to Raper, Odum's writing suffered from its lack of focus. His prose was often circuitous, if not opaque. Raper observed, "he nearly never would let himself get started on anything. He wouldn't delimit himself. He was always dealing in this very confused total."[30] And his questions were often misunderstood as aimed at reform. "I never thought of Odum particularly as a liberal," Raper said, "as much as I did of an exploratory generalist. He was asking questions. He was turning over the rocks to see what was under them. He was not among the Socialists claiming to be liberals. I was not either, but I was nearer to some of them than he was. But in terms of the things that he published and he helped get published, if I see it correctly, he was on the liberal side."[31]

The sociology Raper learned with Odum was modeled on the natural, rather than the historical sciences. By the 1920s, American social science, writes historian Dorothy Ross, had emerged deeply "embedded in the classical ideology of liberal individualism."[32] Raper had grown up among rural farmers who had materially improved their families' lives by combining community effort with practical science. Jeffersonian agrarianism was second nature to him, and all around Arcadia, the handiwork of science and engineering spoke of prosperity and a chance to expand the benefits of democracy. He took his appreciation for the Progressives' accomplishments in Arcadia—building schools and roads—and grafted it at Chapel Hill onto the liberal ideology of modern social science, an ideology whose practitioners felt liberated from the moralism that had bound Victorian reform. By the late 1920s, Raper, like Odum and others at Chapel Hill, had excised the sanctimony and religiosity from social reform. Raper had a modern skepticism toward the zeal of moral crusade. Working with Odum, he developed a sociology that would be useful in combining individual and cooperative goals. Raper wanted to adapt American capitalism, especially as practiced in the South, to its new, modern conditions.[33]

Many sociologists in the 1920s viewed social control in aggressively quantitative terms and approached the idea with an insistence on behaviorist psychology. Yet, rigorously quantitative sociology left little room for the study of change over time. In a world of ceaseless change, the past lost its value for much of modern sociology and history lost its meaning. In the South, however, the past has never been disposable. In Chapel Hill, recognition of the ceaselessness of modernity meant accommodating perpetual change in a culture that remained wedded to the past. Having little tradition of rational (or acceptable) reform, Chapel Hill sociologists, Raper among them, had good reason to transform historical experience into rational control. Raper became a sociologist, rather than a historian, because to a southern farmboy at that time, sociology promised more opportunity for change than did history.[34]

Chapel Hill shared with Chicago both a commitment to social justice and a cultural approach to sociological questions. A sociology that relied on positivism, focusing on existing situations, rather than on the dynamics of change, better served the interest of the status quo. As Ross has written, "The positivist conception of science, with its technical knowledge and manipulative approach to nature, is not easily reconciled with democracy, no more than are 'great factories.'"[35] By the 1920s, Chicago sociology emphasized social control, as conceived by the school's founder, Edward Ross. Social control was integral to the new agenda of liberal reform. In Ross's words, "Social control of individual self-interest meant public control of the private capitalist economy." It was a more radical application of Progressive reform. "Its sway over the mechanisms of the market was intended to be decidedly less gentle." Through Ross, the concept of social control was taken up by activists across the country as a tool for shaping a liberal agenda of reform, although from a supposedly value-neutral and scientific, rather than moralistic, standpoint. In Chapel Hill, sociological studies were seen as a means of clearing the way for a new approach to social planning and civic endeavor.[36]

William Thomas had published the founding document of Chicago sociology in 1912, titled "Race Psychology: Standpoint and Questionnaire, with Particular Reference to the Immigrant and the Negro." It addressed the interplay of social groups in a changing liberal society, an approach that became the trademark of social science in Chicago. It also assumed racial equality. Thomas's study sent graduate students into the neighborhoods of Chicago to develop case studies and accumulate and interpret evidence ranging from objective data to subjective material, including letters and diaries, club records, handbills, and school curricula. This was cultural sleuthing that that owed much to the highly influential anthropological theory of Franz Boas.[37]

Odum took up the Chicago style of sociology and institutionalized it in his own Institute for Research in Social Science. Raper came to it naturally, with his curiosity about people and his knack for interviewing. He began to practice the techniques Thomas pioneered with his barbering, just as he was learning the theory behind them from Odum and others at the institute. By the 1930s, the mass media documentary approach was beginning to appropriate the case study method and the search for cultural clues in personal as well as official corners. The widespread acceptance of Chicago's sociological methods, and its adaptation for use in the new mass media of radio, film, and photo-magazines, made it relatively easy for Raper to bridge the gap between his academic studies and mass market publications.[38]

Chapel Hill sociology was influenced by Chicago's approach, but it was more centrally shaped by Odum's concept of regionalism. Raper was an undergraduate at the time regionalism was taking hold in modernist and liberal circles. Between the World Wars, southern regionalism became part of the broader movement of American modernism. While differing in background and approach, southern regionalists shared with the New York intellectuals and writers of the Harlem Renaissance a critical response to the new mass culture. Politically, they promoted cultural pluralism and artistically they sought aesthetic innovation. What most separated the regionalists from their cosmopolitan counterparts in their response to modernity was their emphasis on place, on the particularities of geography and the way people made their living, in determining culture. As opposed to the universalism of the New York modernists—many of whom were the sons of immigrants, for whom cultivation of a sense of place seemed anachronistic—the southern regionalists cultivated a sense of place as a bulwark against the destructiveness of mass culture.[39]

Regionalism was a signal that modern, mass culture was taking over. Historian Robert Dorman identifies the defense of the region as a sign of the breakdown of the traditional way of life and pattern of American development. Only when the rural, self-sufficient, farm-and-village society, with its ever-receding frontier, had been doomed by urbanized, mechanized, commercialized, mass culture—through the corrosion of what Walter Lippmann called "the acids of modernity"—would intellectuals, artists, and social scientists apprehend a need to foster and protect the old connections.[40]

The regionalists' programs would not be exercises in nostalgia or efforts to legislate back the past, as agrarian writing seemed to advocate. Instead, it would constitute a response to the modern from an attitude rooted in traditional concerns for cultivation and husbandry. Lewis Mumford called the guiding idea "the continuous cultivation and development of all the resources of the earth and of man." Instead of its manifest destiny philosophy of "mine and move," America should harken back to an even older voice and "stay and cultivate." Regionalism aimed to pursue culture and politics as works of the imagination, as Dorman has it, "shaped by the dictates of local tradition and environment, by an organic sense of place." Regionalism envisioned an imaginative, aesthetic approach to social planning working within the context of a particular and scientifically observable place. Odum talked about combining "the poetic and the scientific. It is as if a new romantic realism were needed," wrote Odum, "to portray the old backgrounds and the new trends and processes." Perhaps more than Odum, Raper came to believe that a liberal realism was the only possible antidote for Lippmann's acids of modernity.[41]

Indeed, despite his sharp criticism of southern politics and economics, Raper had no qualms about rooting himself in his homeland. "I am glad that I am what I am," he confided to his journal while at Chapel Hill in 1920. "I had rather say the 'lingo' terms that I use, than to talk perfectly and not have some of the fine old Southern qualities in me. It's better for me to live among a bunch of fellows who say 'plum' bad phrases and speak to each other every time they meet each other than to live among a crowd of correctly-speaking-high-looking fellows."[42]

This emphasis on place was no simple veneer for southern chauvinism. Never before the 1920s had the South undergone such sweeping internal criticism, much of it emanating from Chapel Hill. The commitment to self-examination—for some, objective and scientific, and for others, deeply personal and subjective—made by southern writers, journalists, and social scientists across the region became an integral part of what became known as the Southern Renaissance. Raper and other southern regionalists, from Howard Odum to Erskine Caldwell, defended their analyses and harsh portrayals of southern race mores and policies, and of the social damage caused by the region's politics and economics. They viewed it as a necessary prelude to the changes the South needed to make in both accommodating and tempering modernism.[43]

Raper used regionalism as a double-edged sword, both to protect the various southern folk cultures and to foster radical change in southern politics and economics. In a sense, both had the same aim. His radical politics resulted from a recognition that drastic change was inevitable, and that charting the direction of change would better ensure the survival of traditional folkways. Unlike other elements of modernism, regionalism was determined to make what Dorman called "a home for the older America of the folk in the fragmenting world of the twentieth century, a home not merely metaphorically but literally and concretely."[44]

Odum's and Raper's regionalism was, in the end, quixotic. Chapel Hill regionalism would prove to be as impractical an approach to mass culture and society as the universalist approaches of modernism and communism being practiced in New York. During the course of the 1930s, Raper abandoned regionalist concepts to work both at the grassroots level and with the federal government, leaving regionalism to Odum, who by the early 1940s, had become increasingly detached from the main thrust of the economic and social changes swirling around him. Regionalism, as Dorman writes, "was itself revealed to be a symptom of the passing of the older America, which, after this brief renaissance, 'shrunk back to its own littleness' in the modern world."[45]

In the mid-1920s, Raper had cut his teeth in regional analysis on a study of North Carolina chain gangs. It was a project that, instead of appealing for prison reform on the basis of racial justice—the gangs were exclusively black—concluded that the chain gang was an economically inefficient system, one that was seldom the best option for construction projects. Other researchers gathered data on the economic, political, and legal aspects of the practice of leasing the state's prisoners to contractors building roads. But Raper developed the "human" aspect of the project, through insightful portraits of several members of the chain gang, composed after long interviews with each of the men. His case study of convict Bob Johnson, for example, included such novelistic subtitles as "Bob in the City" and "Bob as a Convict—A Murderer." Raper's prose was visual and interpretive. "Bob Johnson is dark brown, has a narrow, high face and a broad forehead," he wrote. "He is tall and slim and stands erect, and when he walks he has the carriage of a college student."[46] The project itself reflected the way questions of efficiency and an aesthetic attitude embodied Chapel Hill's approach to issues of reform.[47] It also led to incorporating the subjective and personal, individual data in large-scale sociological projects, leading the way to documentary's emphasis on the "human element" in accounts of culture and society. For Raper, the approach came as second nature. Through the chain gang interviews, he found that being a sociologist pushed him to the center of the social forces that were redefining the South. The interviews, he felt, left him "better informed about the criminal justice system than most people ever get to be, unless they are having to learn it the hard way."[48]

Raper's immersion in Chapel Hill sociology also dovetailed with the rise of cultural anthropology. By the time Helen and Robert Lynd published in 1929 their study of "modern American culture," in Muncie, Indiana, called *Middletown*, Odum's institute had commissioned several similar studies. Like *Middletown*, these Chapel Hill case studies explored the interwoven strands of contemporary life in small towns and rural communities. Two years earlier, Raper himself had contributed to *The American Community in Action*, a compilation of similar studies conducted for Jesse Steiner, a Tulane sociologist visiting in Chapel Hill.

Steiner differentiated this new brand of sociological study from the Progressive approach. The previous generation of social scientists, he claimed, had acted as social doctors, diagnosing a community's poverty and setting public standards of health and behavior; these new studies placed "special emphasis upon the interplay of social forces rather than upon social conditions and problems." In doing so, Steiner invoked the sense of organicism that would inform Odum's regionalist approach. "From the point of view of the community organizer," he wrote, "it is essential that there should be an understanding of the nature of the community as well as of the ills to be corrected."[49] This focus on dynamics was a means toward practical solutions. The Chapel Hill modernists admonished the old Progressives: just because you can describe a tree in detail doesn't mean you can prune it well. But if you can figure out how the tree grows, you might be able to make it bear more fruit. Raper, among the moderns at Chapel Hill, was impatient with positivist certainty. He held a modern belief in the rational—it was useful as a best bet, not an absolute. "Apparently," Steiner drolly wrote, "social change goes forward to a very considerable degree more as an indirect response to conscious human guidance." The sociology that resulted aimed to help the South jettison outmoded ways and accommodate itself to the modern condition of change. Modernity would be a moving target and, as Steiner wrote, "community problems may be regarded as a result of failure to make adequate adjustments."[50]

Raper's contribution to Steiner's collection was a study of his hometown of Arcadia. Raper focused on the changing dynamics of town factions, which began with community battles over religious doctrine late in the nineteenth century and, during the second decade of the twentieth, had been fought over related political issues, including raising taxes for education and road improvements. He looked at social forces, rather than at social problems. While he aimed at community improvement, by his mid-twenties, Raper was no Progressive reformer. He started with the assumption of constant change and had come to see conflict as a normal element in a community's dynamic, as the means to reform outmoded practices. His work at Chapel Hill taught him that democracy did not run by consensus, rather, that conflict produced the dialectic that effected change. He analyzed the way a particular religious community conflict was transformed into a political fight. "The scene of the conflict has merely shifted to other interests," he concluded, "and through the contention of opposing forces, advance in the direction of community improvement is made possible." The question he had already begun to ask when Will Alexander brought him to Atlanta in 1926 was how best to use that conflict to steer modernity's changes toward greater democracy.

Working closely with Odum and Steiner, Raper came to believe that perhaps the most important change that modernity had called for was a cooperative approach to social and economic life. He had seen that plantation agriculture was in steep decline and the old, folk culture was passing from the land. Of all the adjustments that social science could offer southerners trying to come to grips with modernity, Raper came to believe the most important was a shift toward the collective and the cooperative. Like Wilbur Cash, he saw a South in the 1920s still too enamored of its frontier ethos. If democracy meant conflict, it also meant collective as well as individual effort. When the frontier closed, the era of rugged individualism passed with it. Raper had seen how civic progress and cooperative effort had worked in rural Carolina. At Chapel Hill, he came to believe that Progressivism had proven the danger and the limitations of unrestrained market capitalism. Raper favored government control over private enterprise because of its accountability to the citizenry. Modernity at its best was a condition of increasing democracy, and cooperative effort was a more forward-looking and modern approach than the market system. Unrestrained capitalism, because it relied exclusively on competition, resulted in a greater and greater inequality of power and resources. In the 1920s, in Chapel Hill, Raper began to believe that in an increasingly mechanized society, capitalism would create an increasingly voiceless citizenry.

In the fall of 1930, a decade after he had first traveled to Chapel Hill, and five years after beginning to apply what he learned there with the Interracial Commission, Raper returned to UNC to take his final oral examination for the doctorate in sociology. He was asked to discuss the work of Emile Durkheim. He described his research for his thesis on the way slavery as a cultural institution varied across the South. He talked about sociological methodology. And he was questioned about his views on race. Even in extraordinarily liberal Chapel Hill, Raper was challenged to defend his view that the races were equal. He was pressured by one of his committee members— the scion of a large plantation family in eastern Carolina, and in Raper's words, a "Negro-phobe"—about his conviction that the differences between whites and blacks could be accounted for by environmental and cultural factors. "He pressed me hard," Raper recalled. "'Surely you don't believe the Blacks as intelligent or as moral as the Whites?'

"I held my ground as best I could by pointing to the difference in expenditures by race for public education and restating the higher incidence of illiteracy among the Black farmers who were landowners, the white primary, no tradition of responsible community participation, and so on, and back of that, slavery."[51]

Raper's answers increasingly irritated his interlocutor. "Didn't I think there were innate and unalterable difference in their mental capacity, in their moral and spiritual capacity, in their very blood, that coursed through their veins? No, I didn't—that I thought, all told, any differences could be accounted for by readily observable environmental and cultural factors, taking into consideration the debilitating effects of the poor nutrition of most plantation workers and the poorer people generally, their thin level of public health services, and so on—in overall, the effects upon the other group of a caste-like society."

The room tightened as the questioning continued. Those committee members who supported Raper's position were reluctant to initiate a confrontation, but T. J. Woofter Jr., showing consummate southern charm, finally lifted the tension. "'Well, Arthur,' he called out, entering the exchange, 'if I understand you, you don't see any real differences between the races?'

"'No, not any that aren't readily accounted for.'

"'I wonder, Arthur,' Woofter continued in a slow, low voice, 'have you ever noticed any differences in their color?'

"There was a spontaneous, big, raucous belly laugh all around," and conviviality apparently settled the issue. Raper was awarded his doctoral degree deep in the Depression at the 1931 commencement ceremonies in Memorial Hall. For many years to follow, Woofter's humor would remain characteristic of a southern liberalism that believed in racial equality but avoided directly confronting the issue whenever possible, counting on quiet gains to avoid reprisals of violence to themselves and their African American fellow citizens. To Raper, though, making speeches about American liberty, while maintaining racial and economic caste systems, was simply not a realistic approach to social change. Through the course of the 1920s, at Chapel Hill and with the Interracial Commission, Raper came to believe that the only reasonable way to take advantage of industrialization and the new mass culture was through the expansion of democracy to poor black and white farmers and industrial workers through greater economic and social opportunity. Raper rode into Chapel Hill a Wilsonian Progressive and left it a New Deal activist. He personified the differences between the largely Republican, Progressive reform of the early twentieth century and the social realism of the Democratic New Deal.[52]

3

THE STRANGE CASE OF THE INTERRACIAL COMMISSION

In the summer of 1928, three thousand mostly white teenagers from all across North America gathered at Kansas City, to convene the International Baptist Young People's Union. "No issue was too small or too great for these young people to discuss," the local newspaper reported. "The relation of the church to industry, the race question, and other social issues received their attention. By far the largest meeting was that conducted by Arthur Raper, on the subject, The Church and Racial Relations.

"Mr. Raper, who is field secretary of the interracial commission, Atlanta, Ga., outlined some of the problems existing between the Negro and white races of this country."

Raper spoke of his conviction that democracy would increase with modernization, and that in the long run, racial tensions would diminish. Then he took questions from the crowd, a mixed bag of queries—fearful, magnanimous, angry, charitable, confused. "Where do we want to get?" asked an exasperated delegate. "Do we want to submerge *all* racial prejudices even to the approval of race intermarriage?" One young woman rose and looked Raper in the eye. "Do you personally feel that you, as a member of the white race, are superior to members of other races?"

"Mr. Raper parried," reported the paper. "He put the question to the audience. Three or four hands were raised to admit feelings of superiority. 'Now let's be perfectly honest,' said Mr. Raper. 'Let's see all the hands of you superior people.' Then about two dozen hands were raised."

The speaker then declared that superiority should only control, so long as it contributes to the welfare of other people. "But who is to determine," came a voice from the audience, "what constitutes a contribution to the welfare of that people?" And so the discussion continued. This convention proved at least that they were not ashamed or afraid to discuss the one greatest national issue.[1]

Raper gathered dozens of questions asked more easily on scraps of paper, programs, and date books than voiced out loud in a filled auditorium. "Are Malados [sic] proud or ashamed of their 'white' blood? Will equality of race tend to mix races—intermarriage?" "Don't you think that all this talk is not so much about *races* as about the economic plane that people live on? Don't the European peasants think the same as the negroes do?" "What organization or movement is the leader representing—to lead us toward a solution of the race problem? In other words *who* is working on this problem, systematically?" The last question, at least, would have been easy for Raper to answer.

"Got any boy like that around here?"

In 1928, Will Alexander was perhaps the most prominent and effective white southerner seen as working on the "race" problem systematically. He had been a graduate student at Vanderbilt a quarter of a century before Raper, on the crest of Progressive reform. He took his degree in the Biblical Department in 1912 and became pastor of a nearby church. During World War I, he worked for the YMCA at army camps, where he combined the roles of chaplain and social worker. At the end of the war, he decided to continue with race relations rather than return to the ministry. His army work had convinced him that, when the Negro soldiers came back from the war, there was going to be trouble in the South because they had been treated more nearly equal in the military and in Europe than in most southern communities. Returning black soldiers were competing for jobs and looking for a greater share of social equality. The need for labor in the war production of northern factories had triggered the Great Migration of blacks outside the South. Social dislocation had increased tension between the races. What could Alexander do to reduce the race friction he saw when black soldiers met whites resentful of the competition for jobs? "Dr. Will" had an extraordinary talent for bringing people together, and, relying on his well-developed list of contacts in southern philanthropy and liberal reform, gathered a group of urban, white and black "moderates." Some were clergy and others social workers and academics; all sought to work out practical ways to diminish the virulence of white backlash. He conceived of the Commission on Interracial Cooperation (CIC) as a temporary measure intended to assist the South through the soldiers' return home. In 1917, he sold the War Department and the YMCA on the idea, which then allowed him to use $75,000 in surplus war funds to finance the commission.[2]

Between the World Wars, the Interracial Commission was the only broad-based, white-sponsored organization of even moderate size in the South dedicated to fairness for African Americans. Born of contingency, rather than mandate, the CIC approach to social change was gradualist and aimed to be pragmatic. It worked through individual assistance and community education, rather than pushing for legislation, to move the South toward greater concern for blacks. Rather than pursuing legal challenges, the Interracial Commission focused on organizing state and local watchdog committees charged with putting out specific fires. Their approach has been criticized for accommodating the Jim Crow South, and some members agreed with the doctrine of separate but equal. But Raper's experience and efforts with the Interracial Commission reveal an organization far more effective than such a judgment would suggest. Raper had already seen how progressive the commission's leader could be. He had first met Will Alexander in Nashville in 1925. "He turned up the first time when I was at Vanderbilt," Raper remembered, "and he began talking about the Negro and white college students and how much we were missing if we didn't get acquainted with and learn how to appreciate and associate, collaborate, with the Negro youth."

Alexander would become Raper's mentor, as influential as Odum. Raper saw in Alexander a man of great energy, intelligence, and fellow feeling, who also knew how to motivate and move people. Raper liked the way Alexander, although a prominent and influential figure, masked his command behind a circumspect manner. Alexander would begin to speak at a meeting or a lecture, for instance, and then stammer and pause, as though drawing his words with difficulty. "When he'd come to a real fine point that he wanted to make, he'd just stutter and he couldn't find the right word," Raper later recalled. "Then *you* would think of what the right word was, and then he would say it, and you'd think—'Gosh, that's a smart man.'" In a sense, that's the way Alexander approached the work of interracial cooperation—by circling in on a problem, rather than bulling into it, giving those involved time to work their own ways through to the right word. In the late 1920s, Raper would assist Alexander in researching, writing, and publicizing data that might assist the white South in moving toward allowing blacks at least economic equality.

Raper had returned to Chapel Hill from Nashville in 1926 to work with

Howard Odum on his doctorate, and Alexander was visiting Odum one spring day. Odum was hustling Alexander around the campus, spinning out ideas as they walked. At one point, they were rushing down a hallway, when Alexander turned to Odum. "Have you got a fellow around here studying about sociology in these brick buildings, who would like to go down to Georgia and study sociology among the people? Got any boy like that around here?" Odum told him Raper might be interested. So they detoured toward Raper's office and poked their heads in. A few minutes later, Raper had agreed to move to Atlanta.

He would continue working with Odum toward his Ph.D., while serving on the CIC staff. Alexander wanted to know how the work he was administering from the commission's offices in Atlanta played out in the rural South. As traveling secretary, Raper would be Alexander's eyes in the field. Alexander pushed Raper to look hard at the black farm families who were leaving the land, and at what was happening to them in the cities where they landed.[3]

"There *is* a reason!"

On a cold, Sunday morning in January, just a few months after he had arrived in Atlanta, Raper boarded a downtown streetcar, headed for a concert at the First Presbyterian Church. He asked for a return ticket as he handed two dimes to the white conductor, who was in the middle of an excited story. The previous night, three black men had been killed when a coal truck they were driving had overturned on an icy road near the end of the streetcar line. The wreckage was still lying along the route. A new passenger offered the conductor another chance to refine the story. He buttonholed the shivering Raper, who didn't want to seem unconcerned, but wanted to find a seat and mull over an article he had just read by M. Ashby Jones on race cooperation and class consciousness. The conductor began the story again for his latest passengers at the next corner as Raper finally made his way to the sole empty seat, opened a newspaper, and tried to warm up.

Soon the car had reached Peachtree Street, where he transferred to a 17th Street car, which dropped him off at the First Presbyterian Church. The concert was part of a full program of discussion and music that began with a sermon by a short, slender, white-haired preacher delivered to five bored-looking college students. This "exhorter of the most fundamental type," as Raper would describe him, spoke of the Bible as the best poetry, the best history, the best biography ever written. The Ten Commandments were the greatest laws ever given. The preacher rubbed his white handkerchief over his forehead and half closed his eyes, as he sighed, "I almost wish I could have been there at the foot of Old Sinai when the mountain was on fire, when a trumpet was heard in the background at first and soon came triumphantly near with its deafening blasts, when God with a thunderous voice, commanded his chosen people: 'Thou shalt have no gods before me.'" After ranging far and wide through the truths of the Bible, the preacher then turned to consider that group of people who called themselves scientists. With as much certainty as he had defended the Bible, he condemned science as a coven of self-important men who do not know anything for sure. The elderly preacher was a fundamentalist Dante, depicting a circle of hell where the vague, insubstantial shadows of scientists bickered over arcane theory.

At last, it was time for the concert. The First Presbyterian was renowned for its pipe organ, and Schubert's "By the Sea" was rendered by Dr. Sheldon. It was worth a long trip on a cold morning. Afterward, another preacher spoke about "Signals." Just as it had recently become necessary for traffic signals to be erected at the city's downtown crossings, correct signals also needed to be erected within the spiritual lives of each citizen of Atlanta. The preacher felt duty-bound to point out to the assembled the true signals—the faith of the fathers and old-time religion. At the end of the service, "when the last prayer had been said in the church, all the people came out as though they had completed a certain task," wrote Raper. "They had that satisfied look that people have when they have finished the dinner dishes or some other monotonous task."

Years later, Raper would tell this story both as a parable that defined his principles and approach and as a cautionary and revealing tale about the tendency toward scientific hubris.

"As I stood before the church looking at the few get into their Lincolns and Pierce Arrows, I saw a street car approaching. I leisurely felt into my pocket for one of the car tickets I had received when I handed the man twenty cents upon mounting the car earlier in the morning. I could not find it in the pocket where I kept my extra tickets. I then felt through every pocket." Once on the car, he emptied each of his pockets. "No sooner did I realize that I had no tickets than I understood why the conductor had been so talkative. It was clear as day why the conductor had gone to such pains to point out the death of the three Negroes on the cold coal truck. I then understood why he began to tell me of it as soon as I mounted, and why he resumed the conversation every time I looked towards him." The conductor's game was to distract his attention from receiving the return ticket, and stick the fare in his own pocket.

At first I felt something like a fish for letting him get by with my thirteen cents, but presently fell upon the idea that it was perhaps worth the both and loss of thirteen cents to really have another concrete illustration of the fact that there is an explanation for every unusual situation. In short, *There is a reason!*

Life is not so complex after all. It can be understood, it can be stated in such concepts that others can know man and never see or hear him—the accomplishments of science are great: the accomplishments of social science can be used. The laws of life can be understood—behavior is a result of a need, whether psychic of physical. The whole morning was susceptible to explanation; the conductor's interest in the death of the Negroes, the fundamentalism of the teacher and the preacher, the men who rode in large cars.

Raper strode like a new man down the avenue to Britlings Cafeteria for Sunday dinner, filled with a feeling "akin to that satisfaction a god must have when something has been created." He walked over to the commission's office to capture the triumph of his realization.

After I had written quite a bit, so that the situation could be vividly seen, so that the cause of the conductor's action would be evident, I decided to go to the window and look out on the masses who lumbered through the world hardly knowing where they were going—just living, not even conscious of life. There was a man, so called, and his body, spirit, and mind had never been beyond the nearest hill. He had no vision, I was thinking. He just exists. He can't see that all life and matter is surging forth in accord with fixed laws, and that man can understand these laws—that man can know what a certain fellow will do in a certain situation.

He sat at the window, marveling about the fixed laws of the universe and the possibility of mankind coming to know them through a kind of visionary of sociology.

Social science would soon be able to run its connections into the dark corners of the earth and with a simple command switch on a light where darkness had reigned supreme—the same thing will happen to immorality that is happening to smallpox, a formula will be effected which will prevent it, the state will require its use. Yes, as I was there thinking of these great advances, I found myself with both hands stuck way down into my coat pockets, and pushing down I could feel the pressure on my shoulders.

Just when I was feeling most triumphant, just when life seemed most capable of explanation—There's a reason for what you do!—just at that time, I felt two little pieces of cardboard in my pocket. There were the two streetcar tickets!

To the end of his life, Raper believed that the universe operates by means of laws, some of which humankind can understand and harness to its benefit. Laws underlie every motion in the universe whether physical or psychic in nature, and by understanding these laws, humankind becomes better able to master its own fate. "Things can be done; the undoable can be realized, the non-understandable can be understood." But the parable of the missing ticket revealed that, although man is a miniature god, he is

very miniature, for his chiefest mistake is that he learns to know a few things and then becomes satisfied with himself and spends his time in categorying the universe to fit his small files, and pitying those who can't understand the life about him: this is man's chief limitation, he shuts himself out of further growth by being too apt with the tool he has created. A ditch digger who is satisfied with his shovel rarely ever invents one that is better.

The parable of the missing ticket helped Raper calibrate to the exact point between faith in the power of science for doing good and an inspired appreciation for how limited are human resources within the immeasurable dimensions of the universe. Raper was a lifelong proponent of Enlightenment science. But he was also a modern, who learned to temper, in all his activism and even through his streetcar exchanges, his confidence that science could predict nature and human behavior with the knowledge that absurdity lay at the bottom of his pockets.

As it would take a man a long time to move the rock at Gibraltar, or perhaps the continuous work of generations of men, and men of differing races and creeds, so would it take a man a long time to understand why the conductor was so persistent in telling me of the death of the Negroes. Or perhaps it would take many men of many races and creeds to thoroughly explain the incident. On the other hand, it might take but one common man for a minute to explain it correctly, just as it takes a farm boy but two minutes to carry a bushel of sweet potatoes from the house to the barn and back.

Be sure, when speaking of the length of time it would take to move a certain rock, that you know how far it extends into the earth. But, when all is said and done: There is a reason—for every motion in the universe, and it is none the less powerful in its force, whether we understand it or not.[4]

Black Southerners and the Dislocations of Modernity

Through the 1920s, the CIC aimed to solve immediate, day-to-day problems faced by black southerners. Alexander, Raper, and the board of the CIC recognized that the commission's practical effectiveness would have been severely limited if they had explicitly endorsed a set of reformist or liberal principles. In its stated goals, the CIC did not advocate racial equality, but sought only to lessen prejudice against blacks. Even the mildest statements the CIC made in the southern press advocating equal treatment for blacks gathered heavy criticism from southern whites through the early 1920s. For its first few years, the commission was wary of newspaper publicity. Reactionary organizations, including the Ku Klux Klan, were already rallying to confront the changes created by the increased social mobility and the industrialization of the 1920s.[5] In fact, Alexander tried to conceal notice of the CIC's work from the general public. It was to be an organization of quiet good works. Soon, though, board members were pushing for an increased measure of publicity that would accrue, not to the commission itself, but to the interracial accomplishments of black and white southerners.[6] Toward that end, in 1922 the CIC hired Robert Burns Eleazer, editor of the Methodist Church's *Missionary Voice*, as its educational director.

Eleazer was from the old school, cautious in his approach, with little appetite for changing tactics on the fly—unlike Alexander and Raper—but he was diligent and exacting. He built a mailing list for the CIC and, by 1925, was sending weekly releases to 1,100 newspapers, including all the southern dailies, religious publications, women's magazines, and all the Negro newspapers in the United States. In 1928, his releases were reaching publications with an aggregate circulation of more than 20 million readers. Historian Ann

Ellis contends that Eleazer's efforts changed the policies of many southern papers.

By the end of the 1920s, Alexander perceived the southern press as having become "much better informed and much more sensitive to the situation than any other group of people." At first, Eleazer's efforts to provide support for African Americans were aimed primarily at the clergy, and he targeted religious conferences and missions. But within a few years, he, Alexander, and Raper saw brighter possibilities for change in working with the press and in the schools than through the ministry.[7]

A former minister himself, Alexander nevertheless felt that southern clergymen had, as Ellis writes, "not been nearly so responsive to the problems of blacks as had women." Most ministers were reluctant to encourage their congregations to challenge the South's racial caste system. In fact, the CIC saw the southern ministry as the "least responsive factor" to their message. "It is the exceptional preacher," read a CIC publication, "who is prepared to lead in combating racial prejudice or even to lend any effective cooperation."[8] So instead of relying on the support of the Baptists and Methodists, the commission began to target a variety of business and social welfare organizations and fraternal and women's clubs and groups.

Alexander was able to tack toward both church leaders and those, such as Odum and Raper, who wanted to apply sociological study and practical application to southern problems. As historian Morton Sosna puts it, "'Practicality' became as much a watchword of the Commission as 'Christianity.'"[9]

By the early 1930s, the CIC had become a major influence in halting the more violent reactions to southern Negroes' efforts to secure their rights and the tensions stirred by mass dislocation and Depression. The CIC helped make it unacceptable to retaliate against blacks for any breach of caste. Without its efforts, the civil rights movement would have had much greater difficulty gaining any momentum.[10]

The commission was also the conduit through which the Rosenwald Fund, financed by Sears, Roebuck, and Company, built some five thousand schools throughout the South. The commission galvanized many communities' efforts to build a Rosenwald school. And the CIC sponsored a great deal of necessary research into southern economic, agricultural, and social conditions, including Raper's own sociological studies, as well as those of Guy Johnson, Roy Steelman, Charles S. Johnson, and Edwin R. Embree.[11]

The commission was founded and largely run by southern whites, but it operated under the principle that blacks would work alongside whites, rather than under their auspices. Black leaders were in fact critical to the CIC's founding and its ongoing policy making, even though they operated in the background. Alexander relied on John Hope of Morehouse College and Charles S. Johnson of Fisk in shaping the direction of the Interracial Commission. Robert R. Moton of Tuskegee was instrumental in the establishment of the CIC, and he spurred Alexander to be more progressive.

Since the civil rights movement, the commission has been pinned with a reputation for having been "more interracial in name than in fact," but blacks were involved not only in the CIC's founding, but also in day-to-day policy-making decisions, providing experience that would pay dividends later. Raper noted that "People like Ira Reid, John Hope, B. E. Mays, all those folks, who later became identified with the first civil rights concerns, were very active in the Interracial Commission. Now I don't mean there weren't people outside—the NAACP [National Association for the Advancement of Colored People], the Urban League, the Negro Women's Association, Association of Negro Women—all of those had their own influences, but I don't think any of them came in direct contact with schools, with police activity, with hospitals and this, that, and the other the way the Interracial Commission did." In the cities of the South, these biracial groups formed standing committees that tried to work out solutions to such problems as inadequate housing for farm families moving to the city, while in both towns and countryside, groups formed on the occasion of a threatened lynching, for example, or when a critical need was seen for a new Negro school.[12]

Alexander also worked closely with Walter White and the NAACP. White, Alexander, and Raper all felt the two organizations were complementary. In fact, Raper saw a symbiotic relationship between the CIC and the NAACP. The two organizations "worked together and also agreed not to work together." For example, they collaborated, using different approaches and styles, to investigate lynchings and, later, to defend the Scottsboro Boys. In the late 1920s, they worked to equalize teachers' salaries throughout the South; the NAACP initiated legal challenges, while the CIC publicized their efforts as a way of educating southern whites toward accepting equitable court rulings. Many southern blacks belonged to both the CIC and the NAACP, but the latter reached few whites in the South. The CIC, however, worked to open white southern opinion to possibility of equality in civil liberties.[13]

This black-and-white management of a civil rights organization marks a turning point from a Victorian concept of helping the disadvantaged to the kind of cooperative and biracial efforts and negotiations that later became integral to the civil rights movement. For the first time, leaders of both the black and white communities came together in a particular locale where trouble had begun and worked together to determine a solution and reduce tensions. New in the history of the South, under the auspices of the CIC, blacks and whites worked on solutions designed for their mutual benefit.

Raper's arrival in 1926 accelerated and expanded this shift in organizational focus from the religious to the civic in Atlanta, where the commission was headquartered, and throughout Georgia. By the early 1930s, Raper had established forums throughout the state intended "to reach the people in local communities who in the final analysis determine racial attitudes."[14] He spoke to the Rotary, Lions, and Kiwanis, to Chambers of Commerce, and to the United Daughters of the Confederacy. Raper had inherited the job from liberal activist Clark Foreman, grandson of the conservative founder of the *Atlanta Constitution*. Foreman's commission work in the early 1920s had pulled him into the orbit of many of the South's most prominent social theorists and race reformers, including Robert Moton, John Hope and his wife, Lugenia Burns Hope, and sociologist E. Franklin Frazier. Raper would eventually follow Foreman's lead. Foreman had quit the commission in 1925, because he worried that the kind of aid it was providing was too dependent on private philanthropy; he favored direct government sponsorship. When the New Deal arrived, it allowed Foreman to develop push for civil rights legislation within the federal government as Roosevelt's special adviser on Negro affairs.[15]

While at the CIC, Foreman had developed in Georgia a network of scattered committees, mostly in the larger communities, ready to act as advocates for black Georgians. All through the late 1920s, Raper stayed in touch with Foreman's committees and helped keep them going. In Albany, for instance, he helped secure a Negro public health nurse. The Athens committee worked with the University of Georgia to establish a summer school for colored teachers. Raper spoke before the Atlanta Board of Education on behalf of keeping the black night schools open, presenting the case as a way "to lessen friction in certain residential areas." In Augusta, he pushed for a matron for the city jail. The Savannah committee worked to raise funds for a Charity Hospital for Negroes. The *Macon News* was persuaded to devote a column or two to the city's black residents. In Thomasville, Raper duly reported, "Legal counsel is being provided for a Negro who accidentally ran down a man some time ago." In Waycross, "a recent interracial mass meeting was held. A modern new building was created for the Negro school."[16]

Much of Raper's work with the CIC followed a direction he had begun to pursue at Vanderbilt in his master's thesis on "Negro Dependency in the Southern Community." In it, he had looked at the economic, political, and sociological factors developed since Reconstruction that constrained southern blacks. Raper based his consideration of race on systemic and environmental causes, and he quoted Du Bois in stating his premise. "When a group of persons have for generations been prohibited from self-support, and self-initiative in any line, there is bound to be a large number of them who, when thrown upon their own resources, will be found incapable of competing in the race of life." He looked at the extent to which blacks had been excluded from the electoral process, and concluded, "It is not surprising that so few Negroes vote, but rather that so many exercise this privilege." Raper likewise studied how the economic dependency constructed by southern agriculture was reinforced in northern industry. He explained, "the social attitudes toward the Negro in the South, which in spite of northern migrations is still his home, inevitably mean that he is not merely given the menial work to do, but also that he is treated more like a domestic than a skilled worker."[17]

Raper took pains to explore the specific ways Negro dependency worked. For example, he interviewed a white, union man in Nashville, who told him why he organized black laborers. "It is to our advantage to get them to organize. For, don't you see, then they can't underbid us; and at the same time we will get the best jobs—for at the same price white workers are preferred over Negroes by white employers and contractors. We want them to organize—it can't lower their wages, and will perhaps raise them, and every time they raise theirs we can raise ours still higher."[18] Raper was drawn to the ironies that ran through the traditions of the southern caste system. In the case of black crime, for instance, he observed that "the Southern public is hard upon Negroes for serious offenses, lenient for minor charges. He is at once more seriously blamed and at the same time more readily excused." He saw ironies, too, in the way blacks could turn segregation into a stronger sense of community and cultural independence.[19]

Right from the start, Raper's calendar grew choc-a-bloc with appointments: Marvin Underwood, a key member of the state's Legal Aid Society; Bishop F. F. Reese, of the influential Christ Church in Savannah; Dr. John Hope, president of the Morehouse College. By the fall of 1926 and through the rest of the decade, Raper wrote editorials, contributed to CIC reports, and addressed a disparate number of groups, from the annual meeting of the Georgia Sheriffs and Peace Officers' Association, to the commencement of the Negro Extension School at State College, South Carolina, and the assembled attendees of Interracial Night, a six-day meeting of the First Congregational Church in Savannah. Most of these dozens of groups and conferences took place in Georgia, but some occurred elsewhere in the Deep South. The Georgia Tech student newspaper reported on a talk by Raper to the Freshman Y Council on science and social policy, titled "Engineers in the World of the Future." "Very popular with his own students Dr. Raper has been a favorite of Tech groups ever since his first program here," ran the article. "He has a large fund of knowledge at his disposal and a broad sympathy for human values."[20]

While speaking and writing widely, Raper was rarely preaching to the choir. Even in Chapel Hill, he was trying to convert a multitude of skeptics and critics. A faculty member in history and government, for example, wrote to Raper in 1928 that he felt certain Raper must have "long since found that the Negro is a negro after all and must remain such in spite of the misguided geniuses who hope to raise him overnight to the position of superiority to the Nordics."[21] To parry criticism, Raper relied on his natural friendliness and openness about his intentions. After a dinner at the home of Dr. John Donald Wade, scion of an old plantation family in Marshallville, Georgia, Raper wrote, "Some of John Donald's friends thought me unkind to accept the hospitality of the plantation families, and then write about what I'd seen and heard about local conditions. This was no problem to me, for I went to them to try to understand the situation, told them what my interests were, and readily shared with them my connections and my thinking about what I was seeing and hearing about the local situation. I thought we needed to analyze the situation, and find some better ways to proceed."[22]

Meanwhile, on the streets of Atlanta, Raper also found himself paying close attention to the nuances of racial etiquette in urban Atlanta and musing over his observations.[23] He kept a notebook with him while he went to lunch or walked the newly crowded city after work.

> Going out on the street car the other day 3 Negroes were sitting on the long-side seat at the back of the car. White people were standing. After a while, one of the Negroes got off the car. More white people got on. One of the remaining Negroes was a well-dressed woman. She got off at the Georgian Terrace. That left one Negro man on the side seat. A very-well dressed white man asked the Negro, "Do you mind if I sit here?" He replied, "No." The white man sat down. Another white man asked the Negro the same thing and sat.
>
> About that time, a white man, standing, looked at the Negro sitting there and nodded him up to give it to a white girl who sat down. The Negro stood. After a while, seats in the front of the car became empty. But, of course, the Negro still stood because whites still sat on the back-side seats. The thoughtless white people kept the Negro from sitting by not moving up into the empty seats in the white section.
>
> If the Negro had refused to rise and give his seat to the white girl, when the white man nodded to him to get up, there would have been words between them, the motorman would have been called and, if the Negro still refused to rise, probably he would have been arrested.[24]

In often-charged public forums, Raper worked out his thoughts on race, sociology, philosophy, and politics. In a speech he gave in 1927 to the Colored Teachers of Macon, for example, Raper articulated his view of activism. It is impossible to make a constructive contribution to race relations, he claimed, unless good intentions and hard work were combined with what he called social vision.

> We want results, but we want only such results as are the product of correct procedure in the light of the welfare of all involved. In effecting satisfactory race relations, as in any type of social adjustment, the welfare of the individual is the essential thing. Social vision is necessary for the preservation of the individual, and unless the people who attempt to make contributions in the field of amicable racial adjustments have social vision their good intentions and hard work will mock them. . . . In this matter of race relations, too many whites are fixed—in a given situation they react rather than think, and although they honestly believe they are fair, the fact is, they are wanting in vision.

By social vision, he meant a sort of double-vision that kept in focus both the individual and the larger society, simultaneously. This was the aesthetic dimension of Raper's modernist sociology. Raper's social vision saw the individual and personal growing within the context of an imaginative conception of the larger community. And that social vision was maturing just as he himself was growing into the partnership of marriage and the context of a family of his own.[25]

"We were in fine fiddle"

Mrs. Maud Henderson was an ex-missionary, a quiet, stately woman of the Old South, who lived at the home of Reverend C. C. Jarrell on Oxford Road in Atlanta and directed the commission's efforts at Women's Work. It was a measure of how far the CIC had traveled during the decade of the 1920s to say that, by 1929, Mrs. Henderson's work had been assumed by Mrs. Jessie Daniel Ames. Ames was a tough-talking, irascible Texan, who relished her crusade against lynching as a way to show that southern women weren't afraid of black men or beholden to white men either. When Raper joined the commission in 1926, he had occasion to visit Mrs. Henderson at the Jarrells'. Jarrell was prominent in Atlanta's ministerial and philanthropic circles. He had studied theology in Germany and Scotland. He was also well acquainted with members of the Candler family, whose Coca Cola fortune was already immense. Secretary of the Methodist Episcopal Church South Hospital Board, Jarrell had headed charity drives, and he had raised money for Emory University, where Raper spoke at student affairs and in sociology and political science classes. The Jarrell family was living in a new house at the end of a streetcar line across from the still almost-vacant Emory campus, half a mile's walk through a forest with azaleas and dogwoods, under majestic oaks and pines.

Raper began to spend more and more time at the Jarrells' when he began to court their only daughter, Martha.[26] She had recently graduated with honors from Randolph-Macon College and was continuing her study of piano. Raper wrote to his sister Blanche, "For the past year she is secretary to her father; takes an active part in church and other orthodox institutions, but with it all, not the least bit stale."[27] He cajoled Blanche into chaperoning the couple on a mountain hike in the summer of 1928. Feeling in "fine fiddle," as he said, the three traveled to Mount Mitchell, near Asheville, picnicking in a meadow, and, at evening, "we found a dark quiet spot by a country road and watched the 'shooting stars' of mid-August." Raper had a romantic sensibility. At Chapel Hill, he had wandered through the lonely outposts of nature and penned melancholy notes to beautiful young women with whom he had barely spoken.[28] But once they met, Martha Jarrell became the woman of his life. In 1929, Arthur and Martha were married at the pink marble chapel of the Candler School of Theology at Emory. They spent their first two months of married life in a woodland house high in the Blue Ridge where, on top of a nearby white pine, a red-and-black scarlet tanager sat each day and sang them a song. In a year, Charles Franklin, the first of their four children, would be born at Emory University Hospital. Just as the nation was sinking into the Great Depression, Raper found himself juggling a demanding work schedule while researching and writing his Ph.D. thesis and confidently starting a new family.

Martha was a smart, inquisitive, and occasionally feisty woman, outspoken in a way that would occasionally embarrass the more buttoned-down Arthur. An early and dedicated proponent of recycling and an ardent environmentalist, even in later life, she was still firing off letters to the *Washington Post*, protesting Nixon's policies. Her sound editorial hand and eye for clear sentences proved to be a great asset to her husband and, by the mid-1930s, Martha was editing all of Arthur's writing.

Their romantic mountain hike had been no lark. Throughout his twenties, Raper was an avid climber in the Blue Ridge west of Salem. In 1924, he helped build a boys' summer camp on Mt. Mansfield, in a beautiful and remote meadow far above Asheville, then worked as its head counselor for the next dozen summers. "I have always liked the mountains; so rocky roads, streams to ford, and camp buildings on a slope were to my taste." He loved to explore. "Where were the good springs? The good places to sleep in times of rain? The best views? The largest clumps of flaming azaleas and the greatest stretches of mountain laurel or pink rhododendron?" And he loved the pioneering. "It's most fun to swim in a lake that you have helped build," he reminisced, "and a tennis game is relished all the more when the ball bounces straight because you had helped clean the rocks off."[29]

Camp Sequoyah called itself "a real camp for real boys," and Raper helped compile its full schedule of nature lore and Bible study, swimming and life saving, archery, riflery, horseback riding, and handicrafts. He had a hand in forming policy. "The first camp year was a combination of developing a camp program and building a camp. These two things fitted together very well," he wrote. "I still have a sneaking notion that the best way to have a good camp is to have the campers help build it." As head counselor, he supervised all programs, planned and headed the rigorous hikes, entertained camp guests, edited the *War Whoop* newsletter, led the Bible study class, and conducted the camp orchestra. He was fascinated not only with nature, but with the exercise of working out new programs as well. "Some of our experiments became fixed parts of the program," he said of Sequoyah, as he would later say of the New Deal, "and others faded out."[30]

At Sequoyah, Raper was planning and leading weeks-long mountain hikes across the highlands in the last years before motor travel made the Blue Ridge accessible to day hikers and auto tourists. The first trips to Mitchell were truly challenging and potentially dangerous excursions. Raper and his campers carried their provisions on their backs, breaking trails atop the landscape. "Later on we used pack horses, and before the decade was gone a truck might bring provisions to Steppe's Gap." He later wrote about the changes he saw over the course of the 1920s. "Some of the best campers in those early years expressed real regret that there was talk of building highways along the mountain ridges," he noted. "They thought this sacrilegious, for up here at least was one area where would be found only those who were strong enough to get there. I shared this feeling with them."[31]

Alongside his summer counseling, Raper made time for several camping conferences, "with a race-relations slant. And conferences galore, here and there in the South. And in and through it all, an interest in what was going on in southern life—especially in the rural areas, as influenced by race and class factors."[32] All the while, his CIC work began to gradually move away from the duties that accrued to the secretary of the Georgia and Florida committees and toward studies of rural life and culture.

"The gadgetted city"

From his first few months in Atlanta, in the fall of 1926, Raper felt surrounded by black and white farm families in exodus, refugees routed by the boll weevil and the collapse of the plantation system. Turned off the land, farm families and wage hands of both races swelled the city, denied their traditional supports, struggling and mostly failing to adjust to an alien way of life.

Near the commission's offices, the Melba Cafeteria was a popular and convenient lunch spot for much of downtown Atlanta in the late 1920s. One day, Raper looked up from his lunch to see a small band of ragged whites creeping up the sidewalk and staring in at the diners at lunch. There was a woman and a man, two girls about eighteen and twenty, and a boy maybe just in his teens. They walked around to the side door, sat down at the first open table, and waited to be approached. Ten minutes passed in wooden silence before a woman seated nearby leaned over and explained that they would have to get up, take a tray, and walk down the cafeteria line. Unaccustomed to being served, they ran the cafeteria gauntlet shyly and awkwardly. When they reached the register, each paid his or her bill separately.

Back at the table, each head bowed as the man asked the blessing. The boy was told to take off his cap. Raper guessed they had come together on the road. An evangelical, fundamentalist convention sponsored by the Church of God was underway in town, and these were "delegates," or better, pilgrims seeking succor as they followed Christ's voice through the radio into the city. "Our respectable churches have almost nobody in them who does not know his way around in city life," Raper reflected afterward, "but these and lot of folks on cotton farms belong to the Church of God. That church is reaching a group which does not know its way around a gadgetted city. They did not look cheap, but uninitiated."[33]

Who would initiate the folks who had drifted into the Melba, or provide some aid while they acclimated themselves to this literally new, urban world? In his early work with the commission, Raper didn't have much time to follow his impulse to pursue this kind of sociological question. "I started out loyally to do what I was supposed to do," he recalled, "to stay in touch with these interracial committees, but shortly I came to the conclusion, 'This isn't too important.' These committees—if there's a crisis, they heave to and do something, usually the right thing, but not always, but when there isn't any crisis, why, there isn't anything very much for me to do. So I began looking.

> See, I'd been at Chapel Hill and the Institute there, and I knew a little something about statistics, so I began looking at this business about all these Negroes that were coming into Atlanta and getting on the welfare business, and most of them—I soon got acquainted with the welfare people in Atlanta. Here was something that was tremendously important, because these people off of these old plantations were just crowding into Atlanta and going on welfare, and here was a real problem. And so I began talking about that and thinking about it.[34]

Raper's questions led him to Ada Woolfolk, who ran Atlanta's Family Welfare Society. Woolfolk supplied the sociological data that Raper was seeing every day in the bursting slums of the black districts and on the downtown streets. She wrote to him, for example, that "a survey of 546 open cases in the Family Welfare Society in January 1927, showed only 148 families where both parents and children had been born and reared under city conditions." She gave him insight into the particular ways modernity was pushing Atlanta's black families into even greater poverty. "The steam laundry is rapidly replacing the general use of the laundress," she wrote Raper. "Better in many ways for the worker and the home, it is [nevertheless] taking from the Negro mother the one type of employment that made it possible for her to supervise the lives of her children while she was earning the where withal for their food and shelter."

In the 1920s, this was the South's most pressing sociological question: What would the collapse of plantation agriculture mean to the thousands of black farm folk who were streaming into the cities? The answer would say much about the future of democracy in a country undergoing rapid urbanization. Soon, Raper had convinced Alexander to let him trace backward from Woolfolk's data and research the reasons for the exodus from farms to cities. "She was telling me about *how* many of these people that she was trying to help had come from that old plantation area, and how little they were prepared to live in the city and how difficult it was to help them," Raper said. "And so we got a study worked out with all the statistical frameworks you could imagine." They chose two counties southeast of Atlanta to contrast. In 1926, when Raper had visited a friend from Vanderbilt named Floyd Corry, who had returned to his family farm in Greene County, he found the worst boll weevil devastation he had ever seen. He found that exodus rates from Greene were among the highest in the South. By contrast, very few rural folk had left the farms of nearby Macon County.[35] These two counties also represented two different approaches and histories. Macon's agriculture was among the most diversified and its farmland some of the least depleted in Georgia. Greene County, on the other hand, had been home to some of the earliest of the Old South, King Cotton plantations. Greene was like an untended cemetery in a sleepy, old town abandoned by those who had forgotten or long since moved away. With Alexander's approval and Odum's encouragement, Raper set about contrasting the two counties as a way to study the effects of the exodus on the racial caste system. Raper remembered telling Alexander,

"Now, we went down there on the assumption that race relations were worse in this county where the people left than in this county where they stayed, but that's not so. Race relations are worse where the plantation is still regnant, and best at the place where it's fallen to pieces. Where it's all fallen to pieces is just the beginning of something, the beginning of realignment and what not." Well, Alexander was tremendously impressed with that. "Here's an idea we had and it doesn't work, does it, Raper?"

It was the kind of problem that fascinated both Raper and Alexander.[36]

The commission changed its focus through the course of the 1920s from solving local and particular problems toward a broader conception of social change, largely as a result of Raper's efforts and Alexander's increasing awareness of the power of the mass media to alter public opinion. Newly developed techniques drawn from publicity campaigns were joined to Raper's documentary sociology, helping pioneer the New Deal—style approach to social planning. The commission likewise pointed the way toward an emphasis on press coverage that would become an integral part of the civil rights movement in the 1950s and 1960s.[37]

Throughout the 1920s, Alexander remained the CIC's backbone. Raper was a bit wary of how heavily Alexander dominated the commission, but, at the same time, saw how much momentum and direction he gave it. Alexander had contacts throughout the region, and he had secured national support for the CIC from the Rosenwald Fund and the Rockefeller Foundation. In contrast with his education director, Eleazer, who steered to an unchanging course day after day, "Alexander made up his mind what was right yesterday, then he looked at it today and wondered if it would have any relevance tomorrow." It was a trait Raper recognized in himself as well. It would serve them both well when the New Deal arrived.[38]

"Every lynching is a small edition of war"

Flexibility made a lot of sense at a time when things were changing so rapidly. Between 1929 and 1930, the number of mob murders across the South jumped dramatically. Since the turn of the century, when southern mobs had lynched 100 blacks a year, along with much smaller numbers of whites, the average had steadily dropped to 17 people a year during the second half of the 1920s. But the number of victims rose from 10 in 1929 to 21 people in 1930—20 African Americans and one recent immigrant. By July 1930, Alexander and the commission had reacted by forming the Southern Commission on the Study of Lynching. George Fort Milton, influential editor of the *Chattanooga*

News, chaired the blue-ribbon panel of 11 influential men—including Odum and Pulitzer Prize winner Julian Harris—chosen from southern newspapers, churches, and universities, 3 sets of institutions with powerful influences on the public mind. Included on the panel were black academics and clergy: Charles S. Johnson of Fisk, John Hope of Morehouse, and Robert R. Moton of Tuskegee.

The founding statement made the commission's goal clear—"to define more clearly the causes of lynchings and to discover more effective means for their prevention."[39] The first action the commission took was to assign Raper to investigate each of 1930's lynchings. He would prepare a set of case studies for publication as part of a public relations campaign designed to show the South that some of its most influential business, educational, religious, and scientific leaders believed that "race intolerance" retarded the chances for economic recovery, prosperity, and democracy. As one lynching after another was reported, a sense of growing crisis pushed the work along. By August, Raper was writing to Charles S. Johnson, the prominent black sociologist, asking for his input. "I realize that I need the suggestions of men like you before beginning this very important and in some ways very difficult assignment."[40] Johnson ended up searching Raper's reports, looking for commonalities among mob murders that could be targeted for legislation and education.[41] He concluded that Raper should emphasize economic relations, public attitudes toward law and lawlessness, and the history of each community's race relations.[42]

Raper had finished a draft of the first case study by the middle of October. In circulating it to the committee, he was also reading a lot of mail from a variety of interested citizens. Some southerners felt lynching would prove immune to analysis. J. B. Lehman, the president of Mt. Beulah College, in Edwards, Mississippi, wrote to warn Alexander, "From the standpoint of reason your commission will find very little. It can not be approached from a scientific study." Lehman went on to reveal the class implications of the crime. "Every lynching is a small edition of war. At present it is a war between the white and colored race, but not so recognized by the colored people. In feudal days it was between the lord and the serf, but not so recognized by the serf. Often a colored man is lynched for an offense of which most of the lynchers have been guilty at some time." To Lehman, and to other cautious white leaders concerned for the peacefulness of their communities, science would only lead to recrimination and increased bitterness between the races.[43]

Raper was running a gauntlet of charged political viewpoints. In November, already deep into the investigations and rushing to write his reports as quickly as possible, Raper nonetheless took the time to write Alexander what amounted to a statement of his political beliefs. Perhaps he needed to ratify to himself where he stood while meeting the demands of a politically progressive, many-headed, and demanding commission pushing to develop an extensive publicity campaign around his research. At the same time, he was picking into the narrowest crevasses in the hearts of the South's most racist and political reactionaries and race killers. "The South is in the throes of a conflict," he wrote his friend, one November night, "between which I would call for lack of better terms 'negativites' and 'positivites'—the latter, a numerical minority, believe that the social problems of the South, all of which are aggravated by the race situation, can be by thorough study and planning worked out to the advantage of all, while the former, still under the control of oratory and ignorance made possible by the more or less undefined fears of the masses of both races, make themselves liable to the continued exploitation of unscrupulous politicians and other astute demagogues, who capitalize upon their fear to secure for themselves personal recognition in public office and elsewhere. The Southern situation is not hopeless, for oftentimes the numerical minority is an effective majority."[44]

As Raper campaigned through the rural South, in Atlanta the commission readied another attack. The idea was to pressure the fault line of the anachronistic, Old South rationale for mob murder. Walter White's *Rope and Faggot* had already skewered the old myth that lynching was justified as a means of protecting white women. Tuskegee had been compiling for years much of the evidence Raper was using to describe and analyze lynching. But *Rope and Faggot*, because it was written by an African American, was dismissed by many whites, who assumed it would be biased in favor of blacks. The commission realized it was critically important for white women and men to lead the fight against lynching.

Jessie Daniel Ames was a determined Texan who wanted to jump down off the pedestal of southern womanhood and call out the southern excuse that lynching protected women from the assaults of black men. By the fall of 1930, with Raper having begun his investigations, the commission formed the Association of Southern Women for the Prevention of Lynching (ASWPL) with "Mrs. Ames" as its leader.

Many of the women who became involved with the association had been working in various church groups. As Raper said, these women had often been denied the opportunity to preach or be active in their churches. So the women's association provided them a good venue. The ASWPL was conceived of as an integral part of the commission's publicity efforts. Through its members, the commission's medium was its message. White, southern women were denying in public forums and in the press that lynching had anything to do with protection, never-mind chivalry. And they had Tuskegee's statistics and Raper's analysis with which to launch their claims.[45]

Raper felt Ames was terrific at inspiring her volunteers and keeping everyone right to the point that lynching did not protect southern women. He also took pride in having provided the results of case study research and statistical, sociological proof behind Ames's claims. "She could then, with security, take the position they took. It couldn't have been taken until that time without somebody taking pot-shots at it."[46] Although their relationship would end several years later in a dispute over her opposition to the Dyer federal lynching bill, Raper felt that Ames and her association played a major role in ending lynching. In stark opposition to the tradition of modest southern womanhood, Ames and her membership stood up and said, "'You aren't protecting us now, Mr. Congressman and Mr. Senator and Mr. Preacher,'" explained Raper. "'If you are going to talk about this any further now, we are going to repudiate you. We're going to do it in public and we're going to call the press on it.' And by gracious, that was the end of it."[47]

The Interracial Commission did not intend to pressure whites on race relations per se, but to develop publicity about social science, which demonstrated that liberalization of the racial caste system would be the best way for the South to ease the Depression and most rationally accommodate the inevitable changes of modernity. Raper and the CIC published several case studies of lynchings in 1931 and 1932, then worked with W. T. Couch at the University of North Carolina Press to publish in 1933 *The Tragedy of Lynching*, a source book and a documentary study, based on sociological methods, of the individual, economic, and racial circumstances of every lynching.[48]

The commission wanted to incorporate information from black witnesses, most of whom would hesitate to talk with a white interviewer. Professor Walter Chivers, a sociologist at Morehouse College in Atlanta, had been raised in Georgia and Alabama. He had practiced social work after earning postgraduate degrees in social science at Columbia and the New York School of Social Work. Among commission members, he was highly respected by both blacks and whites. Chivers occasionally traveled with Raper and worked the black side of town, making his own reports on the news, rumors, information, and perceptions in the black community, while Raper worked the white side and researched town and county records. Once the research was completed, Raper synthesized the reports and wrote the book's text. During their first investigations, Milton complained to Alexander that Chivers's reports were "rather more slip-shod" than Raper's, but Raper always described Chivers's work with praise.[49] At the time and years later, he spoke warmly about the way they worked together.[50]

"There's a snooper here from up North"

Time and again—from Walhalla, South Carolina, and Ocilla, Georgia, and Emelle, Alabama, and Rosedale and Scooba, Mississippi, and Honey Grove and Brazos County, Texas—through the late spring and hot summer of 1930, as the Depression roiled across the baking landscape, news reached Atlanta of another small-town lynching.[51] Time and again, Raper nosed his old Ford out of the city and onto the backcountry roads, a letter of introduction in his pocket from Will Alexander or Howard Odum to the local mayor, sheriff, or county commissioners, and a lot of questions, both simple and extensive, about a lynching that had just taken place.[52] What was the chain of events that led to mob murder? What were the underlying economic and racial motives behind the lynching? Who took part in the lynching? How did the police lose their prisoner to the mob? What kinds of relationships did the victim have with people in the white community and with his black neighbors?

Raper soon found he did not need the official letter. Most often, the town's political, civic, and religious leaders were not talking anyway, certainly not to an investigator for an interracial outfit in Atlanta sent out to dig up trouble.[53] In Thomasville, Georgia, for instance, Raper went to Judge Roscoe Luke, a Baptist evangelical and a prominent figure in town, to ask about a recent lynching. A local tenant, Willie Kirkland, had been dragged around the county courthouse, while the sheriff rerouted traffic. "I took Judge Luke the letterhead of the Southern Commission on the Study of Lynching," Raper remembered, "and said I was one of the researchers for that, and I told him that what we were trying to do for this group of southerners was to find out the causes of lynching, and whether we could reduce them and eliminate them. So I talked with him about fifteen minutes, as much time as he had, about what we were doing and why I was there."

Judge Luke cut such an influential figure in town in part because of his popular radio program. He broadcast, as Raper said, "twenty minutes every day just at high noon, when all the farmers would be at home, you know, eating their beans and what not, and they could listen to the great evangelist. He explained things to them."

Judge Like went on the air soon after talking with Raper. "'Well, you'll be interested to know that there's a snooper here from up North,' he told his listeners, 'and he's agitating about this lynching we had a little while ago.' Well, he says, 'I'm sure that the people of this community don't want to have any meddlers around here interfering in our business and I know that this snooper will find out before very long that his presence is not wanted in this law-abiding, God-fearing community.'"[54]

Faced with this pattern of silence from officials, business leaders, and the clergy, Raper turned to his knack for interviewing, and conducted his studies at crime scenes and on downtown sidewalks, looking for clues as well as for data, developing a kind of gumshoe sociology to get at the facts first, then to analyze the conditions that led to mob violence, and finally to document the authorities' compliance.[55] It was not long before Raper began working undercover. "What I was trying to do was get at the facts of what had happened and you know, you can get very much better information on something like that by stopping and buying five gallons of gas or by going and getting yourself a haircut, or by eating at a little restaurant." He would wait until the lunch crowd had left, then order a hot plate and a piece of pie at an empty lunch counter. "I was just passing through town,'" he would say to the waitress, "and I heard you had a lynching around here." He quickly learned, "if you'll just keep your mouth shut a little bit and say, 'uh-huh' every now and then, why, they'll tell you what they know."[56]

Through the depth of the Depression, in the smallest of hamlets, Raper kept his hair in impeccable trim. He knew firsthand how well the town barbershop served as center of gossip and a cultural barometer, as well as a source for useful information on everything from local cotton prices to the names of lynch mob ringleaders. "Then I would go to the little restaurant, and I would eat something. Then I would go on down the street, eat in another little restaurant, and just talking to people." He'd say, "I'm just going through and I'm just interested in this thing. And heck, they'd tell you. They don't assume you have any attitude different from theirs."[57]

He found the best single source of information in a given town was the local taxi driver, who usually knew exactly who had done what. He often did not have a license, but was a local who could be counted on when someone's car was broken down or Aunt Nancy needed to get to the train station. Raper would often find the driver downtown, introduce himself, and tell him he was curious to see where all the trouble had happened. Raper would say he had his own car, right across the street. "But I don't know where this thing happened, and you do. Would you mind just taking me down there, and just go out there and look around as see what it looks like. Can you go?"

"Well, it's a pretty far piece."

"Okay, well, what will it cost?"

"Oh, six or eight dollars."

"I'll give you eight."

A small-town taxi driver would not see an eight-dollar fare from one month to the next. From that moment on, for the next few hours, Raper recalled, "He was just absolutely open to you."[58]

"You go to Judge Roscoe Luke's, and you see what you get," explained Raper. "Then, you go to the sheriff, and he says, 'Well, why are you asking questions like that?'" With some exceptions, the town's leading preacher would complain, "Well, if you bring a question like that in here, why, you'll split this congregation wide open." "You go to the hardware store, and the owner says, 'Well, you can't talk about that here, why half of the people that come in here would go on down the street to the other fellow.' And they simply don't dare to take a stand."[59]

So instead, Raper would stop in a one-pump gas station on the outskirts of town. He would climb out of the car, mop his brow, and look up and down the road. "Is this Wiggins?" he'd ask as the owner filled the tank and wiped his windshield.

"Yup."

"Didn't I see they had a lynching here a couple of weeks back? Did I see that in the Associated Press a little while ago?"

"That's right."

"Well, what's happening here?" The next thing Raper would know, the owner would have availed himself of the opportunity to tell this stranger about the way his town dealt with black criminals. From gas station to luncheonette to barber shop, post office, garage, and general store, Raper was practicing gumshoe sociology as he pieced together a town's atrocity.[60]

4

THE TRAGEDY OF LYNCHING

"Let's Buy and Read"

By 1930, increased attention to lynchings in the press had made it more difficult for small towns to keep their murderous business to themselves. When local field hand James Irwin was lynched in Ocilla, the *Macon Telegraph* launched an investigation, sending several reporters to town. By the time Raper arrived, a few weeks later, the white community had circled the wagons. "They had gotten sullen," he remembered. "They wouldn't talk. They wouldn't let you in at all, and the blacks wouldn't dare say anything because their lives were nearly on the line, if not precisely on the line."

Raper had spent two days and a night in Ocilla, making his "usual rounds of barbershops, and restaurants, and whatnot, but everyone just clammed up." Storekeepers and old men on the town benches would complain to each other about "'these outsiders coming here from the *Macon Telegraph* stirring up this thing. And we just said we're not going to have anything to do with them.' And when I came in, they said, 'Here's another one we weren't going to have anything to do with.' So I left there just crestfallen," Raper recalled, "and was riding up the road, coming home. I didn't get a single name of a lyncher in my information. I didn't get any information, except that the community had sealed itself off."[1]

As civil rights workers would find out in the early 1960s, fear of media attention made many small southern towns more than difficult to pry information from. Raper was poking into a rural South that was still defending its belief in vigilante justice. Fear often made people dangerous, and in Ocilla, Raper's investigation began to sound like a true-crime story.

"Who are you, anyhow?"

On the dusty road out of town, Raper stopped for a hitchhiker with a tramp's bag on a stick over his shoulder. He said he was going to Texas. Raper thought this hobo might know something about the lynching. Turned out, the fellow knew all about it. In fact, he had taken part in it. After a few minutes' talk, he had warmed to the topic. He reached down into the deep pocket of his overalls and pulled out a fire-blackened toe. He would probably get it ossified. Turned to a stone he could use for a type-end. Or he could sell it.

Afternoon turned to dusk, and all of a sudden, the fellow realized he had been talking a lot. He turned in the seat toward Raper. "Who are you, anyhow?"

"I'm an ethnologist," Raper answered.

"Oh." He paused. "They deal with the Okefenokee Swamp, don't they?"

"Yes," Raper drawled, "and a lot of other things." All through the long course of the Depression, all across the rural backwaters of the South, he never carried a gun.

A well-lighted filling station appeared out of the dark, and Raper quickly turned in. He loudly told the attendant he wanted some gasoline and made a show for the few farmers hanging around the station by pulling out his wallet and loudly telling the tramp, "This is as far as I can take you," before pulling back into the dark road toward home. When he finally reached the house, he was strangely quiet, Martha thought. But she was busy with a friend, and didn't take much notice at first. It took him a while, sitting by the fire, for him to come around to talking about the episode, she recalled, years later. He knew how lucky he had been to have escaped Ocilla unharmed. The young hobo with a bundle on a stick was walking down the country road of an old South whose white folks could swap stories of all sorts with a friendly stranger who shared an accent and a style of speech. Even though it called the tune the South sang in terms of money and power, the North and its ideas still seemed a land far away. In the early 1930s, all of a sudden, the North's opprobrium and control now seemed to come dressed in southern clothes. Far from playing the role of a dispassionate social scientist—or a benign ethnologist—Raper had been pushed by his modern sociology to the brink of an emotionally charged cultural transformation. Lynching was no longer a community's own closely held business, but was now opened wide to wire services, press releases, and scientific investigation.

In a real sense, Raper bet his life that the time had come when it could be safe to bring the backcountry South into the light of the new mass media.[2] Just as, thirty years later, black and white civil rights organizers knew the television camera would follow them to Birmingham and the Delta, Alexander, Odum, Milton, and the rest were confident the press would follow Raper to Cartersville and Plant City. *The Tragedy of Lynching*, published in 1933, appealed to the press for several reasons. Social scientific research had gained increasing cachet in the public mind by the early 1930s, as the search for solutions to the Depression became more urgent. The book was presented not as a jeremiad against lynching, but as a scientifically derived accounting of the heavy price paid by both blacks and whites in the maintenance of southern race relations. Instead of moralizing, *The Tragedy of Lynching* delivered a series of sociological case studies set as detective stories to let the reader come to his or her own conclusions. It was written in a convincing and straightforward, "realistic" style, designed to appeal to modern newspapers and magazines, too.

What made the book news across the country, though, was that for the first time, southern whites themselves cooperated with black southerners to develop a thoroughgoing and reasoned critique of racial injustice. In so doing, Raper, Alexander, and the Interracial Commission were also pioneering in documenting the effects of the Great Migration from its point of departure, as well as the urban crisis it was begetting. These studies anticipated the landmark works of New Deal documentary. Through Raper's writing, the Interracial Commission provided a counterpoint to then-current sensationalized images of the South. *The Tragedy of Lynching* was a scrupulously researched, imaginatively conceived set of stories that told tales of brutal murder and revealed, not a killer or mob, but a set of circumstances that added up, like a collection of clues, to a sociological who-dunnit.

"Let's buy and read"

When W. E. B. Du Bois read *The Tragedy of Lynching,* he felt a sea change taking place in southern race relations. Du Bois was black America's most influential voice and the editor of *Crisis,* its most important publication. In the early 1930s, Du Bois published two reviews three years apart that, between them, showed how far the Interracial Commission had traveled from the cautious good works it had quietly accomplished in the early 1920s to the organization that by the mid-1930s had begun to call for far-reaching changes in southern political policy. It was now an organization deeply involved in a large-scale publicity campaign targeted against the most spectacular form of racial injustice.

Du Bois did not mince words about the CIC. In 1930, he had reviewed a federal report titled, "The Economic Status of the Negro," written by T. J. Woofter, another of Odum's Chapel Hill sociologists and a predecessor of Raper's as research secretary to the CIC. He picked up the term *Woofterism* from the Baltimore *African-American* to mock what blacks had begun to see too often in American sociology and government: well-funded scientific reports on the inequalities in the circumstances of black southerners, complete with sets of suggested solutions, none of which hinted at challenging the political, social, or economic structures that had produced such debilitating conditions. It aggravated Du Bois that a generation of liberal southern whites, like Woofter, intending to help race relations, offered plans for additional agricultural education just as blacks, for lack of political or economic power, were abandoning the South's farmlands by the thousands.

As early as 1903, Du Bois had criticized Booker T. Washington's emphasis on vocational education at a time when low-wage jobs were open to blacks in a range of trades and occupations. That strategy, he argued, would assign African Americans to the status of a permanent underclass. He had no patience at all for a call to finance vocational and agricultural schooling for Negroes during the Great Depression in the 1930s, when whites had begun to hop bells and operate elevators, taking over even the least skilled positions from blacks. "When a southern white man comes to the study of the race problem apparently with the idea of leaving out all 'controversial' matter, and nevertheless calls the results scientific," he wrote of Woofter's report, "then something is being done that is not only wrong but vicious." Woofter's report was indeed intended to help raise the standard of living of the black South without suggesting that the white South cede any of its overwhelming political power or economic strength. To accomplish this trick, Woofter's approach was to look at data, but not at causes or policy or the results of segregation. To Du Bois, this was neither realistic nor objective, and masquerading as objective social science made the report damaging.[3]

Three years later, in 1933, when he read Raper's *The Tragedy of Lynching*, however, Du Bois—along with Walter White in the *New Republic* and Fisk sociologist Charles S. Johnson—recognized the importance of the first critical analysis of southern race relations written by a white southerner. "This is one of the best studies of lynching ever issued," Du Bois wrote in a review titled, "Let's Buy and Read." "Its value lies in the fact that it was done mainly by southern white people. We have often criticized the interracial movement, as led by the Commission on Inter-racial Co-operation," in part, Du Bois said, because "its earlier attacks on lynching seem apologetic; but recently, it has seemed to us to be getting into its stride, and certainly, this study by Arthur Raper, with the assistance of W. R. Chivers, a colored professor in the Department of Sociology at Morehouse College, and other white and colored persons, is epoch-making."[4] To Du Bois, *The Tragedy of Lynching* was the first indisputable sign that southern blacks had dependable allies within the scientific community and within the white South.

Raper had seen that eliminating lynching would necessitate changing the structure of southern society.[5] Although he never used the word *integration*, his convictions about the injustice and unworkability of segregation came through clearly. "It is of momentous interracial import that the Negro and white members of this black belt community are achieving the status of neighbors," as he told a Georgia committee on race relations in 1933. "Neighbors often gossip about each other; they never lynch each other."[6]

Many historians of the civil rights movement have viewed the Commission on Interracial Cooperation largely as a low-key and local orientation of fading influence in its last years, outside the main line of change in southern race relations.[7] But in the mid-1930s, emboldened by the New Deal and by the growing desperation of the Depression, the CIC and the University of North Carolina Press had responded to a growing minority of southern black activists and white leftists by sponsoring both *The Tragedy of Lynching* and *Preface to Peasantry*, Raper's second major work, three years later.[8]

As the Depression deepened, the CIC felt an increased sense of urgency and mission. Lynchings were not only on the rise, but school funding was being cut. Blacks were being pushed out of their jobs, and even off their beaches. Commission member R. H. King wrote Howard Odum in 1932 that "at no time since the World War has the need of a mediatory agency been so imperative."[9] Once the Commission on the Study of Lynching was established in 1930, Raper was not the only controversial voice speaking for the white interracial movement. CIC commissioner Judge Orville A. Park, for example, told white southerners some of the same things. "Unpleasantly Frank Speech Is Made to Kiwanians by New Legislator," ran the headline of the Eastman, Georgia *Times-Journal,* in January 1931, after one of Park's addresses. "State Is Backward, Georgians Are Told." Still, Raper's was the loudest voice, pushing into the most dangerous places.[10]

"'Imperial Bolivar' and what it means"

"About mid-morning of April 23, 1930, Dave Harris, Negro, was lynched near the Waxhall, seven miles north of Rosedale, Bolivar County, Mississippi. He had killed Clayton Funderberg, a seventeen-year-old white tenant, the evening before."[11]

As he did for all twenty-one cases, in the study of the Bolivar lynching, Raper began with the particulars of the incident that sparked the lynching and moved to the broad social conditions surrounding the tragedy. In this case, Harris tended the horses on a cotton plantation near the village of Waxhall, and he sold liquor to the black and white tenants and hands on surrounding farms. He was forty, with a wife and several children, known as a fighter and bootlegger, but considered by local planters to be an excellent worker. Funderberg, a customer of Harris's, was a poor, white tenant, unmarried, a hard-drinking seventeen-year-old who had moved to the area just the year before. Blacks and whites told different accounts of how Harris came to shoot Funderberg. The black version had Funderberg and two friends demanding liquor, telling Harris to add the charge to his unpaid bill. When Harris refused, Funderberg threatened him, and Harris retaliated with a fatal shot. Whites said Harris had stolen groceries from Funderberg, then killed him when confronted with the crime.

In either case, Harris's friends immediately ran off to form a search party. When the deputy sheriff at Rosedale heard of the killing, he looked briefly into the matter. Raper explained, "upon being assured that a large number of people were close on the Negro's trail, the deputy sheriff expressed satisfaction with the way the affair was being handled, and returned to his office in Rosedale." Aided by bloodhounds, two hundred "man-hunters"—composed of migrants and white tenants who had moved to Waxhall in the previous few years—searched through the night and captured Harris the next morning in a corn crib, where he was revealed by another black man, who may have worked with a competing liquor interest. "He was carried directly to the Mississippi levee, a short distance away," reported Raper, "where he was tied to a tree, hands behind him, and his body was riddled with bullets. A plantation owner reports that he heard the fusillade, and is certain there were no less than two hundred shots."[12]

The lynching caused little stir. *The Bolivar County Democrat,* a weekly published in Rosedale, made no mention of the lynching. "The editor, a woman, explained that she did not know anything about the matter until some time afterward; besides it was her policy not to mention things of this kind, since publicity on such matters merely results in a lot of adverse criticism by outside papers," Raper observed. Other papers carried only brief notices of the killings, and nearby Cleveland's *Bolivar Commercial* editorialized against spending resources to track down the mob leaders.[13]

An investigation was held six months later, by which time many of the town's leading whites had forgotten most of the facts concerning the incident. Not surprisingly, no indictments were brought. At the same time, Chivers found local blacks inured to mob violence. In Bolivar County, which averaged a lynching every four years, such occurrences were a part of the normal picture.[14]

Raper rooted the Bolivar killing in its social, economic, and political context. Bolivar was one of the most fertile and populous rural counties in the South. It was called "'Imperial Bolivar' by reason of its wealth and prestige on the one hand and its political self-sufficiency on the other. It is, so to speak, a nation within itself."[15] Raper briefly traced the history of the county to the time when Andrew Jackson secured a 5 million acre tract in the Yazoo Valley, and to when the Choctaws relinquished their claims to these river lands in the 1830 Treaty of Dancing Rabbit. After 1850, the fertile lands along the Mississippi were rapidly opened to plantation development, and levees were constructed to secure the land for cotton. By 1890, the population had reached almost thirty thousand. The ratio of black-to-white residents was three-to-one.[16] As Mississippi's "banner cotton county," Bolivar drew an increasing number of whites from eastern Mississippi and the Alabama hill country during the first decades of the twentieth century. By 1930, the additional white tenants were displacing black farmers and tenants whose ancestors had cleared the swampy river banks, leveed the Mississippi, and built the farms that had driven the county's cotton production. At the turn of the century, it had been possible to ride for miles along the river, from Greenville toward Rosedale, without seeing a white man, but by 1930, a number of planters had begun hiring white tenants and offering them a long-term chance to purchase the land they were working. On the one hand, this new development brought in a broader base of whites who were gaining the opportunity to own their own farms. On the other, it brought an increasing number of migrant white tenants into competition with local blacks for farmland. As historians Stewart Tolnay and E. M. Beck conceive it, "Whites viewed economic success in the New South as a zero-sum game."[17] Whites saw black progress as coming at their own expense. At the same time, the Depression was dropping cotton prices lower and lower, and the county's lack of manufacturing jobs squeezed black tenants even further toward destitution.

Those whites who wanted to displace black tenants saw all around them a system of civic jurisprudence that stirred up their most bigoted impulses. Bolivar's school budgets, for example, clearly reflected the county's official position toward questions of racial equality. In 1930, the county reappropriated to white schools over half of the meager amount designated by the state for the education of Bolivar's black children. As a result, the county spent $42 on each white student for each dollar spent for black students. The official in Bolivar most responsible for protecting the existing social conditions, the sheriff, was the most powerful man in the county. In the depths of the Depression, he made a net cash income in 1930 of $40,000, ten times the salary of the governor of Mississippi. As part of the spoils of office, the sheriff collected taxes, for which he received a commission, and executed court orders, for which he collected fees.[18]

Between 1900 and 1930, seven Negroes had been lynched in Bolivar, six accused of murder and one of rape.[19] The court records showed a consistent pattern of leniency toward black-on-black crime and stern judgments against black-on-white crime. Accordingly, Raper considered Bolivar's white churches—predominantly Baptist and Methodist—weak agents of Christian charity. In fact, no church held a regular weekly service, and black churches had only half the membership that Mississippi as a whole averaged.[20] The church, the law, and the school accepted that the planter should be allowed control of his tenants and wage hands, as tradition had forever dictated. "To all practical purposes a dead 'nigger' is just a worker gone," Raper observed, "and of no concern to the public."[21] In terms of the county's economic structure, Raper wrote,

> The Negro's traditional improvidence is encouraged virtually to the point of a requirement by nearly all white planters, assuming as they do that empty larders are prerequisite to the consistent application of the Negroes' brawn to plantation tasks. On the other hand, a full or half-filled larder may encourage the desire for more self-expression and self-direc-

tion than the plantation system will permit. Dependent Negroes are essential to the delta white man's economic, social, and political demands. This situation accounts for the many conditions of injustice and neglect which Negroes must bear in silence and with such patience as they may.[22]

Through the course of *The Tragedy of Lynching*, Raper's social-scientific realism tails into the sardonic and melancholy, as though to give witness to black sensibility in the face of deprivation. He joins sociological and documentary description and data with a depiction of the quality of mind of the people he is studying, one that mixes the objective and subjective. For example, addressing Bolivar's racial makeup and caste system, Raper concludes the Bolivar case study with a short section on white attitudes toward the county's Chinese immigrants. The last sentence documents the melancholy that Raper found among Bolivar's tenants and farmers, a mood that was becoming in these same years distilled into the blues music that would, improbably, export the sensibility of the Mississippi Delta throughout the world. He wrote:

> Recently in Greenville, thirty miles south, a Chinese boy who married a white girl was forced to leave. This marriage would probably have been permitted to pass, except for the fact that the boy's brother had previously married a Negro. Since that time the white people have held several anti-Chinese meetings, to which Negroes were invited. The Negroes, however, did not attend, and subsequently a white committee waited upon them to ascertain their attitude toward the Chinese. The immediate purpose of the movement was to establish a boycott against Chinese business, in which the cooperation of the Negroes was essential. Somewhat amused and silently unsympathetic with the effort, the Negroes failed to participate.[23]

Raper also presented a set of case studies where lynchings were foiled, but even these studies told of other tragedies. In Screven, a poor, almost wholly rural, Georgia county, precautionary action by the police and judiciary saved a teenaged farm hand, LeRoy Scott, from lynching. Scott had been working alongside his boss, a small farmer. Scott was accused of sneaking away from the fields, and returning to the farmhouse, where he hit the farmwife with an axe and attempted to "assault" their eighteen-year-old daughter. After a days-long manhunt, Scott was arrested and police secured a confession. He was removed to a strong prison in an adjoining county, and later to Augusta to avoid a mob confrontation. The judge brought Scott to trial unannounced, and he was tried and sentenced before the public knew the judicial proceedings had begun. "The sheriff stated his belief that if a public trial had been attempted, the Negro would have been lynched." Instead, Scott received thirty years in the penitentiary.[24]

Nevertheless, Raper concluded, "it may be questioned whether the mob spirit did not at last defeat the ends of impartial justice." He suggested, not surprisingly, that Scott's confession was gained through coercion. The verdict was baffling since neither the farmer, his wife, nor their daughter identified Scott as the assailant, even though he had taken his meals at their kitchen table for the previous month. The farmer aroused the ire of some of his neighbors, in fact, through his defense of LeRoy Scott. In the end, Raper concluded, "The best that can be said is that the Negro was saved from the mob. The worst is that, though unaccused by his alleged victims, he was sentenced to thirty years imprisonment. This case clearly demonstrates that it is the mob, rather than any one particular activity of the mob, which must be eliminated, before impartial justice can be achieved."[25]

"A belated frontier"

Raper saw lynching as the last vestige of the frontier, where civilization had not yet secured a firm foundation for all its citizens. In the famous analysis of historian Frederick Jackson Turner, to whose theories Raper had gravitated while at Chapel Hill, the American frontier had faded into the sunset with the inevitable westward push of civilization. For Raper, lynching was an anachronism that hindered the democracy and rationalism needed to harness science, industry, and media in the modern age. While he warned southerners that "no community is immune from the danger of lynching," Raper quickly came to believe that lynching was a rural crime.[26] He reported that "five of Georgia's six lynchings of 1930 occurred in the southeastern part of the state, the newest and poorest section. Here churches, schools, and a stabilizing tradition are less powerful than in the older communities. In the last decade, this section has been the scene of numerous floggings, with white as well as Negro victims. It is a belated frontier, and one lacking the virility of the typical American frontier."[27] Turner's frontier communities had been dynamic and expansive, but the South's threadbare pockets of belated frontier were backwaters passed over in pioneer movements toward cheaper land and better soil.

Because the commission conceived of lynching as a crime of the farming backcountry, *The Tragedy of Lynching* was organized according to the South's various geographical and agricultural regions. Raper compared their similarities and differences, not only in terms of numbers of lynchings, but in the distinct economic and cultural conditions that contributed to lynchings in southeast Georgia, for example, and to those in Texas, Virginia, Alabama, and Mississippi. His case studies were informed by the historical records and press clippings compiled since 1889 at Tuskegee University.[28] Before going out to investigate the lynchings, Raper spent "weeks and weeks" at Tuskegee, looking for patterns to determine why the crime had increased so dramatically in 1930, so he could place the contemporary phenomenon in the community's historical, social, and economic contexts.[29]

Raper broke down each investigation into three parts. First, he developed a profile of the communities where the lynchings had taken place—the town, its population, economy, political situation, patterns of crime, and religious and civic leadership. Second, he gathered the facts surrounding the lynching itself, including the reported cause of the crime, the efforts made to prevent the lynching, the victim's and the mob leaders' backgrounds, mentalities, education, and standings in their communities. In regard to both the community profile and the circumstances of the lynching, Raper paid particular attention to the local white and black press accounts. Third, he analyzed the reaction of the town to the lynching, the comments of the press, the decisions of the courts through grand jury hearings, and the attitude of leading citizens.[30]

On the scene, though, he adopted the tone of a private detective or a mystery writer. And he took pains to capture the experience of the black community. On November 5, 1930, Raper wrote to Mr. J. L. Grant of Darien, Georgia. "Just now there is one thing in particular I wish you would comment briefly upon. When the fire bell rang shortly after midnight, I imagine several of the colored citizens of the town came out to assist in putting out the fire. I am wondering just what these well intentioned colored people did when they found out there was no fire but rather that a man-hunt was being organized. I would consider it a personal favor if you could tell me just what went on in the minds of the colored people when they found themselves in this situation."[31]

Raper found enough similarities in the pattern of lynchings across the South to conclude that the link between lynching and black-on-white rape was a myth and a cover-up. In most of the cases, violent sexuality played a part only in the ritualistic torture and mutilation of the black victims. Almost 2,500 African Americans had been lynched in the United States from 1889 to 1930, and Raper found that only one-sixth of them had even been accused in the white press of rape. Of the 21 lynching victims in 1930, 5 had been accused of murder, 10 of rape or attempted rape—a higher percentage than any other year in Tuskegee's records—3 of robbery, one of bombing a house, and 2 victims of lynching were not accused of any crime at all. In the course of his investigations, Raper came to believe 2 of those lynched were clearly innocent. In the cases of another 9, the accusations against them had seemed dubious. In 6 cases, the nature of the initial crime had actually been uncertain or in dispute.[32]

"The basic thing we were saying, see," Raper told Daniel Singal, "was that most of the lynchings aren't for accusations of rape and attempted rape, and of those accusations of rape and attempted rape, not nearly all of them are true. That was the big thing we said. That was accepted. There wasn't any flack on that. Chivers and I were very careful. Of course, when you're saying that a man here was lynched for rape, and then you're going to presume he wasn't guilty of rape—that wasn't what he was guilty of, if he was guilty of anything—you have to have your material pretty well in hand."[33]

The victims ranged in age from the late teens to seventy, but most of them were men under twenty-five. Half were married. Many had not identified with any church or lodge. Most of the victims were poor tenants and croppers from broken homes with little formal education. Several were called crazy or half wits by local black farmers.[34] A handful were thought of as "outsiders" by the local Negroes. A couple were prominent Negro businessmen who were resented by poor whites in the neighborhood. But one thing was fairly consistent—sixteen of the twenty-one had never before been to court.[35] Raper chided state and municipal authorities for not offering enough social aid to help these men keep themselves civilized. Many of the poor criminals who ended up lynched were retarded or suffering from a mental handicap, Raper claimed. They were people who could have been helped before a mistake cost them their lives and their town and state their decency.

Raper believed lynching grew out of the racial brooding of a rural community where black and white tenants and croppers were competing with each other to keep their heads above water.[36] By 1930 the Depression was carving to the bone a South that had spent much of the 1920s in an agricultural depression.[37] Raper concluded that the plantation culture itself, with its combination of poverty, poor education, and racism, led directly to mob violence.[38] By all measures, and almost without exception, lynchings occurred in the poorest counties.[39] With some exceptions, the lynchers themselves were most often teenaged boys and men in their early twenties, without property and often unemployed, poor, unattached, and unsocialized. The only lyncher Raper discovered with a college education had been recently released from the State Insane Asylum. From out of the back woods of Depression Alabama, Georgia, and Texas, these were young men "farthest removed from the institutions and agencies determining accepted standards of conduct." To Raper and the Interracial Commission, they provided evidence that American civilization lacked the social conditioning required of a modern, liberal democracy. Their existence challenged the integrity of the American democratic experiment.[40]

In *The Tragedy of Lynching* and the commission's pamphlets, as well as in the innumerable public addresses made by the women and men of its various subcommittees, the CIC warned that lynching contributed to the erosion of democratic institutions. To protect their communities, sometimes their homes, and often their livelihoods, southern officials, as well as black and white clergy, townspeople, farmers, and businessmen, participated in elaborate ceremonies of silence to cover up the barbarous misdeeds of the most irresponsible southerners. Then they paid the bills for a burned courthouse or school and accommodated themselves to the calcification of a community bound by racial and social castes.

So while the lynchers themselves were generally young hotheads and rednecks, the research showed that townspeople of power and position were accomplices to the crimes, in one way or another.[41] Raper observed, "At Scooba, Mississippi, where a double lynching occurred, the two men reported to have organized and engineered the mob from start to finish were leading people in the community and prominently identified with the local church, school, and other community activities."[42] In many of the cases, Raper found he could tie a town's seemingly undirected violence to specific leaders in the white community.

In addition to his statistical analyses, Raper wrote vignettes about the kind of miscreants who gravitated to lynch mobs. He first arrived in Darien,

Georgia, for example, on the morning of September 11, three days after a suspected bank robber, George Grant, had been gunned down by a mob that had stormed the town jail. The first person he talked to in town, over at the barber shop, told him he had been in the mob himself. This young, white fellow, out of work for six weeks, had been living in Savannah when he heard about the lynching. He caught the next bus to get down to Darien before it was all over. "Well, trouble between the whites and blacks has just begun," he explained to Raper, "but things are not so bad yet that niggers need to be robbing banks." He was almost afraid to get off the bus when it pulled into town, though. Everybody he saw had a gun. "Yes," the barber leaned over and chimed in, "but it was a good experience for you."[43]

Raper saw two distinct impulses that sparked the formation of mobs. The disorderly and spontaneous mob of single, farm youths and hotheads looking for trouble were doing the dirty work of the conservative, established, businessman, who told him, "You've just got to have a lynching every so often." Many whites believed the occasional lynching was needed to maintain their town's social structure. "Regardless of the cause of a particular lynching, there were always those who defended it by the insistence that unless Negroes were lynched, no white woman would be safe, this despite the fact that only one-sixth of the persons lynched in the last forty years were even accused of rape."[44] With the drunk and disorderly mob, Raper came to see, "it's a matter of tension and emotion and license, and what not, and it just goes, whoosh. But this orderly mob—it's the drip, drip, drip method. You've just got to have something happening here and something happening there, something happening here, something happening here, so that every Negro knows his life is precarious." Raper was hearing, time and again, that lynching served as social control, maintaining necessary social boundaries.[45]

The drip, drip, drip method exploded in Cartersville, for instance, when a mob pulled a young, black man, John Willie Clark, from his jail cell and lynched him at the fairgrounds east of town. Clark was on trial for killing the chief of police in a late-night altercation. His trial had been prolonged because it had attracted the attention of a black educator who was passing through the town and who had called attorneys in Atlanta to ensure that Clark was appointed a capable defense team. When his lawyers called for Clark to be moved, the judge refused, and local townspeople raided the Cartersville jail. Raper drove down to Cartersville the day after, pulled up to the courthouse, and sat down with two of the town elders. Mr. Hammond told him the lynching was the result of the cussed lawyers from Atlanta fooling with the trial procedures. If it had not been for outside interference, Clark's case would have been handled cleanly. "The prisoner would have received an impartial trial," he explained to Raper, "been sentenced, and electrocuted in short order." His friend was less enamored of the law. "The only objection I find is that they didn't hang him high enough," he said. "Why, his feet weren't three feet from the ground."[46]

Two photo studios were already selling postcards of the lynching. At Morris Studio, Mr. Morris had been pleased he could get such a good shot. He was charging a quarter apiece. Over at Art-Craft Shop, though, they sold them for just a dime. "I didn't want to take advantage of the people at a time like this," the photographer explained to Raper, "so I thought I would sell them for ten cents."

"You know," he continued, "the pictures of that Negro hanging there will do more to reduce crime than anything I know of, and I am glad to distribute the pictures at cost." Warmed by thoughts of the public virtue that his pricing would enhance, the merchant went on to puzzle out why so many lynchings had been needed this year. The trouble was that the "niggers" were no longer willing to keep their places. "This man reported with delight that pictures of the lynching were being sold at Calhoun, Rome, Chattanooga, and various other places, and that he believed it would do a great deal of good." Business was brisk. Raper was only in the store a few minutes, but several people came in for postcards.[47]

"When a man bites a dog, that's news"

Raper found false the old saw that lynchings were needed because the courts did not convict, a point confirmed by Tolnay and Beck's statistical study.[48] On the contrary, the courts were quick to convict accused blacks who brushed against the person, property, or sensibilities of any local whites, particularly when they committed crimes. In most cases, he was able to find out who the mob leaders were, but juries rarely indicted anyone for lynching. Convictions for lynching were virtually unheard of.

Raper soon found that sheriffs beholden to the voters among the mob and its supporters were reluctant to interfere with a lynching party. Some officers were in connivance with the mob. Many asked, "Do you think I'm going to risk my life protecting a nigger?"[49] The record of the courts was equally indulgent. In fifteen of the twenty-one lynchings, the victims were determined to have been killed "at the hands of parties unknown." In only one case was a serious sentence passed against two lynchers.

So fearful were most of the South's clergy of losing the support of their church membership that they refused to challenge their congregations on their assumptions that the Negro was inferior and worthy of little notice. William P. King, book editor and editor of the *Methodist Quarterly Review*, sympathized with Raper, who had written for advice on contacting southern clergy. "It is difficult," he murmured, "as I suspect you have discovered, to get preachers to answer letters."[50] In general, the larger churches were more likely to speak out against lynching, but the ministers of smaller, outlying churches often expressed sympathy with the mobs.

The same was true of many southern newspapers. All the larger dailies denounced lynchings, near or far, but county weeklies and smaller dailies "were inclined to condemn lynching in general, but often justified it in particular instances."[51] Some of the white press, however—while ignoring the commission's call for racial justice—editorialized against lynching on the grounds of modern efficiency and practical morality.[52] "When a man bites a dog, that's news," editorialized the *Macon News*. "When a Negro accused of attacking a white girl, lives to face a Georgia jury, sitting in a courthouse with a judge on the bench and a defense lawyer confronting the state's attorney, that's news." The news was another example that lynching was outdated, explained the paper, because what was in effect a legal lynching would accomplish the same goals without the costly destruction of property. "Georgia courts are perfectly capable of handling this kind of trial. They can do it much more justly than a mob can. They can do it just as effectively and just as impressively and there is no aftermath of disgrace on the community."[53] The *Fayetteville Observer* was among many white papers to frame the issue, not in racial terms at all, but as a question of the rule of law. It noted, "Lynching is a slap in the face to the very majesty of the law, and the law to keep its respect must deal with lynchers in the same manner it would deal with a nest of rattlesnakes."[54]

Raper believed a mob murder ratified a community's hierarchy by allowing dispossessed whites a temporary and sanctioned shake-up of the social order. Raper described the way it worked. "The man-hunt provides an opportunity for carrying and flourishing firearms with impunity, a privilege which appeals strongly to the more irresponsible elements. Moreover, man-hunts and lynchings make it possible for obscure and irresponsible people to play the roles of arresting officers, grand jurors, trial jurors, judges, and executioners. An added attraction is that they often afford an avenue of emotional escape from a life so drab and unilluminated that any alternative is welcomed."[55] Raper saw in lynching a kind of backwoods charivari, a ritualized upsetting of a community's social structure that jeopardized democratic institutions as it ratified its social castes.[56]

"Lynchings and what they mean"

The publicity campaign waged by the Southern Commission on the Study of Lynching saturated the media and was carried throughout the South. Its message was brought to classrooms and church halls and Elks Clubs across the region by dozens of southern women and men. In addition, UNC Press also published another book, *Lynching and the Law*, by James Harmon Chadbourn, in 1933, which traced legal efforts and precedents in the fight against lynching. Although the book received less fanfare and acclaim than Raper's work, it reinforced the message of *The Tragedy of Lynching*. Between 1931 and 1936, Raper also wrote three summary reports printed as pamphlets—"South's Leaders Impeach Judge Lynch," "Lynchings and What They Mean," and "The Mob Still Rides"—and two separately published case studies of lynchings—"The Mob Murder of S. S. Mincey" and "The Plight of Tuscaloosa." Each publication generated press releases and was reported and commented on by dozens of local and national newspapers, magazines, and church publications, whose editors had been cultivated through the 1920s by Alexander, Eleazer, and Odum for the Interracial Commission.[57]

After the formation of the Southern Commission on the Study of Lynching in 1930, these efforts were greatly extended in the white press by the commission's prominent journalists, George Fort Milton and Julian Harris, and in the black press by Charles S. Johnson, R. R. Moton, and John Hope. And when *The Tragedy of Lynching* was published in spring 1933, the Interracial Commission pushed the UNC Press to get the book in the hands of as many reviewers as possible. In addition, because it wanted to reach a broad audience, the committee persuaded Couch to cut the price of books from $4 to $2.50 apiece and paid the difference themselves.[58] More than a hundred correspondents wrote Raper for copies. Letters came from New York, Los Angeles, London, and Washington, from Hampton Institute, Yale, and Chicago, from Greenwood, Mississippi, and Lubbock, Texas, West Palm Beach and Selma, Alabama.[59]

At the time it assigned Raper to investigate the lynchings of 1930, the commission had organized four separate committees on publishing and publeic relations, targeted to the publication of books and pamphlets and to promoting them in southern and northern newspapers and in national, civic, and religious magazines.[60] Eleazer and the committee distributed the case studies as widely as they could. They mimeographed case studies for the social science departments of southern colleges and universities. They prepared a brief historical statement about lynchings detailing the factors shown to reduce its incidence. And they printed pamphlets for church and civic groups, to encourage them to work with police to defuse potential mobs.[61] Couch ran ads in the *Nation,* the *New Republic, Survey-Graphic,* the *Virginia Quarterly Review,* and *Publishers' Weekly,* "which goes to all the book stores and libraries of any importance" in the country.[62]

Copies were sent to a broad and varied list of reviewers in both black and white presses and in the publishing industry, extending from the *Montgomery Advertiser, New Orleans Times-Picayune,* and *Macon Telegraph,* to the *Chicago Tribune, Springfield Republican,* and *Sacramento Bee;* from *Time, American Mercury,* and *New Republic,* to the *Chicago Defender, Pittsburgh Courier,* and *Houston Informer;* from the *Yale Review, Virginia Quarterly Review,* and *Catholic Historical Review* to the *Journal of Negro Education, Crisis,* and Fisk University; from Walter Lippmann to the Supreme Court. Reviews then appeared across the country, from the *San Diego Sun* to the *Boston Globe,* and all across the South, from the *El Paso Herald-Post* to the *Charlotte Observer.*[63]

The Associated Press (AP) became a vital part of the commission's antilynching strategy. As Raper explained, "There were a lot of threatened lynchings prevented after the book came out and after the Association of Southern Women for Prevention of Lynching was formed. They simply watched the Associated Press releases and they had a contact with the AP man in Atlanta and he told them when there was something brewing somewhere. 'This was reported, get your sheriff and see if you can't get this one handled.'"[64]

By the early 1930s, the larger metropolitan newspapers across the country had begun to condemn any community where a lynching had taken place. The effect, Raper felt, was to tighten the silence in small towns. In every single town, he found people opposed to lynching. Often, though, townspeople who were heartily opposed to mob rule remained quiet, loathe to parade their community's shame in the press. Raper came to see that, in that shame, as well as in the fear of reprisal over speaking out, most whites believed that the sooner news of a lynching died the better. Even local blacks felt compromised into silence. "Most Negro property owners," Raper observed time and again, "have close friends among the influential white people, and their properties are generally secure in proportion as this sheltering protection is maintained."[65] Everywhere, he found black and white southerners who would have testified against lynchers if they could have counted on legal protection. Raper became an advocate of federal antilynching legislation in part because he felt it would lead to more indictments and convictions. Federal legislation would allow people to exercise their responsibilities as citizens.[66]

"That was the end of it, and everybody felt relief"

In contrast to the high drama and passions surrounding the mob murders he was investigating, Raper's tone in *The Tragedy of Lynching* was matter-of-fact and declarative, even in its criticism.[67] "In 1930, twenty-one persons were lynched in the United States," begins *The Tragedy of Lynching*. The voice of this scientific presentation has an earnestness of purpose, but in the cool accounting of his prose, Raper sounded more resigned than outraged. "Mobs are capable of unbelievable atrocity," he reported.

> James Irwin at Ocilla, Georgia, was jabbed in his mouth with a sharp pole. His toes were cut off joint by joint. His fingers were similarly removed, and his teeth extracted with wire pliers. After further unmentionable mutilations, the Negro's still living body was saturated with gasoline and a lighted match was applied. As the flames leaped up, hundreds of shots were fired into the dying victim. During the day, thousands of people from miles around rode out to see the sight. Not till nightfall did the officers remove the body and bury it.[68]

In his book on southern liberalism, historian Morton Sosna wrote that "Raper presented every conceivable argument against lynching, ethical, economic, practical, and political."[69] But the absence of a religious argument is conspicuous. Looking at the way the CIC had changed since the mid-1920s, it is important to see that commission's outlook had become secular. Its appeals were to fraternity and equality in economics and politics. There is little sense of an appeal to Christian ideals as such, and nothing of biblical rhetoric in *The Tragedy of Lynching*. Instead, Raper's realism was scientific in tone, sympathetic in feel, and ripe with ironic comment. "At Honey Grove," as he told the story, "the wife of one minister ran to the home of another minister and called to his wife: 'Come, I never did see a nigger burned and I mustn't miss this chance.'"[70]

Because the commission intended this sociological study for a broad readership, George Fort Milton edited Raper's drafts, sharpened his irony, clarified his prose, and streamlined his construction. Milton added a journalist's preference for nouns and verbs over adjectives and adverbs. He subdivided the table of contents to make it more accessible. He cut pompous, ponderous, and prejudicial sentences. "Too much rhetoric," he complained a few times. Leading phrases—"It is of interest to note"—received the red pencil. "The reader will decide whether it is of interest," he told Raper.[71] When Odum wrote to Raper at the end of 1930, "Your style is certainly smoothing up nicely and has quite a kick to it," he had seen Milton's influence at work.[72]

For his part, Raper had to contend with input from four hands: Milton; Julian Harris, who, with a Pulitzer Prize for his work with the *New York Times* and his paternal pedigree, was not about to be outedited; R. B. Eleazer, the Interracial Commission's director of public relations; and Dr. W. J. McGloughlin, president of the Southern Baptist Convention. Raper recalled, "One of the challenges of my life was to get those four men to agree to anything, because each one of them is a prima donna in his own right."[73]

The Tragedy of Lynching was published just as the retrial of the Scottsboro Boys was focusing national attention on the twin problems of lynching and the patterns of the southern judicial system. In March 1931, nine black teenagers had been arrested and accused of raping two white women in a freight car near Paint Rock, Alabama. They were quickly tried and convicted, based on the shaky testimony of the women, and eight were sentenced to death. The Communist Party's International Labor Defense (ILD) initiated a legal and political campaign on their behalf. The ILD first battled the National Association for the Advancement of Colored People (NAACP) for control of the case, then broadcast claims that the accusation represented capitalist oppression and southern class rule. Protests against Alabama justice erupted throughout the country. A retrial was granted in March 1933, during which one of the women recanted her accusation.

Soon after the first trial began, George Fort Milton wrote Raper and predicted the case would become a cause célèbre. In the end, Scottsboro raised the visibility of Raper's work, and the commission benefited from the notoriety of the case. UNC Press's W. T. Couch wrote, for example, in a letter to national magazines accompanying review copies, "In view of the imminence of what appears to be legal lynching in the Scottsboro Case, may I call your attention to the interesting testimony on the prevalence of legal lynching in the South given *The Tragedy of Lynching*."[74] Instead of deflecting attention from the nexus between the controversial case and the commission's work, as Alexander would have done in the 1920s, the Interracial Commission now capitalized on it. And *The Tragedy of Lynching* added a scientific underpinning and a reasonable analysis to the growing sense of many white southerners, their consciences pricked by the blatant injustice of the Scottsboro trial, that the violence in their society against blacks was uncivilized.[75]

"It is the New South itself speaking"

Writing in the *Nation*, Walter White claimed *The Tragedy of Lynching* couldn't have been more timely. Its significance, he said, "lies in the fact that such a dissecting of mob murder could come and has come from out of the deep South. Every person who has been stirred by the Scottsboro and Crawford cases should read the book in order to understand the background of the social, economic, racial, and political forces which have made Scottsboro possible."[76] *The Tragedy of Lynching* exposed usual myths surrounding lynching, White wrote, and it tackled racial myths, too. White also took the opportunity to jab the communist defense of the Scottsboro defendants. He and Raper shared antipathy toward the doctrinaire. Communism would only unite capitalists and white workers in a campaign against the black proletariat, White believed. Much better to rely on practical studies like *The Tragedy of Lynching* than manifestos or theorizing.

Before the review was published, White wrote to congratulate Raper. "Having dealt with the subject myself for so many years I had about reached the stage where I did not believe that any lengthy book on the subject could possibly hold my interest. . . . I am certain that the book is going to do a tremendous amount of good, especially, as I have pointed out in the *Nation*, because it is the New South itself speaking."[77]

The white southern press responded the same way. *The Macon Telegraph* warned, "Unless we are to be branded for all time with the stigma of barbarism, this crime must end. It is not some holier-than-thou Yankee who is telling us of our faults, but leaders among our own people."[78] The southern origins of *The Tragedy of Lynching* could even play on southern chauvinism. The *Columbia State* assured its readers, "The thoroughness of the investigation may be accepted when it is known that it was conducted under a Commission composed of eleven well-known men of the South."[79]

The book's broad and overwhelmingly positive reception indicated the southern press and at least some of the public were willing to reconsider the myths that justified white mob violence.[80] Even much of the rural, southern press endorsed, at least in print, the notion that lynching reflected badly on white civilization.[81] One element underpinning the change of heart was pragmatism. Few white editors were inclined, during the depths of the Depression, to advocate anything that might further isolate the South from the rest of the nation, especially economically. Most southern newspapers of any size carried a news story and an editorial supporting Raper's findings. Both in the South and nationally, virtually all of the notice was positive. Some papers reported the findings as breaking news stories. "Innocent People are put to Death," announced the *Macon News*. "Majority of Mob Murders Preventable, Students of Crime Report," ran a headline in the *Birmingham News*. Raper tallied up the clippings. "Before *The Tragedy of Lynching* had been off the press four months extensive and favorable comment appeared in the American press: more than 60 reviews and editorials in southern white newspapers, 28 articles in Northern newspapers, 12 articles in Negro newspapers, and 27 articles in regional and national magazines."[82]

As if to illustrate literally the cultural distance Raper was crossing in advocating racial justice, even in the northern press, the *New York Times* ran its full-page review alongside a pen-and-ink sketch of three grinning "pickaninnies," dancing and playing banjoes over a caption that read, "Nigger Heaven." Nevertheless, the *Times* was struck by Raper's reasoned and methodical approach. The northern press was by and large as surprised as Walter White and the southern press that a white southerner was capable of producing such a work. The *Times* reviewer claimed, "It would be difficult to praise too highly the careful manner in which the facts are marshaled, the impartiality of presentation, the value of the information assembled for those who would understand the causes of lynching. Here is a source book of genuine worth."[83]

In April 1933, Walter Mills's review of *The Tragedy of Lynching* ran on the front page of the *New York Herald Tribune*'s important and well-read weekly book section, pushing inside *Miss Lonelyhearts*, by Nathaniel West, and Faulkner's *A Green Bough*. Mills viewed Raper's book as background to the Scottsboro case, because it explored the wider tragedy, "more impersonal but more enduring than the immediate tragedy in the court room." He applauded the broader impulse to correct southern racial justice. Written by a southerner and published in the South, the book itself was "a fine monument of the South's own determination to meet its problem."[84] The consensus was that *The Tragedy of Lynching* in itself was an indication that the South was growing more modern in its racial outlook. The *Herald Tribune* had previously run a Lewis Gannett column on the book. After reading Raper, Gannett wrote, "Mobs do not come out of the nowhere. . . . Lynchings are not the work of men suddenly possessed of a strange madness; they are the logical issues of prejudice and lack of respect for the law and personality, plus a sadistic desire to participate in the excitement of mob trials and the brutalities of mob torture and murder." For mob violence, Raper had convinced Gannett, "There's always a reason."[85]

Many of the reviews spoke to the book's documentary character. The *Wesleyan Christian Advocate* commented,

> Objective in its treatment, scientific in its compilation of data, this volume . . . is sensational only as the facts are sensational. It convinces as it shocks. The style is forceful; the arrangement is good. While scholarly in method, it makes an appeal to the general reader. The author illuminates the statistics with telling details. He has an uncanny ability for running on data first hand. This nose for news which makes him so admirable a reporter is combined with a rare skill in evaluation of material.[86]

And the *Mid-Monthly Survey* captured Raper's optimism and his liberal approach to social science. "The note of cheer in the book is the evidence which the analysis contributes to faith in education and the spread of intelligent influence."[87]

A similar comment came in a review by Yale sociologist John Dollard. "The only criticism possible seems to be the impracticable one that it is only one book and not a series of volumes going into still further detail in spreading out before us this fundamental sociological material. It would be very interesting to see what would happen if, in his next study of lynching, Dr. Raper were to take on an associate, trained in dynamic psychology, with the aim of tying the observed material into a significant theory of human nature."[88] Dollard's mention of "dynamic psychology" anticipated his own 1937 classic study of the South, *Caste and Class in a Southern Town*.

Some reviews concentrated on the ghoulishness of *The Tragedy of Lynching*—"This is a gruesome book to read," cautioned the *Dallas Morning News*[89]—

while others called it sociological, and James Weldon Johnson described it as "the most scientific study of the subject yet made."[90] The *Columbia Missourian* caught another paradox. "Although this book resembles a text, with its material outlined and indexed, it is so sincerely and vividly written that everyone will enjoy it."[91]

Alain Locke, the novelist, critic, and cultural analyst, whose anthology, *The New Negro,* inspired the Harlem Renaissance, wrote a "Retrospective Review of the Negro Literature of 1933" for *Opportunity,* in which he considered fiction, nonfiction, and poetry that spoke to the black experience in America. When it came to modern social science, Locke claimed he would trade a dozen detailed historical studies for a single such interpretive study. What social science needed most, Locke said, was the kind of analysis Raper provided, which attended to social forces, attitudes, and traditions, rather than a repetition of facts—although the facts needed fixing, too. Locke pointed to Dabney's *Liberalism in the South,* but singled out for special comment "Mr. Raper's brilliant and fearless study of lynching."[92]

With all its positive recognition, sales of *The Tragedy of Lynching* were poor. Couch put it down to the Depression. None of Raper's books ever became big sellers, however, and no one had expected sociological research to fly off the shelves, no matter how much life was infused into them. More importantly were the reviews themselves. Raper talked in terms of his books' ability to garner notice for its ideas, and for this reason, reviews in the press were perhaps more important than book sales. Raper would say of his books, "They all got a tremendous range of reviews when they came out, which is more important than getting the book around, if you have to choose between the two." He believed that to sell five or ten thousand copies—or even fifty thousand copies—was less important in terms of producing social change than attracting reviews and news coverage that might reach 20 million. "Most people don't have time to read books. They're not going to read books. They're just going to get impressions about this, that, or the other." Not that book publishing wasn't critically important. But publishing could only open a door, not carry people through it.[93]

Looking back from the 1970s, Raper remained certain that *The Tragedy of Lynching* had changed what most whites considered acceptable. The book "meant that Congressmen were no longer, in their filibusters, going to say anything in the world about lynchings to protect white women. That was the end of it, and everybody felt relief," he said. "It was over. They'll have troubles here sometimes, but the basic justification was undercut. It was buried. And that one had to go, before anything much could be done in the field of civil rights."[94]

Apart from the authorship of a white southerner, what made *The Tragedy of Lynching* new was not so much Raper's conclusions, but the way it was designed to appeal to the press, to give this scientific research the widest public notice possible. Couch worked with Raper, Alexander, and Eleazer to develop a publicity campaign to spread notice of Raper's Progressive-minded conclusions to as many people as possible through the southern and national press, including newspapers, magazines, pamphlets, community lectures, and radio. People didn't even have to read *The Tragedy of Lynching*. For the book to have an impact, southerners just had to know it existed. When a white southerner wrote a book that came to the same conclusions as Walter White's, and incorporated White's historical conclusions into a contemporary account, the response was electric.

"A reality of greater authenticity"

Lynching studies were only one aspect of Raper's pursuit of progressive politics through social science conceived in the documentary mode. He was among a number of sociologists who developed a subjective sense of the people they studied, in addition to providing factual accounts of social groups. His approach to sociology, consistent with the goals of documentary, was to make his work accessible to the widest possible public while remaining rigorously scientific. He spoke to local civic groups, conducted radio interviews, taught classes at women's colleges, organized union workers, and then was hired by the New Deal to administer rural development programs. He took pains to serialize his studies in local newspapers and was pleased to see his books displayed at county fairs. He used all these platforms and media to advance a liberal viewpoint that he offered as a common-sense kind of realism.

Raper's realism worked as a tool of political activism and as a modern, aesthetic, and analytic perspective. All through the 1930s, he spread the message that liberalism was part of what it meant to be modern. He told a group of parents and teachers in Atlanta one night that community solutions were inseparable from urbanization. "The Community Chest is the modern city's way of paying for the right of its citizens to work where they please. The modern city does not ignore its defectives; it takes care of them. The modern city aids in the rehabilitation of its inefficient citizens, and also carries on specific programs for preventive work."⁹⁵ *The Tragedy of Lynching* makes the case that lynching was old-fashioned, as well as immoral. By 1933, few editorial writers, even the most prejudiced, any longer wanted to think of themselves as anachronistic. Raper was among a number of liberal southerners who equated racial justice with being modern.

Characteristically, Raper summed up and concluded *The Tragedy of Lynching* by emphasizing dignity and community. "Fundamentally," he wrote, "lynching is an expression of a basic lack of respect for human beings and for organized society." Rather than insisting on personal liberty, Raper stressed the dignity of the individual, and the importance of respect for a collective citizenship was the prime mover of Raper and other New Dealers. Virginius Dabney had outlined the creed in his influential *Liberalism in the South,* published by Couch a year before *The Tragedy of Lynching.* Raper read Dabney with enthusiasm. "An abiding respect for the dignity and worth of the average man is, indeed, an even more essential ingredient of a liberal society than a lively concern for the right of the individual to freedom of thought and action," he had concluded. To Raper, as to Dabney and other southern liberals of the 1930s, a government that respected all of its people, inevitably granted each individual freedom of movement and conscience.⁹⁶

Dabney defined liberalism as instrumental to Raper's generation of Progressives. He viewed it as a politically minded search for a reality of greater authenticity and individuality. "It might be said, indeed," he wrote, "that an individual wins reality for himself only as he takes part in this intense search of the modern age for more genuine and complete liberty."⁹⁷ Raper was guided by his fealty to what he described as a sense of "common humanity." "It does have in common this Jeffersonian democracy," he said. "It has quite as much, I think, of fair play. The brotherhood-of-man business, if it doesn't have fair play and representative government in it, I don't think it stands up very well when the pressure comes."⁹⁸

Raper and the commission "happened into a frame of presentation," as Raper put it, that attracted attention and favorable comment. "Here at last," felt the press, "is a factual presentation of this phenomenon."⁹⁹ Raper's studies of the South aimed to combine accuracy and objectivity with a subjective viewpoint—to achieve immediacy through the telling details, while at the same time analyzing the underlying structure and dynamics of a social condition.

The model Raper embraced had roots in a founding document of the

Chicago School of Sociology, W. I. Thomas's 1912 study, "Race Psychology: Standpoint and Questionnaire, with Particular Reference to the Immigrant and the Negro." Thomas's approach to research was to send students all over the city of Chicago to track down different kinds of evidence in interviews and official records, as well as newspapers, club minutes, school curricula, even handbills and almanacs. Thomas also assumed that his subjects were living within a dynamic society, and he assumed racial equality. In all this, he had been influenced by Franz Boas's conception of cultural anthropology. To Thomas, statistics in themselves were nothing but unknown causal processes. As historian Dorothy Ross puts it, they needed "to be interpreted in the context of the whole life. Thus the life record of case study was the perfect type of sociological material."[100]

Statistics needed to be integrated with sensibility in this approach to modern social science inquiry. Attitudes were explicable only in the context of a whole life, with data gleaned from ephemera, as well as municipal records. Such an approach must have come as second nature to Raper, a sociologist who had "sampled opinion" as he cut hair in his college dorm room. His case studies in *The Tragedy of Lynching*, and the portraits he later painted in *Preface to Peasantry, Sharecroppers All*, and *Tenants of the Almighty*, all reflect Thomas's approach. Raper was not the only writer attracted by this new kind of search for sociohistorical clues in out-of-the-way places. William Carlos Williams developed a similar protocol to vivify his historical imagination for his 1925 study, *In the American Grain*:

> Everywhere I have tried to separate out from the original records some flavor of an actual peculiarity the character denoting shape which the unique force has given. Now it will be the configuration of a man like Washington, and now a report of the witchcraft trials verbatim, a story of a battle at sea—for the odd note there is in it, a letter by Franklin to prospective emigrants; it has been my wish to draw from every source one thing, the strange phosphorus of the life, nameless under an old misappellation.[101]

"A documentary imagination"

The photo project run by Roosevelt's Farm Security Administration (FSA) defined documentary photography in the 1930s. The work of Evans, Lange, Jack Delano, Arthur Rothstein, and a dozen others appeared across the emerging landscape of America's new media, from *Life* magazine to "photoplay" newspapers. FSA photography aimed to document connections among history, sociology, economics, and cultural geography, and to galvanize public opinion around New Deal programs.[102] In Edward Steichen's phrase, the FSA photographs were "human documents."[103] These goals matched Raper's ambitions for his own work. FSA photo editor Edwin Rosskam—who worked with Raper to select photographs for *Sharecroppers All*—emphasized that the best documentary conceived of its subjects organically, rather than as separate pieces of a puzzle. Documentary photography was an aesthetic corollary to the renewed attention to regionalism in the 1930s.

In addition to attention to dynamism and organicism, many influential social science research studies explicitly attended to the strong emotions that inspired them. These studies were intended to not only depict American society, but to contribute to its reform. Important studies of African Americans in southern life, most notably John Dollard's *Caste and Class in a Southern Town* (1937) and Allison Davis's *Deep South* (1941), were influenced by their authors' personal involvement in a particular locality. Dollard, for example, was always conscious of his status as a "participant observer." But he did not approach his interviews in Indianola, Mississippi, as an outsider. Instead, he "settled into the life of the community and was variously defined as a boarder, a friend, a buyer of gasoline, a person with hay fever."[104]

The South of the 1930s was probably the most thoroughly documented society anywhere. For example, at the end of the decade, W. T. Couch, editor of the University of North Carolina Press, documented the authentic in a volume titled *These Are Our Lives*—a collection of direct, first-person stories of working-class southerners, published to extend the writing of sociology to the folk it studied. Because of his own work and Odum's Institute for Social Science Research, Couch staked a claim for the South in the development of this kind of study. "So far as I know, this method of portraying the quality of life of a people, of revealing the real workings of institutions, customs, habits, has never before been used for the people of any region or country."[105]

Through the 1930s, Couch used his press to advance "the writing and reading of popular books, especially of works that will give more realistic views of present-day economic, political, and social life."[106] In 1932, he published Virginius Dabney's *Liberalism in the South* and claimed for it tremendous influence. The next year, he published his own *Culture in the South,* which incorporated the same liberal, antiagrarian perspective that Raper and the CIC held.¹⁰⁷ Under Couch, UNC Press became a major cultural force and the South's most important vehicle of social criticism.¹⁰⁸

The Tragedy of Lynching had all the characteristics of a documentary. As Couch touted it, "This book attracts immediately the reader's attention by virtue of its unique style of presentation. Dr. Raper has not given us merely a compendium of data about the lynchings, but he has given it in such rare and racy style that it grasps the reader from start to finish. . . . This book is thorough in research, graphic in style, fair and unbiased in statement."¹⁰⁹ The even-handedness was not what characterized *The Tragedy of Lynching* or documentary, though. Its "unique style of presentation" was the book's combination of objectivity and "racy" tone—its immediacy, expressiveness, and vividness.

PREFACE TO PEASANTRY

Old South versus New Deal in the Black Belt of Georgia

The first time he saw Greene County, twenty-six-year-old Arthur Raper was sitting on a train headed toward the sea from Atlanta. Past his window streaked pile after dirty pile of sawdust, strewn across the dead landscape as though the detritus of the smoky sky above them. Great expanses of once-fertile soil, once among the oldest and richest plantation land in the cotton South, had been depleted by cultivation, greatly exacerbated by the boll weevil. By the early 1920s, all through the old plantation lands, pines had taken over many of the fields and already grown large enough for saw logs. Soon saw mills were puffing away all over the county. In 1926, when Raper first arrived in Greene, sawmills had become the county's main source of income, where the land had once served King Cotton.[1]

The year before, Raper had lived on the same dormitory floor as a young fellow from a rural Black Belt county in the piedmont southeast of Atlanta, who was working toward a master's in economics. Floyd Corry was quiet and introspective, but he had a lot to say on long walks about his uncle "Punch" Dolvin and his hometown life back in Siloam, Greene County, Georgia. Corry had gone home after graduation, eventually to become the county's school superintendent. After Raper accepted the job in Atlanta with the Interracial Commission, he took the train to visit his friend out in the country.

Corry was home running the store his uncle "Punch" had started, buying up land an acre or so at a time, trying to reestablish his family's fortunes. Floyd's father, W. R. Corry, had been a large planter at the turn of the century, but had lost everything after the boll weevil. Raper recalled, "So now here this young man Floyd Corry that I met at Vanderbilt had in his soul a determination to restore his family to its rightful position, and that rightful position was to be a land owner, have property, be connected with the local bank, to know the sheriff and have him pay attention to him when he talked to him and what not—as goals in an old plantation county."²

Raper was amazed at what he saw in Greene. Old plantation houses were in decay. Fields were overgrown in pines and broom sage. Corry himself lived in a part of the county where small, more diversified farmers still survived on poorer, "white" or chalky soil. But the old plantation tracts, built on what had been the most productive soil in the region, were most often farmed-out ruins.

A decade after the boll weevil first began to plague the rural South, black farmers and sharecroppers were still fleeing the countryside by the thousands, completely unprepared for crowded cities fast becoming resistant to streams of poverty-stricken Negroes. How would a modern, progressive society respond to these refugees from a dying, agrarian past? To Raper, this was the most compelling question facing modern America. The answer would portend the prospects of democracy in machine-age America and throughout the world.

Raper quickly came to the conclusion that Corry "lived right square in the middle of this area where population was leaving the farm the fastest and coming up to Atlanta." From migration statistics he had seen in Chapel Hill, Raper knew that, since 1920, more farm refugees proportionally had fled the stretch of Black Belt between Atlanta and Augusta than anywhere else in the United States. Raper returned to Atlanta to talk with Alexander about Greene County, and about his discussions with Ada Woolfolk, head of Atlanta's Family Welfare Society, who had shown him how many people she was trying to help had come from Greene and the rest of the old plantation counties. According to Woolfolk, 92.2 percent of Atlanta's families on relief had been born outside the city. Three-quarters of those families were from the small towns and open country, mostly in the upper and older end of the Georgia Black Belt. The greatest number of Atlanta's first welfare clients were from Greene, Morgan, and Putnam counties, and others nearby. This was the region that had most suffered the exodus of the 1920s. Greene, along with neighboring Putnam and Hancock counties, had formed one locus of the Great Migration. When Raper compared Woolfolk's data with that of other cities, South and North, he saw American society unprepared for such drastic change. "The cities of the nation can no longer ignore conditions in the rural Black Belt," Raper came to believe, "except at their own expense." Greene County, Georgia, would represent the old plantations from which so many people were still fleeing to the cities as virtual refugees.[3]

Alexander and Raper were determined to contrast Greene with a county where few people had left, hoping to throw into clearer relief the reasons for Greene's great outmigration. Very few farmers had left nearby Macon County, so Raper had his comparison. Was it because race relations were better? Economic conditions? Political opportunities? Farming practices?[4]

Raper told Alexander that he believed he would find race relations to have been worse in Greene, where so many people had left, than in Macon, where they stayed. But he found the opposite. He determined that race relations were worse in younger Macon, where the plantation system had retained some economic vitality. They were better in Greene, where the plantation system had already fallen to pieces. Raper came to see the end of the plantation as the beginning of a racial realignment at a moment when social boundaries were still in flux and the cash economy was then shifting the economic and social exchanges of everyday life.[5]

Raper and Alexander were both fascinated by the dynamic between a people's culture and the way they use their land, in what Raper called "man-land" relations. In the context of Greene County, they concluded that the culture and economy of slavery continued to rule the plantation society into the modern era. Raper wanted to explore the roots of the racial system still so evident in a modified plantation system. Lynching was only the raw edge of the whole process of racial exploitation that the plantation system had inculcated in the Black Belt South. Raper hadn't been in Greene County a month before he could foresee what the Great Migration boded for the modern city. Alexander told him, as Raper recalled, "'Well, whatever you think you want to do. Why, let's talk about it and you can do it.'"[6]

Raper found that plantation agriculture, holding out against modern democracy, was ruining the South's chance to manage a change that would soon be sweeping across the land. The plantation system relied on a workforce that was not only amenable to instructions, but under complete control. Its workers lived in plantation housing, accepted the landlords' and merchants' accounting, and remained landless. Raper saw that the shiftlessness and irresponsibility of both black and white hands—about which owners so often complained—were actually requirements of the plantation system. The viability of the plantation system was threatened when tenants accumulated property or exhibited any independence.

The South's racial caste system ran against the grain of Raper's vision of what was required in a democratic polity. "Democracy," he told a group at the Highlander School, "is superior to other political systems only to the degree that it affords the rank and file of people larger opportunities for growth and responsible participation." Race in the South became Raper's litmus for modernity. The South's race problem moved in retrograde motion from the advances in democracy that Western political philosophy, science, and technology had been propelling the nation toward for two hundred years.[7] The entire system of race relations that entwined southern society made impossible Raper's ideal: a rational application of cooperative action to solve community problems, action that meant greater independence for each individual.[8] For Raper, Greene County represented an example of the living past. Greene would become the location for Raper's most focused sociological and political analysis of the way the southern caste system perverted the promise of citizen participation in democratic government.

Raper used Greene and Macon counties as a laboratory, a practical means of framing some of the major questions of modernity. He asked,

> Why have so many people gone to the cities, and what effect will this transition have upon society? In what ways are the automobile, radio, and motion picture altering the lives of our people? What are the social implications of public schools, of public health programs, of compulsory vaccination against communicable diseases? What is the meaning to society of the fact that the typical worker, who one hundred years ago lived in his own home and made products with his own tools, now lives in a city and works away from home upon machines owned by a man or group of men he has never seen? What are the causes, and what will be the results of the employment of women in industry?[9]

The kind of rural sociology Raper pursued in Greene and Macon was a way to watch the Old South fitfully disappear. But because the region was undergoing such tremendous strain—in economics, politics, and class and race relations—and because change was happening so rapidly, it was also the ideal place to ask, how will the nation respond to a seismic shift from a rural society to urban life?

"The South is facing—who knows what?"

To study the question closely, Raper traveled to the vanishing past, the outer edge of modern life and the core of the Old South, the lonely farm and the one-horse town, a place where he could watch and measure the remains of agrarian America as it disappeared beneath the tide of gasoline and electricity, mass media, and a national, free-market economy.

As the old, southern farming communities vanished, Raper saw the potential for racial violence as drifting into a new channel. After the rash of twenty-one lynchings that swept the South in 1930, the number of mob murders had dropped again, back down to eight two years later. By the mid-1930s, an increasingly urban, white South often turned to the courts—rather than frontier-type violence—but in ways designed to codify in law their control over blacks. Increasingly, by the mid-1930s, the courts were used to reshape political and economic boundaries. In Atlanta, for instance, a group of whites sued to oust black bell men from the city's hotels so that needy whites might take their jobs. Many small-town newspapers, for example, promoted a logical and constructive view of the problem. They advocated the elimination of lynching because, they said, the courts could convict and execute an accused black man more efficiently than a mob, with no damage to property and little outside interference.

Even though the threat of lynching had lessened, Raper was afraid that blacks would eventually respond with violence to the legal and systematic limitations they faced in both the countryside and the city. "The South is facing—who knows what?" Raper wrote to himself in early 1934. Only one thing was sure. "With the landowners and tenants barely holding on to the crumbling plantation system, the traditional rural South seems to be passing out of the picture."[10]

When Raper first traveled to Greene County in 1926, it was already suffering an economic depression. His research convinced him that the source of Greene's poverty—apart from devastation of the boll weevil—was the continuing hold of the traditions of the plantation economy, including its poor soil conservation practices, as well as the social and economic inequalities it had fostered. While to some, most notably the Old South historian U. B. Phillips, the plantation represented the seed-bed of the South's people and its culture, a school for civilization, Raper argued it was a school for dependency.

Stretching along a crescent from Virginia to Texas, two hundred counties across the South formed the Black Belt, where half or more of its people had descended from slaves. By the 1930s, the Black Belt was the ghost of the Old South. America's least democratic region had grown from the remains of the wealthiest and most fertile plantation lands.[11] "Openly justified," Raper observed, "are the terroristic methods used to disfranchise the Negro, and revered is the white primary which legalizes this disfranchisement."[12] To Raper, the plantation retained much of the "master-slave regime." Whether regnant or in decline, the plantation had prepared southern society for peasantry, rather than for the appearance of the traditional, independent American farmer. In fact, Raper claimed, "the majority of the plantation folk are subpeasants—no property, no self-direction, no hope of either." He concluded, "The collapse of the Black Belt plantation system is a preface to American peasantry."[13] The Black Belt South was the Jeffersonian republican's worst nightmare come true.

Greene and Macon counties represented the old and new of the Georgia Black Belt. Greene had been settled soon after the Revolutionary War by pioneers from Virginia and the Carolinas, and it became one of the South's first and most productive King Cotton counties. By 1854, three textile mills churned the Oconee River, which ran the length of the county. One of the earliest cotton plantation counties, Greene was also one of those most devastated by the collapse of the Confederacy, and it had been losing its population for decades. By 1930, the population of Greensboro, the county seat, had dwindled from three thousand people at the turn of the century to two thousand. Greene grew cotton, and corn to support cotton, with minor dairy and poultry enterprises supplementing the home production of some meat and other staples. In 1920, Greene's wealthiest individuals had still been among the largest landowners.[14] In 1934, Greene retained two small textile factories, but pines now spread across most of the old cotton country.

Macon, on the other hand, had not been established until 1837. It was settled largely by the overflow of population from the lower Piedmont counties of central Georgia. When Raper first started his work, Montezuma, Macon's county seat, had a population of 2,200 and Oglethorpe, almost a thousand. Beyond cotton and corn, Macon County also grew marketable quantities of asparagus, melons, pecans, and peanuts. Both counties are formed of rolling hills, both have rivers running their length—the Oconee River and the Flint, in Greene and Macon, respectively—and the climate is much the same in both. Greene covers 416 square miles, with a population density in 1934 of 30.3 per square mile; Macon's population density was 50 on its 332 square miles.

Greene and Macon both ranked below the state average by almost every social, economic, and educational index, including per capita income, number of physicians per person, infant mortality, number of automobiles, and income tax returns. This was the norm for rural Black Belt counties. Raper explained, "Although the whites own more than ninety-five out of every hundred acres, a little over half the rural white families are landless. They live as renters and croppers and wage hands in competition with the Negroes in these same tenure classes." Depressed conditions for both whites and blacks were the logical outcome of a racial caste system.

When Raper first visited the two counties in 1926, neither county had a hard-surface road across it or a single paved street. Few resources in either county were available for public investment. Both ranked below the state average in terms of such social and economic indicators as the numbers of doctors, automobiles, and telephones. In Greene, Raper examined not only the decline of the agricultural economy, but how the decline affected the way its people lived.[15]

Both counties had a mix of soils, creating what were called "red" and "white" lands, and having determined two social structures in each county. Greene's first, great, slaveholding plantations were established in the northern half of the county, where the richer, red soil was found. Smaller farms were established by poorer whites in the remainder of the cheaper, less fertile, chalkier, white lands south of the Oconee. As the large tracts were depleted following the Civil War, and the slaves were converted to wage laborers, the poorer, white land became more valuable by comparison. When blacks were allowed to buy any land, it was almost invariably in the white-land southern section. By the time Raper arrived, the once-fertile red lands of the rich plantations had become the most devastated, and its crumbling plantation houses—mostly occupied by poor white tenants—were most often in worse shape than the meager farms of the few even-poorer blacks who worked the chalky, white-land farms.[16]

Greene, the archetypal, old Black Belt county, established in the late eighteenth century, had reached its peak of development by the middle of the nineteenth century. Macon, much younger, had not been struck so badly by the boll weevil and was not so heavily dependent on the plantation system. Why had Macon County's farming population remained stable, while a third of Greene's population had fled? Raper concluded, the boll weevil had hit Greene County harder than it had Macon, and he examined in detail how this had happened. Also, Greene's older and more firmly established plantation system had more cleanly stripped the soil of its fertility than had Macon's, and thereby forced its sharecroppers off the land. The point he wanted to make was that Greene had suffered longer under a decaying plantation system.

Raper and Alexander wanted to study how life in Greene and Macon counties would change over time, especially under the pressure of social and economic dislocation during the Great Depression. So as soon as he was done checking page proofs for *The Tragedy of Lynching*, in 1933, Raper began driving again to Greene and Macon. Back in the late 1920s, he had visited all the black and white farms in both counties, and he had toured all the schools. As he returned in 1934 and 1935, though, he and Alexander were more interested in seeing the effects of the New Deal on black farm families, so he drove out to see, if he could, every family of black owners, tenants, and croppers in both counties to gather information about them and about their family members who had moved to the city. And he spent a lot of time poking around and just talking with blacks and whites in Greensboro and Montezuma, the two county seats, and befriending a lot of the folks, eccentrics and local leaders, alike, including Floyd Corry's old father, W. R.

"Look here what I found!"

W. R. Corry was a character out of Faulkner. He had grown up the eldest son of a plantation family that had suffered a precipitous decline. W. R. was still accepted in the "best" houses throughout the county and was well connected to its leaders, but by the mid-1930s, he had been reduced to finding, buying, and selling cattle. Now, W. R.'s son, Floyd, was determined to resuscitate the family name and position. His father saw quiet Floyd as a loner, so to encourage a friendship with Arthur, W. R. went out of his way for the young sociologist. Raper would tell W. R.,

> Now, I'm going day after tomorrow down around Liberty and Scull Shoals," which was part of the county where the big plantations had collapsed, "and I'm going to be down there looking for some cattle, and if you want to ride along with me, why, I'll be glad for you to go with me."
>
> You couldn't have bought it, because here was a man who knew everybody, was a member of one of the families, but was doing this rather menial thing of rustling cattle. So he was telling me, when we went by the Armor place or went by the Adams place and got to the Park's Mill and this and that—he told me all about these things, just perfectly candid, you

know, about what was happening. So I began getting that part of the picture from him.[17]

As would be the case throughout his career, Raper combined the anecdotal and the sociological to approach a situation from both the particular and the general at the same time.

Raper's research was a matter not only of science, but of personal diplomacy, too, and he tried to keep an eye out for trouble. He took pains, while researching county records in the courthouse, to be open about his work. He might see some fellow in the courthouse records room who might be curious about this stranger in town who was all of a sudden in his office all the time. "Look here what I found!" Raper he would call over to him, his finger on the page of some ledger or record book.

> Of course, I was in there a lot and people could get suspicious about what in heck is Raper doing here, so when folks would come in to check something, if I could make an easy conversation with them and show them something they'd be interested in, that I was interested in—here's the way I decided to say it—they looked at it. No harm in that, you see. So I was, I thought, being sensible and friendly. So I got that information.

Raper began to fill his notebooks with stories that spoke not only to the social strictures of the small-town, Depression South, but also to his own resourcefulness in turning those strictures to account. After a while, first in 1926, then in the mid-1930s, Raper was able to "sort of come up." He had become acquainted with the school boards, the county commissioners, all the towns' leaders and officials. He became good friends with the sheriff. "And so there would be times when somebody would snipe at Raper a little bit, you know; these fellows would say, 'He's all right.'"[18]

"A radical organization!"

Through the winter of 1934, Raper tramped through one cold, Negro schoolhouse after another, in Montezuma, and Macon City, and Friar's Point, Georgia, where the condition of walls and ceilings offered a ready opportunity, as he said, for the study of geography, meteorology, and astronomy. Up in Chapel Hill, another of Odum's young regionalist sociologists, Guy Johnson, was writing his friend, Robert Eleazer, who directed the Interracial Commission's publicity. "I have been intending for some time to tell you how much I liked the report on 'The Plight of Tuscaloosa,'" Johnson began. His own work, springing from Odum's institute, was in black folk culture, but he followed the activities of the Interracial Commission closely. Given his affiliations, interests, and politics, he could hardly have done otherwise. Johnson had been fascinated by the publicity campaign mounted against lynching around the publication of *The Tragedy of Lynching* and, more recently, Raper's pamphlet analyzing a 1933 lynching in an outlying section of Tuscaloosa, Alabama. Johnson wrote Eleazer elatedly, "It seems to me to be as thorough as anyone could want. I do not see what more the Civil Liberties Union or any other organization could ask for. In fact it is so frank and truthful that it would probably confirm the belief of certain conservative citizens that the Interracial Commission is a radical organization! Please extend my compliments to Arthur Raper for his part in the investigation."[19]

Johnson was himself a bit incredulous at the idea that the Interracial Commission could be seen as radical. And he was right, of course. The Interracial Commission was revolutionary only in its ideals, which were rarely verbalized, except on occasion by Raper. Its official aims were always stated in the vaguest and least controversial of terms as greater cooperation between the races. Through the 1920s and 1930s, the commission never came out against segregation. And the first book it sponsored, *The Tragedy of Lynching*, protested only the most horrible and extreme manifestation of racial bigotry. But it was true that conservatives were calling the commission "communistic." The new Georgia governor, Eugene Talmadge, a Populist demagogue, had taken to lambasting the "red" organization in his official newspaper.[20] In the early 1920s, Alexander and Eleazer had reacted to criticism by withdrawing. By the mid-1930s, Raper had begun work on a second book, developed along with Alexander, that would push the commission's efforts even farther from its first days of genteel intervention.[21]

Preface to Peasantry, published in 1936, focused on the debilitating effects of racial inequalities, particularly in education, that resulted in an ever-more dependent population of both blacks and whites. In the book, a white southerner wrote plainly that the South needed to change its racial caste system or face slow starvation. The New Deal was stirring some of that change, Raper concluded, but its programs often lacked the resources or will to power to do so, and in some cases, most notably the Agricultural Adjustment Act's "plow-up," seemed to fly in the face of an agrarian culture.

"Here's how *we* live"

In each of his books about the South, spanning the 1930s and into the war, Raper tried to make his scholarly research serve in a practical way the farmers he was writing about. And he wrote with the warmth and insight of an insider. While a case could be made that he was working in the tradition of reform literature, Raper's was less a rural sequel to Jacob Riis's account of "the other half," and closer to something like "Here's How *We* Live." Raper criticized southern racial and class hierarchies, while trying to keep from alienating the black and white farmers and working people with whose welfare he was concerned. He knew firsthand about southern folks' capacity for Populist, anticapitalist criticism, but he also knew how skeptical the countryside was about big government. To cite a single of many examples, Governor Talmadge, whose support came from Georgia's white farmers and rural poor, had become one of the New Deal's most vigorous opponents.[22]

As Raper moved from an intense study of lynching to an assessment of the impact of the New Deal on southern blacks, he continued to combine quantifiable facts and human detail in his own adaptation of 1930s documentary. In *Preface to Peasantry*, he would take a picture that would criticize the social, political, and economic structure of rural Georgia, even as he created a portrait of the region that was filled with great warmth for its people.

Preface to Peasantry, like *The Tragedy of Lynching,* would be a social science study, another documentary snapshot. This time, though, it was to be a look at a whole society, at all the dynamics—social, racial, political, economic, and legal—swirling around the transformation of the rural South at the cusp of modernity, where the death of the plantation system had coincided with the plague of the boll weevil, from which a vast, landless underclass was being driven off the land and into the new cities of the industrial age. In its cool and ironic modern language, the encyclopedic *Preface to Peasantry* did what *The Tragedy of Lynching* could not do in its tight focus on mob murder. Beyond its masses of statistics and its controlled, detached tone, *Preface to Peasantry* was a wholesale critique of the system of beliefs at the core of white Southern society.

An integral part of that critique, Fisk sociologist Charles S. Johnson was involved in the shaping and conception of Raper's book, as he had been for *The Tragedy of Lynching*. Johnson agreed with Raper that it should be a comparative study, with Raper updating his findings from the late 1920s to analyze the impact of the New Deal politics on southern blacks and whites. "So far as I know there is nothing in the published literature that approaches this analysis of the agricultural situation in the Black Belt," Johnson concluded. "It is a social document of great importance."[23]

Even Raper's introduction to *Preface to Peasantry* mixed social science research with a tone of intimate connection to the people and land of Greene County.

> I have spent considerable time securing data from the tax digests, court records, and other public documents on file in the courthouses and in the relief offices. I have interviewed all the Negro landowners at their homes, many white landowners, and scores upon scores of wage hands and tenants of both races. I have gone to church on Sunday, hung around the store at night, sat through the picture show and attended the carnival over the weekend; now and then I have had the privilege of tramping after the hounds, or scrambling through the thickets along the Oconee and Flint rivers with farmers turned huntsmen and fishermen. Besides being a lot of fun, these various contacts have provided a basis for an understanding of attitudes and outlooks.[24]

Raper's approach in Greene County fit the imperative of documentary to depict the quotidian. "The Black Belt's way of life is best felt," he explained in *Preface to Peasantry*, "through the little everyday human incidents which may be observed anywhere. Pride is here, and wariness, good-natured humor, hard work, and protracted loafing."[25] Raper was concerned with such issues as the discrepancies in expenditures between black and white schools, for example, and in blacks' treatment in the courts and by the police. But he blended a scientific tone and rigorous quantification of data with a curiosity about how people lived and the ways in which they experienced their lives. He wanted to collect statistics on the education, income, population, and taxes of farmers and townspeople. But he also wanted to see how black croppers and whites mingled around the general store's hot stove as they bragged about their dogs. "We have not neglected specialized studies," Raper explained, "but have often used an episode to convey the meaning of a mass of statistics."[26]

"Upon the pinch of hunger"

Raper was developing this type of analysis right at the tipping point when, in such poor, agricultural counties, the agrarian tradition of household production of food, clothing, and household staples was giving way to a cash economy.

Between Raper's first visits with Floyd Corry and his last observation of New Deal programs, his research measured the changes across the divide between the 1929 Wall Street crash and the implementation of New Deal programs, beginning in 1933. He spent 1927 and 1928 doing fieldwork; compiling and analyzing the information took another two years. Raper first used the data gathered from every farm family, white and black, in Greene and Macon, in his dissertation, "Two Rural Black Belt Counties." He returned to update the data in the summer and fall of 1934.

In *Preface to Peasantry,* Raper posed dozens of particular and comprehensive questions, some statistical and general, others anecdotal and evocative. "What is the annual income of farm families? Do the Negroes live as well as the whites in the same tenure class? What did the planters think of the free distribution of Red Cross flour and cloth? What is the meaning of 'on the county'? Do Negroes and whites sit together around the stove at the Black Belt store? Why is court week so popular? What are the prospects for the future?"[27] Raper was taking as prompts all the questions Howard Odum had been peppering students and colleagues with in Chapel Hill since the early 1920s. Now Odum's most peripatetic disciple was aggressively pursuing all of his questions about society and modernity in the small-town cafes and cotton fields of the rural South.

In *Preface to Peasantry,* Raper offered a compelling argument about what he had learned. "Cotton culture not only has destroyed the soil, but also has resulted in the neglect of a large portion of the population." The plantation system determined that African Americans "were to be 'kept in their place'— a place assumed to be fixed by Holy Writ as forever that of an inferior. For such people, education was not considered important. Schools adequate to make them allies in maintaining a civilization or even an adequate food supply were never provided. These colored people were left in ignorance and poverty."[28] Raper researched and wrote an ethnography of the various subcultures of the population and analyzed the agricultural, economic, and legal circumstances for each county, paying special attention to the relations between the whites and blacks, and the part that race played in everything from school expenditures and land purchases to pick-up baseball games and the way people lined up at the post office.

The book is filled with tables of facts and statistics, but along with an extensive array of sociological data, Raper included a wealth of ethnographic detail that extended down to what folks ate for lunch.[29] From one page to the next, Raper created vivid images to demonstrate the human impact of the numbers, as though he and the reader were approaching a house from a distance and walking right up to the door to look inside:

> Screened houses are very rare, except among the larger owners. Of tenant houses scarcely one in twenty is even partially screened; those occupied by whites make little better showing than those occupied by Negroes. In and out of such houses, the children and flies—often the chickens and pigs—move at will. They are quite open; a mad dog can trot through one of them. Or a tenant mother with a four-day-old baby may awake from an afternoon nap to find in her bed a snake attempting to nurse her full breasts.[30]

He wrote about the bleak, winter months in Black Belt Georgia, its rutted roads clotted with "wagons and trucks filled with the scanty household furniture of landless and unattached families, white and Negro, seemingly motivated by a vague hope rather than an active expectation of finding something better. Their characteristic improvidence was to no small degree simply their adjustment to the demands of a system of farming which insisted that they be landless, that they be servile, and that they be dependent." They were adapting to the system they were living and working within.[31]

Raper saw the migrants as pushed, not pulled, to the city. "The people who left Greene county in 1921 and thereafter were virtual refugees. They were fleeing from something rather than being attracted to something."[32] Often, those who remained were too old or weak to travel and start over. For many, illiteracy tethered them to a home without the written word. Still, by the end of the 1920s a full one-third of Greene's population had fled. From a rural region of fewer than five hundred square miles, Greene's migrants scattered all over the eastern United States, although the majority had remained in the South and Atlanta was by far the most common destination.[33] He explained,

> Many of the migrants left Greene only upon the pinch of hunger. Think of people leaving a Georgia county for the bare necessities of life—a county where peaches, pears, pecans, peanuts, potatoes of two varieties, peas, beans, corn, oats, wheat, molasses, melons, tomatoes, asparagus, and a hundred other vegetables and cereals and fruits can be produced in

great profusion, and where the countryside is well-watered and admirably adapted to livestock farming. The whole economic organization of the county was dependent upon cotton, and when cotton could not be produced everybody suffered.[34]

Raper felt most rural migrants, in the 1920s, had been the "more alert and adventurous individuals leaving home to try their luck elsewhere." By the mid-1930s, though, migrants comprised

> the most dependent and least skilled families (wage hands, sharecroppers, and dependent tenants), who are losing their precarious niche in the cotton economy. What will they do? Will they march on to the county courthouse, the state house, and the national capitol? There is little prospect that they will permanently shuffle down to the swamps and push up on the sides of the gully-washed hills to eke out a bare existence. There is little prospect the present federal "rehabilitation boom" for dependent farm families will be more than a temporary stop-gap operation. No, inevitably and inexorably the stranded rural dweller will gravitate to the urban center, where they arrive as virtual refugees, ill-prepared physically, educationally, politically, socially, and culturally for life there.[35]

What surprised him, though, was that he did not at all find that a greater level of injustice in the older plantation county had led to greater numbers of migrants. When Raper compared Greene's institutions with Macon's, from the standpoint of schools, courts, landlord-tenant practices, and race relations, he could see little reason why more blacks in Macon would want to remain at home. In fact, he judged the treatment of blacks in Macon to be somewhat worse than in Greene. He found only one case in either county where any considerable number of Negroes migrated because of race conflict, and then only after white vigilantes terrorized a neighborhood following a gunfight in which a local black tenant had wounded a white planter.[36] Instead, he found that black folks remained, with tremendous resilience, in spite of the limitations imposed on them in both counties. The boll weevil ended up being worse in Greene, and people left only when they had nothing left to eat.

The reason for the greater migration from Greene was not in the different social conditions; it was in the soil. "It seems clear," Raper reported, "that Macon's cotton output is the most important reason why her population remained relatively stable between 1920 and 1930, while Greene's decreased so much." Macon's soil, he found, had a larger gravel content. It reflected the sun's heat and killed more of the weevil larvae. Beyond that, Macon had fewer acres covered in the sedge, brambles, and pine that offered weevils hibernation.[37]

Although he concluded that the boll weevil was critical to the difference in the two counties' migration rates, Raper instead focused the book on the sociology of the dying plantation. He tucked away the weevil in a chapter on population movements, in the book's midsection, and seldom mentioned it again. The facts surrounding soil content and weevil larvae were not something that he could fix. He chose instead to see Greene County as Macon's cautionary tale, a malignant case farther advanced, and focused on the counties' social inequalities and lack of opportunity. The obsolete plantation system—with its agriculturally destructive over-reliance on cotton and the social injustices that adhered to it—was unable to handle such a blow as the weevil. A more democratic-minded system, using diversified agriculture, would not have thrown its own families off the land they worked. He saw the boll weevil as the straw—"a heavy one, 'tis true"—that broke Greene's back, but Raper believed the county's longstanding social, political, and environmental practices weighed even more heavily in its crash.

Remnants of the "master-slave regime"

Raper also looked at the way remnants of the "master-slave regime" continued to hold sway in Greene and Macon. For example, when black farmers wanted to buy the land they worked and stake a claim in their community, social and personal connections to whites were more important than cash on the barrelhead. A black buyer in rural Georgia needed to be "acceptable," a term that required a multitude of virtues and a paucity of desires. Raper explained,

> It means that he and his family are industrious and that his credit is good. It means that he is considered safe by local white people—he knows "his place" and stays in it. Though it varies somewhat from one community to another and from one individual to another, the definition of "his place" hedges the Negro landowner about by restrictions similar to those which define and enforce the chronic dependency of the landless Negroes: The Negro landowner is an independent Negro farmer rather than an independent farmer. The economic and cultural advantages which the Negro

can secure through the ownership of land are limited by local racial dogmas, which insist alike upon the Negro's submerged status and upon his acceptance of it.[38]

Raper found that nine-tenths of all black owners had bought their land from whites, and "in three-fourths of these cases the white man had taken the initiative—had approached the prospective buyer, advised him to buy, and offered to assist him." He described a typical transaction:

> In Macon County an elderly white owner without heirs said to his only tenant, a Negro: "Now, Herbert, I have just a good one-horse farm here; I want you to work and be smart and save up some money, for when I die I want you to own it." Not many years later the white man died and was buried in the near-by family cemetery. His grave, and those of his parents, are kept in order by Herbert Griffin who now owns the farm.[39]

Paternalism and capitalism were an awkward juxtaposition. It was, indeed, as Raper quotes a white Macon County farmer, a long jump from "my slave" to "my fellow-citizen."[40]

In the end, Raper portrayed the black landowner as the closest thing to a self-sustaining, Jeffersonian agrarian that the South had produced.

> The Negro owner is as near a live-at-home farmer as one finds in the Black Belt: he has hogs, cows, chickens, and a permanent garden. That he is fundamentally correct in having his farm animals and miscellaneous crops is borne out by statements of bankers and merchants, who agree that he is a good financial risk. It is not unusual for a local banker, fertilizer dealer, or merchant, to say he would as soon take this or that Negro owner's personal note as any man's in the county.[41]

Indeed, Raper's study of the racial caste system and black dependency led him to conclude that what whites called shiftlessness was actually black resourcefulness. He saw in black farm folk a determined talent for turning a debilitating system to their advantage. And he mixed economics and psychology in discussing the way the hare was occasionally able to outwit the fox. As Raper said, whites generally considered that "the Negro was inferior," in part because of what they saw as an inherently improvidential nature. "Childlike" blacks were often in a state of chronic debt.

Raper understood that chronic debt not as a moral failing, but a strategy.

For people whose resources were always in jeopardy the most prudent direction was toward security. By attaching themselves to wealthy and influential whites through the medium of debt, powerless blacks were able to purchase their protection. They saw that whites often went to bat for poor blacks who were in their debt. The whites would never see their money again if their debtor ended up out of town, in jail, or dead. The system made it inevitable that sharecroppers would be in debt, but many black tenants managed to spread their indebtedness among several local whites, rather than solely to their landlords. That way, no individual creditor could press too hard for payment of his debt without coming up against the claims of another. Black women who worried about losing their work washing white families' laundry also made sure to establish moderate debt to those families as a form of job protection. In the absence of virtually any legal or governmental resources, many rural, black farm folk developed intricate forms of détente with their white creditors to carve out protection, and occasionally opportunity, for themselves.[42]

Raper saw the Interracial Commission working through a similar kind of stealth and guile. The CIC never issued a critique of segregation, as such, but only of its most obvious effects. Raper considered the word itself a red flag he did not wish to wave. At the same time, in *Preface to Peasantry* he was clear in his descriptions of the damaging effects of segregation on the lives of blacks and the integrity of whites. He observed,

> The white child and the Negro child go their separate ways to school and church and graveyard long before they are old enough to wonder why. They already are separated by the assumption of innate differences, already accept the dogmas which underlie caste distinctions. That the white man and the Negro are fundamentally and inevitably and unalterably different will scarcely be questioned so long as the two races go in opposite directions to recite their arithmetic tables, their reading lessons, their creeds about a loving Heavenly Father, their intentions to emulate a Jesus who called no man common or unclean.[43]

Whites, in fact, hated to face the "Negro question" in the abstract, Raper wrote, but when confronted with a local racial issue, most could not discuss the matter without a measure of excitement, resentment, or rage. "They appear to feel that the attitude which they maintain toward the Negro is, though not a worthy one, an inevitable one, forced upon them by circumstances over which they have no control," Raper explained. "They seem to be in the awkward predicament of being unapologetic in defending a distasteful but inescapable position."[44]

Segregation worked hand in hand with the plantation system to create a culture of dependency and a lack of democratic participation. "The established relation between landlord and tenant has made a puny dictator of the one and a fatalistic plodder of the other. Before there can be any significant change, the tenant must have reason for feeling that he can improve his lot by the application of industry and intelligence; the planter must realize that he has more to gain by ending the present parasitic tenant system than by maintaining it, for the plantation first impoverishes its workers and then disinherits its owners." Raper believed any changes in economic relations between landlords and tenants would mean social and economic changes as well.

Raper looked at community institutions and found an inviolable dividing line. In both counties' cultural institutions—educational, religious, and social—the races were separated absolutely by race. Blacks came together with whites only in certain federal institutions and in some private businesses.[45] Post offices and courthouses were not segregated, nor had a separate legal tender been established for blacks.[46] But that did not prohibit segregated meetings in the general store. When a black farmer had paid for his goods and looked to sidle up to the hot stove, he always sat by a black neighbor. Others would drift in, and the "Negro side" of the stove might reach around two-thirds of the circle. Half an hour later, the "white side" might be two-thirds. "All day long this circle around the stove gradually changes its racial complexion," Raper noticed, "with almost no intermixing of the races. The seating is not prearranged, and doubtless the sitters themselves are unaware of the typical arrangement, which anyone may observe for himself by 'hanging around' a store in the rural portions of either county."[47]

Raper saw Greene's and Macon's most critical dividing lines in their schoolhouses. The data he marshaled to document the disparities between white and black schools was exhaustive and damning, and his descriptions of black schools were withering. "Differentials such as these between urban and rural communities, particularly between whites and Negroes, are so great and so contradictory to the whole theory of public education as to leave one with the feeling that it is incorrect usage of language to write public education without quotation marks." He quoted a Greene County school official's perspective on race, "The Negro should have justice as a human being, but in the light of the kind of a human being he is."[48] And yet, at least, he admitted, in school, blacks were given some modicum of attention, however inadequate.

> In the field of education the presence of the Negro is at least not wholly ignored by local white people—not so in the realms of politics and religion: the politician ignores the very presence of the Negro, except to use him as the subject of jokes and to capitalize on race prejudice; the typical white preacher and churchman . . . ignores the presence of the Negro by preaching and professing theories of the Fatherhood-of-God and the Brotherhood-of-Man which do not include him. The Negro's status in the economic field, too, is even more precarious than in the field of public education.[49]

Raper was most caustic in his handling of race and religion, in whites' use of religious principles to justify racial prejudice. White southerners often claimed the "hewers of wood" passage in the Bible assigned blacks the status of servants.

> It is pathetic to hear a person unaccustomed to reading the Bible or anything else elaborate upon the meaning of this passage and then not be able to find it. And then when he realizes that it says, "And he (Noah) said, Cursed be Canaan"; instead of, "And God in his wrath cursed Ham and turned his skin black," he falls back upon his well-established impression of the meaning of the passage and disposes of the matter by saying that Noah was God's prophet and that the curse was black skin and that he doesn't want to talk with anybody who does not believe in the Bible. The real role of the Bible in this connection was clearly revealed by the young white man who, when asked what the Bible said about the Negro, replied emphatically: "Well, I don't know exactly what it says but I know what it means."[50]

How were the traditional race and class relations changing in response to the new cash economy? The landlord thought of a cash system as a better method of furnishing his tenants because it was cheaper. To the farm tenant as well, some cash meant money for gas and maybe a new outfit. By the mid-1930s, Raper saw the change offering tenant families an additional sense of responsibility. He saw black farm families searching for values and patronizing businesses where they were treated with consideration. Raper observed, "Merchants were quick to realize this, for they knew that when a tenant walked into the store with cash he would not buy unless he wanted to. The one who came for rations might be ignored or put off for an hour or two—he had to stay until he got his order. A tenant with cash in his pockets had a different attitude toward the merchant from one who got rations each week or month—the latter essentially a beggar, the former a buyer."[51]

Raper looked at the family makeup of black and white families in both counties and concluded that the black mother and grandmother bore the brunt of the racial caste system. "The mother in the white tenant household, and even in that of the small owner, is usually the chief burden carrier, frequently working in the fields in addition to doing her housework," Raper explained. "In the planter family, the mother nearly always has heavy responsibilities. Scarcely any farm mother leads an idle or a sheltered life." He recognized that the black mother bore all the same burdens, along with the additional struggle imposed by race in the forms of less stable family lives, meager economic opportunities, and inferior public services and local businesses.[52]

By the late 1920s, the automobile and urbanization were driving southern blacks into the modern era at great speed. In spite of the counties' poverty and Greene's outmigration—not to mention the lack of any paved roads—automobiles were seen by the rural poor as an increasingly important equalizer between classes and races. Raper hoped the automobile had opened a door to a new egalitarianism. Ease of mobility itself spoke to individual choice, rather than community stricture. The poor and the black had begun to share southern roads. "In his car the tenant has a right to half of the road whether he is meeting another tenant, a traveling salesman, or his own landlord," Raper explained. "Only in automobiles on public roads do landlords and tenants and white people and Negroes of the Black Belt meet on a basis of equality."[53] Raper wondered, "Will this make the tenant jealous for rights in other fields? The rapid transportation which the auto furnishes the cotton farmer cannot be ignored, for something important may be taking place when otherwise propertyless white and Negro croppers can climb into their cars, poor though they be, and command half of the road while they ride whither they will and their gas permits, Saturday afternoon and all day Sunday."[54]

Some large landowners carped that the auto made black tenants even more shiftless. Others feared farther-reaching consequences. A white man in Macon proposed the county extend its system of segregation to the establishment of two road systems. He correctly saw that the automobile was necessarily disruptive of Jim Crow. Technology disrupted, rather than abetted, the racial and social hierarchy. Along with the tractor and later, the mechanical cotton-picker, the auto contributed to making an anachronism of the master-slave regime.[55]

Denied recourse to legislative, legal, or economic power, black leaders were creating for themselves cultural roles. Raper reported that Greene's and Macon's black populations established more fraternal lodges and civil organizations than whites, and church membership was higher as well. Both counties' black communities were expected to contribute to their schools, so they organized committees to raise funds for education. The rural black church in Greene and Macon, as throughout the South, was at the center of the surrounding black community. Raper acknowledged the importance of both black and white churches to their communities, but mindful of the conservatism he had encountered in the southern pulpit, he advocated the development of local schools as community cultural centers, serving many ages and purposes.

Of all the ways he charted the ethnography of black-and-white in Greene and Macon counties, Raper was most fascinated by the way blacks turned whites' stereotypes back against them, in the ways the weak tricked the mighty. "The black-face minstrel show is perhaps the most interesting expression of race relations in these Black Belt communities," he observed. He told the story of a black troupe that played the southern minstrel circuit. "Not all black-faced minstrel shows use whites," Raper explained. "Some use Negro actors who poke fun at whites." This particular troupe pitched its tent in a field on the outskirts of Oglethorpe in the fall of 1934. Many of the leading whites in town arrived for the show, bought their tickets from a white woman in a booth, then handed them to another white woman at the entrance to the tent, and sat on benches to one side of a narrow aisle, while blacks sat across the way. A white master of ceremonies took the stage.

> As the curtain rose one saw eight Negroes dancing on the small stage, four dark men with painted mouths and four light women in ballet costumes. Presently the four horn blowers, Negroes too, stopped abruptly and one of the dancers stepping to the edge of the stage announced: "Ladie-es and gentlemen, this first little lady is Miss Irene Jones, next is Joe Gunn, Miss Johnstone, James Kellum, Mrs. Sellers, Sam Baugh, Miss

McGinder and me, Joshua Jennings"—his last words hardly said before the whole troupe was doing a twisting, jiggling dance which was followed by dialogue in which a black boy pleaded for the attention of a mulatto girl, only to be refused with: "Who, me? Why you don't know who I am; my daddy's the largest planter in Georgia." Just then the next skit broke in with some safe subject.

Ten minutes later a Negro man was strolling across the stage singing, "I'll leave my gun at home," if this and that and the other is done, each time pointing out his man; and it seemed quite accidental that he was on the front edge of the stage on the white side of the audience and pointing straight at a white man when he came to the line, "I'll leave my gun at home, if you'll leave my wife alone." Everybody laughed and almost simultaneously, the next dance step was under way with the biggest black man exhorting his associates in good Black Belt diction: "Shake it, black boy; now you darkies is dancin'."

The show rambled along with the attention of the audience quickly and thoroughly transferred after each subtle gibe at the whites.

Finally, in the last skit, one actor pleads, "Daddy! Daddy, do you 'spose the Lord knows how the white folks at 'Mericus, Georgia, treat us niggers?' 'Yes, son,'" his daddy replies. "'He knows, but just don't give a damn!' Suddenly a terrific din arose from back stage, the footlights went out, the actors screamed for help; then a woman struck a match and peered about the stage to find it empty and deathly silent, 'Now, that's a good one on them niggers; they must a thought I had my razor wid me!'" All the people laughed and clapped, and when the music ended, they all left the tent together. "Within a few weeks," Raper added, "most likely, another black-faced show put up a tent at Oglethorpe," a note that caught the still-repeating rhythm of life in the rural South.[56]

"We do our part"

When Raper turned to politics in *Preface to Peasantry*, the overriding criteria he used to judge New Deal programs was this: "Is the New Deal giving rural farmers a chance to become more independent? Will it result in a wider ownership of land, or a further concentration of it? Will it aid in the transformation of the old plantation or will it merely extend its life past the time of its natural and otherwise inevitable death?"[57] The answers to these questions were mixed and ambiguous.

With patriotic enthusiasm for the programs of the newly elected Democratic administration, the windows of storefronts in both counties' towns and villages displayed the National Recovery Act (NRA) placards with its Blue Eagle and slogan, "We Do Our Part." Whatever success the NRA had in Greene and Macon, though, was largely due to whites' traditional loyalty to the Democratic Party. In assessing the NRA's impact on Greene and Macon, Raper pointed out that the minimum wages the NRA established did not cover agricultural workers and domestics, while two-thirds of all southern blacks worked on farms or as household help. When whites were included, three-fourths of Greene and Macon residents were in a position to be helped by the NRA's wage scales.[58] But more than half the remaining one-quarter worked for themselves in small stores, gas stations, and pressing clubs, or else were delivery boys at drugstores and retail establishments working on commission or solely for tips. He concluded, "By the time the various exemptions had been taken most of the Blue Eagles in the store windows of these counties meant just about nothing, except that the proprietors were loyal Democrats and that they liked President Roosevelt."[59]

Wide racial differentials characterized the administration of most New Deal programs in Greene and Macon. Raper found whites on relief fared much better than blacks.[60] Analyzing Greene's Civil Works Administration (CWA) and Federal Emergency Relief Administration (FERA) expenditures, for example, Raper concluded that rural black schools, which were in greatest need of improvement, shared only 8 percent of federal resources.[61] The benefits of the Civilian Conservation Corps (CCC) were virtually limited to whites.[62] The NRA also ended up pushing employers to cut marginal jobs from their payrolls, rather than raise the wages for them. The result was, as Raper wrote, that the NRA was doing for small businesses of the Black Belt what Ford and Taylor had done for big business in terms of maximizing efficiency and return on investment. Wealthy whites and businessmen could no longer afford to hire a few local black men to serve as little else but status symbols. The smaller, hand-processing industries suffered more than mechanized plants, and consequently, laid off more workers. Economic factors dictated the purchase of more productive machines, he concluded, and race demanded that black employees be fired first.

The Agricultural Adjustment Act (AAA) also obtained mixed results after instituting a "plow-up" to reduce the supply of cotton. In the fall of 1934, farmers found themselves, often with misgivings, plowing through their rows of cotton, and receiving a government check for it. Raper approached what seemed to be an absurd, modern intrusion into traditional agrarian culture in three ways, revealing a method he had already well-honed. First, he provided an economic analysis, then he illustrated it with a story that spoke to the strange effect of the new and radical program on the rural farm families and communities. "I might make money by plowing up mine," a cotton planter had told him, "for $15 an acre is not bad; but, you see, I hate to do it. I just like to see things grow, and I've been feeling sort-of funeral-like ever since I signed up for this field."[63] Raper finished with a progressive point about the need for greater diversification of crops and cooperative efforts among farmers. He recognized the importance of taking drastic measures and implementing experimentation on a broad scale, although he wondered whether "we can gain anything in the long run by destroying products even in an orderly fashion." The emergency plan did spike prices, but most of the increased profits went to the largest planters anyway. Raper found that most of the plow-up rebate money returned to farmers found its way into the hands of landlords. Tenants paid half as rent, and then paid the landlord again for advances against his food and supplies. Planters, businessmen, and cotton factors received the lion's share of agency disbursements.[64]

The New Deal programs, Raper wrote, were by and large too timid. The Bankhead Allotment Bill, for example, was a backward-looking response at a time that required systemic change. In an attempt to cap farmers' taxes, the bill fixed a number of bales for different crops that would be tax-free. Because that number was based on the crop production of the most recent, poor years, rather than pegged at the years of its fullest potential, during the second decade of the century, Raper felt the bill would make permanent the depression from which Greene County was just emerging. At the same time, Raper observed the fear of change in the southern power structure. He noted, "The reactions of the planters to the distribution of food and clothing by the Red Cross are symbolic of their fear and subsequent adaptation of most innovations which reach the Black Belt." That is, until the planters discovered that they could take advantage of the Red Cross themselves. In the past, landlords had found it useless to press for payments of the debts of tenants who they knew had virtually no access to cash. But now, tenants with relief checks could be pursued more profitably. Raper noted, "The Red Cross had given the landlords, in sore need of money, a chance to squeeze their tenants drier than they could have done otherwise."[65]

Planters complained that relief promoted gambling, idleness, and vice among the poor and landless, without inculcating in them a sense of personal responsibility. Still, many landlords supported federal assistance. The owner of dozens of black homes in Montezuma found it easier to collect his weekly rents once his tenants had begun receiving government checks. Storekeepers found their businesses growing when more farmers had more cash. And some of the large planters were happy to see relief programs facilitating the shift they themselves were trying to make from the dying paternalism of the plantation system to the cash economy, freeing them from supporting their workers by turning them into wage hands.[66]

Still and all, *Preface to Peasantry* struck a tone of hopefulness about both the efficacy of federal programs and the willingness of these rural southerners to work cooperatively. Raper wrote with confidence, for example, about a county-wide immunization project that saved many poor children from diphtheria. "It was really a county-wide service, for even though a fee of twenty-five cents was asked, any person who could not pay it was served without cost," he explained. "This project seems to demonstrate that a rural county can cooperate with the federal government in serving all the people."

Raper saw that Greene and Macon, along with the rural South as a whole, reaped definite benefits from the New Deal. Even though the South insisted on wage differentials based on race and had the lowest wages under the NRA, the CWA and AAA programs approximated the national standard. Raper believed the "application of national or regional standards has created relative prosperity in the Black Belt and the rural South, the area of the nation's lowest wages and lowest planes of living, by reducing the normal differential between it and the high wage areas." Black and poor white southerners were receiving the short end of the New Deal stick, but because they had been so devastated, the little they received had made a big difference and, by the mid-1930s, the South appeared to be moving toward recovery.[67]

Among the folks in Greene and Macon, there was little consensus about the New Deal programs in general or in particular. Many who favored the cotton-reduction program resented the relief aid, and vice versa. "At almost any place in these counties where people come together," Raper observed, "various reactions to the New Deal and particularly to the relief program will be heard. Some will say that it is ruining labor, others that it is all wrong, or that it is doing some good, or that it is indispensable."[68]

Raper concluded *Preface to Peasantry* with a call for a comprehensive land-use policy, partly as an extension of the regionalist concept. While engaging in a micro-sociological analysis and ethnography of two rural Georgia counties, Raper wanted to set Greene and Macon within the broadest possible context. He offered an orientation toward a systematic approach to greater equality, self-direction, and productivity. The only way for the South to recover was to push past insularity and develop plans that fit within national and international policies. What would it require? According to Raper, "the investment of large sums of public money and an administrative personnel with scientific training and a bold faith in the common man."[69]

"Americans are big exploiters"

All the while he was researching and writing *Preface to Peasantry*, tramping with the hounds and hanging around the courthouse, Raper was also continuing to write reports for the Interracial Commission and pieces for newspapers published across the South, on "Federal Relief in Georgia," "Official Connivance in Lynching," and "The Cotton Plow-up and Cotton Option."[70] With the coming of the New Deal, Raper's writing began increasingly to advocate soil conservation, and in strong terms, he criticized the South's traditional, exploitative use of its natural resources. "Dr. Raper Says Americans Are Big Exploiters," announced the black *Atlanta World*. "Describing exploiters as persons who 'get something for nothing,' Dr. Raper said that Americans have shamefully exploited their natural resources, such as soil and mineral deposits, and that when our lands and resources at home were exhausted we have turned to other places for new fields of exploitation."[71] The *DeKalb Era* reported on a Sunday school talk in which he described the wages of wastefulness. "Dr. Raper, gifted with the rare quality of capturing his audience's attention at the beginning of his talk, made a critical and exposing speech on what Americans of the past and the present have done and are doing to exploit natural resources."[72] At the same time, he continued to study closely how the new, activist government was affecting the economic and cultural status of the descendants of slaves currently caught in a nether world, still not fully emancipated even as they plowed right up to the brink of obsolescence, then jumped or fell into some new world in some strange city.[73]

All through the mid-1930s, Raper continued to speak to small groups and local organizations. Because the South's racial caste system so clearly ran counter to Christian teaching, the Interracial Commission had targeted church and religious groups, and Raper spoke often to church groups of all kinds, including Sunday school classes, women's groups, and youth conferences.[74]

Alexander found women's groups, newspapers, and teachers more responsive to the commission's message than church groups. "It is the exceptional preacher," claimed one CIC pamphlet, "who is prepared to lead in combating racial prejudice or even to lend any effective cooperation." Least cooperative were Baptist ministers, who were under little direct control from their denominational leaders, and under the more certain influence of their white congregations. Eleazer also continued his heavy round of mailings to newspapers and magazines, as well as to high schools and colleges. Dozens of educators took advantage of CIC materials in their classes.[75]

Consistent with the public relations approach, Raper thought of his books as extensions of his lecture audience. "I was writing the books for the same people who had been inviting me to come and talk to them," he said, years later. "That was a pretty broad group out here, many of whom were not convinced, but many of whom were at least willing to listen. That was the group that I envisioned. Here were these folks in the Rotary Clubs, these folks in the Civitan Club, in the Baptist Church and Methodist Church and Presbyterian Church, white and black. They are interested in this stuff. They have asked to hear it. Let us write it down so they can read it."[76] Raper knew well the reactionary nature of much white, southern society, but he tended to lessen the distance he felt between the man on the street or in the field. He certainly emphasized the same themes in his sociological studies and his Thursday night, bean supper talks. "We must get rid of breadlines," he told a "College Night" in Atlanta, in a typical talk. "We must rid ourselves of those foolish notions concerning wealth and private possessions. We should cure millions of the curse of their millions which bring unhappiness to them and unhappiness to countless others. And we must do these things not by revolution, for that is not the way to bring about real constructive changes, but by an ever upward trend toward securing the things that will enable us to live happier lives."[77]

"Hope for the creation of an international mind"

Science and industry might help spur the kind of redistribution Raper spoke about. He admired the way mechanization had lessened the isolation of the farm family, raised its standard of living, and, by so doing, offered to many a new sense of dignity. At the same time, he saw modernity enervating the sinews and drive of pioneer America. Like other regionalists, Raper was troubled by the prospects for an active civic culture in a media- and consumer-driven, industrialized America. He advocated a kind of new folk culture, molded on his own active life, which emphasized doing and making, rather than buying and watching. If Americans could turn their energies to cooperative effort, they would be healthier and less aggressive. "It may be that most of us are eager and unconsciously hoping for more excitement and responsibility than we get," he surmised, in an Armistice Day address he delivered in 1934, speculating on the impulse to war from a regionalist's perspective. "In many respects our present living is out of harmony with our heritage," he explained.

> We do not get our steak from the meat market at the corner, but in the history of the race there was blood in the yard before there was steak on the table. Just lately, we have got away from much of the sober reality of the past: We hire a few people to tramp in the gory muck of the slaughter house, while we eat refrigerated steaks and feel a weakness in the pit of the stomach at the smell of warm blood. Moreover, many of us are employed at tasks which require almost no risk, which involve little personal responsibility, which provide almost no opportunity for creative labor.[78]

If work was to be meaningful, the worker must have a stake in his labor, own his land, share in factory management and profits, render public service. How can we find a substitute for war? Participate in community affairs. Be active. Watch fewer football games, and play yourself. Go to fewer movies, and act in community dramatics. Walk and camp. Americans should preach less and make fewer speeches, and work for more service committees and community forums. Raper insisted, "For the young people a constructive plan for peace will provide for vivacious and vital group games, community orchestras, chorus singing, folk dancing, with a great deal of this carried on in the out-of-doors under the sun, and at night before open fires, with pantomime and costuming playing no mean part."[79]

His energetic idealism ran against the grain of cynicism toward the Great War that had taken hold of the country by the mid-1930s. The Armistice Day talk also gave Raper a chance to develop his sense of rational humanism in an internationalist perspective and to see his own responsibility in that context.

> World peace is a dream which rests upon the assumption that the "consciousness of kind" can be made inclusive; that man can be made to appreciate the unity of humankind. The man who believes that peace is possible is the man who has enough faith in himself to begin to disarm in the

presence of his armed neighbors. He is the man who will go the second mile; he is the man who believes that the other man has the same appetites, pains, fears, joys, and hopes which he has. He is the man who believes that the other man can be made to see things as he sees them. Herein rests the hope for the creation of an international mind. This point of view cannot be achieved by small, weak men. It is the projection of a bold faith in ourselves and will, if anything will, inspire a similar response in the other men.[80]

Like Odum and other regionalists, however, Raper was caught in a contradiction. He was trying to preserve the active life and self-reliance of American folk culture, while using scientific methods to accommodate people to the modern, corporate, industrialized age. Advising farmwives to learn home canning, for instance, Raper was advocating a preindustrial way, even as he was pushing southerners to come to grips with modern conditions and methods.

Like many intellectuals, by the mid-1930s, Raper had begun to define democracy in contrast to the totalitarian systems that had begun to loom over the world. "In our modern world, democracy is the normal political expression where people work together voluntarily, just as some form of dictatorship, whether communist or fascist, is the normal political expression where people work together because they have to." He believed the greatest potential for democracy lay with societies that produced and distributed goods and services cooperatively.[81]

Raper conferred on New Deal liberals and sociologists the status of new pioneers. "The study of sociology is challenging because of the world in which we live; because of the adjustments which have to be made. There is no more free land in the west; our physical frontiers have been reached; the real pioneers of the future will doubtless be those persons who devote themselves to the questions involved in the necessity of our living together upon the lands and resources which we now have." Sociology would synthesize the data of more particularized and arcane disciplines to develop plans that communities could adopt as a modern, common-sense approach to its social problems.[82]

Federal intervention in rural social and economic life increased dramatically under the New Deal, and social science was enlisted throughout to help direct the incursion.[83] The Bankhead-Jones Farm Tenant Bill of 1936 implemented Raper's practical approach to sociology. In 1934, Alexander met with Henry Wallace and Rexford Tugwell to develop strategies for federal intervention in the tenancy crisis. Based on Raper's research in Greene and Macon, as well as work by Charles S. Johnson, Alexander recommended that the Department of Agriculture purchase land currently held by insurance companies and federal land banks. The idea was to subdivide designated lands to separate farms, then sell it to landless farmers and tenants already working the land. The federal government would make loans and offer twenty- or thirty-year mortgages at low interest. A supervisory agency would help these new homesteaders to diversify their crops and improve production. Wallace persuaded Senator John Bankhead of Alabama to introduce a bill with such provisions in February 1935.[84]

Alexander and Raper were convinced that only a program of tenant ownership would help the tenancy problem, but Tugwell felt that ownership programs should come later. He wanted to focus instead on establishing government-run resettlement communities that would offer more immediate benefits to the most needy families. Even so, Alexander continued to press for passage of the Bankhead-Jones bill in the 1936 session of Congress, using as evidence a short book by Charles S. Johnson, which Alexander had sponsored and edited. *The Collapse of Cotton Tenancy,* designed to appeal to the general reader, buttressed Alexander's and Raper's argument in favor of tenant ownership.[85] *Preface to Peasantry,* in turn, became a way to follow up some of the questions raised by Johnson's own conclusion that the land, economy, and culture of the plantation system was in serious trouble.

"Just sit still, Raper, something's happening"

Raper felt the work he did in Greene and Macon counties contributed to Alexander's appointment as Rex Tugwell's chief administrator at the Resettlement Administration (RA), and later, as director of the Farm Security Administration (FSA). Soon after Roosevelt's inauguration, Alexander was pressing federal agencies to gain for southern blacks a more equitable share in New Deal programs than they had ever shared in their public services. So he encouraged Raper to spend a lot of time looking at how the programs were working. Alexander became a southern prod to the administration, pushing it to improve its distribution of resources to African Americans. Raper became Alexander's way of measuring that distribution. "I was out and about in the rural parts of the South," Raper explained, "and knew a tremendous number of people, and very quickly could get the dope, as it were, on how the programs were working." In this way, academic social science served New Deal reforms.

Raper found Alexander often on the phone with Tugwell, Clark Foreman, and other New Deal administrators. And he saw that the new Department of Agriculture had a welcoming attitude toward informed critics. One day, during their drive for passage of the Bankhead-Jones Farm Tenant Bill, Raper was sitting in his boss's office when Alexander turned from the phone and said, "Just sit still, Raper, something's happening." Henry Wallace, Roosevelt's secretary of agriculture, was calling. He was asking Alexander to come to Washington to be his alter ego, as he called it, the deputy director of the RA.

On the one hand, Alexander could become a strong voice within the Roosevelt administration for African Americans and the South.[86] On the other, the Interracial Commission would be left without his leadership at a point when the future of southern race relations was uncertain, and the Communists had loudly entered the field by appropriating the defense of the Scottsboro Boys in 1933. Worsening conditions were making southern race relations even more brittle, and if Alexander left Atlanta, the CIC would likely be weakened.[87]

"Now what do I do?" Alexander asked.

Raper said, "You go."

"Well, what happens to these things here?"

"What happens to them doesn't make too much difference," Raper said. "They'll work better if the thing goes right in Washington. If it doesn't go right in Washington, we can't do anything anyhow."

"What they need in Washington is not a technician but a philosopher," Raper told him. "So you go to Washington."[88]

Before long, Alexander had developed a strong connection between the Interracial Commission and the Department of Agriculture. He loaned Raper to the Federal Emergency Relief Agency (FERA), for example, to study how federal relief funds were being distributed in Georgia. Raper spent eight months, beginning in August 1933, analyzing the new government's exhaustive sets of statistics. The data led him to three conclusions. Most rural people on relief were white. In more than 80 percent of the counties, whites received more money than blacks. And although blacks comprised 37 percent of Georgia's population, only 17 percent of CWA teachers were black. Du Bois called the report excellent and quoted from it. Clark Foreman said it showed a keen eye.[89]

Alexander called Raper his ear to the ground. Even after he left the Interracial Commission for Washington, Alexander relied on Raper to let him know how federal policy was working in cotton rows and courthouses across the South. Alexander's move would strengthen the federal government's knowledge of the field and improve the way its programs were working. For example, Raper looked at several Settlement Projects in southeast Georgia for the FSA.[90] When Alexander left, however, the loss of his vision and drive weakened the CIC irreparably. Its high-water mark had been the first half of the 1930s, with its campaign against lynching, its legal work, and Raper's various analyses. After Alexander's departure, the Interracial Commission no longer wielded the kind of force that could mount a full-scale assault on lynching. For the next few years, it was a collection of individual activists. When Howard Odum took over as director of the CIC in 1937, he turned it to regionalist revival and race was virtually forgotten. Black organizations had rendered the Interracial Commission obsolete. Or rather, by completing the groundbreaking work it had set for itself, the CIC had rendered itself obsolete. Black activists, Du Bois foremost among them, had begun to take the lead in southern race relations and in working with northern, liberal groups. The approval of socially prominent southerners and the white scientific and academic community had considerably eased the way for black leadership in the 1940s to create a more visible and militant push for civil rights. But Alexander's departure from the CIC was a sign that white, southern liberalism had moved to a larger and more potent stage.

"The next year a little larger, and so on"

Raper's ample home life reflected little of the storm and struggle of his work. The first of the Rapers' four children, Charles Franklin Raper, had been born in May 1930. Harrison was born two years later, Jarrell in 1934, and Margaret in 1937. The family's modest bungalow in a green neighborhood of Decatur was not far from the CIC's downtown Atlanta office. A trellis over the doorway, a white, picket fence, fruit trees in the backyard, and a tire swing on a big, old oak. Decatur's weekly paper came to report on Raper's speeches and books as a favorite son made good. His family became a model of his advocacy of the active life. Each of the children played an instrument, often together with Martha and Arthur. She worked as a free-lance editor and supported his work and politics. "It keeps a man on his toes," he would say, "to have a wife who's keener than he is."

While writing *The Tragedy of Lynching,* Raper had taken a part-time appointment at Agnes Scott College, a white school for the daughters of wealthy Atlantans, near their neighborhood. Before long, Raper was raising eyebrows on campus because he was bringing his students face to face with the problems they were studying. He took his student-debutantes to the bloating and squalid neighborhoods of Atlanta. They made field trips to old plantations to study soil erosion and farmed-out gullies. They counted Atlanta's empty storefronts and charted the growth and blight of its neighborhoods through the course of the 1930s. With Martha as a chaperone, he took his class of young white women overnight to Tuskegee.[91] He took them to see the way smoke from the Tennessee Copper Works had killed the land for a hundred square miles, musing with them on the approach of modernity. As they drove across treeless Ducktown, Tennessee, the road was littered with billboards, colorful pictures of new appliances outlined against the scorched earth. "One wonders," he offered his class, "whether these and other products, which strive for profits through the exploitation of natural resources and the deception of society, are not as ruinous as the fumes from the Tennessee Copper Works."[92]

He had arrived on campus in 1932 to find little interest among students for sociology. "I had a very small class," he remembered, but found "the next year a little larger, and so on." By the time he left in 1939, Raper's class had become the largest elective at Agnes Scott. From the mid-1930s on, Raper's classes, tying together social and political science, liberal activism, and economics, attracted all the campus leaders.[93]

Raper also attracted the attention of the local chapter of the Ku Klux Klan and Mrs. J. E. Andrews, the voluble and powerful head of the Southern Association of Women for the Preservation of the White Race, who wrote her members that Raper was making Agnes Scott girls available to black men. He decided against courting the publicity of a libel suit. But when the college administration began to pressure him to stop emphasizing race in his study of southern society, he quit his position. He had made certain his family did not rely on his small salary from Agnes Scott, because he knew his job would always be precarious.

Still, through the 1930s, he had been able to conduct a class in a white, women's college in Atlanta that questioned the deterministic ideas about race and class ingrained in the white South, while ignoring the traditional prohibitions clustered around race. Soon, he was working with Gunnar Myrdal, the Swedish social scientist, who was heading the Carnegie Corporation's groundbreaking project on race in America. In 1940, just a year later, he would be sitting down to tea with Myrdal and Mrs. Andrews at her home in Atlanta, hearing her talk about the dangers to the purity of white women posed by New Deal integrationists. Myrdal had wanted to meet with representatives of every political persuasion throughout the South. In his lilting Swedish accent, he responded to her speech by asking his hostess whether she was familiar with the Freudian theory that held that an individual's neuroses are a direct result of an erotic fascination with the object of their fear. Raper was soon driving Myrdal fast toward the Alabama line with a frequent eye in his rearview mirror.

As the long-expected World War II finally broke across Europe, Raper would play field guide to the engaging, gregarious, direct, and ceaselessly energetic Myrdal through the strange, foreign land of the American South, while helping to research the most influential book ever published on U.S. race relations. A dozen years later, Thurgood Marshall would acknowledge how the Supreme Court's decision in *Brown v. Board of Education* had been based in part on *The Negro in America,* the findings published by Myrdal, whose most prominent contributions were made by Du Bois, Charles S. Johnson, and Raper. For Raper, his travel through the Depression South with the irrepressible and meticulous European scientist, legislator, and researcher would furnish him with a view of the South that pushed him even farther toward an international perspective.

NEW DEAL INTERMEZZO
Brer Raper in the Briar Patch

One day, in October 1934, Will Alexander called Raper into his office and asked him to help out with a job on a New Deal project in rural Putnam, another Black Belt county southeast of Atlanta, from which large numbers of black farm families had left for the city. Gay Shepperson, the state's chief of Federal Emergency Relief Aid (FERA), needed a favor. Tracts of failing farmland were being retired to forest, and a hundred families, most of them black, were being moved to more suitable land. Alexander told him, "Go and see how you can help out with the move."[1]

Raper met with Shepperson and agreed to survey the families about their health, education, and work skills, so FERA could place them knowledgeably. Then he hired a staff of five workers. Two of them were white: Raper's friend from Vanderbilt, Floyd Corry, and his uncle, "Punch" Dolvin. And three were black: Ethel Cochran, a trained social worker; V. A. Edwards, a graduate of Morehouse; and Clyde Williams, a teacher at Fort Valley Junior College. Black and white were guaranteed the same salary. That was new to Corry and Dolvin. So was the way Raper used polite titles when he talked with Cochran, Edwards, and Williams. New and strange, but so was a paycheck for $200 a month.

Meanwhile, Raper had peppered Shepperson with questions about the logistics in Eatonton, Putnam's county seat. "You would be wasting your time to go early and scout the town," she had told him. The County Relief Office was on the second floor of an old commercial building in the middle of the downtown block, looking across the town square and past its somber Confederate monument to the county courthouse and its own statue of local son Joel Chandler Harris, beloved author of the Brer Rabbit tales. "Just show up at nine Monday morning," Shepperson said, "and one of my agents will set you all up. Don't you worry. Everything has already been arranged."

At seven-thirty Monday, Raper pulled into town and parked up the street from the square. He saw Clyde Williams's car, already parked in front of the office. Unlike Shepperson, Williams was no expert. But he was from these parts, and he knew what these people thought was strange. He wanted to be on hand early.

"Hello!" white folks called to each other, as they met on the way to the bank and the luncheonette and the courthouse. "Who is this dressed-up nigger in a shiny car?" No one could imagine. "Goodness, here come two more, and one a woman," they said when Cochran and Edwards pulled up across from the square. Soon after, Corry and Dolvin showed up together, in another respectable automobile new to town. Raper, too, another stranger dressed in suit and tie, collected his staff when the office opened at nine.

Mr. Johns was in charge of the office. He was a local fellow, not a social worker, who filled in and kept the office open now and again. He didn't know anything about the project, but if Miss Shepperson had said they could start this morning, then that would be just fine with him. Mr. Johns did not bat an eye when Raper brought him around to meet the staff, including "Miss Cochran." All Mr. Johns could tell Raper was, the chief here just took the train to Chicago last Saturday to take a special social work training course, and his secretary had just been transferred.

The men took off their coats in the growing warmth of the day and arranged the sparse furnishings in three unused rooms upstairs. They pushed a table and chair to the center room for Raper, flanked by rooms for the blacks and the whites. Before long, the staff drove off toward the first interviews. Raper wanted to meet folks around town and make sure they knew what he was doing. He found the county agent in his office and told him about the project. "Watch out," replied the agent. "There's a squabble going on between the relief office and the folks over at Land Utilization." Both were federal offices, and each felt it had a better claim to jurisdiction over the families being moved. Farther down the street, Raper heard more about the fight from some fellows in Forestry Service. The mayor was at the druggist shop, and he chimed in. Raper ran into a neighbor from Decatur, now a storekeeper in town, talking with the hardware-store owner. They brought up the fight, too.

"Hey, why don't you come on over for dinner tonight?" his old neighbor offered.

Raper begged off. "I need to meet with my staff as they come back in from the interviews," he explained.

"Then come over later," said the neighbor.

"Some of these folks might very well be pretty late," Raper told him. "Let's make it another time."

The next morning, driving into town, the mood seemed different. The air was a little sharper, as though the season had turned overnight. Along Main Street, it was quieter than it had been the day before. Now the old neighbor was very busy at his store. It wasn't that the work was trouble. The client families were happy to cooperate. The staff was doing a good job. In the office, the work quickly brought them together. Information, advice, and chitchat bounced back and forth across the desks and between the offices. It all seems very hopeful, Raper thought. Here were families who, while having to leave their homes, were being interviewed by government workers of their own race to help them make the move as easy as possible.

Still, by the time the staff met Wednesday morning, they were talking about the chill in town. Ethel Cochran, heading out to her first interviews, turned on the stairway. "I don't need any bad luck today," she told the group. "I'm heading over to Lynch, down below Murder Creek."

"I guess not," Raper called out, as the others laughed and clattered toward the door.

An hour later, Raper heard the heavy steps of several men climbing the stairs. Settling into chairs around Raper's office, the three delegates told him they had come to inquire as to who were these dressed-up niggers? And how was it that each of them was driving a good car when there were so many white people needing work? And where were you born, they wanted to know. Where did you go to school? Who are you married to?

Raper talked about the project. "I hired black staff workers," he told them, "because they might make the black farm families they were interviewing feel more comfortable." They shook their heads and seemed satisfied. At least they did not have much more to say, and before long they were heading back down the stairs. Raper looked up, saw it was noon, and grabbed his coat. He was supposed to meet the county agent for lunch.

Raper already knew the town's restaurant. Today, the few tables were filled with men who had all kept their hats on. A few white farmers and some of the cotton mill workers on the west side of town were a little upset about the black workers, the agent told Raper in his office after lunch. The story had gone around town that Ethel Cochran had pulled up at the town's filling station and asked the owner to put air in a tire without buying any gasoline. The indignant owner had refused. The agent himself thought hiring black staffers was a good idea, and he had helped map out the routes the interviewers would travel. "I guess it will soon blow over," he said.

Raper had planned to do some interviews himself that afternoon, but now he decided to stick around town. Mid-afternoon, he was back at his desk, when a group of men down in front of the building called up through his open window. "We want to know what these dressed-up niggers are doing here," they demanded. When he joined them on the sidewalk, the crowd grew, and Raper's explanation began to ripple outward, as other whites walked up and were filled in by the first group. He could feel he was making headway.

Negro workers were interviewing only Negro families, he kept repeating, now louder and louder. Yes, white workers would interview white families, and some Negro families, too. No, the cars belonged to the Negroes themselves. Yes, each was paying for his own gas and oil. The sidewalk began to overflow, and Raper said, "Let's move across the street to the square." Then the matter got out of hand.

A leader emerged. The scion of a prominent family, speech-slurring drunk, had bullied his way to the center of the circle and told them all he did not like the idea of dressed-up niggers driving good automobiles being paid by the government. "As a taxpayer, I don't mean to tolerate it." His conviction raised up a growling assent from the crowd. It didn't make any difference how well-trained the black workers were. White people needed jobs.

The drunken scion was sobered somewhat by the agreement he had stumbled into. Sensing the groundswell, he became magnanimous. "Tell us in your own words," he bade Raper, "just why it was these dressed-up niggers are here on a government assignment instead of white people." Raper responded at length, and surprisingly, he seemed to understand. It seems reasonable, he agreed, that black field workers could come nearer getting the truth from people like themselves about their health, about the kind of work they had done, about where they would like to live.

After a lengthy discourse, the scion stopped short, tottering on the crest of the crowd's momentum, rose up again, and demanded, "Now, why is it you say you are using these here niggers? Did you say it was because they were trained?"

"Yes, that's the reason we are using them."

"Does that mean they've got a lot of education?"

"That means they're well educated."

The drunken man began to smell blood. "Do you mean to tell me that any nigger, however much education he has, can do a better job than a white man can do, even if he didn't have no training?"

"Yes, with the right training Negroes can do a better job than white people can do without training."

The scion gathered himself up for the coup de grace, looked Raper in the eye. "Young man!" he intoned to the outer ring of the swelling crowd in a voice cracking with earnestness and indignation. "Do you mean to tell me that these educated niggers of yours can do a better job than I could do?"

"I hired the best people I could find for this particular type of work."

"I demand a direct answer to a direct question," he shot back, as though honor-bound to pursue the line of discourse.

"Yes," replied Raper. "I'm sure they can."

The growing crowd turned noticeably darker. When Raper repeated the same arguments for hiring black workers, they were met with hostility, as though they had become excuses or ways of obscuring the real point. Whatever fringe of generosity the folks in the crowd may have had for their black neighbors was dissipated in their recognition of the wider economic implications for the white South. Others in the crowd began to orate. Raper managed to duck out under the crossfire of competing speechifying and found the mayor behind the counter at his drugstore.

The mayor told him how Mr. Johns had come over from the Relief Office on Monday night and asked a few of the boys downtown whether they had yet met "*Miss* Cochran." Whether he meant to or not, Mr. Johns gave the Land Utilization Office a way to stir up some big trouble for the Relief Office. The Land Utilization Office played on white resentment of governmental strings to federal money. On Monday night, his staff had made Raper feel hopeful for the usefulness of the project. Just two days later, he was finding that even New Deal agencies could stoop to race-baiting in the Depression South.

The mayor suggested a special meeting of the city council, to convene at five o'clock. Raper got in his car and drove out to Milledgeville, twenty-five miles away, to call Shepperson. He knew from experience that small-town switchboard operators had big ears for what local people wanted to hear. No, said Shepperson, her office had no way of doing anything about the situation at Eatonville. Raper raced another dusty hour to make it back to town by five.

Four of the five city councilors advised that Raper "withdraw" Cochran, Edwards, and Williams. They told Raper they liked him personally and thought what he was doing was important. Why not go ahead with the project by letting the black workers go and hiring some local whites? He thanked them for their suggestions but assured them that if he finished the work, it would be with his present staff. They were surprised at his failure to agree to their seemingly natural suggestion. Then they told him frankly they could not vouch for the ability of the police to protect the black workers.

There is only one thing to do, Raper thought. He returned to his office and waited, alone in the falling light, for the others to return from their interviews. At sundown, Corry and Dolvin came in talking excitedly. Their eyes had been opened by the work. They had never seen anybody as poor as the folks they had been interviewing. When Edwards came in, Raper told the three of them he was going to close down the project. He told Corry and Dolvin to sit tight at the hotel until he sent for them.

An hour later, Raper walked Edwards across the town square to his car. Edwards would join Williams at their boardinghouse out in the black side of town. The now-empty street had darkened past twilight. Raper stood and watched Edwards's red taillights circle around the statue of Harris and disappear behind the old brick courthouse. Raper liked the Uncle Remus tales. He liked the way big blustering critters were regularly outmaneuvered by the weak and wily.

As Raper walked back slowly across the square to his office to wait for Ethel Cochran, three men appeared out of the dark. "We want to talk to you, man to man," one said, "about the Negroes working out of the Relief Office." He told Raper he worked for the Land Utilization Office, and they all walked over and sat down on the base of the Confederate monument. "We want to make sure there is no real trouble," the man said.

It turned out this man lived with the scion's family. "He is determined to get these here Negroes out of town tonight," the fellow warned Raper, "and he wants whites hired in their stead. Until just recently, I was a businessman in Indiana," he explained, "a practical man, without racial bias." He confided to Raper that he was simply trying to solve a problem. A reasonable man would comply. Raper told him he would not comply, got up, and tramped slowly back up the stairs to the empty Relief Office to wait.

He sat silently at his desk, alone in the bare room. A single drop-light shone over his head. Before long, one car after another pulled slowly up the quiet street and parked at the curb outside his window. Finally, he heard the door open downstairs and a tired footfall climb the stairs.

Ethel Cochran came in apologizing for being late. Her last family needed help with the paperwork to qualify their crippled child for public assistance. Raper cut her off. Both sides of the street had filled with cars. Some white people, he told her, were going to see to it that white supremacy was protected. She breathed deeply. "What do we do now?"

A shout rose up from the sidewalk. Silhouetted in the doorway at the bottom of the stairway stood the drunken scion, wobbling slightly under the influence of righteousness. He wanted to make it clear that he still thought Raper was a reasonable man. But that time was passing. "I will be down shortly," Raper told him from the top of the stairs. He turned to Cochran. She agreed the best thing to do was drop the project and leave.

The sight of Raper and Cochran leaving the office together pushed back the men littering the sidewalk. Raper opened the passenger door of his car for Cochran and asked her to stay inside. Then he turned back to the small knot of a crowd. At the foot of the steps with the scion was the Indianan who, as Raper wrote later, "had come to appreciate the Southern white man's point of view in a very short time." Two or three of the men stepped up to remind Raper that they had been very patient. Words simply weren't going to be enough much longer.

Just then, Corry walked up, returning from the hotel to check on Raper. At his quick steps up the dark sidewalk, the momentum of anger hung fire for a moment. Raper turned immediately to Corry. "Take Ethel's car and drive over to her rooming house with her," Raper told him. Then he pointed to the scion and the businessman. "Why don't you fellows come with me?" he said and pointed to his own car. "We'll all go together and tell the black workers they need to leave town right now."

The two cars slowly circled the town square, the dark courthouse, and the silhouette of Joel Chandler Harris, then soon passed from the wide, paved downtown streets to the narrow dirt roads that led to "Colored Town," where Cochran roomed, and Edwards and Williams were waiting. Both cars shone their headlights at the old house, while a few dim lights down the street popped on, and Cochran stepped nervously across a shaggy lawn through the headlights' glare to the front steps. Edwards and Williams had come out onto the porch, and Cochran pulled them inside the house. Raper waved over Corry, who left Cochran's car running and got in the backseat beside the businessman.

Long minutes passed through a thin breeze and the heavy rumble of idling autos. Edwards, Williams, and Cochran clattered back onto the porch, hunched with luggage, clambered down the stairs, and quickly crossed the lawn to their cars. Three trunk lids slammed down like shotgun blasts across the yard. Raper pulled out slowly and snaked back down the dirt road toward the county highway, where he picked up speed and headed toward Milledgeville.

Across the county line, he slowed and pulled into heavy gravel on a roadside shoulder. Cochran slowed, too, but kept going, honking as she passed Raper's car, followed by the others, blaring their horns, too, in turn, as they disappeared into the darkness, like birds flying out of a thicket or rabbits escaping a briar patch. In a moment, the road was empty and black. Raper slowly turned around and began the drive back to Eatonton.

Now the scion and the businessman could call off their fellows and relax. "Good thing for them niggers they turned tail when they did," one said. Their job had been done for them. "Another couple of hours," they told Raper and Corry, "and those niggers still would have left town, for sure, but a body could safely wager they would not have looked quite so healthy." Raper nodded at Corry.

He dropped the two off at their cars downtown, then drove to the hotel with Corry to check in with Dolvin before heading to bed. In the morning, after breakfast, he saw Corry and Dolvin off before heading over to the druggist's to tell the mayor the project was done. Before noon, he was on a weary road back to Atlanta. "I let the South knock me down all right," he thought.

Interracial projects went just fine when he had been given a chance to lay the groundwork, first among white and black workers, and then with the locals and officials in the towns where they were working. But in Putnam County, he found how fast Georgia towns could close around any breach in the social structure. And Raper, the staunch Roosevelt Democrat, found that, in a turf war, New Deal agencies could turn to race hate as quickly as a Talmadge or a Bilbo. The New Deal opened some doors for him, but not others. Still others were trap doors. To work on the ground in the Depression South, Raper found a race activist needed not only optimism and sympathy, but cunning, too, and a sharp sense of danger, to outmaneuver its hungry wolves and blustering hounds.

6

"THE DIVINE RIGHT OF THE COMMON GOOD"

In the middle of September 1936, Raper was driving through flat fields of Delta cotton, fast by the levee south of Clarksdale, toward the new cooperative farm near Hillhouse, Mississippi, when he spotted a long line of pickers stand up straight, all together, and look across the field. Slowly, they started to step across the rows, dragging their cotton bags with them, toward a roar that reached across the field.

"It was one of the early Rusk pickers," Raper recalled, years later. He pulled his Ford into the farmyard, and found an older, black sharecropper watching the machine. "Well, if that thing works, they ain't going to need us here," he told Raper, sagaciously. "And it looks to me like it's going to work." Raper believed that technology had a tremendous influence on social structure. Not only did he agree with the 'cropper that mechanization would eliminate agricultural labor and disrupt traditional farm life, but he also saw its blade cutting the other way; he was convinced that industrialization would make more and more city folk into a new kind of sharecropper, saddled with the risk, but without a stake in ownership.[1]

"A clever mechanic arrangement" was Raper's laconic impression of the first cotton picker.[2] "The cooperators did not believe it would work, but hoped it would and hoped it wouldn't." They didn't necessarily think they'd be thrown off the farm if the machine worked, but there would be little need for more farmers in the future. That was for sure. The picker's first pass down a row had netted about a third of the cotton, but the stalk still stood upright, and the cotton in the bag was clean. The machine ran back and forth up the same row a half dozen times without damaging the plant. Then, Raper saw the operator stop halfway up a long row, jump down, and adjust the machine.

From then on, it picked up half the cotton on each stalk. Raper wrote to Will Alexander in Washington. "It was very pathetic and hopeful, too, to see the pickers drop their sacks to come up to see the mechanical picker, or carry their sacks to come up to see the mechanical picker, or carry their sacks on their shoulders and come across the rows to the picker! 'Well, now we'll see.' Much staring, anxiousness, a kind of blurred electrical situation."[3]

"The most hope I have seen anywhere"

Still, with all the uncertainty mechanization was engendering, Raper could report to Alexander, "The most hope I have seen anywhere along the way is the Eddy Farm. The people began in late March and now have a good crop of cotton, perhaps 215 bales on 275 acres. Much of the land needs to be cleared of ten-year-old cottonwood trees."[4] The Delta Cooperative Farms had been staked by Sherwood Eddy of the national YMCA. The Delta Co-op consisted of two landholdings owned by the cooperative's board and black and white tenants who worked the land in Bolivar and Holmes counties, in the Mississippi Delta. First, in 1936, the co-op farmers tried to farm two thousand acres in Bolivar named for Rochdale, England's pioneering cooperative farm. When the land proved poor for cotton, they bought an additional tract of 2,800 acres in Holmes County in 1939, the site of a prosperous antebellum plantation known as Providence, which in the middle of the Depression lay fallow and desolate. The overhead for the Delta Co-op farms was small—the acreage had come cheap—and everyone involved was motivated, by Depression, dislocation, and their ideals, to develop a new kind of pioneering.

Most of the Delta Co-op's thirty black and white tenant families were from eastern Arkansas, victims of the landowners' backlash against the Southern Tenant Farmers Union (STFU). The farms were run by half a dozen idealistic young Christian Socialists, as historian John Egerton has called them. On the original board, besides Eddy were theologian and activist Reinhold Niebuhr, black sociologist Charles S. Johnson, F. D. Patterson, H. L. Mitchell, president of the STFU, Howard Kester, Dr. William Amberson, Lane Treadway, and John and Mack Rust, inventors of the cotton picker Raper had first seen on the Rochdale farm.[5] The farm director, Sam Franklin, was a preacher's son with a gift for the practical. Will Alexander sent Raper and others to survey the Delta Co-op, analyze its efficiency, and look for effective procedures to apply in turn to federal resettlement projects.[6] Raper's involvement began about the same time he started thinking about the ideas that would go into his next book, *Sharecroppers All,* the culmination of his work in the rural South, and before long, he became a member of the board as well.[7]

"The Delta Cooperative Farm," Raper wrote Alexander after his first trip, "is a very interesting development. The families there are working hard, and are beginning to sense the advantages which will accrue to them through cooperative efforts. The crops are good. The management has made common sense adjustments in the areas of economics and race factors. The whole project is characterized by something of a religious fervor which may serve well to maintain morale among the lowly ex-sharecropper families who live there."[8]

The "cooperating" families lived in well-maintained frame houses built of wood cut and milled on the farm, with sanitary wells and privies. Houses for whites stood in a row, two hundred yards north of the black farmers' similar houses. A community house had been erected in between. Raper did not notice much social contact between the races, but he did observe a show of respect. As members of the STFU, most of the families had been driven off the plantations of eastern Arkansas, and they knew each other's troubles. At the co-op, Raper noted, "The families seem to have very little race consciousness and take each other as people to a marked degree. White sharecroppers 'Mr.' Negro men with ease and dignity."[9]

Raper was always interested in the character of leadership in any project, as well as the cultural notions of the rank and file. "Sam Franklin, man in charge," Raper observed, "is a christian idealist with good horse sense. The whole outfit is rather impelled with his religious zest. Many volunteer people have been there this summer to conduct daily vacational [sic] Bible classes, etc., to work on the farm, to help with recreation, etc." The board and management were a coalition of Christian activists and socialists skeptical of religion but glad for the chance to put their political beliefs into practice. "Those who are not overt churchmen are overt non-churchmen," Raper told Alexander. "A funny thing to see, but they get along because they all agree that the farm must be a success."[10] Raper admired the zeal he saw in the co-op's "churchmen," but only as it offered practical benefit. "I have no real faith in religion as now organized in the South," he confided to Charles Johnson. "The type Sam Franklin lives will surely put him in the martyristic position sometime; on the other hand, it may have some potency in terms of the real situation."[11]

After that first visit in 1936, he wrote a long piece for the *Presbyterian Sur-*

vey to promote cooperative farming. "Because of the primary importance of the human factor, the program of the Delta Cooperative Farm had rightfully earned widespread attention." Because the "cooperators" were acquiring equity through their labor, Raper claimed for them two or three times as much work as tenants or sharecroppers typically produce. "The reason is that they have become vitally interested in the success of the project, that they are encouraged to utilize initiative and resourcefulness. They have come to feel that they can determine their destiny, and they are responding to the opportunities offered them." To Raper, this experiment indicated that "a similar response could be secured from the vast majority of the South's landless farmers, if constructive procedures for them were worked out." But what kind of constructive procedures? And who would determine how they were worked out?[12]

Raper himself was torn about how he thought the Delta Co-op should be run. Ideally, it should operate as a scientific experiment, he told Charles Johnson. That is, nothing should be done that could not be reproduced elsewhere. But the fact that it was a pioneering venture that needed to fit within the prevailing economic system precluded such an idealistic approach. Trial and error appeared more practical. Racial tension had developed because the biracial character of the farms offended the social mores of the surrounding communities. That most of the families had been in the STFU made them further suspect to white locals. "The situation presents a dilemma," Raper wrote the board in 1938. "If the prevailing pattern is too violently resisted, much of the time will be consumed in handling racial details and, if the venture goes on, it will induce a martyr complex on the part of all concerned. On the other hand, if we yield on the racial issue at unnecessary points, merely to facilitate the economic aspect of the experiment, we lose an important value of the experiment. Since white and Negro agricultural workers are in contact in natural situations throughout the South, it would be an artificial and unreal experiment that did not include them. The point would be to demonstrate the workableness of a new personal basis of relations within the pattern of race."[13]

The co-op ran on an ad hoc principle of "inter-racial justice" that fell short of integration. "The two communities determined to live separately," Raper wrote, "and to be separate in a social life. They would come together and cooperate, however, in the economic development of the farm." He quoted Eddy's approach to race. "The Negro is doubtless the acid test of America's principle of democracy. For no country has any more democracy than it is willing to grant to its weakest and poorest citizens." Still, the official policy was wait-and-see. "The policies on the Delta Cooperative will be conservative and patient. They will be non-violent and constructive," according to Eddy. "The aim of this Delta Farm is to provide a favorable environment and see how the Negro farmer will respond. Thus far most of them have made good."[14]

Raper returned a number of times. In the spring of 1938, he traveled again to the delta and continued to be impressed with the co-op's progress. "Without question, there are certain dramatic and news-worthy stories at the Farm," he wrote to Alexander. "The families are very much better dressed, look better fed, and have developed in their corporate undertaking. Not all roses by any means: the land at Rochdale is difficult to cultivate and the farm at Providence is not safe until a creek, which runs across one end of it, has been kept within bounds."[15] The same year, Eddy also reported positively on a tour the board had recently taken of the new farm at Providence. "Here we found the first ten families already settled, working without supervision on their own initiative and under their own elected council. We inspected their fine crops of cotton, corn, potatoes, vegetables and almost complete self-subsistence farming, already far advanced within less than three months." The co-op's farm families, many of them black, "were making more and enjoying a richer life," Eddy claimed, "than would be possible if each had the traditional 'forty acres and a mule.'"[16]

In spite of the optimism, everyone knew that the old plantation system would be a weak platform on which to build a successful cooperative. Farmers, management, and board members all realized that the project would take a great deal of experimentation with crops and livestock and with varied methods of production, harvesting, and marketing. And yet, pressures mounted to see fast results. In spite of Eddy's positive words, the farms had required repeated infusions of new funds. And they were pinched in many other ways. The doctor and nurse and the co-op's clinic had begun offering medical care to surrounding tenants, for example, reluctantly draining resources from the farms. Eventually Amberson charged Eddy with being positive to the point of dishonesty and dictatorial in his management of the board.[17] In 1942, the board folded the Delta Co-op and consolidated its resources on the Providence Farm, until local, white backlash against the rise of civil rights activism finally ended the operation in the 1950s.[18]

"For many regionalists in the 1930s," writes historian Robert Dorman, "the need to factor the transformation of industrialization, the force of tradition, and the demands for social justice required a somewhat different configuration for rural reconstruction, one tending away from the proprietary individualism of 'many owners' and toward a full-fledged cooperatism and collectivism. Arthur Raper tentatively took this further step beyond the lingering neo-republican prejudices of the Odum group with his call for 'democratic cooperative endeavor' in *Sharecroppers All*." For Raper, the Delta Cooperative Farms would become another way of testing out on the ground the ideas he would soon publish in *Sharecroppers All*.[19]

Near the end of his life, Sam Franklin was still wondering why the Delta Co-op had failed. A few months before Raper's death in 1979, Franklin got in touch and asked what Raper thought about it, forty years later. "It was inevitable," Raper told him, "that the operations of the farms in Mississippi would be problem-laden, for the land of each was far from ideal, and, yet more important, that the farm families on them had over a period of years been schooled in disinheritance, and that the damaging results of this disinheritance to personality could be overcome only by constructive programs operating over decades at least. And that this was nearly impossible in a cultural situation that reinforces the continued disinheritance of the nether group as then defamed in Mississippi." Such conditions were enough to overcome what Franklin called "the dedication of the Farm members, volunteers, staff members, and others, who gave so much to the project."[20] To Raper, the lesson of Delta Cooperative Farms was that cooperative endeavors required sustained political, economic, and social will over the course of generations. Faith in democracy meant sustaining that will over the course of many rocky years.

"Mister, I can figure"

Late in the hot summer of 1937, Raper and Floyd Corry spent a month driving the length of the South. Raper wanted to assess the work of a dozen or so Resettlement Administration (RA) projects, as well as see some cooperative efforts that seemed to signal a move away from the plantation system. He promised to send Alexander reports on the projects, and on local attitudes concerning labor conditions—his notes always included an assessment of sociological factors along with agricultural conditions—"and maybe a suggestion or two. This jaunt," he wrote Alexander, "will be of real value to me."[21]

Heading west at the burnt end of August, Raper and Corry drove down highways roiling with tumbleweed into the heart of the Dust Bowl. From the car they saw abandoned tractors sunk into barren cropland. They saw good homes in small towns, their yards given over to thistle. They pulled into Keyes, Oklahoma, with sand in their eyes and throats and shoes, and they saw fine dirt piled a foot high across the floors of several of its barns. The druggist downtown had shoveled his sidewalk to reach his store. Raper talked with a number of small farmers whose "pretty places" had turned to dust. "Ground sinks beneath feet in many places," Raper scribbled in his notepad. "Many roads impassable. Fences covered with dust almost to top. You can look across the fields and see dirt sliding over itself near the horizon—an uncanny thing to watch; you see bleak and deserted, leaning farmhouses, with sand piled two to six or more feet deep around some of the walls; expansive fields, covered with nothing but thistle or tumble-weed."[22]

They were driving down a dusty highway in eastern Arkansas, heading toward Memphis, when Raper saw a hobo up ahead hitching a ride. He pulled to the shoulder.

"I see you're on the road," Raper offered, as Corry jumped in back and the white farmer settled into the passenger seat.

"Yes, I'm on the road."

Raper had learned to let a lot of silence pass with farmers. After a while, the farmer said, "Mister, you know why I'm on the road? I'm on the road because niggers can't figure in Arkansas."

"Wait a minute. How is that?"

"I'm on the road, and I have a family, and I'm off of the farm over in the bottoms of Arkansas," the man told him. "See, I can figure, and I wasn't wanted." It turns out, the man had worked a farm for years. "I had come down from the hills and replaced a colored family, and we were getting along alright. And then things got tougher and tighter. When the owner had started taking a larger share, the fellow told him, 'Mister, I can figure.' After that, the owner simply wouldn't have me. He went and got a nigger who couldn't figure. And I'm here on the road."[23]

"A little too rambunctious and communistic"

The first southern sharecroppers to organize for protection worked in Arkansas, where the plantation was newer and least-well established, having been opened to cotton production at the time of the Great War. "There was a new life style which was comparatively free of the paternalism," H. L. Mitchell observed. "The master-slave society had not fully developed in Arkansas." Mitchell was a child of the rural poor himself who became a school teacher and a homegrown socialist in Tyronza, Arkansas. He met with black and white farm workers who had been evicted, recruited a few socialists from around the region, and formed the Southern Tenant Farmers' Union (STFU) in 1934 to protest inequities in the Agricultural Adjustment Act (AAA) program. The AAA had left it to owners to disburse crop-reduction payments to their tenants. Without government enforcement, though, the owners kept the lion's share. The STFU also criticized AAA programs for exacerbating the displacement of tenants, a point Raper frequently made as well. Odum's Chapel Hill institute provided the documentation that proved, as Mitchell said, "that the STFU wasn't just a group of agitators, foreign or otherwise, who were stirring up trouble."[24] Roosevelt responded to the growing political momentum by establishing the RA, with Rex Tugwell as its head and Will Alexander as deputy administrator, to address the needs of the rural poor.[25] In the fall of 1936, Tugwell convinced Secretary of Agriculture Henry Wallace to see conditions in the Deep South for himself. Wallace traveled the South with Will Alexander and C. B. Baldwin with a copy of *Preface to Peasantry* in his suitcase, shocked by the poverty of the Black Belt. The destitution of the South began to gain more press, and the STFU was adding to membership rolls. By 1937, the union had attracted thirty thousand members through six states. Significantly, and dangerously, a third of the members were black.

The STFU was a political powder keg. It endured tremendous repression, including beatings and intimidation, from the owners over tenants' and sharecroppers' attempts to organize. The atmosphere surrounding the STFU was dangerous and repressive. Raper knew an investigator who had interviewed policemen like Chief Deputy Ward of Caruthersville, Missouri, about a lynching in nearby Sikeston. "They shot that son of a bitch three or four times," Ward told him. "They should have shot him ten." The problem with due process, he opined, was that "sometimes you can't wait. It's better to do it right there."[26]

The STFU attracted further attention in a March of Time newsreel in August 1936 that showed Mitchell in his second-floor office in downtown Tyronza and countered his popular image as a rabble-rouser. Years later, Mitchell told a conference at Chapel Hill that, one day not long after the newsreel, he had been sitting at his desk, when a brisk-talking young-looking fellow walked in. He looked across the desk and demanded, "Are you Mitchell?"

"Yes," he said, and waited through a long pause. "I didn't know whether he was going to shoot me or what."

"Where is your cage?" he finally asked.

"I didn't know what he meant," said Mitchell, "and I just looked at him."

"I have been over in Eastern Arkansas," said the man, "and they told me over there how bad you are. So I was sure that you would be in a cage, and I would have to pay 25 cents just to see you."

"He has been my good friend ever since," Mitchell laughed. "He is a real social scientist. He has written books, and made many surveys and reports. He has also helped in land redistribution all over the world—Japan, the Philippines, and other countries, but they have never let him redistribute the land here in the South. He is Arthur Raper."[27]

As the Depression ground on, and he saw southern blacks and white farmers fall farther into poverty, Raper became more outspoken in his speeches, even to conservative audiences. He stood before a Civitan Club's Luncheon Meeting in January 1937 and told the tradesmen and small businessmen who filled the Atlanta Athletic Club, "Anyone who looks realistically at the typical American business man must see that he still thinks it is 'good business' to get more from the earth and from society than he puts back. Such a system doubtless served our ancestors well in their hurried conquest of the American continent, but it fails now to provide the purchasing power needed to distribute our available goods and services."[28]

Japan had torn a page from our history in their treatment of Manchuria, he told them, "and Italy has memorized enough North European policy to confound the leading nations of the League of Nation in explaining her 'rights' in Ethiopia." American exploitation of resources included the dispossession of the Indians and the treatment of blacks. "Throughout their stay in America, the Negroes have been exploited economically, politically, and culturally," he explained to the silent tables of Civitans. "We continue to pay them low wages and to restrict their work opportunities, keep them away from the polls, divert sizable public funds from their educational and health programs to ours, employ none of them in the courthouse and city hall, permit mobs to lynch scores of them with impunity, laugh at black-faced minstrels, and repeat ludicrous stories about Negroes which serve to rob them of their essential humanity."[29]

His critiques were not always appreciated "realistically," even by those on the left. A few days after the Civitan Club speech, Raper received a word to the wise from Witherspoon Dodge, self-styled leader of "Radio Church, A Liberal Institution." Dodge told him he had not heard very good reports about the speech. "As a friend, I am slipping it to you that some of the nut-heads thought you were a little too rambunctious and communistic. Of course I like company, especially good company, but I don't want you to run the risk of jeopardizing the valuable liberalizing service that you are rendering. Hence, if there be need, calm down the fire and put on the brakes a bit."[30]

It had become clear to Raper, though, that the only hope for a democratic way of life in America was for blacks and working-class whites to gain participation in the political process. As the world moved toward another World War and the number of "patriotic" organizations began to rise, Raper believed that no one could depend on his or her civil rights until everyone had been granted their own civil rights.[31] So he did not put on the brakes a bit. Nor did he confine his criticism to southern venues.

In 1941, Mitchell invited Raper to New York to speak at the Amsterdam Hotel on behalf of National Sharecroppers Week. "The United States is a long road," he told the well-heeled gathering. "Wall Street is at one and a sharecropper cabin at the other." Then, as he recalled, "I proceeded to tell the brothers in New York that there was some relationship between the croppers' cabin and their own affluence, which was all around me that night. They were hoping to get $100 from everybody that night, and $1,000 from some. I emphasized the deprivation of those chaps that lived down at the end of the road in the sharecropper cabin, and most of the people liked it, but some of them didn't like this idea of saying that part of the reason there was so much wealth in New York was that they had been able to skim it off of such wide areas in such devious ways sometimes, and sometimes not devious, but anybody who's a creditor can always bitch a little bit, or more, when you get around where the accumulation takes place."[32]

In spite of his radical message, Raper found himself being "received handsomely" in intellectual circles, and by fair-minded citizens in every town and city in the South. He was convinced by wide experience, as well as his own temperament, that "people knew that something ought to be said about the racial situation, and about the sharecroppers situation, and the poor white situation." Looking back from the 1970s, he himself found this acceptance almost unbelievable, given prevailing views on racial and class agitation. Nevertheless, "between the thirties and the forties, there wasn't any platform in the South that I wasn't asked to appear on, except the Ku Klux Klan and the Knights of Columbus. But the DAR, the United Daughters of the Confederacy—even they had to have Raper come for some reason or another."[33] He booked ten speaking engagements a month through all of 1936 and 1937. No one was surprised at the content of his speeches. "They didn't invite me because they didn't know anything about what I was doing," he recalled. "They knew about what I was going to say, but they wanted me to come." People all over the South did not themselves want to say out loud that change was needed. "They knew their barns would get burned if they said too much, or pushed the local mores too far. But they, themselves, I think, were wishing and hoping that somehow or other the situation could develop in which they could be more free." He told historian Walter Jackson, "I simply cannot explain it other than on the basis that there was a residual of what I would think of right-thinking and right-feeling." White liberals across the region used him as a vehicle for their own aspirations of a more just South.[34] "They didn't want to sink our boat," Raper said about many white southerners he met throughout the decade. "They very definitely didn't. They weren't quite satisfied with what we were doing, but"—he was certain of this—"they sort-of wanted somebody to do it. They wanted somebody to press up here and have some association with Negroes. Treat them like people. They wanted it done. *They didn't want to do it.*"[35]

"Mr. Raper entertains sociology students"

"In the late afternoon," began a story of a class trip in the Agnes Scott *Agonistic*, "the group gathered around an open fire and enjoyed hamburgers, peanuts, potato chips, marshmallows, fruit, crackers, and coca-colas." By 1936, Arthur was often inviting his students home, while Martha and the children helped with musical entertainment. The visits were not, however, without their educational components. "After supper," continued the *Agonistic,* they sat on logs around the fire while several members of the class reported on books about the family in the Middle Ages. Lulu Ames presented several interpretations of typical family situations at different periods of history, and Frances Belford and Sarah Johnson gave book reports."[36] At his home, in the classroom, walking barren cotton fields, or in Atlanta's ghetto, Raper made sure his students came away from his classes with the sense that the world didn't have to work in one particular way.

He had begun to make similar points on the air as well, using occasional short talks on the Agnes Scott program on an Atlanta radio station. In the mid-1930s, he had become, in a low-key way, an advocate for sociology as an aid to greater egalitarianism and democratic action through government. Social science required vision toward that end, he said in his addresses. He "wanted to focus attention upon the fact that for the social scientist to be effective in this modern world of hard-surfaced roads and skyscrapers, automobiles and motion pictures, telegraphs and radios, loudspeakers and gaudy billboards, surpluses and bread lines, he must possess something of the insight and character of those constructive religious and social leaders who have emerged now and then across the centuries." And sociology required a hard shell, too, for the hardships a practitioner might find who traveled the Depression South preaching racial equality. "He must make his contribution in a world where entrenched special interests will frown on him and destroy his teachings, if they can. And all in a short-sighted attempt to safeguard for themselves the advantages which they now happen to have."[37]

The 1938 *Silhouette,* Agnes Scott's yearbook, was dedicated to "Arthur F. Raper, a sociologist who lives by practical theories, rather than as an advocate of theoretical practices . . . A teacher whose classes are continually increasing because of the reputation for sincerity and honesty and enthusiasm in presenting his subject."[38] But in spite of the *Silhouette,* in spite of the marshmallows and coca-colas, reactionaries kept an eye on him, and through the late 1930s, placed increasing pressure on the school's administration concerning his beliefs and his field trips to slums and gouged farmland and black colleges. He could see the handwriting on the wall, and in the spring of 1940, before the pressure grew too great, he quit. He had always taught only part-time, because he didn't want to rely on it solely for support. Ever since Roosevelt's election, it had been easier for liberals all across the South to find more support in Washington than to seek it out at home. By the late 1930s, with the Interracial Commission drying up, Raper gravitated to the only safe place for a southern radical and began working more and more for the New Deal.

"Can you serve us?"

While Raper and Corry had been wiping the sand from their eyes in Dust Bowl Arkansas in September 1937, the RA became the Farm Security Administration (FSA). Secretary of Agriculture Henry Wallace had considered the RA's resettlement and construction projects as nearly complete, and Roosevelt believed a new agency would be needed to help carry out the recently passed Bankhead-Jones Farm Tenant Act by lending money to farm tenants and developing land utilization plans. Wallace named Will Alexander to head the new agency. And Alexander continued to use Raper as his eyes in the field, first for the RA, then with the FSA. It was under the new FSA auspices that Raper had headed west. By 1937, he was traveling more for the FSA than the Interracial Commission. The following summer, Roosevelt would issue his devastating *Report on the Economic Conditions of the South* and make his famous pronouncement of the South as the nation's number one economic problem, trying to resuscitate the effort to redress the region's poverty.[39]

By then, Raper had released his last publication on lynching. In 1936, the Commission for Interracial Cooperation (CIC) published a pamphlet, "The Mob Still Rides, A Review of the Lynching Record, 1931–1935." Starting where *The Tragedy of Lynching* had left off, Raper charted the way the number of lynchings had dropped to a just a few in 1931 and 1932, then rose again, to twenty-eight in 1933 and twenty in 1935. "The optimism of ten years ago is waning," Raper wrote. "Lynchings are not fading naturally from the American scene; the mob still rides."[40] Now, though, more headlines in the southern press referred to the need for aid to blacks. By 1936, partly due to Raper's and the CIC's influence, lynching had become tied in the public mind more directly to civil rights and education. The headlines had begun to read "Negro Education Urged of South" and "Racial Exploitation Blamed in Lynchings."[41]

By 1937, 65 percent of southerners supported a federal antilynching law, according to Gallup. In fact, a higher percentage of southerners wanted to see a federal bill than respondents on the West Coast.[42] By then, most members of the Interracial Commission favored federal legislation. Raper's experience in the field told him that only federal protection would make small-town whites feel safe enough to speak out and identify mob members.[43] The biggest opponent to a federal role was Jessie Daniel Ames, head of the CIC's women's campaign against lynching, who remained committed to states' rights and, as Raper saw it, the continuation of segregation.[44] "Insisting that her woman's group was the most effective means of combating racial violence," writes Ellis, "she confided to a friend that her position was 'far from popular with the Commission.'" In a few years, their disagreement over federal involvement would spill into acrid testimony before a congressional subcommittee.[45]

As the new FSA was inaugurated, Alexander passed the directorship of the

CIC to Howard Odum in an attempt to change direction and broaden the perspective of the commission, as Odum saw it, by adopting his regionalist orientation, emphasizing agricultural rehabilitation, the coming of industry, labor and public administration, in addition to race relations. The South was a different place than it had been in 1919. To Odum, the increasing complexity of southern problems required that the commission cast a wider net to capture the economic and political factors that determined race relations. At the same time, Will Alexander had begun to feel, as did Raper, that the gradualist philosophy in race relations increasingly appeared bankrupt. Raper was caught between white CIC staff members who opposed integration and the black activists he worked with who now called for nothing less than an end to segregation. Odum's CIC did pursue a campaign against the poll tax and white primary and worked to repeal laws that disfranchised blacks. But the commission had lost the support of many black activists who saw that greater militancy had become a more effective means toward equality than education of whites. But before militancy could become possible, blacks had needed an organization of white southerners to help prepare the ground with the middle class of the white South, on the basis of scientific evidence and "realistic," common-sense thinking. But by the late 1930s, the Interracial Commission's position of advocating for black rights within the Jim Crow system had already served its purpose.[46]

Within a few years, once the country had begun a fight for democracy abroad, it became impossible for southern liberals to avoid the question of segregation. The contradiction between the support of legal segregation and the fight for equality throughout the world had become too great, and the Interracial Commission cracked under the pressure. Odum succeeded in changing its name to the broader, and more amorphous, Southern Regional Council, and the Commission on Interracial Cooperation was drowned out by the war and dwindled to an end in the middle of 1943.[47]

Through the late 1930s, Raper himself was operating between the older approach of quiet accommodation and the growing militancy of young black activists. His own way of bending Jim Crow was to ignore him resolutely, whenever possible, practicing a policy that a later generation would describe as, "Don't ask, don't tell." Private companies had begun to covet the African American market, but these businesses did not want to lose the white market by standing up for integration. So, for example, Raper took it upon himself to book the train reservations for black scholars and activists when they visited the Interracial Commission's offices in Atlanta. "And here now was an interesting thing happening," he chuckled, remembering the scenario. The ticket sellers at the Pullman offices in Atlanta knew the Interracial Commission brought in both blacks and whites from all around the country. But when Raper would walk over to make reservations for Mary McLeod Bethune, for example, they would not ask him, "Is Mrs. Bethune white or is she black?" And when Mrs. Bethune turned up, she was a fait accompli. She already had her reservation. No one raised a fuss. They all knew whom he was buying tickets for. Company policy still prohibited blacks from riding on Pullmans, but everyone knew they rode the cars. "They wanted them to. They wanted our business."[48] Raper's point was, "If the Interracial Commission had gone to the Pullman Company in writing, and said, 'We want to have this meeting. We're going to have it every year, and smaller groups in between. This is our clientele. These are the people we want to bring here. Can you serve us?' It would have been in the record. They would have had to say 'no.'"

But Raper never gave them a chance to say no, and Pullman backed down rather than stand openly for segregation. "And our folks came and went in dignity," he said, with some satisfaction. "It wasn't a completely open society; it wasn't a completely closed one either, unless someone stood on his rights and said, 'I don't want to ride a Pullman, unless it's publicly announced that I'm going to ride it two days ahead of time, and put in the paper.' Well, if that's what he had to do to enjoy a ride in the Pullman, we didn't have any way of servicing him." With a decade of experience as a racial activist in the Jim Crow South, Raper had learned the system and quietly enjoyed being able to play it so well.[49]

He even tried, whenever he could, to turn the opposition against itself. On a Sunday in February 1936, for example, Raper drove down to Barnesville, Georgia, to speak at the First Methodist Church on "The Cause, Curse, and Cure of Farm Tenancy." The Reverend Nath Thompson had attracted the watchful eye of the Klan. The church was filled. By then, Raper's work had become well known among the far right. The Klan's attention later focused on Raper's teaching at Agnes Scott, but in 1936, the group wanted to accumulate damning evidence of Raper's dangerous points of view, and sent a stenotypist to record his Barnesville speech. Raper told her that the only way he would allow her to record his speech was if she would send him a copy of her full transcript. After a bit of hesitation, she agreed.

A few minutes later, he was telling the parishioners, and the stenotypist was duly recording, "If we believe in Christianity, if we believe in the brotherhood of man, in representative government, in continuation of the home, in democratic institutions—if we believe in building and making money instead of destroying, for ourselves and for others, if we believe in hope and health and decency, in conservation of soil fertility, our greatest natural resource, and in promotion of human welfare, we must solve this problem [of tenancy farming]. It can be faced and solved."[50] When the transcript arrived in the mail soon after, Raper took it to a printer and developed a twenty-five-page pamphlet, "The South's Landless Farmers." The CIC eventually distributed more than twenty thousand copies throughout the South of a progressive land-management publication initiated through a "contribution" by the Klan.[51]

All through the 1930s, Arthur and Martha Raper's family was growing—to three boys and, last, a girl, and they initiated them all to music making, as well as the hiking, camping, and nature study Arthur loved so well. When the first two boys, Charles and Harrison, were six and seven, he took them on a two-day hike to an old haunt in the Blue Ridge, high above Asheville. On the way home, they stayed the night at a pioneer's log cabin, listening to a tumbling mountain stream. "A great deal of poetry," he wrote a friend, "along with unwiped noses and stumped toes."[52]

But hardly any aspect of his life escaped Raper's bent toward organizing and leadership. Every summer, the young Raper family spent time at Lake Junaluska, high above Asheville, where he ran a Methodist summer conference program and brought Charles S. Johnson, for example, to speak on race relations, and C. T. Carpenter, the STFU's attorney, to talk about unionizing. "We talked about race and lynchings and farm tenancy and peonage and the high interest rates of the small loan sharks," Raper recalled. "We talked about all the major questions that came along." Because his speakers were so topical, he was able to book the prime weeks and attracted crowds of three or four thousand a night.[53]

"A wonderful sort of love feast"

Never mind that many of his remedies distributed aid inequitably or displaced those he was trying to help. Franklin Roosevelt had developed a broad, popular appeal for his groundbreaking programs in liberal social engineering. The AAA, for example, may have inadvertently favored the large landowners and left the short end of the stick to the small farmer and tenant, but who was offering them even as much? The fact is, the federal government was now helping poor and working-class families of both races in the cities and on the farms of the South, and allowed thousands of others to stay in the middle class. This swelling of support, all across the nation, stamped by Roosevelt's landslide victory in the 1936 election, emboldened racial activists across the South toward a show of strength, the declaration of a new political force. The 1938 Southern Conference on Human Welfare (SCHW) was not a labor union, but it sought to organize a collective. Instead of working for a specific trade or association of workers, the SCHW tried to establish a union of liberal activism on behalf of African Americans and the dispossessed of the South. Many liberals thought it too brash a declaration, including Odum and Ames in Chapel Hill. But to Raper, after years of driving the South to speak at one Odd Fellows Hall after another to silent rooms full of skeptical shop owners, it was a sign of progress and a comfort as well. The SCHW was a meeting of 1,500 southerners, black and white, labor unionists and governors, state officials and U.S. senators, social scientists and socialists. As John Egerton wrote, the South had never seen such a gathering of progressives a s the Birmingham meeting.[54]

"The right people met there," Raper declared, "and they met for the right cause. It was one of the most spontaneous upwellings of hope I think I have seen in the South or anywhere else. And at that first meeting, people were having their say." The conference was unusual in many ways. Because it was organized so quickly, he said, "it had in some ways the seeds of its own undoing in its unstructured nature. Most meetings by the time they get that size have had years of experience and growth and development, but here it just gets together, and it afforded opportunities for people who had designs to begin to working their way."

He called the conference "one of the most serious efforts ever made in the South to deal realistically with all of the region's major problems. The attendance, the nature of the discussions, and the active participation of the delegates suggest an awakening of Southern people to their own conditions, and the need for constructive programs. It is hopeful when college professors, newspaper editors, government officials, industrialists, and labor leaders sit down and talk together."[55]

The conference was filled with criticism of federal efforts, but it was organized by New Dealers, from the president himself to the conference chairman, Louise O. Charlton, an Alabama federal judge appointed by FDR. Even though the legislative phase of the New Deal had ended, as historian Patricia Sullivan observes, its political consequences were still much at stake. Many in the Roosevelt administration "maintained that the fate of New Deal reform would depend largely on what happened in the South."[56]

Following the release of the *Report of the Economic Conditions of the South* in 1938, in which the president identified the region as "'the Nation's No. 1 economic problem," Roosevelt had suggested a conference of southerners to address the concerns raised by the report. The result was the SCHW, whose first meeting was held in Birmingham over Thanksgiving week of the same year. Birmingham attracted 1,200 political leaders, labor activists, academics, and journalists, one-third of them black. For the first time in the South, its liberals met in a show of strength. Because of disagreements between liberals and radicals, the SCHW was longer on rhetoric than accomplishment, beyond its subsequent campaign against the poll tax. It was dogged by conservatives and reactionaries because of its union tinge, the presence of a handful of Communists, and its implicit hostility toward Jim Crow. From the start, the SCHW was tainted by charges of promoting racial equality. While leaders did not intend to take a stand on segregation, Frank Graham, who presided over the conference, acknowledged the feelings of many in his keynote address. "The black man," he said, "is the primary test of our democracy and Christianity."[57] Raper had expected trouble. "We were in the vanguard," he recalled. "We were saying that we had to have some interracial meetings. We were going to have interracial meetings in Birmingham. It put the town on its edge and it was sort of a warning, a red flag of danger as it were, to people in the South that here was a group that wasn't dependably orthodox. Particularly on the race issue." Not that Raper minded at all. "I thought we'd been orthodox quite long enough," he explained. "And if we had a meeting, and it was a logical thing for Negroes and whites to be at it, there ought to be a place where we could meet."[58]

The second day, the issue caught fire. Eugene "Bull" Connor, spurred by reactionary whites, interrupted the conference to enforce the city's segregation ordinance that prohibited a mixed audience in the municipal auditorium and threatened arrests if participants continued meeting in mixed groups. Leaders mollified Connor by splitting the auditorium, with blacks sitting on one side and whites on another. "A lot of us," said Raper, "felt that this isn't the way it should have gone, and it mustn't go this way the next time. And where can we meet? How can we do it?" Had he been on the executive committee, as he was for the second meeting of the conference, he would have voted to disobey the ordinance.[59]

Connor's intimidation became international news when Eleanor Roosevelt herself, late for a meeting, took an open seat on the "Negro side" of the auditorium. A few minutes later, she was told by a Birmingham policeman that she was breaking the law. Delegates said she picked up her chair and plunked it in the middle of the aisle. She declined to follow up with a statement of her beliefs, but that meant little in the face of the tale's symbolic importance to conservatives and liberals alike. In practical terms, the SCHW's subsequent resolution never to meet again in a city where segregation was mandated opened the door to a whole range of economic boycotts in support of social reform.[60] As Raper said later, "The action of the Conference which secured the most notice in Birmingham and outside was the resolution condemning the enforcement of Birmingham's racial segregation law, and its instruction to the permanent Conference officials that this matter be kept in mind when selecting places for future conferences."[61]

Beyond Graham's and Eleanor Roosevelt's addresses, the speakers included Lucy Randolph Mason, Clark Foreman, and Charles S. Johnson. Raper spoke on a panel addressing tenant farming with John H. Bankhead, H. C. Nixon, George Mitchell, and Donald Comer. They drafted a resolution seeking to extend more AAA benefits to farm tenants, to expand the FSA and the Bankhead-Jones Farm Tenant Bill, and to support experiments in producers' cooperatives and subsidized rural housing. And they participated in panel discussions dealing with, according to Raper, "farm tenancy, constitutional rights, suffrage, unemployment and labor problems, child labor, women wage earners, prison reform, housing education, health, race relations, freight rates, and youth problems."[62]

To Raper, the conference was a gigantic workshop in political organizing. It served to help a thousand disparate liberals from dozens of different fields to think together about specific programs of action to pursue in Congress and the courthouse, as well as on the factory floor, in the city slums, and in wasted fields. "The resolutions of the Conference dealt with literally every phase of Southern life," he said, and offered examples. "The states were urged to pass wage and hour laws to supplement federal statutes, and to support Southeastern governors in their fight to eliminate freight rate differentials. Public defenders in the various states were recommended to provide free legal counsel for the poor—farm tenants and wage hands in rural areas, and members of low-income groups in cities."[63]

The conference endorsed Social Security and petitioned Congress to extend its services to farm laborers, domestics, and other groups not then reached, many of them black. They advocated uniform election laws, as well as the removal of the poll tax. Bibb Graves, the governor of Alabama, present at the meeting, was asked to extend clemency to the remaining Scottsboro prisoners.

Historian Morton Sosna writes about a spirit at Birmingham that held together people who elsewhere would be fighting. "Thus Arthur Raper and Bibb Graves, the Governor of Alabama, both lent their names to the Conference, though Graves, who had been instrumental in upholding the conviction of the Scottsboro boys, held racial views poles apart from those of Raper." But by talking about economics, Raper could implicitly advocate racial equality while breaking bread with Graves.[64]

Much of the usefulness of the SCHW, in Raper's view, was the way it posed crucial questions, similar to those he himself had been asking for years.

> What are the welfare needs of the South? To what extent are they economic, political, racial? What part should be played by local community, state program, and federal government? What part by industrialists, labor leaders, educators, churchmen? Can adequate programs for human welfare be achieved in the South now? If not, why not? If so, by what programs, and through what agencies?[65]

Perhaps he was thinking back to the tent revivals in Arcadia when Raper described the Birmingham meeting as "an exaggerated expression of change in the South.[66] Here was a revival, a bush-shaking, something that just jumped up." Maybe he still saw many bricks in the wall and felt himself well-measured. His was not the only exuberant reaction. Virginia Durr called it "a wonderful sort of love feast." Even those with more reason for skepticism were pleased. Black poet Sterling Brown was at least hopeful. "The hind wheel may be off and the axle dragging, but the old cart is hovering along."[67]

Late 1938 had seemed a particular moment of possibility, when the South's business interests could agree with the region's social critics and political progressives that change was needed.[68] Modern meant something similar to both, and businessman and Progressive were finally done with the past. The urban press presented the Birmingham meeting in a positive light. Much of white Birmingham was embarrassed in front of the nation by police enforcement of the segregation ordinance on Mrs. Roosevelt. Many were dismayed by the prospect of an economic boycott.[69] Charles Johnson noted that Birmingham had held biracial events in the past and suggested that "other interests inimical to the Conference's program found it convenient to use the race issue, in the ancient manner, as the most effective means of confounding or perhaps nullifying the proceedings." Nor had reactionary whites been reluctant to call for an investigation of the conference by the House Un-American Activities Committee or to call it communist, and both sides took to the press. The *Atlanta Constitution* ran a story soon after, "Welfare Officials No Reds; Dr. Raper, Educator Replies to Charges That Communists Instigated Southern Conference."[70]

"It was evident," Raper was quoted as saying, "that there were certain elements in Birmingham who didn't like us to be in that city. There were lots of police around, but none of the conference delegates ever asked for this protection. It appears to me the complaints are coming from persons who disliked the prominence and the number of New Dealers present." In addition, "Dr. Raper also pointed out that labor and farm tenant problems were discussed, which might also have 'annoyed certain elements.'"[71] Raper himself was not thrown by the presence of a dozen or so Communists at Birmingham, although he disliked the way the Communists worked, for the same reason he had disliked the pacifists he had met at Chapel Hill.

As an advocate for social equality, he was often accused of being a Communist, but Raper was acutely skeptical of the doctrinaire. Back in the early 1930s, he had spoken against war in principle, but he always held out the option of self-defense, and, as events turned out, was a wary, but not unwilling, supporter of the fight against fascism. He had quickly grown cynical about communist participation in the Scottsboro trial because of the way it shut down dialogue. In Raper's view, the Party had moved in on the trial, pushing out the Interracial Commission, as well as the National Association for the Advancement of Colored People (NAACP) and others. "We either had to work with them," he told Jackson, "or else you had to pull out. They would not give you a chance. I tried. I tried very hard to work out some kind of a collaborated exchange of ideas with them so that we could work together with them."[72]

He remembered a meeting one night to set up a provisional committee in support of the Scottsboro Boys at the Labor Temple in Atlanta. The Communist Party had taken control of the defense at that point, and they had already decided every aspect of the committee. "Now I've been in a lot of conferences and a lot of committees," Raper said, "and I've helped write a lot of reports, but we came away from there that night thoroughly convinced that we were expected to be rubber stamps for that little guy that had been sent in there from somewhere." The organizer had been instructed on exactly what to say and do. "You could just sense the minute that you went in," said Raper. "He could not decide anything. He could not do anything himself but blabber his memorized lines, and his instructions—he was not anything within himself." Raper's revulsion about this kind of direction was visceral. "I thought of him as sort of a pitiful little fellow when the evening was over." The Communist Party, he saw, adopted a cause that had already been growing, then took it over and ended discussion. "I haven't yet learned how to work with Communists," he said, years later.[73]

Notwithstanding his antipathy to the character of the party, Raper was glad for the Communists' presence in the South. Establishing the far left of the political spectrum, the Communist Party helped broaden debate against the region's cacophony of reactionary conservatism. Raper felt the Communist Party presented southern voters a wider range of viewpoints from which to choose. It gave the great majority in the middle more room to think.

Many others were more concerned about communist participation. Odum feared the Communists were behind the Birmingham meeting and refused to attend. He saw the conference as competition for his own plans, according to Raper. And, Jessie Daniel Ames, as Morton Sosna phrased it, "likewise rejected the mystique surrounding SCHW."[74] Many delegates saw the SCHW as moving a step ahead of the Interracial Commission, but Raper did not see it exactly that way. The conference was "talk-oriented rather than action-oriented," he said. The CIC was already doing in a quieter way many of the things the conference wanted to accomplish, but without getting stuck on the issue of segregation.[75]

While Ames may have considered the conference a rival, Raper, along with many of the SCHW participants, agreed with Lucy Randolph Mason that "the South cannot be saved by middle-class liberals alone," as she told the Birmingham conference. "They must make common cause with labor, the dispossessed on the land, and the Negro. Some may find it too shocking to have the other three so articulate about their needs. But this is the basis for progress in democracy, economic justice, and social values in the South."[76]

To Raper, one of the SCHW's most hopeful signs was the fact that it did not consist solely of people like himself and Odum and Ames and Alexander. He agreed with Jesse O. Thomas of Atlanta, who "suggested that the reason the Birmingham Conference dealt realistically with the Southern racial situation was 'the fact that the majority of the delegates were hand-laborers and not the white collar professional interracialists.'" What they did not so well understand, said Thomas, was that "the power of the Birmingham police superseded the authority of the church, that the Negro still transcends in importance all other Southern considerations. 'Of human welfare, churches, Christianity, and the Negro,' Mr. Thomas concluded, 'the greatest of these is the Negro.'"[77]

Raper never got over the suspicion that Odum felt Raper's activism compromised his research. Odum had approached him about joining the faculty at Chapel Hill as a junior member; Raper told him he would come only on the same basis as Guy Johnson and H. C. Nixon. "Maybe I was pretty big britches," Raper admitted to historian Walter Jackson, "but I would not have any reason to do any differently now." Skeptical of his activism, Odum wanted Raper to prove himself first as a bona fide social scientist. "Then we will decide what to do with you, buster,' is how Raper phrased it. "But I had something else I could do and wanted to do." Odum knew the quality of Raper's research as well as anyone. Why should he have to take a back seat on the basis of his politics and activism? So he turned Odum down. And once he became involved with the SCHW, there was no turning back. It meant the possibility of working with Odum had passed, which also meant he would never be offered a full-time post at any southern university.

"I had taken a very active part in the Southern Conference on Human Welfare. Odum was a little shy of that. Alexander was a little shy of that. Even Charles S. Johnson was a little shy of that." The SCHW developed just at the time the CIC was shifting toward Odum's Southern Regional Council. Just as the shift was being made, and Odum was finally gaining the larger platform he had wanted for researching and implementing his ideas on regionalism, the SCHW came along—with Odum's own president, Frank Graham, lending tremendous legitimacy—and rendered the CIC as somewhat anachronistic. Odum and Alexander felt the SCHW would be a flash in the pan, but they were afraid, as Raper saw it, "that it was just draining off what they had said would be the solid core of this shift that they were going to bring from the old Commission on Interracial Cooperation over to a more genuinely social science-oriented interracial organization."[78]

"They just simply did not like me too much for being actively involved in that," Raper believed. "I guess they thought I ought to know better." Regardless, he never regretted his association with the conference. It was vibrant, he said, and clearly democratic. Odum's Southern Regional Council "was being done a little bit in the closet. It was going to come out all right, but there was not going to be very much public participation, and there wouldn't be very much public knowledge of it, until it was all set up. I just sort of liked the openness of the Southern Conference."[79]

The next time the SCHW met two years later in Chattanooga, Raper was one of the convenors, and he received "assurances that all sessions, big and little, could be held interracially—and this was done, by local authorities keeping their promise of 'openness' during the days of the conference." The meeting itself, though, was "largely just sort of pandemonium," he said. "I had the feeling that the meeting that we started with in Birmingham had sort of gotten confused with international interest and national labor emphases, and labor training activities and what not, and I simply didn't know very much about that.... The Deep South origin and thrust that was in the first one was somehow or other dissipated or sidetracked." The third conference, held in Nashville in 1942, looked beyond the war. Only five hundred delegates attended, most were black, and the majority affiliated with organized labor. The SCHW also organized a number of local units, the most important headquartered in Washington. Dr. George Johnson, head of the law school at Howard, and Russell Smith, who was in charge of the department of information for the Department of Agriculture, asked Raper to head the chapter, but by then, Raper had begun to have questions about the SCHW leadership, and he passed on the offer.[80] The conference, he said later, "broke on the point of whether or not the leadership was independent or whether it was controlled by the Communists. And I think it was pretty much controlled. I mean they just moved in on it."[81]

"The bright tin roof on the cotton tenant's cabin"

One of the Chapel Hill sociologists' most important articles of faith was that rational planning on a regional basis would enable the South to retain and control its own resources. Constructing an economic bulwark against the control of northern industry and capital would lessen the South's social and racial conflicts. Raper followed Odum in examining patterns of colonialism and analyzing its effects on race relations on rural sociology and urban growth, on industry and agriculture, and on violence and patterns of social change and dislocation. In talks and addresses through the 1930s, and in his 1941 book, *Sharecroppers All,* he depicted his thought on the South's colonial status through one of his favorite tropes, the tin roof of the sharecropper's cabin. In so doing, he characteristically resolved an abstraction, the dynamics of an economic and political system, into a specific and vivid image.

> Nowadays the bright tin roof on the cotton tenant's cabin epitomizes the South's place in the nation. It reflects the exhaustion of local forests from which shingles were once rived; it emphasizes the unbalance between urban and rural economies, for the tin roof was made on machines driven by fossil fuels but paid for by cotton grown in the sun by hand. The price of the roof decreased scarcely one fifth during the depression, cotton over half—the price of the roof was protected by monopoly and tariff, the price of cotton by neither.
>
> The tin roof also sheds light on the urban South, for the raw materials used in its manufacture may have been loaded and crudely processed in the Birmingham area. But Southern industry and labor receive only a small part of the sale price, the Birmingham tasks and pay being limited largely to the unskilled and semi-skilled phases of its production. Even if the roof were made from first to last in the South, the ownership and control of the operation most likely would be centered outside the region, with tribute siphoned off in the form of interest and profits.[82]

Raper pushed the argument in an audacious direction, though, and demonstrated how similar was Odum's new scientifically oriented moderation to the old southern rationale for its own failures. While he agreed that the region was an economic colony of Wall Street and northern industry, Raper was convinced the South's race and class problems were largely the causes, rather than the results, of its colonial status. The South was an agent of its own subservience. Like all regionalists, Raper believed that better education would lead to better jobs and higher standards of living for black and white southerners but, unlike the more moderate regionalists, including Odum, Raper did not believe that education replaced politics, nor that planning could take the place of participation.[83]

Raper emphasized equally the South's own exploitative class relationships and the North-South relationship, and he spent most of the 1930s working directly in a variety of political arenas to ameliorate the region's homegrown inequalities. To Raper, modern social organizations always combined local and national issues and relationships, and he felt it naive to think that one would take care of the other. He said it at Rotary Clubs and academic conferences, in magazine articles and in *Sharecroppers All:* the divisions of race and class—as much as northern colonialism—depressed the wages of all southern workers and kept the South's economy moribund.

"The full picture involves regional as well as national policy and politics," Raper wrote, "for the ease with which the South has been victimized by tariffs and colonial status is dynamically related to her political ineffectiveness in the national Congress for the past several decades. From race and attendant class demarcations stem the South's economic feudalism, one-party system, white primary, and poll taxes. The result has been the disinheritance and disfranchisement of nearly all the Negroes, a majority of the whites, and of the region itself in national affairs."[84]

Would Odum have agreed with Raper that the peculiar social relations the white South defended so tenaciously only served to maintain its political impotence? If so, chances are he would never have written it nor debated it at a Wednesday luncheon meeting of the Macon Chamber of Commerce. It is no wonder that Raper came under fire of the writer Donald Davidson. The sociology that to Raper enabled a realistic approach to the modern age was to Davidson part of the dehumanizing materialism of industrial capitalism. Nor were any of the other Nashville Agrarians inclined in any case to renounce a claim of southern victimhood by acknowledging the region's own role in its decline. On issues of race, the Agrarians deferred to the opinion of their avowed inferior, the poor white southerner. Confronted with a world changing under their feet, the Agrarians threw up their hands at any question involving the role of African Americans in an increasingly industrialized world; Davidson and Allen Tate wrote that changes in blacks' social standing would never be accepted by the average white southerner. Meanwhile, Raper was speaking with white shopkeepers and merchants in Milledgeville and on the radio from Atlanta that changes in race relations were critical to the South's economic recovery.

Conservatives saw the development of the sharecropping system as a response to a set of particular agricultural conditions and a rational accommodation worked out by competing actors in a free-market economy. Planters aimed to retain their control over labor, and instituted Black Codes, which legalized and rationalized serfdom for the former slaves. Meanwhile, the freedmen insisted on becoming wage earners, just as they had expected citizenship. Even when the Black Codes were declared illegal, the landowners were unable to pay wages. The negotiated "compromise" between planters and labor was that the freedmen accepted a reduced wage along with a share of the crop, on the one hand, and planters accepted the payment of wages in return for control over tenants' sources of food and supplies. Sharecropping was seen as a textbook compromise, in which neither side received all it wanted, and both sides profited from the other's concessions. Because the classic economic model gave no consideration to the conditions under which sharecropping developed, the relative positions of power between planter and freedman, or the abuse of that power, Raper considered this view both naive and self-serving.

The Nashville Agrarians, among other moderates and conservatives across the South, believed that once economic conditions improved, racial justice could be sought, in some appropriate measure. Raper and others on the left, including W. E. B. Du Bois and Charles S. Johnson, saw an improvement in racial equality as the precondition that would stimulate the southern economy.

"A Sociologist in Eden"

From Nashville, Donald Davidson had fired a broadside at *Preface to Peasantry* from the deck of the *American Review*. "A Sociologist in Eden" is a statement of the Agrarians' antipathy toward the most "extreme" of the Chapel Hill social scientists, pitting the figure of the literary humanist against the purveyor of cold facts. In his essay review, Davidson recalled his own visits to Macon County, "a beautiful land, a land of long-leaf pines and water-oaks and red earth beneath skies of ever-changing color. And the people are the best of all." But now he realized, in mock chagrin, "how feeble my conception of the all-seeing eye of sociology! I now discover that the wise serpent, the Light-Bringer himself, was in that region before and after my visit, not for purposes of temptation so much as to focus upon Eden the central blaze of a high-powered social-scientific investigation."[85]

Sociology was modernizing and generalizing Davidson's very particular Southland. Traveling from humanism to sociology, he claimed, quoting Tennyson, "'The individual withers, and the world is more and more.'" Not that sociology in itself did not have its place, he said. But in this case, it was clear that Raper's sociology intended to disrupt the pas de deux of southern race relations, one that finely balanced "the old feeling of white responsibility and of black loyalty and devotion."

Davidson said Raper was wrong for believing that mechanization would supplant "the deft and special process of chopping cotton—in which thinning, weeding, cultivating, and replanting go on together—can only be done efficiently with a hoe." The survival of the plantation was a sign of its continuing vitality and resilience. Raper was applying urban standards to a rural South he knew nothing about. Raper did not realize, for example, that "relations between the two races are generally peaceful, partly because the white man, after long experience with the Negro, is indulgent toward him, thinking him to be a less responsible person than a white man." In the end, for all his literary sophistication, Davidson, in his politics, fell back on the standard southern complaint against outside meddling, even against a Carolina farmboy.

"One ought, I suppose, to be charitable with the errors of a man of Mr. Raper's earnestness and ability," Davidson mused, "but how can charity hold out against such garblings and wild imaginings?" When Lillian Smith offered Raper a chance to respond in the *North Georgia Review*, he declined. With resolve toward magnanimity, he recommended the review to a friend, saying he was "flattered that he thought my book deserves such lengthy attention."[86] Davidson paid Raper more attention than any of the other Agrarians did— "and more attention than I paid him and his associates."[87]

Meanwhile, in the spring 1937 number of the *North American Review*, Raper had written as though in reply. "We Southerners know the answers to our race problems," he began, with mock solemnity. "We learned them from our leaders—politicians, educators, churchmen, landlords, industrialists. They have assured us that the answers grew out of the very natures of the two races, and that they have become revered Southern institutions simply because they are right." "The South Strains toward Decency" is a satirical primer on southern race relations. If a white man is orthodox in his beliefs, he is a "real Southerner," he explained. Any critic is a "'nigger lover,' and in charity may be considered honest though deluded; if he becomes effective in his desire to change race relations, he very probably will be called the worst name the community knows, Bolshevik, Communist, or Fool." The harangues of southern patriots "have tried to make it appear that any reasonably liberal person, who believes in treating the Negro like a human being, was a paid agent of Moscow." But the times had begun to change, he observed. "In press, magazine, radio, and book we find things which are out of harmony with what we've been taught." Popular culture, as well as scientific research, has begun to make southerners feel confused about the way they preach Christianity and practice bigotry, for example, about their conviction of white supremacy and the achievements of Jesse Owens and Joe Louis. Whereas Davidson considered blacks as a side issue, Raper felt that the direction of southern race relations would determine the future of the South in the modern era. A few southerners had begun to see, he said, "that a philosophy which neglects Negroes also neglects white people, while one which protects all the white people will also protect the Negro." Either the South begins to strain toward decency in race relations or, by discounting great blocks of its people, it will "fall a frustrated and helpless victim of its own disharmonies."[88]

But several years later, Raper did respond in greater depth, and ironically, largely to agree with Davidson. "He cannot relate," Davidson had complained of Raper, "the shabbiness of tenant houses to the glorious upsurge of the Empire State Building or realize that the thirty or forty cents a day paid to the Negro hadn't may, in a sense, represent what is left when tribute has been paid to Detroit, Wall Street, and the American Federation of Labor." In a sense, *Sharecroppers All* would agree with Davidson's view—minus the crack at labor—that a single highway connected Wall Street and Tobacco Road. While he disagreed wholeheartedly with the Agrarians on social and racial issues, Raper's fears about the consequences of industrial capitalism, expressed in *Sharecroppers All*, were equally as deep.[89]

"There is certainly dynamite in his book"

Through the course of 1938, while FDR was declaring the South the nation's number one economic problem, and the SCHW was taking shape, Raper and Ira De A. Reid, an African American sociologist at Atlanta University, were in the field, assessing the changes in southern society that would become *Sharecroppers All*.[90] Consonant with Roosevelt's theme, the idea they started with was that the southern economy was "a chronic problem in which certain drastic and fundamental changes are taking place in the life of the people."[91]

In January 1938, Raper described their project, formulated under the auspices of Will Alexander. "Pressures from within and without the rural South affect the role and status of its rural dwellers. The processes of urbanization, mechanization, immigration, nationalism, government assistance and regulation—all these definitely influence the farm folk, particularly the tenants, wage hands, and casual laborers. For while the man who grows cotton or tobacco by hand works with products truly international, he lives within a community excessively provincial. . . . The present study will seek to portray the life of Southern rural dwellers, with emphasis upon any recent changes." As their research developed, they began to see that the sharecropping system was not limited to agriculture, so their research began to extend to the new urban South. Raper wrote to W. T. Couch early on that "quite clearly, the manuscript starts off where *Preface to Peasantry* ends—the better to lay a rural plantation background upon which to discuss the urban expressions of the plantation economy, no less than the impact upon the region's caste and class structure."[92]

All through their research on the way race worked in the Depression South, Raper and Reid were required, as a pair of interracial colleagues and friends, to negotiate their way through the system they were studying. Raper remembered having to choose carefully where to stop for lunch. "Once they were going to segregate us when we went on the Pullman from Durham to Greensboro," Raper recalled, "and I said, 'No, wait a minute here—Dr. Reid and I have been over to Chapel Hill at a conference, we've got some papers we need to work on, and we want to work together on them.' And we did."[93]

Through the course of their travel and writing, Raper tried to interest a commercial publisher in *Sharecroppers All*, but once again, Couch ran the only press willing to take a chance on a book that was politically to the left of the most progressive of Roosevelt's policies at a time when a widespread southern conservative reaction was beginning to turn back many New Deal programs. In fact, as the project developed, Raper and Reid came to believe that the "sharecropping" system was endemic to American capitalism, and determined to say so.[94]

Even for Couch this was a dark and unsettling thesis, as it was for several people who evaluated it for the Press. S. H. Hobbs, in Chapel Hill's Department of Rural Social Economics, was of two minds about the manuscript. "Raper has a very biased leaning towards the under-privileged classes," he complained. "There is no question but that everything he says is true but it is all on the negative side." Hobbs feared the effect of such a book on peaceful race relations. "I may be wrong about my conclusions but I have heard Raper speak several times and I feel that from his speeches and from this manuscript he doesn't miss much of advocating things that are highly repugnant to Southerners and to people outside of the South."[95] Judge Orville Park, a friend of Raper's from Macon, was supportive, but somewhat backhanded in his recommendation. "I believe that the picture as drawn in *Sharecroppers All*, as dark as it is, is not overdrawn. I think it is accurate. . . . Concrete examples rather than statistics and abstract statements make the work unusually readable and plants the thought in the mind so that it will not be easily forgotten." Park also agreed with the other readers in feeling that "maybe the Negro's unfortunate status was perhaps a little over emphasized. Since Dr. Reid, the co-author, is himself a Negro this is to be expected." In the end, the best he could muster was a backhanded recommendation.[96]

Alexander himself wrote to Raper, a bit shaken by the manuscript. He recognized Raper's particular style and called his colorful descriptions of the lives of a sharecropper couple "the best piece of writing you have ever done. . . . I seem to be standing on the inside of the mind of this tenant and looking out on the world as it went by. I was much moved by it." His reaction to the overtly political and proscriptive text that followed was a different story. "It seems to me the material lacks unity, and I think, in a sense, it lacks significance. One had the impression, aside from the first beginning, you had on hand some left over material and wanted to use it in a book lest it spoil setting in the cupboard!"[97]

Lucy Mason was an enthusiastic reader, however, and offered to help promote the book. She wrote Couch, "Ever since I saw you that day at the Atlanta luncheon, I have intended writing to urge you to publish Arthur Raper's book because I think it is needed and will fill a place that is still empty. . . . As you know, Dr. Raper has a wide following among civic and social groups in the South and is also well known through his writings in other sections of the country. I recall seeing a number of good reviews of *Preface to Peasantry* when I was living in New York. If the new book is published, I will make it my business to write Bruce Bliven of the *New Republic,* Paul Kellogg of the *Survey,* and a number of other editors who I know in the North, asking their special interest in securing adequate reviews."[98]

Perhaps the most insightful reader's comments were from Margaret Haygood. The conclusions of *Report on the Economic Conditions of the South* and the Birmingham Conference "seem mild," she wrote, in comparison with those of *Sharecroppers All.* "Perhaps it is fortunate that Mr. Raper no longer has a job in a Georgia college to lose, for there is certainly dynamite in his book." At the same time, the manuscript, she told Couch, "makes a good case for the fitness of sociologically trained people for the task of interpreting validly the results of social research to the general public in an almost inspirational manner."[99]

Couch had seen poor sales follow the publication of *The Tragedy of Lynch-*

ing and *Preface to Peasantry,* in spite of the publicity they garnered. And he foresaw an even more paltry return on *Sharecroppers All.* While the manuscript was being edited, in July 1939, Couch suddenly got cold feet and wrote Raper to say he was pulling the book out of production. Meanwhile, Raper had been anxious to see his timely research released as soon as possible. He had understood that the book would be published with all due speed. "Frankly," he replied, "I am sort of dazed."[100] Couch argued that if he were going to take a chance on such a volatile book, with such meager prospects for sales, he wanted financial support. The threat of canceling the book was Couch's way of getting Raper to approach Odum, once again, for a subsidy.[101] For his part, Odum responded enthusiastically and collegially. In spite of Couch's claims of his parsimony, Odum routinely subsidized the books his institute published through UNC Press. And he told Raper not to be discouraged by Couch. "You will find all of these university presses hard taskmasters, most of them harder than ours."[102] Still, Couch dragged his feet on the project, and the book was not published until midway through 1941, marring its timeliness. Raper understood the difficulty, however. "It's a little bit disconcerting to some people who are looking to foundations for money . . . when you say that people who drive taxis, people who sell insurance, people who work in five-and-ten cents stores, people who run filling stations, they are essentially sharecroppers, they are sharing in the risk without sharing in the control. And Odum knew it. But, the Institute for Research in Social Science underwrote the publication of that book."[103]

Sharecroppers All: A Modernist Jeremiad

In *Sharecroppers All,* Raper would analyze the practical experience he had gained working with the SCHW and the other southern social and agricultural experiments of the late 1930s.[104] "The Southern Tenant Farmers Union and the Delta Cooperative Farm," he writes, "further demonstrate that white workers and Negro workers can be made to understand that they compete with each other for work and, consequently, must work together in labor organizations and cooperatives lest their separate efforts be cancelled by the traditional playing of race against race." About the Birmingham meeting, he observes, "The attendance, the nature of the discussions, and the active participation of the delegates suggest an awakening of Southern people to their situation and the need for unified efforts. From first to last there was evident a striving for democracy in the conference. Everything was subject to adjustment in the light of the wide range of interests represented, yet there was a remarkable degree of harmony, clearly resting on a broad spirit of tolerance and appreciation." And he tied the conference to *Sharecroppers All*'s theme. "From the outset it was evident that the South's basic problems were all tied up with regional and national politics, and that economic factors, illegitimatized by the racial nexus, lie at the root of the South's political and social structure."[105]

Sharecroppers All is a modernist jeremiad. The pioneers' unbounded opportunities had been spent, although many southerners continued to act as though they still lived under primitive conditions, which demanded only that each American work hard, save, and let others do the same. "We still hold to the old view, we fear change lest we lose our privileges. We still speak of inalienable rights, see only ourselves, and disregard the consequences to the many and to the group as a whole."

America needed to make the leap from a frontier society of rugged individualists to an industrialized nation of cooperative effort and the recognition of limitations. The pioneers' philosophy of life had made their skills powerful in their hands. They were "practical anarchists," who had left behind the divine authoritarianism of church and king. "In religion, the Protestant Reformation made *him* supreme; in economics, the laissez-faire doctrine proclaimed his own advantage first; in politics, Locke's theory of the right of revolution placed political sovereignty within himself." But now, America needed to reconstruct its prevailing philosophy. "We shall have to rethink our economics and our human relations," Raper exhorted. "We are no longer opening up a virgin continent. We have already done that. It could happen only once."[106]

Nevertheless, the typical southerner still thought it was good business "to get more from the earth and from society than he puts back. Such a system doubtless served well the transplanted Europeans in their hurried conquest of the American Continent, but it fails now to conserve natural resources and to provide the purchasing power needed to distribute the available goods and services."[107] Before we wreak any more devastation on ourselves and our land, wrote Raper and Reid, we must recognize that we are "in the midst of a wilderness of transition" from a hand-hewn and individualistic life to the modern world of machines and cooperative endeavor.[108] In the twentieth century, the ethos of the individual had outlived its usefulness. The evidence was plain to see. "America's unexcelled rates in lynchings, homicide, kidnapping, and unemployment are the product of no deep and dark mysteries. They are as American as the cotton plantation, as the dominating and aggressive population elements, as the acquisition of wealth through exploitation of natural resources and people, as the chain store and the assembly line."[109]

The country desperately needed to mature—to turn from values spun out of abundance, to a modern view that prized conservation of its people and resources and democratic planning for the future. "Some of us realize that we can no longer seek each separately his own personal welfare but must unite to make the welfare of all a prerequisite for the welfare of each."[110] In a short time, America had opened a continent. Now, it was time to conserve what was left, even as science and industry was offering more and more means by accelerating the expenditure of resources. "We have made powerful machines; we must learn how to use them. We are mastering the science of matter; we must become masters, too, in the realm of social control." But Raper was advocating conservation to a nation with resources to burn, which would propel itself out of a decade of Depression through a vast expenditure of resources for war production. He wanted to combine technology and conservation, even as science and industry were daily offering more and greater means to accelerate the expenditure of resources. Nevertheless, Raper's main argument was that the traditional American ethos of individuality should be superseded by scientifically informed, cooperative action. "We have asserted our divine right as individuals; now we must recognize our dependence upon each other—the divine right of the common good." The bridge across was liberalism.

Raper co-authored *Sharecroppers All* with Ira De A. Reid, whose contributions seem to have been mostly in research.[111] The book developed themes Raper had established in *The Tragedy of Lynching* and *Preface to Peasantry*, as well as in his talks and speeches. The language was similar, and his metaphors were cut from the same cloth, although here his prose is more essayistic, less explicitly empirical, than in his previous books. The approach is still documentary. "We have not neglected specialized studies," he wrote, "but have often used an episode to convey the meaning of a mass of statistics."[112]

While its commentary was often biting, the book itself tried to be friendly. There's a charming, innocent quality to the cover's line drawings of rural cabin and urban factory. Spread through the book are thirty FSA photographs. The people they depict, while poor, look steadfast, plainspoken, and dignified. Dorothea Lange photographs of a wagonload of determined farmers and a broad-shouldered, black farmer plowing through the late afternoon light. A John Vachon photograph of a housewife in trim kerchief cleaning a kitchen table filled with canning jars, captioned, "FSA's rural rehabilitation has demonstrated that a pressure cooker makes all the difference in next winter's diet." A crowded street of dark cabins with scowling roofs and porches, photographed by Walker Evans. A Marion Post shot of an older, white man in a trim uniform, gamely hefting two large suitcases toward an open car door, trying hard at a new job; as the Depression dragged on, one hotel after another had replaced its black bellhops with whites. "Unemployment is the greatest monopoly now held by the Negro," read a caption. "The turpentine barons bleed the trees and move on." Many other captions, though, caught nostalgically the pioneer spirit as it disappeared. "Lest We Southerners Forget—how to quilt." A white blacksmith at a forge: "Lest we Southerners forget—how to sharpen a plow point." A farmhand in overalls holding open the mouth of a black horse, while a white man in expensive suit and tie leans in to look in its mouth: "Lest we Southerners forget—how to tell a horse's age." Chapters titled "Fur Coats and Frayed Collars," "Arid Aristocracy and the New Wealth," and "Brown Faces and Bright Lights" softened the text's radical criticism.

Raper expanded the trope of feudalism he had explored in *Preface to Peasantry* in stating the theme of the book—that American capitalism, if it continued to restrict citizens from participating in democratic action, would betray the promise of greater equality of opportunity.[113] Uncontrolled industrial capitalism would become increasingly stratified and socially deadening.[114] "The roots of America's new peasantry lie in the concentrated ownership and control of wealth, be that wealth in farm lands, forests, fossil fuel reserves, factories, stores, or mortgages. Taken broadly, a plantation is a plantation whether in the rural or urban community, whether simple and hoary as the cotton plantation or complex and shiny as the chain store."[115]

"For the real meaning of the term 'sharecropper' look to such matters as low wages, insecurity, and lack of opportunity for self-direction and responsible participation in community affairs." A sharecropper is anyone who shares in the risk without sharing in the control.[116] Raper examined how "the wearers of fur coats and frayed collars, too, are the urban counterparts of plantation wage hands and sharecroppers." He showed how wages were being kept down in many subtle ways. "Employers frequently prefer girls who live at home, for these, they say, make more stable workers. The girl's family is really supplementing the employer's wage scale, but to the girl it is an opportunity to look nice; she feels better toward everybody and everybody feels better toward her. So, why not get a job, even if the check is small. . . . But many a woman must support herself and dependents in competition with the girl who is merely earning her allowance."[117]

Sharecroppers All was also a eulogy delivered over the withered body of King Cotton. Through the history of the South, cotton had migrated from northeast to southwest, from old plantations to new. Because land was cheap and slave labor had to be maintained whether working or not, planters cultivated their fields as intensively as possible, then abandoned them when they were farmed out and used their slave labor in winter to clear the forests for new fields.[118] The South could support the plantation system when America was expanding and foreign markets were growing. By the turn of the century, though, other countries had begun to produce cotton by the millions of bales and the full extent of Old South farmland had been exploited. And a newer competitor threatened to sweep the field. "In 1939," Raper explained, with portent, "World Fair visitors gaped at durable nylon hose satisfyingly fitted to shapely legs, saw dresses of spun glass washed and wrung dry, heard of even more fantastic developments. Many 1940 Fair visitors are wearing nylon hose, looking expectantly at the glass frocks and the synthetic fabrics."[119]

The book looked at the way the South employed race and class—using tools that included the land-tenure system, one-party system, white primary, and poll taxes—to build a highly stratified society without any of the stability of true feudalism. Overall, *Sharecroppers All* was more anthropology than economics. Raper and Reid studied the effects of the New Deal on agriculture for the ways its programs changed southern culture. Agriculture and economics were social issues, symbiotic with politics.

The political force that drove down wages and values combined the small-town xenophobia of American patriotic organizations with national, corporate interests. "The so-called 'un-American trends' in our national life," Raper observed, "are talked about most frequently by patriotic organizations and representations of big business." The southern patriot "dislikes outsiders, meddlers. He is afraid of agitators, afraid they will tamper with the meaning of white skin, afraid they will dislodge him from his precarious economic perch, afraid he will lost his status of at least being 'better than the Nigger.' To escape dropping to the level of 'the man farthest down,' the industrial Southern white worker will cooperate with the management in the expulsion of all outside influence, of all radical influences from whatever source if he sees in them a threat to his job." In spite of all this, Raper wrote, the southern farmer turned mill worker does not think of himself as a member of the proletariat. "He was a farmer, a capitalist, without money 'tis true, but still a capitalist who sometimes hired labor and who always had debts and cherished the chance of profiting by a rise of the market." His political ally, the corporate tycoon of contemporary business, compared with the plantation slaveowner in his mutual devotion to states rights and a narrow constitutionality as a means of avoiding public control.[120]

"Surely," Raper concluded, "there can be no excuse other than greed or ineffective business organization for chronically low wages." But he wanted to make clear that not everyone who raises hard questions for southern industrialists calls himself an agrarian. "Some very plain and practical people stop to wonder whether industry as now operated in many Southern communities, particularly the smaller towns, is of any real benefit." A southerner did not have to choose between the rapacity of industrial capitalism or nostalgia for the past.[121]

"That foremost bugaboo of the South, 'social equality'"

Race continued to be the South's bête noire. The region's greatest problem was whites' assumption of the biological inferiority of blacks. Far from reflecting biology, wrote Raper, the forces that were moving blacks farther downward as the Depression dragged on were wholly economic. *Sharecroppers All* argued that economics pulled down, first blacks, then whites too, in work on the farms and in the growing cities as well. "Today's attitude is reflected in the comments of a planter who, when driving his friend through a small town, saw a group of Negroes sitting in front of an empty store and a group of overalled whites hanging around a filling station half a block down the street. 'These,' he said, 'represent the Johnson grass of our people. And as long as those whites keep these Negroes humble, we'll keep them both poor.'"[122]

The black southerners' biggest problem was that economics had finally caught up with the myth of race, as Raper put it, and legislation was following economics, pushing African Americans out of more and better-paying jobs and farther into peonage, poverty, and unemployment. After the boll weevil had driven rural blacks to the city through the course of the 1920s, the Depression came along to siphon off the few urban occupations blacks had carved out for themselves through the course of the 1930s. By the time Roosevelt arrived in Washington, Raper wrote, "all across the South, the whites are moving rapidly into fields of employment formerly looked upon as 'Nigger' work."[123] The Depression had turned over to whites many service jobs—bellman, bootblack, and elevator operator. "The day of squeamishness has passed," Raper observed. "It is a far cry now from the pungent phrase, 'A Southern white man will curry a mule but he will not brush a gentleman's coat.'" Many blacks were faced with the choice of accepting lower wages or being replaced by whites and losing their incomes altogether. The effect, Raper wrote, was to drive down wages for blacks *and* whites. Blacks were also first to be replaced by new machinery. In addition, the pressure of "'patriotic' organizations makes it fashionable to employ whites."[124] And if an African American acquired a job of higher social status, Raper wrote, he was placing himself at greater risk of replacement.

As urban unemployment rose, many southern municipalities began to legislate the color line to engineer more jobs for whites. A Florida city passed an ordinance, for example, restricting black building tradesmen from working in the white section of town. Ordinances were passed in Georgia to prohibit black barbers from serving white women and children.[125] The burden of these racial and economic inequalities, wrote Raper, fell disproportionately on the black woman, who was being legislated out of laundry and domestic service and had become, "through no fault of her own, the South's economic and social problem #1a. Exploited socially, sexually, and economically to a greater extent than any woman of the Western World, she becomes the veritable index of the South's insecurity and inadequacy. Men, machines, and manners have given her the least gains of all people in the struggle for survival."[126]

Technological change and the depressed economy cut black women out of a tremendous amount of work within just a handful of years. By the early 1930s, under pressure of the Depression, many of Atlanta's white wives and mothers were using washing machines or doing their own laundry. The income earned by generations of the city's black laundresses had almost disappeared. At the same time, though, the white South's caste system was confronting new decisions by the Supreme Court that challenged the white jury system. Raper anticipated the collapse of legal segregation, while studying how its cultural aspects were becoming ever-more refined and desperate.

The color line shaped and regulated southern life and society, and the politesse of racial etiquette extended to class distinctions. Leaflets posted by the Ku Klux Klan in Miami's black district before an election in 1939 read like a bilingual notice, clearly intended for two distinct classes. "Respectable colored citizens are not going to vote tomorrow. Niggers stay away from the polls. KKK."[127] Raper was fascinated by the mystery of caste. He wrote about the concept of social equality—"that foremost bugaboo of the South"—as though it were a ghost bumping around in the attic. And still nobody wanted to climb the old stairs with a lantern to see about the banging.

What does social equality even mean? Everyone knew, he wrote, but no one knew. He told the story of the American Legion district meeting somewhere in the South at which a contingent of Negro Legionnaires arrived. They stood at the door of the meeting hall, and waited at attention to be announced. With all pomp, they were welcomed, then shown seats in the rear of the room. At the podium, the post commander called upon one of the black delegation for remarks. Their commander rose and conveyed the appreciation his men felt for the opportunity to serve in a legion that embraced *all* veterans. This is our only concern, he assured the assembly. We are not interested in "social equality." The white Legionnaires applauded heartily, leapt up, and paraded the Negro Legionnaires into an anteroom where they all sat down for a celebratory dinner. Raper summed it up fairly unscientifically, "It is a complex code—this one of race."[128]

Sharecroppers All took a picture of American agriculture at the tail end of traditional family farming, when new farm machinery and corporate capital led to the large-scale growing operations and the creation of agribusiness. By the early 1940s, half of the biggest cotton farms in the country were already on huge tracts in California and Arizona. In spite of the Depression, the number of tractors in Texas, for example, jumped from 37,000 in 1930 to 99,000 eight years later. Raper looked at industrial agriculture anthropologically as well, and he saw it as a completely different kind of endeavor.

"This new kind of farming is not a 'mode of life,'" he explained, "but the operation of open air factories."[129] Immediate evidence indicated an even greater degree of economic migration and social rootlessness. Modern trucks and fast highways made possible the advent of migratory labor for chopping and picking cotton. "As the plantations on the best lands become mechanized, the demand for part-time workers increases. With a surplus of labor within trucking distance, plantation owners no longer need to maintain workers throughout the year. Tradition will retard this change in some areas, but there is no antidote for tradition so effective as economic pressure." Modern meant science that could save rural folk from poverty, disease, and isolation. But modern also meant "the commercialization of almost everything—soil fertility, forests, fossil fuels, scenic spots, homeownership, mother's days, and on down the list to funerals."[130]

Raper would not end on a downbeat, though. He concluded by reaffirming the ability of science and education, powered by democratic action, to solve the South's social and agricultural problems. But there is no prescription beyond that profession of faith, and *Sharecroppers All* ends the way the New Deal ended—reaffirming its liberalism, but offering no blueprint or timetable for achieving it. Even though federal legislation had to run the gauntlet of state governments, which could alter or cancel its programs, sometimes at will, Raper believed only federal authority could change the social and economic structure of the South.[131]

"I am glad that I can not live much longer!"

Theodore Langdon Van Norden put down his copy of *Sharecroppers All* and picked up a pen. "I am glad that I can not live much longer!" he lamented in a letter to Raper. Van Norden had been born in the Deep South and spent his early boyhood in Dixie during Reconstruction, although his family was from the North and he had been brought up a Republican. "A number of recent books—by Percy, Cash, Dabney, etc.—have alarmed me; and now you make me feel that I prefer Reconstruction with all its poverty to conditions immediate and to come."[132]

Many thought the book focused too much on the negative, but Raper responded to a critical letter from Donald Comer with a disavowal characteristic of Cassandra. "I am sorry if it seemed to you that we had painted the picture dark," he wrote Comer. "Maybe you did not spend as much time on the last chapter as you did on the earlier ones. I am by no means a confirmed pessimist or fatalist."[133] Even his mother, Julia, wrote him a terse postcard typical of the uncertain view Raper's family had begun to take of his radicalism. "Received your book and are enjoying reading it," she began. "We seem to like it more than the others. Wish you the best of luck with it. Remember me to all the family. Thanks for the book. Mother."[134]

To many political radicals and race activists, however, the book's prescriptions were just right. Walter White wanted to help advertise and market the book and offered to mail six hundred brochures that encapsulated its research and conclusions.[135] And Lillian Smith wrote a glowing letter of congratulations.[136]

John Ford's *Grapes of Wrath* had been such a success in 1939 that Hollywood began looking for more dispossessed Joads, and Raper was amused by, but not dismissive of, the offer of movie agents Lichtig & Englander to shop around *Sharecroppers All* to the studios. They had seen the *New York Times*'s glowing review in February 1941. He talked with Alexander first, then responded as he did to most initiatives, by looking for a way to make it work. "I believe the book does do for the southeast something of the same type of thing that *Grapes of Wrath* did for the 'Oakies' and 'Arkies,' with the difference, of course, that the latter is purely novelistic while our materials are factual with much episodical material and portraiture." He thought a movie might be built around the old sharecropper couple he used to personalize the social forces he was describing in the book. Seab and Kate eke out a living on a once-fertile, now-dying plantation and, like all 1930s documentary, gave the book a sense of immediacy and a way for readers to feel what the system must feel like. While his materials were a kind of factual portraiture, as he claimed, Raper did not have John Steinbeck's or Ford's facility for creating particularized, dramatic situations or sustained, compelling narratives. He saw Seab and Kate "in turn move about in the crumbling big house where they live," but the story between them is missing. In the end, none of the Hollywood studios took a chance on a movie in which the villain is a system of dispossession and "the people" do not necessarily persevere.

7

AN AMERICAN DILEMMA
"'Human Nature' Is Changeable"

Through the late 1930s, Raper continued to find ways to popularize activism and social science, most often in conjunction with New Deal agencies and programs. He joined the board of the National Sharecroppers' Fund, for example, and later, the National War Labor Board, and he served as executive secretary of the Council on a Christian Social Order.

He became a prominent member of the Georgia Citizen's Fact Finding Committee, in 1938, an endeavor that Jonathan Daniels enthused was maybe the state's most important event since Sherman. "For Georgia itself is preparing to march," he wrote, taking up the banner in *Survey Graphic*. Instead of having the facts of their poverty described to them by northerners and scientists, Georgians themselves researched their own conditions in a homegrown sociology. Daniels explained, "Georgians will take the facts about themselves more readily from those who are native participants in their civilization than from itinerant reformers whose intentions may be excellent but whose own sense of superiority is at least equal to their good will." The faith informing such a study, as Daniels wrote, was "belief in the ultimate wisdom of informed self-government." The research was meant to mix social science and politics. "This does not mean that the committee is a conventional pressure group pushing a fixed program," he explained. "But neither is the committee coldly scientific in its attitude."[1] The committee published facts both to bolster pride, on the one hand, and to make Georgians think about change, on the other. "Georgia tops the list of states for production of watermelons, peanuts, pimiento peppers; stands second in peaches," read one brochure sent around the state. "Georgia spends less on education per pupil than any state in the union except Arkansas." "Georgia stands among the top states in church membership," reported the brochure, before informing its readers that "Georgia discriminates against Negro children."[2]

Still, despite Raper's devotion to egalitarianism and unfettered democracy, he distrusted the new forms of popular culture built on consumerism and broadcast through the modern media. "You can hardly believe how excited everybody is with *Gone with the Wind*," he wrote to Guy Johnson in December 1939. Atlanta had rolled back the years for a four-day fete surrounding the movie's premier. Buildings throughout the business district had built false fronts to remember the 1860s, and streetcar conductors, doormen, waitresses, and elevator operators wore Confederate uniforms and period costumes.[3] Amid the hoopla, Raper had attended a luncheon of Atlanta's Inquiry Club, with some twenty-five academic and business guests, including officials of Georgia Power and Coca-Cola.

"I suggested that a giant Klan parade be staged in connection with the festivities," Raper wrote, "and that the *Atlanta Journal* (with well-known Klan background . . .) should sponsor it. I was talking with Pope, of the *Journal*, and told him that I believed 10,000 more Yankees could be attracted down here at least $25 a head (to the city of Atlanta, hotels, etc.) if, when the ladies put on hoop skirts, the men would put on pillow cases and sheets." Unlike many white Atlantans, Raper could not separate magnolias and mint juleps from slavery and white supremacy.[4]

By 1939, Raper was still traveling the South as much as ever, but the trips were to visit projects of the Farm Security Administration (FSA) and experimental cooperatives with Gunnar Myrdal and to research "Race and Class Pressures." The fundamental issue of race still drove many of his trips, but Raper's lynching research was over, and travel for the Interracial Commission had dried up. In early March, for example, he was in Mississippi at the Delta Cooperative Farms. Later in the month, he was in Chapel Hill to talk with Couch about *Sharecroppers All,* then back to UNC in April for a conference at the Institute of Human Relations, then back again in May for his first meeting with Gunnar Myrdal, after which they traveled together to Atlanta. Over the Fourth of July, Raper drove from Richmond to Mississippi to meet Myrdal again and show him the Delta Co-op.[5]

"The Negro in American society"

Race in America was such an emotionally charged issue that when the Carnegie Corporation decided in the late 1930s to fund an exhaustive analysis, it sought the most detached perspective it could. Instead of going to New York or Chapel Hill or Tuskegee for its scholarship, the corporation sought the proverbial man from Mars, a social scientist from a nation with "no background or traditions of imperialism which might lessen the confidence of the Negroes in the United States as to the complete impartiality of the study and the validity of its findings." Of course, the most knowledgeable American researchers would be enlisted, but in part to provide themselves cover from conservative criticism, the corporation looked for a director of research from a nation "of high intellectual and scholarly standards," wrote the corporation's president, Frederick Keppel, but with no legacy of race conflict. "Under these limitations, the obvious places to look were Switzerland and the Scandinavian countries, and the search ended in the selection of Dr. Gunnar Myrdal, a scholar who despite his youth had already achieved an international reputation as a social economist, a professor in the University of Stockholm, an economic adviser to the Swedish government, and a member of the Swedish Senate." When the corporation extended its invitation extended to Myrdal in the summer of 1937, it specified that the most comprehensive study of race ever conducted in America "be undertaken in a wholly objective and dispassionate way as a social phenomenon."[6]

Myrdal had arrived in New York in September 1938, and he quickly decided that the project would be very different from what Keppel had in mind. Because blacks were so integral to the nation's identity, Myrdal knew he needed to conduct, not a study not of a subculture, but of American society as a whole. And the study would be clear about its values—in fact, Myrdal instructed his researchers, including Raper, to be clear about their beliefs. There was no such thing as a wholly objective and dispassionate perspective, Myrdal believed, although Raper would come to see how deftly Myrdal would assume the mantle of the detached, scientific observer when it helped him advance his ideas.

Within a few weeks, in October 1938, Myrdal started out on a two-month exploratory journey through the southern states, accompanied for part of the trip by Ralph Bunche and Raper.[7] Myrdal's approach matched Raper's emphasis on fieldwork. In fact, Frederick Keppel, Carnegie's chairman, advised Myrdal to begin, not by reading the existing literature, but by traveling, to see the country with his own eyes.[8] The following summer, Myrdal was ready to prepare a detailed plan, and the various "scholars and experts" he had enlisted to analyze specific aspects of race in America began their own work.

Raper, Odum, and Alexander were on Myrdal's list, along with pioneering anthropologists, Melville J. Herskovitz, Ruth Benedict, and Franz Boas; leading sociologists, including Robert Park, Charles S. Johnson, John Dollard, Hortense Powdermaker, Rupert Vance, and Guy Johnson; and a number of other prominent figures, including Du Bois and White, Clark Foreman, and Alain Locke. Many of them, including Raper, prepared monographs specifically for the study.

Soon after arriving in New York, Myrdal had gotten in touch with Odum and with Alexander, among others, who told him to contact Raper. They hit it off right away. "He was a grand and glorious guy to work with," Raper recalled with enthusiasm. "One of the most resourceful I've ever seen."[9] For their parts, neither Odum nor Alexander was excited about Myrdal's project. Raper surmised they felt the study should have been done at Chapel Hill. Perhaps they envisioned an organizing body similar to the Southern Commission for the Study of Lynching. Maybe, after years of struggling to fund even simple projects, they resented Myrdal's carte blanche. Myrdal wrote Alexander to gain Raper's release from his Commission for Interracial Cooperation (CIC) duties. "I anticipate that his contribution, although not formally done for the commission, will be very much a contribution to things which are near your heart. In fact, he told me that you and he had often discussed making such a study of the policy situation in the South, the court procedure and the whole realm of extra-legal pressure upon the Negro group."[10] The more Raper talked with Myrdal, the more he felt they understood each other. "He was interested in what I could do," Raper said, "and I was interested in what he wanted me to do." To Raper, Myrdal's project dovetailed perfectly with his work with the Interracial Commission.

Encountering American race relations, Myrdal decided he must first find his bearings and construct a system of social coordinates. Like Raper, he anchored his perspective in the American ideals of equality and liberty, rather than on its examples of injustice.[11] Although the social system he was studying was foreign to him, Myrdal's own approach was in fact consistent with that of American documentary realism. *"Throughout this study,"* he explained, *"we will constantly take our starting point in the ordinary man's own ideas, doctrines, theories and mental constructs."*[12] Myrdal's and Raper's interests both centered on the methods by which white dominance were asserted, although both were also drawn to questions of black agency. "Under all circumstances," Myrdal wrote, "in fact even in slavery, the attitudes and activities of the Negro people do, to a certain extent, influence the attitudes and policies of the white majority group in power, as account is taken by the whites of the Negro's reactions." Even with the prevailing power structure so heavily skewed toward white control, the values of American and southern society are "the product of a two-way interracial relationship." For this reason, Myrdal concluded, "*the Negro problem is an integral part of, or a special phase of, the whole complex of problems in the larger American civilization. It cannot be treated in isolation.*"[13] In spite of this, Myrdal saw white Americans as tending to see the "Negro problem" as separate from the rest of society.

Like Raper, Myrdal believed that the "Negro problem" existed because of a complex of forces at work in American society at large. "Establishing this integration is thought to make the analysis more realistic." Since his work with Odum and Steiner in Chapel Hill, Raper had been familiar with studies of social dynamics, where the arrows of influence pointed both ways. "The relationship between American society and the Negro problem is not one-sided," wrote Myrdal. "The entire structure of American society is itself greatly conditioned by the presence of the thirteen million Negro citizens. . . . New impulses from the Negro people are constantly affecting the American way of life, bending in some degree all American institutions and bringing changes in every aspect of the American's complex world view."[14]

Myrdal agreed with Raper that technology and industrialization were creating the huge changes in southern race relations, technology by serving as the engine of urbanization and industrialization by eroding traditional social structures. But so were New Deal agricultural programs, by shifting the structure of southern agricultural economy, not through a constructive, long-range reorganization, but rather by inadvertently pushing black and white sharecroppers and tenants off the land. By altering the economics of the cotton plantation system, these programs had struck at the root of the ideology of racism, the need for a permanent farm peasantry. The decline of King Cotton allowed other forces to weaken the caste system.[15]

Myrdal also placed the South's agricultural policies in the context of the World War that was doing so much to change America's perspective on race relations. He looked to a postwar world in which agricultural economies and agrarian societies might be considered from local, national, and also international perspectives. In this way, Myrdal also foretold the importance of an internationalism that would shape the second half of Raper's career.[16]

Myrdal and Raper both believed in the capacity of social science to advance rational self-government. They both subscribed to Enlightenment values and the welfare state. "In social engineering," Myrdal wrote, the social sciences "will retain the old American faith in human beings which is all the time becoming fortified by research as the trend continues toward environmentalism in the search for social causation. In a sense, the social engineering of the coming epoch will be nothing but the drawing of practical conclusions from the teaching of social science that 'human nature' is changeable and that human deficiencies and unhappiness are, in large degree, preventable."[17]

Myrdal ended *An American Dilemma* with an affirmation of his liberal belief in the value of government action. The fault in a given political situation lay not with the existence of government per se. "These institutions regularly direct the individual toward more cooperation and justice than he would be inclined to observe as an isolated private person," Myrdal concluded. "The fault is, rather, that our structures of organizations are too imperfect, each by itself, and badly integrated into a social whole." What was needed was more science and more government, not less. The Swedish social democrat and the Jeffersonian modernist were in accord. The sooner America realized that the day of the rugged individualist was over, the sooner its "Negro problem" would be solved.[18]

"Race and Class Pressures"

Raper's own three-hundred-page monograph for Myrdal, "Race and Class Pressures," completed in June 1940, considered a critical intersection between the races. Whom among official, white America did blacks most often come into contact with? Raper studied the symbolism and reality of black relations with the police and the various systems of jurisprudence.[19] Raper's sociology of law enforcement and the court system examined the points where urban blacks and white Americans most often met. Who becomes a policeman? What work did they do before they became cops? What were their official and casual relationships with blacks? Had they killed any blacks? In what specific ways did the courts serve the system of racial caste system? How did Jim Crow work in prison? What extralegal pressures supplemented the legal system? Raper talked Myrdal into allowing him to commission a series of short studies on particular issues and situations critical to African Americans in the late 1930s. He wrote about racketeering and vice in Atlanta, the eviction of sharecroppers, particularly in Arkansas and Missouri, the intimidation and violence growing out of New Orleans's longshoreman strike, legal and illegal controls in a typical plantation community, the coercion of labor organizers, and the resurgent Ku Klux Klan. His experience had shown him it was imperative, Raper told Myrdal, that black researchers be hired for the work in black communities. So he contacted Walter Chivers to work on the rackets and Ira De A. Reid, with whom he had worked closely, as well as Bettina Carter, Alvin Jones, and John Mclachlan. Myrdal was an unheard-of source of support and funding.[20] "Raper, you know that business better than I do," was Myrdal's response to his request. "And so, why don't you just decide and do it. Here's the money."[21]

Early in his career, Raper had been wary of interpretation in reporting his research, but he became more comfortable with it as the 1930s progressed. Myrdal pushed him further toward stating his own personal beliefs. "Our general purpose in this study," he instructed all his writers, "is to make a comprehensive, well-rounded, interpretative analysis of the social position and relationships of the Negro in American society." Myrdal's memorandum made it clear he was not looking for an encyclopedia of African American life in America. "Quite impractical, and perhaps not very important, would be an effort to prepare a compendium of all knowledge about the Negro," he wrote.

> This is *not* our purpose. However, though the report will not be all-inclusive as regards "facts," it should be quite complete as regards major "insights." All of the main vortexes of social life should be thoroughly explored to the end of defining and interpreting the relations of Negroes to American culture. In short, once our report is completed, none should be able to say that there are important "problems" or "relationships" or "insights" which we have overlooked.[22]

In another sense, though, Myrdal's approach was familiar to Raper. Like Odum and Jesse Steiner, Myrdal emphasized the importance of constructing a comprehensive picture of the dynamics of social forces, with attention to the agency of each group of social actors. Not only did the dominating structure and processes of American society largely determine the position and experiences of blacks, but African Americans helped shape the pattern of the wider culture as well. Like the Chapel Hill sociologists, Myrdal had an organic conception of sociology that required consideration of the parts and the whole at the same time. "The study," Myrdal explained, "might properly be conceived, therefore, as an effort to interpret American culture from the viewpoint of the nation's most disadvantaged racial minority."[23]

Myrdal's instruction to make clear statements of value freed Raper to state his conclusions with greater force than he had in his studies for the CIC. "Myrdal was very strong on saying that you had to give your value premise," Raper recalled. So he became expansive in his analysis, rather than limiting his exposition to the points of his research. "It was a little bit more comprehensive," he explained. "I could go ahead and say whatever I wanted to say about the situation in general, instead of having to be limited because of my own insights to a more restricted field."[24] After a decade of working and writing for the Interracial Commission, Raper felt he had "boxed the compass," so to speak. "I wanted to go ahead and say it."[25] Years later, he would consider his year with Myrdal, grounded on what he had earlier done with Alexander, a summation of all his work in the South, "a challenging opportunity to put on paper my choicest observations and thinking."[26]

Conservative backlash to the New Deal had gained steam by the late 1930s, and in the face of the growing threat of war in Europe, Raper saw the nation drawing inward, creating unlikely alliances of reaction. "The Jeffersonian adage that people are governed best when governed least has been picked up by the economic royalists who fashioned themselves into a Liberty League, backed by the Chamber of Commerce no less than by the small farm owner who hired a man now and then and stands to win or lose with the rise or fall of the cotton or wheat markets. And so far, to the Americans the least Government is still the best," he observed, "except for the propertyless man who needs a job, and the propertied man who wants favors such as vagrancy laws, franchise rights, injunctions, and so on."[27]

Raper gave fuller rein to sarcasm and cultural criticism than he ever had before. "Finding ourselves in confusion," he wrote about the national scene, "we put up more flagpoles, make the children take the oath of allegiance daily, proclaim Americanism and threaten any other 'ism' which raises its head. All of which emphasizes the shift toward political control once economic dislocation becomes serious."[28] By now, Raper's sense of hypocrisy had become fine-tuned, and he tied it to the dynamics of a social situation. He posed the question, "Where do the rackets begin?" and then answered it pointedly. "Though the answer to this question is clear enough to the middle-class moralist, who lives in the restricted residential district, it is not so clear to the man who lives in the slums. The slum dweller's contacts with private business leave him no clear cut distinction." To Raper, as to the new generation of urban blacks, morality seemed beside the point when its judgments supported a skewed system.[29]

Raper looked in detail at those officials designated to carry most of the weight of southern race relations—"the Southern policeman who has been awarded this crucial position in the caste society." To Raper, the cop on the beat stood not only for civic order, but also as the embodiment of the whole set of social customs associated with white supremacy. Especially in the South, a transgression of caste that aggrieved any white individual was conceived of as an aggression against white society and, indeed, as a potential threat to every other white American. "It is demanded that even minor transgressions of caste etiquette should be punished," wrote Raper, "and the policeman is delegated to carry out this function. Because of this sanction from the police, the caste order of the South, and even the local variations of social customs, become extensions of the law."[30]

Raper studied the police force in more than a hundred towns and cities all across the South, and the conclusions he drew were clear.[31] "Probably no group of whites in America have a lower opinion of the Negro people and are more fixed in their views than Southern policemen." It was not just that most police forces were comprised of officers with a minimal education, wrote Raper. "In many small cities almost anyone on the outside of the penitentiary who weighs enough and is not blind or crippled can be considered as a police candidate. Even the formal police training is usually very deficient." What is more, southern policemen were looked down upon by the middle class, who nevertheless expected them to uphold the prevailing social structure.[32]

Raper's judgments were harsh. Often, "the cop is dumb, uneducated, unreasonable, and is in consequence weighted down by an inferiority complex that demands somebody to be better than." This was as heated as Raper ever became. "The average bluecoat has the reasoning powers of a child and carries a chip on each shoulder," he wrote. "Unfortunately for the Negro, he is the natural foil for such a mentality." But he recognized the poses that policemen assumed for the sake of race. "The cops aren't as tough as they act," he observed. "Cussing the niggers and offering to plug them are sometimes just ways of showing your stuff to the other boys on the force. They represent the only universally popular sentiment and the only issue on which you can be sure where the other officers will stand. Underneath, many a policeman is more kind hearted than he dares admit."[33] At the same time, Raper saw signs of change in the new civil service systems that were being initiated, even in the South. These systems would not only raise the educational level of policemen, but also allow them greater independence from local influence. Raper was convinced that reform of the southern police system was critical to improved race relations. "Ideally," he wrote, "the policeman should be something of an educator and a social worker at the same time that he is the arm of the law."[34]

Raper carried the analysis into the southern court and prison systems, where he found, to no surprise, that black defendants were handicapped, as were poor whites, in meeting the costs generally required for litigation or an adequate defense. But the black man or woman accused of a crime involving a white adversary encountered the additional and heavy burden of solidarity that allied the white citizenry and its judiciary. Raper found, however, that in criminal cases, the black defendant did not always run into presumption of guilt. A central conviction in the cluster of beliefs that composed white supremacy was based on the assumption that blacks were preternaturally disorderly and lacked the most basic moral sense. Officialdom, then, showed great indulgence toward black-on-black violence and crime, as long as African Americans "not act it out in the presence of whites," Raper observed, "'not right out on the street.' As long as only Negroes are concerned and no whites are disturbed, great leniency will be shown in most cases." He saw the patriarchal traditions of the plantation continuing to influence heavily the judicial system in the late 1930s. Raper pointed, for example, to "the undue importance given white 'character witnesses' in favor of Negro offenders. The South is full of stories of how Negroes have been acquitted or given a ridiculously mild sentence upon recommendation of their white employers with whom they have a good standing." As partial remedies for all these official manifestations of white supremacy, he advocated the establishment of legal aid agencies throughout the South. He applauded efforts to extend federal police standards to communities. To further curb lynching, he suggested that the national wire services send reporters to the scene when any trouble was first reported. In all cases, his recommendations emphasized regional or national efforts, rather than local solutions, in part because larger efforts would generate more publicity. In terms of public attitudes toward African Americans, Raper was beginning to see a change from opposition to apathy.

> It is the author's observation that, in principle, the average white Southerner is no longer prepared to defend racial inequality of justice. Much of the judicial discrimination against Negroes in the South seems to be backed or tolerated by public opinion because of carelessness and ignorance in regard to the Negro, rather than by an intentional and considered

aim to discriminate. As far as public opinion is part of the problem, the task is, therefore, mainly one of adult education. White people must be taught to understand the damaging effects upon the whole society of a system of justice which is not equitable.[35]

In addition to providing fresh data to document racial discrimination, Raper pushed further in analyzing and commenting on the psychology of race than he had in his previous work. "It is astonishing to observe," he wrote, with newly emotional rhetoric, "how far to the background these problems are pushed in America, and how deep the common ignorance of them is even in the higher classes. Most people discuss crime as if it had nothing to do with social conditions and was simply an inevitable outcome of personal badness."[36]

"Race and Class Pressures" also included an extensive report on lynching, from which Raper drew heavily on his findings for *The Tragedy of Lynching* and his subsequent studies for the Interracial Commission through the mid-1930s. But his research for Myrdal pushed further in considering the psychological aspects of mob murder.[37] Raper and Myrdal wanted to make certain that lynching was seen as only the most egregious among an entire spectrum of repressive methods. In fact, legal repression was much more common and its cumulative effects on "white morals and Negro security are greater."[38] Lynching, Raper claimed, was a reflection of white fear of the Negro. "The low level of education and general culture in the white South is another important background factor. Allied with it is the prevalence of a narrow-minded and intolerant, 'fundamentalist' type of Protestant evangelical religion." Beyond these elements, he believed the isolation and boredom of rural backwaters helped to kindle many lynchings.[39]

In addition to quantification, analysis, and psychology, Raper continued to employ significant detail in narrative descriptions of the day-to-day, emotional landscape of black and white southerners as they lived out the intricate patterns of race and class and gender. "Funny to the white people," he observed, at the start of a story that combined documentary and parable, "are the situations in which Negro men can get themselves, but the greatest levity comes when Negro women are involved," he observed, disconsolately, before telling the story of eighteen-year-old Bertha Nelson, who one day stood timidly before the judge of the Atlanta Police Court, accused of stealing fruit at the municipal market.

While the judge was writing the sentence on her card—$12 or twenty days—he turned with mischievous eyes to the arresting officer and said, "Is that big black cell downstairs empty?"

"Which cell, Your Honor? That pitch dark hole in the ground?"

"That's right. The one with the alligator in it."

"Yes, Your Honor. I think it's empty."

"Well, you run down there are reserve it for Bertha."

While this farce was carried on, Bertha stared stolidly and impassively ahead, and dignity lay in a young Negro girl in front of the bench rather than in the snickering judge behind it.[40]

As the Depression meandered through the 1930s, and official inequalities continued unabated, Raper's sarcasm increased its bite, in spite of his continued professions of objectivity.

"Does it do you good to call them niggers?"

It had not taken long for Myrdal to recognize what Raper had been seeing all his life: America, and especially the South, encompassed an extraordinarily wide range of behaviors and attitudes about race. In fact, for a short time in the fall of 1938, they discovered how wide a range, while they traveled together, along with Ralph Bunche, engaging and provoking all kinds of southerners from black professors to redneck deputies.

From the time he had been an undergraduate at Chapel Hill, clipping his classmates' hair in his room in Old West, Raper had prided himself on his interviewing skills. He had a disarming way about him that put many different kinds of people at ease and made them ready to talk. He could jump in with a leading insight or story to keep a conversation rolling. He could wait out a reluctant interview, when he had to, and leave a silence hanging like a prod. And he had practiced those skills with scores of different people, in settings that ran from congenial to threatening, all across the South. But Raper marveled at Gunnar Myrdal.

No one had ever treated white southerners the way Myrdal did, and for the rest of his life, Raper would remember his days with Myrdal down to the last detail. "I've seen a lot of people interview folks, and I've done a good deal of it myself. But Myrdal, here was a new dimension for me." Myrdal could get away with conversation that no American—North or South—could consider making. He took advantage of his status as a European, and his foreignness was treated by normally skeptical southerners with simple curiosity. Raper recalled a prime example. "We get down to Lowndes County, Alabama, and he says, 'Let's go talk to the sheriff.'" They bustled up to his office, and Myrdal seated himself in a chair across from the sheriff, and started right in. "I'm Gunnar Myrdal. I'm from Sweden. We have nearly no Negroes in Sweden. I just wonder. I'm trying to understand—I'm here studying for the Carnegie people about race relations in the South—and I just wonder if you would tell me this. Why is it you're so afraid of them?"[41]

"Leading questions, just right to the gut," laughed Raper. "Now, if I had asked that question, the man would have said to me, 'You're baiting me,' having a Southern drawl somewhat. If I'd been from the North and asked it, why, I'd have been cursed for meddling. But here comes a Swede." Myrdal played the innocent abroad, and his apparent lack of guile made his blunt questions palatable. He was simply wondering about this situation, and would the sheriff set him straight? "And the man sat there for two hours," said Raper, "and explained to him about why they didn't want their daughters to marry niggers." The sheriff explained why he had to shoot one every now and then. He told him why they had to lynch one every now and then and make a public spectacle. And why plantation owners had to rig their commissary books the way they did, and on and on. And when he was through, Myrdal graciously thanked him very much. He had been most helpful.[42]

"I saw him do that over and over again." Myrdal emphatically did not, as Raper said, "come around to it after you had gotten through with the family, and the weather, and this, that, and the other. He came right straight to the point. "'Why do you call them niggers? Do they like it? Does it do you good to call them niggers?' He asked them all." While in Macon, Georgia, soon after he arrived from Sweden, Myrdal had noted that "a policeman slapped a Negro girl for skating on the sidewalks in the business section. When no ordinance could be found for holding her for skating, she was changed with disorderly conduct and arrested. The Negro Citizens Club was raised to fight the case. She was convicted but sentence suspended. For the sake of race relations the good whites advised the case not be agitated further and 'the good Negroes agreed.'" Such stories fascinated Myrdal, as well as Raper, because they pointed to the intersection between official policy and social mores.

Alongside his pose of innocent curiosity, Myrdal had honed a keen ear for irony and hypocrisy that greatly appealed to Raper.[43] In Tuscaloosa at the tail end of the 1930s, Myrdal, traveling with Raper and Ralph Bunche, asked the sheriff what steps he would take to prevent a lynching. "He said he would go to the mob," Myrdal noted afterward, "and talk to them in a friendly way, along such lines as this: 'I will see to it that the nigger gets a speedy trial and the justice you want.'" Myrdal, Raper, and Bunche were canvassing the South just at the moment before southerners came to expect criticism from any outsider. In just a few years, the openness with which the official South acknowledged and explained Jim Crow to a stranger would disappear, and even a man from Mars would have been met defensively, and with skepticism.[44]

"You ought to run for governor"

Raper had undergone an appendectomy just a few weeks earlier, but he did not want to miss the chance to travel with Myrdal and Bunche when they came to Atlanta in November 1939. He hoped to join them for a grassroots look at the politics and culture of race in Georgia and Alabama. They spent a long day in Atlanta, then had dinner at Raper's house in Decatur and drove the couple of hours to Greene County. They planned to visit John Donald Wade, the southern Agrarian and professor of English, who lived near Greensboro, before traveling to Macon, Tuskegee, and Montgomery. Myrdal wanted to meet everybody in Atlanta.

First thing, he interviewed Dr. Evans, Imperial Wizard of the Ku Klux Klan. Next was Mrs. J. E. Andrews, who chaired the Society for the Preservation of the White Race. Andrews also wrote for the rabid *Atlanta Woman's World* and Eugene Talmadge's *Statesman*—often accusing Raper of making white girls available to black men, based on the evidence of an Agnes Scott field trip to Tuskegee Institute. Meantime, Raper and Bunche waited for Myrdal with Martha at home.

"In the late afternoon," Raper recalled, "when he returned from the interview with Mrs. Andrews, he was very greatly excited." Andrews had begun talking about white girls and Negro men. "After she had repeatedly said overtly and insinuatingly that the practice was very widespread, Myrdal demurred and asked whether she knew white women who had conducted affairs with black men. Andrews kept firing back that it was much too widespread. "To make his point more strongly," Raper explained, "he stopped her and said, 'Well, have *you* ever had intercourse with a Negro man?' This, he said, at first non-plussed her, and then she became very, very angry and could hardly go on with the interview."

Myrdal explained all this over dinner to an incredulous Raper, and afterward, as Bunche charmed the Rapers's eight-year-old Harrison with a long string of bedtime stories, before they packed up and drove over to Greene. They parked in front of the Delaney Hotel on Main Street in Covington, and Myrdal and Raper registered. Bunche drove off with the car to head for the black undertaker, who in nearly any small, southern town was the one home that was certain to have room for a lone black traveler. Myrdal and Raper decided to go out and find something to eat.[45]

As they walked up the quiet main street, now close to midnight, Myrdal began to question Raper. "Why don't you run for governor here?" he demanded. "At first I laughed," Raper recalled. "He kept pressing the matter, saying that even though at first a Southern liberal would not perhaps get very many votes, that there was no other choice except for folks like me to get into politics. We talked about this at some length, and every time the subject was shifted to something else, shortly he would be back again insisting upon the importance of liberals taking an active part in politics."

Early the next morning, Bunche picked them up after breakfast, and all along the drive, they passed and talked about the "crumbling plantation homesteads, shabby tenant cabins, and gulleys." In Greensboro, Myrdal talked with a number of county officials, and he grilled Wade West, the county tax collector, responsible for interpreting Georgia law and determining who was eligible to vote. In the meantime, Bunche talked with black leaders in town. When he matter-of-factly used the front door of the Colonial Terrace boardinghouse to find Myrdal and Raper, the black servants became nervous, but Mrs. Calloway, the proprietress, did not say a word. She trusted Myrdal's standing.

Later in the day, they drove out with several officials to a convict camp and were met by Warden Smith, who hosted a steak dinner for Myrdal. "There was friendly conversation of ten or fifteen minutes in the yard," Raper remembered, "as the convicts came in from their road work on trucks and were put in their quarters for the night. Presently a man announced that dinner was ready. Warden Smith said, 'Well, let's all go in and eat.'" The convivial group stood to convey themselves into the warden's reception room, where the table had been laid with white linen and silver, and steaks from the county's best butcher were fried in rich butter. Hamp McGibony, one of the county commissioners, turned and suggested that perhaps Bunche would "best be served separately." Through his life, over and over, Raper saw that whites would go a long way toward integrating a given social scene if no one said anything about it. But once the question of Bunche sitting down to dinner was voiced out loud, the warden was committed to Jim Crow. If the issue had not been raised by one of them, they all would have ignored it. But after McGibony spoke up, the warden could not condone the breach of segregation. The bitterness with which Raper later in life told the story seemed to show the guilt he felt at having sat down to steak while Bunche was turned away. Bunche, though, later talked about treating the incident with scientific detachment, compassionately, as a chance to talk, unmediated, with a roomful of black convicts, eating in chains, who slept in iron cages.

They got back late to Colonial Terrace and found that Martha had been trying urgently to reach them. Mrs. Andrews had finally decided to take action against Myrdal for his indiscreet question, and her friend, the sheriff, told her it was indeed a chargeable offense. So she swore out a warrant to arrest the Swedish scientist and senator. Raper and Myrdal quickly called Colonel Faust, the county's leading lawyer, who told them the Greene County sheriff would have no choice but to serve the warrant. "Gunnar turned to me," said Raper, "and asked what I thought the court would do in case they did arrest and try him. I told him, it was my thinking, on the basis of what he had told me, that it was highly unlikely that an Atlanta jury would do other than find him guilty." The whole problem, he told him, "was more or less in keeping with things we were up against all the time." At that, Myrdal said they needed to leave, as fast as possible. "The arrest and trial would be international news," Myrdal told Raper. "The study would be ruined."

They immediately called Floyd Corry, who drove them to meet Bunche, who was staying with one of the town's black doctors. As they sped off toward the state line, Myrdal talked about his deeper appreciation for the intricacies and raw emotions surrounding southern race relations. Long into the dead of night, they crossed the Chattahoochee River into Alabama and out of harm's way. Raper wryly noted that nowhere along the long ride or through the excited talk "did Gunnar reiterate his insistence that I run for governor."

While Bunche went to spend the night at Tuskegee Institute, Myrdal and Raper registered in a small hotel in town. "All tired out," Raper remembered, "we went to bed with the roosters already beginning to crow." Ten o'clock the next morning, Myrdal stomped in from his connecting room, yelling about Runnymede. "'Now Raper, tell me what in the hell does Magna Carta say?'"[46]

"Well, Gunnar, it says you can not be arrested without a warrant," Raper told him, "but Mrs. Andrews *has* a warrant.'" Raper remembered, "We talked then at some length," despite his fatigue and the pain of his recent surgery roused by exhaustion, "about the means by which civil rights and personal liberties can be wholly ignored by a manipulation of the court procedures by persons intent upon using the court to further their racialistic interests." It was as clear to Myrdal as it was to Raper that the courts themselves served those racist interests.[47]

Myrdal felt less enthusiasm for the project at Tuskegee than anywhere else. His direct approach was not what black academics and administrators had come to expect of white liberals. At the end of the next day, in Haynesville, a few hours from Montgomery, Raper had finished his interviews and looked around for Myrdal, first in the court house offices. Then he stepped across the street in the growing dark, where he found Myrdal in a little cafe drinking a coke with a small group of white men. He was asking them about local race relations, and something Myrdal had said was finding vocal disagreement.

Quickly, the whole group became tense with excitement, and the fellows wanted to step back and find out why he was here in town. He was handling it well, thought Raper. Just then, as dusk turned to black, Bunche drove up in their car. A few more fellows left the cafe to stand around the group on the sidewalk. Raper moved close to Myrdal and suggested they start back to the hotel. A black driver was a common sight in Haynesville, but an obviously educated, well-dressed black man would have been very strange to the fellows from the cafe. Raper swept Myrdal into the car, and Bunche took off. Soon they saw the lights of a car behind. Bunche sped up. So did the other car. Bunche drove faster and faster until the other car finally fell farther and farther behind, then turned around, in the black backcountry of Alabama, far indeed from the Swedish Senate in sunny Stockholm.

In Montgomery, they talked with black leaders about the ways they were kept from voting. The meeting went on until midnight, when Myrdal and Raper went to their downtown hotel, while as custom dictated, Bunche drove off for the night. Raper was exhausted and crawled off to bed. Myrdal wanted to head downstairs to the hotel bar. "Raper, you know I always like to go drink beer with the folks," Myrdal told him. "I'm going down for a beer with these fellows, and see what's on their minds."

An urgent knock woke Raper in the middle of the night. It was Myrdal, who burst in and began pacing up and down the room as Raper pulled on his clothes. "Now," Myrdal started on a long peroration, "I'm an internationally known social engineer!" He spoke insistently. "I have something of a reputation in this field." He was, as Raper put it, somewhat in his cups—not too deep—but he had been drinking. These conversations over drinks, when folks were most relaxed, were especially significant, Myrdal was saying. And the way the fellows downstairs talked about the blacks in town filled him with questions. Stopping at the foot of Raper's bed, Myrdal threw up his hands. "I'm working here with the Carnegie Corporation," he told Raper, with an exaggerated tone of patience. "I am supposed to have a solution for this race situation here in America, but I simply do not see one."

"Well," said Raper, rubbing the sleep out of his eyes, "it is something of a dilemma, now, isn't it?" And Myrdal took hold of the idea, as if to say, here's a concept I can use to frame my report. "He was in a dilemma that night," Raper recalled, years later, "and he saw the racial situation as a dilemma that night." A few hours later, Raper left Myrdal and Bunche, taking the train back to Atlanta, wistfully, and with more than a little concern, while they kept driving west, the cultured black writer and the Swedish social scientist, buttonholing everyone they met to talk about the taboo of race in the heart of the Deep South.

"It was a bleak day for Raper"

Raper had told Myrdal he wanted to make some comparative observations from cities where race was a lesser handicap. Walter White and others at the Urban League sent Raper north to Buffalo, then Cleveland and Dayton. He was surprised when White did not suggest Boston or Cambridge—"No, no. We have trouble there"—but instead upstate New York and Ohio.[48] Raper's brother Cletus lived in Cleveland and was well informed about civic government. So Raper would talk during the day with judges and police chiefs, then head to Cletus's house and talk through what the officials had told him at night.[49] He interviewed and observed policemen and court officials in Dayton and Buffalo, too. The day his research in Buffalo was done, Raper was feeling good about the work. He had a few hours to spare before his overnight train left town. Dan's Restaurant was a local spot that came well recommended, and Raper found himself sitting down to dinner at what turned out to be a black strip club that catered to whites and interracial couples.

In his subsequent report, he sounded less in his element than in any other scene he ever passed through, from Tampa to Baghdad. He duly noted that he had talked to the waitresses about "any number of other things which I felt would be pertinent to my general interests." As he did everywhere, Raper also set the scene, as delicately as possible. "Several numbers," he advised, "were calculated to stimulate spent glands. The most intense exhibition was a dance called 'The Dance That Caused John the Baptist to Lose His Head.'" Because the waitresses were amused by this white southern sociologist studying the natives way up in Buffalo, he felt, they were particularly open about the circumstances they found themselves in. "Our conversations were continued somewhat intermittently between the floor show acts," he noted. "During the evening, ice clinked as I drank my ginger ale and other people paid for Dan's more or less expensive beverage."[50] This trip north produced the first sets of systematic observations Raper had developed outside the South. Although he was not charmed by winter along the Great Lakes, he did not mind the unfamiliar territory. It gave him a chance to apply what he had learned at home in very different circumstances. And the wider perspective was exciting.

On his way north to Buffalo, in February 1940, Raper had appeared as an expert witness before a Senate committee debating the Van Nuys Anti-Lynching Bill at the request of Walter White.[51] Tom Connally, of Texas, chair of the committee, was displeased to see a white southerner appear on behalf of the bill. Connally felt that he himself well represented the southern point of view. "And the southern point of view was that 'we didn't want any interference with administrative matters in the southern states,'" Raper said later. "Particularly on race." Connally tried to establish that Raper wasn't a real southerner, and when that failed, to accuse him of being under the influence of Walter White and "militant Negroes."

Connally peppered Raper with questions about recent lynchings, then continually interrupted him throughout the grilling. By the time Connally was through, Senator Neely of West Virginia took the floor to suggest that in the future witnesses be allowed to finish their sentences. Knowing that Raper had ended his study of lynching in 1936, Connally insisted on hearing the specifics of murders in the previous year or two, and about recent incidents in which local action had prevented a lynching. One minute, Raper said, Connally was floundering, trying to prove Raper was not bona fide, and the next, a sheaf of papers was presented to him, and he honed right in on specific questions about recent lynchings. And when Raper could not answer, Connally mocked him. "How about that, Mr. Expert?" Most disheartening was Raper's conviction that Connally's strategy—that sheaf of papers—had been fed to him by Jessie Daniel Ames as a way of protecting her own turf in the fight against lynching. "It was a bleak day for Raper," he wrote later, "the long grilling Connally made effective by the betrayal of an associate."[52]

Historian Jacqueline Dowd Hall, researching a book on Ames, pressed Raper, late in his life, about Ames's possible motivation for sinking his testimony. Ames was opposed to federal legislation, because she had built her career on local action. "That's the area in which she had had status. That was in the area in which she was somebody. She was nobody at the federal level. She was somebody when she had to talk to these women in these states, and she had to get in touch with them by telephone or get in touch with them by telegram, and she could do it. But this other, she simply could not weather." Before the hearing, Ames and Walter White had already disliked each other. If Ames's career was tied to the local level, White's was tied to the federal. "When they came together!" said Raper, shaking his head. After the debacle, though, "Walter wanted me—and it was perfectly clear what she had done—he wanted me to make a statement about it. And I said, 'No, no, I'm not going to do it.'

"He says, 'We can put that old bitch in her place.'

"I said, 'No, no, no. We aren't going to do it. I'm not going to have anything to do with that. And don't you do it either. You've asked me to come here, and I've come. And we saw what happened, and it wasn't what we wanted to happen, but it's what did happen.'" Raper, who always prided himself on his preparation, was terribly embarrassed by his testimony. Later in the year, Ames wrote a letter to Connally congratulating him on the success of a filibuster against the bill. Walter White came by a copy and published the letter. Raper and Alexander had always chafed at Ames's brusque manner and lack of diplomacy around the office and in her work. Connally's attack made him see red. Raper had seen internecine fighting ruin many well-meaning organizations, though, and he refused, even through his shame, to criticize a comrade-in-arms.[53]

Through the spring of 1940, with war having broken open across Europe, Raper sent telegrams to Georgia's senators, Walter George and Richard Russell, imploring them to remain level-headed and continue to promote liberalism. "Europe has no choice now but fight. We can still avert catastrophe. Let us pioneer a sensible way: Feed the hungry, treat the sick, employ the idle, teach the young, deflate the over-powerful, ease the economic tension of the world by adjusting our tarriff [sic] and currency to stimulate exchange of goods. Let us invest three and a half billions in domestic and international well-being." He was worried, as much about the potential for totalitarianism in the United States fueled by patriotic right-wingers as by Hitler and Mussolini.[54]

"One's as important as another"

When it was finally published in 1944, *An American Dilemma* had an immediate and lasting impact. Of course, it quickly gathered a tremendous number of critics. While the far left claimed it did not go far enough in connecting racism to the capitalist system, conservatives called it communist. Historian Stephen J. Whitfield observed that Myrdal was quickly "tagged a 'notorious Swedish Communist' (he was in fact anti-Communist), a 'Red psychologist,' and an 'alien anthropologist' (he was in fact an economist). He was often called 'Dr. Karl Gunnar Myrdal,' the full name that he never used, because the first name was the same as Dr. Marx's."[55] Nevertheless, many historians and social critics came to echo the judgment of historians William Cooper and Thomas Terrill, who asserted, "*An American Dilemma* is the single most important book ever written about American race relations, a source and stimulus for the civil rights revolution in the post-World War II South."[56] A decade later, the Supreme Court cited its findings in their ruling on *Brown v. Board of Education*. In large measure, much of its influence came from its powerful statements of principle and values that abandoned the moderate course most white liberals had charted in an effort to keep the peace. These assertions were reflected in Raper's bold contributions. Myrdal's book began with the premise that, as Raper stated, "people are people, and that one's as important as another, and that if we don't devise ways and means to see that none of them are handicapped and all of them are given development opportunities, the South and the nation will pay the bill. That was the end of it." Raper had been reluctant to state so clearly in his writing his own perspective on race, and neither Odum nor Alexander had pushed him to. "How are you going to guide this person who's going to read this thing?" Myrdal had demanded.[57] The genius of the Carnegie Corporation's choice of a foreign social scientist to lead the study was that Myrdal was not motivated by the idea of reducing racial tensions, as was the Commission on Interracial Cooperation. Rather, he took as his goal the task of measuring the practice of race relations in America against its principles of equality.[58]

Raper was approached several times to expand and publish his monograph, "Race and Class Pressures," which he had prepared for Myrdal. Samuel Stouffer, of the University of Chicago and Myrdal's editorial board wrote him, "May I say, off the record, that all of the members of the Committee felt that your study of extra-legal pressures should serve as one of the most valuable in the entire project in aiding Dr. Myrdal. . . . It clearly has the potentialities of being an extremely valuable book for the public to have."[59] Alexander and Guy Johnson both urged him to turn his contribution into a book. Myrdal himself took time out from compiling the dozens of manuscripts and research reports he had received to write Raper. "I have had very much use of your manuscript; indeed, next to Ralph's voluminous studies, more of yours than of any other memorandum," Myrdal wrote. "I think it would be highly valuable if you, in the future, got the necessary time to write a comprehensive and penetrating study of the faltering system of justice in the South."[60] Raper was certainly interested in building "Race and Class Pressures" into a book but, especially given his record of poor sales, he would need to find the funding himself. As late as 1945, though, he was writing Charles S. Johnson to ask whether the Rosenwald Fund might be able to help with the costs. But by then, the moment had passed, and a book on the way Jim Crow worked in court and prison and at the sheriff's office in the postwar South no longer seemed so relevant.[61]

"How does one go about getting a job, anyway?"

Just as Raper was pushing hard to wrap up his research and writing for Myrdal, in June 1940, Will Alexander wrote him to say he needed to start looking for work. The Interracial Commission would not sponsor any more research projects. It was as sure a sign as anything that the CIC was folding its tent. Odum's time was stretched among many endeavors, in Chapel Hill and elsewhere, and without Alexander's leadership, the commission was stagnating. Ames was continuing her work, but now in the face of opposition from her own colleagues, including Raper, who felt the antilynching campaign needed congressional legislation. Eleazer's publicity had dwindled. Alexander's imaginative conception of how to use research had always fueled Raper's work. It still did, but once Alexander had taken the job with Rex Tugwell, Raper's research was directed from Washington, rather than Atlanta. Once Myrdal had returned to Sweden and he had finished "Race and Class Pressures," Raper was left high and dry.[62]

Raper wrote back to Alexander in June, with an uncharacteristic plaintiveness in his tone. As resourceful as he had been in making money when he needed to, whether cutting hair or mowing hay, Raper had no experience in developing a career per se. Alexander and Odum had plucked him out of a graduate-student's office in sleepy Chapel Hill, and fourteen years later, all through the Great Depression, he had never been out on the street. "How does one go about getting a job, anyway?" he asked Alexander. "Any suggestion you have along this line will be greatly appreciated. As you know, I never flirted with other work since I came with the Commission. I have been interested in what I was doing here, and not on the outlook to go elsewhere."[63]

In July, Raper also wrote Guy Johnson, who had spent a harried year with Myrdal in New York. "As you perhaps know, the Commission is about to the end of its row—barring, of course, unexpected happy developments. More than this, it is perhaps desirable that the research part of the program be liquidated first. Quite baldly, I shall need to get some permanent connection within the next few months. My last fifteen years, in fact ever since I have been grown, has been so thoroughly satisfying and challenging that I have never spent any time thinking about new alignments."[64] Johnson could offer no reassurance. He explained to Raper,

> One of the men on our staff was saying one time that he thought that some of us white interracialists profited by fat jobs which were made possible by race prejudice and the plight of the Negro. I should have said—but I held my tongue—that we also take a great risk in that we bar ourselves from other good jobs. There are certainly some rather desirable university places in the South where you would be considered too radical to be acceptable because you have been in the field of race relations.[65]

All through the 1930s, as southerners felt the continuing pinch of the Depression, many complained about relatively well-heeled academics and speechmakers making a good living by criticizing the white South. In Raper's case, the truth was that it was never easy to make ends meet.

Nevertheless, his job worries were short-lived. As soon as he finished "Race and Class Pressures," Raper was approached by the Department of Agriculture's Bureau of Agricultural Economics (BAE), which was developing federally funded cooperative programs in agricultural counties around the country. He received a new but familiar assignment. Largely as a result of Raper's previous studies, the BAE had decided on Greene County, Georgia, as the site of a two-year rehabilitation program. He was hired to administer the program and also observe its effects on the county. By October 1940, Raper was writing Guy Johnson that he was glad for "the opportunity to live away out in the rurals eight miles from the county seat." Once again, he was leaving a desk and an office in an old brick building and going down to Greene to live out among the people.[66]

8

WAR AND CHANGE

"Is It Coming This Way Now?"

By the start of the 1940s, whites in Greene County were feeling a tangible change, as though the ground beneath many of their assumptions had begun to shift. Sooner or later, some said, the country would go and fight Hitler. But that was only the half of it.

James G. Boswell commanded a presence among the county's shop owners, businessmen, and large farmers, who drove in each week from Siloam and Union Point and Penfield to convene the Greensboro Lions Club. Boswell was one of Greene's biggest planters, and he knew everybody in town. He saw the way Washington was preparing for war, even in Greene County. And he saw a different handwriting on the walls of the courthouse and police station. At a Lions luncheon, one winter day in 1940, Boswell pushed back his chair, stood up at his table, and turned to address his friends and neighbors. Raper, a member himself, heard the room go silent.

"Now, look here, fellows," Boswell began. "We just as well better get ready to do some new things in Greene County." Everyone knew him as a practical man. He had come to an important new conclusion about what constituted good, common sense. "This school situation isn't going to stay the way it is." Boswell told them what they already knew, but couldn't yet say themselves. "This jury situation isn't going to stay the way it is," he said. "This voting situation isn't going to stay the way it is."

Boswell was saying the previously unthinkable, and the white folks who ran things in town put down their forks and glasses. "You could hear a half of a pin drop," Raper thought. Boswell appealed to the business sense of white Greene County. Momentum is all on the side of change, he told them. If we keep fighting for segregation, we are fighting to keep business down. They were wasting their time and money on a losing battle, and besides, they needed the customers. The cash economy had changed everything. It had finally split open the plantation system, freeing the owners from support of their sharecroppers. But it also freed black farm families to spend only where they were treated well. When Boswell moved to sit back down, no one stood to argue. A few years earlier, he would have fired the room with incredulity. Now, Raper marveled, "there was no harangue," and no Lions moved to defend the status quo.

Raper had returned to Greene County to look at how the New Deal had worked on the ground in the rural South. And over the course of the next year and a half, he saw that, just as they were accepting the new tools of mechanized farming, many of Greene's whites were beginning to believe they would be better off accepting the break-up of segregation—that is, Raper said, "if they were going to be awake and realistic."[1]

He had found himself standing at a surreal crossroads in rural Georgia, where stories of the Confederacy were mixing with radio news of a second World War. In the summer of 1942, he would drive his old Ford through a plume of dust to a sharecropper's home in the county's red-clay cotton farms. He stopped in front of the cabin, slammed the car door, and stood for a moment, mopping his brow. The old farmer called out from his porch, "How's the war?" his rocking chair groaning beneath him in the heat. Greene County was a place, Raper had found, where Sherman's march was still a living presence. Raper climbed the old porch steps, as the farmer wondered aloud, as though asking about both the past and the strange future, too, already at his door. "Is it coming this way now?"[2]

For two full years, beginning in the fall of 1940, Raper, his wife, their four children, and Martha's great-aunt App'm lived in an elderly plantation house out in the country, seven miles from town, while he crisscrossed Greene's towns and all its farms, black and white, administering and studying the programs of the Farm Security Administration (FSA). His old friend from Vanderbilt, Floyd Corry, offered them the old plantation house owned by his uncle J. B. "Punch" Dolvin. Corry's Uncle Punch had cut a large figure in the county and, at his death, left a rambling manse of high ceilings and spacious porches. The Rapers left their tidy bungalow in increasingly suburban Decatur, and they soon filled the barnyard with a cow and a calf, chickens, dog and cats, and the little white horse that the boys and Margaret all grew to love. The Rapers' daughter and their three sons milked the cows and pitched hay, and they all learned the violin or the trumpet or the flute, so the family could play music together in the evenings. "All about us," Raper would write, "have been farm and sawmill folk, owners and workers, who have been affected in one way or another by the county-wide farm program and by the world situation. We listened, tried to help." Almost immediately, Arthur and Martha were in hot water with white neighbors, who quietly complained they were "ruining" their cook by paying her too much.[3]

"See the wheels go around"

Raper had landed back in Greene County after finishing his work for Myrdal, because, by 1940, he found the pickings for a white liberal in the South to be slim. He had quit Agnes Scott the year before to write "Race and Class Pressures." Will Alexander had been in Washington for years now, and the Commission on Interracial Cooperation was a husk of what it had been.[4] And Raper felt Odum's institute was past its heyday. Beyond that, Raper had already turned down Odum's offer of a faculty position at Chapel Hill. By the start of the 1940s, Raper felt at the end of an era, in part, because he saw that "things in the South were sort of running out." The once-energetic fields of regionalism and white southern activism had lost steam. The center of gravity pulling all the planning and activist initiatives was, of course, the New Deal. Raper's return to Greene County as a result of his joining the Department of Agriculture was actually his first big step out of the South, as it turned out, and into the national and international arenas.

Over the years, Raper had been offered jobs, from union organizing to Black Mountain College, but he felt he wanted to work out a new direction through his own initiative. "So I got some blanks," he told historian Daniel Singal, "and I filled out one of these God-awful applications for employment with the federal government." He had already been invited to work for several federal agencies and rejected each offer. What he wanted was a chance to apply federal clout to local problems, so Raper took a job as a rural sociologist for Carl Taylor's Bureau of Agricultural Economics (BAE), right after he'd submitted his work for Myrdal in June 1940. At first, Raper's projects had one foot in the FSA, but as the agency became increasingly vulnerable to congressional criticism, he stayed home more and more at the BAE. Raper was working on what soon was termed "rural life," which combined analysis of the economics of agriculture with study of the various forms of culture that supported, and were supported by, American farming. Taylor encouraged this application of sociology to economics, this mix of the human element with quantification. Taylor was himself familiar with Greene County, and he approved Raper's idea of going back again to study the way the Unified Farm Program (UFP), merging efforts of the BAE and the FSA, was working out.

The UFP was a new initiative, developed in 1939 under Roosevelt's secretary of agriculture, Henry Wallace. The program chose representative agricultural counties around the country as models in coordinating the services of federal, state, and local aid and educational agencies in support of family farms. Raper advocated for Greene as one such model county, and he convinced Carl Taylor, his boss at the BAE, to send him back for ten months to study the effects of the program and help with administration of services.[5]

Returning to Greene in September 1940, Raper was officially a participant-observer to the UFP. At the time, unlike Odum's institute, the UFP was in its heyday. Through his work with Ada Woolfolk and the Family Welfare Society, Raper had come to believe strongly that the kind of problems created by the black migration he had studied both going and coming, from Greene County to Atlanta, could be realistically addressed only by an interlocking network of local, state, and federal agencies. The problem was not simply agriculture or rural economics or urban housing or even Jim Crow. He imagined a holistic approach to a set of overlapping issues that had been left by a long river of migrants whose problems polluted its banks all along its length, before emptying into the city. He found encouraging the fact that folks in Greene had responded to their failing agriculture by trying new crops and forming new organizations. Their willingness—or perceived need—to innovate told Raper that the county might very well be amenable to modern government planning. Through the UFP in Greene, Raper was able to lock together local studies, regional analyses, and national intervention. The number and range of agencies he worked with in Greene from 1940 to 1942 shows the extent of federal involvement even in the rural heart of states' rights conservatism in a county that also offered support to the staunchly anti-Roosevelt governor, Eugene Talmadge. Greene's agricultural agencies liked the idea of government help, and Democratic Senator and New Deal supporter Richard Russell pushed the legislation, along with the county's congressional representative, Paul Brown. Raper had advocated with Will Alexander on behalf of Greene. Because of its long history of sociological, agricultural, and economic study, it was a natural choice for the program.

So the new direction he intended sent him a third time to Greene County.

To Raper, though, the nature of the work made a big difference, because it gave him the independence to follow his interests and it offered an opportunity to become an activist analyst. "I was nominally under Alexander's supervision when I was down there," Raper recalled, "but actually I was doing my own thing, as it were. And he liked it and he just came down and looked at me, didn't tell me to do anything different than what I was doing." As it did for many New Dealers, the federal government offered Raper a tremendous opportunity for innovation and independence.

The UFP would include everything from teaching soil conservation methods, to recommending ways for people to balance their diets, to improving black and white schools, to encouraging community participation in local issues.[6] Raper himself was drawn to studying how federal policy worked on the local level, and to take a hand in implementing it, too. Raper tacked among the FSA, the Civilian Conservation Corps, the County Agent for the Agricultural Adjustment Act, the County Health Program, soil conservation agencies, the FSA School Program, and the National Youth Administration. "One can participate in policy making," he wrote to Ira De A. Reid, his collaborator on *Sharecroppers All,* soon after returning, "and one is close enough to the bottom of the structure to not only see the wheels go around but know how they turn in the direction and the rate they do."[7]

"Finding out their sorrows and their secrets"

A year to the day from the end of his work on *An American Dilemma,* in the summer of 1941, Raper wrote Gunnar Myrdal from his new office in Greensboro. "Now that I am here in the country quite at the end of the American road, racially and economically, I am picking up some of the best factual data I have ever got."[8]

"I can quite see you walking around in Greene County," Myrdal replied, "talking kindly to everybody and finding out their sorrows and their secrets."[9] At the same time, the program gave him a chance to study all the varied and integrated dynamics of a local culture, the way he had been taught back at Chapel Hill by Odum and Jessie Steiner. The program served five hundred farm families, mostly sharecroppers, called rehabilitation clients or "rehabs."

Now Raper was working for the federal government on programs he had advocated for in *Preface to Peasantry.* Martha Raper remembered the character of her husband's peculiar days back in Greene.

One afternoon, Daddy listened to a landowner explain why the FSA ought to drop more of the families who were behind in their payments, and when he got home a landless man was waiting to talk with him. He had been asked to leave the farm program for "lack of cooperation." He admitted he was way behind with his payments, but he claimed he had done the best he could, and he didn't know where to turn. And so went Daddy's days, listening to anybody's and everybody's story.[10]

Raper was always listening to everybody's stories, as well as gathering data. As a social scientist and a government official, working simultaneously on the federal and local levels, he listened for the particular as well as the aggregate.

When he had first studied Greene in the late 1920s and early 1930s, Raper saw the county as mired in the nineteenth century. He had described the residue of worn-out economic and agricultural systems. But now, Raper was impressed by the balance Greene was just then striking between lingering agrarianism and modernity. He noted right away, for example, that instead of convening in lodge halls and churches, black students now attended twenty new public school buildings scattered throughout the county. Now, three-fourths of their teachers had college educations. After just a few weeks back, in September 1940, he stopped his car along a wild, lonely stretch of road and found a spot to write up some observations.

"When I began to write these notes, sitting on a rock at the old Willis place," he jotted to himself, "the weather was all quiet, except for the low rustle of grass, magnolia, and mulberry leaves, and crickets of early fall. And now as I finish these notes all is quiet again. In the meantime, a shiny two-motor airplane streaked across the sky reminding one that Atlanta is to the west and Augusta to the east. Fast by the kitchen stove in Judge Stock's old house, the elderly Negro man—stooped and limp—sits with legs apart, the easier to spit through a hole in the floor."[11] Returning to Greene in the early 1940s, the county's strange, new juxtapositions and contradictions engaged Raper's taste for irony, his imagination, and his politics.

He was fascinated to see new Tenant-Purchase homes built with federal financing alongside tumble-down slave quarters. "The new order had come; the old order remained," he wrote in *Tenants of the Almighty*. "Some people liked the new, hoped it could last; others liked the old, hoped it would not pass." Raper and Taylor were confident that enough liked the new, and that, in spite of its affection for Talmadge, Greene was open to change. This optimism was based on the way the county had cooperated with the Agricultural Adjustment Act's crop controls. "One year after another the farmers of Greene had voted on crop limitations," Raper reported. "In the spring of 1938 a total of 996 votes were cast, and all but thirty-eight favored the program. In the soil district election that year, only thirteen out of 239 landowners voted against it." Raper concluded that Greene's farm folk had shown they were willing to cooperate with the federal programs.[12] "Some very thrilling things are happening here," Raper wrote his friend, writer and newspaperman Tarleton Collier, after just a few months back in Greene, "also many typical little ones which tend to pile up along race and class lines. I have an office in Greensboro just across the street from the new auditorium on the first-floor of the Brown Building: open fires, and magnolias right by my window." His excitement was over the way the county accepted and prospered by government intervention. "Our experiences with the landless black folk all about us further confirms us in our faith in the importance of programs which provide opportunities for the disinherited." When he addressed a crowd of wealthy Democrats in New York's Roosevelt Hotel during National Sharecroppers Week in March 1941, Raper outlined how he saw liberalism working. He told them Wall Street was at one end of America's long road and Greene County was at the other. The human residue of a system of exploitation of the latter by the former was apparent in the wealth at the Hotel Roosevelt and the poverty of rural Georgia.[13]

The solution, he told them, was government that worked both top down and bottom up. "There is urgent need that the various farm programs be continued and that the services of the Farm Security Administration and related agencies to aid the landless farmer and migratory laborer be refined and extended." He stipulated with emphasis, "This basic program, from above down, can be most constructive only as there are organized groups of farm workers to help determine the types and quantities of Federal and state services which shall be provided for them and their children." The money and power and education provided by the federal government had to be coordinated and particularized by the farmer in his fields. This was why the UFP was so important to Raper. It was the first serious attempt to yoke federal power to community participation. "People are of first importance in a democracy," he told the group. "And democracy is superior to other political systems in the degree that it affords the rank and file of people larger opportunities for growth and responsible participation." The UFP, Raper hoped, might become the practical means of working out his most fundamental belief.[14]

Many of the observations Raper made in Greene during the early 1940s had little to do with agricultural economics per se or with the effectiveness of government programs. He wrote whole series of character sketches. "Yes, we give her a dollar a week," he quoted Floyd Corry's wife, talking about her maid, and herself, and the sociology of the racial caste system as well. "She's young and not really able to do anything but wash dishes, sweep, and help keep up with the baby. Now that my cook's gone she's a real help. What I'm afraid of is that she will stop work and go back to school." In a dynamic sense, these documentary vignettes of "rural life," as literary as they were accurate, had everything to do with rural sociology. Raper consistently looked for the ways that agricultural economics and government programs worked their ways into the tiniest capillaries of people's lives.[15]

"The FSA is a grand mess." Raper induced an elderly planter into philosophic expression, and through him drew a sketch of rural conservatism in the New Deal South. "It has ruined the niggers," was the reason why. "Now mind you, I like the FSA, I am all for the principal aim of the FSA." The problem with it was that it ran counter to the workings of human nature. "Every individual has a limit to his capacity to take in and understand new things," the planter believed. "The FSA has carried some of them so far beyond their capacity that they have just decided that the government is going to take care of them anyway, so they act accordingly." Even if the aim of the FSA was true, he believed, the pace of government change was too fast. It hurt those it was trying to help. "The FSA has harmed a good many of their clients by destroying their morale and initiative through pampering them. You can't change people's living conditions too suddenly—they can't stand it. Some of these people have had so little for so long that they can't seem to grasp the idea of the program and realize that they have to pay for these things." Now that his tenants had gotten used to free rations, they wouldn't even come up to the house for them. Now the same tenants who had once appreciated their rations just sat around and waited for them to be delivered.[16]

Critics had objected that the program seemed more concerned with social than economic values. And Raper acknowledged that the UFP was indeed focused on social engineering. "The FSA," he made clear, "has tried to put human values first, and the materialistic phases of the program have been geared to the development of more adequate human beings, as persons and as members of communities." Social values were in fact integral to its objectives.[17]

Raper speculated on the psychology behind the county's racism and the conservative economic perspective of even its poorest whites. "Perhaps nothing makes white farmers here feel more kindly toward Negroes than for Negro farm labor to be available when white farmers want it," he explained. "The presence of this Negro labor did more than increase the farming operations of the white farmers; it afforded them satisfying evidence that they were still in position to command the services of the Negro." Occasionally, though, Raper had to face the fact that he did not quite understand the entrenched conservatism of rural dwellers. "'Now, don't misunderstand me,' is a common expression, 'the government has helped some people who deserved it, but it's ruined a lot more than it has helped.' You listen and wonder as earnest self-supporting farmers look you straight in the face and say that once a man works for WPA he's worthless as a farm laborer, and once a family gets on the FSA they will never be good tenants again."[18]

"It is no accident that the benefits of the New Deal have been spread thinnest among the small independent farmers," Raper wrote. "Rather, it was by design, for these live-at-home farm families throughout the nation, as in Greene County, have been the most self-sufficient group in our whole economy." The FSA felt the small, landowning farmer could weather hard times better than anyone else—the large commercial farmers or the landless tenants and wage laborers, and even better than the industrialists who had surplus stocks of goods going to waste or factory workers faced with unemployment. After all, it was the Jeffersonian agrarian who had survived all the various vicissitudes of the nineteenth century. Why wouldn't the yeoman survive the twentieth?[19]

"The live-at-home farmer's neighbors knew he had staying qualities, and so did the government experts. Most of the activities of the U.S. Department of Agriculture in Greene county, as throughout the South and the nation, are designed to get all farmers to follow in the well-worn footsteps of the family-size farmowners who have always grown their food and feed at home." The war would come to emphasize maximum production and push the trend toward agribusiness. Over the next few years, Raper would sit in congressional hearings; he heard programs designed to assist the family-sized farm lumped with New Deal social programs and retired in favor of aid to large-scale, high-production agricultural operations. "Diversified farming was not begun in response to a government program," Raper explained. "It was begun by farm families themselves. The solid sense of such a way of life on the land caused the federal and state governments to promote it." In fact, Raper believed that the New Deal's agricultural policies, as played out in Greene County, in spite of their shortcomings, pointed the way to a republican system with genuine reciprocity between governed and government. That is, Raper saw the federal policy that was flowing out of Washington as one that had first been distilled from the experience of the counties themselves. "It has not yet been proved that Thomas Jefferson was wrong when he pointed to the small independent farmer as the backbone of a democratic society," Raper wrote. By the end of the war, however, many policy makers' sense of such a way of life, as well as the promise of democratic action it offered, had given way to the enticements of agribusiness.

"What experiences have you had with the watermelon?"

Raper filled his day-to-day work in Greene with meetings of all sorts. One day in May 1941, for example, he invited a few FSA and county officials over to his office to talk about whether Greene's farm families were gaining anything, in terms of their diets, by way of the government programs. Mrs. Wheeler, the FSA district home supervisor, arrived, along with Mr. Thomas, the FSA farm supervisor. Alla Maze Bailey, the county social worker, attended, along with a nurse and half a dozen home supervisors; all except Louise Allen were white women. Getting this group together gave Raper a chance to help mold FSA programs at their most basic and critical level, asking whether the government was delivering nutritious food to people who needed it. At the same time, Raper was using the meeting to practice the kind of sociology he had been honing for fifteen years, which mixed analysis of broad economic and political trends with particularized and anecdotal cultural information. In some pantheon of the New Deal, Raper might well have played the figure of a minor deity, the personification of the participant-observer.

Alla Maze Bailey spoke up to report on a Home Demonstration Club meeting she had recently attended. Each of the dozen or so club members were supposed to answer the roll by calling out the name of a new vegetable she had just planted that year. Only a few, it turned out, could name one. A farmwife had called out parsnips. "I was surprised," admitted Bailey, "to hear one woman give 'carrots' as being new to her."

Raper felt suddenly circled by an awkward silence when he asked, "What experiences have you had with the watermelon?"

"I just associate watermelons with nigras," offered one of the home supervisors, timidly.

"Some day," Raper replied, "somebody is going to show that watermelons contain vitamins, and that they like them for more reasons than the fact they don't have to be cooked." By the same token, he went on, "There is something back of their desire for tobacco. The nicotinic acid is known to ease the effects of pellagra. Perhaps their craving for watermelons and tobacco is an effort to balance off life." Further, he saw war preparation might open opportunities for social programs. The country's defense program would serve the sake of preparedness if it created a national standard for health that could be used in peacetime to ensure a good diet for all Americans. Then he mused a bit about how he felt his neighbors at the Punch Dolvin place seemed to feel the government aid they had been receiving would turn out to be as temporary as the Rapers themselves. In *Preface to Peasantry,* he had warned about the staying power of the plantation, the way it continued to suck the marrow of so many southerners. Now, though, he felt a victory had been won. Even if its odor still lingered through the countryside and in the cities, the plantation itself was finally gone. "Mr. Punch is done," he could tell the assembly of new government workers who had crowded into his office in May 1941. "Just about all the Mr. 'Punchs' are gone."[20]

Still, there was much work to be done to raise the level of education that would help propel more democratic action. With few exceptions, even the best-educated families read little more than the occasional best-selling novel. Most people hardly read anything other than the weekly newspaper. Few people in Greene would read a book of sociology, least among those who might most benefit from it. Concerned that Arthur's work would not amount to much in Greene itself, Martha suggested he publish installments in each week's *Herald-Journal.*

With the same impulse of combining local and global perspectives, of contributing directly to people's lives while providing sociological analysis, Raper introduced in the *Greensboro Herald-Journal* a series of articles, each of which visited another of Greene's family farms and emphasized what he saw as its achievements, all in the course of delivering a weekly homily on husbandry and conservation. In September 1941, for example, Raper wrote about a family who lived out near the Macedonia Baptist church four miles northwest of

Penfield. "The I. C. Elders," he claimed, "have found an answer to their farm problem. The answer is diversification. With them it used to be cotton, more cotton, and still more cotton; but now it is chickens, eggs, sour cream and cotton."[21] Another profile advanced another Progressive idea. "It has been said that a person who works somebody else's land is not much interested in the future value of the property," Raper wrote. The Thompsons were a good example of how private ownership was an excellent stimulus to conservation.[22]

After a couple months of articles, Raper dipped an oar into new waters. "Thus far," he explained, "all the families who have appeared in this column have been white families. We thought it would be well enough to see what the colored farmers of Greene county are doing; so this week we will tell you about the family of Robert McWhorter, who lives one and one-half miles west of Bairdstown." McWhorter had started out as a sharecropper. Within three years he was able to buy his own work stock and become a renter. Once the UFP arrived in the spring of 1939, he signed up with the FSA and took out an $800 "rehabilitation loan" to finance his farm. Soon after, he secured a $2,500 Tenant-Purchase loan, which enabled him to buy his 140-acre farm.

The McWhorters were just the kind of family Raper's father would have pointed to, back in Davidson County, North Carolina, when he told the teenaged Arthur that if their black neighbors were given an equal chance, they would make good citizens. Raper explained that McWhorter, his wife, and their nine children had taken over a rundown property and transformed it into an efficient, productive farm, growing cotton, corn, peas, beans, kudzu, peanuts, cane, wheat, and oats. From a fine, half-acre garden by the farmhouse the McWhorters harvested sweet potatoes, watermelon, and a range of greens and vegetables. What's more, the truck the McWhorters recently bought would help them pay for their farm within ten years.[23]

Raper's desire to encourage local readers, however, shows in the choppiness that mars *Tenants of the Almighty*. It is clear that Raper wrote much of the last third of the book with newspaper columns in mind. And the study is compromised by his intention to praise both Greene's farmers and New Deal officials in the paper each week. "With well laid plans in their heads," he reported, for example, "and deft hands willing to work, the members of the Garden Club—with their servants—in a day or so transformed the auditorium into a place of beauty and good taste."[24]

The problem with the UFP itself was that it was reaching only those who, like the McWhorters and the Elders, had already gotten a leg up on their own.

What troubled Raper was "we weren't getting down to the bottom of the barrel." Most of the aid was going to those farm families who had already obtained a certain level of success. So, he helped design a sort of remedial program for the poorest farmers in Oglethorpe County, next to Greene. It would involve much more intensive supervision, and families were expected to take longer to get on track with their gardens, canning, and so forth. Raper claimed that a number of national leaders were interested in seeing how the Oglethorpe experiment would progress. By 1942, though, as Raper was evermore convinced of the effectiveness of this kind of comprehensive assistance program, the exigencies of war helped the growing conservative impulse in Congress to put the brakes on any government initiatives unrelated to defense. By the middle of 1942, he recognized, "the politics in Washington which had created the FSA had turned and destroyed it." By the time the family left the old Punch Dolvin place for a new home outside D.C. in the fall of 1942—Raper's final leave-taking from Greene—the handwriting was already on the wall.[25]

Raper had met economist Paul Taylor while Taylor was traveling and researching the South with his wife Dorothea Lange for a project that would eventually become the classic study, *An American Exodus*. Compared with Taylor, Raper was naive about the resilience of the family farm. "It is plain that with advances in agricultural techniques the country requires fewer farmers rather than more," Taylor had concluded. "Further, the income of agriculture is not great enough to support more people adequately." By the late 1930s, Taylor and Lange, unlike Raper, no longer believed the small family farm had a viable future. Raper seemed constitutionally unable to reach Taylor's conclusion that the family farmer, currently being displaced by the machine, would need to abandon his farming altogether and take work in industry. "Industrial expansion alone offers hope of permanently raising agricultural income to high levels," Taylor argued, "and of employing at good standards the population produced but unneeded on the farms." Government assistance should be in the form of aid to help farmers make the transition.[26]

"I was home with very little cash"

While he was involved in all Greene's government initiatives, Raper was also recruited to advise on wages in textile and sawmills and furniture making, as part of a committee named by the Wage-Hour Division.[27] He traveled to Washington for committee hearings in the spring and summer of 1941 and, in a letter to Guy Johnson in Chapel Hill, was typically sardonic. The largest mill owners had been arguing in favor of maintaining a low minimum wage as a way to help the small mills to stay in business during their hard times. "I have come to observe," ran his mock report, "as how the more successful industrialists have a deep concern for the well-being of their smaller brothers. At times in these hearings the milk of human kindness stands so deep that cream begins to rise on it. Somehow I wish the larger employers could remember their concern for the little fellow when they get back home." Raper showed that, time and again, he was alert to the cant proffered by the privileged. Sometimes his response was tactful or private; other times it was more emphatic and less diplomatic.[28]

Raper's work on wages took him to Puerto Rico, where he met with railroad owners and workers as the official U.S. "Public Representative." It was a trip that said a great deal, not only about Raper's politics, but also about the way the family was forced to live in order to accommodate those politics. The wealthy of Puerto Rico, charming and gracious, hosted Raper in their mountain homes and in-town villas to gain a favorable ear. He told the owners he would spend only as much time with them as he did with the workers. For their part, the workers could hardly find time or money to take him to lunch, so his "socializing" was limited. But as usual, he found the owners revealed more of their politics at home than they did in committee. One evening, once they realized that Raper was not about to lecture or denounce them, their conversation drifted into the usual complaints about the unreliability and intractability of their laborers. The talk reminded Raper of a favorite topic among wealthy southerners, the "sins and wickedness," as he called it, of the lower classes. Finally, hoping to stir the pot a bit, one of the well-dressed owners turned to Raper and wondered how this talk sounded to the "Public Representative" at the wage-and-hour conference. "What would you do about such people, Dr. Raper?" he inquired. Raper hesitated for a moment in the shadow of his official status. "If all that you are saying is true," he finally replied, "maybe you should just grind them up into hamburger."[29]

Meanwhile, Martha was straining even more than usual to keep the family finances together. "At that time and for many years I was the bookkeeper and bill payer," she said, looking back from the 1970s with great equanimity about the difficulties Arthur placed on her shoulders. Scrupulous as he was about the data for his research, Arthur was a mess about keeping track of his own money. "So I was the one who was aware of how slim was our balance at the bank in Greensboro," she said. "Maybe we might even overdraw, as we had done so many times before, especially when checks written during trips did not get entered into the check book." Raper wrote a check to cover the weeks-long trip to Puerto Rico, and as Martha remembered, "As so often before, I was home with very little cash." The truth was, Arthur had left her with no money to spend. She attacked the problem head on.

"To Mr. Hamp's store, I took what surplus eggs we had from our hens, and sold them for cash." She took the money, then asked the clerk, with tremendous embarrassment, whether she might charge some groceries. Then she took the cash to a filling station and bought some groceries, before returning home in humiliation. "The clerk very courteously did not raise an eyebrow," she said, "at this performance of selling eggs for cash and then charging groceries. Perhaps other people had done the same thing at times? But I thought he was just being polite about my predicament." The Rapers paid out the bill at Mr. Hamp's store at the end of the month, and that was the end of that. "But I never forgot it," wrote Martha, at sixty-four years of age. "Obviously." While Arthur was making sarcastic and tough-minded rejoinders in a Puerto Rican palace, Martha was at home, feeling the pinch of the near-poverty he had asked his family to endure.

His children, too, certainly suffered because of Raper's liberalism. When the family moved outside Washington, a couple of years later, Raper would remark on the stereotyping his children faced from their teachers for their southern accents. But he never mentioned their problems in Greene County schools. "Our little boys are inordinately happy with a big oak which we have cut and piled up for firewood," Raper wrote his friends Jack and Irene Delano, who had spent several weeks in Greene. "They do not want to ever leave the country."[30] Irene saw their lives differently. She had grown to love the four children dearly, and she remembered their troubles well. Raper would not give in to bullying, she said. As a result, his children led a very tough life in Greene. She saw them suffer the shame of their father being fired as a Sunday school teacher because he mixed politics with religion. But that was the least of it. Several times, in fact, for the sake of Raper's social views and actions, the boys were stoned on their way to school.[31]

"Some of these rumors were true"

The resistance to Raper's work focused squarely on race. During the dog days of the summer of 1941, the *Greensboro Herald-Journal* ran a note in its courthouse column about some suspicious activity in town and its quick resolution. "The Grand Jury investigated the rumors that have been coming from the office of Dr. Raper," the paper reported, "and found that some of these rumors were true. Dr. Raper admitted himself some indiscretions and promised that this will not occur again."[32]

One day, the week before, Raper had arrived at his downtown office about noon. His secretary rushed over and told him two men from Sheriff Wyatt's office had come in several times with a subpoena for him. Raper thought it must be about that fellow over near Lloyd Rhodes's place, who had been caught stealing meat. When she told him they were also looking to subpoena his assistant, Carolyn Blue, Raper knew it was something else altogether. He had heard about all the talk currently circulating through the county about his peculiar "social views." Here, as elsewhere, Raper was used to hearing accusations about the nature of his work. Not long before, for instance, Hamp McGibony, one of Greene's county commissioners, had pulled him aside and told him that word around town claimed he had been recruited by the commissioners to fix the black man on a level with the white.[33]

Belle Huey was a white teen in town who had received some spot work through the National Youth Administration. She had spent a few days on Raper's project, and he knew already she was dismayed about the way Raper addressed the blacks who worked in the office. Once Raper heard Belle Huey had appeared before the Grand Jury, he put two and two together.

Raper walked across Main Street to the courthouse, found Sheriff Wyatt, and told him he was ready any time to appear before the Grand Jury. He passed from one office to another, intent on appearing nonchalant, looking for Deputy Tugell, who had his subpoena. He found the usual courthouse crowd of clerks and officials strangely surly and incommunicative. Once he had found Tugell and served himself, Raper walked up the street and ate an anxious lunch, waiting for the afternoon session to begin. First called was Belle Huey, who testified again. Then Sheriff Wyatt was called. Miss Atkinson, who had also worked on and off in Raper's office, appeared in the hallway with an older woman and an elderly man, both obviously tense. The man leaned into a group of fellows sitting at another bench to ask if they knew anything about a Dr. Raper. Raper jumped right up and introduced himself. "I don't want to see *you*," the old man replied, and he stomped off down the hall.

Two more women in Raper's office were called to testify. The second,

Francis Bowen, was with the Grand Jury for less than a minute. She passed Raper on her way out and bent to tell him, "I just told them, I didn't know who paid you." A friend of his, Ed Downs, arrived and was called for a long testimony. He came out in good spirits and nodded to Raper. Carolyn Blue testified for fifteen minutes, and as she passed him on her way out, she told Raper, "Nothing to it." Finally, as he recalled, "I heard the welcome word. 'Dr. Raper is wanted.'"

Forty or fifty people from around the county, many of them farmers, some of them friends, sat leisurely around the courtroom. Solicitor-General Baldwin conducted the hearing, laboriously intoning a report that several complaints had come from Raper's office about the cordial way he had received blacks. "Now, Doctor," he advised Raper, "you know this is the South, and we don't want to have any trouble here.' Baldwin talked on at length, but to Raper, it seemed he had little to say. He loudly proclaimed his own interest in "the nigger." All good southerners shared his interest in their black neighbors. Notwithstanding these warm sentiments, the white folks of the South simply would not stand for social equality, Baldwin told Raper, indignation lifting his voice loud enough to fill the last row of the courtroom. "You know what I mean," he offered, conspiratorially, "niggers marryin' white girls, eatin' together, and mixin' and minglin' like that."

At the conclusion of Baldwin's performance, Raper asked him, what do you want to talk with me about?

"Well, Doctor, there have been a lot of reports coming out of your office. We have had a lot of witnesses in here, and we wanted to give you a chance to make a statement about it."

Raper then challenged him to say what allegations, specifically, he was talking about. Baldwin backpedaled. "Well, some of the things we've been told, we've found out are not true." Then the jury foreman jumped. "Quite a few of the things we've learned are not so." And another member spoke up, "Now, Doctor, I just want you to know this thing has been made to appear a whole lot worse than it is." Raper told them he was glad to hear it. But he still wanted to know what the allegations were.

"Well, Doctor," replied Baldwin, puffing himself up to his full height. "We wanted to know whether you are a member of any organizations proposing social equality and whose purpose it is to overthrow the government."

Raper assured him he was a member of no such organization and asked whether anyone had claimed he was. No, replied Baldwin. Raper wanted to know, then why did you ask me about it?

Baldwin launched into a detailed statement about southern race relations, concluding that "all this federal program is making the nigger restless. You know what I mean. This wage and hour stuff, old age assistance, surplus commodities, and all the rest.

"Now we want the nigger to have his rights," he assured Raper, "but we are not going to have any of this equality stuff. The niggers are feeling more independent and they have got to be watched." His speech delivered, Baldwin again turned conciliatory. "But you say you're not a member of any organization for social equality or to overthrow the government."

Raper told the Grand Jury he himself was an employee of the federal government, and he had never been questioned about his loyalty. He said he was glad they had invited him to come before them. I am more interested than anyone else that the Grand Jury knows who I am, he continued, and what I am doing. To Raper, the members of the jury looked uneasy, and they seemed unsatisfied about his responses, afraid the point was being lost. At that point, Baldwin, too, seemed to sense he was losing control, so he cut right to the chase. "Doctor, do you believe in niggers and whites going to school together in Greene County?" Raper replied that he had never mentioned any such thing. Raper asked whether anyone had told the jury that he had advocated integrated schools.

"Why, no," said Baldwin, "they haven't."

Then why did you ask me? Raper wondered aloud.

"Well, Doctor, we just wanted to know."

Just then, a member of the jury spoke up from the back corner of the jury box in an agitated voice. "But you do believe in social equality, don't you?" Raper ignored the voice and turned to Solicitor Baldwin and Foreman White. "Gentlemen," he pointed out, "I came here in good faith and am anxious to give you any specific information you want."

"Well," confided Baldwin, "it's been reported by several people who've come before us that you have called niggers 'Mr.' and 'Mrs.'"

Raper assured him he had indeed used titles and would explain why. "My use of titles grew out of wholly southern experiences, and in connection with southern organizations and programs." The use of titles is standard practice, he explained, in the Georgia Council of Social Welfare, the Atlanta Community Chest, and among the faculty of Agnes Scott, Emory, and Georgia Tech as well as with leaders of Atlanta's black community. "Of course in my work with the Inter-Racial Commission, I used titles. All of the members of this all-southern organization had followed this policy from the outset." He elaborated on racial etiquette in the new urban South. It was awkward *not* to use titles when white and black church groups conferred, and within interracial professional circles.

Raper always played the southern card in these kinds of situations, happy to produce his bona fides. To the consternation of conservatives in Greene and across the region, Raper could never be called a carpetbagger or an outside agitator, although his opinions and actions were equally radical and just as foreign to the southern mainstream. "My use of titles was of the best southern traditions," he told the Grand Jury, before launching into his own background.

"I married the daughter of a North Georgia Methodist preacher," he began with a typically southern genealogical litany, "whose maternal grandfather, Dr. John S. Moore, taught Latin at old Emory, and his father-in-law had drawn the designs for and built the Merrimac." The jury looked ever more perplexed. "I mentioned this only to say that I have often at the dinner table and elsewhere, in conversation with Mrs. Raper's father and mother, heard them use titles in speaking of Negroes, and that was in Atlanta. So whatever your estimate may be of the use of titles, the practice is not un-southern."

This seemed to satisfy most of the jurymen. Baldwin, though, anxious not to appear soft on race, took the opportunity to point out the danger of using titles with blacks. The practice encouraged them to rise above their place. "For example, Doctor," he patiently explained, "we don't want any mixin' of white boys and black girls. Just suppose you needed $1,000 and a nigger told you he would give it to you, if you would take his black daughter out to a party that night?"

Raper, just as patiently, told Baldwin he had never borrowed any money under those circumstances, nor had he ever heard of anyone else doing so. He turned to Foreman White and asked if he could make another statement.

Raper explained what he was doing in Greene, and talked about the federal programs in the Southeast. He told them about his previous studies, including the work that became *Preface to Peasantry*. One of the effects of the book was that the Department of Agriculture hired Raper to return to the county in 1940 to develop a model program linking agricultural assistance and social service. He told them Greene County had been an exemplary choice for the model program, not only because the need was great, but also because the leadership of the county could be counted on to help work out and carry through agreed-upon programs. "We all know," he concluded, "how correct I was in my estimate of your leadership here."

Baldwin told Raper he was impressed with the program in Greene County. In fact, he wished it were operating in Morgan County, where he lived. "Doctor," intoned another juryman, "we appreciate your interest in the county and the assistance you have been able to render us. We hope you will continue to help us."

"That is my intention."

As the hearing was concluding, another juror spoke up. "What kind of study is this you are making?"

"A comprehensive study of the whole county."

"Well, what all does that include?' Baldwin asked.

"Well, it includes everything. Historical materials, as well as facts about present-day social, economic, political, educational, and health conditions."

"Oh, well, then. I guess you'll report on this Grand Jury investigation?"

"Well," Raper answered with a laugh. "I'm supposed to tell the whole story."

The investigation had been conducted to gather political ammunition for prototype demagogue Governor Eugene Talmadge in his fight to roll back New Deal programs. Most of the jurymen were clearly Talmadge supporters. Raper suggested that while he was in Greene County, he would refrain from introducing blacks to Greene County whites using titles. He was primarily interested in helping the people of Greene County, Raper told them, and if they felt he could do this best by leaving off titles for blacks, he would do it out of deference to their wishes. He did not tell them that he also promised to himself he would now leave off titles for everyone, white and black. The Grand Jury said such a promise made the matter entirely satisfactory.

"The hope was then expressed that I would continue to work in behalf of Greene County," Raper recalled, years later. "I assured them that I would as I left the Grand Jury room." But he did not say which of them he would continue to work in behalf of.

In the meantime, through the rest of his time in Greene County, he found new ways to circumvent the racial mores, while protecting his New Deal programs and pushing without directly challenging white attitudes. When half a dozen of his white friends from around town gathered in Raper's office, for example, to hear the black poet and humorist Sterling Brown recite his work, they all felt comfortable, because Raper had lugged in a big, bulky box of a tape recorder. They weren't just mixing socially, but participating in a documentary project. That way, the technology gave his white friends free rein to mix with this black friend. On the old tapes made that day, along with the whistle of a Georgia Railroad train through an office window can still be heard the hearty chuckling of Raper's friends—the sheriff, the county commissioner, the school superintendent, and the rest—at Brown's funny verses and pointed racial jibes at whites.[34]

Raper was fascinated by these surprising changes and the *pas de deux* of the races as they danced through a variety of social tableaux. The first October back in Greene, he was drawn to the mix at the county fair. "One wonders what are the explanations of the free and easy manner in which Negroes and whites mix and mingle at the County Fair and the stilted hardness of segregation in all the full-time institutions." The constant seemed to be the intrigue that whites had for blacks, even pursuing their own fun. "Again and again one was impressed with the observation that white people like to see Negroes in holiday mood. Here again we approach an explanation of the attraction of Negro minstrels to white audiences and get some hint of why Negro night clubs are particularly popular with the sporting element of the white community." Whites always seemed pleased to crumble the cake of racial custom at the county fair. It seemed to Raper they could rebake it all the easier the next day at work.[35]

"I don't care now whether Hitler takes this country"

Working as adjuncts to the Talmadge administration, the members of Greene County's Grand Jury had raised a bastion against social change. The hearing on the threat of racial equality, which Raper represented, was the official expression of the fears of Greene County's whites. And those fears were increasing as whites' racial attitudes were turned in on themselves, both at home and overseas. The fight against Nazism prompted insistent questions about southern racism. And the assumed logic of time-worn prejudices wilted into absurdity when patriotic southerners fought in the Pacific. "Many white soldiers and sailors from Greene are finding themselves in a strange world," Raper wrote. It was a world in which white southerners were facing death with Filipinos, Chinese, and other brown- and yellow-skinned people. Raper could not ignore the fact that sometimes homegrown racism won out. "One mother," he recounted, "reports that her pilot-son compares the complexion of the pilot in the other plane with his own and brings him down if it doesn't match. 'But suppose he is one of our dark-skinned allies?' comes the quick inquiry. 'Oh, well, he'd rather take a chance on bringing one of our bunch down by mistake than leaving one of theirs up there.'" Clearly, though, this was not a view that would any more much advance southern interests, white or black.[36]

Even in downtown Greensboro, whites were astounded by the change in their black neighbors. As Raper observed, "Some new ideas are seeping into the field of entertainment." New ideas that had whites wondering why all of a sudden, for the first time in their lives, they found themselves uncertain about their neighbors.

As though Boswell's plea to the Greensboro Lions had been a prophecy, as well as a caution, at the end of 1940, two local businessmen built the New Greenland Theatre right in the middle of downtown Greensboro. Folks would not wait until the Depression ended to enjoy the pleasures of big-screen movies and air conditioning, and they built and equipped a theater that would suit a town twice the size. Opening night was a big affair. The hall was filled to capacity, with two hundred blacks seated in the large balcony. The whole town, it seemed, leaned back in the comfortable new seats and enjoyed the feature film.

When the lights came up, an elaborate ceremony began. The master of ceremonies, County Commissioner Hamp McGibony, set a mirthful tone with a speech full of humor and good spirits. He recognized townspeople and farmers from the audience, both on the ground floor and in the balcony. He said he hoped they would continue to be "well beloved" of their community. Then he introduced speaker after speaker to the cheering hall. "Each congratulated the community and the owners on the completion of the beautiful theatre," recalled Raper, "called attention to the spacious balcony and the traditional good conduct of the colored people in the old Greenland Theater across the way." Toward the end, old John Calloway took the stage. There was not much left to talk about, he said, since McGibony had stolen his thunder. His predicament, Calloway told the crowd, reminded him of the old joke about "our old nigger and a mule." You see, he said, the mule doctor had given the old nigger a straw and some medicine to blow into the mule's mouth. The next day, the mule was no better, but the nigger was all sick, because the mule blew first.

The story was typical enough, but as soon as Calloway started in, though, the balcony began to rumble. Downstairs, Raper heard an "audible resentment" welling from above. One voice called out. "Callin' us 'niggers' again!" Another answered, "Let's get out of here, and stay out!" Each time Calloway used the word *nigger,* dozens of black folks rose from their comfortable, new seats and clattered down the stairs and out the door. The clamor of their exit was so loud the folks below could hardly hear the end of the joke. Whites who had lived in Greene all of their lives were amazed. "Since when can't we call them nigger?" asked one woman afterward. "Why, we've done it all our lives!"

The next evening, the balcony was almost empty. The owners were anxious. They had counted on black patrons to fill their big house. Some whites became angry that blacks had forgotten their place. Others were afraid of race trouble if the balcony stayed empty. One and all among Greensboro's blacks denied leading the exodus from the balcony. Whites, though, were quick to point to the influence of the Negro Civilian Conservation Corps (CCC) camp and the few black supervisors who were helping to administer the UFP. Many black moviegoers declared that they had not left, or that their neighbors had pushed them along down the stairs. Like the Great Migration itself, "an Exodus without a Moses," wrote Raper, "it was, so far as the white public could learn."

Within a few weeks, however, the balcony had begun to fill again, and talk of race trouble died back down. Blacks went back to the movie house because it was their most exciting amusement. And some of the community's black leaders had recommended returning, as a way to forestall any chance of race trouble. The temperature did indeed drop below what Raper called "its low boiling point." But why had blacks walked out in the first place? They had, indeed, been referred to as "niggers" all their lives. Few explained why they had left. "It makes a fellow feel heavy down in his heart to be called that," said one man. What was new about that, though? Another did articulate a new thought, an increase in his sense of social importance. He told Raper he "didn't mind being called a nigger by white people when he worked for them, for he figured part of his pay was for that, but he didn't like to be called a nigger or otherwise made uncomfortable when he paid out his own money for an evening of relaxation at the movie." Here was a new recognition of self-worth and personal dignity. Greene's racial conservatives were absolutely right. In the New Greenland Theatre, in late 1940, this black man had indeed forgotten his place.[37]

Other black folks went further. One view was, "We oughter had a lot of rocks." Another said, "I wish I meet him out on a dark road by himself." And others connected Greensboro with the war. "It made me feel like this," said a young woman. "I don't care now if Hitler or anybody takes this country. It would be worth what ever we get to see these mean, white people get what's due them, and it couldn't be much worse." Not everyone in the black community agreed with the boycott, for a variety of reasons. Some were embarrassed. "Our people don't know how to appreciate nothing," complained one woman. "I stayed myself. If I had left, what other show could I have went to?" Blacks did not have their own movies, and she did not see any hope of building their own theater. A black man Raper spoke with told him he simply liked the show. "We don't have any other place to go and enjoy ourselves," he said. But his friend disagreed. Did *he* regret the boycott? "Sure don't. I don't hate to do. I hate to go back."

Greene County's blacks did go back to the movies, but old John Calloway never told the same joke again to black people. By the start of the war, Raper saw some of Greene County's whites trading in their racial caste system for air conditioning. They wanted a big, modern theater, and to get it, they would treat blacks with dignity.

As Boswell and Raper both saw, even the older generation of black southerners was being pushed into changing their lifelong relationships to whites by Greene's new circumstances of modernity and war. Near his office one day, not long after the theater walk-out, Raper overheard an exchange in a downtown store. A white woman working in the store saw an old black man of long acquaintance. "Sam," she called over to him, "I hear the colored folks walked out of the show the other night?'

"I wasn't there," replied Sam. "I don't know." Remaining noncommittal had served generations of black southerners in any situation that stirred with potential conflict. The incident at the theater, though, and others like it, had begun to push even older black folks to choose up sides.

"If you had been there," the white woman persisted, "what would you have done?"

"I reckon," replied Sam, "I'd a done the same thing they did."[38]

9

TENANTS OF THE ALMIGHTY
"Uncle Sam Is My Shepherd"

The first time Margaret Mead traveled the Deep South, she stopped in to stay with the Rapers at the Punch Dolvin place. Over dinner, Arthur and Martha asked what had most impressed her about the Black Belt. "Well, as I see it," the famous anthropologist was quick to answer, "most white people spend much of their time not being Negroes. Whenever two different groups live close together, I've found each puts great importance in not being like the other." Mead analyzed everything in sight, Raper remembered. Her influence fit well with his own observations, and Raper's vignettes of black farm life are as literary as they are sociological, with a precise knowledge about these people that most whites hardly saw.

"Black men and women walked the white roads at night," he wrote as though he had tramped the back roads with them, "whistling, talking, humming in minor keys. They seemed happier at night, maybe just freer." As Mead had done, Raper considered the verbal defenses required of southern blacks in the elaborate system of caste. He took the example of the ubiquitous black refrain, "Yah, suh." What did it really mean? After a few months at Punch Dolvin's, "we began to see that it could mean three things. One, I am listening respectfully to what you say. Or second, I understand what you have told me. Or third, you are exactly right; that's just what I think. Maybe there are other degrees of meaning. We began to think that we could sometimes tell from manner and tone of voice which was the real meaning of Yas'suh or Yas'm."[1] The real meaning was contextual and deflective, a trial balloon flown to see which way the wind was blowing, as a way of adjusting to the direction.

To employ Mead's anthropological eye, Raper said he carried the stimulation of her visit when he wrote the captions for Jack Delano's documentary photographs in *Tenants of the Almighty*. Delano was one of Roy Stryker's Farm Security Administration (FSA) photographers, along with Dorothea Lange, Walker Evans, Arthur Rothstein, and a dozen others, who traveled the country during the late 1930s documenting the effects of the Depression and the vanishing small-town life of America. Raper extended acknowledgment in the book to Mead, as well as to Howard Odum and Ira De A. Reid.[2] Will Alexander, Raper wrote, had "always encouraged us to look deep, think straight, and write plain." And he thanked Roy Stryker and Delano, "one of the expert photographers of his staff."[3] The way Raper described Delano's approach to his work in Greene County echoed similar accounts of Stryker's other photographers as they pursued documentary realism across the entire country. Raper reflected, for example, that "Jack took pictures of the Lamb residence," the Greensboro's wealthiest family, "inside and out, and of granny woman Lucy Anne's cabin, inside and out, but not of scar-disfigured Lumma Dell. Jack liked to make pictures of things about which something could be done."[4]

To Delano's boss, Stryker, documentary photography was a tool and ally of social science and liberal politics. In fact, historians Carl Fleischauer and Beverly Brannan argue, sociology was for Stryker at the foundation of documentary photography. Stryker was a sociologist himself, a disciple of Rex Tugwell at Columbia, and he later followed Tugwell to the New Deal's Resettlement Administration (RA), and on to the FSA, where Tugwell was Roosevelt's director. In the mid-1920s, Stryker compiled illustrations for Tugwell's *American Economic Life,* a prototype documentary project that tied photography with sociology, economics, history, cultural studies, and geography. Stryker eventually came to know and work with numerous social scientists, including Caroline Ware, Helen and Robert Lynd, and Odum, as well as Raper. What tied all of these figures together was what Raper would later come to admire in Delano's work. Each wanted to provoke change. This was certainly not an approach shared by all sociologists or all photographers. Ansel Adams had famously grumbled to Stryker about the social and political intentions of his art form. "What you've got aren't photographers," he chided. "They're a bunch of sociologists with cameras."[5]

At the FSA, beginning in 1935, Stryker gathered together a shifting group of photographers who did indeed consider themselves, at least in part, as sociologists with cameras. Stryker instructed his photographers to prepare for their photo assignments by reading analyses of local social, economic, and geographical conditions. Besides Delano's, the photographs of Walker Evans, Dorothea Lange, Arthur Rothstein, Marion Post Wolcott, and a dozen others appeared across the emerging landscape of America's new popular media, from *Life* magazine to innumerable Sunday newspaper supplements. These photographers all drew paychecks from federal agencies to take pictures, not only of morale boosters, but of the failures of government policy and the economic destitution that had gripped the nation.[6]

Raper had begun corresponding with Stryker about *Sharecroppers All*, which used photos from a number of FSA photographers, including Lange, Evans, and Post. To Stryker, Raper's proposed book followed the typical formula, a text ornamented with a few photographs. He felt it would have benefited by integrating word and picture in a photo-book, documentary approach. "I am sorry that it was not possible to use more of the photographs," Stryker had written Raper. "I believe I told you once that you write awfully good captions." By the winter of 1941, with Raper studying Greene County again, Stryker proposed an idea. "Soon someone or some group will need to do a pictorial and graphic presentation of the problems in the Southeast," he wrote Raper. "This should not be a 'picture-book.' It should be dramatic and appealing, yet accurate. I am afraid of the word 'picture-book,' but this publication would of necessity be very much on the visual side. You should do the captions." The approach perfectly fit Raper's own impulse to write, not for sociologists, but for as large a readership as possible. Stryker promised to send a photographer to document Greene County. "We will have a photographer working in that general section some time this spring. I will keep in touch with you," he told Raper. "I have not forgotten the intelligent cooperation Marion Post received from you last year."[7]

"It was always a very delicate matter"

A year after the family had moved back to Greene, while he was drafting what would become *Tenants of the Almighty*, Raper wrote to Bill Couch at UNC Press. He wanted to let Couch know why he was publishing his next book with Macmillan, which wanted to pick up on the notoriety that *The Grapes of Wrath* and *You Have Seen Their Faces* had established for sharecropping. "We plan to present a good number of FSA photographs," Raper explained to Couch, "some pictorial statistics and maps, and a text on sixth or seventh grade level. The point of view of the report is that of a story for Greene County from the inside, rather than a typical social scientist's study about a rural county for a university audience." That point of view also pushed farther into the territory of documentary than Couch could afford to go—in its extensive use of photograph—and in the way Raper phrased in everyday language a quasi-populist anthropology.[8]

Jack and Irene Delano arrived at the Punch Dolvin place in late April 1941, and the Delanos and Rapers quickly became fast friends. Irene was an artist who sketched for the family, and Jack recorded for the Raper children a reel-to-reel tape of his own songs accompanied by his wobbly guitar. The couple took a special interest in twelve-year-old Harrison, and Jack gave him a camera. "They did him good," Raper said at the time. "They did us all good. They shared our faith in Greene County's poorer people."[9]

Raper provided Delano with a comprehensive and sociological context for the photography. Raper's knowledge—and his own documentary eye—helped Delano gain an understanding he never again experienced on a shoot. "But in the first place," said Delano, "it gave us a chance to know Arthur Raper, who was a remarkable man." Many of the photographs Delano took were not taken with his FSA assignment in mind. Instead, they originated with Raper's interests and relied on his savvy at playing the cultural norms of the rural South. "For example," Delano remembered, "the FSA had nothing to do with the county jail, but it was only because Arthur Raper was there with us that we were able to get in the county jail to photograph the inside of that place and the prisoners, and the way they lived, and so on. I think both Irene and I learned a tremendous amount about what the South means, the attitudes in the South, from our few months' stay in Greene County during this project." The assignment influenced all of Delano's subsequent work in the region.[10]

Raper showed the Delanos how the typical southern town encompassed—even within the white community—violent bigotry, Christian charity, apathy about race, and a view of blacks as customers. "You had to have an understanding of what the whole community was like, the whole social structure," explained Irene Delano, "because it varied tremendously." Raper had gained hard-won experience in how to negotiate among the many crosscurrents of small-town viewpoints and passions and social strictures that comprised the Black Belt South. "It was always a very delicate kind of thing," said Jack. "Arthur himself was under tremendous attack," said Irene. They both saw right away that Raper's Progressivism "didn't go very well with some of the people in the South," as Jack phrased it. "They also knew he was writing a book. And writing a book about a county in the South is always suspect because you don't quite know what they're going to say in that book." Raper was the subject of much back-fence scrutiny, and the Delanos saw how word would make its way around town when Raper was seen, for example, shaking hands with a black man.[11]

In spite of antipathy toward his views and the grapevine surveillance, Raper managed to maintain good relations with most of Greene's citizens. "He was a very, personally, a very warm and sympathetic type of person," Jack explained, "and obviously a Southerner. I mean, you couldn't take him for anything but, so that he was able to accomplish a great deal. Although, as I say, it was always a very delicate matter whether he was going to be able or not going to be able to do certain things." Delano saw that the entry Raper provided was not simply a matter of knowing the right folks to contact, but of being able to take the temperature of a room and having a sharp sense of timing. "For example," Delano explained, "it's true that we did get into the county jail and we did take the photographs. Somehow or other, Arthur wangled that, but while we were there we had the feeling that we had better do this and do it fast because we didn't know whether they meant it or not in the first place." Both socially adept and intimately familiar with the way the southern caste system worked, down to its smallest patterns of behavior and expectation, Raper knew how to enter the crevices between Jim Crow strictures and open up situations that maybe had never existed before—situations that racial habits had not settled—then rush into the vacuum before anyone could object.[12]

Raper's update two weeks after Delano arrived gave Stryker a sense of the variety they were aiming for. "This week we are picking up *must* shots," Raper wrote him, "such as an abandoned factory site in a literally abandoned part of the county. In which abandoned corner, incidentally, we found a good brace of oxen and cart, atop of which was a man—part Cherokee Indian—wearing a derby hat. Or yesterday we went with our leading citizen, Judge James B. Park, to his old home-place." As an invited guest, Delano would take photographs of the Greensboro Lions Club the following Tuesday night. As Raper described it, diversity was not a policy but an attempt to see the world for what it was. "When it clears soon we will try a rather interesting interracial picture, for that kind, too, is needed if the Report is to be realistic."[13]

Raper's approach fit perfectly with the new direction that Stryker was establishing for the FSA's documentary. When the agency was first organized, in the mid-1930s, the focus had been on documenting the need for government action. Photos of dust bowl victims, Oakies in migrant camps, displaced sharecroppers, and tenants living in squalid hardship formed the nucleus of the file in its first few years. By the early 1940s, though, Stryker was assigning his photographers to shoot community studies. They documented American towns, not in crisis, but in their normal routines—and with an air of impending change. The intent of the FSA file had changed from providing evidence that rural poverty required immediate government action to the documentation of small-town America before it passed away. What had started with urgency for change ended with a different urgency—for preservation—mixed with a tinge of nostalgia for the old permanence. Raper had always been more interested in cultural studies than exposés, anyway, and so he naturally helped Delano move in Stryker's new direction. "The same was true about meeting the people in the county seat in Greensboro"—Raper provided Delano with entry to the county's power structure—"the editor of the newspaper, the mayor, the deputy, the sheriff, all the various people who made up the community and were the opinion-making group of the community." Irene Delano marveled at how comprehensive Raper's knowledge was. "Arthur had worked in that county for one or two years before we came and he just knew practically every individual in it," she remembered. "He had organized all the material for his books, so that by teaching us as we were working, we got—I mean not just little pieces that happened to interest us visually as we went through, as did happen in some places—but we were able to just kind of go through the whole community like a dose of salts, you know, and do every aspect of it."[14]

Raper had spent years honing this integrated, dynamic approach to community studies that so well fit Stryker's new direction for New Deal documentary photography. But as Arthur was introducing Jack and Irene to Judge Park and "Preacher" Parrott and the deputies at the county jail, the New Deal was facing legislative and fiscal attacks that would soon eliminate both the FSA photographic unit and federally financed community studies. Raper would quickly come to see federal emphasis shift from integrated social studies of rural communities to measurements of agricultural production suited to a free-market orientation. Government studies of "rural life," whether visual or sociological, were passing from the scene as rapidly as was rural life itself.

"We have a pile of quotable phrases"

All through 1941, Raper spent a good deal of time out in Greene's fields. By the middle of summer, he had completed hundreds of interviews throughout the county to canvas opinion of the various government programs. "We have a pile of quotable phrases," he reported to Stryker in mid-summer, "which can be used in text and in captions."[15]

Delano returned in the fall to photograph the county at harvest time, after Greene's farm wives had finished canning fruits and vegetables for the winter using their new government-issued steamers. Many women were proud to have their picture taken with their hundreds of cans lined up across their long kitchen tables. October was also when the county fair was held. Raper insisted to Stryker that Delano document the caste system at its weakest point, in its least-rigid circumstance. "Of all the times of the year to take pictures here," Raper exhorted Stryker, "to get all the people in relaxed mood—is during the Fair. Jack will be literally intoxicated with the possibilities and will get some groupings and poses that will make everybody in your office glad he was here. It is, in short, the only institution and activity that has not been made colorless by segregation. It is vibrantly alive."[16] But by September 1941, Delano was all booked up, and Stryker had to work hard to find time for him in Greene County. "Unfortunately," Stryker wrote Raper, "he got mixed up in a lot of defense jobs which just have to get done." Stryker groused, "these defense jobs seem to have a terrible insistence."[17]

By the following spring, 1942, Stryker was explaining to Raper that his photo unit survived only by hiring out to other federal agencies. Conservatives in Congress had begun to question the need for nonessential social services in time of war, so Stryker tried to save his photographers' jobs by sending them to take pictures of B-17s and machine-gun assembly lines.[18]

That summer, Stryker's section photo editor, Edwin Rosskam, traveled to Greene County to work with Raper on choosing and arranging Delano's photographs. Rosskam had developed a concept and presentation of pictures that fit the goal of sociological presentation. Instead of trying to contain a subject within a single, dramatic shot, documentary photography worked best when it developed the context of the subject through a series of pictures. "When photographers think of assignments in story terms, they are likely to cover cultural relationships and processes more fully than if they simply pursue single images." Rosskam had begun refining the double-page spread the year before Raper returned to Greene County and began *Tenants of the Almighty*. The spread became a format in which, as he wrote, "word and image complemented each other." The ideal result was a kind of cubist's realism, a multifaceted view of a community that tied together all its strands.

Rosskam's goal was to accrete a photo file that contained, as he wrote, "the most gay and the most tragic—the cow barn, the migrant's tent, the tractor in the field and the jalopy on the road, the weathered faces of men, the faces of women sagging with household drudgery." Rosskam made clear the multipurpose and ecumenical intentions of documentary. "They are all here," he said of Americans, "photographed in their context, in relation to their environment. In rows of filing cabinets, they wait for today's planner and tomorrow's historian."[19]

Implicit in the documentary photography of the 1930s is the same sense of sturdy optimism that underlay all of Raper's work. Stryker always remembered Tugwell's advice, which mirrored Raper's approach as well in considering dignity a part of documentary realism.[20] "Roy, a man may have holes in his shoes, and you may see the holes when you take the picture. But maybe your sense of the human being will teach you there's a lot more to the man than the holes in his shoes, and you ought to try to get that idea across."[21] Raper's documentary sociology shares with the FSA photography a major flaw as well. As Lawrence Levine points out, the FSA "paid more attention to regional and folk than to popular and mass culture. While these documents attest to America's complex, ethnic, regional, and cultural heterogeneity, they are less successful in depicting the growing uniformity and standardization."[22] What is equally true is that the New Deal initiatives—including those of Raper and Stryker's documentary team—employed as many of these uniform and standardized products and processes, in particular, the most modern technologies of communication, to create a progressive vision of America. Unintentionally and ironically, the impression created by the FSA's documentary photography, and of Raper's own form of documentary realism and sociology, is one of a rural America being overtaken by an increasingly commercial and urban, standardized and affluent modern society.[23]

For *Tenants of the Almighty*, Raper, Delano, and Rosskam constructed a series of spreads—forty in all—that fill the first one-quarter of the book. The spreads not only provide context for the text but also suggest political points. As many blacks appear as whites, and most of the spreads include both. Ten years earlier, shots of black and white schoolhouses in *Preface to Peasantry* had made a decided point about the inequality of educational funding for blacks. In *Tenants of the Almighty*, by contrast, pictures of blacks and whites are as often joined to suggest a sense of community and their underlying similarities. The way Raper used photographs in *Preface to Peasantry* had much in common with Jacob Riis's exposé, *How the Other Half Lives*. *Tenants of the Almighty* is not at all a documentary accusation, however, but instead tells a story of improvement through photographs whose realism aimed to appeal to both bootstrap conservatives as well as advocates of government planning.

In *Tenants of the Almighty*, Rosskam often set two photos across a spread to create an instructive juxtaposition. One spread shows two Greene County residents in their own gardens, shot from the same perspective, as they bend to their work. The thin, black farmer in his dark overalls contrasts with the stocky white woman wearing earrings and a light print dress. The similarity of their postures, though—beneath the differences the two photographs imply—binds them in a politics that suggests the equality conferred by working the land.

Another spread opposed matching portraits of married couples. Delano pokes fun at Mr. and Mrs. Harold Lamb, owners of the Union Manufacturing Company, who sit stiff and prim on their Victorian sofa, daintily turning the pages of an old photo album, while across the tapestry hung above them, like erotic thought-bubbles over their heads, nubile harem girls dance sensuously through a Middle Eastern bazaar. Opposite is an earnest portrait of the Carl Lingolds, who worked in Lamb's mill. The clean-cut young couple stand, a little shy, but comfortable and proud, in a cotton dress and clean overalls, in front of their clean, simple hearth, among photos of family. Above the Lingolds' heads is a framed poem, "Greetings to Mother," and a Roman-style profile of President Franklin Roosevelt.

The photo that opened the book, facing the frontispiece, is Delano's portrait of the elderly and distinguished Dr. T. B. Rice, the county historian, its antiquarian and a lifelong observer of Greene's political scene. Delano shoots him sitting in his rocking chair before his hearth, as though afloat among his heirlooms. Aged painted portraits of a stern-looking couple, both of whom bear strong resemblance to Rice, share with him the photograph equally. The past is a living presence in the Black Belt South. From its very first image, *Tenants of the Almighty* creates the sense of being paused at a cusp, a tipping point, where the strength of the modern pulls against the weight of the past, a momentary equipoise between city and country, between the agrarian and industrial Americas.

All through *Tenants of the Almighty*, in both text and captions, Raper used "we" to mean both the black and white people of Greene. His captions were vividly inclusive. Beneath a photograph of black farmers, Raper wrote, "Our hands and feet know the feel of this land, and of trace-chains, plow handles and hoe handles, of washboards and cotton to pick. Black feet on the red land of Greene, black feet on the white lands—in the field by day and along the roads and paths at night." When had a white southerner ever taken a comradely and egalitarian tone in assuming a black voice?

By largely eschewing dialect, his voice gives greater dignity to his subjects. "I hope of course that some people outside of Greene County will be interested in our report," Raper wrote in the *Herald-Journal*. "I am most interested, however, in the Greene County audience, for from the outset I was writing it primarily for Greene County people."[24] Raper's conceit in *Tenants of the Almighty* was that he was constructing a homegrown documentary.[25]

Most of the 1930s documentary photo-books aimed for photos and text to carry the book equally. In his review of *Tenants of the Almighty*, Tarleton Collier praised the "smooth, occasionally poetic and always historically rich narrative," and was quick to add that "these photographs by Jack Delano are no less notable than the text." While it shared the same approach, superficially, as the most famous of the 1930s photo-books, Raper and Delano's *Tenants of the Almighty* contrasted sharply with the best-selling *You Have Seen Their Faces*, by photographer Margaret Bourke-White and novelist Erskine Caldwell, published in 1937.

Bourke-White had worked extensively for *Fortune* and *Life*, photographing the new icons of the coming machine age—gleaming turbines and imposing factories—with drama and energy. The cover of the first issue of *Life* was a Bourke-White in which the massive, newly constructed Hoover Dam loomed like the backdrop of a Wagnerian opera. Caldwell, of course, was notorious for his sensational novels of southern destitution, preeminently *Tobacco Road*, which was so successful in depicting southern poverty as depravity that it became a smash Broadway play. The poor, rural white and black southerners Caldwell and Bourke-White photographed and interviewed came across as suffused in the light of a mindless bathos, as though parading their afflictions. Caldwell wrote his captions in a condescending dialect that purported to reconstruct the photo subjects' thoughts.

Delano's and Raper's photos and captions are much less heated than Bourke-White's and Caldwell's, but carry an immensely greater sense of fellow-feeling between author and subject. Raper and Delano rejected the theatricality of *You Have Seen Their Faces* in favor of a more modest documentary realism. In *Saturday Review,* Jonathan Daniels recognized the approach and the temperature of *Tenants of the Almighty.* "Factually, Mr. Raper has done the job excellently. Pictorially also in the fine photographs by Jack Delano with which the book begins, the Greene County story is made clear. Somehow, however, while the book gives us all the facts, it remains a document rather than a drama." Drama or document, it was material that needed public attention.[26]

The appendices of *Tenants of the Almighty* reflect Raper's documentary impulses as well and showed Raper's attempt to gain a purchase on a multivarious reality by gathering and synthesizing as many different kinds of "facts" as possible—sociological, economic, and deeply personal and subjective facts: statistics on the number of slaves owned in Greene and on crop loans, but also wedding stories, poems, and the types of goods sold in the stores. Aiming to add depth to his portrait of Greene's people, Raper brings together different types of information and orders of knowledge to convey emotional states and the sense of individual personalities.[27] In its review, the *Greensboro Herald-Journal* caught the book's documentary spirit, its combination of fact and feeling. "*Tenants of the Almighty* is the best job of reporting that Raper has done," wrote Wayland Hayes, who praised its "maximum of clear facts in historical perspective. This does not mean that facts are cold. On the contrary, they come from the hands, faces, words and records of human beings as they live on a 'small patch of the earth' in Greene County, Georgia."[28]

Raper had admired Rosskam's choices and arrangements of photographs for Richard Wright's *Twelve Million Black Voices,* which was published in the fall of 1941, just as Raper was driving Delano and his cameras around Greene County. Raper wrote to Stryker that he wanted to accomplish something similar with the photographs in *Tenants of the Almighty.* He, too, wanted to tell a long and broad history with the help of pictures from the FSA file.

In the late 1930s, Wright had begun writing the story of African Americans from slavery through their exodus to the cities of the North and South. Though literate and a Marxist, Wright wrote in a folk dialect, and the effect was portentous, oracular, and inauthentic. His dialect was as far from the voices it claimed to speak through as Caldwell's hillbilly ventriloquism.[29] Wright was successful, though, in making a case for the New Deal as one of the most positive and hopeful occurrences in the history of black America. Wright and Rosskam prompted William Shands Meacham, in his review of

Twelve Million Black Voices for the *New York Times Book Review,* to conclude that "the Roosevelt Administration has done more to further the second emancipation of the Negro than any since the Civil War. . . . This is not the story Mr. Wright started out to tell, yet almost all the excellent photographs selected for his book by Edwin Rosskam came from the files of the Farm Security Administration." Meacham saw that these documentary photo-books were a way to lead readers to see new connections between community and nation in a modern American society.[30]

Let Us Now Praise Famous Men, published two years earlier than *Tenants of the Almighty,* in 1941, is the most literary and inventive book in the canon, a surrealistic documentary whose reemergence in the 1960s spoke to a common taste for the absurd in the everyday. Writer and journalist James Agee and FSA photographer Walker Evans had traveled to the farthest backwaters of southern poverty and Depression on assignment for *Fortune,* the Henry Luce precursor to *Life,* a pioneering magazine of documentary photography, as well as business journalism and social commentary. In the early and mid-1930s, the glossy *Fortune* published features that documented in text and photography the poverty and social dislocation of the Depression among factory workers, miners, and farm laborers. Bourke-White documented the logging industry of Quebec and Maine, and *Fortune* readers looked at pictures of lumberjacks and their families saying grace at humble tables, gaunt in their clean, meager homes. When Agee submitted an article on southern sharecropping, though, the editors were unhappy. It was much too long. It was too self-referential for journalism. And it was politically incendiary. So Agee went on writing and expanding his prose before finally publishing his photo book just as the country was turning toward war. As was the case with *Tenants of the Almighty,* sales were dismal.

Both *Let Us Now Praise Famous Men* and *Tenants of the Almighty* are structured with a gallery of photographs by a member of Stryker's FSA team, followed by a painstaking study of a particular place. While Raper and Delano used aesthetic techniques to create a work of documentary, Agee and Evans created a work of art that places the documentary in the service of the subject.[31] *Let Us Now Praise Famous Men* is about Agee's voice and consciousness, before it is about sharecropping. Its prose is self-conscious, poetic, ambiguous. It is a work of literature that sits on a shelf between the novel of subjectivity and a history—between, say, *The Sound and the Fury* and *The Grapes of Wrath.*

Agee insisted that the book was document, not art but, protestations aside, Agee's prose was extremely high-toned, and it did not try to please. Raper's and Delano's aesthetic ran the other way. Raper and Delano share with Agee and Evans their books' structure, and of course their subject, but Agee and Evans are antipolitical, while *Tenants of the Almighty* begins with politics. *Let Us Now Praise Famous Men* made hyperbolic demands on its readers as it worked to harmonize readers with the author's voice, with a single consciousness seeking to bridge its distance from a distant world. There is nothing self-conscious about *Tenants of the Almighty*. With its authorial "we," *Tenants of the Almighty* wanted its readers to consider it written by Greene County's folks themselves.

Raper's conception of documentary meant that his book should appeal to the broadest possible audience, and its intended readership were those people whose photographs filled its pages. When Raper began publishing his observations in the local newspaper, soliciting readers' comments, the *Greensboro Herald-Journal* ventured that it might be "the first government report that had ever been submitted to the people of a county for them to check upon its accuracy and adequacy."[32] Raper arranged for copies of his reports to be distributed throughout the county, from extension agents to union representatives. Black and white school officials asked for five hundred copies each, so they could develop curricular materials, using photos and captions for the lower grades and text chapters for the upper grades.[33]

Raper's impulse to write for the broadest possible readership was born of his Progressive political aims, but it also ensured the book's liberalism would be ecumenical and inclusive, not narrowly doctrinal. Raper's first intention was to understand and depict how people felt about the Unified Farm Program (UFP). But his instinct for context compelled him back into what he called "a full study of what had happened to the people in the county over the years." The history of Greene County would have influenced greatly the way people reacted to the new program. Before long, he was researching the area's natives, its eighteenth-century English settlements, the Indian wars, the crowning of King Cotton in the 1830s and 1840s, Civil War and Reconstruction, time-merchants and Populism. "In a single generation," he wrote about early Greene County, "the Indians had been driven out and slaves from Africa outnumbered the white people. To the landed Whites, accumulation and security was becoming a profession." The first half of *Tenants of the Almighty* became a people's history of the American South.[34]

Raper challenged orthodox southern historiography in many ways. He claimed the antebellum prosperity of the plantation system had eaten itself from inside, creating a dependent population antithetical to democracy and destroying the fertility of the soil by over-reliance on cotton.[35] The Civil War hastened, but did not cause, the South's decline. Raper's Reconstruction was completely unlike the one described in standard southern histories. "The slaves were free and had the ballot. But they had no economic resources, no way to escape chronic dependency, no reasonable hope for the coveted forty acres and a mule. And so as wage hands and sharecroppers, they could not prevent the use of political power to regulate their economic and social conditions."[36]

Raper's history pointed out the hypocrisy of the wealthy landowners in the 1870s, who objected to funding public education when Greene's indebtedness was far less than its revenues. "It will be remembered that it was during the decade of the 1870's that the county's population increased over one third and that some merchants built fine new homes."[37] Raper wrote about the campaign of 1894, when local townsfolk carried Tom Watson on their shoulders to the speakers' platform in Greene's courthouse square and listened to him talk about "laws which would give all classes, the rich and the poor, the white and the black man, equal justice." Young Watson even wooed Greene's black voters by promising free schoolbooks. Raper painted a mostly courageous portrait of the Populist movement in their fight against the banks, corporations, and railroads. "Many people in Greene thought they at last had 'treed the varmints that had been carrying off our chickens.'"[38] Still, Raper acknowledged, "the poorer Whites wanted to be in political control, but more than that they wanted recognition from the well-to-do Whites. Political harmony among the Whites of Greene was achieved in the early 1900's by depriving the Negro of political participation, as it had been achieved just after the war by the re-establishment of White supremacy, and before the war by the defense of slavery." The lesson Raper draws from the Populists, though, is that success in political liberalization and the modernization of the South clearly required advances in civil rights for African Americans. Throughout its history, Raper saw, southern agriculture had been deviled by race. Most whites were never quite willing to do all the work for themselves, he claimed, but they were never able to get blacks to do it for them efficiently.[39]

In part, Greene's history was a series of cautionary tales that pointed out the problems that can result from a lack of social and agricultural planning.[40] In the second half of the book, he returned again to Greene's race relations since the Great War, to the boll weevil and the slow decay of the plantation system. And after all the history and background, he addressed the work and perceptions of the UFP and showed the difference planning can make in enhancing democracy.[41]

Raper worked hard to include as many sources of information as he could. "Everybody helped us compile this story of Greene—county officials, representatives of the various agencies in the Unified Farm Program, and most of all the farmers and townspeople themselves, white and colored, men, women, and children."[42] He tried to understand each viewpoint. Doing his research in the Greensboro records, he took the time to type out several single-spaced pages of an address delivered April 2, 1868, from "the White people of Green County, Georgia to the Colored people of the same county," an amalgamation of amicability, intimidation, and racial *realpolitik* that advocates a joining of racial forces to stave off the economic and political domination of the North.

> It is to our interest to be friendly with you for we expect to live with you always. It is also to your interest to be friendly with us, for the same reason. You will always live with us. You cannot get away from us, and we cannot get away from you. . . . We wish now to caution you against a great danger. Strangers from the North have come among us, and have endeavored to get you all together into a black man's party without saying whether their motives are good or bad, we wish to say to you, that if you allow yourselves to be formed into a black man's party, you will force us to form ourselves into a white man's party. . . .
>
> You must recollect that when it comes to the final struggle, you will have not only the Southern people to contend with, but all the white people, both North and South.[43]

Raper also incorporated such nontraditional sources as his friend, the nonagenarian ex-slave Alfred "Preacher" Parrott, the Uncle Remus of the Punch Dolvin place. Preacher Parrott had lived in the little town of Siloam all his life. "Belonged to the white folks in slavery times," he said, in Raper's caption, accompanying his portrait, sitting comfortably in a rocking chair at home.

I worked, plowed in slavery time for my master. And I'm thankful to be here and be with the guv'ment. They give me bread to eat, they give me clothes to wear, they give me coffee to drink and I'm thankful fur it. Don't know how we'd git along if it wasn't fur the gov'ment helping us old people in this country. You see the guv'ment is better able to take care of me now than I am to take care of myself.[44]

"The logical next step"

Raper looked at Greene's history for signs of the future. He used Greene's past to push his claim that a more democratic culture was prerequisite to the kind of modern, cooperative agriculture that most suited America's new, industrialized economy. He found articles and letters in local newspapers that pointed to the dominance of cotton as ruinous to soil quality.[45] And as a way to root New Deal social policies in the traditions of the past, Raper found in the records writers who had advocated cooperatives and conservation. "The things which have been done are not new. The roots of the UFP go far back into the checkered history of Greene. In 1800 Joel Early left specific instructions in his will for the care of his orchards and fields. Thomas Stocks was first president of the Southeastern Agricultural Society in the 1840's, and in the 1850's Judge Garnett Andrews spoke of the severe erosion of the soil."[46] Raper reported that the lesson offered by the failure of early efforts at cooperative farming had shown that more co-ops were needed, rather than fewer.

As early as 1923, an editorial in the *Herald-Journal* had said that cooperatives should be the "watchword of the farmers." Some time after the dairymen's association was organized, a small cooperative creamery was set up. But it was too little and too poorly managed to compete with the larger creameries, and so went out of business after a few months. Its failure did not make the local paper despair of cooperatives as a way out.

> Cooperatives can scarcely be developed overnight to function in one lone field of a community's activities. The abandonment of the creamery helped demonstrate that more cooperation was needed, and that the cooperative here should have been effectively related to cooperatives elsewhere. Developing cooperatives among farm tenants and wage hands is most difficult, not easy among large landowners who are accustomed to having farm tenants and wage hands do as they say.[47]

The difficulty with establishing co-ops, Raper wrote, was due not to the cooperatives themselves, but to the plantation system that had fostered a tradition of shiftlessness among farmers, "where propertyless Whites have little tradition of participation, propertyless Negroes almost none."[48]

As he had done in *Preface to Peasantry,* Raper again diminished the role of the boll weevil in assessing the exodus from Greene. Instead, in *Tenants of the Almighty,* he saw the outmigration as a call for higher incomes for farmers, soil conservation measures, and better housing and education. The UFP was the mechanism the FSA had designed as a response to these needs. Raper ticked off the social and agricultural progress it had made, including

> an increase of soil-building crops, terraced fields, strip farming. Kudzu and sericea were planted in waterways and on spent hillsides, and eroded lands were retired to forests. New farm dwellings were built, old ones repaired, sanitary privies installed. Screens were put at windows and doors, pumps in wells. There were new barns, too, and permanent fences, pastures cleared and fertilized for additional cows and calves. More brood sows and fattening hogs, brookers for baby chicks, and crates full of eggs for the market. Bigger sweet potato hills, larger gardens, pressure cookers by the hundreds and glass jars by the hundred thousands. New schoolhouses and vocational buildings, better-trained teachers, hot lunch programs, a county library and a bookmobile. School children examined, lined up for "shots" by public nurses. Public clinics for expectant mothers, and for well babies; clinics to get rid of syphilis; clinics to keep from having diphtheria and typhoid.[49]

The UFP was the extension of forward-thinking ideas that Greene's citizens had often advocated, and it was the corrective of the retrograde policies and customs bred by slavery and King Cotton. "And so the Unified Farm Program is the logical next step," he concluded, with an unusual rhetorical flourish. "It marks a new day—in an old calendar."[50]

In *Tenants of the Almighty* Raper tried to humanize the work of the numerous federal agencies that had become active in Greene, from the Federal Land Bank and the Rural Finance Corporation, which dated from the Hoover administration, to the dozen or so New Deal organizations, including the Civilian Conservation Corps (CCC), the Works Progress Administration (WPA), the Forestry Service, and the Farm Credit Administration. By placing them in the context of Greene's history, Raper wanted to integrate these federal services, "with their long, high-sounding names," into the fabric of the county. He wanted to ease local fears about the new, active role the federal government was taking in county affairs. "Services hailing from Washington were becoming as much a part of Greene's history as the first bridge across the Oconee, or the county's first cotton gins and mills."[51]

Woven throughout the book is a paean to the Jeffersonian agrarian. "There is deep satisfaction in a good garden close to the house," he wrote, as though in Latin on the virtues of the Roman republic. "On this patch of earth a farmer and his wife perform nobly. Here they stir the land most hopefully, for here they conserve and replenish the soil gladly. Here they deal justly with the Almighty, and here they reap abundantly." And he went on to tie such virtues with the New Deal. "The making of good gardens has been an essential part of the Farm Security Administration's work in Greene county. Ride along with an FSA supervisor on a spring day, observe the gardens of the 'government farmers,' gardens not yet four years old. Look at them now. See with what pride the family takes you through the garden gate."[52] Raper claimed that the family farmer had been given the short end of the stick by federal programs because he was deemed the most resilient of Americans. As the most self-sufficient segment of the population, independent farmers could longer withstand hard times. But of course, Raper was arguing that a modern, industrialized society—in the form of New Deal programs—could invigorate the self-sufficient family farm just as American agribusiness was rendering the agrarian obsolete. Reading *Tenants of the Almighty* now, Raper's paean to the family farm sounds like an elegy.

In *Tenants of the Almighty*, by advocating a personal approach to aid, Raper answered criticism that government handouts had "ruined" farm workers by giving them something for doing nothing. His bureaucrats would know the names of the citizens they served. His conception of government aid was the establishment of a contract between the society and each of its citizens. State and federal agencies would serve not only to instruct and advise, but in a sense to act as money managers for struggling or delinquent families. This economic, as well as social, contract required responsibility on the part of both parties, and "an increased measure of self-direction for the client is the essence of his contract with the government."[53] To fulfill Raper's conception of assistance, large bureaucracies would be required to devote an extraordinary level of attention to citizens' particular characters and circumstances to assure both dignity and responsibility.

"Uncle Sam Is My Shepherd"

Raper recorded a response to federal initiatives among Greene's farmers that by and large was extraordinarily positive. He asked scores of farm families to speculate on where they would be if the government programs had not arrived in Greene County. "Over and over God and Washington were linked together. 'There would have been some po' hongry folks,' was a typical answer." Greene's poet laureate, as appointed by Raper, responded in verse. "Yea though I walk through the valley / And shadow of death to stay here / But as long as Uncle Sam hold everything / No evil will I fear."[54]

He found the best way to convince readers of the extent and importance of federal assistance was to take them for a long drive out to the lonely backwaters of the county in search of a farm the government had not yet found.

> Don't stop at the house where you see a privy, a fenced garden, and black-framed screens on the windows. Without stopping you know that family is one of the 500 working with the FSA. Be adventurous. Try not to get lost. Keep going until you come to some side road that is a thread through the woods, not even a mailbox to mark it. See what's at the end of that road.

He wrote about a conversation with an old woman who lived deep in the pines at the end of that road. "Has the government got down here?" he had asked her.

"No, sir," she told him firmly. She rarely had a chance to talk to anyone, was suspicious of a stranger, and was slow in her answers. "No," she did not receive an old-age pension. Although, come to think of it, she did get some grits and other food from the Surplus Commodities office sometimes. And the County Welfare Office had given her two dresses. And government nurses had given her boys typhoid shots. Her grandson is the first child she ever raised who rode to school in a bus and had a hot lunch. One of the county midwives had delivered her granddaughter's baby. And some time back, they had received a check from the government for their cotton.[55]

Raper placed the new, activist government in the fabric of contemporary southern life and assigned it as strong a pull as the Civil War or the boll weevil. "What is this new personality of 'government' in Greene county?" he asked rhetorically. "It no longer means just the police or the postman. The people speak of being 'on the government' and 'off the government.' They speak of 'government farms,' 'government chickens,' 'government men.' They say: 'We belong to the government'; 'The government never turns us down.'" The phrase "before the government came" had now become as customary as "back in slavery times" and "before the boll weevil" had been before it. Raper felt a new era rising.[56]

"The Boswell of Greene County"

Virginius Dabney, reviewing *Tenants of the Almighty* in the *New York Times Book Review*, called Raper the Boswell of Greene County.[57] Tarleton Collier saw *Tenants* as a microsociology. "It is the story of a program that is working in a single county and that may work for revitalization of an entire region."[58] Jonathan Daniels, in the *Saturday Review*, wrote, "Mr. Raper has in a sense made a new sort of book about the remote results of centralized government." Its liberal viewpoint was well received, even locally. "The story leaves us feeling very differently," editorialized the *Herald-Journal*, "from the congressmen who are recklessly attacking the FSA and other Administration measures intended to better the lot of underprivileged Americans."[59]

"What can be done?" asked John Chamberlain, in his *New York Times* review. "Mr. Raper, a devout supporter of the Farm Security Administration, sees the land coming back as the family-size farm produces its own vegetables and fruits and builds up the soil by judicial use of legumes, lime and phosphate rock." Chamberlain smelled a storm of retrenchment approaching Washington and was disappointed that Raper did not address the prospect of rain in the forecast. "Rehabilitation in the Nineteen Thirties has been carried out by government aid. And the aid has helped, for the simple reason that here, for once, political power has been used to increase the average man's social power. But as the New Deal mood evaporates, the future of Greene County will depend on the average man's ability to conserve his own social power when government support is withdrawn. Can the average man use his brains this time? Mr. Raper does not say."[60]

"Two Years to Remember"

All the time he was writing *Tenants of the Almighty*, Raper had another, even more unconventional, project in the works. For their last Christmas at the Punch Dolvin place, in 1943, Raper presented the family with a homemade book about their lives in Greene County. He had pulled aside fifteen-year-old Charles on Christmas Eve and bade him draw pictures of the old well and the windmill at the plantation, their neighbors and some of their cows, to make into a picture book, "an intimate record of what went on in & around our house, an abandoned plantation headquarters on a dirt road ten miles from the county seat town where we lived for two years." But just as he used Greene County to develop a microstudy of social, racial, agricultural, and economic trends in the Black Belt, he used his family's own experiences for broader sociological study. He went so far as to list "Two Years to Remember" with the American Sociological Society on its census of current research projects. "This cultural-anthropological study is both narrative and analysis," he reported. "An attempt has been made to convey the social realism of a plantation neighborhood in a readable form. The whole range of neighborhood life is set forth in considerable detail, showing how traditional landlord-tenant relations and racial identity affect the every-day behavior of each of the socio-economic elements of the neighborhood's population; and also how such matters as diets, work habits, health practices, pastimes, family organization, and the roles of church, school, and politics are influenced by class and race factors."[61]

The book is remarkable, if not convincing, for its attempt at cooperative authorship. Raper did not use the first-person singular in any of his books. In fact, he eschewed writing "I" even in handwritten notes to himself. And in "Two Years to Remember," he staked an intentionally indefinite point of view in telling his family's stories. Instead, he disguised his voice, forfeiting clarity of perspective to include Martha and the children as well. "If the reader is sometimes uncertain who is telling the story, that's as it should be," he declares, "for it is written from *within* the family." He wanted to do the impossible—write a sociological study and create a folk document in one, trying to push the role of participant-observer simultaneously to both its farthest extremes. Could a social scientist participate in folk culture from the inside? A few years later, he tried to interest publishers in what he called a sociological manuscript. "An inside-the-family story like this," he claimed, "shows life as it then was and becomes a historic document, much more valuable for present day students than if it had been written initially for publication." If a text is not written for publication, is it a truer cultural artifact? In a larger sense, he was asking what in the 1930s was a question of some urgency: what is the relationship between a modern, industrial, and media-driven society and the folk cultures of the past?

More than family stories, "Two Years to Remember" is filled with anecdotes that illustrate the invisibility of blacks to whites within the Black Belt's caste system, anecdotes that are both anthropological and literary. A white neighbor came for a visit and told Raper he lived just up the road, "the first house on your right up here." Raper was stumped, because he knew the first few cabins were occupied by black families, until he realized the neighbor's phrase implied the first white landowners' house. White folks did not count blacks' cabins when giving directions.

Raper revealed his own religious and political beliefs through family stories, too. "Every Sunday we attended Sunday School," he wrote, "and shortly Daddy was asked by Mr. Bryson to spend five minutes just before the lesson explaining the Golden Text. More embarrassing to Daddy was being asked to lead the prayer. He does not mind praying, but he rather likes to do his praying in his own way, which seems to be without out-loud words." As always, Raper uses Christianity to open questions of ethics and a New Deal social consciousness. As alternate Sunday school teacher, Raper found biblical precedents "for things he thought the local people should be thinking about." Paul had held fast to that which was good, and he took on new endeavors and challenges. Noah dared stand up in the face of local criticism. Jesus called no man common or unclean, and He made people better through His faith in them. "Mother said it usually took her all day Monday to get over Daddy's Sunday School teaching enough to endure being a privileged white lady."

Raper wrote about endless discussions of politics around the kitchen table.

> "Fact is," Daddy said as he resumed his talk with Mother, "there is a sort of equity in human affairs. The more we mistreat people, the more we fear them; and the appetites of the overfed are not nearly so good as of the hungry, and nobody is so afraid of a fair distribution of food and power as those who know they have more than their share...."
>
> Daddy wasn't through—sometimes it seems like he never gets through—and so he went on talking, with only Mother listening. "In the long run, I guess, we all just about pay our human debt in full: It is tough on a man to be a slave, maybe tougher to be a master, for the master saddles himself with the maintenance of slavery, while the slave hopes for freedom. The landless man may favor everybody's having a farm of his own, and the man who has been treated unjustly yearns most for justice."[62]

He wrote about taking a break from chopping wood to sit for a few minutes at the table while Martha was baking pies. "Tell you what," he exclaimed. "Let's take the kids and App'm and ride around the county tomorrow afternoon and let you know what is going on." He jumped up and walked over to the big table where Martha was pouring filling into the pies. "They're doing a lot of other things around here, too, that some people thought couldn't be done," Father told her, "Maybe I'm kind of silly, but I always want the family, especially you, to know what I'm working at and interested it."

"'Bless your heart,' said Mother, and she kissed him, her floury hands stretched down behind her. 'Let's go tomorrow. The kids will love it.'" With that, Raper wrote, he went back to his chopping.[63]

"Something fundamental may be happening"

All the time he was chopping wood and trudging behind a mule plow on the old Punch Dolvin place, Raper was seeing how the mass media had infiltrated the lives of the most rural farm families. And he noted how they were adapting modernity to their own needs and circumstances. "After I got the radio I stopped the paper," said one farmer. "I can't read right good and it's better to sit down when I'm tired and listen to the radio. Radio does my reading for me." The radio had already become a fixture at the county courthouse and the crossroads store. Entertainment from throughout the wide world lay across the fields at a neighbor's home. "Here were programs at the turn of the dial, hillbilly music and Fibber McGee and Molly, Bob Burns, Amos 'n Andy, and Lum 'n Abner. When the war came the regular news broadcasts became popular over night. Interested in the news and wanting to hear the President's speeches, many another family without electricity made the down payment on a radio and set of batteries." True to form, Raper was optimistic that the new mass media would offer an opportunity for greater democratization.[64]

"Something fundamental may be happening when a landless man, in an unscreened house that leaks when it rains, turns on his battery-radio. He is now interested in world news, and in what people are saying about the conduct of the war, and the prospects for peace." Modernity meant, in part, that lack of education need not be an obstacle to community participation. "Without ever having dipped into the indirect world of books and magazines and newspapers, and not uncommonly without a vote now, he sits there by his own fireplace with his wife and children about him and hears the voices of earth's leading men and women say common-sense things about the most basic human desires and needs."[65]

Raper was also watching the new welfare state change the traditional southern mindset. He had a sharp eye for the human response to the New Deal. "A Negro mother may doubt the value of sending her children to school," he wrote, for example, "may think they will get along with the white folks better without an education. But she wants a birth certificate filled in for her new baby. She thinks it would be a sad oversight for her baby to grow up and be kept out of the army or a good job just because his birth certificate had not been filled in. She couldn't fill it in, nor could her husband or the midwife who was there when the baby was born. A week later the husband, embarrassed as only a proud father can be, asked a neighbor if he would come up to the house and 'send in a record of his baby to the government.'"[66]

"And that's no baloney"

Sharecroppers All was finally published at Chapel Hill after the family had been in Greene several months, and Raper continued to push for publicity. Because *Time* had just run a review of another study of the South, Wilbur Cash's *Mind of the South*, Earl Brown could not talk his colleagues into making space for Raper's book.[67] An editor at *Life*, Brown had heard Raper speak at a 1940 conference on lynching at Tuskegee and approached him about publishing some of his research for Myrdal's project. But Raper was holding off from using any of "Race and Class Pressures" until after *An American Dilemma* was published. Raper sold Brown on Greene County, though, and Brown would end up pushing to publish a special feature on the changes in rural Georgia in *Life*, with Raper writing the story and directing a photo shoot. But that initiative, too, fell through from another strange failure of timing.

Life liked Raper's optimism. The story out of Greene County would not be another *Grapes of Wrath* depicting the plight of the sharecropper. Instead, Brown was attracted to Raper's findings of positive change, and *Life*'s upbeat approach meshed with Raper's aim of promoting the good work of the UFP. "Here are a few facts which will contrast with the materials you will find in the chapter on Negro schools in *Preface to Peasantry*," Raper wrote Brown his first fall back in Greene. Seven new teachers had been hired since the UFP program started in 1938. "Well over half of the old schools had already been replaced."[68] Brown sent Eliot Elisofon, a veteran photographer, to Greene, just after Delano had left the county. Through the fall of 1941, Raper was working simultaneously with both Brown and Stryker, with both *Life* and the FSA. Stryker was glad to see *Life* had become interested in the kind of study Raper could provide in Greene, and he offered use of Delano's photos.[69]

As he had done with Delano, Raper took Elisofon to PTA meetings and national defense committees. He had him shoot the automobile repair classes at a black vocational school. "There you have the sons of Negro tenant farmers becoming expert in auto mechanics," Raper told Brown, and added, importantly, "under the supervision of a local Negro mechanic. The Elisofons will have the names of all these folks." Raper, always interested in historical context, explained, "but I want to emphasize that the names involved—Kimbro, Moore, Armour, Baugh, and Wright—are each and all prominent antebellum planter families." Raper was happy with the racial balance he was able to achieve with Elisofon's photographs. "We all genuinely appreciate the fact that *Life* has elected to do part of its story on Negro education here," he told Brown. Raper was surprised at the coverage. He had always been able to generate good publicity, whether through the auspices of the Interracial Commission, his standing at Chapel Hill, or his research with Gunnar Myrdal. But this was entirely new. "At first I frankly shuddered," he wrote Jack Delano about Brown's idea of featuring "Negro education"; he was fearful of a blithe condescension. He had been taken aback by a hugely popular national news magazine finding in his work an upbeat story on race in the Black Belt South.[70]

But Raper recognized the opportunity and bent over backward to develop a photo-documentary for *Life,* revolving around old friend "Preacher" Parrott, the ex-slave and minister who, in his nineties, worked a little bit around the Punch Dolvin place and was now glad to be on a "government farm." In turn, Brown was impressed by Raper's art direction. "I say this in all sincerity," he wrote Raper, "I was infinitely more confident that we would get a real and worthwhile story after you consented to help us out than I was before I saw you. And to be comforted with the knowledge that you are getting the proper steer on a story is quite often more than half the battle." As did so many people, from farmers to academics to politicians, Brown quickly grew to trust Raper's judgment and character. "A real guy like you can't ever do any wrong in so far as I'm concerned," Brown wrote Raper. "And as long as there are guys like you I know our battle for Democracy will go on until victory is won. And that's no baloney."[71]

The feature, slated for mid-December 1941, was abruptly canceled, of course. The new crops of Greene's family farmers and the new government schools for black children were swept off the pages of *Life* by Pearl Harbor. Greene's story would never be rescheduled. Sharecropping, and the plantation system and, indeed, much of agrarian America had just made a quiet and abrupt exit from the national stage.

10

"BUT WHAT *IS* THE AMERICAN WAY?"

One day toward the end of the war, Raper was driving with Herb Prior, whom he worked with in Oklahoma, between Shawnee and Stillwater, when they saw a sailor up ahead on the roadside. "Just don't like to pass up a uniform," Prior said, as he pulled off and turned around to clear a space on the back seat.

The sailor was traveling on leave from the West Coast to his small hometown east of Little Rock, and as they rode along, he began to talk about himself and his family. His father was a tenant farmer. He would go to see him first. But he also wanted to get on over to the tuberculosis sanitarium in Boonville to see how his two children—seven and five—and his wife were getting along.

He did not know what he would do after the war, but he surely was glad he went ahead and joined up. He had found work as the second cook at the sanitarium after moving his family in. He had resented the way the superintendent had tried to get him deferred. "Once you let somebody like that get you deferred, they just about own you," he explained from the backseat. "You've got to do as they want, or they'll turn you in." Not that the training in the Navy had been easy. It was tougher than he had expected, but he never regretted his decision. "I didn't want to stay out bad enough to be anybody's slave." Raper was fascinated, through the course of the war, by the stories of why people joined up. What convinced southerners—including thousands of whites, who saw themselves as unregenerate rebels and cussedly independent—to abandon their suspicions about the federal government and fight for the United States? As he usually saw it, the prime mover, among many mixed motives, was most often money and the economics of the South.[1]

When *Life* finally got around to publishing a feature on the rural South, six months after pulling the Greene County story, the article focused on small-town Americanism. Patriotism had tapped a giant reservoir in the hinterlands. The South, said *Life,* sent a particularly high proportion of its boys to fight, and the nation owed "The Fighting South" a debt of gratitude for the fervor of its patriotism. Raper was quick to write and correct them. "Why didn't you acknowledge the underlying truth about the South's excessive number of peace-time volunteers, namely: that our poorer families are large and that work opportunities here during the 1930s were scarce? It is a fact, and all students of Southern conditions know it, that our young men found enlistment in the Army and Navy the best job—often the only job—open to them." As always, Raper derived social attitudes largely from economics. He never became swept up in the emotions of war. He was certainly concerned about postwar prospects for democracy in Europe and Asia and Africa, but he was anxious about the potential of American patriotism to erode the civil rights of blacks and whites at home, too.[2]

It had been only a couple of years since Gunnar Myrdal had harried him in his hotel room in Greensboro with the preposterous notion of Raper's running for governor. Only another social scientist could think that a man might get elected in Georgia by ranking socioeconomics over patriotism. Over the next few years, while in Washington, Raper would learn a few lessons in hardball politics from conservative southerners who saw the war as an opportunity to grab the reins back from the Roosevelt Democrats by teaming up with northern business interests under the imprimatur of wartime emergency.

Raper and Carl Taylor, with whom he began to work in the Department of Agriculture, and those others in the federal government who wanted to weld social science planning to legislative power, no longer held the political capital of the early New Deal years. Raper saw firsthand how liberal politics and social science were beaten by economic and social conservatism. Racial gains were being made and reaction setting in. Sociology was pushed by the war to measure productivity, rather than assess character and values, and so rejuvenated positivism. Federally funded cultural studies did not seem so important in the face of World War, and conservative Democrats and Republicans played the politics of patriotism to kill off many of the remaining New Deal programs and their soft-science projects. The Farm Security Administration (FSA) held on for a while, and its photo section took assignments documenting defense work, as Raper had heard from Roy Stryker, but the FSA was reformed into the Office of War Information and the photographic mission was finally dropped.

During the war, conservatives began to hand liberals their hats. For two years after leaving Greene County, Raper was able to build on his experience doing community studies and to manage a federal program, the Rural Trends Project, that established dozens of cultural listening posts around the country to take the pulse of small-town and farming America. By the end of the war, though, that project was gone, too, and Raper had no place left to go. Blacks were taking the lead as the movement for civil rights took a more militant tone, and white speakers on race were in much less demand. While not yet completely eradicated, lynching had moved out of the purview of white philanthropy. And once the war had ended, no U.S. organization, public or private, was looking to fund another study of disparities among Americans.

"One of the most terrifying days of my life"

Through the summer of 1942, Arthur and Martha had worked day and night, set up on the porch of the Punch Dolvin place, editing *Tenants of the Almighty,* before packing up the family and moving to Washington, where he would begin work for Carl Taylor's Rural Trends Project, in the U.S. Department of Agriculture's (USDA's) Bureau of Agricultural Economics (BAE). Raper saw the program as a way to expand the kind of cultural sociology he had practiced in the South to fit the whole nation, to give the federal government a chance to tap into the work and perspectives of rural America. While in D.C., Raper also continued to work with Stryker and Rosskam, who helped push *Tenants of the Almighty* through Macmillan's publishing process as quickly as possible, even in the face of war.[3]

Since his first trips to Washington in the late 1930s, Raper had portrayed himself as a southern fellow who wasn't about to be overwhelmed by the big city. He retained a certain southern skepticism. "One thing is distinctly bad about Washington," he had complained to Guy Johnson one July day in 1941. "Those rooms are so well air conditioned that when a fellow comes back to the real South he is poorly equipped for the continued heat."[4] It rankled him that his children's deep accents were ridiculed in school. Never mind they had been roughed up in southern schools because of his own politics. The family bought a brick bungalow in the Westover section of Arlington and, with the war looming, Martha organized a day-care for newly working mothers. "The crayons go in the middle of the table and you take *one,*" she observed one day soon after setting up shop. "That has to be said a dozen times each time the little ones color. How futile and unhappy is the acquisitive instinct! The child who is intent on getting and keeping has no chance to use what he has. And when one seeks too hard, the others think they want to hoard, too. Then nobody has time to enjoy anything. Only contests for more." Characteristically, Martha used her own work to think about human nature, to try to discover inherent potential for cooperation.[5]

Arthur tried to get used to a daily half-hour commute and a bureaucratic regime, as difficult as that was for a man who had once fled Chapel Hill's brick buildings for a chance to be out among the people. Although everyone was as helpful as could be, "the first day at the office was one of the most terrifying days of my life," he said, belying his years spent poking into race across the Deep South. He would come to make an often-uneasy peace with government work. But just as it seemed the whole country was beginning to move to the suburbs, the Rapers would move back to the land. Soon after the war ended, they purchased the old farmhouse in Vienna, on thirty-seven rolling acres, an hour west of Washington, where Arthur and Martha would live—between overseas missions—for the rest of their lives. With his typically southern flair for the slyly humorous, Raper named the place Slope Oaks, and insisted that visitors said the name slowly enough to get the joke.[6]

Everyone still pitched hay and helped with the animals. Home was a working farm, but now the children went to the most modern high school in Virginia. Raper soon bought himself a Cub tractor, as well as various mowers and mechanical cultivators, but the family talked him into keeping old Dobbin, too, because, as they boys pointed out, "his traction is very much better than that of the tractor." They all worked in the garden, and Margaret had her own plot on the side, and a farmstand out on the road from which she sold five-cent bunches of radishes. Raper continued to think of family in relation to the larger community. He went to the funeral of a local boy killed in the war and went home thinking about the priest's brief talk. There is no love of God aside from love of family, he remembered him saying. And there is no love of family aside from love of country.[7]

Jarrell and Harrison were stars of the Fairfax High School Band. Jarrell played the piano, and Harrison the violin, although he also doubled on string bass when the Rapers formed their own dance band. Twelve-year-old Margaret played the baritone horn. And Harrison was good at holding a harmonica for little Charles to blow while he played a nice, little guitar. Within a few years, Charles would spend a summer at Arthur's old haunts above Asheville, breaking the dawn each day as Camp Sequoyah's bugler.

"Both our parents play instruments," Harrison told the *Washington Post* in a feature on the family's virtuosity. "Our whole family is musical."[8] Musical or otherwise, something was always happening among the family's "goodly sized crowd," as Raper loved to call it. "There is no point," he wrote his siblings, "describing the great range of other noises they make, almost none of which are harmonized." From his family's home in Arcadia to his own in Vienna—and even in his dorm room at Chapel Hill—Raper always lived among the bustle of talk and organized chaos.[9]

"But what *is* the American way?"

In the late 1930s, a group of pacifists had approached Raper with a declaration against all wars. They had heard his outspoken opposition to the Great War and, increasingly, about the coming conflict. To their surprise, Raper refused to sign. He could not rule out a fight in self defense, he replied, and he could imagine cases where war was justified. He looked at war as a pragmatist, not as a pacifist. War was to be avoided, if at all possible, as a waste of lives and energy and goods, a mostly unnecessary exercise in misery. But a nation sometimes did find itself in a situation where eschewing war cost more in terms of lives or freedoms. In such situations, citizens might seek ways a war might be turned to advantage.

Raper had already been looking ahead to the meaning of the new war, and by doing so he further developed his own sense of American democracy. "We Americans again prepare to defend our way of life," he mused to himself the month before Pearl Harbor. "But what *is* the American way? How many of us can subscribe to the unrivaled words of our own Declaration of Independence?" His thoughts ran alongside the arguments black activists would make in the coming months and years. "The present world crisis forces us to turn the spotlight inward. Are we serious when we say we want democracy? When we proclaim, 'I believe in fair play'?" As always, Raper attached thought to action in his conception of democracy, instead of leaning on individual liberty.[10]

The American way had always been more than the right to free expression, he claimed. It had been a stimulant to endeavor, to reaching across to the Pacific, creating the organizational machinery of a continental republic, and filling the needs of a populous and variegated nation. Americans had pioneered in the physical sciences. For the first time in history, material goods had become abundant, in large part due to American business acumen and adeptness at the exploitation of resources. "Our captains of industry and finance have their monuments," wrote Raper in mock tribute, "in steel rails and in copper wires stretching across a continent, in the clouds of dust churned up even on back country roads, and in the skyscrapers of every city where corporate wealth has gravitated through combines and mergers." Americans had become shrewd about how to organize businesses and make goods. Could they now learn to be fair in dealing with each other?[11]

America required the same kind of shrewd thinking about how a society could maximize its democracy. For the sake of its democracy, the United States needed to develop a social science to organize itself as a commonwealth, to discover how to most wisely distribute its human and natural resources. "Tomorrow, he will point out the new ways which are worthy of use in the further building of our democratic life." This active, warm-blooded sociology was related to America's heritage of pragmatism and its ideals of democracy. "Only then will our democracy become the thing we have dreamed of, the thing our Jeffersons and Lincolns and Wilsons lived for, the thing we should now defend from all who would ignore or destroy it." Sociology must become an organic part of the American way.[12]

Raper remained as convinced as ever that social science would become the modernist means for planning the future. In the months after Pearl Harbor, in fact, Raper hoped the war itself might become a way for social planning to enter the national bloodstream. Raper postulated that the American way works best in peacetime, but the country could make use of war planning to prepare an advance in social planning after the peace. American sociology, engineering, and business acumen could turn barracks construction into low-income housing. "We now build army tanks and bombers, cartridges and guns for ourselves and our allies. Tomorrow Europe will need farm carts and wagons, milk trucks and locomotives, and the poorer people of the earth—inside and outside this nation—will bless America for wider use of telephone and electric lights." Military planning could become social and economic planning.[13]

World War II was pushing into overdrive the transformations brought about by industrialization, an activist federal government, and the mass media. Before the family had moved to Washington, ten months after Pearl Harbor, Raper described the way modern warfare figured in the thoughts of

Greene's farm families. "The influences of the war are reaching down powerfully to the last man and woman. Men who cannot read and write now need to know their ages and birthdays when they register in the military draft." He had overheard one young mother tell another, "'Better blow out your lamp when you hear a plane at night. Just to be sure no bomb is dropped on your house.'" The other woman, in turn, "inquires about bombs, hears how they are dropped from airplanes, and faints when she understands how readily her house and family could be blotted out. And who is there to condemn the overwhelming fear of an illiterate landless voiceless mother when she first realizes the full measure of defenseless death that modern science may have in store for her and her family." Raper saw in the remnants of the Old South an almost surreal world of change.[14]

"A world in which bombs fall upon cities from planes four miles high, and out of sight, and piloted by farm boys who but a few months ago walked between the handles of one-horse plows. A world in which the news of earth's greatest battles are heard an hour later over the radio even by people who never learned to read or write. A world in which fear of death and faith in the future are compounded in terrifying and hopeful ways." A world in which social planning would be needed now more than ever. By the end of the war, however, Raper felt his vision of sociology slipping away. It had become clear that the American Way would not be socially planned.[15]

With Taylor's Rural Trends Project, Raper had found an ambitious program of community and cultural assessment, working in cities across the country to find out from the people affected by government programs just how they worked. Then to suggest programmatic, and presumably legislative, changes in policy. It was a chance to gain quick feedback on government initiatives, while also providing data to see how rural cultures changed over time. "An attempt is being made," Raper wrote, "to describe the *why* of the *what* in the local situation so well that reasonably trustworthy predictions can be made as to the range of local reactions to any specific proposal which might be brought up. In short, the objectives are to describe current conditions so correctly in terms of backgrounds and emerging situations that the future becomes not wholly a guess." The project had gotten off the ground just as the war broke out.[16]

"We decided that we could help the government understand what the rural people were thinking about," Raper explained. "Agriculture was written pretty large in our program." As always, though, agriculture and society and politics ran together. Through agriculture, Taylor's group could get at what undergirded the culture of the various regions. The project included seventy-two counties, selected as representative of the diversity of America's rural ways of life and forms of livelihood. Corn counties and cotton, wheat, and fruit counties of all sorts were chosen, as were Mexican counties and Black Belt, Swedish, and Polish counties. The idea, to Raper, was to "stratify that county and get representative people that you'd stay in touch with week after week about what they were going to plant, what they were going to buy, who they wanted to stay out of the draft, as it came on closer to the war, and this, that and the other." If you knew what was going on in these seventy-two counties, Taylor reasoned, then you'd know what was going on in the rural United States.[17]

Taylor and Raper had started out trying to answer questions about what "representative" meant. How large a sampling of individuals, families, and organizations would be needed to make accurate generalizations for a whole county? And how large a sampling to define national trends?[18] They wanted to determine how a community's institutions worked to learn about its informal groups, its class lines, its system of social stratification. In addition, they wanted to contextualize all the data they collected, especially because much of the data was in the form of "attitudes," which they believed could not be interpreted except in their cultural and social settings, and then only fully through layers of conversations accumulated over time.[19] In fact, the objective of the project was to contextualize community questions as a way to provide more responsive government. Implicit was the recognition that government programs introduced into rural communities would be successful only in proportion to how well they fit the general social and cultural backgrounds of the county's people. Through a web of agricultural and community studies, Raper intended to look at all of rural America the way he had looked at Greene County.

The project was originally sold in part as a help to the war effort. Its sociologists would look at manpower adjustments, including the employment of women and girls in production plants. They looked at how fast farmers were adjusting to new crops and methods, as well as patterns of consumer spending. In addition, they wanted to assess small-town attitudes toward government initiatives and toward minority groups.[20] The field staff members were instructed to make certain they were getting information from representatives of all elements of the community. They needed to find the appropriate people to talk with about each different ethnic and racial group, religious group, farm tenure group, and socioeconomic group. They were told to deal openly with all their informants. In no case should they appear as though they were interested in only one particular point of view or that any perspectives were less than valid.[21]

Twenty-four rural sociologists fanned out across the country to make observations in the seventy-two counties, in what was the nation's largest-ever analysis of rural America. Raper ran the project for Taylor, using his own experience to develop guidelines for their reconnaissance and reports, then working with each sociologist, intending to produce, in a sense, six dozen Greene County studies, but now with uninterrupted data and feedback. "I had a grand time," he recalled warmly, "running all over the United States. Each of these fellows knew his own area pretty well, and I in turn let them tell me what they knew." He soon acquired a good feel for the comparative approach to sociological research. He found he could put together numerous comparative studies by setting similarly developed data from, say, Lowndes County, Georgia, and Watertown, North Dakota. What was more, he felt he could develop a solid record of predictability. "We began pretty soon calling the shots on what the farmers were going to do, and the Department began using our stuff pretty heavily."[22] In its first year, and due to its experimental character, everyone involved thought of the project as a work in progress. "Hopefully, the Trends Project is still in the experimental stage," Raper wrote in the second year. In reality, though, it was never far from the end.

Raper made certain he spent a lot of time on the road, seeing for himself the way the country was changing, taking innumerable notes. On the night train from Washington to Chicago in mid-June 1943, he woke up in Indiana and watched the farms roll through the morning mist. "There were many tractors in the fields," he noted, "seldom a horse."[23] He loved movement itself, and many of his descriptions are closer to travel writing than sociological census. "From Salt Lake onto Ogden the plateau continues," he wrote of a trip out West, "and now it is late dusk with the red still in the west and the moon peeping between the gaps of the snow topped mountain range to the east. Off to the west across the Lake the distant mountain peaks can still be seen against the pale lines in the evening sky."[24] He always kept an eye out, though, for the way work and landscape intersected. Driving through New Hampshire's hills and hollows near the end of the war, he spied several modest works of art. "As we crossed this stream on a new concrete bridge we saw just above it a very primitive looking stone bridge of two arches. The bridge is built of large pieces of granite fitted together in such a way that the two arches have stood without mortar. And now considerable-sized trees are growing on the sides of the bridge. It is built slightly curving upstream to stand the pressure of flooded waters. A very beautiful piece of machinery and a real monument to skill and hard work."[25] Raper's war years were spent between so many monuments to yesterday and an increasingly industrial tomorrow, standing at the edge of a hundred fields watching a half-dozen mechanical cotton pickers moving up and down the rows, each run by a single man doing the work of a hundred.

"This all went to pieces in the years that followed"

Raper soon found that documentary social science couldn't last a fight with the politics of retrenchment. He would come to look back on the Rural Trends Project and say, "This all went to pieces in the years that followed."[26] The holistic, cultural approach of the project looked at race relations and class issues as integral to a region's agricultural and economic conditions, especially in a "plantation civilization," as Raper called the South. Not everyone, however, agreed that to look at farming, the project needed to be so thorough.

At the end of 1944, one of Raper's researchers in Mississippi, Frank Alexander, filed a report that included an assessment of race and class in developing a discussion of the Delta's cotton. Alexander showed the connection between a highly stratified society and the cotton culture, complete with a thorough analysis of the racial caste system that was detailed down to the practice of white landlords taking black mistresses.

For their parts, Raper and Taylor had both read the draft of Alexander's "Cultural Reconnaissance Survey of Coahoma County, Miss." and planned to offer it as a model for the other counties' reports. Alexander had done a careful, factual job, in Raper's words, and had followed the approach and format they had all agreed on. A draft made its way to the Mississippi State Agricultural Extension Office for review. Instead of responding directly to the draft, though, the extension service had turned it over to Mississippi Congressman Jamie L. Whitten. The next thing they knew, Whitten was up in arms. He loudly expressed a significantly different perspective on the appropriateness of commentary about interracial sex in a government study on agriculture. Mississippi had been slandered, Whitten claimed, and he was going to see to it that no more cultural studies were made in his state, or anywhere else the

USDA spent its money.²⁷ In competition for funding with the Rural Trends Project and the BAE, the Agricultural Extension Office had dealt its rivals what turned out to be a fatal blow by turning the draft over to Whitten. As he had in the South, Raper once again found that governmental bureaucratic in-fighting could become an ally of local demagoguery and political reaction.²⁸

Whitten, whom Raper dismissed as "a very pure, small, moralistic man," was not going to stand for such government waste.²⁹ Beyond ensuring the elimination of funding for cultural studies, Whitten also pushed to prohibit the funding of local land-use planning as well. The extension office saw such planning as yet more competition for funds.³⁰ Alexander's draft had indeed run far afield of agriculture, but to Raper, "trouble arose not from the fact that he hadn't told the truth, but rather because he had put on the line truths that white Mississippians would not then tolerate."³¹ What Alexander wrote was common knowledge, Raper felt. Whom did it surprise? To Whitten, being forthright was not the point. Who cared about common knowledge when economic stability and honor were at stake?³²

For the rest of his life, Raper believed that this had been a watershed moment in American history. If the United States had supported the medium-sized and small farmer during the early 1940s and into the postwar world, Raper was convinced, both rural poverty and urban blight would have been blunted or stopped. If agricultural policy had been less oriented toward agribusiness and maximum production, and instead aimed to strengthen the country's rural cultures and farming communities, the migration of blacks to the cities, as well as the white rush to the suburbs, would have been better managed and less destructive. "The big farmers hopefully would not be so big, nor so burdened down with investments in machines and supplies, nor have so poisoned the land, and air and water," he wrote, looking back from the early 1970s. "And the smaller and medium-sized farmers would be more numerous, more secure, and with mostly greater hope for the future. And the inner cities and the suburbs would be less crowded, less fearful, and so more relaxed and with a better America in their expectations." In the end, Raper's kind of documentary sociology, with its human face and "telling feeling," was abandoned by Washington for a statistical and economic-minded approach to agriculture and rural development; agricultural data was gathered in order to increase production in the interests of large producers. Small-town and rural culture could take care of itself.³³

As he traveled the United States during the war, Raper had wanted to see mechanization in hopeful terms. He recorded a far different outcome. "Farm machinery, if small enough, or if used jointly by family-size farmers, can increase the security of the family-size farm. Up until now, however, there has been a rather distinct tendency for new farm machinery to be accompanied by greater specialization of farming activities. This increased specialization, in turn, has in general increased the size of the farm unit and therefore caused a decrease in the number of farms as in the Mid-West and in the Plains States, or it has been accompanied by more of the farm work being done by hired labor as on the West Coast and in some of the specialty crop areas along the Gulf and in the eastern states." Raper himself must have known how unlikely his suggestions for preserving the small farm sounded.

By the mid-1940s, with no real solution for the loss of traditional agrarian values, the Old Left had already begun its long ebb. "One of the few ways farm land can be kept at a reasonable level in prosperous times," he argued in 1948, "is for the farm owners in an area to agree among themselves to offer the land for sale only to *bona fide* farm operators and at prices they believe it fair to ask of a family whom they expect to have as long-time neighbors. This is suggesting that farm owners put community values above immediate money values—there is in fact no other certain way to have a community in which the security of the family-size farm is assured." By the late 1940s, such liberal, agrarian sentiments would come to sound less like populism or cooperativism than communism.[34]

In spite of the governmental turn against cultural studies, Raper and Taylor and a small number of New Dealers continued to develop projects where they could, and right through the 1940s, Raper continued to watch the washing away of American folk culture. But to work on cultural studies, Raper and Taylor had to moonlight. With Martha, Raper wrote "Guide to Agriculture, U.S.A.," a publication for foreign farmers interested in American farming. And in 1949, along with several other BAE staff members they rounded up, Taylor and Raper compiled a textbook survey of American rural sociology for Knopf, working nights, weekends, and holidays, for months on end. *Rural Life in the United States* became a standard text in sociology departments around the country. Before long, Knopf had requested a revision, and Raper and Taylor made the changes their sections needed. But most of the other contributors had abandoned their work on agriculture, so the update was canceled, the text was soon out of date, and the royalty checks quickly stopped arriving. "Too bad," Raper concluded, "especially for Taylor and me!"[35] Especially so, since they had intended it as the start of a new direction and momentum for the field. Their survey had looked at seven different farming areas in the United States as separate cultural regions. The goal had been an ongoing, comprehensive cultural anthropology of American rural life.[36] To Taylor and Raper, the fact that farming was becoming more integrated with urban and suburban America was all the more reason to pursue rural sociology. Because farm life had become less isolated by the late 1940s, it was in greater need of studies that documented the dynamics of integrated pursuits in labor, business, and social relations.[37]

Some of their most ambitious ideas never got off the ground. Raper and Taylor wanted to use the observations of the Rural Trends Project to write a study of rural migration, both black and white, in the face of increasing industrialization. They wanted to analyze patterns of America's urbanization through the first half of the twentieth century. Who were the migrants and where did they go? What was the impact on the communities they left and the cities where they landed? How did mechanization drive this migration?[38] The same questions Raper had asked in Greene County through *Preface to Peasantry* were still valid to ask of the country as a whole. Similarly, too, he would again look at the way political demagogues continued to stymie the cooperative efforts of independent farmers and laborers. Race and class would figure prominently.[39] This would have been Raper's easiest book to write. Instead of working by himself or with a partner, he would have access to all the data already compiled by the Rural Trends Project. But with the statistical approach in ascendancy, the idea was soon shelved. Nevertheless, in 1949, he was still giving talks with titles such as "Significant Trends in Rural Life," that detailed not only the steadily decreasing proportion of Americans who lived on farms and the increasing commercialization of agriculture, but also the weakening of farm associations and the dissipation of folk beliefs and folk arts and skills, in favor of the practice of scientific and standardized methods. Along with these findings, it was clear to Raper that rural standards of living were on the rise.[40]

The Last of the Mohicans

Raper became profoundly ambivalent about mechanization. His data clearly showed that machines in farming meant more cotton grown per family, which meant better houses, better medical care, more conveniences, and more access to civic organizations and government agencies. On the other hand, it was equally indisputable that fewer families would be needed on the best lands. "Some may look at this whole cotton situation and say it is wrong for people to be pushed off the land, and that therefore the mechanization of cotton production should not be permitted," Raper offered. "But there is no more reason to put restraints on the mechanization of cotton production now than there was to have stopped the use of machinery in factories, or of steam locomotives on the railroads, years ago. No one, I think, would argue that shoes should be produced by hand, that wheat on the Plains should be cut with a cradle, or that automobiles should be made in a blacksmith's shop by one or two mechanics. Cotton is simply one of the last great enterprises to be mechanized." Real problems were being caused by industrialization, but great problems had resulted from lack of mechanization—small farms, low incomes, child labor, irregular school attendance, poor housing, credit farming, excessive soil depletion, inadequate medical care for a great proportion of the lower-income families, could all be helped by developing greater production through machines.[41]

Raper did not see mechanization itself as the root of the problem. The issue was how to control it. "The real question we face when we look at the mechanization of cotton production is the same question we are up against in the general use of our machines and technologies, namely, how can we make modern machines and technologies serve human needs more effectively?" The worst case would be the poor continuing to be pushed off the farms and into the ghettos, while completing the depletion of the land and rural cultures. The best-case scenario would be to use mechanization either to prepare those who leave for industrial occupations or to help restore the soil and improve the lives of those who would remain on the land.[42]

Between 1930 and 1945, farm ownership grew at the smaller and larger ends of the scale. More very small farms were bought during the Depression and war. The total number of farms under 3 acres doubled during those 15 years, and farms from 3 to 9 acres increased by almost half. Farms of more than 500 acres also increased. But farms of intermediate size—the backbone of the prosperous family operation—decreased in number. The balance was clearly tipping toward the largest farm operators. The largest 5 percent of farms in the United States produced one-third of the value of the nation's agricultural goods. These were the farms where mechanization was in greatest use. Raper could only forecast the obvious. "The very success of the use of machines and modern technology may result in a still further concentration of the American farm enterprise into fewer hands." Farmers had become dependent on cash incomes and less interested in what Raper called live-at-home farming. The emotional value farmers put on their land seemed to be waning, he averred, as farming had become more a business enterprise and less a way of life.[43]

Raper had hoped that mechanization would be a boon to democracy. By using light farm machinery, the independent family farmer would be able to plant, cultivate, and harvest larger crops; diversification would be easier to accomplish. The ideals of Jeffersonian agrarianism could be achieved in modern America, ironically, because the use of light farm machinery would allow the independent family farmer to plant, cultivate, and harvest larger and more different crops. More small farmers, black and white, would be able to purchase their own stakes, live more comfortably, and be more responsible citizens. Raper saw a future of American farmers, both black and white, as modern-day agrarians, the hardest labor of their husbandry accomplished not by slaves, but on tractors.[44] In his exhortation, however, Raper was actually writing the yeoman's epitaph. Machinery was industrializing the processes of agriculture, rather than serving a way of life or a foundation of republican government. The predictions Raper made in *Tenants of the Almighty* about the resilience of the family farm had turned his Greene County folk into *The Last of the Mohicans*. By the end of the war, Raper understood that the American agrarian was indeed obsolete—and the modernist sociology that had served it had been abandoned by Congress.[45]

Raper continued to speak and write on race, through the end of the 1940s, but instead of lynching and disparities in education, the issues revolved around industrialization and internationalization. At the end of the war, for example, the Associated Negro Press asked for his assessment of how the South's increasingly mechanized agriculture would affect race.[46] The issue of southern race relations started to overlap with foreign relations, and the State Department began to use Raper's experience to help answer some new questions. India wanted to turn toward cotton, rice, and tobacco, for instance, and students wanted to study these crops in southern colleges and universities. But agricultural officials wanted to know, would dark-skinned Indians be accepted on southern campuses?[47] To Raper, the question went right to the heart of the new, postwar world, and it was a question that would not be easily answered. "Indian students will need to be prepared to protect themselves from those who are too friendly as well as those who are not friendly enough."[48] To Raper, the fact that foreign students on southern campuses would be caught in a political cross-fire between the two was a sign that, in the immediate postwar world, the South still had a long way to climb toward modernity.

On a cold morning in the late winter of 1944, Raper woke up in a hotel room in Minot, North Dakota, as far from the South as he had ever been. He shook off another of what he called his sociological dreams. A world away, Raper had left the Mississippi Delta just the day before, and his dreams were sifting through the new disorientation of long-distance air travel.[49] He had woken in Minot from a scene back home. In his dream he had been sitting in his old cabin-office out in the pine woods, when a young, black farmer walked in and asked to sign up with Raper for a chance to work. Raper checked his records, talked with him about the kind of work he wanted, and signed him up. The man went away happy.

Soon the owner of a big plantation filled his doorway. "Well," he drawled at Raper, "you signed him up didn't you?"

"Yes, he qualified alright."

"And you called him 'Mister,' too, didn't you?"

"Yes, I did."

"Well, we don't like for you to call niggers 'Mister.'" He paused before making his point. "Fact is," he told Raper, "you are making a living by calling niggers 'Mister,' and treating them the way you do. And we don't like it."

"Why don't you like it?"

"Well, we don't."

"No, you don't," Raper agreed. "And the reason you don't is that you've been making a living off them all these years by not calling them 'Mister!'"[50]

A few nights later, he dreamed he stood in the home of an elderly kinsman, who owned his own fruit farm. Three of his pickers, young, American-Indian men, came into the room and said that, as representatives of the workers' benefits association, they wanted to bargain about their wages.

"Do what!?"

They repeated their request. Raper's kinsman became exasperated with what he considered their impertinence. Finally, he stepped back, drew a pistol, and fired at the three of them, who scrambled out of the room and ran from the house. Raper ran, too, but veered off around the house, instead of following the others. He knew he should have stayed with the old man, but he realized as he woke that he was more sympathetic to the Indians, and he didn't really mind if his elderly kin knew it.[51]

In his work he found that the wide and strong web of people and organizations who had supported racial and social justice in the 1920s and 1930s had become diffuse. The Commission on Interracial Cooperation had changed its name when Howard Odum became director, and its focus changed from race to regionalism. Many white people who had listened sympathetically and worked with Raper through the Depression were now scared by the increased militancy not only of young blacks, but of whites, too, as efforts at social and racial justice raised the specter of communism. Raper's own field of rural sociology was withering away as fast as the family farms he had studied. In his dream, Raper had rejected the class assumptions of his kinsman and run, but he did not run alongside the workers he felt bound to. By the end of World War II, Raper would often wake up feeling he was running alone, and to somewhere unknown.

To his surprise, though, as soon as the war was over, Raper found that the United States, having cut its cultural studies of rural America in the interests of agribusiness and in the name of fiscal prudence, was to make such work an integral part of the reconstruction of Japan. As part of the Allied Occupation, Raper would travel to Japan three times between 1947 and 1950. The skills he had honed in the South, now obsolete at home, became useful to General Douglas MacArthur, who personally sought him out to advise on the postwar transformation of feudal Japanese society. The democratization of rural American culture was of little concern anymore. The front lines of black southerners' battles had moved to the cities. In the countryside, Americans felt that prosperity itself was doing the work. Postwar Japan was a different story, though, and carefully planned change and analysis was the order of the day.[52]

A "New Deal" for Japan

Raper's brother, John, had become a renowned biologist at Harvard, and during the war found himself working on the Manhattan Project. He had built a reputation as an innovative scientist capable of pioneering in the new field of radiation biology, and was recruited to the Plutonium Division in Chicago and then to Oak Ridge. Soon after Hiroshima and Nagasaki, he had come to definite convictions, from the perspective, as he said, of "a lay scientist involved in the fringes of this epoch-making development." He told Arthur and

Martha he felt Truman's decision to attack without warning was extremely questionable. We can only accept the consequences, he counseled, "with the best conscience that we can muster, muttering military expediency the while." Knowing he had Arthur and Martha's sympathy in the sentiment, John worried about whether the country would accept its new responsibility. The United States must face up to its action, he said, by placing itself under house arrest. We must share the technology of the bomb and internationalize future nuclear research. A multinational regulatory body should license both materials and processes. Otherwise, he was ready to return to Cambridge.[53] For his part, Arthur's organic regionalism—his sense of wheels within wheels—had always run the gamut from the local community to the region to the nation and on to the global. John's letter tugged insistently at Arthur's old Wilsonian sentiments and gave a new urgency to his globalism.[54]

Japan's great agricultural leap began within months of surrender, and by 1950 the transformed nation had transferred 5 million hectares from wealthy landowners to tenant farmers and worked a major democratization of the former empire. The Japanese recognized that, through the land reform project, their nation had become a modern society. "Such rapid development had never been dreamed possible before the war," wrote sociologist Masaru Kajita, "nor had it been even imagined that Land Reform would play such a significant part in the rapid formation of the democratic and modern social structure." Because of land reform, community relations no longer conformed to traditional roles of deference and obeisance, and patriarchal control, even within the individual households of rural Japan had become fainter, in turn.[55]

Early in May 1947, Raper flew from island to barren island across the Pacific, landed in Tokyo at five in the afternoon, and once in his hotel, found some stationery to write his family. "What a city, and what a situation," he started. "The industrial areas, scattered out over wide areas are little more than rubble, with chimneys left standing—more and smaller and more slender factory chimneys than ours." The Japanese looked stunned and uncomfortably obedient as they taxied U.S. Army jeeps, carried bags, and waited on Americans with the Occupation forces. "I hope the over-all impression we made on these maturing men and women is that we are a very decent and worthwhile kind of people. Some of our people here would certainly give them that impression. Others I'm sure will not." It would become a preoccupation of his for the next fifteen years, through any number of Third World nations: the way Americans comported themselves as representatives of the world's foremost democracy, and how they were seen by the people who truly looked up to them.[56]

During that first trip to Japan, Raper was part of a team of Americans called to consult on four areas as part of a Japanese brain trust: banking, taxation, cooperatives, and land reform. Raper spent a couple of months traveling to villages, observing the land reform program, and talking about it with as many people as he could. A year later, MacArthur asked Raper to return and review the progress of land reform. The first time to Japan, he showed up dressed as usual. Traveling the South had suited Raper's bent toward rumpled attire. But by his second trip East, he had learned to shine his shoes, he said, and he reported at MacArthur's headquarters wearing pressed trousers and a fresh collar and tie. He had even combed his hair. He thought his sharper appearance was the reason why MacArthur's adjutant assigned him the rank of brigadier general.[57]

In all, Raper surveyed Japan three times, for a total of six or seven months, enough time to be impressed by the capacity for change in a unified and motivated country. The way he had in *Preface to Peasantry,* Raper charted changes in farm implements, co-ops, farm credit and debit situations, religious organizations, community organizations, political parties, schools. The result of his review was a short book, published under the imprimatur of the Supreme Commander of the Allied Powers. *The Japanese Village in Transition* was a detailed analysis of the changes that had been made in thirteen rural villages, from north to south, over a year and a half, in the wake of the Allied Occupation. The thirteen villages covered each major geographical region and type of agriculture.[58]

Raper's approach was to study the interactions among families, local communities, and national organizations in a Japanese regionalism. These interactions were shifting rapidly because of a number of thoroughgoing changes, including the enfranchisement of women and direct elections, the establishment of farmers' and fishermen's cooperatives, a revision of the educational system, and the withdrawal of tax support for religious organizations.[59] On his first visit, Raper traveled with five Japanese social scientists and two Americans, a part-time anthropologist and a sociologist. When he returned to analyze the changes wrought by the overhaul of Japanese society, his team was more formidable, including four American anthropologists and sociologists, five Japanese sociologists, and map-makers, agricultural economists, and translators.⁶⁰

Even as American social science was withdrawing to the laboratory and the institute during the postwar years, Raper stuck with his old approach, as a participant-observer, aiming to meet as many different kinds of people as possible. "I've been measuring my success as an investigator of rural institutions by the number of times I take off my shoes in a day." That way, he saw the dynamics firsthand, taking part in a village meeting, for instance, where ten men sat talking around a plain and simple, horseshoe-shaped table—landlords, tenants, and small farmers. Now and then an inspector stood to introduce a new topic, and occasionally a man stood up, shoeless on a straw mat in the back of the room. "So far as I could see," Raper recalled, "here was the democratic process at work; all having their say, and then voting." This was the kind of scene for which, later in life, Raper always felt nostalgic. "One landlord was a picture," which he found charming. "Small, chubby, old wing collar and tie, and all smiles."⁶¹ Though he was just another American while in Tokyo, "I'm somebody out in these villages," Raper wrote his family shortly before returning to them. "You should see the mayors of the villages, making certain that I'm in the preferred spot—the *highest* seat, a la Margaret Mead." Soon, he would be back at the BAE. "And what a slapping back into place is ahead for me—oh, well, I'll need something to remind me that everybody else wants to be in the highest seat, too."⁶²

His assignment had turned out to be not only land tenure, but determining what changes should be made in village culture, "to implement the shift," as he phrased it, "from the old feudal Japan to the new democratic country that the Occupation forces would like to make it." With a small team of specialists, he spent a few days in each village—talked with the village leaders and typical families, copied data from the village records, made base maps, took dozens of photographs, toured the schools and temples, and visited hundreds of village households. "Everybody was cordial and cooperative," he noted, "from the village headsman to the smallest farmer." One evening's party ended with rice whiskey, beer, and saki. "Many got rather high; the singing was lusty and screechy, and a rousing 'Banzi!' for me at the end."⁶³ Another night in a remote village, Raper sat with a dozen or so young people to see what was on their minds. They asked him two questions. "Are farm machines everywhere in America?" Most seriously, though, they wanted to know, "Is it true what we hear about the treatment of minority groups in America?" He would come to find that it was not easy to travel too far, at home or abroad, without being faced with the same questions.[64]

A Model for Developing Countries Everywhere

Before he returned to the States, following his second trip, in January 1948, Brigadier General Raper scheduled an audience with Supreme Allied Commander MacArthur, who asked what progress he had seen. Raper read a list of eight or ten items, adding little in the way of interpretation. MacArthur broke in to express his appreciation of the work. Raper broke back in to tell him how many farmers had asked him for more technical assistance. Raper told him he saw such assistance as safeguarding the progress of the land distribution, and he recommended that an experienced specialist in agricultural extension should be part of each military and governmental team.

The new, small land owners were becoming stable elements in their communities, Raper told him, and they had become more interested in politics and protecting the gains they had made. MacArthur was obviously interested. Raper told him about a Taiwanese official who had buttonholed him about Japanese land reform. If the nationalist Chinese could launch that kind of program, he had told Raper, the Communists would be stopped dead in their tracks. MacArthur nodded thoughtfully, so Raper told him how important it was for the United States to take care of its friends. He told MacArthur that liberal organizations among the Japanese should not be considered as enemies of the Occupation, because many were allies in the Occupation's strike at the heart of Japan's feudal social relations. He told him that American-led agrarian reform would ease difficult international situations around the world. MacArthur, in turn, as Raper remembered, "spoke of the great influence land ownership has had on the French people, and generalized broadly that the ownership of the land was a basic consideration in the stabilization of any civilization." Raper was learning from MacArthur how to use national security concerns and anticommunist policy as cover for actual democratization accomplished on the ground.[65]

To his surprise, Raper found the military officials in charge of the Occupation and land reform talking and acting as thought they would get along well with Henry Wallace or Harold Ickes or Will Alexander. "This occupation government has the leftover of the New Deal in a rather hopeful degree," Raper wrote home. "They talk of democratic values, of planning, of being proud when the under-fellow begins to express himself—and that it is not bad for people who are gaining their new freedom to be a little extravagant, in fact that is to be expected."[66] Even during the Roosevelt years, Raper had always had to struggle with conservative political and social forces to accomplish his cultural analyses and progressive initiatives. In Japan, on the other hand, New Deal–type policies were being carried out in cooperation with a willing populace, whose moneyed interests had been defeated, and with the full governmental and military support of the Allied Powers. In Japan, he was able to say to industrialists, "Oh, no. You must take care of your workers first. If, later, the machines are needed, you will get them." He was at the center of the greatest and most successful democratic state-building project in history, a model for developing countries everywhere.[67]

Raper understood the philosophy of Japanese land reform this way. For centuries, landownership had provided the foundation for Japan's powerful feudal families. In the years leading up to the war, tenants had repeatedly agitated for more widespread landownership and greater equality in their relations with landlords. Japan's militarists developed rural support by promising land reform (even as they simultaneously assured the large landowners that they would retain their holdings). After the war, the Allied Occupation picked up the tenants' dissatisfaction and determined to break the old feudal pattern as a way to launch democratic programs. As Raper saw it, the State Department realized that the Japanese countryside could move toward personal responsibility and free enterprise only in proportion to their ability to acquire their own farms. The Occupation had every reason to displace the feudal landlords. The result, according to Raper's analysis, was that the single greatest change in the lives of rural Japanese was land reform.[68]

The idea behind the land reform was to replace Japanese feudalism with a system that fostered a more democratic way of life. Reform covered everything from the break-up of large land-holdings to the extension of credit for small farmers. Raper found that in only eighteen months, Japanese village life had become much more self-directed. Land was already much more widely available, and community decisions were being made by the villagers themselves. The Occupation did insist, though, that the mechanization of Japanese farming be implemented with an eye toward enhancing cooperativism, rather than corporatization.[69]

The values the Allied Occupation overlaid onto Japanese land reform were those of the New Deal. The dignity of the individual and the family were emphasized. Cooperative efforts were assisted. Distribution of ownership was spread widely among those who worked the land. Family farming was nurtured. By the late 1940s, those values also included the belief that the introduction of mechanization should be planned. Machines that simply facilitated larger holdings were discouraged and then blocked from use.[70]

The Occupation was driven by liberals and leftists, according to historian John Dower, "who had been associated with Franklin D. Roosevelt's progressive New Deal policies—policies that were already falling out of favor in Washington before the war ended." These newly discounted policies, however, were the engines of Japan's transformation. "What made the occupation of Japan a success was two years or so of genuine reformist idealism before U.S. policy became consumed by the Cold War," Dower posits, "coupled with a real Japanese embrace of the opportunity to start over." America's political and economic control was combined with Japanese desperation and a desire for reform that had begun during the 1930s. "One might say," Dower writes, "that the last great exercise of New Deal idealism was carried out by Americans in defeated Japan." In postwar Japan, Doctor Win-the-War had improbably turned back into Doctor New Deal. Just as improbably, Raper had found himself studying a people who were changing as he watched and talked and took off his shoes yet again, and a feudal society was turning into a humane, progressive, and efficient nation.[71] He had marveled at the way war marshaled resources and motivated a whole society in a way that social concern never could. In Japan, though, he was seeing just how military and political organization, operating on both national and local levels, could set priorities and guide reconstruction to transform a society.

During Raper's first visit in the summer of 1947, many tenants had been afraid to acquire land, anxious not to cross their former landlords. By the time he returned, in late 1948, not a single new farm owner told Raper he would have preferred remaining a tenant. Everyone expressed great pride and satisfaction over having become a modest landowner. And the leaders of all the villages he visited were amazed that so comprehensive a reform could have been achieved in so short a time. Land reform was carried out largely through what Raper called "one of the most significant adult educational efforts ever launched," and through direct village-directed elections to local commissions on land sales. Having represented workers on New Deal labor boards, Raper was accustomed to seeing the makeup of labor commissions determine the outcome of the negotiations. In Japan, half of each local land reform commission was composed of farm tenants, with the remaining members drawn from owner-farmers and large landholders. The election of such commissioners gave the Occupation its first chance to establish the mechanisms of democracy. As many as two hundred thousand men, in rural villages across Japan, participated in the process. A third of them were drawn from farm tenants who never would have expected to exert such control over the land they had worked all their lives. The Japanese land reform was exactly what Raper had wanted to accomplish in the American South. He was able to watch how effective democratization could be when unified community action and national legislative planning came together.[72]

Less than three years after their unconditional surrender, Raper found, the Japanese were experiencing a mood of optimism buoyed by the new junior high schools, by numerous small machines, by more livestock, and by the opening up of new land for small farmers all over the country.[73] He saw that women could now vote. Raper saw that village heads were being elected by popular vote, rather than through the traditional village assembly. He saw improved local school systems. He considered such changes at the village level toward greater democracy to be especially significant, because the village was Japan's most important locality and functioning group.[74]

Once he realized during the war that American yeomanry had become a lost cause, Raper took his hope overseas to try to develop traditions of democratic action in agricultural communities throughout the Third World. Beginning with his work in Japan, Raper started a new career, exporting social planning to Asia, Africa, and the Middle East. Regionalism for farm families in America had expired, but not for those throughout the Third World. The concerns of the newly surging U.S. civil rights movement kept moving toward urban affairs, as Raper had predicted it would, while the South's black migrants crowded into unprepared and hostile cities. By the end of World War II, Raper's skills and know-how were in greater demand in rural communities overseas than in the newly urbanizing and suburbanizing South. So he split the rest of his career between his agrarian haven in Piedmont Virginia and a multitude of regionalist projects in the only places they remained viable—the Third World.

11

THIRD WORLD, COLD WAR

"I Wasn't Going to Play Cloak-and-Dagger"

Through the course of the 1950s, Raper undertook assignments in two dozen countries, from French Indochina to Sierra Leone. He was in Taiwan during the McCarthy hearings, he was in Saigon during the Korean War, and later, during the Freedom Rides, he and Martha were working in the delta of the Ganges.[1] Raper saw his work as stretching overseas the long line of community development projects that Americans had always engaged in, from Puritan towns to frontier settlements and Populist cooperatives, and from agricultural extension to the Farm Security Administration. What would have happened, he wondered, if Reconstruction had actually addressed community development? The goal of "forty acres and a mule" had died a quick death. Raper wanted to resuscitate and modernize the concept for the small farmers of the Third World.[2]

At the midpoint of the twentieth century, and reaching his own fifties, Raper felt the need to sit down one day at his typewriter and remind himself why he felt it was worthwhile working for a federal bureaucracy. He had the chance to deal with large issues and influence national policy. Although that influence had been continually diminishing, the federal government still offered an activist the best means to accomplish change. More than ever, he still felt sociology's greatest challenge was to retain its essential scientific character while continuously adjusting to political necessity. Raper believed that social science, by its nature, was not meant for the laboratory, but that its findings demanded political implementation.[3]

His list of drawbacks was longer. Raper was struggling in postwar America with the role of bureaucrat and the public's growing resistance to government experts. "I think the thing that disturbs me here is that there is a tendency to blanket us as equally grasping and unnecessary." Political change undercut the stability of his projects and the objectivity he tried to bring to his work. And he chafed at the impersonality and red tape. He knew he was losing the battle to hang on to the kind of intense, engaging fieldwork he had known his whole career. He saw that Will Alexander had retired to his farm near Chapel Hill, and Howard Odum had long since withdrawn from activism. No more the nation's underpinning, rural America was becoming a memory. And with it went any real semblance of regionalism.[4]

Apart from the political troubles that Raper's cultural studies had encountered, scholarly interest in regionalism was in decline, and with the stress on consensus that would develop in the 1950s, social divisions, in terms of class, race, or region, began to attract less attention. In the social sciences, regional issues began to seem outdated. To Raper, though, focus on the local remained as important to democracy as national issues. His response was to leave the consensus-minded United States and pursue regionalism throughout the Third World.[5]

By 1952, Carl Taylor's staff at the Department of Agriculture was one-third the size it had been when Raper had joined him ten years earlier. Half that time, Raper himself had been focusing on the Third World. Even when back in Washington, he was often out on loan to another agency, writing about Asia. Back in Washington, Raper began using his experience working with Roy Stryker, Edwin Rosskam, Dorothea Lange, and Jack Delano to develop orientation sessions for foreign-service personnel to prepare them for what they would encounter overseas, particularly in rural work. In 1951, he had made a film about rural development around the world, with such subtitles as, "The dignity of the agriculturist," showing farmers as social and economic equals within the panoply of American occupations. He pointed out the importance of the American farmer as a producer of food and a consumer of industrial products. He emphasized the respect the farmer received from other social groups. And he demonstrated the critical services provided the farmer by local, state, and federal governments.[6]

Even as the small farmer he celebrated was disappearing from the American landscape, Raper himself lived the ideal he had documented for Asians on his farm in Virginia. In orientation sessions, he would say to foreign visitors, "My knowledge of the American farmer is of a practical nature, for I have had the opportunity to observe farm life first-hand in many parts of the country, and I was reared on a farm, and am now living on a farm of thirty-seven acres, twenty miles west of Washington." He liked to tell them that "as usual, I helped do the farm chores before I came to the office this morning."[7] Meanwhile, his focus continued to shift overseas.

He worked sporadically on trends in rural America, charting its continual decline.[8] He compiled health studies in New York and Mississippi, gathering data on how farm families made use of medical care.[9] And he worked with Martha on such projects as "Guide to Agriculture, U.S.A.," an orientation manual for foreign visitors to rural America. It seemed they were the only ones still interested in the subject. He went on loan to the State Department to oversee a series of documentaries for eleven countries, from Turkey to Indonesia.[10] He became a program evaluation analyst, a job that stood midway between a cultural anthropologist and an agricultural extension agent. He became a source of information about indigenous cultures, rather than a policy-making, administrative officer. From the first, he considered it critical that he be seen by nationals as a neutral party, rather than a representative of U.S. interests or policies.[11]

When the chance came, it made sense to move to the U.S. International Cooperation Administration (USICA), which later became the U.S. Agency for International Development (USAID).[12] There, for the rest of the decade, he worked exclusively on international projects, either in foreign missions in Taiwan, Vietnam, Pakistan, Iran, Iraq, and Libya, or in Washington, developing information about these nations for American officials traveling overseas. And he began to see his work in the Third World as another way to demonstrate that, as he wrote, "there is no real basis for a lack of faith in poor people." Especially after the heady experience of Japanese land reform, he attributed the postwar prosperity of the 1950s to New Deal democratization and faith in the dispossessed, rather than to agribusiness and the corporatizing of America.[13]

In 1951, Raper began making consultation tours to Southeast Asia and the Middle East to advise U.S. missions throughout the region on ways of increasing aid to villagers and farmers. He soon began to run into other kinds of problems to add to his list of "negatives." He chaired a conference on village and national cultures for the Far East Division of the U.S. Mutual Security Agency, attended by a number of leading social scientists, including Carl Taylor, Glenn Taggert, and Donald Stone. After the first day, the group recommended that a senior social scientist be attached to each of the five nations in the region. Raper contacted five colleagues, including Ira De A. Reid, who agreed to serve.¹⁴ "I left the States in high spirits," Raper remembered, "and remained on cloud nine as I went from one country to the next and 'sold' my man to the Mission Director." The high spirits evaporated as soon as he arrived home and found that, because of their liberal activism, none of the five had passed security clearance. What's more, Raper was forbidden from telling any of them why their appointments were canceled. Tell them the project has been abandoned, he was instructed, or make up another kind of story. "The truth must not be told them," he recalled, sardonically, "lest it damage them professionally." Nonetheless, Raper was not willing to create a subterfuge. "I wasn't going to play cloak-and-dagger with Ira Reid," he said.¹⁵ "Together we were deeply sad that McCarthyism, then at its height, was taking so heavy a toll!" Raper's goal had been to transfer his experience with southern regionalism to the Far East, but by the early 1950s, once-benign regionalism had become politically dangerous.¹⁶

Raper's plan had been to regionalize the kinds of reports he had developed for Japan and Taiwan, and for that matter, Greene County. Recognizing the interdependence of Asia, he wanted to link regional studies throughout the entire western rim of the Pacific. Then social science would be able to help planning, from the local level to the regional, from village projects to geopolitical strategies. On the verge of getting underway, the plan was swallowed by anticommunism.¹⁷

Raper called it a booby prize when, instead, he was sent to Taiwan to establish a pilot program in community development for the Nationalist Chinese. His own aim was to demonstrate what a social scientist could do in an official planning capacity and then resurrect the idea of regional planning. But by 1954, after two years of work, Raper realized the time had passed in Southeast Asia when he could think realistically about region-wide initiatives. Not only was he fighting anticommunism, but sociology had also turned further away from the cultural approach and toward statistical-minded, quantitative research.¹⁸

Raper still managed to involve himself, as project evaluation adviser, with initiatives far from rural agriculture. In Taiwan, for instance, he met with officials at the Taipei Pedicabmen's Union, whose six thousand members made it the largest craft union in the country. He analyzed its democratic organization and its labor and theft insurance policies. And as the union's newspaper observed, "Dr. Raper pays much attention to our members' wages and income, and conditions of living."¹⁹

The biggest difference Raper recognized between American farm families and those in Asia was that U.S. farmers played a conscious role in their national, political life. Not only did rural Americans vote and organize to promote their own interests, but farmers also engaged with both public and private scientific and educational organizations and agencies. Similar kinds of organizations existed in the Third World, but the number of farmers who could participate was so much smaller, and they had little chance to take part in their nations' cultural and social institutions and affairs. He also saw that the most stable farming communities in America were those where social distinctions were least prominent, where landownership was most widespread, and where young people had expectations to succeed on their own farms.[20]

All through the 1950s, long after McCarthy was gone, Raper's studies faced the opposition of Cold War policy makers. Much of his work was conducted in tense political arenas. For instance, Raper was sent as a community development adviser to the U.S. mission in the Philippines. Ignored by the director, Raper found something else to do. He worked with the Philippine military on *The Rural Philippines,* a two-hundred-page report based on his studies of Japan and Taiwan, and on a project to document the barrios' poor public services.[21] President Elpidio Quirino, afraid of the criticism it would engender, secreted the book away in a warehouse. Quirino's opponent, Ramon Magasaysay, snuck it out of hiding. "Vote for me," Raper remembered Magasaysay saying, "and these unmet needs will be met." *The Rural Philippines* was a significant factor in Magsaysay's subsequent victory.[22]

At the same time, Raper found that subterfuge and surveillance were not new to the Cold War, when he learned his conversations at the Birmingham Southern Conference on Human Welfare had been bugged. Back in 1938, Raper had been driven home from Birmingham with Ira Reid, Ralph McGill, editor of the *Atlanta Constitution,* and Tarleton Collier, a columnist with the *Atlanta Georgian.* They ended up philosophizing as they drove through the night. What does the South do now? they mused. What does America do now? Raper held forth to that "marvelous audience" at great length. We are not taking anywhere near full advantage of the potential of our people, he told them. If and when we begin to take such advantage, we will devise some tests to determine who among our students, black and white equally, had a good ear and could play the violin well. Who was interested in and would make a good physicist? Who would make a good doctor? "We were going to get these people; we were going to educate them. If their parents didn't have money to educate them, we'd educate them at public expense," he remembered. "I had never talked about it before. I didn't ever talk about it after that one night."[23]

Fourteen years later, Raper was heading for Taiwan. First, he had been cleared for top secrecy, and then USAID changed its mind and canceled his project.[24] He was ushered in to see an agent named Barber, who sat leafing through Raper's dossier, thick with documentation concerning his interracial work. As he sat behind his desk and slowly turned the pages, Barber asked, "Now, Dr. Raper, is it true that you think that children ought to be educated in college at public expense?" Barber repeated Raper's whole conversation, point by point, as he had spun it out across the late night drive out of Birmingham. Either the car was bugged, Raper concluded, or the driver was spying on them. Barber told him he was not safe on the "race situation. I said, 'What evidence do you have that I'm not safe on the race situation?'" Barber repeated a story one of Raper's Slope Oaks neighbors had told him about Raper's efforts to upset the racial balance of the community. Raper told him the story had originated with a man in the neighborhood, who had suffered with a history of mental problems and had recently committed suicide. Barber decided to rescind his cancellation of Raper's project, and Raper's interracial activism became a dead issue. And five years later, once *Sputnik* had shocked the nation, Raper found his advocacy of public-assisted higher education was no longer a problem, either.[25]

"We appreciate your comments"

Driving all his Third World work was Raper's belief that what America had most to offer was its example of how a once-rural country could pull together its disparate peoples and form a nation built on self-determination. Especially in countries where different and often-hostile groups had been sewn together by colonial boundaries, the American example of a polyglot success, said Raper, "was a matter of high relevance." In Japan, Raper had seen the Allied Occupation place the full force of America's economic, technological, and military strength behind a social and political revolution in the service of democratization and prosperity. But the strategic aim of aiding Japanese self-determination in the late 1940s was rendered increasingly obsolete for the rest of the Third World through the course of the 1950s. Raper saw American intervention in the Third World turn toward supporting and extending existing power structures. The focus of the military-industrial complex changed from nation-building and social planning to military assistance and police training programs.²⁶

He would come to think a lot about a minute's exchange in an hour's meeting in the fall of 1955 in Tehran. An Indian, working in a village development program, wanted clarification concerning American policy from the director of the U.S. Overseas Mission (USOM) to Iran. Mr. Goswami pressed Director Gregory for answers by offering some advice. The first question the USOM needed to ask itself, offered Goswami, was this: "Is our program lessening the gap between the landlords and the peasants, or is it making it greater?" Gregory told the curious Goswami he had asked the wrong question. The United States did not focus on landlords and peasants but, rather, on officials, and with a specific intent. "The policy of the U.S. government is to *support* friendly governments, not to *change* them."²⁷

Goswami had suspected as much, but he wanted to be certain, so he pushed further. "The purpose of the U.S.-aid program must be more than that," he countered. "The intention of the American people is clearly more than that. The genius and tradition of the American people is toward freedom and opportunity for all."

Gregory was unambiguous. "We are here to aid and support friendly governments."

Goswami was emboldened by Gregory's being so forthright. "If that is *all* U.S. aid is here for," he parried, "then it has no business in Asia, and Asia will be better off without it. Forgive me for being so direct. I do not want to seem rude, but this is a matter of first importance."

"Well, I've been pretty direct, myself, but sometimes it is good to be able to be so." Gregory was as solicitous as he had been clear. "We appreciate your comments," he told Goswami, and Raper remembered the conversation swiftly moving on to other matters.²⁸

Through the course of the following year, as he continued traveling through Iran, Iraq, Syria, and Jordan, Raper came to view American foreign policy philosophically. Now that the United States was the strongest nation in the Free World, he reasoned, with historical perspective, "it is not surprising that it should be making an effort to maintain the peace in ways that leave its position intact. Such is the history of strong nations." Raper would run into the same problem through the course of the Cold War 1950s, trying to establish mechanisms for democratization and community planning throughout in the Middle East, in nation after nation where the State Department wanted its officials to maintain existing power structures and troubleshoot anything that jeopardized the status quo.[29]

Raper worried about the impressions that U.S. officials were making among the rural poor of the Third World. "The greatest single weakness in our foreign program is not lack of administrative efficiency," he wrote in 1954. "We are not inefficient as a people. On the contrary. The weakness of our foreign program is that too often it is manned by the wrong kind of Americans. Intelligent, capable, alert, and patriotic, in so far as they understand the genius of our country, still they throw away with one hand what they try to build with the other, because they are within themselves people who seek and desire power, conquest, and superiority."[30]

Aggressive officials are not unpatriotic, Raper wrote, nor are those who hire them. But he saw too many Americans who were filled with the need to satisfy their own ambitions; they did not fit in among the people to whom they were sent. The self-important American was no help to the foreign service. On the other hand, "If your spirit longs for real communication between people, in the free give-and-take of equals interacting with equals, then you are qualified to work for democracy." The key was to develop an understanding of the psychology of colonialism, which had shaped the thinking of Third World people as thoroughly as it had in the American South.[31]

By the early 1960s, he was recording a modern parable born of an opinion poll taken of villagers' problems. "The first villager said his main problem centered around 'too little water and the residues of the Colonial System.' A second villager answered: 'Too much water, and the residues of the Colonial System.'" Whatever had been liked or disliked about European colonialism stuck to Americans, too, at least until Asians saw reasons why they should separate the white European from the American. Raper had seen in the South the same pattern. "The resentment and admiration that combine in a nation's attitude toward Americans do not come wholly from their experience with Americans, nor do they stem entirely from its previous experience with Europeans," he observed. "It springs first of all from their experience with each other, daily, throughout their lives. Human beings easily project onto the foreigner whatever resentment they feel toward the upper classes of their own societies." The answer, in Asia, as it had been in the American South, was greater self-determination for more people.[32]

To Raper, it was critical that American help in the Third World be extended humbly. Afghanistan, for instance, bore the burden of a tragic history.

"There is at present not one single enterprise in Afghanistan which comes up to the level of hundreds of enterprises in Afghanistan two thousand years ago," he observed. "So, when you work on community development matters in Afghanistan there is this historical influence which reaches through into many a situation, and most dynamically I presume in the personality structure of the people themselves." He was already intimately familiar with a region stifled by gradual decline, which knew the tragedy of defeat. "How does one behave, when one is the poor and unsuccessful descendent of more prosperous forebears?"[33] This meant that American advisers needed to work against their own cultural grain. In the United States, getting ahead meant seeing what needed to be done first, then convincing one's colleagues to follow. In the Third World, an American adviser needed to see just as quickly what must be accomplished but, as Raper wrote, "he needs to hold his tongue longer, sometimes for days, to give the country operator an opportunity to discover the answer for himself, and articulate it, and so become the more effective as a result of his sense of achievement." He knew the way northern reformers had been seen in the South, and winced at the way cocksure Americans behaved in the Third World.[34]

In the South, Raper had insisted on working as part of an interracial team to gain a more sympathetic view and more comfortable cooperation from his black subjects, and he used the same approach overseas. In Taiwan, for example, he brought mainland Chinese and Taiwanese to work together, just as he had worked years before with Walter Chivers on *The Tragedy of Lynching*. To Raper, an interracial approach—what he called a balanced research team—was a requirement for an adequate scientific job.[35] He had believed in blacks and whites working together in the South, and Raper's work in the Middle East reflected a similar perspective on integration.

He traveled to Syria, Lebanon, Iraq, Egypt, and Jordan, but he refused invitations to Israel. "I wanted very much to go to Israel but decided not to go." In Arab countries, he was often asked whether he had been to Israel. "I wanted to stay within communicating reach with the Arab," he said, years later, "and I saw that if I said I'd been to Israel, there'd be a damper put in there. I thought I could be most effective with the Arabs if I could tell the truth, and said I hadn't been to Israel." Had he once crossed over to work in Israel, Raper felt strongly he would have been seen as another pro-Jewish American when he returned to the Muslim countries. As it was, he worked, now and again, through the mid-1950s for the American Friends of the Middle East, analyzing ways to improve the region's agriculture.[36] During these trips, he saw the conditions endured in the Arab refugee camps in Syria, Lebanon, and Iraq. "I have not been surprised at any of the unrest resulting therefrom," he wrote, "and the end is not yet!" Years later, he recalled driving "by the edge of the large camp on the slope above Jericho one evening a little after sundown, and some teen-age boys began throwing rocks at our car, and I realized how volatile the situation was, for here were spirited people with nowhere to go, for their leader, the Mufti, in Jerusalem, insisted that none of them accept opportunities to improve their lot outside of the camps, for to do so would weaken the claim of the group as a whole to their basic human right to go back home!"[37]

"Life is doubly convincing after crossing the Syrian Desert"

In Asia and the Middle East, signs of progress were seldom as visible to Raper as they had been, not only back home in Arcadia, but even in the South of the early 1930s, with its sadistic lynching and grinding Depression, its wholesale exodus and reactionary demagoguery. Albeit slowly and painfully, and in part because of federal pressure, efforts in the South had finally yielded results. The Middle East was a more difficult challenge, requiring a more difficult logic. The story that made the rounds of American officials in Beirut in the mid-1950s may have been apocryphal, but it gave true measure to the horror American officials felt about the region. Chuck Wright, an adviser assigned to Libya, was traveling in Egypt with another American. In the streets of Cairo, they happened on a beggar woman with a baby whose eyes were rimmed with flies. Wright's companion moved to brush away the flies, but the mother shielded the child's face. The flies crawling over the infant's eyes had already satiated themselves on the baby's tears. "If you shoo the ones that are there now," the mother admonished, "the hungry ones would come." More than a cautionary tale, the story was a meditation on the futility of good intentions where the smallest change was feared. Not only were social and economic problems overwhelming. The intractability of the Third World's hardships was exacerbated by inhospitable climates. The South had its own intense summer heat, of course, but the Middle East was often inhumanly hot. On the way from Tehran to Beirut in 1956, Raper observed that "life is doubly convincing after crossing the barrenness of the Syrian Desert."[38] By then, he had seen enough to make some generalizations about the Third World.

Most often, sovereignty was concentrated in the hands of a king or strong man who held all the political and economic power, from the generalissimo in Formosa to the shah of Iran. (The most successful Third World countries during the 1950s—India, Pakistan, Egypt, Turkey, the Philippines—had elected new presidents in the past few years.) Most officials were paid so poorly they engaged in graft to make ends meet. Time and again, Raper had seen, for example, agricultural inspectors expecting to be paid tribute by the villagers the government was paying them to distribute seed to. Across the regions, farmers and governments were anxious to buy the newest agricultural machinery, but Raper saw most farmers and officials feel resentment toward Americans and Europeans for having to "keep their shiny new gadgets in operation," as he said. In so many ways—from traffic to politics—the Middle East forced on Raper a sense of unmanageable chaos. He had assumed the American drive to expand was universal, and regarded with dismay the masses of poor people living in the cracks of their society's crumbling walls, making a living by refixing old shoes or selling flowers from coffee cans, without any conception of improvement. In Asia and North Africa, he walked, ate, and slept among unimaginable odors. He saw people drink and bathe from streams foul with excrement. In India, Ethiopia, and Afghanistan, people hoped to live into their thirties.[39] He asked, at Mutual Security Agency conferences through Southeast Asia, "How can we get people who are accustomed to a status-quo way of life to cooperate in programs of induced change?" Trained and inclined to study societies in dynamic flux, Raper was flummoxed by Third World cultures of stasis.

The problems he experienced, though, were certainly not solely related to the indigenous cultures. In 1953, for example, the Mutual Security Agency was having difficulty defining its Southeast Asia program objectives. The agency's stated goal in Vietnam was to improve relations but, as one of its economics advisers admitted, such an ideal "may at times appear to be in conflict with our rearmament and strategic materials objectives." Conflict also existed within the State Department. Many pushed for policies aimed at fostering stability in Third World nations friendly to the United States. Others, like Raper, who pushed for a greater degree of effective democracy in these countries, found it tough to battle both local conditions and opposition from within the agency.[40]

Iran was his most difficult assignment. The shah had instituted his own grandiose land reform while Raper was stationed in Tehran, "and to demonstrate his interest in democracy," Raper noted, "he had an opposition party organized." The Japanese and Taiwanese reforms Raper had participated in resulted in substantial changes. But Raper saw the shah's land reform as a sham. Everything was handled from the throne, down to the number of obedient peasants who appeared promptly at the Marble Palace to be told of their good fortune in being granted a tract of village land. At the same time, the best village lands and water rights were sold to the shah's friends; these sales concentrated the shah's wealth in the fast-growing urban centers of Iran, especially in Tehran. Raper had already seen similar effects in the South, where cash had been drained from an agricultural region, transferred from village land to city property.

While the reform was underway, the shah asked a friend to form an opposition party. This friend contacted Raper about becoming an adviser. Raper checked with the U.S. ambassador, who cleared him for the project. Raper said he was available. "And that was that—seemingly all he wanted was a paper organization."[41] Beyond all that, factional fighting among the U.S. Overseas Mission staff and between the United Nations and Iranian officials was set within a regional context of in-fighting among Iranians. "Seemingly each faction knew what it didn't want done," Raper observed, "but not how it could cooperate with any other faction to get done what it wanted to do."[42] What possibility remained for democracy in such a situation? What hope was there for someone trying to break down institutionalized poverty? Years later, Raper mustered the kindest description he could in calling his time in the Middle East and South Asia challenging. "To no small extent, we were trying to do the impossible, and we were in a hurry." Small exigencies and bureaucratic justifications bumped aside experiments and pilot projects.[43]

While advising in Iraq in 1955, Raper received a communication from Washington marked "secret," in which he was directed not to talk with Iraqi officials and contractors about the community development projects he was working on. Instead, he was to become yet another trouble-shooter. Any planning was to come from above. He found himself a fill-in for the community development adviser in Iraq during the run-up to the Suez Canal Crisis, when the United States faced down Britain and France. He perceived almost unanimous Iraqi resistance to the American presence.[44]

In spite of all the difficulties, Raper continued to advocate for a balance among local control, regional initiatives, and national direction. All his experience with Third World officials convinced him again that modernity required such a balance. A meeting in Washington with a group of Turkish officials proved the point to him. In a windowless, air-conditioned room on the fourth floor of the State Department building, they sat around and asked Raper how social improvements were accomplished in America. Each answer found its way to some national or governmental organization, and often to a powerful lobby in Congress. How was it that the children of building tradesmen could afford to go to high school, and even to college? "The answer," Raper remembered, "identified the national labor organizations, Social Security, and the great religious and civic organizations that have promoted general and vocational educational interests, and advocated labor-management cooperation. Or, if they inquired about the highway system, our answer soon involved Federal Aid to the States for roads, with the Central Government picking up the larger part of the cost for the new limited-access interstate highways." They were not satisfied. They wanted to hear how they could accomplish such things under their own conditions. How could discussions about the American Interstate System help them link Istanbul with their remote villages? They broke for coffee, and Raper began thinking about Arcadia. When they filed back into the room, he had written on the blackboard, "Education, Health, Communications, Household Facilities, Making a Living, Agricultural Services, Group Activities, Pastime Activities, Outside Contacts, Security, and Human Relations." The rest of the afternoon, Raper talked about the self-help democratic processes he had grown up with in Davidson County. "No sooner had we begun this discussion than the visiting Turks began nodding appreciatively—what we were saying did relate to their current situations in Turkey; our illustrations were applicable to their own developmental needs back home." And Raper had seen, once again, how progress and democracy necessarily combined individual and local initiatives with national policies and resources.[45]

"A funny-looking woman was in town today"

In between his assignments, and through the years of Little Rock and Selma, Arthur and Martha enjoyed the solace and accomplishment of the family farm. Much later, he would look back on their days at Slope Oaks with extraordinary nostalgia, not only for the simplicity, but also for the pleasure of self-sufficiency the farm held for him. "Wake up with the birds, breakfast on day-old eggs and raw milk," he recalled. "For lunch, mainly vegetables and fruits and home-made cottage cheese. Maybe snatch a brief afternoon nap.

Take a swim in the spring-fed pond. Eat a leisurely dinner of stew or steak or fish with corn and potatoes and a salad from the garden. Ready ourselves for the church choir on the 'morrow. Feel the cool of the evening, and then fall asleep as night's silences deepen—having done during the week the work in two downtown offices and around the place, so that there be yet other such days."[46]

At the start of the 1950s, the couple was still driving to one or another regional band concert, sitting front and center, craning their necks to see Harrison almost off-stage left at the end of a seventy-piece orchestra and Jarrell, who occupied the end chair at the extreme right. "Maybe," Arthur mused to his family in a round-robin letter, "we will never be as proud again." At the time, he was president of the Fairfax High School Band Boosters Club, and he bragged about making enough money to present brand new uniforms to the thirty-seven members, with leftover funds to finance a few extras the following year. "This thing is all very immediate and real," he told his folks. "Tonight our group puts on a square dance at the high school. Wish all of you could be there."[47]

Moving through Asia and the Middle East, Martha had often felt out-of-place and cut off from her family. "A funny-looking woman was in town today," she wrote in a self-styled parable from Taiwan. "I was the funny-looking woman, and I drew a crowd wherever I went. Always many children and sometimes adults stared unabashedly at my short tightly waved grey hair and pale face." They were spending the summer of 1953 touring the island, while Arthur met with village officials and observed agricultural and social conditions. Martha fought the urge to rue each day they spent in Taiwan. "What can one person, or two people, do to change a human situation that would be worth leaving one's not-quite grown children a half a world away?—being bitten by mosquitoes and being too hot all the time?—tossing restlessly at night on a bed-roll on the floor, trying not to remember that a large roach may crawl along any minute?"[48]

For the remainder of Arthur's overseas career, Martha returned to Washington often, once to attend Harrison's wedding, and at other times because her health had become an issue. A bad back left her at Slope Oaks for much of the rest of the 1950s. When she was gone, being alone and concerned about her health, Raper plunged into his work and wrote frequently. "Don't like for my Martha to be sick," he wrote, once she had left Taiwan for Virginia, "and trust the next letter to say you are feeling ever so much better."[49] Arthur was often overseas, though, and busy when he was home.

Neither poor health nor the social decorum of the 1950s, though, was changing Martha's own outspoken views. In 1952, Arthur, alone in Taiwan, was surprised and taken aback when he picked up a copy of *Time* and saw a letter to the editor, in which Martha took Carl Jung to task for diminishing the importance of sex to spirituality. The previous issue had taken up Jung's conception of religion. "Jung objects to acknowledging that religion is related to the sexual emotions," Martha wrote. "But to some people it seems reasonable and satisfying to feel that the Creator and the creativity in man are akin." Bashful Arthur felt a bit ticklish about Martha's attack on what she called "the pervasive secrecy about sex—our own iron curtain." A resolute Freudian, Martha was not about to let Jung claim religion was more exalted than sex. "A more tolerant observation of Freud would suggest that he was only trying to help disturbed people get their genital impulses re-established to a wholesome place in their philosophy of life. Suppose he was a little belligerent and tactless about it—he was pioneering, he had a hard row to hoe. He may be excused if he did not finish discovering all that humanity will come to understand in the years ahead." She herself felt kinship with smart, determined people who did not mind breaking a few eggs for a just cause. After a brief flurry of embarrassment over her letter, Arthur quietly told her he stood behind her views. Or at least behind her in stating them.[50]

Beginning with *Tenants of the Almighty*, Martha had helped Arthur with editing and organizing, and by the mid-1950s, the couple had become a team. To prepare for a conference in Bangkok, for instance, they worked together, evenings, weekends, and holidays, to draft and polish several talks. Martha herself took pleasure in writing, even if sometimes it was a substitute for being with her family. "Let us celebrate the return of the typewriter with a carbon-copy letter," she wrote their children in 1956. Helping Arthur's work overseas and writing her moved-away children, Martha was home alone more and more. Eventually, she landed a job with the Educational Television and Radio Center in Washington. They were both in their fifties, now, and it began to seem time to cut back on the twelve-hour plane flights and cold, bug-infested mattresses. Arthur was feeling the need to spend more time with her, and he felt less momentum in his work than ever before.[51]

By the mid-1950s, Raper was beginning to feel he might as well stay home. Besides, he said, communications in Asia and the Middle East were so slow that messages from Tehran to Baghdad, for example, were expedited by passing them through Washington. Martha needed to stay close to home to help her aging father, and Arthur, on a tight leash by the State Department, was becoming more and more circumscribed. "Back home in the States in early 1958 I was at something of loose ends."[52] By the end of the year, he had found a niche as acting chief of the Orientation and Counseling Branch of the Office of Personnel, where he stayed the next four years, preparing USAID officials for overseas assignments and debriefing them on his return. He organized a "Grand Central Station type of operation," shuttling as many as a thousand personnel a year in and out of Washington.[53]

Windmills in Pakistan

By the spring of 1962, Raper had been back in Washington long enough to find the office-bound orientation work "taxing." Out of the blue, the chance to join the Comilla Project came up. Before they knew it, in their sixties, the Rapers were once again flying to Asia, living in the delta of the Ganges. The Pakistani government had approached Michigan State University (MSU) and the Ford Foundation for development assistance it could not obtain from the U.S. government. By the early 1960s, private foundations and universities were more interested in studying social change than was the State Department.

Comilla was one of two Academies for Rural Development—east and west—that Pakistan had established to reform its agriculture and modernize its rural societies. Raper had met the director of East Pakistan's Academy, Akhter Hameed Khan, while working in Dacca as regional community development adviser.[54] A mutual friend, Ed Schuler, whom Raper had known from Carl Taylor's old USDA office, had gone on to take part in the MSU project. "He wanted me to come out, and so we went out," said Raper. The decision could not have been as simple as that, but Raper was clearly glad to abandon office work. Close to retirement age, he was still looking to get out among the people and tilt at the same kinds of windmills he had faced in the South during the Depression. He found more than a few such windmills in Pakistan.

Comilla, near Dacca, was a 100-square-mile piece of the great deltaic plain of the Ganges, or more accurately, of a confluence of the Brahmaputra, Megna, Ganges, and Triputanes, rivers forever forgetting their banks and wandering across the horizon. A hundred miles from the coast, none of the land rose more than 30 feet above sea level. In this monsoon-wracked floodplain lived one of the densest populations in the world, 1,700 people per square mile, four-fifths of them rural. Nine out of 10 men eked out a rice crop on acre-sized plots. Villages were built on each spot of dry land, and every path and road was a causeway. Homes were built of bamboo, thinly plastered, thatch-roofed. A 300-year-old levee system tried to push back a river that had come to be called "Comilla's Sorrow." The annual flood was followed by a dry season that, within a few weeks, would bake the soil until it was too dry to till. The irrigation needed to farm had been impossible to organize among villagers so accustomed to having so little that they feared the sacrifice necessary for cooperative effort. The men farmed, and they met in the marketplace to drink tea in crowded stalls. Women were rarely seen outside their homes, like ghosts in flowing, white *burqa*. The Islamic calendar dictated each village's passage through the year. The region averaged a school for every three villages. Curricula combined the British system, little changed since the 1830s, and 1,600-year-old lessons from the *Quran*. Along with the burdens of nature, Comilla suffered, too, from its proximity to the Partition line between India and East Pakistan, five miles from Comilla town, which divided a single agricultural unit and ecosystem, making difficult the political organization and economic potential of an organic region.

In spite of all this, Raper found the Comilla Project appealing. Its approach to rural agriculture and society was consistent with his own ideas about democracy. The academy relied on local *thanas*, approximate to counties, to work out and test its experimental programs. The project counted on the voluntary participation of villagers and their cooperation with government officials. It required those government officials to leave the city and walk the fields with the farmers they were serving. The Comilla Academy, like Raper, considered the function of government, in fact, to educate, as well as regulate. At the same time, this approach implied a faith that the people would trust the government's policies long enough to give them a chance to work. In spite of a record of failure throughout the region, the project insisted on establishing cooperatives for rice and for capital. The project coordinated village-wide, *thana*-level, national and international resources, as though it were an Asian version of Odum's regionalism. Comilla focused on the practical and experimental, rather than the doctrinaire. As Raper explained, "The Comilla approach is not so much a formula for development as it is a formula for *finding* a formula for a development program to fit a particular area."[55] He could have been talking about his own career in the South and the way the New Deal worked.

When he described the government farms and demonstration plots the academy ran, he could have been talking about the Farm Security Administration. The pragmatic, American influence was no coincidence. Khan had specifically sought to draw on the tradition of the American land-grant college. And in both Raper's experience and the approach of the Comilla project, private-sector businesses played little part in social change or rural development. Technological innovation and equipment, for example, were introduced by government and nonprofit agencies. Other than such large-scale industries as mills, factories, and railways, Raper saw business as following modernization, rather than driving it. Once Comilla's farmers began earning capital by saving through their local cooperatives, then merchants would begin moving to the villages, the tail on the dog of modernization. Raper saw Comilla, as a whole, as a research project in rural sociology; the mission of the academy was to provide social science insights to Pakistani officials responsible for rural development.[56]

In spite of the obvious differences, Raper saw the Pakistani peasantry he worked with the same way he had seen southern sharecroppers—as potential agrarians. In some ways, the sociology of the delta of the Ganges was similar to that of the Depression South. Most of the people were poor, unhealthy, and powerless in the face of political and economic circumstances. This was certainly not the first time Raper had written about a place, as he described Comilla, "where people fear change lest their tenuous hold on what little they have be broken." He recognized that "the average Asian villager, far from being indifferent to change as he is often portrayed, given quite feasible conditions—of incentives, knowledge, organization, and supplies—is a canny and hard-driving entrepreneur, ready for swift innovation." As always, Raper saw the dynamism of a situation, even in the backwaters of the ancient East.[57]

Raper spent two years in Comilla, with Martha joining him for part of the time, and they did everything possible to make the project "a very real experience." The couple spent Christmas 1963 in the village of Ranir Kute and, as usual, turned a holiday away from their own family into an occasion for communion. They strung lights and shiny trinkets on a cedar tree tricked up to look like a pine, and at dusk on Christmas Eve, hosted Catholic nuns, Baptist missionaries, and Peace Corps volunteers, along with local Hindus and Muslims. The Buddhist reverence for all living things was also strong in Comilla, and as farm animals wandered the crowded alleys and streets of the city beyond their home, the party sang "Silent Night" in a dozen different accents.[58]

By the fall of 1964, the couple had moved to East Lansing, where Raper was writing up his findings in *Rural Development in Action*, his last study of modernity coming to the rural countryside.[59] The book itself, he wrote in the preface, is a documentation of the work of the academy. By now, though, the intimacy of Raper's documentary approach was gone. Driven by its mission, as defined by MSU and the Ford Foundation, *Rural Development in Action* lost the subtle outrage of *Preface to Peasantry* and *The Tragedy of Lynching*. His warm-blooded sociology had become a blueprint for development, efficient and comprehensive, but drier, more distant, more bureaucratic in tone and structure. Raper preached respect for the rural poor, and his sympathies remain with them but, not surprisingly, *Rural Development in Action* had little of the empathy or bonhomie that filled his early books with knowing wit and the telling detail of the lives of southern farm folk. Documentary had become documentation, administered through a triumvirate of governmental, academic, and philanthropic bureaucracies. The Comilla book incorporated the lessons of Greene and Macon counties, of the Delta Co-op and the Birmingham Conference, then applied them in a committee-driven text that, for all its good intentions, ended up sounding generalized and somewhat pedantic. And besides, these villagers were people he did not know so well as the black and white farm families he had grown up among in the American South. The details of particular people's lives that suffused and vivified his earlier books were missing.

So how did the Comilla Project contribute to the emergence of Bangladesh? Raper felt its greatest benefit was that the project gave villagers the belief that they could work cooperatively. He pointed to their high rate of participation right through the 1960s in regional public works programs. As he had done with Robert Eleazer and Will Alexander in the 1930s, Raper sent reports and publications to a long mailing list of people interested in development. But MSU's project director, Richard Niehoff, reined him in. Raper found the results of social science research were no longer the stuff of news releases.[60] Nor did the *Rural Development in Action* create much of a stir. It certainly did not sell well. By 1974, three years after the bloody establishment of Bangladesh, Raper was hoping the academy's lessons would be rediscovered. In spite of the book's initial obscurity, he wrote to the publisher, Cornell University Press, that he still felt it was "the most adequate formula that has emerged for basic rural development in depressed areas; and surely future scholars will unearth it, though buried now as it is beneath the staggering problems of survival in South Asia, and especially in Bangladesh."[61] He knew that wishful thinking might be coloring his perception. "Let history say whether it is valid," he demurred. All he knew for certain was that by working for the agricultural people of the Third World, he was doing what he could for the majority of humankind.[62]

"That's where the big show is"

Back in the United States, Raper combined his two careers during the next couple of years, while at MSU, writing about Comilla and taking a new look at race in America. He had kept a hand in southern politics and American race relations throughout the 1950s and 1960s.[63] Back in 1952, when Adlai Stevenson's running mate, John Sparkman, was seen as a voice of southern liberalism, the *New Republic* had asked Raper to take up again the old question of whether a new, socially changed South had finally risen.

In "Is There A 'New South'?" Raper explained that the New Deal had allowed more tenants to buy their own land, and it had financed a good deal of civic construction. But it had not delivered a new South, because the region was still being run by the same people. Now, though, the irrefutable hand of industry had finally created a true revolution. In the face of all previous, premature announcements, Raper now proclaimed a truly new South, "because cheap hand labor—the one thing more than any other that gave distinctive character to the old South—is no longer indispensable in the region's agriculture." Science and technology had finally broken the hold of the plantation South.

Industrialization had changed the rest of the nation, of course, but its impact on the South was most dramatic, because the region had been the last mechanized. When the war ended, the South was still only harvesting half a percent of its cotton mechanically. Five years later, it was harvesting 17 percent by machine, ten times as many bales. The number of combines more than doubled, milking machines quadrupled, and corn pickers increased more than 600 percent. As a result, well over half a million tenants left the farm during the course of the 1940s. As part of such change, the South's standard of living was clearly rising. "One of the characteristics of the New South is that it is more afraid of poverty than of work," Raper wrote. He had always felt that way, but now, southerners' work led more directly to reward. Hope was now less necessary than machinery.[64]

His early teaching on race had begun to show its effects. He received a letter, for example, from Charles Lawrence, chair of the Sociology Department at Brooklyn College in the 1960s and 1970s and a high-ranking Episcopalian.

Lawrence had graduated from Morehouse and Columbia. He had been a public school teacher in Atlanta during the 1930s, when he had often met with Raper at meetings of the Interracial Commission and functions of the Atlanta Intercollegiate Council. He had taken Raper's summer school class at Atlanta University. He wrote his master's thesis under the supervision of Ira Reid, while Reid and Raper were writing *Sharecroppers All*. "My main intellectual and scholarly interests have continued to be in the area of organized movements for social change," Lawrence told Raper, "as well as family sociology, reflecting the early influence of people like Ira Reid, W.E.B. Du Bois, Walter Chivers, and yourself." It would not have been lost on Raper that he was the only white on the list. He would never have admitted to it, but this would have been a point of pride.[65]

All through the 1950s, Raper had been ready to go home and take up the study of race again. In 1956, he had met an old friend in Tehran and talked about old times. Gunnar Myrdal urged Raper to pick up his research on blacks in America the previous time they had seen each other, in the early 1950s. Again, in Tehran, he pressed his point. Myrdal wrote to Charles Dollard, former head of the Carnegie Corporation, to see whether he might be able to develop funding for an update of Raper's work on *American Dilemma*. Myrdal had always felt Raper's analysis of the way blacks were treated by the southern police and court system was a highlight of the book, especially in the way Raper had set official discrimination in its wider economic and social setting.

"When we now met again it was natural that I came back to my old idea," Myrdal wrote Dollard, "and I was very happy to find Arthur responsive." Raper was ready to take a year off and write a new book on the dynamics of southern race relations. The corporation was not interested, though, reflecting perhaps the distance philanthropy had traveled between the late 1930s and the mid-1950s in terms of liberal faith in broad-based and activist social science research. To Raper, it seemed the moment had passed when an organization of white liberals could mount an extensive project on race in America. From sociological studies, race had moved to the courts and the schools, to bus stations and lunch counters and picket lines. Social science studies were no longer in a position to use the mass media to broadcast knowledge to aid conciliation. By the mid-1950s, everyone knew what the American dilemma was. But now, there was little faith that liberal sociology could tell the country how to fix it.[66]

Even into the late 1960s, though, Raper himself had lost none of his own belief that social science could ally with government to fashion a reasonable society. In 1968, he wrote a new preface for a reprint edition of *The Tragedy of Lynching*. "Racial exploitation in many other forms continues to plague us. May not the overall situation improve as one segment after another of the problem is delineated, fully researched, and programmed for corrective action by appropriate leaders?"[67] Throughout the decade, he took aim at the rapidly moving target of race.

In 1966, he taught a seminar at MSU called "Current Status of Race Relations." As usual, he was excited by the dynamism of the situation. "Goodness knows what comes next," he wrote at the time, "and when and how this new surge towards freedom and participation will end. Before things settle down into some sort of new system, I think the more stable elements of the white and Negro groups in numerous communities will have worked together closer than they had ever thought they would need to, just to keep the lid on the volatile urban slum-backgrounded young groups."[68] He thought the future would consider Lyndon Johnson the prime mover of change in American race relations. A year before Martin Luther King Jr. was killed, Raper predicted he would soon galvanize the inner city.

Raper had spent a lifetime studying the people of the countryside, all the while seeing America's center of gravity shifting to the city. In Greene County's exodus of the 1920s, he had foreseen the hemorrhaging ghettos. In the mid-1960s, he was predicting the most vital leaders of the 1980s and 1990s would come out of the inner cities. Raper believed, all through the violence of the civil rights and antiwar movements, that the children of the ghetto would become agents of positive change, because they had the most to gain by the hard work it would take to accomplish.[69]

Raper was not by temperament a man-the-barricades radical, but his rationalist's conception of societal dynamics left a lot of room for political extremism. Just as he had felt that Communists in the 1930s had formed a useful counterweight to right-wing elements, he saw the need for civil disobedience in the face of southern reaction. When the mavericks, as he called them, set the outer limits of the discourse, then more conventional people gained greater latitude to push for change. "That's where the real thing is," he said. "That's where the institutions are. And that process can be increased and made more effective if we've got these outer limits." Still, while he "ain't agin' 'em," he did not march for civil rights. Maybe if he had been younger, but then again, maybe not. He sent money to King and to the freedom riders, but he never joined a sit-in. He never criticized the movement, but he was not part of it. "I guess the basic philosophy here is, let's see what the truth is—what the possibilities are—and then let's see how to tell the truth in an acceptable manner. You can tell it in a way that you cut yourself off from having any chance of having any influence. That's where the big show is. That's where the human race show is." Through the civil rights movement, Raper proved himself no Romantic revolutionary. He again showed himself as a modernist heir to the Enlightenment, who supported the militants, but whose faith in change focused on the center.[70] He saw evidence in the late 1960s that "in this drop-out group, there is an abundance of life. But who can speak for it, much less guide it?" He was somewhat puzzled by such violent change occurring without plan.[71]

Militancy did not fit Raper's style or his approach to work. The New Left and the civil rights movement appealed to his sense of justice, but the volume hurt his ears. He could not help but be wary of a decade that moved so fast its details had become a blur. When his son Harrison sent him a copy of *The Autobiography of Malcolm X,* Raper's response was characteristic. "Somehow it gets at the larger truths," he wrote, "while quite clearly careless with some of the smaller ones." He recognized the *Autobiography* as a valuable document. But he could not find in it the kind of detailed and broad-based cultural analyses he himself had honed. Social science had retreated to the campus, while the political underground had gone mainstream. And besides, the times themselves were a bit too emotionally tangled for him.

Raper was warm and personable, but at a certain distance, and he always shrank from emoting. He had been uncomfortable, for instance, when Lillian Smith, back in the 1930s, had cried on his shoulder. "All my life I've more or less fended people from throwing their personal problems at me," he said, sitting in his living room at Slope Oaks. "Martha tells me I'm heartless. I think we need some psychiatrists, and psychoanalysts, and counselors, and what not. I just don't want to be one. I have helped some people. Some people have helped me. I can do it, and I do it if I need to. But I don't take any satisfaction." His lack of militancy on race was not a measure of changing views. He never changed his mind on race. Theatrical, dramatic, and impulsive, filled with actors who played to the back row, the times themselves moved Raper to the sidelines. By the late 1960s, he found himself not an opponent of change, but somehow out of his element.[72]

12

BACK TO THE LAND

> "No ideas but in things."
> WILLIAM CARLOS WILLIAMS

Once he had finished the Comilla book, after five years in Pakistan and East Lansing, Arthur and Martha finally returned to Slope Oaks in June 1967. This time the move was permanent and undertaken with Edenic intent—to fish, garden, and pitch a little hay to a few animals. Raper looked ahead to "piddling about," as he said, "writing on episodic matters as the occasion arose." But it was a different America they were resettling themselves into during the Summer of Love. One day, just a few weeks home, Raper found himself thanking a band of hippies living in an old farmhouse up the road who had, with anarchic joy, helped him corral a steer that had broken through his fence.[1]

Through the early 1960s, the Rapers had rented out Slope Oaks to a succession of tenants, none of whom had been interested in pursuing agriculture or husbandry in what was becoming a Beltway suburb. Arthur and Martha turned up the long, curving drive toward their old home and into a chaos of honeysuckle vines and poison ivy, poke berries, and briars. The fields were long-unmowed, the fence rows down, the garden obliterated. The elderly house had grown shabby. With Martha's back too bad for her to help Arthur, it took him a year to revive the farm.

He had seen a doctor about a skip in his heartbeat when they first returned from Comilla. After getting the farm back in shape, though, he was "pleasantly surprised that it did me good to work hard." The skip was gone, and he felt fit as a fiddle. "Now the place is in about the best shape it's ever been in," he boasted afterward, "and I like to keep it that way."[2]

By then, he was finding himself occasionally called to account by curious family and liberal friends about the nature of his work with the State Department. Raper always insisted that he had been busy overseas only with community development, glad for the chance to do something constructive in government service. He certainly saw the dimensions of the vast military assistance programs in Taiwan, in the Philippines and Southeast Asia, and in Iran and other Near East and North Africa countries. He was in Iran when the shah's American-run police training program was launched; the chief was a neighbor in Baghdad. But he did his best to work independently. "I had my own work," he claimed, "cherished the opportunity to do it, and hoped to do it so well that that part of the program would be continued and expanded." In terms of garnering official support for democratization, though, Raper had been forced to fight for every gain.[3] Often, for example, he would help develop basic programs in agriculture and public health, then national leaders would begin to feel threatened enough to force cutbacks. Sometimes, he had found he could help out programs for a time mostly by working on a limited, local basis. "When I look back," concluded the old, New Deal rationalist, from the other side of the 1960s, "I find I have nearly always worked at matters that were but barely tolerated." Such toleration was practiced not only by the Third World nations themselves, but by the State Department as well, perhaps as window dressing it could point to as principled work.[4]

The summer Jimi Hendrix set the Star Spangled Banner on fire, Raper sat in the cool shade of Slope Oaks and ventured that the counterculture was simply trying, with pharmacology and new media, the same things younger generations had always done.[5] He was not convinced the world was changing so fundamentally or drastically. "And who knows," he foresaw, "but that even the Hippies of today will nearly all become stable, middle class parents of tomorrow? It's an age-old pattern for the elderly to be sure the younger generation is headed for the ditch—and a small percentage of the 'farthest out' youth in every generation has destroyed themselves in their determination to find fulfillment." Maybe the youth of the 1960s would incur more casualties than most generations. "Perhaps, logically, a larger price will be paid for whatever new dimensions of body, mind, and soul that the present crop of youngsters are achieving," but, he demurred, "stress and strain, even the trauma experienced, may jolly well prepare them for a more imaginative and productive maturity than would otherwise have been possible."[6] Crisis is action oriented, he believed.

Raper stood up in church and told his dismayed, fellow parishioners in the days of race riots and war protests that crisis was fuel for necessary change.

"It was when the world wasn't in crisis that mankind thought it could accommodate itself to slavery, to racial superiority, to the caste system, to inequality between the sexes, to disfranchisement, to the theory of the divine right of kings." In Raper's mind, crisis was accountable to good, old-fashioned American pragmatism. "Shrink not from controversy, but rather study the situation, decide what you think is right, take your stand and hold it," he preached, "that is, so long as it seems the best course, but always know as you learn more you may modify your position. Yes, there's room for compromise, for accepting the rule of the majority, for the minority always has the challenge to make itself the majority at the next testing time! And a next testing time always lies ahead!" Crisis was the stuff of life. Be glad for it, he told his fellow church members. Be ready for it, and move ahead.[7]

Like his own patron saint, Thomas Jefferson, Raper never lost his taste for social change, even in the moment of bloodshed and upheaval. In fact, he entered retirement feeling a certain kinship with the disaffected youth. The way he saw it, his work with the Interracial Commission, the cultural studies he conducted under Carl Taylor, the Comilla Project, were all countercultural. "All my life," he said, "I've been working at non-establishment things." He had not been defensive about it in his own youth. He was not about to change his tune now, just because the music had gone electric.[8]

"I Like to Live at Slope Oaks"

Raper found it fitting to finish his life's work on what he called an "intensive mini-farm operation." He had seen his whole career as oscillating between close, detailed work in small locales and summary work in large regions, moving between sample, micro-projects and extensive application of the findings from those projects. Now, he could concentrate on close study of nature around him while continuing to think about the larger questions of politics and environment and race, although from a greater distance, through the *Washington Post*, the news magazines, and television.[9]

Arthur and Martha had chosen the farm in Oakton, back in the late 1940s, largely because of its abundant water, and much of the work they did in the early years involved turning it to account for irrigation and, just as important, for swimming and fishing. Over the years, they and the boys had terraced the hillsides, lined the road to the house with dogwoods, and built sheds for the tractor and the cows.[10] By the late 1960s, they had achieved a fine balance among their crops. And Arthur spent his days working within that balance.

"I feel successful," he explained, "when I can arrange things so that if it rains when the hay is down, there is some compensatory gain, like the corn or beans coming up to a better stand." By planning for the variations in weather and season, he modulated his work, while keeping an even course through the year. If he needed to mow the lawn more through a wet spring, then he would not have to worry about irrigating the fields, and he knew his dozen steers would be gaining weight faster. Everything was a trade-off. If it was so dry that he needed to hook up the pump for water for the steers, well, then he could mow and rake the fields more easily than when the soil was softer. He did not use pesticides or commercial fertilizer.[11]

Arthur grew his white hair long, like Walt Whitman, and he grew a full beard, part southern gentleman, part aging radical. He made it a matter of principle to mix hard work with pleasure. When he and Martha, and maybe a couple of kids, went for a swim on a hot summer day, he always made certain to carry down to the pond a couple of pails, so he could water the garden on the way back to the house. The equipoise he achieved at Slope Oaks not only increased his crop yields. He could feel the balance of nature itself in his sinews and under his fingernails. As he had back home in Arcadia, he was working within that balance. "All during the summer, late spring and early fall," he wrote, "there is scarcely an hour that I do not estimate the up-coming weather. So many things to wonder about. If it rains tomorrow, we'll not need to water the azaleas and fruit trees we planted this spring. If it does not, we will." And all year round, Slope Oaks at close range offered an array of small beginnings and transitions, countless manifestations of dynamism.[12]

Slope Oaks was the regionalist's dream in miniature, offering the integration of self and place that Brook Farm had sought a hundred years earlier and the hippies down the road were still aiming for. For Raper and the regionalists, and the transcendentalists before them, the farm was an open book, rooted in reality and conceived imaginatively, a lesson plan for the attentive learner. Neighbors liked to say their children loved to visit the Rapers because, every time, they came home having learned something new and interesting.[13]

Over the next few years, Martha and Arthur settled themselves in to Slope Oaks like the snow that drifted snugly around the farmhouse in the winter of 1973. "It's now nearly Christmas," Arthur wrote to his family, "and we are nearly snowed in, but so far we have had electricity and oil and firewood; and there's plenty of hay in the barn to throw to the horse and steers; and places for our dog and cats to keep warm." Both were in their seventies, but he still felt ashamed to admit he needed the neighbor boys to shovel the paths and pitch enough firewood up on to the porch to keep the stove hot, to push the old couple's car up the last bend in the drive, where the solid shadow of the barn left patchy, stubborn ice. He spent more of his time noting the dates the winter birds returned, and watching how the geese flew in from the northeast and turned a dogleg left, before fading away to the south in a scramble of furious honking.[14]

In *Tenants of the Almighty*, Raper had included appendices that presented a mélange of data for Greene County. Statistical charts sat across the page from recipes for wedding cakes, though, and tall tales of Civil War valor and tragic melodrama complemented columns of figures on farm wages and tenancy rates. In all his best work, as in the best documentary work of the 1930s, facts merged with imagination. The "human document" was what many like-minded modernists had called realism during the Depression, but it had not sprung out of thin air. One day at Slope Oaks, Raper sat at his desk and copied a page of Whitman.

> When I heard the learn'd astronomer,
> When the proofs, the figures, were ranged in columns before me,
> When I was shown the charts and diagrams, to add, divide, and measure them,
> When I sitting heard the astronomer where he lectured with much applause in the lecture-room,
> How soon unaccountable I became tired and sick,
> Till rising and gliding out I wander'd off by myself,
> In the mystical moist night-air, and from time to time,
> Look'd up in perfect silence at the stars.

Raper was himself a "learn'd astronomer," but long before their last years at Slope Oaks, his view of life was equally informed by wandering in the mystical night-air, and from time to time, looking up in perfect silence at the stars.

Raper himself picked up writing verse, and wrote a number of pastorals about Slope Oaks that relied on a litany of specific names to conjure the abundance of nature. Back in the 1930s, he could not pursue the gathering of sociological data without investing the process with emotion and imagination. Now, in his retirement, he turned the tables. He could not pursue poetry without the hard fact of the physical world. "No ideas but in things" was the dictum of his contemporary, William Carlos Williams, another modern realist who looked at the world clearly, while conceiving of it imaginatively. To celebrate the feel of the world around them, he began his last writing project, a little paean, "I Like to Live at Slope Oaks," a booklet of writings and sketches about the farm, a journal of rough-hewn, agrarian pleasures. Like Williams's, Raper's tone is objective. He wrote field notes as odes. He had spent his whole life naming the world and by doing so, reconceiving it for himself and his fellows.

> The trees are here, all about us, and
> The shrubs, vines, berries, and vegetables.
> Here, too, are the animals, large and small, and
> Birds of many sizes, colors, and songs.
> The free-flowing springs, the pond, and
> The creek down front; and out
> From the house on all sides
> Open fields, hills and hollows.
> And in and through it all, the seasons—
> Rain and snow, wind and sunshine,
> Nights when the stars twinkle, and
> Nights when "the lightning walks about."[15]

Near the end of his life, in another poem, Raper finally defined his religious belief. He could understand the need for faith in the face of an unconcerned universe. But faith ran against the foundation of his rationalism.

> As it seems to me—
> there can hardly be any logic
> in a special dispensation creation.
> Yes, hard as it is for me to think
> of a Universe without
> time and space perimeters,
> It's harder yet for me to think
> of one with them.

Intellectual honesty compelled him to acknowledge and maybe celebrate the frightening unhumanity of the universe, which served to throw him back on helping his fellows, rather than fashion a spiritual comfort. Besides, after his teenage crisis of faith, Raper was never much interested in questions of metaphysical intention. He had always been impatient with questions built on speculation or foregone answers.[16]

He began to sever his professional ties, giving up his seat, for example, on the board of the National Sharecroppers Union. But he and Martha joined the local Methodist church, although they found themselves "not always saying fully all we think," he admitted, "for such it seems is the price of harmonious relations." Raper was still always ready to travel. He took his last trip to Chapel Hill in 1971, where he was treated as a venerable personage, like some New Deal relic. He teamed up with H. L. Mitchell to talk to the history honor society about union organizing in the Depression. He spoke to a seminar, whose members found it hard to believe he had grown up with enlightened racial views. Raper welcomed various "degree-getting researchers, who stop by now and again to look through some of my files and talk with me, often tape recorded, [with] the transcriptions usually coming back to me for my files."

He was interviewed by doctoral students, among them Jacqueline Dowd Hall, who would in years to come lead another generation of Chapel Hill progressives, in her research on his old nemesis, Jessie Daniel Ames. To Hall, Raper exuded integrity.[17] Daniel Singal remembers Raper's graciousness. "He is certainly one of the most admirable human beings I ever met." Raper had a singular ability, Singal observed, to live in the present in spite of the accomplishments and intensity of his long career. "Arthur had an immense feeling of satisfaction about how he had lived his life. He knew that he had done the world a great deal of good and thus did not need to dwell on it."[18]

Raper's old friend, FSA photographer Jack Delano, was shocked to be rediscovered in the 1970s as a piece of Americana, and he was skittish about the publicity. Raper, though, was always ready to talk about his work with the Interracial Commission and the New Deal, because he knew modernist liberalism was still so obviously useful. Raper was always happy for a chance to extend the lessons of the New Deal into the Nixon, Ford, then Carter years. In fact, he expected the attention of history.

The impulse of Depression America to document itself, to show the future of life at the dawn of the modern age, reached its apogee in Raper. For years, he worked assiduously on his files—boxes and boxes of all sorts of materials compiled with the same scrupulous intent he had used in all his sociological studies. The personal element in the files—drawings and sketches of the Punch Dolvin plantation and Slope Oaks, college diaries and love letters to Martha, tape recordings of family reunions and photographs of Dorothea Lange talking with farm folk—serves to round out the history of the times, to add intimacy and emotional resonance to copious factual information. He created a documentary of the southerner as a New Deal liberal. Knowing how unusual his career had been, he proved, through accurate documentation and intimate detail, the existence of white southerners at the cutting edge of modern political theory, while also working on the ground for social and racial justice. When historian Walter Jackson traveled from Harvard to Slope Oaks and became incredulous that Raper had learned racial equality in the cradle, Raper could open his files. He could look it up.

He arranged to donate his papers to University of North Carolina's Southern Historical Collection, and then spent his last years at Slope Oaks currying his files as though grooming them, which indeed he was. He would inscribe messages in the margins of long-ago, cryptic letters to decode their intentions to the future. True to the goal of 1930s documentary, Raper's files are filled with hard facts and vivid, intimate detail.

During the last years at Slope Oaks, through the late 1970s, he filled the files with reminiscences and travel journals and, increasingly, clippings to document the interests of a New Deal philosopher in winter. He took up all the social and political topics of the time. Vietnam dismayed him, partly because its failure struck root. Vietnam was a New Dealer's nightmare. He said he came late to recognizing it as a mistake, because he had given the benefit of the doubt to those whom he saw as well-intentioned federal administrations each with access to the best and most comprehensive information and technology in the world. He followed Watergate, of course, and his dismay turned to anger with Nixon's pardon. "Mr. President," he wanted to ask Gerald Ford, "does it not now strike you as ineptness on your part that up to a few days before former President Nixon resigned you thought him innocent of any crime?" And more to the point, he wanted to know, "Is it not self-serving on your part to claim the correctness of your pardon of your predecessor on the grounds that resigning the Presidency 'in shame and disgrace' rightfully relieves him of the due process of the law?" Raper could not condone in any way leniency for Nixon's breach of public trust.[19]

The roots of Watergate lay, he felt, in a disparity of wealth among citizens that inculcated a hierarchical pattern of thinking. Big, hierarchical organizations—whether corporate, governmental, educational, or religious—were directed from the top down, their orders carried out by officials below. That is how bureaucrats survive and prosper, he concluded. As long as the management at the top is resourceful and vital, everything works. Otherwise, obedience becomes essential, and democracy is in peril. Ordinary people become the instruments of their superiors. They become susceptible to following orders they would otherwise find objectionable. They feel responsible to authority, but not to the consequences of the actions the authority dictated.

Raper had seen the way it worked during the Cold War. And he still saw it now, in microcosm, through the top-down organization of his own church, Oakton United Methodist. The fellowship, in a "Crusade for Progress" development drive, was being maneuvered and directed by a visiting church-affiliate expert, one who knew enough to identify his plan for church advancement with God's own work and who saw in any counter-ideas a hint of blasphemy. The result was a lack of input from individuals acting on their own initiative. The effort made enough money, Raper granted, but "what will be the larger and deeper results may not be so clear." Through all the Slope Oaks years, Raper remained as skeptical of religious hypocrisy as he had been when white preachers had blocked his work for the Interracial Commission. In 1974, he watched a big, new, all-white, Mormon Temple rise in Maryland. "A Temple of Opulence or Affluence," he would call it, driving by.[20]

He picked up the *Post* one morning in the winter of 1971 and stopped at the headline, "Sharecroppers Are Almost Gone From Miss. Cotton Farms." Yes, he thought, but, just as during the Depression, many people are still sharecroppers, in the cities and towns of America, north, south, east, and west.[21]

A few years later, the farm life he had known was being called "organic." He wrote the *Washington Post* to advocate for it as a practical alternative to commercial methods with their chemical fertilizers. Organic farming was the way to reinvest the small farmer in a healthful approach to agriculture.[22] At the same time, he could not help but see the current practice as having become a bit precious. He looked at an ad for a training center in organicism that promised, "We're really punching holes in the big corporations," then scrawled across the top, "Somehow or another, there's too little humility here!" He practiced organicism himself, but shied away from separating it out from traditional farming, as though reluctant to admit it was just a niche interest now, taken up by farmers on a different track from the rest of agriculture.[23]

"Complicated business, isn't it?"

"Complicated business, isn't it?" he wrote to his brothers and sisters about the disappointments of liberalism and the political issues of the 1970s. "And so is life complicated business. And we've each got to do with it the best we can." The one truth he wanted to hold on to was this belief. "In proportion as we deal fairly with ourselves and everybody else, we'll feel better, fear other people less, and have more hope for the future." Hopefulness still made him feel better about life, and he still kept faith that answers could be found to continuing problems. "No, let us not shy away from realities of life's complexities, but rather understand and appreciate them." And hard work still made him feel better, too. "Remember," he reminded himself, "food always tastes better after having done some real work and perspired a bit. If you find Christmas dinner a little uninteresting because you've stood around too much, eating nuts and candy; I'll tell you what to do—go out and rake leaves from eleven to one o'clock and then come in and, wash up, and sit down to a banquet!" When he looked at the progress of democracy over his lifetime, though, Raper felt double-crossed by the complexities of technology.[24]

He had been wrong in believing mechanization would bolster the family farm. Before the war, he reflected, it had seemed as though technology would answer many of the questions of social inequality as well as lagging production. And he foresaw America making its technology available to the world. He had been wary about opening Pandora's Box, but traditional farming left too many limits on social change. By the mid-1970s, however, he felt let down. "How far from adequate in our estimates we were," he acknowledged, "is now being proclaimed on TV, radio, and in our morning papers."[25] American invention was nearly miraculous, Raper always believed. But now, the consequences of that invention were pushing themselves past technology's intentions. The amounts of energy needed, the waste, the pollution fouling the soil, air, and water, and the tension and noise. Now, he was skeptical about the big philanthropic organizations and even the federal government seriously tackling anything as critical as auto pollution. He saw such organizations now as protecting big-oil interests. "To some considerable extent, our know-how experts have often performed as lackeys of big business and big government." Look at "agribusiness and the industrial-military-communication-energy complex. Look, too, at who it is that employs our ranking consulting and lobbying firms, to say nothing of our highest paid lawyers, PR experts, and think tankers." Even higher education was now integral to the push toward profits over stewardship, too, through the funding and direction of big business and government. "Our great institutions of learning have not been so much bought off," he argued, "as just plain used."[26]

Not only Americans, but people around the world had begun "to wonder if our know-how experts really knew what they were doing." Where was there a serious and committed Commission on Interracial Commission to agitate for fair housing practices? Or a Birmingham Conference on healthy foods or clean air? Or New Deal–type initiatives for developing alternative energy? Raper's faith in government and philanthropic action had soured.[27] He had always looked back on his childhood in Arcadia, glad for his father's insistence that his children get out and get ahead. At the end of his own life, though, in the middle of the energy crisis of the 1970s, Arthur had begun to wonder whether, in view of the ecological problems coming into focus, his mother would still have agreed to abandon her dream of Moravian communitarianism and the husbandry of their family farm.[28]

Science itself had helped spoil the land and exacerbate inequality. And yet, in spite of everything, science was also the only means of making things right. "I am still an optimist," Raper said, "but not an easy one."[29] He never despaired of his liberal sociologist's belief that actions have demonstrable causes, however difficult they may be to uncover. "Why do most of us most of the time drive above the speed limit, and ride singly to and from work?" he mused. "Why are assembly-line workers getting teed-off with their jobs? Why do people shop-lift? There are causes for all these things that can be found out, and then programs for their correction can be developed. It will be cheaper to do these things than not to do them." The difficulties lay not with technology per se, but with the masters of science who had dictated the preeminence of the profit motive.[30]

Martha retained her own liberal fire. She was already sick of the backlash against big government that followed the end of the Great Society. "I am tired of reading articles," she wrote to the *Washington Post* in 1974, "about government funded research grants that are described as ludicrous by the writer." Such complaints provided "good reading, but not very good thinking." What was so wrong with spending $70,000 to study the body odor of Australian aborigines, when we were spending $9 billion on cosmetics, perfumes, and deodorants? Who did that money help? Only manufacturers and advertisers "who work so hard to make consumers' self-esteem more and more fragile and more and more susceptible to useless 'needs.'" An inquisitive rationalist herself, Martha "would be glad to know why some people who don't bathe at all, because they don't have any water at all, still don't smell bad at all. How come?" People were not using their imaginations to consider the possibilities of scientific knowledge. They were simply too angry about paying taxes to think. "If you can get mad enough, you don't need to think at all. Great relief, but poor solution.

"Well, two can play the get-mad game," scolded Martha. "I'm mad, too.

"I'm mad about my *non*-tax money. How much energy and raw materials go into making, packaging, and shipping 'food' items that are not worth eating, but dressed up in dyes and flavorings so they'll look good and taste good, and who cares whether they give people heart attacks and cancer?" She was angry that her non-tax money funded sweetheart deals for corporations and payoffs to government officials for business favors. "We are paying for all of that every time we buy something." Her point was, "The more they can get us to blame the government, the bureaucrats, the Congress, each other, the poor, anybody at all, the less apt we are to see what is really going on."[31] Martha expressed her skepticism about corporate America and modern society in everything from letters to verse. "Instant coffee, instant tea; / Instant ease and luxury. / When the piper is to pay / Charge it to another day." And that other day would be made more difficult by the lack of faith in government to solve social problems inculcated by the anti-tax tide rising around her in the 1970s.[32]

Through much of their retirement, the only time Martha's back did not hurt was when she was standing. Still, she helped Arthur polish the Comilla manuscript, while she kept up her own reading and letter writing. But her health kept the couple tethered to the farm. Arthur continued to hope medical science would find help. In spite of her back, Martha spent a lot of time attending meetings of Methodist Women's groups and the League of Women Voters. She ran errands for a family of farm folk from the Virginia hill country who had moved in up the road. And physical therapy was a constant. Margaret and the boys, and their spouses and children, came and went for holidays and summers, but Charles's own family was now in Macon, Georgia, and Jarrell, a cardiologist, was living in Pennsylvania, across the Haverford College campus from Harrison, who had grown up to become a conductor and composer. A Taiwanese boy they had befriended in the early 1950s stayed with the couple at Slope Oaks off and on, through the early 1970s, helping out with the chores. Same with a young African student who lived with the Rapers and worked in the fields with Arthur. One winter day, Arthur wrote a typical invitation to a friend. "We've got snow here now, about nine inches, and more forecast," he began. "Truth is, I like cold weather, but not too much of it. We've got plenty of good oak firewood, close to the house, for we had to cut down one of our biggest trees. The one tree yielded more than seven cords of firewood—yes, we've got plenty, so come and we'll sit by the fire and talk as long as you like."[33]

In a terse hand, Raper started a journal entry, "May 9, 1970. And then it happened—The Cub tractor turned over on me at 5:12 P.M. I was taken to the Emergency Rooms at Fairfax Hospital, and later in the evening to George Washington University Hospital, where I stayed until June 27, when I came back to Slope Oaks." He had possessed extraordinary health and tremendous energy throughout his life, through some exorbitant work schedules and all the prodigious rigors of near-constant travel through the whole of the South, and across the United States and much of the Third World. Now, in the succor and quiet of Slope Oaks, he began to fear his decline. He had made it a point of pride to manage the farm machinery as well as he had the livestock and crops themselves. The tractor accident was a portent of age. It announced the start of the war he knew he must lose.[34]

He was guiding the Cub along the side of a ditch when it pitched over and threw him down in the ditch before rolling in after him. Enough weight fell on him to break his pelvis in four places, most seriously near the ball-and-socket point in his right leg. After many X rays and consultations, the doctors decided not to operate, but to let the bones slowly heal back together. He ended up in traction, flat on his back, for six weeks.

"He is in pain, of course," Martha observed, "but will not complain. When people ask how he is, he says he is mending slowly. Neighbors and friends and the children have been wonderful." Harrison and Jarrell drove in the very next day and shuttled back and forth to help.[35] The lack of mobility severely tested his patience. Martha sent notice to Ahkter Hameed Khan, who would have known well what she meant by writing that "it means a lot to him to help, at least verbally, in keeping the place going. He enjoys the visits from the grandchildren at the hospital, and shows them how he can work the gadgetry that keeps his leg in place." He felt somewhat better when he was able to manage the care of the farm through instructions to the boys on how to keep the fields mowed and maintained. He came home "double-crutched," as he said, gradually moved to a single crutch, then a cane, which he continued to use, off and on. As soon as he could get on his feet, he had Charles rig him a seat and a hand-hold so he could climb back up on the Cub. "Yes," Martha wrote to the children, resignedly, "the same tractor that fell over on him."[36]

Charles called Arthur's seat the "Director's Module." Before long, he had talked some of the neighborhood teens into working with him again. He pushed against his age the only way he knew. He bought a few more steers. And "after a year or so," he proudly claimed, "things were again getting back to normal." The antidote for old age, as for everything else, was work. Work carried Arthur and Martha both, year after year, through the quiet of Slope Oaks, through an increasingly distant America.[37]

"Odd-man-out"

When the Smithsonian organized an exhibit on the Great Migration in the late 1970s, they called Raper to come and consult. George McDonald, a historian from Duke, was supervising the furnishing of a "Sharecropper House," which had been moved to the site from Bowie, Maryland, to show the younger generation the southern roots of urban blacks. Raper showed up at the museum with a copy of *Preface to Peasantry* in his old briefcase and an Interracial Commission pamphlet, "The South's Landless Farmers," to offer some concrete data on the construction and furnishings of farm dwellings by tenure and race. He took one look at the house and was disappointed. It was "way above" the typical tenant shack, he thought, especially so for the lower South.

Raper had arrived at lunchtime, when the museum was nearly empty and those few stragglers ambled through the halls with little interest in anything. McDonald was nowhere to be found, and the neighbors Raper had planned to meet had not yet arrived. He was left to stand alone at the ersatz tenant house, his own thoughts bouncing around the air-conditioned silence like flies following the handful of bored tourists. "I felt like the odd-man-out, or the fifth wheel, or something else out of place." He had looked ahead to the day as a new experience, maybe a new perspective on his life's work. He ended up, when McDonald finally arrived, pulling out some old photographs and commandeering the passersby like a circus barker talking the rubes into his sideshow.

He went home and typed McDonald a seven-page, single-spaced epistolary report, recommending what he very well knew a "typical lower South sharecropper house of the 1925–35 period" to be. He drew the connection between sharecroppers and urban slums, just as he had with Ida Woolfolk, working for Will Alexander in the 1920s. He went on to characterize the typical sharecropper by landholdings, diet, medical services, transportation, and treatment by courts and police, drawing on data he had analyzed for New Deal agencies and Gunnar Myrdal. And, as always, his depiction of rural southern society was documentary and dynamic.

In spite of "The Law," despite bloodhounds and chain gangs, black farmers had wrought creativity from oppression. "There were in the croppers' houses the fiddle, the banjo, the guitar, and human voices that could sing halleluiah to make you want to shout, a lullaby to put you to sleep, and blues so mournful you didn't know how to cry aright!" Here had been a chance to create a three-dimensional documentary in the world's most visited museum, and Raper found himself strangely unable to take a hand.[38]

He brandished the photos at tourists and demanded to know whether they would like to live in a house like this? "But that was at best," he adduced with restraint, "a strained and highly tenuous relationship, almost a confrontation." Through his whole life, Raper had never used confrontation as a form of education. Education was ennobling, partly because it pushed toward greater perception of reality. But now, Raper felt that, not only the Smithsonian but the whole of the century, was pushing away from the vivid reality of his life's work. No matter how hard Raper might try to change the exhibit, what he saw as the past could not be re-created. Documentary meant immediacy, not retrospection. Time itself had ruined any chance of getting at the truth of the thing.[39]

Not until both were well into their seventies did Arthur and Martha face up to their age and began to close the circle. In 1978, Arthur finally sold their old horse, Apache, and the last couple of steers. When he watched them being driven down the long drive, he thought for sure he would go back in the house and have himself a cry. But he tried to look at it realistically. He knew he could no longer expect to safely care for them. "Oh, yes, I could have continued to throw some hay to them, and put feed in their feed boxes," he wrote himself. "But I wasn't up to anything beyond these bare routines, and I learned long since that one can never fully anticipate what may happen with anything that is alive." He came back in the house and sat down for a minute or two, sad but dry-eyed. "There are some things that can't be changed: your age, parents, where you were born, your sex, color of your hair, and eyes, etc., and these things that can't be changed are best accommodated to. That's the reason, I guess, I didn't cry when the animals were sent away." The boys had prevailed upon their father to keep the young Apache, way back in the early 1950s, when he first bought the Cub tractor, because of the horse's superior traction, as they explained to him. The sale of Apache made it clear now that, as with everything else, Raper needed to accommodate himself to that most complete of all changes, his own mortality.[40]

"Left in their usual good order"

Soon after, in the middle of a bright, early spring day in 1978, Arthur found himself looking up at the sun through the still-leafless trees and wondering whom the siren was for. A rescue car wailed up the long drive, followed by an ambulance, a fire engine, and another emergency truck. "Where's the patient?" he managed to ask, as he rose to his feet. Starting to clamber on his own into the rescue car, before the crew jumped to help him, Arthur was whisked to the hospital.[41]

He had woken from a noon nap with a steady pain in the center of his chest, shooting up his neck and ringing into his jaws and ears. For over a year now, he had known the drill. He placed a nitroglycerine tablet under his tongue and wait for relief. For the first time, though, the distress only worsened. After ten minutes, he took another tablet. Five more minutes, and he called to Martha for help. The first time he had been hospitalized for chest pains, in January 1977, they were told it had been a "near heart attack," and he had spent three weeks in Fairfax Hospital. Now, though, it was clear that his heart was giving way.[42]

He came home to Slope Oaks determined against slowing down, resolute against invalidism, and his body, which had served him so well through seven decades, agreed to this last demand. He spent his last year on the farm, caring for the garden, entertaining friends and an ever-growing family, still giving interviews, telling old stories, looking out on the Carter years. "This is indeed a wonderful time in which to live," he wrote at Christmas 1978, "and too bad that we oldsters can't stay around long enough to see what happens." The next summer, on a Friday evening in August, he had just driven to Dulles to pick up a grand-daughter flying in from Scotland when he collapsed and suddenly died.[43]

A week later, Harrison sealed his father's files—his life's documentary, prepared for the people of the future—with his own testimony to his father's completeness, as though writing an ode to Arthur's impulse toward the organic. "His still-ample (though recently reduced) garden, fruit trees, large mowed area around the house, barns and out-buildings, tools, and the garden gate were left in their usual good order," Harrison dutifully noted. "The following pictures, taken by grandson John Raper, attest to this." Indeed, the lush fecundity of summer abounded in a set of snapshots that fit together to form a panoramic vision of pastoral cultivation. Harrison knew it was unnecessary to add a note on Arthur's papers. But his father's own scrupulous reporting required the son to testify, "His files were equally up-to-date."[44]

Of course Arthur had planned his funeral in advance, and while he left many of the decisions on music and psalms to the family, he wanted someone to read "Good Gardens," a passage from *Tenants of the Almighty*.[45] It was as though, written midway through his career—halfway along the path—Raper had already reprised his whole life.

> There is deep satisfaction in a good garden close to the house. On this patch of earth a farmer and his wife perform nobly. Here they stir the land most hopefully, for here they conserve and replenish the soil gladly. Here they deal justly with the Almighty, and here they reap abundantly.
>
> The young mother on the arm of her husband walks first to the garden. Here little feet first make tracks in loose soil. Here the child first sees seed planted, waits for the rows of new sprouts, sees the spaces between filled with other sprouts—learns that beans and beets have to be protected from weeds and grass. A farm child learns to keep the garden gate shut against the chickens and pigs long before he knows anything about war or politics.
>
> Year after year, the garden yields up its dishes for those who tend it. Then one afternoon an old man, too feeble to reach the fields or even the barn, hobbles out of the garden and closes the gate behind him. In a few days the neighbors gather, their faces sad, their voices low. The old man's last tracks are in the garden.
>
> That garden could have been across the road, or on the other side of the house. The real meaning of a good garden anywhere is that we could make gardens almost everywhere.[46]

Just a few months later, right before Christmas, Martha had a massive stroke while she slept and slipped into a coma, then died three days later. Margaret, Harrison, and Jarrell were with her. The same day, a letter from Newport News arrived in the mail for Arthur. The graceful handwriting began with an introduction and admission of a revelation.

> As a student, my name was Elsie West, and as product of comfortably complacent Virginia aristocracy, I entered college at sixteen with what is sometimes known as "tunnel vision." I now perceive you to have been decades ahead of the times, and am glad that you have lived to see a number of social changes that were then regarded as visionary.
>
> Because of your courageously unorthodox teachings, I finally broke out of the "mold," and learned to make my own considered judgments on matters of pride or principle, so that I could emerge as a mature adult.[47]

Elsie Duval had taken her sociology degree and followed a happy and successful career, thirty-five years in southern community services. "While there are still a few 'Rednecks' in my life, it is largely to your credit that I have been able to stand firm whenever I hold an unpopular view. Actually, it was not so much a matter of what you believed was right or wrong which impressed me in youth, but rather that you taught me, for the first time in my life, to THINK for myself." She had gone to Agnes Scott believing that lynchings and chain gangs were like ghost stories invented to scare young white girls. "You made me believe the unbelievable," she wrote, still in amazement after all the years at the depth of her change. "We were invited to your home to sit around a campfire and discuss issues which we never talked about in our own homes." In her hometown near Atlanta, there had been no high school for blacks at all. Raper introduced her for the first time to college-educated African Americans. "In 1937," she wrote to Raper, "you had arranged for dialogue between our class and one at Atlanta University, and I was very angry when parents of other students protested so violently that the meeting was cancelled."[48]

Looking back across her long life, West was savoring her own amazement at her turn from privilege to commitment. She wrote page after page, searching for a way to describe what Raper had given her. Dynamic, she realized, finally. Dynamic was the approach he had given her to carry through work and life. Dynamic was the way she had seen the world ever since.[49]

NOTES

Introduction

1. Walter Lippmann, letter to Howard Odum, April 23, 1930, Southern Historical Collection (hereinafter SHC), Howard W. Odum files.

2. Robert Wiebe, *The Search for Order, 1877–1920* (Westport, Conn.: Greenwood Press, 1967).

3. John Steinbeck, *The Grapes of Wrath* (New York: Viking Press, 1939); Richard Wright, *Twelve Million Black Voices* (New York: Arno Press, 1969).

4. Frank Freidel, *F. D. R. and the South* (Baton Rouge: Louisiana State University Press, 1965), 66–67.

5. Carl Fleischhauer and Beverly Brannan, eds., *Documenting America, 1935–1943* (Berkeley: University of California Press, 1988), 28.

6. *New York Times Book Review,* May 14, 1933, 3.

7. In *Preface to Peasantry,* Raper was concerned with such issues as the discrepancies in expenditures between black and white schools, for example, and in blacks' treatment in the courts and by the police. But he blends a dispassionate tone and rigorous quantification of data with a curiosity about how people lived and the ways they experienced their lives. "Who owns the land?" he asks, in a series of questions that present the scope of *Preface to Peasantry.* "What is the annual income of farm families?" But then he goes on to ask, "Do Negroes and whites sit together around the stove at the Black Belt store? What are their pastimes?" To his sociology, Raper added anthropology.

8. Richard King writes that "Cash, along with Arthur Raper and Ira De A. Reid in *Sharecroppers All* (1941), attributed the South's problems to its intense individualism, growing out of the frontier experience, and saw the need to devise new political and social strategies now that the frontier had disappeared." Richard King, *A Southern Renaissance: The Cultural Awakening of the American South, 1930–1955* (New York: Oxford University Press. 1980), 153.

9. Robert Dorman, *Revolt of the Provinces: The Regionalist Movement in America, 1920–1945* (Chapel Hill: University of North Carolina Press, 1993), 267.

10. Dorman, *Revolt of the Provinces,* 267.

11. Virginius Dabney, *Liberalism in the South* (Chapel Hill: University of North Carolina Press. 1932), 422–423.

12. *Atlanta Constitution,* May 30, 1936.

13. Raper, "The Southern Conference for Human Welfare, First Meeting—Birmingham, Alabama, November 20–23, 1938," undated manuscript, SHC folder 947.

14. Singal contends that southern modernists "resolutely looked inside their own minds to find the dynamics of southern identity, and with equal resolution researched the subjective states of the people they were writing about." Raper, writes Singal, was "a summation of the Modernist cultural movement in the South of which he was a part." Daniel Singal, *The War Within: From Victorian to Modernist Thought in the South, 1919–1945* (Chapel Hill: University of North Carolina Press, 1982), 263, 338.

15. Caroline Ware, ed., *The Cultural Approach to History* (New York: Columbia University Press, 1940), 299.

16. Gunnar Myrdal, *An American Dilemma: The Negro Problem and Modern Democracy* (New York and Evanston: Harper & Row, 1962 [1944]).

17. Arthur Raper, *The Tragedy of Lynching* (Chapel Hill: University of North Carolina Press, 1969 [1933]), ii.

18. Raper, videotape interview conducted by Sue Thrasher, Peter Wood, and Larry Goodwyn, April 24–28, 1978, SHC 3966/2. John Egerton, *Speak Now Against the Day: The Generation Before the Civil Rights Movement in the South* (New York: Alfred A. Knopf, 1994); Patricia Sullivan, *Days of Hope: Race and Democracy in the New Deal Era* (Chapel Hill: University of North Carolina Press, 1996).

19. Historian John Egerton writes, "During a ten-year period beginning in 1933, at least a dozen volumes of illustrated regional interpretation appeared. Among them, in addition to the [Erskine] Caldwell and [James] Agee books, were Julia Peterkin's *Roll, Jordan, Roll*, a descriptive study (with Doris Ulmann's photographs) of black residents on some old South Carolina plantations; Clarence Cason's *90 Degrees in the Shade*, a native Alabamian's gentle but forthright call for social reform (photographs by James Edward Rice); H. C. Nixon's *Forty Acres and Steel Mules*, an ex-Agrarian's late-thirties acknowledgement of the necessity for modernization; Richard Wright's *12 Million Black Voices*, subtitled *A Folk History of the Negro*; and Arthur Raper's *Tenants of the Almighty*, another account of the plight of sharecroppers. The Nixon, Wright, and Raper books all featured Farm Security Administration photographs." Egerton, *Speak Now Against the Day*, 147.

20. Lillian Smith, letter to Raper, February 6, 1941, SHC folder 103.

Chapter 1. Progress in Arcadia

Epigraph is from Blanche Raper, "Poem by Blanche Raper," Raper family genealogical paper, privately published.

1. Jesse F. Steiner, ed., *The American Community in Action: Case Studies of American Communities* (New York: Henry Holt, 1928), 266.

2. Jack Raper, personal communication, August 14, 2002.

3. Raper, "On the Crest of Forming Waves," unpublished manuscript, May 1976, 252, SHC folder 548.

4. Raper, "On the Crest of Forming Waves," unpublished manuscript, May 1976, 252, SHC folder 548.

5. Adelaide L. Fries, *The Road to Salem* (Chapel Hill: University of North Carolina Press, 1944), v, vi; Daniel Singal, "Interview with Arthur Raper," January 18, 1971, SHC folder 363.

6. Singal, "Interview with Arthur Raper," SHC folder 363.

7. Jessie F. Steiner, ed., *The American Community in Action: Case Studies of American Communities* (New York: Henry Holt, 1928), 267.

8. Raper, "Arcadia," SHC folder 14.

9. Raper, "Arcadia," SHC folder 14.

10. In the early years of the century, during Raper's childhood, North Carolina adopted a number of Progressive measures, most notably involving railroad regulation. C. Vann Woodward, *Origins of the New South* (Baton Rouge: Louisiana State University Press, 1951), 380–381.

11. Raper, "Arcadia," SHC folder 14.

12. Steiner, ed., *The American Community in Action*, 265.

13. Steiner, ed., *The American Community in Action*, 270, 264.

14. Steiner, ed., *The American Community in Action*, 271–272, 275.

15. Steiner, ed., *The American Community in Action*, 277.

16. Raper, "Arcadia," SHC folder 14.

17. Luther E. Raper, "Daily Diary of Luther E. Raper," unpublished manuscript, September 27, 1914–December 31, 1917, SHC folder 1.

18. Raper, "Family letter, December 23, 1973," SHC folder 444.

19. Raper, "The Revival," unpublished manuscript, March 19, 1923, SHC folder 1.

20. Raper, "The Revival," unpublished manuscript, March 19, 1923, SHC folder 1.

21. Raper, "The Revival," unpublished manuscript, March 19, 1923, SHC folder 1.

22. Raper, "The Revival," unpublished manuscript, March 19, 1923, SHC folder 1.

23. Raper, "A Cruel Necessity," unpublished manuscript, dated "1913, '14, or '15," SHC folder 1.

24. Raper, "When we went back home," unpublished manuscript, October 18–November 6, 1973, SHC folder 438.

25. Singal, "Interview with Arthur Raper," 21, SHC folder 363.

26. Singal, "Interview with Arthur Raper," 36, SHC folder 363.

27. Jerome E. Brooks, *Green Leaf and Gold: Tobacco in North Carolina* (Raleigh: Division of Archives and History, North Carolina Department of Cultural Resources, 1997); Raper, "Statement at Howard's Retirement Party," speech delivered January 27, 1973, SHC folder 420.

28. Raper, "Statement at Howard's Retirement Party," SHC folder 420.

29. Raper, "Statement at Howard's Retirement Party," SHC folder 420.

30. Singal, "Interview with Arthur Raper," 12–13, SHC folder 363.

31. Raper, "On the Crest of Forming Waves," unpublished manuscript, May 1976, 252b, SHC folder 548.

32. Singal, "Interview with Arthur Raper," 12–13, SHC folder 363.

33. Raper, "Statement at Howard's Retirement Party," SHC folder 420.

34. Singal, "Interview with Arthur Raper," 14, SHC folder 363.

35. Singal, "Interview with Arthur Raper," 14, SHC folder 363.

36. Raper, "When we went back home," October 18–November 6, 1973, SHC folder 438.

37. Singal, "Interview with Arthur Raper," 36, SHC folder 363. Davidson County included a high percentage of farm owners, as opposed to farms operated by tenants, relative to North Carolina in general. In 1910, for example, those who owned their own farms comprised 77.8 percent of Davidson County farmers; the number of owner-operators throughout all of North Carolina comprised only 57.3 percent of the total number of farms. The average size of farms in Davidson County tended to be larger than in the state. Thirty percent of farms in North Carolina were 20 to 49 acres, 25 percent were from 50 to 99 acres, and 17 percent were from 100 to 174 acres. At

the same time, only 23 percent of farms in Davidson County were from 20 to 49 acres, while 30 percent of farms were from 50 to 99 acres, and 23 percent of farms were from 100 to 174 acres. Davidson County had significant acreage in corn, wheat, hay and forage, cotton, and sweet potatoes, in addition to tobacco. *Thirteenth Census of the United States*, vol. VII: *Agriculture 1909 and 1910* (Washington, D.C.: U.S. Government Printing Office, 1913).

38. Morton Sosna, "Personal interview with Arthur Raper," April 23, 1971, 3, SHC folder 370.

39. Raper, "Statement at Howard's Retirement Party," SHC folder 420.

40. Singal, "Interview with Arthur Raper," 36, SHC folder 363. In 1900, Davidson County's population consisted of 20,229 whites and 3,174 black residents; *Twelfth Census of the United States, 1900* (Washington, D.C.: U.S. Government Printing Office, 1903).

41. Singal, "Interview with Arthur Raper," 36, SHC folder 363.

42. Singal, "Interview with Arthur Raper," 79–80, SHC folder 363.

43. Raper, "Arcadia," SHC folder 14.

44. Steiner, *The American Community in Action*, 265.

45. Steiner, ed., *The American Community in Action*, 278.

46. Raper, videotape interview by Sue Thrasher, Peter Wood, and Larry Goodwyn, Vienna, Va., April 24–28, 1978, SHC folder 3966/2.

47. Raper, "Growth of Internationalism," unpublished course paper, March 3, 1924, SHC folder 8.

Chapter 2. Modernism, Chain Gangs, and Five-Cent Haircuts

1. The war allowed Raper to attend college. After 1917, land that had previously been selling for $35 was producing a tobacco crop that grossed $350 per acre. Frank Raper could then afford to replace Arthur's labor with hired help.

2. Raper was proud of his financial resourcefulness. Idling at his desk one day, he jotted, "I have been to a friend's room. He tells me of his hard work to stay in school. I remember my own lot and smile within when I remember that I can easily make from $.80–$1.00 each hour of my spare time." Raper, "A Cruel Necessity," February 3, 1923, SHC folder 1.

3. Raper, SHC folder 424; Daniel Singal, "Interview with Arthur Raper," January 18, 1971, SHC folder 364.

4. Raper, "Beliefs, 108-'B'-Grimes, 5/2/23," SHC folder 7.

5. Dorothy Ross, *The Origins of American Social Science* (Cambridge: Cambridge University Press, 1991), 165.

6. Daniel Singal, *The War Within: From Victorian to Modernist Thought in the South, 1919–1945* (Chapel Hill: University of North Carolina Press, 1982), 119.

7. Singal, "Interview with Arthur Raper," January 18, 1971, SHC folder 363.

8. As John Egerton writes, "Frank Porter Graham gave his university unexcelled progressive leadership without directly confronting the volatile issue of segregation." John Egerton, *Speak Now Against the Day* (New York: Alfred A. Knopf, 1994), 132.

9. Raper, "The Rise of Individualism," March 10, 1924, SHC folder 8.

10. Raper, "I'se des a livin'," undated notes. SHC folder 12.

11. Raper, "On the Crest of the Forming Waves," May 1976, SHC folder 548.

12. Raper, videotape interview by Sue Thrasher, Peter Wood, and Larry Goodwyn, Vienna, Va., April 24–28, 1978, SHC folder 3966/2.

13. Singal, "Interview with Arthur Raper," SHC folder 364.

14. Raper, May 11, 1924, SHC folder 725.
15. Singal, "Interview with Arthur Raper," SHC folder 363.
16. "Raper Discusses Negro Question," *Daily Tar Heel,* December 1, 1925.
17. Quoted in "Upon the Retirement of Arthur Raper from Federal Service," SHC folder 265.
18. Singal, "Interview with Arthur Raper," SHC folder 364.
19. Raper, "Youth judges race relations," SHC folder 26.
20. Ellen Fitzpatrick, "Caroline F. Ware and the Cultural Approach to History," *American Quarterly* 43 (1991): 173–198.
21. Frederick Jackson Turner, quoted in John Roper, *C. Vann Woodward, Southerner* (Athens: University of Georgia Press, 1987), 69.
22. Singal, "Interview with Arthur Raper," SHC folder 364.
23. Walter Jackson, "Interview at Slope Oaks," April 13, 1977, SHC folder 576. Raper didn't complain about a lack of rigor. Of thirteen master's students, in the fall of 1925, only six finished. "Pretty stiff going," he admitted. Singal, "Interview with Arthur Raper," SHC folder 364.
24. Raper, "Negro Dependency in the Southern Community" (master's thesis, Vanderbilt University, 1925), SHC folder 20.
25. Singal, "Interview with Arthur Raper," SHC folder 364.
26. Singal, "Interview with Arthur Raper," SHC folder 364.
27. George B. Tindall, "The Significance of Howard W. Odum to Southern History," *Journal of Southern History* (August 1958): 307.
28. John Shelton Reed, personal communication, August 15, 2002.
29. "When younger sociologists, many of them his disciples, began moving beyond mere description to analyze specific southern problems like lynching, mill villages, and sharecropping with an eye to drawing causal connections and assigning responsibility, Odum could encourage but not join them." Singal, "Interview with Arthur Raper," SHC folder 364.
30. Singal, "Interview with Arthur Raper," SHC folder 364.
31. Jackson, "Interview at Slope Oaks," SHC folder 576.
32. Ross, *The Origins of American Social Science,* xiii.
33. The Progressivism of Odum, of Woodrow Wilson and Theodore Roosevelt, had emphasized what John Roper called a "triptych of progress, moralism, and culture." The special character of American Progressivism was in the way it focused on stewardship over social life and personal behavior, and the gentle sway with which it tried to steer the market economy. By the middle of the Depression, C. Vann Woodward, among other liberals, felt that sway was "too gentle to mitigate the ravages of what he called 'unrestrained capitalism.'" Roper, *C. Vann Woodward,* 70. Where the Progressives "traffic in moral absolutes," in Richard Hofstadter's famous phrase, Raper's undergraduate study of history took a relativist's and anthropological approach to culture and society. Hofstadter quoted in Roper, *C. Vann Woodward,* 72.
34. Renato Roggioli considered that a modernist historical consciousness rested on a sense "of belonging to an intermediate stage, to a present already distinct from the past and to a future in potentiality which will be valid only when the future is actuality." Carl Jung agreed, "Today is a process of transition which separates itself from yesterday in order to go toward tomorrow. He who understands it, in this way, has the right to consider himself a modern." Roggioli and Jung quoted in Ross, *The Origins of American Social Science,* 311.
35. Ross, *The Origins of American Social Science,* 252.
36. Ross, *The Origins of American Social Science,* 232–233, 235, 236.

37. Ross, *The Origins of American Social Science*, 351.

38. "When Thomas analyzed the autobiographical document he printed and tried to deal adequately with the complexity of a single life, his interpretive sense came visibly into conflict with his positivist aims. Attitudes, he said, could not be taken from isolated instances, but needed to be interpreted in the context of a whole life. Thus the life record or case study was 'the *perfect* type of sociological material,' far more so than statistics, which were, 'taken in themselves . . . nothing but symptoms of unknown causal processes.'" Ross, *The Origins of American Social Science*, 355.

39. Charles Reagan Wilson, *The New Regionalism* (Jackson: University Press of Mississippi, 1998), x.

40. Walter Lippmann, *Preface to Morals* (New York: Macmillan, 1929); Robert Dorman, *Revolt of the Provinces: The Regionalist Movement in America, 1920–1945* (Chapel Hill: University of North Carolina Press, 1993). Dorman sees the regionalist impulse as still active, if transformed. "The region, it was hoped, would provide the physical framework for the creation of new kinds of cities, small-scale, planned, delimited, and existing in balance with wilderness and a restored and rejuvenated rural economy. In all of these applications, then, regionalism must be considered not only as a critique of modernization, and not only as a noteworthy contribution to the historic dialogue over pluralism, but also as marking a significant stage in the still-unfolding history of conservationism, preservationism, urban planning, and environmentalism."

41. Dorman, *Revolt of the Provinces*, 22–25.

42. Raper, "My Southern Accent," unpublished notes, SHC folder 13.

43. Considering Howard Odum, Michael O'Brien captures the ambivalence of regionalists' attitude toward modernity. "Like Frederick Jackson Turner, Odum was concerned that urbanization would make America a class society. Regionalism might hold the line, or even reverse the trend, by pitching institutions of geographical control against class divisions. It was, he wrote, 'a symbol of America's geographic as opposed to occupational representation; of popular as opposed to class control.' Odum wanted the South to defy and moderate modernity by drawing together." Michael O'Brien, *The Idea of the American South, 1920–1941* (Baltimore: Johns Hopkins University Press, 1979), 80–81.

44. Dorman, *Revolt of the Provinces*, 24.

45. Dorman, *Revolt of the Provinces*, xii, xiii, xiv.

46. Raper, "Life History of Bob Johnson," in Jesse Steiner and Roy M. Brown, eds., *The North Carolina Chain Gang: A Study of County Convict Road Work* (Chapel Hill: University of North Carolina Press, 1927).

47. "At the present time, the wider use of road machinery makes it extremely doubtful whether unskilled convicts who must be worked in a compact group under guard can any longer be profitably employed in road building. As for road maintenance, the evidence is conclusive that the chain gang is entirely unsuited for such work. From the economic point of view, it is highly essential that the counties devise some better method of segregation and connecting the able-bodied offender." Steiner and Brown, *The North Carolina Chain Gang*, 124.

48. Raper, "Family letter, December 23, 1973," SHC folder, 444.

49. "In a very real sense," Steiner goes on to assert, "the fundamental approach to an understanding of the community and its problems is through a study of the process of social change." Steiner and Brown, *The North Carolina Chain Gang*, 3.

50. Steiner and Brown, eds., *The North Carolina Chain Gang*, 6, 7.

51. Raper, "My Final Oral Examination," SHC folder 716.
52. Raper, "My Final Oral Examination," SHC folder 716.

Chapter 3. The Strange Case of the Interracial Commission

1. Raper, unpublished notes, July 14, 1928, SHC folder 50; Wilma Dykeman, *Seeds of Southern Change* (Chicago: University of Chicago Press, 1962).

2. Daniel Singal, "Interview with Arthur Raper," January 18, 1972, 99, SHC folder 364; John Egerton, *Speak Now Against the Day: The Generation Before the Civil Rights Movement in the South* (New York: Alfred A. Knopf, 1994), 47.

3. Singal, "Interview with Arthur Raper," SHC folder 363.

4. Raper, "There is a reason!" unpublished manuscript, January 16, 1927, SHC folder 15.

5. Nancy MacLean, *Behind the Mask of Chivalry: The Making of the Second Ku Klux Klan* (New York: Oxford University Press, 1994). *The Statesman*, the official newspaper of Georgia Governor Eugene Talmadge encapsulated the conservative view of the CIC. "The spearhead of the movement in Georgia to tear down the social barriers between the races is an organization known as the 'Commission on Interracial Cooperation.' . . . It has been prolific in issuing pamphlets, circulars, and other tools of propaganda designed to influence public opinion and serve as guidebooks for those who preach, and those whom the sponsors seek to convert, to its infernal experiments in racial equality.'" Ann Wells Ellis, "The Commission on Interracial Cooperation, 1919–1944: Its Activities and Results" (Ph.D. diss., Georgia State University, 1975), 277.

6. Ellis, "The Commission on Interracial Cooperation, 1919–1944," 222.

7. Ellis, "The Commission on Interracial Cooperation, 1919–1944," 229–231.

8. Ellis writes, "The pulpit was the 'least responsive factor' to the Commission's program. Especially among the Baptists, whose ministers were under little direct control from the denominational level, there was a lack of cooperation. Alexander and other CIC officials perhaps tended to judge ministers especially harshly since the South's treatment of the Negro and Christian principles were so plainly in conflict, but the fact remains that ministers on the whole were not as interested in interracial work as they might have been." Ellis, "The Commission on Interracial Cooperation, 1919–1944," 249.

9. Morton Sosna, *In Search of the Silent South* (New York: Columbia University Press, 1977), 86.

10. Ellis, "The Commission on Interracial Cooperation, 1919–1944," 381.

11. Singal, "Interview with Arthur Raper," 102–104, SHC folder 364.

12. Egerton, *Speak Now Against the Day*, 48; Singal, "Interview with Arthur Raper," SHC folder 364; Sosna, *In Search of the Silent South*. Sosna goes on to argue that the commission deliberately misled southern blacks to keep them in a subordinate position. The truth of the matter was that blacks had very little voice in the organization, and their main function was to lend an aura of Negro support for the Interracial Commission's activities. He notes that in 1934, there was only one paid Negro in the organization, and no blacks worked in the commission's Atlanta office. But Raper, for his very visible part, actively recruited and worked alongside black sociologists, authors, and speakers whenever he could. His notebooks and diaries are filled with meetings with black ministers, educators, and teachers, 106–107.

13. Ellis, "The Commission on Interracial Cooperation, 1919–1944," 367, 368, 369, 371.

14. Ellis, "The Commission on Interracial Cooperation, 1919–1944," 254.

15. Sullivan, *Days of Hope*, 25, 32.

16. Raper, "General Report of the Secretary of the Georgia Committee on Interracial Cooperation, Presented at the Annual Meeting, Atlanta, Ga., May 11, 1928," SHC folder 23. Raper reported numerous efforts on behalf of individuals in trouble. Here are two examples:

> A colored boy in the Atlanta jail was fleeced out of approximately $400 by various shyster lawyers who promised to defend him. When the boy's money was gone one of his older brothers secured a lawyer who appeared before the judge and got the youngster released on condition of good behavior. It is this jail case which led to efforts to secure a public welfare worker at the jail.
>
> The colored operator of a small motion picture show of Atlanta proved to be the victim of unionized labor on one hand and the motion picture monopoly on the other. He could not afford to employ a union operator. At the same time he could not qualify to become an operator himself. A city ordinance requires the signatures of two motion picture operators on an applicant's blank to make the applicant eligible for the examination. Efforts are being made to remove this technical restriction which virtually excludes colored people from operating motion picture machines.

Raper and the various committees also worked on gaining access for Negroes into local hospitals. The commission widely circulated Raper's report of the story of Julia Derricott, a Fisk University student, who was in an automobile accident on the highway between Atlanta and Chattanooga. She was refused by a local hospital in north Georgia, and later died, possibly because she wasn't hospitalized quickly enough. Singal, "Interview with Arthur Raper," 105, SHC folder 364.

17. Raper, "Negro Dependency in the Southern Community" (master's thesis, Vanderbilt University, 1925).

18. Raper, "Negro Dependency in the Southern Community" (master's thesis, Vanderbilt University, 1925).

19. Raper, "Negro Dependency in the Southern Community" (master's thesis, Vanderbilt University, 1925).

20. Raper, "Interracial Cooperation is a Necessity in Georgia," *Georgia State Teachers' Herald*, Fall 1926, SHC folder 50.

21. Fletcher Greene, letter to Raper, April 28, 1928, SHC folder 767.

22. Raper, desk calendar, SHC folder 23.

23. Ada Woolfolk, "Case Work with Dependent Negro Families in a Southern City, Family Welfare Society, Atlanta, Georgia," "about 1928," SHC folder 24.

24. Raper, "Miscellaneous observations of Arthur Raper's," SHC folder 716.

25. Raper, "The Significance of the School Teacher in Effecting Amicable Racial Adjustments," SHC folder 21.

26. Raper, desk calendar, SHC folder 23.

27. Raper, unpublished notes, July 8, 1928, SHC folder 23.

28. Raper, desk calendar, SHC folder 23.

29. Raper, desk calendar, March 9–April, 1927, SHC folder 23.

30. Raper, "Early Days at Camp Sequoyah," SHC folder 157.

31. Raper, "Early Days at Camp Sequoyah," SHC folder 157.

32. Raper, desk calendar, March 9–April, 1927, SHC folder 23.

33. Raper, "Miscellaneous observations of Arthur Raper's," SHC folder 716.

34. Singal, "Interview with Arthur Raper," SHC folder 364.

35. "Floyd Corry, who later became superintendent of schools in Greene County, . . . was about as poor as I was, and was living on the same hall with me, and he was working for a Master's in economics which he got the same year I got my Master's in sociology, 1925. . . . I came to the conclusion that he lived right square in the middle of this area where population was leaving the farm the fastest and coming up to Atlanta." Singal, "Interview with Arthur Raper," 57, SHC folder 363.

36. Singal, "Interview with Arthur Raper," 58, SHC folder 363.

37. In addition to the print media, the commission sponsored occasional radio broadcasts. As Ellis writes, "Eleazer felt as early as 1929 that radio could be used to reach the 'mass mind' and there were several discussions about arranging programs, but the general Commission never undertook any series of broadcasts. . . . The Commission might have utilized radio broadcasts far more extensively than it did, but there were perhaps several reasons why it chose not to do so. For one thing, few southern station owners were willing to risk alienating their audiences with discussions of such a controversial and emotional issue as race relations. If a station agreed to carry a program, the Commission then had to locate a sponsor since the CIC and most state commissions lacked the funds to pay costs, especially of a series of programs. The radio was also an uncertain educative medium, since people could simply choose not to listen to a specific program; face to face presentations to civic and religious groups provided captive audiences and an opportunity to reply to hostile questions." Ellis, "The Commission on Interracial Cooperation, 1919–1944," 251, 252.

38. Singal, "Interview with Arthur Raper," 106, SHC folder 366.

39. Commission on Interracial Cooperation, "Southern Leaders Impeach Judge Lynch, High Lights from Report of Commission on The Study of Lynching," pamphlet published in 1931 by the Commission on Interracial Cooperation, SHC folder 27.

40. Raper, letter to Charles S. Johnson, August 12, 1930, SHC folder 27.

41. Charles S. Johnson, letter to Raper, January 23, 1931, SHC folder 781.

42. Charles S. Johnson, letter to Raper, March 2, 1931, SHC folder 781.

43. J. B. Lehman, letter to Will Alexander, September 20, 1930, SHC folder 788.

44. Raper, letter to Will Alexander, November 18, 1930, SHC folder 780.

45. By 1938, even southern congressmen in their filibusters against a federal antilynching bills no longer defended mob murder as protecting white, southern womanhood. "Indeed," as Morton Sosna argues, "they argued that the decline in lynching indicated that local authorities were satisfactorily dealing with the situation." Morton Sosna, "In Search of the Silent South: White Southern Liberalism 1920–1950" (Ph.D. diss., University of Wisconsin, 1972), 105.

46. Jacqueline Dowd Hall, for the Southern Oral History Program, "Interview with Arthur Raper," January 30, 1974, SHC folder 449.

47. Southern Oral History Program, "Interview with Arthur Raper," January 29, 1974, SHC folder 447.

48. In his introduction to *The Tragedy of Lynching*, George Fort Milton echoed Raper in declaring his belief that lynching was the failure of communities to accommodate to and avail themselves of modern, liberal society. "Until America can discover and apply means to end these relapses to the law of the jungle, we have no assurance that ordered society will not at any moment be overthrown by the blind passion of a potentially ever-present mob." George Fort Milton, "Introduction," in *The Tragedy of Lynching* (Chapel Hill: University of North Carolina Press), 1933.

49. Milton, letter to Will Alexander, November 14, 1930, SHC folder 780.

50. "[Chivers and I,] we went separately," Raper explained. "Sometimes we'd go down together, except we had these durned separate coaches, you know, but we'd sometimes go about the same time. We'd sometimes see each other after we got into, say, Tuscaloosa or somewhere, but usually not. Usually I went in and did what I could do and he went in and did what he could do. We got back to Atlanta or Memphis or somewhere agreed to and we sat down. Sometimes we went back again to check on certain things. I'd find things that he'd want to check in, and he'd find things that I'd want to check on." Singal, "Interview with Arthur Raper," SHC folder 365.

51. Raper, "Miscellaneous editorials on lynchings taken from white papers in Georgia, 1930–1931," SHC folder 774. In most cases, the CIC learned about lynchings by radio broadcast or newspaper report. Although its reliability wavered, radio and the southern press was a more comprehensive source of information than law enforcement agencies or governmental channels. In terms of gathering information, as well as disseminating it, the media was as essential to the commission's work as were the town, county, and state records Raper used to develop sociological portraits of the locale of each crime.

52. In Alabama, Raper traveled with a letter from Governor Bibb Graves to the state's law officers. "I will be glad for you to give him any information that would not jeopardize any case now pending." Bibb Graves, letter to Arthur Raper, October 25, 1930, SHC folder 798.

53. "In the United States between 1885 and 1900 there was an average of 162 persons lynched each year; between 1900 and 1920 an average of 77; from 1920 to 1925 there was an average of 46 persons while from 1925 through 1930 there was an average of but 17 persons lynched each year." Arthur Raper, "Address to a conference of Georgia sheriffs and peace officers," May 28, 1931, SHC folder 27.

54. Southern Oral History Program, "Interview with Arthur Raper," January 29, 1974, SHC folder 447. Although Raper identified his background as clearly as did his southern accent, to Luke, Raper was "from up north." Luke assumed Raper was a frontman for northern liberals, Communists, or Jews.

55. In lynching after lynching, local investigations were concluding that death had been meted out "at the hands of parties unknown." He quickly found that the parties were always known. "Anytime you see that phrase, 'parties unknown,' in a southern community, you know that they've perjured themselves right to the limit," he said. "In a southern community, you know what happened. Particularly these people who control everything. They know." Southern Oral History Program, "Interview with Arthur Raper," January 29, 1974, SHC folder 447.

56. Walter Chivers worked the same thing, although "Chivers didn't have to be quite so careful about not getting anybody worked up," as Raper explained laconically, "because the Negroes were more opposed to lynching than the whites were." Raper, videotape interview by Sue Thrasher, Peter Wood, and Larry Goodwyn, Vienna, Va., April 24–28, 1978, SHC folder 3966/2.

57. Raper, videotape interview by Sue Thrasher, Peter Wood, and Larry Goodwyn, Vienna, Va., April 24–28, 1978, SHC folder 3966/2.

58. Raper, videotape interview by Sue Thrasher, Peter Wood, and Larry Goodwyn, Vienna, Va., April 24–28, 1978, SHC folder 3966/2.

59. Southern Oral History Program, "Interview with Arthur Raper," January 29, 1974, SHC folder 447.

60. Raper, videotape interview by Sue Thrasher, Peter Wood, and Larry Goodwyn, Vienna, Va., April 24–28, 1978, SHC folder 3966/2.

Chapter 4. *The Tragedy of Lynching*

1. Raper, videotape interview by Sue Thrasher, Peter Wood, and Larry Goodwyn, Vienna, Va., April 24–28, 1978, SHC folder 3966/2.

2. His black informants were in greater jeopardy than he ever was, according to Martha Raper. "It wouldn't be you that would get stepped on, it would be one of them." Singal, "Interview with Arthur Raper," January 18, 1971, SHC folder 364. Raper said, "I could have gotten any number of people killed when I was investigating lynching, particularly Negroes, just by being a little careless and a little blabbermouth." Morton Sosna, "Personal interview with Arthur Raper," April 23, 1971, SHC folder 370.

3. "He speaks of vocational guidance, but it is soon clear what he means by that. He means keeping the Negro in his place, curbing his ambition, preserving him, as in the Atlanta experiment which he lauds, as a domestic servant. There isn't the slightest intimation in Mr. Woofter's discussion that there are any numbers of Negro youth who have ability and talent for law, medicine and dentistry; for the work of the scientist and artist." W. E. B. Du Bois, "Woofterism," *Crisis* 82 (March 1931), SHC folder 771.

4. W. E. B. Du Bois, "Let's Buy and Read," *Crisis* (July 1933), SHC folder 37.

5. Stewart Tolnay and E. M. Beck confirm the connection between cotton culture and southern race violence. "Perhaps it is reasonable to think of the cotton culture as representing a constellation of factors including arrangements of land tenure, a strong dependency on cotton as the primary cash crop, and a reliance upon black labor. To be sure, many blacks died at the hands of white mobs outside the boundaries of the cotton culture, yet it is unmistakable that the demographic, social, and economic conditions that defined such a culture were important factors influencing the likelihood of lethal violence directed toward southern blacks." Stewart E. Tolnay and E. M. Beck, *A Festival of Violence: An Analysis of Southern Lynchings, 1882–1930* (Urbana and Chicago: University of Illinois Press, 1995).

6. Raper, "Report of the Secretary of the Georgia Committee on Race Relations to the Annual Meeting," March 15, 1933, SHC folder 34.

7. Under Odum's directorship, the name of the organization was changed to the Southern Regional Council, and race was all but subsumed within concern for planning the region's economy.

8. Jacqueline Dowd Hall writes about this minority: "As the Depression deepened and the threat of fascism intensified, moreover, the voices of black radicals were amplified, and white leftists throughout the country came increasingly to see racial and regional diversity as the hallmark of American democracy, a source of national resiliency, and a seedbed for social change." Hall claims that the southern regionalist movement as a whole pushed to the left in the mid-1930s and became influential in the New Deal's cultural policies. Jacqueline Dowd Hall, "Women Writers and the 'Southern Front,'" *Journal of Southern History* 69, no. 1 (February 2003): 8.

Here were influential, white southerners conducting scientific studies advocating that Congress legislate southern questions of race and economic justice as part of U.S. national policy. In 1925, Woofter had written a textbook that characterized lynching as primarily damaging to "white civilization," as Morton Sosna explained it, "and referred to the Dyer [federal] anti-lynching bills of 1922 and 1924 as 'partisan and sectional' and thus foolhardy measures." Raper would testify before Congress on behalf of the same kind of federal bills.

9. R. H. King, letter to Howard W. Odum, May 12, 1932, SHC, Howard W. Odum papers.

10. Morton Sosna, *In Search of the Silent South: Southern Liberals and the Race Issue* (New York:

Columbia University Press, 1977); Julian Harris, "State Is Backward, Georgians Are Told," *New York Times* wire story published in the *Eastman, Ga., Times-Journal,* January 15, 1931, SHC folder 774.

11. Raper, *The Tragedy of Lynching* (Chapel Hill: University of North Carolina Press, 1933), 94.

12. Raper, *The Tragedy of Lynching,* 95.

13. "That the lynching occurred in the First Judicial District is to be deplored. To investigate the matter, however, would be entirely futile. No hope of conviction could be entertained, in view of local sentiment. Such occurrences are reflections on the citizenship, rather than on the small force of peace-officers." Raper, *The Tragedy of Lynching,* 96.

14. Raper, *The Tragedy of Lynching,* 97.

15. Raper, *The Tragedy of Lynching,* 98.

16. In 1890, the population of Bolivar County was 29,970, of which 89.2 percent were African American. In 1920, the population was 57,669; 82.4 percent were African American. In 1930, the population was 71,051; 74 percent were African American. More than 200,000 acres each year were planted in cotton. Corn was the only other crop grown, and it was cultivated in support of the cotton system. Raper, *The Tragedy of Lynching,* 98, 99.

17. Tolnay and Beck, *A Festival of Violence,* 247.

18. Raper, *The Tragedy of Lynching,* 98, 99.

19. Raper, *The Tragedy of Lynching,* 102. In terms of the percentage of lynching victims accused of sexual assault, the figures for Bolivar are consistent with the rest of the region. Of all the lynchings across the South during the forty years prior to 1930, approximately one victim in six had been accused of rape.

20. "In 1926 only 23.5 percent of the county's Negro population over fifteen years of age held church membership, while in Mississippi as a whole their church membership was equal to 47.8 percent of this age group." Raper, *The Tragedy of Lynching,* 104.

21. Raper, *The Tragedy of Lynching,* 105.

22. Raper, *The Tragedy of Lynching,* 106.

23. Raper, *The Tragedy of Lynching,* 106.

24. Raper, *The Tragedy of Lynching,* 459.

25. Raper, *The Tragedy of Lynching,* 462.

26. Commission on Interracial Cooperation, "Southern Leaders Impeach Judge Lynch, High Lights from Report of Commission on The Study of Lynching," pamphlet published in 1931 by the Commission on Interracial Cooperation, SHC folder 27. "Almost no place in these United States can assume that it is without lynching danger," Raper wrote in 1933. "Within recent years, lynchings have occurred in all types of communities, from the capital city of Tennessee, with its more than 150,000 inhabitants, strong social set-up, and well-organized police force, to McIntosh County, Georgia, with less than six thousand inhabitants, rudimentary social organization, and two constables." Raper, "The High Cost of Lynching," unpublished manuscript, 1933, SHC folder 33; Frederick Jackson Turner, "The Significance of the Frontier in American History," reprinted in *Rereading Frederick Jackson Turner* (New York: Henry Holt & Co., 1994 [1893]).

27. Raper, *The Tragedy of Lynching,* 5.

28. Southern Oral History Program, "Interview with Arthur Raper," conducted by the Oral History Seminar, January 29, 1974, SHC folder 447.

29. Fitzhugh Brundage argues that Raper did not account for change in the patterns of lynchings over time and by region. "Raper argued that mobs flourished in isolated, backward communities such as those that dotted the vast expanse of south Georgia. And yet mob violence had

been chronic when the same region had been undergoing rapid development and could not, in any real sense, be described as stagnant or back ward." For the most part, though, the communities where lynchings occurred were in isolated pockets by-passed by rapid development. W. Fitzhugh Brundage, "Introduction," in *Under Sentence of Death: Lynching in the South*, ed. W. Fitzhugh Brundage (Chapel Hill: University of North Carolina Press, 1997), 1–16.

30. Raper, "Revised Tentative Outline for Case Studies of Lynchings," November 5, 1930, SHC folder 789.

31. Raper, letter to J. L. Grant, November 5, 1930, SHC folder 800.

32. Tolnay and Beck, *A Festival of Violence*, ix.

33. Singal, "Interview with Arthur Raper," January 18, 1971, SHC folder 365.

34. Raper turns this information into a call for the South to provide "sufficient educational opportunities and adequate institutional care for her population." Raper, *The Tragedy of Lynching*, 4.

35. Raper, *The Tragedy of Lynching*, 3, 4.

36. Tolnay and Beck portray lynching as an integral part of the southern economy and the class structure that emerged as a replacement for slavery during the 1870s and 1880s. That new system remained more or less intact until the early decades of the twentieth century. During this era, blacks were lynched when it served the economic interests of well-to-do or poor whites. They were particularly vulnerable when violence benefited more than one class of southern whites.

"Although the pursuit of King Cotton persisted after the Great Depression, rural class relations were altered substantially, and the structural arrangements that had given rise to the lynching phenomenon began to fade. In addition, increasing farm mechanization created a superfluous rural work force, black and white, which fled the countryside and the South in search of better opportunities. The cotton economy changed irrevocably. The use of wage laborers gave landlords greater control over the work force, who could be hired when needed and let go when the work was done. . . . As the social and economic foundation that had supported the use of mob violence began to crumble, lynchings continued to decline in frequency and became increasingly uncoupled from the southern rural economy." Tolnay and Beck, *A Festival of Violence*, 244.

37. "In approximately nine-tenths of them the per capita tax valuation was below the general state average as was also the per capita bank deposit. In three-fourths of the counties the per capita income from farm and factory was below the state average, in many cases less than one-half; in nine-tenths, fewer and smaller income tax returns were made per thousand population than throughout the state. In over two-thirds, the proportion of farms operated by tenants was in excess of the state rate; and in nearly three-fourth of the counties, automobiles were less common than in their respective states." Raper, *The Tragedy of Lynching*, 6.

38. Tolnay and Beck also indict the cotton culture, concluding that economic factors were critical elements motivating lynchings. Tolnay and Beck, *A Festival of Violence*, 251.

39. According to the research of Tolnay and Beck, lynchings were more frequent in areas with larger concentrations of white tenants. "For white farmers, tenancy was the bottom rung on the agricultural ladder. It was supposed to be a status reserved for poor black farmers. Whites were supposed to be owners of land rather than tillers of someone else's soil. However, white tenancy grew sharply during the late nineteenth and early twentieth centuries, forcing more and more farmers to the margins of southern agriculture. They were clinging desperately to that marginal position along with their black neighbors, who were also tenant farmers. With virtually no legitimate claim to economic superiority, poor whites resorted to mob violence in order to shore

up the caste line that represented a claim to superiority based on the color of their skin." Tolnay and Beck, *A Festival of Violence*, 253.

40. Raper, *The Tragedy of Lynching*, 1.

41. "At various times, lynchings served the economic interests of all whites," Tolnay and Beck conclude. "When the economic fortunes of marginal whites soured (e.g., because of shifts in farm tenure or swings in the price of cotton), violence against blacks increased. Either out of frustration or with more instrumental motives in mind, whites responded to economic stress by terrorizing blacks." Tolnay and Beck, *A Festival of Violence*, 221.

42. Raper, *The Tragedy of Lynching*, 11.

43. Raper, preliminary report to the Southern Commission on the Study of Lynching, October 2, 1930, SHC folder 800.

44. Raper, *The Tragedy of Lynching*, 20.

45. Singal, "Interview with Arthur Raper," SHC folder 366. Tolnay and Beck also found that "Southern blacks were vulnerable from more than one direction. The white elite was willing to see the black community terrorized when it served the elite's purposes, for example, to exert control over workers or to drive a wedge between struggling blacks and whites. and poor white dirt farmers were equally willing to resort to violence when their meager claim to social superiority was at risk when their economic fortunes waned." Indeed, they write, "one of the reasons that the gruesome and shameful practice of lynching was so common and so tolerated is probably because it had the potential to benefit all classes of whites." Tolnay and Beck, *A Festival of Violence*, 255.

46. Raper, preliminary report to the Commission for the Prevention of Lynching, October 2, 1930, SHC folder 795.

47. Raper, preliminary report to the Commission for the Prevention of Lynching, October 2, 1930, SHC folder 795.

48. "Our findings are not kind to the popular justice explanation for lynchings, despite its popularity among whites during the lynching era. Time after time, mobs expressed frustration with cases in which expected guilty verdicts were not rendered or in which sentences were more lenient than anticipated. . . . In fact, however, we could find no systematic evidence of a linkage between the level of mob activity and the actions of the formal criminal justice system. In both temporal and spatial senses there was little relationship between lynchings and the frequency with which blacks were marched off to the gallows." Tolnay and Beck, *A Festival of Violence*, 248–249.

49. Raper, *The Tragedy of Lynching*, 13. Nevertheless, Raper met with law enforcement groups when he could. When he addressed the Georgia Association of Sheriffs in 1931, he suggested they agree with neighboring counties to respond to each other's mob threats; arrange to bring in leading citizens to advocate on behalf of the law; and remove the potential victim of lynching to another county or a strongly defended jailhouse. Raper, "Address to a conference of Georgia sheriffs and peace officers," May 28, 1931, SHC folder 27.

50. William P. King, letter to Raper, November 28, 1930, SHC folder 781.

51. Raper, *The Tragedy of Lynching*, 23.

52. Much of the press, looking to the economy, was concerned that southern communities be perceived as attuned to modern business interests. Many newspapers editorialized for better race relations and against mob murder as a way to keep the federal government from passing antilynching legislation. By 1930s, middle-class public sentiment had changed. An increasing num-

ber of southern towns, where a lynching had taken place, held public meetings to denounce the outrage. As Fitzhugh Brundage writes, "That these meetings were often organized by local Rotary Clubs, Chambers of Commerce, or newspapers is hardly surprising. These self-appointed guardians of their communities' reputations took it upon themselves to assure the rest of the state that their communities, with the exception of a lawless minority, were committed to the rule of law." W. Fitzhugh Brundage, "Lynching in the New South: Georgia and Virginia, 1880–1930" (Ph.D. diss., Harvard University, 1988), 284–285.

53. *Macon News,* December 24, 1930, SHC folder 774.

54. Editorial, *Fayetteville Observer,* April 29, 1930, SHC folder 774.

55. Raper, *The Tragedy of Lynching,* 8, 9.

56. Bertram Wyatt-Brown connects lynching with the rites of charivari, descended from medieval festivals of public atonement, whose "chief aim was the protection of traditional values and conventions against forces outside as well as within the community. . . . The [accused] malefactor not only suffered for his crime in such rituals, legal or otherwise; he also served as an offering to the primal, sacred values of common folk." Bertram Wyatt-Brown, *Honor and Violence in the Old South* (New York: Oxford University Press, 1986), 210, 213.

57. Within a few months of its founding, the Southern Commission of the Study of Lynching was actively deterring potential lynchings. On September 30, 1930, for example, Alexander wrote to the members and friends of the CIC about a notable success. "Yesterday afternoon a mob gathered about the jail in Huntsville, Alabama, threatening to lynch a Negro suspected of murder. A member of our Commission living in a nearby town promptly called the Commission's Atlanta office and reported the situation. The office immediately got in touch with the Governor of Alabama and with ministers and leading citizens of Huntsville, urged that everything possible be done to avert the danger. At 10:30 last night we received a wire saying that the crisis had been safely passed, and the morning paper tells of the determined and successful stand made by the officers and soldiers.

"Whether our efforts in the matter contributed at all to the satisfactory outcome, we do not know. At least we did what we could. The point of this letter, however, is to suggest that the prompt action of our Alabama friend was just the sort of service needed in every such situation, in order that public opinion may be effectively mobilized against anarchy and the breakdown of civilization." Will Alexander, letter to Raper, September 30, 1930, SHC folder 788.

58. On January 30, 1932, Raper wrote to Couch: "Relative to advertising this lynching report, I should like to have from you, at your convenience, a list of the publications and persons to whom you will send it. In many of the larger Southern communities to which you will be sending copies, we can, perhaps, help by sending to you names of people in these communities whom, from experience, we know to be particularly interested in race relations, lynching, etc." He says he's sure the members of the commission, including its black members, would also be glad to assist you in placing your regular review copies in the hands of interested people. Mr. Milton, Mr. Harris, and others, know personally many of the news writers and magazine editors in the country." Arthur Raper, letter to W. T. Couch, January 30, 1932, UNC Press Archives, Subgroup 4: Author/Title Publication Records, Raper, A. F., *The Tragedy of Lynching.*

59. Raper, letter to W. T. Couch, April 5, 1933, SHC folder 36.

60. George Fort Milton, letter to Raper, July 23, 1931, SHC folder 787.

61. Couch also wanted the Interracial Commission to publish a newsletter, thinking it would be a good way to raise funds. Raper told him that they'd thought about it, but it had never gotten

off the ground, for one reason or another, although it would be something they would like to pursue. W. T. Couch, letter to Arthur Raper, January 7, 1933. Raper, letter to W. C. Couch, January 10, 1933, UNC Press Archives, Subgroup 4: Author/Title Publication Records, Raper, A. F., *The Tragedy of Lynching*.

62. Couch, letter to C. C. Regier, November 7, 1932, UNC Press Archives, Subgroup 4: Author/Title Publication Records, Raper, A. F., *The Tragedy of Lynching*. Raper, letter to George Fort Milton, July 23, 1931, SHC folder 787.

63. Alexander, letter to W. T. Couch, March 29, 1933. "Reviews and Newspaper Comments on '*The Tragedy of Lynching*,'" UNC Press Archives, Subgroup 4: Author/Title Publication Records, Raper, A. F., *The Tragedy of Lynching*.

64. Singal, "Interview with Arthur Raper," 105, SHC folder 364.

65. Southern Commission on the Study of Lynching, "Lynchings and What They Mean," pamphlet published by the Commission on Interracial Cooperation, 1932, SHC folder 32.

66. Morton Sosna, "Interview with Arthur Raper," April 23, 1971, SHC folder 370.

67. By contrast, Walter White's denunciatory *Rope and Faggot*, published in 1929, had made even white liberals defensive. Liberals were also cool to White's call for federal antilynching legislation. They believed that white southerners would end lynching themselves, once they realized that it injured whites, as well as blacks. Sosna, *In Search of the Silent South*.

68. Raper, *The Tragedy of Lynching*, 6–7.

69. Morton Sosna, "In Search of the Silent South: White Southern Liberalism 1920–1950" (Ph.D. diss., University of Wisconsin, 1972), 101.

70. Raper, *The Tragedy of Lynching*, 12.

71. Raper, draft report to the Southern Commission on the Study of Lynching, 1932, SHC folder 828.

72. Howard W. Odum, letter to Raper, December 10, 1930, SHC, Howard W. Odum papers.

73. Singal, "Interview with Arthur Raper," SHC folder 365.

74. W. T. Couch, letter to the editors, *Survey Graphic*, April 11, 1933, UNC Press Archives, Subgroup 4: Author/Title Publication Records, Raper, A. F., *The Tragedy of Lynching*.

75. Dan Carter, *Scottsboro: A Tragedy of the American South* (Baton Rouge: Louisiana State University Press, 1979). On June 23, 1931, George Fort Milton wrote to Raper: "I hope you will get all the information you can about the Scottsboro case, for it looks as though it is going to become a *cause celebre* almost of the magnitude of the *Sacco Vanzetti* affair. Should this turn out this way, our commission ought to have a very accurate body of facts regarding the matter so that if it does seem that these young Negroes are not guilty, we can make vigorous protest against their execution." George Fort Milton, letter to Arthur Raper, June 23, 1931, SHC folder 784.

76. Walter White, "Why We Lynch," *The Nation*, May 17, 1933, SHC folder 37.

77. Walter White, letter to Raper, May 9, 1933, SHC folder 30.

78. "Our Lingering Barbarism," *Macon Telegraph*, April 15, 1933, SHC folder 36.

79. Editorial, *Columbia State*, April 23, 1933, SHC folder 36.

80. The way southern newspapers covered and commented on lynchings was critical to, and indicative of, the way whites thought about blacks and the way they conceived of the South. It was through the press, as historian W. Fitzhugh Brundage observed, that "lynchings became critical to the larger debate about southern race relations." W. Fitzhugh Brundage, "Lynching in the New South: Georgia and Virginia, 1880–1930" (Ph.D. diss., Harvard University, 1988), 19.

81. "Media support for lynching waned during the 1930s," write Tolnay and Beck, "as newspa-

pers increasingly abandoned their role as apologists for mob violence and became cheerleaders for economic development in the 'New South.'" Tolnay and Beck, *A Festival of Violence*, 240.

82. Sosna, *In Search of the Silent South*, 32–33. "Innocent People Are Put to Death," *Macon News*, Georgia, April 9, 1933. "'Judge Lynch' is on the spot in South, Majority of Mob Murders Preventable, Students of Crime Report," *Birmingham News*, Alabama, April 18, 1933, SHC folder 36. Raper, "Preface to the reprint edition," *The Tragedy of Lynching* (Montclair, N.J.: Patterson Smith, 1969 [1933]), ii.

83. C. McD. Puckette, "Getting at the Truth in the Lynching Problem," *New York Times*, book review section, 3, May 14, 1933, SHC folder 38.

84. Walter Millis, "Social and Racial Forces Behind Lynching, Out of the South Comes This Excellent Study of Its Tragic Problem," *New York Herald Tribune*, April 30, 1933, SHC folder 36.

85. Lewis Gannett, "Books and Other Things," *New York Herald Tribune*, April 8, 1933, SHC folder 36.

86. Carolyn Pierce Dillard, "The Tragedy of Lynching," *Wesleyan Christian Advocate*, June 23, 1933, SHC folder 37.

87. "Lynching and Its Cure," *Mid-Monthly Survey*, June or July 1933, SHC folder 37.

88. John Dollard, "The Tragedy of Lynching," *The American Academy of Political and Social Science* 178 (March 1935): 226, UNC Press Archives, Subgroup 4: Author/Title Publication Records, Raper, A. F., *The Tragedy of Lynching*.

89. "Southerner Looks Into Causes of Barbarism Known as Lynching," *Dallas Morning News*, May 21, 1933, SHC folder 36.

90. James Weldon Johnson, letter to Will Alexander, May 7, 1933, SHC folder 30.

91. "Study of Mob Action Reveals and Analyzes Causes of Lynching," *Columbia Missourian*, April 29, 1933, SHC folder 36.

92. Alain Locke, ed., *The New Negro* (New York: Albert & Charles Boni, 1925); Locke, "Retrospective Review of the Negro Literature of 1933," *Opportunity*, January 1934, SHC folder 37.

93. "There are several reasons for this slow sale. The prime reason is that everyone now is hard up and bookstores are not buying to stock anything for which there is no active demand. The book is getting excellent reviews—front page in the *Herald Tribune* Books this week, full page in *New Republic*, and a number of others in media of lesser importance, all of which are extremely favorable." Six months after publication, little more than five hundred copies had been sold. W. T. Couch, letter to Raper, January 7, 1933. Raper, letter to W. T. Couch, January 10, 1933. Raper, letter to W. T. Couch, March 11, 1933. Couch, letter to Raper, April 28, 1933. Couch, letter to Roger N. Baldwin, September 19, 1933. UNC Press Archives, Subgroup 4: Author/Title Publication Records, Raper, A. F., *The Tragedy of Lynching*.

94. Singal, "Interview with Arthur Raper," SHC folder 365.

95. *Georgia Tech*, "Arthur Raper Tells P.T.A. of Community Chest Work Along Social Service Lines," April 27, 1932, SHC folder 50.

96. Virginius Dabney, *Liberalism in the South* (Chapel Hill: University of North Carolina Press, 1932), 415.

97. Dabney, *Liberalism in the South*, 422–423.

98. Singal, "Interview with Arthur Raper," SHC folder 365.

99. Singal, "Interview with Arthur Raper," SHC folder 365.

100. Dorothy Ross, *The Origins of American Social Science* (Cambridge: Cambridge University Press, 1991), 355. Raper was strongly influenced by the approach of Robert Park as well. As W.

Fitzhugh Brundage observes, "Early sociological explorations of lynching had a clear intellectual debt to sociologist Robert Park's theory of collective behavior. Park saw human society as made up of interdependent individuals and groups who were divided by competition for economic and political dominance but were held together by shared values and purposes. When social controls, which served the vital function of softening the competitive struggle for existence, weakened, Park predicated that collective violence became more likely." W. Fitzhugh Brundage, ed., *Under Sentence of Death: Lynching in the South* (Chapel Hill: University of North Carolina Press, 1997), 6.

101. William Carlos Williams, *In the American Grain* (New York: New Directions Books, 1956 [1933]), frontispiece.

102. With a file of tens of thousands of photographs, the project didn't always succeed, as Maren Stange observes. The most mawkish and sentimentalized FSA photos forgot about context and instead idealized, rather than particularized, their subjects. Maren Stange, *Symbols of Ideal Life: Social Documentary Photography in America, 1890–1950* (New York: Cambridge University Press, 1989).

103. Carl Fleischhauer and Beverly Brannan, eds., *Documenting America, 1935–1943* (Berkeley: University of California Press, 1988), 4–5, 9. William Leuchtenburg, "The Achievements of the New Deal," in *The FDR Years: On Roosevelt and His Legacy* (New York: Columbia University Press, 1995), 267.

104. John Dollard, *Caste and Class in a Southern Town* (New Haven: Yale University Press, 1937), 20. "Several of the most celebrated and enduring nonfiction books about the South to come out of the 1930s and 1940s were characterized by an unconcealed personal perspective," writes John Egerton. "Among these more or less unconventional works of remembrance and belief and history are W. J. Cash's *The Mind of the South*, Lillian Smith's *Killers of the Dream*, Richard Wright's *Black Boy*, Erskine Caldwell's *You Have Seen Their Faces*, James Agee's *Let Us Now Praise Famous Men*, Clarence Cason's *90 Degrees in the Shade*, Saunders Redding's *No Day of Triumph*, Stetson Kennedy's *Southern Exposure*, Zora Neale Hurston's *Dust Tracks on a Road*, and William Alexander Percy's *Lanterns on the Levee*." John Egerton, *Speak Now Against the Day: The Generation Before the Civil Rights Movement in the South* (New York: Alfred A. Knopf, 1994), 630.

105. W. T. Couch, ed., Federal Writers' Project, Works Progress Administration, *These Are Our Lives* (Chapel Hill: University of North Carolina Press, 1939), ix.

106. Couch, letter to Frank Graham, April 19, 1934, SHC, UNC Press Archives, Series 1: General Files 1934, Subgroup 2: Directors Records.

107. Couch, letter to Louis R. Wilson, September 16, 1932. SHC, UNC Press Archives, Series 1: General Files 1932, Subgroup 2: Directors Records.

108. William Cooper and Thomas Terrill, *The American South: A History* (New York: Alfred A. Knopf, 1991), 652.

109. UNC Press release, UNC Press Archives, Subgroup 4: Author/Title Publication Records, Raper, A. T., *The Tragedy of Lynching*.

Chapter 5. *Preface to Peasantry*

1. Arthur T. Raper, *Preface to Peasantry* (Chapel Hill: University of North Carolina Press, 1936), 211.

2. Daniel Singal, "Interview with Arthur Raper," January 18, 1972, SHC folder 364. Floyd Corry would later become the county's school superintendent.

3. Raper, *Preface to Peasantry*, 197, 198–199.

4. Morton Sosna, "Personal interview with Arthur Raper," April 23, 1971, SHC folder 370.

5. Alexander would turn around and relay Raper's information to Rex Tugwell and others at the Department of Agriculture. "Alexander was a remarkable fellow," Raper told Daniel Singal. "He'd keep me talking sometimes for half an hour or maybe two hours about what I'd found, what I'd seen, who I talked with, what they said. And then he would make a speech the next day and take the essence of everything I had gotten and give it." Singal, "Interview with Arthur Raper," SHC folder 364.

6. Southern Oral History Program, "Interview with Arthur Raper," January 29, 1974, SHC folder 447.

7. Jack Kirby defines the Old South plantation system as modern, because it was tied to a global economy with metropolitan capital and management through sophisticated transportation systems. By the early 1930s, in the breakdown of its old plantation system, coupled with the lack of new capital or machinery, the Black Belt had begun to collapse into a premodern economy. Jack Temple Kirby, *Rural Worlds Lost: The American South 1920–1960* (Baton Rouge: Louisiana State University Press, 1987).

8. Raper, "The Highlanders—A Challenge to Democracy," no date, SHC folder 48.

9. Raper, "Why Study Sociology?" unpublished manuscript in Raper's files, SHC, University of North Carolina at Chapel Hill, 1933, 1–2.

10. Raper, "Some things to think about now, and hard," dated early 1934, SHC folder 40.

11. "Greene and Macon counties exhibit the disfranchisement which characterizes the 'Solid South,' for not only do scarcely any Negroes vote, but less than half of the whites. In 1932, the largest poll on record, the total presidential vote in Greene was a number equal to but 35.0 per cent of the whites of voting age; in Macon 49.8 per cent. Less exciting elections draw hardly half this many." Raper, *Preface to Peasantry*, 170.

12. Raper, *Preface to Peasantry*, 5.

13. Raper, *Preface to Peasantry*, 4. He went on to draw out the analogy. "European feudalism, however, cultivated permanence in its society and the husbandry of its natural resources. The plantation system was built on speculation and flux in a seeming rush to expend, and the Southern planter, unlike the noble, often moved his seat of operations from exhausted land to virgin soil, and regularly discarded the least satisfactory workers in his search for more desirable ones, always enforcing upon them economic and cultural dependency." Raper, *Preface to Peasantry*, 4.

14. "Ownership of land correlates with total wealth at a level of 0.864 (significant at the 0.01 level), although the correlation differs by race for reasons examined below. The pattern of large landholding indicates a striking difference, though, not only in the amount of acreage held, but in relation to family ownership. In sharp contrast to the black landholding pattern, the same names of whites appear again and again in county tax records, and the same names were most often located within the same district. I assume that many of the largest white landowners were members of families that included numerous landholders, based on the records of farms owned by people with the same land name within the same district, indication these farms were part of long-established, inherited plantation lands. By contrast, Greene's wealthiest blacks were individual, rather than family, landowners who bought their own property. Raper's records for 1934 indicated that only five out of seventy-three black landowners had inherited their land; the rest had acquired land through individual purchase from whites or other blacks." Louis Mazzari, "Greene County, Georgia, in 1920: Portrait of a Black Belt county during the Great Migration" (unpublished graduate paper, University of New Hampshire, 1999).

15. Raper, *Preface to Peasantry*, 18.

16. Raper, *Preface to Peasantry*, 91.

17. Singal, "Interview with Arthur Raper," SHC folder 364.

18. "Then the historian, Dr. T. B. Rice—he was a druggist doctor, the county historian—for some reason he took a liking to me and to the secretary working with me, Miss Blue from Macon County, Alabama, where Tuskegee is, and he just gave us everything in the world he had, all of his files. He had a tremendous number of these little episodic items that he'd picked up about Greene County here, yonder and there, and he made all those available to us, which we duly mentioned in *Preface to Peasantry* and in *Tenants of the Almighty*. Singal, "Interview with Arthur Raper," SHC folder 364.

19. Guy B. Johnson, letter to Robert Eleazer, January 8, 1934, SHC, Guy B. Johnson Papers.

20. Talmadge was correct to claim in the *Statesman* that the CIC "has been prolific in issuing pamphlets, circulars, and other tools of propaganda designed to influence public opinion and serve as guidebooks for those who preach, and those whom the sponsors seek to convert, to its infernal experiments in racial equality." Quoted in Ann Wells Ellis, "The Commission on Interracial Cooperation, 1919–1944: Its Activities and Results" (Ph.D. diss., Georgia State University, 1975), 277.

21. Raper said that when he joined the CIC in the mid-1920s the accommodationist philosophy was perhaps foremost, but "the longer I stayed there, the more it shifted to the other side, and perceptively so." Quoted in Ellis, "The Commission on Interracial Cooperation, 1919–1944," 367, 368.

22. "Despite his popularity with the rural people, Talmadge had little insight into the problems facing Georgia farmers," according to Kenneth Coleman. "He believed that by hard work and thrift alone a person could master his own fate; he opposed programs calling for greater government spending and economic regulation. Such views, especially during the Great Depression, ignored the plight of tenant farmers as well as many landowners." Kenneth Coleman, ed., *A History of Georgia*, 2nd ed. (Athens: University of Georgia Press, 1991).

23. Charles S. Johnson, letter to W. T. Couch, May 7, 1934, UNC Press Archives, Subgroup 4: Author/Title Publication Records, Raper, A. F. *Preface to Peasantry: A Tale of Two Black Belt Counties*.

24. The dictates of Raper's sense of realism led him to steer a difficult course between frankness and sympathy. "We wanted to tell the truth. I didn't want to leave off anything in this story. But neither did I want to tell it in any kind of abrasive way, if there was a way to tell it that wasn't abrasive. . . . And I don't know a much greater challenge that a person has, if he has some body of data, than that—because just to ram it in somebody's face, and then have him call you damned fool and walk off and you're through and they're through, just the satisfaction of one emotional spurt, doesn't weigh anything, in my better moments, in comparison with having the data there, let them go back and look at it—every time they look at it, they'll come out at the same place." Singal, "Interview with Arthur Raper," SHC folder 364.

25. Raper, *Preface to Peasantry*, xiii.

26. Raper, *Sharecroppers All* (Chapel Hill: University of North Carolina Press, 1941), v.

27. Raper, *Preface to Peasantry*, 8–9.

28. Raper, *Preface to Peasantry*, xv.

29. "A great number of the local white people and Negroes who happen to be in town without lunch eat at the store, making their meal of soda crackers and sardines, potted ham, and Vienna sausage or cheese, along with a bottle or two of Coca-Cola or other carbonated drink. Candy is often used as dessert for a repast of this kind. White people and Negroes sit on opposite coun-

ters or on the same counter and talk freely while eating their 'tin-can' lunches." Raper, *Preface to Peasantry*, 384–385.

30. Raper, *Preface to Peasantry*, 65.
31. Raper, *Preface to Peasantry*, 217–219.
32. Raper, *Preface to Peasantry*, 191.
33. "Six times as many Greene County migrants were living in Atlanta as in any other city, and eight times as many lived in Georgia as in any other state." Raper, *Preface to Peasantry*, 195.
34. Raper, *Preface to Peasantry*, 206, 208.
35. Raper, "Lynching and Racial Exploitation," unpublished manuscript, dated 1933, early 1934, SHC folder 33.
36. Raper, *Preface to Peasantry*, 208.
37. Raper, *Preface to Peasantry*, 209, 210.
38. Raper, *Preface to Peasantry*, 122.
39. Raper, *Preface to Peasantry*, 122, 123.
40. Raper, *Preface to Peasantry*, 168.
41. Raper also painted a portrait of an acceptable black farmer, however, that was not altogether flattering. "At a Republican mass meeting held in the Macon County courthouse to which whites and Negroes were invited, a very astute property-owning Negro rose to answer the accusation that the federal government was doing nothing to help the rural Negro. He said the great need of the rural Negroes of Macon and surrounding counties was more potatoes and peanuts and corn and chickens and cows, rather than algebra, rhetoric, philosophy, and Latin. 'We need,' said he in closing, 'more food and better houses, not more books and bigger books. You know, I like substance better than sound: I like a whole lots better a fellow who says 'dem taters' and has some, than a fellow who says 'those potatoes' and has none.' His remarks were enjoyed almost beyond measure by the local white people, most of whom went there to see what 'niggers' and white Republicans could talk about. The speaker is the kind of Negro who votes most often in the rural Black Belt." Raper, *Preface to Peasantry*, 170.
42. Raper, *Preface to Peasantry*, 162.
43. Raper, *Preface to Peasantry*, 371.
44. Raper, *Preface to Peasantry*, 372.
45. "The only institutions which serve both races in Greene and Macon counties are commercial or governmental in nature; the institutions operated to improve, enlighten, and enrich the body, mind, and spirit serve the races separately." Raper, *Preface to Peasantry*, 165.
46. "Negroes and whites use the same stores and banks because they have the same kind of money. They use the same post office and courthouse because they have the same government.

"Even though the post office is sometimes referred to by Negroes as 'the white folks' post office,' they demonstrate that they trust it more than any other institution serving both races in the Black Belt community. They often buy money orders for mail order houses; they send and receive letters containing discussions which would not be tolerated if known by the local white community. Their confidence is seldom violated. The United States Post Office is practically immune to the dominant local white assumption that the Negro's rights are nowhere outside the reach and control of white public opinion." Raper, *Preface to Peasantry*, 280–281.
47. Raper, *Preface to Peasantry*, 276.
48. Raper, *Preface to Peasantry*, 165.
49. Raper, *Preface to Peasantry*, 347–348, 349.

50. Raper, *Preface to Peasantry*, 165.

51. Raper, *Preface to Peasantry*, 177.

52. "When her sister or daughter dies she takes the small children and rears them; when the family moves to another tenant house she puts up new clothes lines and clears the path to the spring or well and chops the weeds from the back door. When the busy season comes she prepares breakfast for the entire family, and, often leaving a small baby at the house with a young child, works until the middle of the day when she returns to the kitchen and prepares a hasty meal for her family. She goes back into the field in early afternoon and works until almost dark, returning to prepare supper and put tired children to bed. When the crop is poor she takes in additional washing or finds some neighbor who will give her a day's work now and then; when there is no work which she must do in the field or away from home, she gets out the family wash and attends to her housework, which usually includes the cultivating of whatever garden the family has and often the chopping of the wood for the stove. When 'hard times' force the family to leave the home county, the father goes ahead to find work while the mother waits for word to come; then with bundles of belongings she gets her children on the train for a place where she hopes for an easier life but does not always find it." Raper, *Preface to Peasantry*, 75.

53. Raper, *Preface to Peasantry*, 174.

54. Raper, *Preface to Peasantry*, 87.

55. Raper, *Preface to Peasantry*, 175.

56. Raper, *Preface to Peasantry*, 392.

57. Raper, *Preface to Peasantry*, 180.

58. Raper, "The Southern Negro and the NRA," CIC report, no date, SHC folder 42.

59. Raper, *Preface to Peasantry*, 237–238.

60. Raper, *Preface to Peasantry*, 259.

61. Raper, *Preface to Peasantry*, 311.

62. Raper, *Preface to Peasantry*, 263.

63. Raper, "We are in the depression. What has sociology to offer?" SHC folder 34. Another story Raper told was about the aversion landowners felt to plowing up their cotton. We might, with understatement, call it counter-intuitive for those who "year in and year out had been taught above everything else to treat the cotton plant with respect.

"The following case, from Greene County, is typical: A planter got in his automobile one mid-afternoon and rode to the plantation where his six tenants were waiting for him under a chinaberry tree at the corner of a cotton field. He placed a cord 210 feet long in the hands of two tenants and told them to stretch it across the ends of the rows. That measured one side of one acre. The man at the far end marked the place by knocking his heel in the soft ground and moved on another length of the cord. This time, when he marked the spot by pulling up a handful of cotton stalks, a glum look came over the tenant at the other end of the cord—it was his cotton. Five lengths carried them to the corner of the field, where the man at the back swung across the rows to take the lead, and now having got beyond his own cotton, marked the end of the cord five times with a green pyramid of pregnant stalks. Turning back up the other end of the rows for five cords and then down the rows for five cords, to the starting point, the party measured off the twenty-five acres to be plowed up.

"As he left the field, the planter told them that he was expecting to receive final instructions any day and he would let them know when to plow it up. The tenants looked out over their twenty-five acres of good cotton without any show of pleasure and without any suggestion that they would do other than follow their landlord's instructions.

"In low tones, one tenant said to another: 'You know, I ain't never pulled up no cotton stalks befo', and somehow I don't like the idea.' 'I been feelin' sorter funeral-like all afternoon,' said another. A third relieved their gloom somewhat by suggesting: 'Let's swap work that day; you plow up mine, and I'll plow up yours.'" Raper, *Preface to Peasantry*, 244–245.

64. Raper, *Preface to Peasantry*, 245.
65. Raper, *Preface to Peasantry*, 256–257.
66. Raper, *Preface to Peasantry*, 269.
67. Raper, *Preface to Peasantry*, 272.
68. Raper, *Preface to Peasantry*, 267.
69. Raper, *Preface to Peasantry*, 406–407.
70. During the early and mid-1930s, Raper was also busy setting up the annual meetings of the Council on a Christian Social Order, as its executive secretary.
71. *Atlanta World*, "Dr. Raper Says Americans Are Big Exploiters," April 12, 1936, SHC folder 732.
72. *DeKalb Era*, "Dr. Raper Addresses Sunday School Body Here, Agnes Scott Professor Criticizes Destruction of Natural Resources," August 8, 1935, SHC folder 732.
73. In 1934 alone, Raper wrote articles, including "The Southern Negro and the NRA," and reports, including "A Rural Negro Community." He also taught a class at Gammon Theological Seminary and Atlanta University on "Race Relations" and facilitated women's political groups.
74. In Texas during the 1920s, Jessie Daniel Ames and her volunteers appeared before the Presbyterian Synod, the Mission Conferences and Annual Conferences of the Texas Methodists, Presbyterian Conferences for Negro Women, as well as various mission schools in Dallas and Houston, among many other groups. Robert Eleazer, who directed the CIC's publicity, cultivated the editors of young people's religious magazines, offering them various program materials, and contributed literature for special undertakings such as the Southern Methodists' "Youth Caravan." Ellis, "The Commission on Interracial Cooperation, 1919–1944," 233–238.
75. Ellis, "The Commission on Interracial Cooperation, 1919–1944."
76. Walter Jackson, "Interview at Slope Oaks," April 13, 1977, SHC folder 576.
77. *Atlanta World*, "'College Night' Is Brilliant; Raper Stirs Throng," April 29, 1935. SHC folder 51.
78. Raper, "War and Peace, The Past War and the Threats of Future Ones," Armistice Day address at the Haygood Memorial Church, November 11, 1934, SHC folder 43.
79. Raper, "War and Peace, The Past War and the Threats of Future Ones," Armistice Day address at the Haygood Memorial Church, November 11, 1934, SHC folder 43.
80. Raper, "War and Peace, The Past War and the Threats of Future Ones," Armistice Day address at the Haygood Memorial Church, November 11, 1934, SHC folder 43.
81. Raper, "Philosophy of Cooperative Action (A little think piece–1935–Raper)," unpublished manuscript, SHC folder 42.
82. Raper, "Why Study Sociology?" WSB Radio transcript, March 4, 1934, SHC folder 40. Raper went on to define his sense of the difference between sociology and history. "Briefly, history seeks to find out what actually happened and how it came about; while sociology seeks to explain the nature of the social process involved in causing the particular instances studied by history. That is, history seeks to interpret; sociology seeks to explain. Incidentally, just as the most

stimulating historians utilize the sociological method, the most vital sociologists have a general appreciation of the most important data of history and the other social sciences."

83. William Leuchtenburg writes, "If one examines the experience of the American farmer between 1932 and 1939, one is struck by the enormously increased involvement of the national government. Though the Department of Agriculture had been very active since the late nineteenth century, it had never been so intimately concerned with the everyday life or the economic welfare of the farmer. Under the New Deal this changes dramatically. (By the way, the developments I have been describing should not necessarily all be though of as good. Whether the subsidy program has been a success, whether public housing projects are well conceived, whether intellectuals ought to be so involved in government are all debatable questions.)" William Leuchtenburg, "The Great Depression and the New Deal," in *The FDR Years: On Roosevelt and His Legacy* (New York: Columbia University Press, 1995), 230.

84. Ellis, "The Commission on Interracial Cooperation, 1919–1944," 316–317. The Bankhead-Jones Farm Tenant Bill remained too radical an idea to many of Roosevelt's fellow Democrats from the South, and it was never pursued as vigorously as Alexander and Raper had hoped.

85. When the Bankhead-Jones bill was passed the following year, the Resettlement Authority, and later the Farm Security Administration, shifted the bill's funding toward Alexander's more moderate vision of facilitating land sales to small farmers, rather than Tugwell's plan to create cooperative farm communities.

86. "Alexander was tremendously concerned that the Negro share more equitably in these programs than the Negro had normally shared in the public services in the South, so he found it very convenient to let me spend a lot of time looking at how these programs were working, and I did very gladly, and we got the materials together and then sent it to Washington." By the time Roosevelt was elected, Alexander was already well-practiced in serving as what Raper called "the channel, the prod, as it were, the Southern prod to the administration to shore up its performance with reference to the Negro group, and I was out and about in the rural parts of the South and knew a tremendous number of people, and very quickly could get the dope as it were, on how the programs were working." Not surprisingly, given Roosevelt's predilection for turning to critics for advice, Alexander was offered a federal post in 1935. He would continue to direct the commission while working in Washington as head of the Farm Security Administration. His channel became for Raper an official's voice in Washington. At the same time, Alexander's departure from Atlanta signaled not only the commission's decline, but reflected the shift in emphasis, with regard to America's social policy, from private philanthropy to federal intervention.

87. John Egerton, *Speak Now Against the Day* (New York: Alfred A. Knopf, 1994), 95.

88. Singal, "Interview with Arthur Raper," SHC folder 364.

89. Raper, "Federal Relief in Georgia," unpublished government manuscript, March 1934, SHC folder 41.

90. "Alexander knew how to use a staff associate—let him go out and get significant data, turn it over to Alexander and answer his few clarifying questions, and he'd make it his own; he'd get up and talk about it like he himself had collected the information personally." Raper, "When we went back home," unpublished manuscript, November 1977, SHC folder 548.

91. Raper also used the Agnes Scott position to advance his speaking engagements. "I was introduced, I suspect, one-third of the time at the places that I went to speak, as Professor of Sociology at Agnes Scott College, rather than Research Secretary of the Interracial Commission." No matter, he never made any bones about the content of his speeches. "They knew what I was

going to talk about. I was going to talk primarily about the stuff I had gotten as Research Secretary at the Interracial Commission, . . . which was the lynchings, and which was the soil erosion . . . and man-land-relation matter." Walter Jackson, "Interview at Slope Oaks," April 13, 1977, SHC folder 576.

92. Raper, "When we went back home," unpublished manuscript, November 1973, SHC folder 438.

93. Jackson, "Interview at Slope Oaks," SHC folder 576.

New Deal Intermezzo

1. This episode is drawn from Raper's field notes: Arthur Raper, "Putnam County, Georgia—Oct. 1–4, 1934," unpublished manuscript. SHC folder 880.

Chapter 6. "The Divine Right of the Common Good"

1. Arthur Raper, "Notes on trip to Hillhouse, Mississippi, and Eastern Arkansas," September 11–14, 1936, SHC folder 910.

2. Raper quickly saw the inevitability of machine agriculture. "It's my observation that when a machine had been perfected to the place where it will mechanically do the job, that you can't have labor abundant enough or cheap enough to keep hand labor out there. The owners simply won't use them. Now I know the typical USDA farm line; namely, that labor was so high, was the reason we brought in the combine, and labor was so high and scarce that the owners had to pick cotton with machines. That is not so. The combine came in right after the depression. The cotton picker came in not all together at scarce labor times. Whenever you get a good machine that will do something dependably, tenants' cabins are in the way, untrained people are in the way, and you can't make them cheap enough and available enough to be used." UNC History Honors Society, "Transcription of Statements by Arthur F. Raper and H. L. Mitchell," unpublished manuscript, January 29, 1974, SHC folder 448.

3. Raper, letter to Will Alexander, September 25, 1936, SHC folder 48.

4. Raper's kind of cooperative Progressivism was at work throughout the New Deal. The WPA travel guides provide numerous examples of New Deal applications of cooperative effort, scientific planning, and government resources. "The *Wisconsin Guide*," its foreword explained, "like all the others published under the auspices of the Work Projects Administration, is a product of cooperative effort by numerous writers working to a definite plan under the supervision of a State Director and the National Director."

5. Raper believed that the Rusts themselves hoped to demonstrate at the Delta Co-op "that their mechanical cotton picker can serve, rather than displace, agricultural labor." Raper, "Farm Tenancy and the Delta Cooperative Farm," *Presbyterian Survey* 27, no. 8 (August 1937), SHC folder 64.

6. Sherwood Eddy, letter to members of the Delta Cooperative Farm, May 3, 1938, SHC folder 914b.

7. John Egerton, *Speak Now Against the Day* (New York: Alfred A. Knopf, 1994), 126–127.

8. Raper, letter to Will Alexander, September 25, 1936, SHC folder 48.

9. Raper, letter to Will Alexander, September 25, 1936, SHC folder 48.

10. All through his career, Raper made a point of talking with the widest range of people he could find, often challenging those he interviewed to think through their opinions. The first

Delta Co-op trip was followed by the same kind of reports of interviews he eventually ended up conducting across the United States and throughout the Third World. "Next I talked with a self-made banker, W. W. Campbell. He was quite interested in the whole situation. He had been raised on a poor farm in the hills—yes, he had noticed that the poorest people lived on the richest land, but he had never thought of it before. He now 'lives on' the plantation system, but he feels that the farmers ought to own their land. When I suggested corporately owned lands he shied a bit. The obvious answer was he could see how small individual owners would fit into the system of rural and town economy which his bank serves, or lives off, or exploits as the case may be. Cooperatives, etc., looked rather strange to a man who owns stocks and bonds and deals with them, corporate wealth. Why must the farmer remain the easy mark for all who would get more out of him than they give him in return. 'Well, you may be right,' he said, 'maybe you are, I've just not thought of that side of it.' This discussion arose in our talk about the Bankhead-Jones Bill, and its provisions for cooperatives and corporately owned farms. There are not any more good reasons for cutting up a 2,000 acre farm into twenty acre farms than there are for giving each employee of the American Telephone and Telegraph a few telephone poles on a little telephone company. The best way to do both, if we would provide a purchasing power to use the goods we need, is to leave the unit large through provisions for corporate ownership, collective ownership; that is, social responsibility put on property values created by society's needs and/or wishes.

"Reverend Hayden, pastor of the local Forrest City church, was with me at the interview. He agreed with me and also with the banker. It was clear that he wanted to help the tenants and landlords by some genuine changes no less than he wanted to remain quite in the favor of the planters so long as the present exploitative system is followed." Raper, letter to Will Alexander, September 25, 1936, SHC folder 48.

11. Raper, letter to Charles S. Johnson, October 25, 1938, SHC folder 101.

12. Raper, "Farm Tenancy and the Delta Cooperative Farm," *Presbyterian Survey* 27, no. 8 (August 1937), SHC folder 64.

13. Charles S. Johnson and Raper, "Personal Note for Trustees' Meeting, November 1, 1938," November 1, 1938, SHC folder 918.

14. Raper, "Farm Tenancy and the Delta Cooperative Farm," *Presbyterian Survey* 27, no. 8 (August 1937), SHC folder 64.

15. Raper, letter to Will Alexander, May 6, 1938, SHC folder 914b.

16. "Memorandum for the Trustees' Meeting of the Delta Cooperative Farm," October 25, 1938, SHC folder 74.

17. "Memorandum for the Trustees' Meeting of the Delta Cooperative Farm," October 25, 1938, SHC folder 74. Dr. William Amberson accused Eddy at a board meeting, then fired off a letter of resignation from the board, complaining about Eddy's economic management, and claiming, "Never before have I seen with such blinding clarity the essential and irreconcilable conflict between the scientific and the ecclesiastical approach to social problems. Never before have I become so deeply committed to the scientific search for knowledge as opposed to all other methods." William R. Amberson, "Statement to the Board of Trustees of the Delta Cooperative Farms, Inc.," February 22, 1939, SHC folder 920.

18. Egerton, *Speak Now Against the Day*, 127.

19. Robert L. Dorman, *Revolt of the Provinces: The Regionalist Movement in America, 1920–1945* (Chapel Hill: University of North Carolina Press, 1993).

20. Raper, letter to Sam Franklin, March 2, 1979, SHC folder 717.

21. Raper, letter to Will Alexander, May 27, 1937, SHC folder 731. Raper visited the resettlement projects in all these states. Projects included, for example, a land-use program for 12,000 acres of eroded crop land in northwestern Kentucky; a cooperative project in which housing was constructed for 80 farm families, each on its own tract of land; and construction of houses for 350 low-income farm families, with 200 of them for blacks. Raper, "Project Description," unpublished manuscript, June 11, 1937, SHC folder 911.

22. Raper, "Unarranged Notes—Dust Bowl," unpublished manuscript, September 6–23, 1937, SHC folder 901.

23. UNC History Honor Society, "Transcriptions of Statements by AFR and H. L. Mitchell," January 29, 1974, 10, SHC folder 448.

24. UNC History Honor Society, "Transcriptions of Statements by AFR and H. L. Mitchell," January 29, 1974, 8, SHC folder 448.

25. As Patricia Sullivan writes, "The STFU, in conjunction with its sympathetic supporters in the Roosevelt administration, succeeded in broadening the debate over federal farm policy and compelling the government to address the issues of rural poverty and displacement." Patricia Sullivan, *Days of Hope: Race and Democracy in the New Deal* (Chapel Hill: University of North Carolina Press, 1996), 58–59.

26. Sullivan, *Days of Hope*, 43; Frank McCallister, "Report on Caruthersville, Missouri, Investigation, Highly Confidential, Not for Publication," unpublished manuscript, 1938, SHC folder 922.

27. UNC History Honor Society, "Transcriptions of Statements by AFR and H. L. Mitchell," SHC folder 448.

28. Raper, "Civitan Luncheon Meeting," address presented at the Atlanta Athletic Club, January 12, 1937, SHC folder 49.

29. Raper, "Civitan Luncheon Meeting," address presented at the Atlanta Athletic Club, January 12, 1937, SHC folder 49.

30. Witherspoon Dodge, "Letter to Arthur Raper," January 16, 1937, SHC folder 56.

31. Raper, unpublished handwritten notes dated "Late 1930s and early 1940s," SHC folder 716.

32. Raper himself was often skeptical of northern critics. "In general, the white people farthest removed from the Negro are kindlier in theory and harsher in practice, while those in close contact are uncompromising in theory but quite humane in specific situations." Raper, "Youth judges race relations," unpublished manuscript, undated—late 1920s, SHC folder 26.

33. UNC Oral History Seminar, "Interview with Arthur Raper," unpublished manuscript, January 29, 1974, SHC folder 447.

34. Walter Jackson, "Interview at Slope Oaks," April 13, 1977, SHC folder 576. "Interview with Arthur Raper, conducted by the Oral History Seminar for the Southern Oral History Program," 11 and 29, SHC folder 447. Raper always said northern audiences were not as receptive to his findings. They would listen, he said, "if somebody wanted their emotions twitted and wanted to talk about 'these poor black folks down there, and how damnable they're being treated by this and that and the other,'" he explained. "But if we came around to *Sharecroppers All* and those theses, don't you see, that bothered them more than it did the southerners." "Interview with Arthur Raper, conducted by the Oral History Seminar for the Southern Oral History Program," 11 and 29, SHC folder 447.

35. Singal interview with Arthur Raper, 78–79, SHC folder 464.

36. "Mr. Raper Entertains Sociology Students," *Agonistic,* October 25, 1936, SHC folder 52.

37. Raper, radio address, "Agnes Scott Program," WSB radio, March 18, 1936, SHC folder 48.

38. Raper, untitled notes, February 9, 1979, SHC folder 669.

39. David L. Carlton and Peter Coclanis, eds., *Confronting Southern Poverty in the Great Depression: The Report on Economic Conditions of the South* (Boston: St. Martin's Press, 1996).

40. Commission on Interracial Cooperation, "The Mob Still Rides," pamphlet published 1936, SHC folder 45.

41. "Negro Education Urged of South," *Birmingham News,* March 16, 1936. "Racial Exploitation Blamed in Lynchings," *Palm Beach Times,* March 16, 1936, SHC folder 45.

42. Stewart E. Tolnay and E. M. Beck, *A Festival of Violence: An Analysis of Southern Lynchings, 1882–1930* (Urbana and Chicago: University of Illinois Press, 1995), 202.

43. Raper told historian Jacqueline Hall, "I had seen, practically everywhere I had been, people who would have been glad to have been asked questions under protection, who perjured themselves if they didn't answer them correctly, they would have answered them correctly because, 'this is my duty.' And they would have done it." Jacqueline Dowd Hall, "Interview with Arthur Raper," January 30, 1974, SHC folder 449.

44. According to Raper, Ames "felt that lynching and all matters generally was of concern to the local authorities, to the states, the districts and the counties. It did not go to the national level. It stopped." Hall, "Interview with Arthur Raper," January 30, 1974, SHC folder 449.

45. Ann Wells Ellis, "The Commission on Interracial Cooperation, 1919–1944: Its Activities and Results" (Ph.D. diss., Georgia State University, 1975), 103–104. Jacquelyn Down Hall, *Revolt Against Chivalry: Jessie Daniel Ames and the Women's Campaign Against Lynching* (New York: Columbia University Press, 1979).

46. Ellis, "The Commission on Interracial Cooperation, 1919–1944," 340.

47. Ellis, "The Commission on Interracial Cooperation, 1919–1944," 159.

48. Morton Sosna, "Personal interview with Arthur Raper," April 23, 1971, 63–64, SHC folder 370.

49. Raper told Sosna, "I think that just to discuss [segregation] and ask people whether or not they should do it, they would have told me not to do anything. I wouldn't have made any of the speeches I made. I wouldn't have worked on any of the things I've done. I wouldn't have published any of the books that I published. I'd have been told to leave every one of them off. . . . You perhaps can go on and do it and they'll accept it. . . . I know you can't ask if you can do it. They'll tell you 'no' every time, because there's some scared guy over here that if he hears about it, why he'll object. And you're reporting to him, and you're beholden to him, and you're kind of building yourself up by getting yourself as a very secure Southerner in his eyes. I never did raise the question of whether to do it or not." Sosna, "Personal interview with Arthur Raper," SHC folder 370.

50. *Barnesville News-Gazette,* "Dr. Raper makes stiring [sic] address on ills attending tenant farming," February 28, 1936, SHC folder 44.

51. Raper, "The Cause, Curse, and Cure of Tenancy," address transcribed by M. H. Hansell, SHC folder 44.

52. Raper, letter to Mrs. Carter, August 10, 1938, SHC folder 732.

53. Jackson, "Interview at Slope Oaks," April 13, 1977, SHC folder 576.

54. Egerton, *Speak Now Against the Day,* 184.

55. Raper characterized the conference as "easily the most representative and diverse group of

Southerners ever to spend four days discussing Southern conditions. Ranking officials from several states were there along with Mrs. Roosevelt, U. S. Congressmen, representatives of the Works Progress Administration, the Farm Security Administration, the National Youth Administration, and other federal agencies. Participating also were sheriffs, jailers, probation officers, and petty court officials. Then there were newspaper owners and editors, columnists, and feature writers. A number of college presidents, deans, professors, and college students were in attendance, as were also leaders from the public schools. Scattered among the group were ministers. . . . Responsible local and regional labor leaders of the C.I.O. and A. F. of L. were present. . . . On hand, too, were ex-sharecroppers evicted for union activities, labor union leaders who had been manhandled.

"Adding still further variety to the delegates were two or three hundred representative Negroes: educators, ministers, government officials, labor leaders and on through the same varied list as the whites, except as Negroes are automatically excluded for some activities because of race. Of all the occupational groups in the South, industrialists and ministers had fewest representatives at the Conference." Raper, "The Southern Conference for Human Welfare, First Meeting, Birmingham, Alabama, November 20–23, 1938," unpublished manuscript, SHC folder 947.

56. Sullivan, *Days of Hope*, 98–101.

57. Raper, "The Southern Conference for Human Welfare, First Meeting, Birmingham, Alabama, November 20–23, 1938," unpublished manuscript, SHC folder 947.

58. Daniel Singal, "Interview with Arthur Raper," January 18, 1971, SHC folder 364.

59. Singal, "Interview with Arthur Raper," SHC folder 364.

60. William Cooper and Thomas Terrill, *The American South: A History* (New York: Alfred A. Knopf, 1991), 654.

61. Raper, "The Southern Conference for Human Welfare, First Meeting, Birmingham, Alabama, November 20–23, 1938," unpublished manuscript, SHC folder 947.

62. Raper, "The Southern Conference for Human Welfare, First Meeting, Birmingham, Alabama, November 20–23, 1938," unpublished manuscript, SHC folder 947.

63. Raper, "The Southern Conference for Human Welfare, First Meeting, Birmingham, Alabama, November 20–23, 1938," unpublished manuscript, SHC folder 947.

64. Morton Sosna, *In Search of the Silent South: Southern Liberals and the Race Issue* (New York: Columbia University Press, 1977), 122.

65. Raper, "The Southern Conference for Human Welfare, First Meeting, Birmingham, Alabama, November 20–23, 1938," unpublished manuscript, SHC folder 947.

66. Raper's belief in the New Deal coalition of blacks and working-class whites had its roots in his father's brand of Populism and Mr. Frank's faith that the common denominator of disinheritance would overcome race prejudice, lead to political and economic leverage, and increase opportunities for more folks to work their own farms and become solid citizens.

67. Sullivan, *Days of Hope*, 98–101.

68. In *Days of Hope,* Sullivan considers the SCHW as a watershed event, an indication of a bolder effort taking shape in southern race relations. "Seasoned by the popular democratic impulses of the New Deal and the labor movement, the founding of the SCHW in 1938 marked a significant departure from the interracial movement born in the aftermath of World War I. Several former and longtime participants in the CIC, like Arthur Raper, Clark Foreman, and even CIC founder Will Alexander, embraced the SCHW as a natural extension and continuation of the work begun by the CIC. But for others, the SCHW's close ties to the Roosevelt administration, its efforts to

build a political program with mass appeal, and its resolution not to hold segregated meetings ran against the grain of southern liberalism and the interracial movement." The SCHW separated traditional southern liberals from those advocating racial equality. "During the SCHW founding meeting, Mark Ethridge, editor of the *Louisville Courier-Journal*, convened a small group to consider Howard Odum's plan for a new regional organization. A follow-up meeting, consisting mostly of journalists and academics, met in Atlanta, with Charles S. Johnson present as the sole black participant. Countering the perceived militancy of the SCHW, the group reaffirmed its commitment to slow, carefully moderated change and declared, 'Since our conditions are products of a long existent economy, remedial action will require a relatively long period of time.'" Sullivan, *Days of Hope*, 163.

69. Egerton, *Speak Now Against the Day*, 292. After fighting for its life during the first several, overheated years of the Cold War, the organization finally disbanded in 1948. By then, Raper was working in Japan and Taiwan.

70. *Atlanta Constitution*, "Welfare Officials No Reds; Dr. Raper, Educator Replies to Charges That Communists Instigated Southern Conference," November 27, 1938, SHC folder 946.

71. *Atlanta Constitution*, "Welfare Officials No Reds; Dr. Raper, Educator Replies to Charges That Communists Instigated Southern Conference," SHC folder 946.

72. Jackson, "Interview at Slope Oaks," April 13, 1977, SHC folder 576.

73. Jackson, "Interview at Slope Oaks," April 13, 1977, SHC folder 576.

74. Sosna, "Personal interview with Arthur Raper," 122, SHC folder 370.

75. Singal, "Interview with Arthur Raper," SHC folder 364.

76. Sullivan, *Days of Hope*. Raper was not as interested in peaceful race relations per se, as Odum or many other southern liberals, but instead with constitutionality. He told a story about John Hope that spoke about his own perspective.

"The Atlanta Christian Council, which was more conservative than the Interracial Commission was, pushed hard to get an agreement with the Negroes that if they would set up a certain street somewhere that the whites would then let the Negroes come up to there: that that would save these bombings when blacks went over into white neighborhoods, you know.

"Well, John Hope would never agree to that. They said John Hope was unreasonable. John Hope was right, because what John Hope would have done is that he would have relinquished his claim on equality under the Constitution. He would have said: 'Well, this segregation is all right.'

"He said he would not do it. He was correct, and not the fellows who were pushing for peace and harmony, like getting a line established up there where the demarcation was to be." Jackson, "Interview at Slope Oaks," April 13, 1977, SHC folder 576.

77. Raper, "The Southern Conference for Human Welfare, First Meeting, Birmingham, Alabama, November 20–23, 1938," SHC folder 947.

78. Jackson, "Interview at Slope Oaks," April 13, 1977, 60–61, SHC folder 576.

79. Jackson, "Interview at Slope Oaks," April 13, 1977, 60–61, SHC folder 576.

80. Raper and Ira De A. Reid, *Sharecroppers All* (Chapel Hill: University of North Carolina Press, 1938), 258. "I did this because at some of the recent chapter meetings Clark Foreman and others seemed to be to be responding to forces outside themselves, and unknown to me. They often did things differently from the way we in committee meetings had decided. Later on, I was glad I had sensed when it was that the leadership of SCHW was drifting into the hands of the Communists. There was never a southwide meeting of the SCHW again, and after some months, the Wash-

ington Chapter, too, became inactive. Naturally I wonder, maybe a bit vain: if I had taken the chairmanship of the Washington chapter, if we could have kept it a viable activity? And if so, could the Southern Conference have continued to function? It would have been very difficult at best for many liberals naturally leaned toward Henry Wallace's presidential candidacy, and his overly zealous political promoters went out and got votes from any, we repeat any, source they could." Raper, "When we went back home," unpublished manuscript, October 18—November 6, 1973, SHC folder 438. Egerton, *Speak Now Against the Day;* Sullivan, *Days of Hope.*

81. Singal, "Interview with Arthur Raper," SHC folder 364.

82. Raper and Reid, *Sharecroppers All,* vi—vii.

83. Richard King, *A Southern Renaissance: The Cultural Awakening of the American South, 1930–1955* (New York: Oxford University Press, 1980), 48.

84. Raper and Reid, *Sharecroppers All,* vii.

85. Donald Davidson, "A Sociologist in Eden," *The American Review* 8 (November 1936–March 1937): 177–204.

86. Raper, letter to Felder Frederick, December 30, 1936, SHC folder 49.

87. Raper, handwritten note, August 8, 1976, SHC folder 49.

88. Raper, "The South Strains Toward Decency," *North American Review* 243, no. 1 (Spring 1937): 106–122.

89. Davidson, "A Sociologist in Eden," 177–204.

90. Raper, "The Changing Status of Southern Rural Dwellers, A Study of Current Economic and Social Adjustments," January 6, 1938, SHC folder 101.

91. Ira De A. Reid, letter to Raper, March 2, 1938, SHC folder 99.

92. Raper, letter to W. T. Couch, March 24, 1939, UNC Press Archives, Subgroup 4: Author/Title Publication Records, Raper, A. F., *Sharecroppers All,* 1 of 2.

93. Sosna, "Personal interview with Arthur Raper," 34, 36, 37, SHC folder 370.

94. Raper and Reid, *Sharecroppers All,* 232.

95. S. H. Hobbs Jr., letter to W. T. Couch, March 16, 1939, UNC Press Archives, Subgroup 4: Author/Title Publication Records, Raper, A. F., *Sharecroppers All,* 1 of 2.

96. Orville A. Park, letter to W. T. Couch, March 31, 1939, UNC Press Archives, Subgroup 4: Author/Title Publication Records, Raper, A. F., *Sharecroppers All,* 1 of 2.

97. Will Alexander, letter to Arthur Raper, March 1, 1939, SHC folder 99.

98. Lucy R. Mason, letter to W. T. Couch, June 22, 1939, UNC Press Archives, Subgroup 4: Author/Title Publication Records, Raper, A. F., *Sharecroppers All,* lot 2.

99. Margaret Haygood, "Comments on *Sharecroppers All* by Arthur Raper and Ira De A. Reid," February 8, 1940, UNC Press Archives, Subgroup 4: Author/Title Publication Records, Raper, A. F., *Sharecroppers All,* 1 of 2.

100. Raper, letter to W. T. Couch, July 24, 1939, UNC Press Archives, Subgroup 4: Author/Title Publication Records, Raper, A. F., *Sharecroppers All,* 1 of 2.

101. Couch wrote Raper what is essentially a long blackmail letter. The book would cost at least $2,500, and Couch wanted Raper to secure at least $1,800 from Odum to guarantee its publication. "If in my efforts to find ways to finance the work of this organization I had had from sociologists here and elsewhere a small fraction of the enthusiastic support which I have given to sociologists when they have come to me with proposals of books, then there would be no financial obstacle to our publishing your manuscript. To be specific, if Mr. Odum is interested in our publishing for you he can manage it quite easily. Now if you put the problem to Mr. Odum as I am

putting it to you, you not only will not solve this problem, but will make additional serious difficulties. It is clear you do not realize the powerful position which Mr. Odum holds. The fact is that he has not turned his finger in years to help us get financial support, but, on the contrary, has created obstacles, and expressed to me most extreme discouragement of my efforts.

"I cannot be certain, of course, of the terms under which Mr. Odum would be willing to help us, but my experience with him over a period of fourteen years indicates that he would be willing to help only on terms which would destroy the Press." W. T. Couch, letter to Arthur Raper, UNC Press Archives, Subgroup 4: Author/Title Publication Records, Raper, A. F., *Sharecroppers All*, 1 of 2.

102. Howard W. Odum, letter to Raper, September 11, 1939, SHC folder 100.

103. UNC Oral History Seminar, "Interview with Arthur Raper," January 29, 1974, SHC folder 447.

104. Another element of his increasing radicalism was Raper's labor activism at Highlander Folk School. During the mid-1930s, he conducted workshops on labor issues at Highlander, in the Appalachians of Tennessee. Established in 1932, with help from Will Alexander, and funding from Reinhold Niebuhr and Sherwood Eddy, Highlander tried to establish the regionalists' ideal of combining the preservation of southern folk culture with Progressive politics concerning race and class. The school intended to draw from working-class and farming families, but had trouble attracting students, because many rural mountain families were reluctant to send their daughters to a school with a left-wing reputation. And besides, many wondered why their children should go away to learn skills they could still learn at home. Still, the school attracted many of the region's social activists, and Raper was able to sustain many of his contacts in part through his workshops at Highlander.

Indicative of the lines that intersected at Highlander, in its library was a volume of *Preface to Peasantry*, inscribed from Walter White to Hugo Black. Raper used his Highlander workshops as a way to think out loud about politics. "People are of first importance in a democracy," he told a group at the school. "And democracy is superior to other political systems only to the degree that it affords the rank and file of people larger opportunities for growth and responsible participation." Raper, "The Highlanders—A Challenge to Democracy," unpublished manuscript, no date, SHC folder 48.

105. Raper and Reid, *Sharecroppers All*, 257–258.

106. Raper and Reid, *Sharecroppers All*, 214.

107. Raper and Reid, *Sharecroppers All*, 209.

108. Raper and Reid, *Sharecroppers All*, 141. Raper saw evidence that the changes taking place in the 1930s were the most far-reaching in history. "The field tools used by the typical tenant farmer would not seem strange to Moses and Hammurabi," he wrote. Southern sharecroppers were last of the line of American agrarians. Raper and Reid, *Sharecroppers All*, 21.

109. Raper and Reid, *Sharecroppers All*, 141.

110. Raper explained, "In frontier days the American family's security was attained largely through the mutual-aid practices within the local neighborhood. The size and complexities of the modern community render security impossible except through responsible personal participation in a centralized government equally jealous of the welfare of all the people. Uncle Sam has little choice but to secure the active interest of the South, as it is to the South's advantage to have the interest and assistance of the nation in its programs for self-improvement." Raper and Reid, *Sharecroppers All*, 140.

111. "Ira de A. Reid and I did jointly bring out *Sharecroppers All*," Raper told historian Walter Jackson. "It was a thoroughly joint effort." The prose style and the organization are very similar to that of Raper's other books, though, and particular figures of speech appear elsewhere in Raper's writing. My own sense is that the writing and organization was mainly Raper's. Jackson, "Interview at Slope Oaks," April 13, 1977, SHC folder 576.

112. Raper and Reid, *Sharecroppers All*, v.

113. Walter Prescott Webb was another regionalist who used the trope. In fact, Raper copied out a section from *Divided We Stand*, in which Webb compared medieval and modern feudalism. Originally, the system was intended to provide order in a chaotic society. "The sole motive of the American feudal system," on the other hand, "has been the economic one of making profits." Raper, "From *Divided We Stand*, by Walter Prescott Webb, pp. 56-59, 1938," unpublished manuscript, 1938, SHC folder 854.

Robert Dorman observes about the Chapel Hill regionalists, "By thus pointing to the essentially coercive and exploitative 'arrested frontier pattern' of the Southern economy, the Odum circle attempted, in sum, to reendow words like *aristocratic* and *feudalistic* with all the negative and antiexceptional connotations that by rights they should have in a New World context, signifying not romance and gentility, nor the sectional 'communities of interests' that Webb and Davidson assumed, but the 'differentials' of a 'stratified society,' the 'stern class lines' of 'social hierarchy.'" Dorman, *Revolt of the Provinces*, 184.

114. "Certainly the material disinheritance of the stranded population in the poor-land sections is no more harmful to personal integrity or hurtful to community standards than that lack of realism in the rich land areas and wealthy cities which makes much of the physical abundance there socially sterile." Raper and Reid, *Sharecroppers All*, 59.

115. Raper and Reid, *Sharecroppers All*, 48.

116. Raper and Reid, *Sharecroppers All*, v, vi.

117. Raper and Reid, *Sharecroppers All*, 191, 183–184, 185.

118. Raper and Reid, *Sharecroppers All*, 28, 29.

119. Raper and Reid, *Sharecroppers All*, 32–33.

120. Raper and Reid, *Sharecroppers All*, 224, 212, 178, 182.

121. Raper and Reid, *Sharecroppers All*, 180, 162. As Dorman writes, Raper "tended to shunt the issues of racism and nativism together with the problem of class oppression, believing as did many artists and intellectuals of the 1930s that the power underlying 100 percent Americanism was primarily economic." Dorman, *Revolt of the Provinces*, 239.

122. Raper and Reid, *Sharecroppers All*, 79.

123. Raper, "Some things to think about now, and hard," dated early 1934, SHC folder 40. Raper occasionally wrote short think pieces to work out an idea he had been puzzling with while on the road.

124. Raper and Reid, *Sharecroppers All*, 91, 97–98.

125. Raper and Reid, *Sharecroppers All*, 120.

126. Raper and Reid, *Sharecroppers All*, 104–105.

127. Raper and Reid, *Sharecroppers All*, 77. Raper addressed the two-ness of African American life in terms of class. "The Negro with education and means lives in two worlds. In one he is a 'colored gentleman,' in the other he is a 'nigger.' As he walks across the campus, he is a person of importance; but when he gets on the street car he has 'a place.' In a downtown department store he is the member of an 'inferior race' until he reaches the counter where the clerk appreciates his

purchases. Or he stands in the pulpit of his church, the most revered of men, only to become a 'nigger' four blocks up the street when his car bumps into the one ahead of him." Raper and Reid, *Sharecroppers All*, 87.

128. Raper and Reid, *Sharecroppers All*, 81–82.

129. Raper and Reid, *Sharecroppers All*, 30.

130. Raper and Reid, *Sharecroppers All*, 44.

131. Raper and Reid, *Sharecroppers All*, 265. "Experience has found no more effective method of coping with these discriminatory practices"; Raper and Reid, *Sharecroppers All*, 138. Raper stuck with his premise in *Sharecroppers All*, right into the 1970s, when an article in the *Washington Post*, titled "Sharecroppers Are Almost Gone From Miss. Cotton Farms," could make him think, "Yes, greatly reduced in the cotton South, especially on the best land. *But* there are lots of *sharecroppers* in non-farm enterprises, North, South, East, and West"; *Washington Post*, "Sharecroppers Are Almost Gone From Miss. Cotton Farms," January 25, 1971, SHC folder 717.

132. Theodore Langdon Van Norden, letter to Raper, August 9, 1942, SHC folder 100.

133. Raper, letter to Donald Comer, October 7, 1941, SHC folder 100.

134. Julia Raper, letter to Raper, January 13, 1941, SHC folder 100.

135. Walter White, letter to Raper, February 14, 1941, SHC folder 100.

136. Lillian Smith, letter to Raper, September 23, 1941, SHC folder 100.

Chapter 7. *An American Dilemma*

1. Jonathan Daniels, "Georgians Discover Georgia," *Survey Graphic, Magazine of Social Interpretation*, March 1939, SHC folder 78.

2. Daniels, "Georgians Discover Georgia," *Survey Graphic, Magazine of Social Interpretation*, March 1939, SHC folder 78.

3. *Atlanta Constitution*, "Atlanta to Recall War, Four-Day Fete Set for 'Gone With the Wind' Premiere," December 11, 1939.

4. Raper, letter to Guy B. Johnson, December 15, 1939, SHC folder 924.

5. Raper, "Appointments 1939," unpublished manuscript, 1939, SHC folder 86.

6. Gunnar Myrdal, *An American Dilemma* (New York: Harper & Row, 1944), xlix.

7. Myrdal, *An American Dilemma*, li.

8. In his author's preface to the book's twentieth anniversary edition, Myrdal goes on to say, "I was shocked and scared to the bones by all the evils I saw, and by the serious political implications of the problem which I could not fail to appreciate from the beginning." Myrdal, *An American Dilemma*, xxv. For background on Myrdal's project, see Walter Jackson, *Gunnar Myrdal and America's Conscience: Social Engineering and Racial Liberalism, 1938–1987* (Chapel Hill: University of North Carolina Press, 1990).

9. Myrdal, letter to Raper, May 5, 1939, SHC folder 924.

10. Myrdal, letter to Will Alexander, June 1, 1939, SHC folder 924.

11. Myrdal, *An American Dilemma*, lx, lxi.

12. Myrdal, *An American Dilemma*, lxxiv.

13. Myrdal, *An American Dilemma*, lxxvi.

14. Myrdal, *An American Dilemma*, lxxvi, lxxvii.

15. Myrdal, *An American Dilemma*, xxviii.

16. Myrdal, *An American Dilemma*, 270.

17. Mydral, *An American Dilemma*, 1023.

18. Myrdal, *An American Dilemma*, 1023.

19. "Race and Class Pressures" also included an extensive report on lynching, from which he drew heavily on his findings for *The Tragedy of Lynching*, and his subsequent studies for the Interracial Commission through the mid-1930s.

20. Raper, "Proposed Study for September to June," unpublished manuscript submitted to Gunnar Myrdal, June 1, 1939, SHC folder 1006.

21. Daniel Singal, "Interview with Arthur Raper," January 18, 1972, SHC folder 365.

22. "In fact," Myrdal told his contributors, "no type of research is so defenseless against biases as the ostentatiously pure fact-finding research. In our critical survey of the literature we will have occasion to illustrate the methodological weakness even from the present point of view of the type of scientific approach which is frequently referred to as the 'naïve empiricism.' . . .

"Only from specific valuations can it be ascertained whether a social situation should be deemed to be in 'balance' or 'disbalance,' 'harmony' or in 'disharmony,' and whether a social change is a 'disturbance,' an 'adjustment' or an 'accommodation.'" Gunnar Myrdal, "Intra-staff memorandum on Chapter B in the introductory section," undated, SHC folder 1012.

23. Gunnar Myrdal, "Memorandum to staff members and collaborators," February 8, 1940, SHC folder 1008.

24. Walter Jackson, "Interview at Slope Oaks," April 13, 1977, SHC folder 576.

25. Jackson, "Interview at Slope Oaks," April 13, 1977, SHC folder 576. Singal, "Interview with Arthur Raper," January 18, 1972, SHC folder 365.

26. Raper, "On the Crest of Forming Waves," unpublished manuscript, May 1976, 252, SHC folder 548.

27. Raper, "Race and Class Pressures," unpublished manuscript prepared for Gunnar Myrdal's *An American Dilemma*, June 1, 1940, 297–298, SHC folder 90.

28. Raper, "Race and Class Pressures," unpublished manuscript prepared for Gunnar Myrdal's *An American Dilemma*, June 1, 1940, 331–332, SHC folder 90.

29. Raper, "Race and Class Pressures," unpublished manuscript prepared for Gunnar Myrdal's *An American Dilemma*, June 1, 1940, 331–332, SHC folder 90.

30. Myrdal, *An American Dilemma*, 535.

31. As part of his research, Raper tactfully surveyed fifty southern chiefs of police to compile all kinds of data, from how many blacks their officers had shot to whether they used the term *bad nigger*. Most of the materials for "Race and Class Pressures" were gathered from direct observation and from current newspaper reports. In all, Raper's submission to Myrdal included six or seven hundred pages of appendices.

32. Myrdal, *An American Dilemma*, 538–539, 540, 541.

33. Raper, "Police," unpublished manuscript, January 1940, SHC folder 1058.

34. Myrdal, *An American Dilemma*, 544.

35. Raper, "Police," unpublished manuscript, January 1940, SHC folder 1058.

36. Myrdal, *An American Dilemma*, 557.

37. Raper returned to most of the towns where he had studied lynchings to chart the changes in the police and legal systems since the early 1930s, and he revised the studies he had compiled for Alexander at the Resettlement and Farm Security administrations.

38. Myrdal, *An American Dilemma*, 561, 562, 560.

39. Myrdal, *An American Dilemma*, 564, 563.

40. Raper, "Race and Class Pressures," unpublished manuscript prepared for Gunnar Myrdal's *An American Dilemma*, June 1, 1940, 103–104, SHC folder 90.

41. Singal, "Interview with Arthur Raper," January 18, 1972, SHC folder 365.

42. Singal, "Interview with Arthur Raper," January 18, 1972, SHC folder 365.

43. Singal, "Interview with Arthur Raper," January 18, 1972, SHC folder 365.

44. Gunnar Myrdal, unpublished notes, November 17, 1939, SHC folder 924.

45. Raper, "Lest I Forget," unpublished manuscript, November 10, 1949, SHC folder 172.

46. Raper, "Lest I Forget," unpublished manuscript, November 10, 1949, SHC folder 172.

47. Raper, "Lest I Forget," unpublished manuscript, November 10, 1949, SHC folder 172.

48. In October 1939, he had written Walter White. "Now the more I think of it the more it occurs to me that the assignment which I have just about falls squarely in the middle of the field of the NAACP's activities," he explained. "I do want, before preparing the final report in the early spring, to have exposed myself to such a gold mine of information which your file is." Raper, "Appointments 1939," unpublished manuscript, 1939, SHC folder 86.

49. Singal, "Interview with Arthur Raper," SHC folder 365.

50. Raper, "Buffalo, New York, Notes on Dan Montgomery's restaurants," February 9, 1940, SHC folder 1026.

51. "I kept saying that there were people all over the South who would like to give testimony as to who did the lynching if they could be protected, that they would be relieved to have a framework within which they were under oath as a citizen to tell the truth about what they knew about a particular lynching. They know it and they'll tell it if a framework can be provided in which they aren't exposing themselves legally or personally and individually. They will. So I said I thought the federal anti-lynching legislation was the right thing. . . . it was from the point of view of providing a framework within which this fellow here who wants to tell the truth and who doesn't like people being lynched and would like to say 'Get rid of it.'" Morton Sosna, "Personal interview with Arthur Raper," April 23, 1971, SHC folder 370.

52. Raper, "When we went back home," unpublished manuscript, October 18–November 6, 1973, SHC folder 438.

53. Jacquelyn Dowd Hall, "Interview with Arthur Raper," January 30, 1974, SHC folder 449.

54. Raper, telegram to Walter F. George and Richard B. Russell, May 24, 1940, SHC folder 92.

55. Stephen J. Whitfield, *The Culture of the Cold War* (Baltimore: Johns Hopkins University Press, 1991), 23.

56. William Cooper and Thomas Terrill, *The American South: A History* (New York: Alfred A. Knopf, 1991), 654.

57. Singal, "Interview with Arthur Raper," SHC folder 365.

58. At the same time, *An American Dilemma* owed a large debt to the CIC. Raper's work, which was so critical to Myrdal's manuscript, was informed almost entirely by his research for the CIC. "Race and Class Pressures," as Raper saw it, "sort of rounded out, in broad outlines at least, my earlier research efforts—and such merit as it may have rests largely upon my earlier opportunity to get a rather comprehensive picture of the relation of race to economics and politics." Raper was grateful, he wrote Alexander, for "the opportunity you gave me to do the research and write the report on mob violence, the Black Belt counties, the adjustment downward since 1930 (the *Sharecroppers All* manuscript), and last of all the chance to work with Myrdal on the 'Race and Class Pressures,' which if I mistake not, is the best piece of work I've done." Raper, letter to Will Alexander, June 11, 1940, SHC folder 92.

59. Samuel A. Stouffer, letter to Raper, September 13, 1941, SHC folder 924.
60. Gunnar Myrdal, letter to Raper, July 29, 1942, SHC folder 924. Guy B. Johnson, letter to Raper, August 6, 1940, SHC, Guy B. Johnson papers, series 2.2.
61. Raper, letter to Charles S. Johnson, September 18, 1945, SHC folder 924. Raper, letter to Guy Johnson, November 17, 1941, SHC, Guy B. Johnson papers, series 2.2.
62. Myrdal later returned in March 1941 to New York, where he wrote and synthesized the compendium, which the Carnegie Corporation published in 1944.
63. Raper, letter to Will Alexander, June 11, 1949, SHC folder 92.
64. Raper, letter to Guy Johnson, July 31, 1940, SHC, Guy B. Johnson papers, series 2.2.
65. Guy B. Johnson, letter to Raper, August 6, 1940, SHC, Guy B. Johnson papers, series 2.2.
66. Raper, letter to Guy Johnson, October 24, 1940, SHC, Guy B. Johnson papers, series 2.2.

Chapter 8. War and Change

1. Morton Sosna, "Personal interview with Arthur Raper," April 23, 1971, SHC folder 370.
2. Raper, *Tenants of the Almighty* (New York: Macmillan, 1943), 351.
3. Raper, *Tenants of the Almighty*, x.
4. Raper missed working with Alexander. "The truth is," he wrote him in 1941, "I am beginning to feel quite too far removed from your counsel." Raper, letter to Will Alexander, January 21, 1941, SHC folder 100.
5. Raper, *Tenants of the Almighty*, x.
6. Raper, *Tenants of the Almighty*, 234.
7. Raper, letter to Ira De A. Reid, November 8, 1940, SHC folder 100.
8. Raper, letter to Gunnar Myrdal, June 3, 1941, SHC folder 924.
9. Gunnar Myrdal, letter to Raper, November 25, 1941, SHC folder 924.
10. Arthur F. Raper and Martha J. Raper, "Two Years to Remember and Other Writings," unpublished manuscript, August 1977, SHC folder 143.
11. Raper, "Greene County Notes," unpublished manuscript, September 19, 1940, SHC folder 111.
12. Raper, *Tenants of the Almighty*, 187.
13. Raper, letter to Tarleton Collier, February 22, 1941, SHC folder 103.
14. Raper, unpublished handwritten notes dated "Late 1930s and early 1940s," SHC folder 716.
15. Raper, "Domestics: School Children," unpublished manuscript, September 26, 1940, SHC folder 111.
16. Raper, "An Adverse Point of View, Factors Impeding Progress," unpublished notes, undated, SHC folder 992.
17. Raper, *Tenants of the Almighty*, 287.
18. Raper, *Tenants of the Almighty*, 326–327.
19. Raper, *Tenants of the Almighty*, 326–327.
20. Raper, unpublished meeting notes, May 20, 1941, SHC folder 96.
21. Raper, "The Family Size Farm," *Greensboro Herald-Journal*, September 5, 1941, SHC folder 97.
22. Raper, "The Family Size Farm," *Greensboro Herald-Journal*, December 12, 1941, SHC folder 97.
23. Raper, "The Family Size Farm," *Greensboro Herald-Journal*, October 31, 1941, SHC folder 97.

24. Raper, *Tenants of the Almighty*, 341.

25. Raper and H. L. Mitchell, transcription of conversation taped by the University of North Carolina History Honor Society, January 29, 1974, SHC folder 448.

26. Dorothea Lange and Paul Taylor, *An American Exodus: A Record of Human Erosion* (New York: Reynal & Hitchcock, 1939), 153–154.

27. *Atlanta Constitution*, "Georgians Are Named on New Mill Pay Body," March 13, 1941, SHC folder 95.

28. Raper, letter to Guy B. Johnson, July 2, 1941, SHC folder 115.

29. Martha J. Raper, "Note by MJR on Arthur's trip to Puerto Rico," unpublished notes, January 1942, SHC folder 116.

30. Raper, letter to Jack and Irene Delano, November 29, 1941, SHC folder 97.

31. Richard K. Doud, personal interview with Jack and Irene Delano, Rio Piedras, Puerto Rico, June 12, 1965, Smithsonian Archives of American Art.

32. *Greensboro Herald-Journal*, "Grand Jury Presentments—July Term, 1941, of Greene Superior Court," August 8, 1941, SHC folder 976.

33. Raper, "Race Relations," unpublished manuscript, September 20, 1940, SHC folder 111.

34. Raper, "Greene County Grand Jury Investigation of 'Dr. Arthur Raper's Office,' July 1941," unpublished notes, July 29, 1941, SHC folder 976; Raper, "Sterling Brown," SHC folder 3966/2.

35. Raper, "Greene County Fair," unpublished manuscript, October 26, 1940, SHC folder 112.

36. Raper, *Tenants of the Almighty*, 348.

37. Raper, *Tenants of the Almighty*, 338–339.

38. Carolyn Blue, unpublished notes for Raper, January 23, 1941, SHC folder 976.

Chapter 9. *Tenants of the Almighty*

1. Raper and Martha J. Raper, "Two Years to Remember and Other Writings," unpublished manuscript, August 1977, SHC folder 143.

2. For her part, Margaret Mead told audiences that, if they wanted to understand the South, they should read Raper's books, especially *Tenants of the Almighty*. They would find a great deal of "compassionate detail, the kind of information that needed to be absorbed by those who would develop constructive programs for the South." Raper, "Remembering Margaret Mead," unpublished manuscript, November 15, 1978, SHC folder 657.

3. Raper, *Tenants of the Almighty* (New York: Macmillan, 1943), ix.

4. Raper and Martha J. Raper, "Two Years to Remember and Other Writings," SHC folder 143.

5. Carl Fleischhauer and Beverly W. Brannan, eds., *Documenting America, 1935–1943* (Berkeley: University of California Press, 1988).

6. Stryker had the most trouble managing Evans, his most brilliant photographer, but least amenable to the idea of visual sociology. Alan Trachtenberg, "Reading the File," in Fleischhauer and Brannan, eds., *Documenting America*.

7. Roy Stryker to Raper, February 5, 1941, SHC folder 96.

8. Raper to W. T. Couch, September 9, 1941, UNC Press Archives, Subgroup 4: Author/Title Publication Records, Raper, A. F., *Sharecroppers All*.

9. Raper and Martha J. Raper, "Two Years to Remember and Other Writings," unpublished manuscript, August 1977, SHC folder 143.

10. Richard K. Doud, "Personal interview with Jack and Irene Delano," Rio Piedras, Puerto Rico, June 12, 1965, Smithsonian Archives of American Art.

11. Doud, "Personal interview with Jack and Irene Delano," Rio Piedras, Puerto Rico, June 12, 1965, Smithsonian Archives of American Art.

12. Raper often spoke with regret about the visit to the Greene County jail he had made with Ralph Bunche and Gunnar Myrdal. Their hosts had planned a fine meal, and because Myrdal's presence and project was so unprecedented, Raper expected that Bunche would be allowed to dine with the rest if Raper could nonchalantly arrange Bunche's entry without making it an issue. When one of the jail officials voiced the question to the group, "What about Dr. Bunche?" then Jim Crow came into play, and Bunche was dispatched to eat with the prisoners. Raper was frustrated at not having moved quickly or smoothly enough into what he thought was a crack in Jim Crow to have kept the question from being raised and Bunche from being humiliated.

13. Roy Stryker, letter to Raper, May 7, 1941, SHC folder 96.

14. Doud, personal interview with Jack and Irene Delano, Rio Piedras, Puerto Rico, June 12, 1965, Smithsonian Archives of American Art.

15. Raper, letter to Roy Stryker, July 30, 1941, SHC folder 96.

16. Raper, letter to Roy Stryker, September 19, 1941, SHC folder 96.

17. Stryker, letter to Raper, September 22, 1941, SHC folder 96.

18. Stryker, letter to Raper, May 29, 1942, SHC folder 96.

19. "The newspicture is a single frame," explained Stryker, "ours a subject viewed in series. The newspicture is dramatic, all subject and action. Ours shows what's back of the action. It is a broader statement—frequently a mood, an accent, but more frequently a sketch and not infrequently a story." Fleischhauer and Brannan, eds., *Documenting America*, 9.

20. "An affirmation, not a negation," is how Stryker phrased his conception of documentary realism. Trachtenberg, in Fleischhauer and Brannan, eds., *Documenting America*, 64.

21. Lawrence W. Levine, "The Historian and the Icon: Photography and the History of the American People in the 1930s and 1940s," in Fleischhauer and Brannan, eds., *Documenting America*, 38.

22. Levine, "The Historian and the Icon," 39.

23. Trachtenberg, in Fleischhauer and Brannan, eds., *Documenting America*, 68.

24. Raper, *Greensboro Herald-Journal*, August 7, 1942, SHC folder 117.

25. Raper, *Tenants of the Almighty*, plate 22.

26. Tarleton Collier, "For Those The South Baffles," *Louisville Courier-Journal*, August 1, 1943, SHC folder 137; Jonathan Daniels, "The Lord's Plantation," *Saturday Review*, June 26, 1943, SHC folder 137.

27. Raper, *Tenants of the Almighty*, 365–387.

28. Wayland J. Hayes, "Planning in the 'Grass Roots,'" *Greensboro Herald-Journal*, no date, SHC folder 132.

29. Raper to Roy Stryker, November 29, 1941, SHC folder 96.

30. William Shands Meacham, *New York Times Book Review*, "The Bitter Saga of the Negro," November 23, 1941, SHC folder 987.

31. "I must say to you, this is not a work of art or of entertainment, nor will I assume the obligations of the artist or entertainer, but is a human effort which must require human co-operation." James Agee and Walker Evans, *Let Us Now Praise Famous Men* (Boston: Houghton Mifflin, 1941), 111.

32. *Greensboro Herald-Journal*, "early September 1942," SHC folder 117.

33. Raper to Carl C. Taylor, November 10, 1942, SHC folder 118.

34. Raper, *Tenants of the Almighty*, vii, 97–98.

35. "The family-size farmer—the Jeffersonian ideal—lost his first round in Greene to the slave plantation system, which rose to its height in the 1840's. The plantation remained regnant for the next two decades, though in the late 1850's it began to wane. It was not being displaced. It was weakening from within through the loss of soil fertility and the loss of planter security. It was being censured from without by unyielding critics and threatened by national politics." Raper, *Tenants of the Almighty*, 58.

36. Raper, *Tenants of the Almighty*, vii, 97–98.

37. Raper, *Tenants of the Almighty*, 106.

38. Raper, *Tenants of the Almighty*, 119–120.

39. Raper, *Tenants of the Almighty*, 129.

40. "Landowning and landless ones alike operated on a yearly basis, each trying to get as much as he could out of the other, and out of the land. Every year stood on its own bottom. No plan for the decade or for the century." Raper, *Tenants of the Almighty*, 89, 90.

41. Raper, *Tenants of the Almighty*, vii, 28. Raper also leavened the politics with comforting and familiar tidbits of history that old-timers would take pleasure in recalling. "The big world kept pushing in on Greene. Ice was shipped in from Atlanta, with express charges of $1.00 per hundred pounds. Lemon, strawberry, and sarsaparilla were then the standard drinks. The folks of Greensboro had their first taste of Coca-Cola when on Memorial Day 1890 local druggist T. B. Rice dispensed ten gallons of 'Candler's coffee.'" Raper, *Tenants of the Almighty*, 106.

"The first phonograph, as reported by the *Herald-Journal*, appeared on the streets of Greensboro in 1892; the man exhibiting it 'reaped a harvest of nickels from those who wanted to hear the songs, speeches, etc., from this mysterious contrivance.' The first embalming was done this same year. Five years later telephones were installed, and druggist Rice soon became the local 'telephone man.'" Raper, *Tenants of the Almighty*, 109.

42. Raper, *Tenants of the Almighty*, viii.

43. Raper, *Tenants of the Almighty*, 89. The admonishment went on to reason: "We know that we are the stronger party and we can afford to be magnanimous. We offer to you the right hand of friendship. We do not think you are qualified to vote. We know you are not qualified and so do you know it. Still at present you have the right to do it. We acknowledge that right. If you choose to vote with these few Yankees who are trying to make use of you for their own purposes, you can do so. But you may depend upon it no good will come of it."

44. Raper, *Tenants of the Almighty*, plate 46.

45. Raper claimed he found numerous examples of this kind of notice in the Grand Jury presentments. "Attorney James Davidson of Greensboro addressed a letter to the January, 1911 grand jury pleading for the continuation of the tick eradication programs. 'Are Farm Conditions Worse in Greene County Than Thirty Years Ago?' he asked. 'They are,' he said. 'In truth, we have no prosperity . . . what percent of the actual tillers of our soil own their farms, what proportion live in painted houses or give other evidences of possessing those small comforts that change a struggle for existence to a satisfied living? The condition of the man on the farm is worse than it was thirty years ago . . .

"'What brought about this condition,' he asked—and answered, 'All cotton and the tenant system.' He told of the rich soils the first settlers in the county found, how the trees were chopped down, 'piled into heaps and burned.'" Raper, *Tenants of the Almighty*, 143–144.

46. Raper, *Tenants of the Almighty*, 209.

47. Raper, *Tenants of the Almighty*, 172. Raper referenced a recent trip Will Alexander had taken

to survey Denmark's cooperative farm. "Less than one hundred year ago the great bulk of Denmark's farm people had been in much the same situation as the tenants and wage hands in the Southeast. The Danish farmers themselves, through cooperative programs, had multiplied the number of farmowners, eliminated illiteracy, improved their health, and developed an international market for their high-grade farm products. In short, the Danes had made a garden of their little country. [Alexander] expressed the belief that the same kind of advancement could be made in the Southeast, and that the program being developed in Greene county was an effort to move in that direction." Raper, *Tenants of the Almighty*, 205.

48. Raper, *Tenants of the Almighty*, 268.
49. Raper, *Tenants of the Almighty*, 207–208.
50. Raper, *Tenants of the Almighty*, 210.
51. Raper, *Tenants of the Almighty*, 230.
52. Raper, *Tenants of the Almighty*, 233–234.
53. Raper, *Tenants of the Almighty*, 257.
54. Louisiana Dunn Thomas, "Uncle Sam is My Shepherd," unpublished poetry, quoted in Raper, *Tenants of the Almighty*, 270.
55. Raper, *Tenants of the Almighty*, 320–321.
56. Raper, *Tenants of the Almighty*, 322.
57. Virginius Dabney, "Georgia's Doughty Stepchildren," *New York Times Book Review*, July 18, 1943, SHC folder 137.
58. Tarleton Collier, "For Those The South Baffles," *Louisville Courier-Journal*, August 1, 1943, SHC folder 137.
59. Wayland J. Hayes, "Planning in the 'Grass Roots,'" *Greensboro Herald-Journal*, undated, SHC folder 132.
60. John Chamberlain, "Books of the Times," *New York Times*, June 18, 1943.
61. Raper, letter to the American Sociological Society in response to its "1944 Census of Current Research Projects," December 1944, SHC folder 142.
62. Raper and Martha J. Raper, "Two Years to Remember and Other Writings," 106–107, SHC folder 143.
63. Raper and Martha J. Raper, "Two Years to Remember and Other Writings," 44, SHC folder 143.
64. Raper, *Tenants of the Almighty*, 349–350.
65. Raper, *Tenants of the Almighty*, 349–350.
66. Raper, *Tenants of the Almighty*, 350–351.
67. Earl Brown, letter to Raper, February 23, 1941, SHC folder 94.
68. Raper, letter to Brown, November 22, 1941, SHC folder 97.
69. Roy Stryker, letter to Raper, December 11, 1941, SHC folder 96.
70. Raper, letter to Brown, December 4, 1941, SHC folder 97.
71. Brown, letter to Raper, December 15, 1941, SHC folder 97.

Chapter 10. "But What *Is* the American Way?"

1. Arthur Raper, "Sharecropper Brimm is now in the Navy," unpublished notes, March 8, 1945, SHC folder 1075. Raper would look at the war as a way to educate rural folks about the world at large, as a way to prepare Americans for an international perspective that he hoped would fol-

low the peace. "People who seldom read magazines and may never have had a map of the world in the house are now vitally concerned in world conditions, and would study a picture map of the world as never before in their lives. This interest of theirs affords our government an excellent opportunity to help them learn something about the world whose peoples are now involved in war—someday equally involved in the character of the peace.

"The map could be distributed by sending one to the Postmaster in each town of three people or more with the request that he put it up in the post offices, or give it to a merchant who would like to display it in his store-front window." Raper, letter to Mr. Odegard, July 18, 1941, SHC folder 116.

2. Raper, letter to A. W. Barton, July 3, 1942, SHC folder 116.
3. Raper, letter to Carl Taylor, November 10, 1942, SHC folder 118.
4. Raper, letter to Guy Johnson, July 2, 1941, SHC folder 103.
5. Raper, untitled and undated notes, SHC folder 147.
6. Raper, letter to Carl Taylor, November 10, 1942, SHC folder 118.
7. Raper, family letter, October 19, 1948, SHC folder 171.
8. *Washington Post,* dated "spring 1940," SHC folder 92.
9. Raper, letter to family, May 29, 1946, SHC folder 161.
10. Raper, "Late 1941," unpublished manuscript, November 1941, SHC folder 98.
11. Raper, "Late 1941," unpublished manuscript, November 1941, SHC folder 98.
12. Raper, "Late 1941," unpublished manuscript, November 1941, SHC folder 98.
13. Raper, "Late 1941," unpublished manuscript, November 1941, SHC folder 98.
14. Raper, *Tenants of the Almighty,* 351.
15. Raper, *Tenants of the Almighty,* 363.
16. Raper, untitled and undated manuscript, SHC folder 133.
17. Raper, "A Prohibition on 'Cultural Studies," unpublished manuscript, dated "Early February 1945 (as recollected October 1973)," SHC folder 151.
18. Carl C. Taylor, "General Memorandum No. 69," U.S. Department of Agriculture, Bureau of Agricultural Economics, September 25, 1943, SHC folder 118.
19. In addressing the method of accumulating such conversational information, Raper described at the time his own long-honed approach. "The major methods used thus far have been that of the observer getting acquainted with living conditions in the county, and in a more superficial way in the surrounding areas, through a study of historical backgrounds, the use of available statistics, an understanding of the character of the population, their organizations, institutions, and values. Repeated observations have been made in each county, where possible by the same observer, and these basic sociological materials have been brought to bear in interpreting the meaning of the information collected." Raper, untitled and undated manuscript, SHC folder 133.
20. Conrad Taeuber, "Rural Life Trends," U.S. Department of Agriculture, Bureau of Agricultural Economics, August 19, 1942, SHC folder 117.
21. Taeuber, "Rural Life Trends," U.S. Department of Agriculture, Bureau of Agricultural Economics, August 19, 1942, SHC folder 117.
22. Daniel Singal, "Interview with Arthur Raper," January 18, 1971, SHC folder 367. For example, Raper was able to quickly forecast that the prosperity of the war economy would not be swallowed up by inflated land prices and big-ticket purchases, the way it had after 1918. At the end of World War II, "most of the farmers' extra money now is being used to pay off debts, as a re-

serve to produce the next crop, to secure better livestock, to have more comfortable clothes and houses, and to buy war stamps and bonds to help their kinsmen and friends in the armed forces." Raper, "Rural Life Trends, Pittsylvania County, Va., Report No. 3," March 1943, SHC folder 120.

23. Raper, "Detailed notes on Raper's Western Field Trip," unpublished manuscript, June 1943, SHC folder 1971.

24. Raper, "Enroute—Los Angeles to Cheyenne via Salt Lake City," unpublished notes, November 1944, SHC folder 739.

25. Raper, "From Laconia, N.H., to Northampton, Mass.," unpublished notes. April 1944, SHC folder 1071.

26. Singal, "Interview with Arthur Raper," SHC folder 367.

27. Raper, "A Prohibition on 'Cultural Studies,'" unpublished manuscript, dated "Early February 1945 (as recollected October 1973)," SHC folder 151. The Rural Trends Project was forced first to cut the number of counties it studied from seventy-two to thirty-six, before it was finally eliminated altogether.

28. Raper, "A Prohibition on 'Cultural Studies,'" unpublished manuscript, dated "Early February 1945 (as recollected October 1973)," SHC folder 151.

29. According to Richard F. Fenno Jr., who interviewed Whitten at the end of the 1950s, midway through a fifty-five-year career in the House, the Charleston, Mississippi, Democrat conceived of his role, as a longstanding member of the House Appropriations Committee, as holding things down. "He spoke about his job as 'press down,' 'hold the line,' 'keep the lid on,' 'sit on people,'" noted Fenno. "He noted that he was 'pliable' but that he had to sit on people across the board." Richard F. Fenno, "Research Interview Notes of Richard F. Fenno, Jr. with Members of the U.S. House of Representatives, 1959–1965. Interview with Rep. Jamie L. Whitten (D-MS)," June 1, 1959, National Archives and Record Administration, Records of Congress. www.archives.gov/records_of_congress/oral_histories/fenno/whitten_1959.html.

30. Singal, "Interview with Arthur Raper," SHC folder 367.

31. Raper, "A Prohibition on 'Cultural Studies,'" unpublished manuscript, dated "Early February 1945 (as recollected October 1973)," SHC folder 151.

32. "I personally know of the truth of all he wrote," wrote Raper, "and so did Congressman Whitten. . . . I attended one or more annual meetings of the Farm Bureau in Coahoma County, Miss. (and elsewhere in the Deep South), listened to what was said and not said, and saw there were no Negroes present; I heard white men tell of their colored mistresses, saw the pale skinned offspring, some of whom were publicly acknowledged by their fathers and halfbrothers (I saw both of these latter in Greene and Macon Counties, Georgia, in the 1920s and 30s)." Raper, "A Prohibition on 'Cultural Studies,'" unpublished manuscript, dated "Early February 1945 (as recollected October 1973)," SHC folder 151.

33. Raper, "Where Has U.S. Agriculture Gone Wrong?" unpublished manuscript, March 1972, SHC folder 717. Writing about Howard Odum, Michael O'Brien sketches the turn toward quantitative sociology that had overtaken Raper as well. "By the late 1930s, the comforting theory hastily absorbed in his youth had been challenged by a changing profession of sociologists. His peers and juniors were less interested in social involvement and more involved in particularist scholarly investigation. Grand theory was no longer very respectable, unless it came marked with a European label. The new temper was strenuously positivist, the instinct was to take one thing at a time, the mood was skeptical of the old Hegelian assumptions. The mold into which Odum, with little thought, had poured his mass of statistics and plans, was broken. Few seemed to mind

if the pieces were left on the floor. The old obsessions of Darwinian theory with nature, conflict, and geography were deemed less germane than the internal mechanisms of advanced social organization. Odum's nostalgic faith in the inherent strength of the farm began to make little sense to a generation raised on city blocks." Michael O'Brien, *The Idea of the American South, 1920–1941* (Baltimore: Johns Hopkins University Press. 1979), 92–93.

34. Raper, "Influences Tending to Destroy the Family Type Farm," unpublished manuscript, dated "mid 1948," SHC folder 168.

35. Raper, "On the Crest of Forming Waves," unpublished manuscript, May 1976, SHC folder 548.

36. At the same time, Raper and Taylor realized that the different areas had begun to blend and that the peculiar character of rural life was now less distinct in the face of growing suburbanization.

37. Carl C. Taylor et al., *Rural Life in the United States* (New York: Alfred A. Knopf, 1949).

38. Raper, "Nearly Quittin' Time," unpublished book proposal, undated, SHC folder 167.

39. Raper, "Nearly Quittin' Time," unpublished book proposal, undated, SHC folder 167.

40. Raper, "Significant Trends in Rural Life," address delivered at the Midwest Conference on Rural Life and Education, Lincoln, Neb., March 31, 1949, SHC folder 171. That rise had already begun to mean a great deal to rural America. "One thing the automobile and the radio certainly do is provide us with the ready means for forgetting some of the handicaps of hand labor," Raper wrote. "The shabbiness of things weighs on us less when the radio is going, and the louder it goes the more certain we are to get our thoughts off our immediate surroundings. . . . Besides there are many really good programs, and we find out about a lot of things all over the world—makes us feel we are right in the middle of things, and we like that feeling. Moreover, for many of us without much education, it's just simply easier to get the news from the radio than from the paper; and when we're tired we can just sit there and listen, and rest. . . .

"What we do know about autos and radios may make a lot of difference to us in the years ahead as the mechanization of cotton production increases—may make it easier for some of us who have a bent that way to stay on cotton farms, and may make it easier for some of the rest of us to get work elsewhere if we leave the farm." Raper, "Better Rural Living in the Postwar Period, The Old Cotton South in Transition," address to the Fifty-Fifth Annual Farmers' Conference, Tuskegee Institute, Ala., December 12, 1945, SHC folder 156.

41. Raper, "The Role of Agricultural Technologies in Southern Social Change," *Social Forces* 25 (October–May 1946–1947): 28

42. Raper, "The Role of Agricultural Technologies in Southern Social Change," 29.

43. Raper, "Tensions in American Agriculture," address delivered to Methodist Federation of Social Action, Kansas City, Mo., December 28, 1947, SHC folder 166.

44. Raper raises a poignant plea for the future of yeomanry. "Is it not reasonable to hope, and expect, that the same sound earthy judgment that led some families to develop live-at-home farming will now rise up from among their children to point the way for farm people today? Certainly there is no group closer to the earth, no group better qualified to do their share of the world's work, no group better prepared to live and let live. If the small live-at-home farmer will learn to cooperate with his fellow small farmers he can sell his produce at an equitable price, buy his supplies on a fair market, use light labor-saving machinery, pay for the essential community services, live reasonably well without exploiting the labor of any man, be an [sic] good husbandman and leave fertile fields to the next generation." Raper, *Tenants of the Almighty*, 334.

45. Raper, *Tenants of the Almighty*, 331–332, 333.
46. Claude A. Barnett, letter to Raper, September 18, 1945, SHC folder 156.
47. Robert T. Ogden, letter to Raper, December 12, 1945, SHC folder 156.
48. Raper, letter to Robert T. Ogden, January 16, 1946, SHC folder 156.
49. Raper was just becoming accustomed to air travel. Later that month, he would write about this new experience. "The even hum of the motors gives confidence as we leave the ground. So too does the unconcern of the passengers, and the occasional little kindnesses of the air hostesses. Only now and then does anyone of the 20 passengers look out of the windows. They all seem to be seasoned travelers. And to them I may seem seasoned too, but actually I am all excited over being up in the air, excited over the scene outside my window, for from here you can look at things from the middle of a sphere." Raper, "As I Ride, in flight from St. Louis to Washington," unpublished notes, March 31, 1944, SHC folder 1071.
50. Raper, "A Sociological Dream," unpublished notes, March 1944, SHC folder 147.
51. Raper, "A Sociological Dream," SHC folder 147.
52. Singal, "Interview with Arthur Raper," SHC folder 367.
53. John Raper studied the way radiation worked on different animals. As his mentor and older brother Kenneth later wrote, John discovered, among other research, that "on the basis of absorbed energy, gamma rays were 1.75 times more effective than beta rays in producing lethality. Out of this exploratory work . . . came a man chastened by the experience and frightened by the implications of what he had learned." Kenneth B. Raper, "John Robert Raper," *Bibliographical Memoirs*, vol. 57, National Academy of Sciences, 1987.
54. Kenneth B. Raper, "John Robert Raper," *Bibliographical Memoirs*, vol. 57, National Academy of Sciences, 1987.
55. Masaru Kajita, *Land Reform in Japan*, Agricultural Development Series, 2 Agriculture, Forestry and Fisheries Productivity Conference, no date, SHC folder 1114.
56. Raper, letter to Martha J. Raper, May 4, 1947, SHC folder 1096.
57. Singal, "Interview with Arthur Raper," SHC folder 367.
58. Raper, "Initial Conference with Village Leaders," unpublished notes, November 1948, SHC folder 1112.
59. Raper, "Some Recent Changes in Japanese Village Life," *Social Forces* 16 (1951).
60. Raper, "Some Recent Changes in Japanese Village Life," *Social Forces* 16 (1951).
61. Raper, letter to Martha J. Raper, May 15, 1947, SHC folder 1096.
62. Raper, letter to Martha J. Raper, May 23, 1947, SHC folder 1096.
63. Raper, "Suke Mura," unpublished notes, December 22, 1948, SHC folder 1109.
64. Raper, unpublished and undated notes, SHC folder 1095.
65. Raper, "Interview with General MacArthur," unpublished manuscript, January 11, 1949, SHC folder 173.
66. Raper, letter to Martha J. Raper, May 12, 1947, SHC folder 1096.
67. Raper et al., *The Japanese Village in Transition*, General Headquarters, Supreme Commander for the Allied Powers, Natural Resources Section, Tokyo, Japan, 1950.
68. Raper, "Some Recent Changes in Japanese Village Life," *Social Forces* 16 (1951).
69. Raper, "Initial Conference with Village Leaders," unpublished notes, November 1948, SHC folder 1112.
70. Masaru Kajita, *Land Reform in Japan*, Agricultural Development Series, 2 Agriculture, Forestry and Fisheries Productivity Conference, SHC folder 1114.

71. John W. Dower, "A Warning from History," *Boston Review* 28, no. 1 (February–March 2003): 6. Japan was undergoing the kind of societal introspection that the Depression had engendered in southern regionalists and New Dealers. Dower writes, "There are moments in history—fleeting occasions of opportunity—when people actually sit down and ask, 'What is a good society? How can we bring this about?' Winners in war do not ask this of themselves. Winners tend to say we won, we're good, we're righteous, what we did was just, now it's time to get back to business and build on our strengths. But losers—certainly in the case of Japan—are under more compulsion to ask what went wrong and what they might do to make sure they don't fall into the same disasters again."

72. Raper, "Some Recent Changes in Japanese Village Life," *Social Forces* 16 (1951): 3–16. John Dower concurs with Raper. "The reforms that were introduced in the opening year and a half or so of the occupation were quite stunning. They amounted to a sweeping commitment to what we now call 'nationbuilding.' The Americans introduced in Japan a major land reform, for example, that essentially took land from rich landlords, eliminated widespread tenancy, and created a class of small rural landowners. The argument for this was that rural oppression had kept the countryside poor, thwarted democracy, constricted the domestic market and fueled the drive to control overseas markets. We introduced labor laws that guaranteed the right to organize, bargain collectively, and strike, on the grounds that a viable labor movement is essential to any viable democracy. We encouraged the passage of a strong labor standards law to prevent exploitation of workers including women and children. We revamped both the content and structure of the educational system. In all this the input of Japanese bureaucrats and technocrats was essential to implement such reforms, and serious grass-roots support was basic to their survival." Dower, "A Warning from History," 6.

73. Raper, "Suke Mura," unpublished notes, December 22, 1948, SHC folder 1109.

74. Raper, "Some Recent Changes in Japanese Village Life," 3–16.

Chapter 11. Third World, Cold War

1. Arthur Raper, untitled and undated notes, SHC folder 729.

2. Raper, "The Role of Pilot and Demonstration Projects in Community Development Work," unpublished memorandum, undated, SHC folder 421.

3. Raper, letter to Carl Taylor, April 26, 1950, SHC folder 189.

4. Raper, letter to Carl Taylor, April 26, 1950, SHC folder 189.

5. Charles Reagan Wilson, "Introduction," in *The New Regionalism,* ed. Charles Reagan Wilson (Jackson: University Press of Mississippi, 1998).

6. Raper, *This is Rural U.S.A.,* unpublished film script (International Motion Pictures Division, U.S. Department of State, Office of Information, U.S. Department of Agriculture, 1951), SHC folder 195.

7. Raper, "Backgrounds of American Rural Life," government publication marked "orientation of foreign visitors," undated, SHC folder 189. The Japanese, in particular, were impressed with Raper's help and appreciative of U.S. aid. One group of officials wrote Raper in 1952, "We are much obliged to you for the kindness you extended us when we visited you during our recent trip to your country. We are glad that we enjoyed a very useful trip thanks to your goodwill. After three months' stay in the United States, we returned safe and sound to Japan on January 11.

"It is our pleasure to find that the general conditions of Japan we see and hear about after some four months' absence are steadily improving, which we believe is largely owing to the continued support of your country. The Japanese people are earnestly looking forward to the day when, with the ratification of the Peace Treaty, they may become a member of the world's free nations and thus make contributions, however small as they may be, toward the world's welfare so as to make up for their past misdeeds." Kiyoshi Okuhara, Saburo Miyaki, and Toqhinobu Tomizuka, letter to Raper, February 8, 1952, SHC folder 1113.

8. Raper, "On the Crest of Forming Waves," unpublished manuscript, May 1976, SHC folder 548.

9. Raper, family letter, March 24, 1950, SHC folder 727.

10. Raper, "On the Crest of Forming Waves," SHC folder 548.

11. Hubert G. Schenck, Mutual Security Agency memorandum, March 24, 1953, SHC folder 1137.

12. Raper, "On the Crest of Forming Waves," SHC folder 548.

13. Raper, "Overcoming the Greatest Obstacle," unpublished manuscript, October 30, 1943, SHC folder 134.

14. Raper, "On the Crest of Forming Waves," SHC folder 548.

15. Daniel Singal, "Interview with Arthur Raper," January 18, 1971, SHC folder 367.

16. Raper, "On the Crest of Forming Waves," SHC folder 548.

17. Raper, "On the Crest of Forming Waves," SHC folder 548. Raper was never able to find out why he had passed security himself, in spite of a thick dossier on his race and political activism.

18. Singal, "Interview with Arthur Raper," SHC folder 367.

19. Ch'ang Tung, *A Periodical of Taipei Pedicabmen's Union,* September 8, 1953, SHC folder 1156.

20. Carl C. Taylor et al., *Rural Life in the United States* (New York: Alfred A. Knopf, 1949), 325.

21. Singal, "Interview with Arthur Raper," SHC folder 367.

22. Raper, "On the Crest of Forming Waves," SHC folder 548.

23. Singal, "Interview with Arthur Raper," SHC folder 367.

24. Singal, "Interview with Arthur Raper," SHC folder 367.

25. Singal, "Interview with Arthur Raper," SHC folder 367.

26. Raper, family letter, November 22, 1974, SHC folder 482.

27. Raper, "As best I remember," unpublished notes, February 1, 1956, SHC folder 241.

28. Raper, "As best I remember," SHC folder 241.

29. Raper, "Some ruminations about Technical Aid," unpublished notes, August 1956, SHC folder 720.

30. Raper, "Needed—Better Screening of Overseas Personnel," April 1954, SHC folder 1154.

31. Raper, "Needed—Better Screening of Overseas Personnel," April 1954, SHC folder 1154.

32. Raper, "Residues of the Colonial System," unpublished notes dated 1963, SHC folder 714.

33. Raper, "Rural development complications," unpublished manuscript, May 1957, SHC folder 1177.

34. Raper, "Some ruminations about Technical Aid," SHC folder 720.

35. Singal, "Interview with Arthur Raper," SHC folder 367.

36. Singal, "Interview with Arthur Raper," SHC folder 367.

37. Raper, "On the Crest of Forming Waves," SHC folder 548.

38. Raper, "Tehran to Beirut," unpublished notes, 1956, SHC folder 1164.

39. Raper, "Some notes based on a decade of overseas observations," unpublished notes, dated "late 1956," SHC folder 721.

40. Mutual Security Agency, unpublished notes from the Conference on National and Village Cultures," March 14–15, 1952, SHC folder 1136.
41. Raper, "On the Crest of Forming Waves," SHC folder 548.
42. Raper, "On the Crest of Forming Waves," SHC folder 548.
43. Raper, "On the Crest of Forming Waves," SHC folder 548.
44. Raper, "On the Crest of Forming Waves," SHC folder 548.
45. Raper, "A case study of democratic procedures in rural development—A personal document," unpublished manuscript, March 1965, SHC folder 291.
46. Raper, "I Like to Live at Slope Oaks," unpublished manuscript, September 1976, SHC folder 560.
47. Raper, family letter, March 24, 1950, SHC folder 727.
48. Martha J. Raper, unpublished notes, August 1953, SHC folder 1154.
49. Raper, letter to Hubert G. Schenck, August 5, 1952, SHC folder 1137.
50. Martha J. Raper, letter to the editor, *Time*, March 7, 1955.
51. Martha J. Raper, family letter, March 17, 1956, SHC folder 1165.
52. Raper, "On the Crest of Forming Waves," SHC folder 548.
53. "On the Crest of Forming Waves," SHC folder 548.
54. Raper ended up placing Ahkter Hameed Khan among his pantheon of activist mentors. "I've been very fortunate to work with Will Alexander, to work with Myrdal, to work with Ahkter Hameed Khan, to work with Carl Taylor." Khan had been a Cambridge-educated civil servant in India who resigned his position in 1945 to work as a laborer and locksmith to learn about the working class. Later, he taught in Delhi and was principal of the Comilla Victoria College in 1958, when he was approached to direct the Comilla Rural Development Academy, to which he devoted his energies until the creation of Bangladesh in 1971. Singal, "Interview with Arthur Raper," SHC folder 367.
55. Raper, *Rural Development in Action* (Ithaca: Cornell University Press, 1970), 267.
56. Raper, "Pakistan Academy for Rural Development at Comilla, East Pakistan," address to AID Mini-conference on Interrelationships of Population, Agriculture, and Rural Development Programs, delivered December 8, 1970, SHC folder 358.
57. Raper, *Rural Development in Action*, 1.
58. Raper, *Rural Development in Action*, 1.
59. Raper, "Some Thoughts at Christmas," family letter, December 22, 1974.
60. Raper, "On the Crest of Forming Waves," SHC folder 548.
61. Raper, letter to Cornell University Press, October 22, 1974, SHC folder 480.
62. Raper, "On the Crest of Forming Waves," SHC folder 548.
63. The years Raper was overseas coincide with the most dramatic changes in the history of American race relations. In the mid-1960s, Myrdal considered that "the changes in American race relations from 1940 to 1962 appear to be among the most rapid and dramatic in world history without violent revolution." "Social change and the Negro problem," in Gunnar Myrdal, *An American Dilemma* (New York: Harper & Row, 1962 [1944]), xlii, xliii, xliv.
64. Raper, "Is There A 'New South'?" *New Republic* (August 18, 1952), SHC folder 943.
65. Charles Lawrence, letter to Raper, February 27, 1979, SHC folder 670.
66. Gunnar Myrdal, letter to Charles Dollard, April 2, 1956, SHC folder 712.
67. Raper, "Preface to the reprint edition," in *The Tragedy of Lynching* (Montclair, N.J.: Patterson Smith 1969 [1933]).

68. Raper, family letter, July 11, 1966, SHC folder 727.
69. Raper, "Over and over again," unpublished manuscript dated 1967, SHC folder 716.
70. Morton Sosna, "Personal interview with Arthur Raper," April 23, 1971, SHC folder 370.
71. Raper, letter to Harrison Roper, February 10, 1966, SHC folder 304.
72. Sosna, "Personal Interview with Arthur Raper," SHC folder 370.

Chapter 12. Back to the Land

Epigraph is from William Carlos Williams, *Paterson* (New York: New Directions, 1992 [1946]), 6.

1. Arthur Raper, "On the Crest of Forming Waves," unpublished manuscript, May 1976, SHC folder 548.
2. Raper, "I Like to Live at Slope Oaks," unpublished manuscript, September 1976, SHC folder 560.
3. Raper, family letter, November 22, 1974, SHC folder 482.
4. Raper, family letter, November 22, 1974, SHC folder 482.
5. Hendrix's performance at the 1967 Monterey Pop Festival was a defining moment, emblematic of the 1960s counterculture, perhaps the opening salvo in a barrage that would culminate two summers later at Woodstock. Raper, "Over and over again," unpublished manuscript, 1967, SHC folder 716.
6. Raper, "The Increased Use of Drugs by Youth," December 13, 1970, SHC folder 717.
7. Raper, "The matter of crisis," address delivered at the Oakton United Methodist Church, October 8, 1967, SHC folder 314.
8. Sue Thrasher, Peter Wood, and Larry Goodwyn, videotape of Raper, April 24–28, 1978, SHC folder videotape 3966/2.
9. Raper, "I Like to Live at Slope Oaks," SHC folder 560.
10. Raper, "I Like to Live at Slope Oaks," SHC folder 560.
11. Raper, "On the Crest of Forming Waves," SHC folder 548.
12. Raper, "I Like to Live at Slope Oaks," SHC folder 560.
13. Raper family genealogical paper, privately published, undated, 70.
14. Raper, family letter, December 23, 1973, SHC folder 444.
15. Raper, "I Like to Live at Slope Oaks," SHC folder 560.
16. Raper, "Prologue for Man's Nuclear Age (for Georgia Springer and Bill Finger)," in Raper and Martha J. Raper, "Two Years to Remember and Other Writings," unpublished manuscript, August 1977, SHC folder 143.
17. Jacqueline Dowd Hall, personal communication, University of North Carolina, Chapel Hill, August 20, 2002.
18. Singal, e-mail, July 10, 2002.
19. Raper, unpublished notes, October 18, 1974, SHC folder 480.
20. Raper, unpublished notes, November 1973, SHC folder 443.
21. *Washington Post*, "Sharecroppers Are Almost Gone From Miss. Cotton Farms," January 25, 1971, SHC folder 717.
22. Raper, "Our hope still lies in science and technology," unpublished manuscript, May 1, 1978, SHC folder 629.
23. *Harper's Weekly*, "Dirt Cheap," January 17, 1975, SHC folder 496.

24. Raper, "Some Thoughts at Christmas," family letter, December 22, 1974.
25. Raper, "On the Crests of Forming Waves," SHC folder 548.
26. Raper, "Our hope still lies in science and technology," SHC folder 629.
27. Raper, "Statement at Howard's Retirement Party," address at the Alamance Country Club, Burlington, N.C., January 27, 1973, SHC folder 420; Arthur Raper, "When we went back home," unpublished manuscript, October 18–November 6, 1973, SHC folder 438. By the late 1970s, he could see why much of the public had become cynical about the effects of technology, although he continued to hold on to a faith in science. "A couple of decades ago some of us thought our recently gained scientific and technological know-how held the answers to many if not most of mankind's problems, whether in developed or developing countries. And then with the passing of the years, and much to our chagrin, we realized that while we could make all kinds of things and influence people, we were using much too much irreplaceable energy and leaving too many of our people without meaningful remunerative employment and so caused many, many people here in our own country and around the world to wonder if our know-how experts really knew what they were doing—and thus a credibility chasm emerged in our civilization, augmented by various and sundry credibility gaps here, yonder, and there. . . .

"The question is: to what extent has the objectivity of the services of our know-how experts been colored by the interests of their employers and administrators? What differences would there be in their services if their monetary and psychological pay came from less top-side financial and political sources?" Raper, "Our hope still lies in science and technology," unpublished manuscript, May 1, 1978, SHC folder 629.
28. Raper, "On the Crest of Forming Waves," SHC folder 548.
29. Uneasy as he was, Raper continued to see progress, even if glacial, toward egalitarianism. At his most pessimistic, he never succumbed to a vision of dystopia. The future would have more equality than the past, because it would become less oriented toward profit and the individual consumer than toward the community. He speculated in 1970 that "our great, great, great grandchildren will surely look back in wonder upon the Twentieth Century, especially the middle half of it. For it was then that a small proportion of the human race, perhaps not more than one-eighth of the Earth's 3.6 billion people in 1970 ('Most of the people of the United States, a sizeable proportion of those in Canada, Europe and Japan, and a very thin upper class elsewhere.') had the personal use of a tremendous amount of human and physical energy. We refer to the automobile and truck, tractor, radio and television, refrigerator and deep freezer, running cold and hot water, central heating and air conditioning; and beyond these, ready access to airplanes, telephones, and the mass production of a vast array of goods and services tailored to the use of the individual consumer." Raper, "A Unique Period in Human History," unpublished manuscript, November 1970, SHC folder 717.
30. Raper, "Our hope still lies in science and technology," SHC folder 629.
31. Martha J. Raper, letter to the *Washington Post,* April 6, 1974, SHC folder 455.
32. Martha J. Raper, "Memorial Service for Martha J. Raper," Oakton United Methodist Church, Oakton, Va., December 29, 1979, SHC folder 704.
33. Raper, letter to Richard Ward, February 17, 1979, SHC folder 669.
34. Raper, untitled, handwritten note, May 9, 1970, SHC folder 345.
35. Martha J. Raper, letter to "Nina and Lady Ruth," May 27, 1970, SHC folder 345.
36. Martha J. Raper, letter to Akhter Hameed, May 18, 1970, SHC folder 345.
37. Martha J. Raper, family letter, July 4, 1970, SHC folder 346.

38. Raper, letter to George McDonald, April 24, 1978, SHC folder 625.
39. Raper, "'Sharecropper House,' at Smithsonian Institution," unpublished manuscript, April 20, 1978, SHC folder 625.
40. Raper, "The Increased Use of Drugs by Youth," December 13, 1970, SHC folder 717.
41. Raper, "Off to the Hospital Again," unpublished manuscript, April 13, 1978, SHC folder 624.
42. Raper, "Off to the Hospital Again," unpublished manuscript, April 13, 1978, SHC folder 624.
43. Raper, "The end of an era, and no tears," unpublished manuscript, December 20, 1978, SHC folder 663.
44. Harrison C. Roper, "An Afterword," unpublished manuscript, August 16, 1979, appended to Arthur SHC folder 704.
45. Raper, "Suggested Memorial Service for Arthur F. Raper," April 25, 1979, SHC folder 703.
46. Raper, *Tenants of the Almighty* (New York: Macmillan, 1943), 233.
47. Elsie Meehan Duval, letter to Raper, December 3, 1979, SHC folder 704.
48. Elsie Meehan Duval, letter to Raper, December 3, 1979, SHC folder 704.
49. Elsie Meehan Duval, letter to Raper, December 3, 1979, SHC folder 704.

BIBLIOGRAPHY

Manuscripts

Johnson, Guy B. Papers, Southern Historical Collection, University of North Carolina.
Moravian Archives, Winston-Salem, N.C.
Odum, Howard W. Southern Historical Collection, University of North Carolina.
Raper, Arthur F. Papers, Southern Historical Collection, University of North Carolina.
University of North Carolina Press Archives, University of North Carolina.
Vance, Rupert B. Papers, Southern Historical Collection, University of North Carolina.

Interviews

Hall, Jacqueline Dowd, personal interviews, July 2002.
Raper, Julis Jack, personal interviews, August 2002.
Reed, John Shelton, personal interviews, August 2002.
Singal, Daniel, e-mail communications, July 2002.

Published Primary Sources

Carlton, David L,. and Peter Coclanis, eds. *Confronting Southern Poverty in the Great Depression: The Report on Economic Conditions of the South.* Boston: St. Martin's Press, 1996.
Davidson, David. "A Sociologist in Eden." *The American Review* 8 (November 1936– March 1937): 177–204.
Du Bois, W. E. B. "Woofterism." *Crisis* 82 (March 1931): 81–83.
Federal Writers Project. *These Are Our Lives.* Ed. W. T. Couch. Chapel Hill: University of North Carolina Press, 1939.
Kajita, Masaru. *Land Reform in Japan.* Agricultural Development Series, 2 Agriculture, Forestry and Fisheries Productivity Conference, no date.

Myrdal, Gunnar. *An American Dilemma: The Negro Problem and Modern Democracy.* New York and Evanston: Harper & Row, 1962 [1944].

Raper, Arthur, and Ira De A. Reid. *Sharecroppers All.* Chapel Hill: University of North Carolina Press, 1941.

Raper, Arthur, and Martha J. Raper. "Two Years to Remember and Other Writings." Unpublished manuscript, August 1977.

Raper, Arthur, et al. *The Japanese Village in Transition.* General Headquarters, Supreme Commander for the Allied Powers, Natural Resources Section, Tokyo, Japan, 1950.

Raper, Arthur. "Daytona." In Jessie F. Steiner, ed. *The American Community in Action: Case Studies of American Communities.* New York: Henry Holt, 1928.

Raper, Arthur. *Preface to Peasantry.* Chapel Hill: University of North Carolina Press, 1936.

Raper, Arthur. *Rural Development in Action.* Ithaca: Cornell University Press, 1970.

Raper, Arthur. *Tenants of the Almighty.* New York: Macmillan, 1943.

Raper, Arthur. *The Tragedy of Lynching.* Chapel Hill: University of North Carolina Press, 1933.

Steinbeck, John. *The Grapes of Wrath.* New York: Viking Press, 1939.

Steiner, Jesse F., ed. *The American Community in Action: Case Studies of American Communities.* New York: Henry Holt, 1928.

Steiner, Jessie F., and Roy M. Brown, eds. *The North Carolina Chain Gang: A Study of County Convict Road Work.* Chapel Hill: University of North Carolina Press, 1927.

Taeuber, Conrad. "Rural Life Trends." Washington, D.C.: U.S. Department of Agriculture, Bureau of Agricultural Economics, 1942.

Taylor, Carl C., et al. *Rural Life in the United States.* New York: Alfred A. Knopf, 1949.

Terrill, T., and Jerrold Hirsch, eds. *Such as Us: Southern Voices of the Thirties.* Chapel Hill: University of North Carolina Press, 1978.

U.S. Congress, Senate, Committee on the Judiciary. *Crime of Lynching, Hearings,* Senate on H.R. 801, 76th Congress, 3rd session, 1940.

U.S. Government Printing Office. *Thirteenth Census of the United States, vol. VII: Agriculture 1909 and 1910.* Washington, D.C.: U.S. Government Printing Office, 1913.

U.S. Government Printing Office. *Twelfth Census of the United States, 1900.* Washington, D.C.: U.S. Government Printing Office, 1903.

White, Walter. *Rope and Faggot.* New York: Arno Press, 1969 [1929].

Wright, Richard. *Twelve Million Black Voices.* New York: Arno Press, 1969.

Secondary Sources

Abbott, Berenice. *Changing New York.* Ed. Bonnie Yochelson. New York: Museum of the City of New York, 1997.

Agee, James, and Walker Evans. *Let Us Now Praise Famous Men.* Boston: Houghton Mifflin, 1960 [1941].

Appleby, Joyce, Lynn Hunt, and Margaret Jacob. *Telling the Truth About History.* New York: W. W. Norton & Co., 1994.

Ayers, Edward L. *The Promise of the New South: Life After Reconstruction.* New York: Oxford University Press, 1992.

Barr, Peter. "Becoming Documentary: Berenice Abbott's Photographs, 1925–1939." Ph.D. diss., Boston University, 1997.

Berger, John, and Jean Mohr. *Another Way of Telling.* New York: Pantheon Books, 1982.

Blum, John Morton. *V Was for Victory: Politics and American Culture During World War II.* New York: Harcourt Brace Jovanovich, 1976.

Brooks, Jerome E. *Green Leaf and Gold: Tobacco in North Carolina.* Raleigh: Division of Archives and History, North Carolina Department of Cultural Resources, 1997.

Brundage, W. Fitzhugh. "Lynching in the New South: Georgia and Virginia, 1880–1930." Ph.D. diss., Harvard University, 1988.

Brundage, W. Fitzhugh, ed. *Under Sentence of Death: Lynching in the South.* Chapel Hill: University of North Carolina Press, 1997.

Bryant, Jonathan M. *How Curious a Land: Conflict and Change in Greene County, Georgia, 1850–1885.* Chapel Hill: University of North Carolina Press, 1996.

Caldwell, Erskine. *Tobacco Road.* New York: Scribner & Sons, 1932.

Caldwell, Erskine, and Margaret Bourke-White. *You Have Seen Their Faces.* New York: Modern Age Books, 1937.

Camus, Albert. *The Rebel: An Essay on Man in Revolt.* New York: Alfred A. Knopf, 1967.

Carter, Dan. *Scottsboro: A Tragedy of the American South.* Baton Rouge: Louisiana State University Press, 1979.

Cash, W. J. *The Mind of the South.* New York: Alfred A. Knopf, 1941.

Chadbourne, James H. *Lynching and the Law.* Chapel Hill: University of North Carolina Press, 1933.

Clayton, Bruce. *W. J. Cash: A Life.* Baton Rouge: Louisiana State University Press, 1991.

Coleman, Kenneth, ed. *A History of Georgia.* 2nd ed. Athens: University of Georgia Press, 1991.

Cooper, William, and Tom Terrill. *The American South: A History.* New York: Alfred A. Knopf, 1991.

Couch, W. T., ed. *Culture in the South.* Chapel Hill: University of North Carolina Press, 1934.

Curtis, James. *Mind's Truth: FSA Photography Reconsidered.* Philadelphia: Temple University Press, 1989.

Dabney, Virginius. *Liberalism in the South.* Chapel Hill: University of North Carolina Press, 1932.

Degler, Carl. *In Search of Human Nature.* New York: Oxford University Press, 1991.

Dollard, John. *Caste and Class in a Southern Town.* New Haven: Yale University Press, 1937.

Dorman, Robert L. *Revolt of the Provinces: The Regionalist Movement in America, 1920–1945*. Chapel Hill: University of North Carolina Press, 1993.

Drake, Willmarth W. *The New Frontier, based on American Regionalism, by Howard W. Odum and Harry E. Moore*. Chapel Hill: University of North Carolina Library Extension Publication. Vol. VI, no. 1, October 1939.

Dykeman, Wilma. *Seeds of Southern Change*. Chicago: University of Chicago Press, 1962.

Egerton, John. *Speak Now Against the Day: The Generation Before the Civil Rights Movement in the South*. New York: Alfred A. Knopf, 1994.

Ellis, Ann Wells. "The Commission on Interracial Cooperation, 1919–1944: Its Activities and Results." Ph.D. diss., Georgia State University, 1975.

Emerson, Ralph Waldo. *Selected Writings of Emerson*. Ed. Donald McQuade. New York: Modern Library, 1981.

Fitzpatrick, Ellen. "Caroline F. Ware and the Cultural Approach to History." *American Quarterly* 43 (1991).

Fitzpatrick, Ellen. *History's Memory: Writing America's Past, 1880–1980*. Cambridge, Mass.: Harvard University Press, 2002.

Fleischhauer, Carl, and Beverly Brannan, eds.; essays by Lawrence Levine and Alan Trachtenberg. *Documenting America, 1935–1943*. Berkeley: University of California Press, 1988.

Fogel, Robert William, and Stanley Engerman. *Time on the Cross: The Economics of American Slavery*. Boston: Little, Brown, 1974.

Foner, Eric. *A Short History of Reconstruction, 1863–1877*. New York: Harper & Row, 1990.

Fox, Richard Wrightman. *Reinhold Niebuhr*. Ithaca: Cornell University Press, 1985.

Fox, Richard Wightman, and T. J. Jackson Lears. *The Power of Culture: Critical Essays in American History*. Chicago: University of Chicago Press, 1993.

Franklin, John Hope. *From Slavery to Freedom: A History of Negro Americans*. New York: Alfred A. Knopf, 1967 [1947].

Freidel, Frank. *F.D.R. and the South*. Baton Rouge: Louisiana State University Press, 1965.

Fries, Adelaide L. *The Road to Salem*. Chapel Hill: University of North Carolina Press, 1944.

Fullinwider, S. P. *The Mind and Mood of Black America: 20th Century Thought*. Homewood, Ill.: The Dorsey Press, 1969.

Gaston, Paul M. *New South Creed: A Study in Southern Mythmaking*. New York: Alfred A. Knopf, 1970.

Giddens, Anthony. *Making Sense of Modernity: Conversations with Anthony Giddens*. Cambridge: Polity Press, 1998.

Giddens, Anthony. *Modernity and Self-identity: Self and Society in the Late Modern Age*. Stanford, Calif.: Stanford University Press, 1991.

Giddens, Anthony. *The Consequences of Modernity.* Stanford, Calif.: Stanford University Press, 1990.

Goodrich, Lloyd. "Edward Hopper." *DoubleTake* 24 (Spring 2001): 46–47.

Graebner, William. *The Age of Doubt: American Thought and Culture in the 1940s.* Boston: Twayne Publishers, 1991.

Hall, Jacqueline Dowd. "Women Writers and the 'Southern Front.'" *Journal of Southern History* 69, no. 1 (February 2003): 8.

Hambourg, Maria Morris. *The New Vision: Photography Between the World Wars.* New York: Metropolitan Museum of Art, 1989.

Harris, J. William, ed. *Society and Culture in the Slate South.* London and New York: Routledge, 1992.

Harris, J. William. *Deep Souths: Delta, Piedmont, and Sea Island Society in the Age of Segregation.* Baltimore: Johns Hopkins University Press, 2001.

Hughes, H. Stuart. *The Sea Change: The Migration of Social Thought, 1930–1965.* New York: Harper & Row, 1975.

Hunt, Lynn, ed. *New Directions in Cultural History.* Berkeley: University of California Press, 1989.

Hurley, F. Jack. *Portrait of a Decade: Roy Stryker and the Development of Documentary Photography in the Thirties.* Baton Rouge: Louisiana State University Press, 1972.

Hurston, Zora Neale. *Dust Tracks on a Road.* Philadelphia: J. B. Lippincott Co., 1941.

Jackson, Walter A. *Gunnar Myrdal and America's Conscience: Social Engineering and Racial Liberalism, 1938–1987.* Chapel Hill: University of North Carolina Press. 1990.

Karanikas, Alexander. *Tillers of a Myth: Southern Agrarians as Social and Literary Critics.* Madison: University of Wisconsin Press, 1966.

Kazin, Alfred. *On Native Grounds: An Interpretation of Modern Prose Literature.* New York: Reynal & Hitchcock, 1942.

Kelley, Robin D. G. *Hammer and Hoe: Alabama Communists during the Great Depression.* Chapel Hill and London: University of North Carolina Press, 1990.

Kennedy, David. *Freedom from Fear: The American People in Depression and War, 1929–1945.* New York: Oxford University Press, 1999.

King, Richard H. *A Southern Renaissance: The Cultural Awakening of the American South, 1930–1955.* New York: Oxford University Press, 1980.

Kirby, Jack Temple. *Rural Worlds Lost: The American South, 1920–1960.* Baton Rouge: Louisiana State University Press, 1987.

Lears, T. J. Jackson. *No Place of Grace: Antimodernism and the Transformation of American Culture, 1880–1920.* New York: Pantheon Books. 1981.

Leary, Helen F. M. *Centennial History of Davidson County.* Raleigh: Edwards and Broughton, 1927.

Leuchtenburg, William. *Franklin D. Roosevelt and the New Deal, 1932–1940.* New York: Harper & Row, 1963.

Leuchtenburg, William. *The FDR Years: On Roosevelt and His Legacy*. New York: Columbia University Press, 1995.

Levine, Lawrence. *The Unpredictable Past: Explorations in American Cultural History*. New York: Oxford University Press, 1993.

Lewis, David Levering. *W.E.B. Du Bois: Biography of a Race, 1868–1919*. New York: Henry Holt, 1993.

Lippmann, Walter. *Preface to Morals*. New York: Macmillan, 1929.

Locke, Alain, ed. *The New Negro*. New York: Albert & Charles Boni, 1925.

MacLean, Nancy. *Behind the Mask of Chivalry: The Making of the Second Ku Klux Klan*. New York: Oxford University Press, 1994.

Madden, David, ed. *Proletarian Writers of the Thirties*. Carbondale: Southern Illinois University Press, 1968.

May, Henry F. *The End of American Innocence, A Study of the First Years of Our Own Time: 1912–1917*. New York: Alfred A. Knopf, 1959.

Miller, Dan B. *Erskine Caldwell: The Journey from Tobacco Road*. New York: Alfred A. Knopf, 1995.

Novick, Peter. *That Noble Dream: The "Objectivity Question" and the American Historical Profession*. New York: Cambridge University Press, 1988.

O'Brien, Michael. *The Idea of the American South, 1920–1941*. Baltimore: Johns Hopkins University Press, 1979.

Odum, Howard. *An American Epoch: Southern Portraiture in the National Picture*. New York: Henry Holt, 1930.

Odum, Howard. *Southern Pioneers in Social Interpretation*. Chapel Hill: University of North Carolina Press, 1925.

Pells, Richard H. *Radical Visions and American Dreams: Culture and Social Thought in the Depression Years*. New York: Harper & Row, 1973.

Percy, William Alexander. *Lanterns On the Levee*. New York: Alfred A. Knopf, 1941.

Phillips, U. B. "The Central Theme of Southern History." *American Historical Review* 24 (1928): 30–43.

Potter, David M. *People of Plenty: Economic Abundance and the American Character*. Chicago: University of Chicago Press, 1954.

Rodgers, Daniel T. *Atlantic Crossings: Social Politics in a Progressive Age*. Cambridge, Mass.: Harvard University Press, 1998.

Roper, John. *C. Vann Woodward, Southerner*. Athens: University of Georgia Press, 1987.

Ross, Dorothy. *The Origins of American Social Science*. Cambridge: Cambridge University Press, 1991.

Roszak, Theodore. *The Making of a Counter Culture: Reflections on the Technocratic Society and Its Youthful Opposition*. Garden City: Doubleday & Co., 1969.

Schulman, Bruce J. *From Cotton Belt to Sunbelt: Federal Policy, Economic Development, and the Transformation of the South, 1938–1980*. New York: Oxford University Press, 1991.

Singal, Daniel. *The War Within: From Victorian to Modernist Thought in the South, 1919–1945*. Chapel Hill: University of North Carolina Press, 1982.

Sitkoff, Harvard. *A New Deal for Blacks: The Emergence of Civil Rights as a National Issue*. Vol. I: *The Depression Decade*. New York: Oxford University Press, 1978.

Smith, Lillian. *Killers of the Dream*. New York: W. W. Norton Co., 1949.

Sosna, Morton. "In Search of the Silent South: White Southern Liberalism 1920–1950." Ph.D. diss., University of Wisconsin, 1972.

Sosna, Morton. *In Search of the Silent South: Southern Liberals and the Race Issue*. New York: Columbia University Press, 1977.

Stange, Maren. *Symbols of Ideal Life: Social Documentary Photography in America, 1890–1950*. New York: Cambridge University Press, 1989.

Stott, William. *Documentary Expression and Thirties America*. New York: Oxford University Press, 1973.

Sullivan, Patricia. *Days of Hope: Race and Democracy in the New Deal Era*. Chapel Hill: University of North Carolina Press, 1994.

Tindall, George B. "The Significance of Howard W. Odum to Southern History." *Journal of Southern History* (August 1958).

Tindall, George B., ed. *The Emergence of the New South, 1913–1945*. Vol. X: *A History of the South*. Baton Rouge: Louisiana State University Press, 1967.

Tolnay, Stewart E., and E. M. Beck. *A Festival of Violence: An Analysis of Southern Lynchings, 1882–1930*. Urbana and Chicago: University of Illinois Press, 1995.

Trachtenberg, Alan. *Reading American Photographs*. New York: Hill and Wang, 1989.

Trachtenberg, Alan. *The Incorporation of America: Culture and Society in the Gilded Age*. New York: Hill and Wang. 1982.

Turner, Frederick Jackson. "The Significance of the Frontier in American History." In *Rereading Frederick Jackson Turner*. New York: Henry Holt & Co., 1994 [1893].

Wald, Alan M. *The New York Intellectuals: The Rise and Decline of the Anti-Stalinist Left from the 1930s to the 1980s*. Chapel Hill: University of North Carolina Press, 1987.

Ware, Caroline, ed. *The Cultural Approach to History*. New York: Columbia University Press, 1940.

Welty, Eudora. *Photographs*. Jackson: University Press of Mississippi, 1989.

Westbrook, Robert. *John Dewey and American Democracy*. Ithaca: Cornell University Press, 1991.

Whitfield, Stephen J. *The Culture of the Cold War*. Baltimore: Johns Hopkins University Press, 1991.

Wiebe, Robert. *The Search for Order, 1877–1920*. Westport, Conn.: Greenwood Press, 1967.

Williams, William Carlos. *In the American Grain*. New York: New Directions Books, 1956 [1933].

Wilson, Charles Reagan, ed. "Introduction." In *The New Regionalism*. Jackson: University Press of Mississippi, 1998.

Wilson, R. Jackson. *In Quest of Community: Social Philosophy in the United States, 1860–1920*. New York: John Wiley, 1968.

Woodward, C. Vann. *Origins of the New South*. Baton Rouge: Louisiana State University Press, 1951.

Woodward, C. Vann. *Tom Watson: Agrarian Rebel*. London: Oxford University Press, 1938.

Wright, Richard. *Black Boy: A Record of Childhood and Youth*. New York: Harper & Bros., 1945.

Wyatt-Brown, Bertram. *Honor and Violence in the Old South*. New York: Oxford University Press, 1986.

INDEX

AAA. *See* Agricultural Adjustment Act (AAA)
Adams, Ansel, 239
Afghanistan, 294–95, 297
African Americans. *See* Blacks
Agee, James, 11, 249–50, 330n19, 346n104, 367n31
Agnes Scott College, 4, 139–40, 159–60, 163, 203, 216, 232, 326–27, 352n91
Agrarianism. *See* Jeffersonian agrarianism; Nashville Agrarians
Agricultural Adjustment Act (AAA), 115, 129–30, 131, 156, 164–65, 167, 218, 220
Agriculture: and agribusiness, 187, 223, 279, 319; and A. Raper's Slope Oaks farm, 12, 13, 266, 288–89, 299–300, 310, 312–18, 321–25; and blacks' ownership of farms, 29, 36, 112, 121–22, 225, 347n14; and boll weevil, 69, 110, 112, 120, 121, 185, 254; and Comilla Rural Development Academy in Pakistan, 302–6, 312, 376n54; and cooperatives for farmers, 150–54, 180, 191, 253–54, 353n5, 353–54n10, 368–69n47; and debts of farmers, 370–71n22; and electricity for farmhouses, 11–12, 27; and F. Raper's farm, 15–16, 20, 25, 27, 332n1; and future of small family farm, 226, 257, 273, 372n44; in Greene and Macon counties, Ga., 69–70, 106, 107, 111, 112–13, 120–21, 219–20, 368n45; in Indiana, 271; in Japan, 280–86; mechanization of, 149–50, 175–76, 187, 215, 274–79, 284–85, 306, 319, 353n2, 353n5, 372n40; in Middle East, 296; in Mississippi, 83–84, 340n16; New Deal programs for, 115, 129–31, 135–37, 156, 160–61, 164–65, 194, 220, 222–23, 255, 352n83; and North Carolina crops, 332n37; and organic farming, 318; and "plow-up" of crops, 115, 129–30, 350–51n63; and Rural Trends Project, 269–75; and size of farms, 276, 331–32n37; statistics on, 276, 331–32n37; and tobacco production, 25, 33, 332n1; and Unified Farm Program (UFP), 217–26, 232–33, 250, 252, 254; and women's work on farms, 135, 244, 350n52. *See also* Cotton production; Tenancy

Airplanes, 373n49, 378n29
Alabama. *See specific cities*
Alexander, Frank, 272–73
Alexander, Will: as Commission on Interracial Cooperation (CIC) founder and director, 5, 6, 23, 33–34, 48, 52–53, 58, 70; and Delta Cooperative Farms, 151, 153; and Denmark's cooperative farm, 368–69n47; education of, 52; at Farm Security Administration (FSA), 5, 136, 161, 352nn85–86; and Highlander Folk School, 360n104; and mechanized agriculture, 150; as mentor for Raper, 33–34, 53, 211–12, 239, 364n58, 365n4, 376n54; as minister, 23, 52; and Myrdal's *American Dilemma*, 193; Progressivism of, 33–34; Raper's first meeting with, 54; and Raper's "Race and Class Pressures," 211, 364n58; and Raper's research on Macon and Greene counties, Ga., 69–70, 108; and Raper's *Sharecroppers All,* 177, 189; and Raper's studies of New Deal impact, 137–38, 154–55, 161, 347n5, 352n86, 352n90, 363n37; at Resettlement Administration (RA), 136, 137, 141, 156, 211, 352n85; resignation of, from Commission on Interracial Cooperation (CIC), 138, 161–62, 211, 352n86; retirement of, 288;

389

Alexander, Will (*continued*)
    and Southern Commission on the Study of Lynching, 70; and Southern Conference on Human Welfare (SCHW), 171–72, 357n68; and tenancy crisis, 136; and Unified Farm Program (UFP), 218. *See also* Commission on Interracial Cooperation (CIC)
Amberson, William, 150, 354n17
American Dilemma, An (Myrdal): conclusion of, 195, 207; funding for, 191–92; Myrdal's travels for research on, 140, 203–7; publication of, 210, 365n62; and Raper's "Race and Class Pressures," 191, 195–201, 210–11, 261, 363n19, 363n31, 364n58; Raper's work on, generally, 5, 11, 140, 193, 203–8, 307, 376n54; research approach for, 192, 196–97, 363n22; researchers involved in, 11, 140, 193, 196; research for, in North, 207–8; twentieth-anniversary edition of, 362n8; updating of Raper's work on, 307; and visit to Greene County jail, 204–5, 367n12
American Friends of the Middle East, 295–96
American Review, 175–77
Ames, Jessie Daniel, 65, 72, 161, 165, 170, 209, 316, 351n74, 356n44
Andrews, Garnett, 253
Andrews, Mrs. J. E., 139, 140, 203, 205
AP. *See* Associated Press (AP)
Arkansas, 150, 151, 155, 160, 195
Associated Negro Press, 277
Associated Press (AP), 94
Association of Southern Women for the Prevention of Lynching (ASWPL), 72–73, 94, 161
Atlanta: blacks' migration to, 67–70, 107–8, 217, 349n33; Christian Council in, 358n76; conductor's game in, 55–56; deaths of blacks in coal truck in, 54, 55–56; education of blacks in, 61; Family Welfare Society in, 68–69, 107, 217; *Gone with the Wind* in, 191; Myrdal in, 140, 203–5; newspapers in, 61, 132, 169, 191, 291; poverty of blacks in, 69; racial etiquette in, 63–64; racketeering and vice in, 195
Atlanta University, 177, 307, 327, 351n73
Atomic bomb, 279–80
Autobiography of Malcolm X, 309
Automobiles, 19, 25–26, 29, 31, 126–27, 142, 319, 341n37, 372n40

Bailey, Alla Maze, 223
Baldwin, C. B., 156
Baldwin, Solicitor-General, 230–33
Bangladesh, 305, 376n54
Bankhead, John H., 136, 167
Bankhead Allotment Bill, 130
Bankhead-Jones Farm Tenant Bill, 135–37, 161, 167, 352n85, 354n10
Baptists, 17, 51–52, 59, 84, 133, 335n8. *See also* Religion
Barbering, 28, 34–35, 44, 186, 201, 332n2
Beck, E. M., 84, 91, 339n5, 341n36, 341nn38–39, 342n41, 342n45, 344–45n81
Benedict, Ruth, 193
Benton, Thomas Hart, 6
Bethune, Mary McLeod, 163
Birmingham, Ala., 98, 166–67, 169, 171
Black, Hugo, 360n104
Black Belt, 110–11, 238. *See also* Agriculture; Greene County, Ga.; Macon County, Ga.
Black Codes, 174
Blacks: agency of, 193–94; attitudes on inferiority of, 63, 123–24, 185, 199; automobiles for, 126–27; class issues of, 361–62n127; courts' convictions of, for crimes, 91, 92, 199–201, 342n48; crime by, 62, 84, 91, 199–201; cultural organizations for, 127; and Delta Cooperative Farms, 152–53; disfranchisement of, 1, 62, 111, 162, 174, 184, 206–7, 347n11; education of, 61, 80, 84, 118, 124–25, 231, 245, 260–62, 361–62n127; employment of, 69, 185–86; exploitation of, 132–33, 157–58; families of, 126, 350n52; as farm owners, 29, 36, 112, 121–22, 225, 347n14; and meaning of "Yah, suh," 238; migration of, to urban areas, 1–2, 40, 52, 67–70, 79, 107–8, 217, 254, 273, 286, 349n33; military service by, 52; and minstrel show, 127–28, 157; and movie theater in Greensboro, 235–37; needs of, in Macon County, Ga., 349n41; and New Deal, 129, 136–38, 231, 352n86; "nigger" as term for, 201–3, 221, 230–33, 235–37, 363n31; and police, 198–99; and political parties, 12; population of, 29–30, 340n16; poverty of, 69, 118; Raper's use of titles for, 231–33, 278; Raper's work with black researchers, 141–48, 162–63, 177–79, 196, 204–5, 335n12, 367n12; religion of, 29–30, 127, 340n19; and Southern Conference on Human Welfare (SCHW), 357n55; and unions, 62, 156; voting rights for, 368n43. *See also American Dilemma, An* (Myrdal); Civil rights movement; Commission on Interracial Cooperation (CIC); Lynching; Race relations; Segregation; Tenancy

Bliven, Bruce, 179
Blue, Carolyn, 229, 230
Boas, Franz, 43, 103, 193
Bolivar County, Miss., 82–85, 150, 340n16
Boll weevil, 69, 110, 112, 120, 121, 185, 254
Boswell, James G., 214, 235, 237
Bourke-White, Margaret, 247
Bowen, Francis, 230
Brannan, Beverly, 239
Brooklyn College, 306–7
Brown, Earl, 261
Brown, O. E., 39
Brown, Paul, 217
Brown, Sterling, 234
Brown v. Board of Education, 140, 210
Brundage, W. Fitzhugh, 340–41n29, 343n52, 344n80, 345–46n100
Bryan, William Jennings, 26
Bunche, Ralph, 192, 201–4, 206, 207, 367n12
Bureau of Agricultural Economics (BAE), 212–13, 216–18, 265, 273, 274, 282

Caldwell, Erskine, 45, 247, 248, 330n19, 346n104
Calloway, John, 235–36
Campbell, W. W., 354n10
Camp Sequoyah, 66–67, 267
Capra, Frank, 6
Carnegie Corporation, 191–92, 207, 210, 307, 365n62
Carpenter, C. T., 164
Carter, Bettina, 196
Cash, Wilbur, 7, 8, 48, 261, 329n8, 346n104
Cason, Clarence, 330n19, 346n104
CCC. *See* Civilian Conservation Corps (CCC)
Chadbourn, James Harmon, 93
Chain gangs. *See* Prison chain gangs
Chamberlain, John, 257
Change. *See* Social change
Charlton, Louise O., 165
Chase, Harry Woodburn, 41
Chattanooga News, 70–71
China, 295
Chinese immigrants, 85
Chivers, Walter: career of, 73–74; influence of, on Lawrence, 307; and Myrdal's *American Dilemma*, 196; research on lynchings by, 74, 81, 88, 295, 338n50, 338n56
Christianity. *See* Religion; *and specific churches*
Churches. *See* Religion; *and specific churches*

CIC. *See* Commission on Interracial Cooperation (CIC)
Civilian Conservation Corps (CCC), 129, 218, 236, 254
Civil rights movement, 2, 70, 79, 138, 265, 286, 287, 308–9
Civil Works Administration (CWA), 129, 131, 138
Clark, John Willie, 90–91
Coahoma, Miss., 272–73
Cochran, Ethel, 141–48
Coleman, Kenneth, 348n22
Colleges. *See* Education; *and specific colleges and universities*
Collier, Tarleton, 220, 247, 291
Colonialism: and South, 1, 4, 172–75, 294; and Third World, 294
Columbia University, 41, 239, 307
Comer, Donald, 167, 188
Comilla Rural Development Academy, 302–6, 312, 376n54
Commission on Interracial Cooperation (CIC): Alexander as founder and director of, 5, 6, 23, 33–34, 52–53, 58, 70; Alexander's resignation from, 138, 161–62, 211, 352n86; and black leaders, 60–61, 335n12; and clergy, 23, 59, 133, 335n8; cooperative biracial efforts by, 60–62, 336n16; criticisms of, 115, 335n5, 348n20; decline of, 211–12, 216; and Department of Agriculture, 137; and disfranchisement of blacks, 162; and Du Bois, 6, 79–80, 81; and education, 59; Eleazer as education director of, 34, 58–59, 70, 93, 94, 101, 114–15, 211, 337n37, 351n74; end of, 162; and federal antilynching legislation, 161; focus and goals of, 33–34, 58, 59, 70, 79–80, 95, 115, 138, 162, 170, 210, 279, 348n21; funding for, 53, 70; lynching publications sponsored by, 6, 73, 81, 89, 115, 161; and media, 34, 58–59, 70, 93, 114–15, 337n37; and NAACP, 60; and name change to Southern Regional Council, 162, 279, 339n7; Odum as director of, 138, 162, 279, 339n7; purpose of, 52–53; and Raper's *Preface to Peasantry*, 81; Raper's speeches sponsored by, 51–52, 63, 64, 101–2, 132–33; Raper's work with, 4, 6, 48, 54–77, 211–12, 232; and Scottsboro Boys, 97, 169; and segregation, 123, 170; and Southern Commission on the Study of Lynching, 70–74; and tenancy, 164. *See also* Alexander, Will; Southern Commission on the Study of Lynching

Communist Party: in China, 283; Raper on, 169–70, 308; and Scottsboro Boys, 96, 137, 169–70; and Southern Conference on Human Welfare (SCHW), 166, 169, 170, 172, 358n80; White on, 97
Congress and antilynching legislation, 73, 95, 161, 208–9, 337n45, 339n8
Connally, Tom, 208–9
Connor, Eugene "Bull," 166–67
Conservation of people and resources, 182. *See also* Environmental issues
Cooper, William, 210
Cooperatives for farmers. *See* Agriculture
Copland, Aaron, 6
Cornell University Press, 305
Corry, Floyd: and arrest warrant for Myrdal, 205; career of, 337n35; and FERA study, 141, 142, 146–48; Greene County farm of, 69, 106–7; maid of wife of, 221; and Raper family's home in Greene County, 215; and Resettlement Administration (RA) study, 154–55; at Vanderbilt, 69, 106, 337n35
Corry, W. R., 106, 113–14
Cotton production: and agribusiness, 187; in Bolivar County, Miss., 340n16; and decline of plantation system, 184, 194; in Greene County, Ga., 69–70, 83–84, 120–21, 368n45; and lynching and cotton economy, 339n5, 341n36, 341n38; mechanization for, 149–50, 175–76, 276, 306, 372n40; migratory labor for, 187–88; and "plow-up," 350–51n63; and soil erosion, 253. *See also* Agriculture; Plantation system
Couch, W. T.: and Dabney's *Liberalism in the South*, 102, 104; and Odum, 41; and proposed newsletter from Southern Commission on the Study of Lynching, 343–44n61; publications written and edited by, 104–5; and Raper's *Preface to Peasantry*, 180; and Raper's *Sharecroppers All*, 178–80, 191, 359–60n101; and Raper's *Tenants of the Almighty*, 240–41; and Raper's *Tragedy of Lynching*, 73, 93–94, 96–97, 100, 105, 179–80, 343n58, 345n93. *See also* University of North Carolina (UNC) Press
Council on a Christian Social Order, 190, 351n70
Counterculture, 310–13
Courthouses, 114, 124
Courts: and control over blacks, 110; conviction of blacks by, 91, 92, 199–201, 342n48; and legal aid agencies, 199; lynchers not convicted by, 91–92, 340n13; and Raper's "Race and Class Pressures," 199–201, 206, 207; and white jury system, 186
Crime: by blacks, 62, 84, 88, 91, 199–201; courts' convictions of blacks for, 91, 92, 199–201, 342n48; and lynching, 88. *See also* Lynching
Criminal justice system. *See* Courts; Law enforcement
Crouse, Julia. *See* Raper, Julia Crouse
Cultural anthropology, 43, 103
Cultural history, 10
CWA. *See* Civil Works Administration (CWA)

Dabney, Virginius, 9, 100, 102, 104, 257
Daniels, Jonathan, 248, 257
Daughters of the Confederacy, 14, 61, 159
Davidson, Donald, 9, 174, 175–77, 361n113
Davidson, James, 368n45
Davidson County, N.C., 331–32n37
Davis, Allison, 104
Davis, Elisha and William, 16
Delano, Irene, 228, 241–46
Delano, Jack, 103–4, 228, 238–39, 241–43, 247, 248, 261, 262, 288, 316
Delta Cooperative Farms, 150–54, 180, 191, 353n5, 353–54n10
Democracy: and American Way, 267–69; and conflict, 31, 48; importance of people in, 220–21; in Japan, 282, 283–84, 286; Jeffersonian, 102; and lynching, 86, 89; and modernity, 48, 51; and plantation system, 108–9, 251; and race relations, 38–39, 71, 152–53, 158, 166, 339n8; and segregation, 124; and technology, 277; in Third World, 297–99; totalitarian systems versus, 135, 210; and Wilson's internationalism, 32
Denmark, 368–69n47
Department of Agriculture, U.S., 136, 137, 172, 212–13, 216, 222, 232–33, 264, 288, 347n5, 352n83. *See also specific agricultural agencies and programs*
Depression. *See* Migration to urban areas; New Deal
Derricott, Julia, 336n16
Developing countries. *See* Third World
Dewey, John, 35
Disfranchisement. *See* Voting
Documentary. *See* Photography; *and specific titles of Raper's works*
Dodge, Witherspoon, 158
Dollard, Charles, 307

Dollard, John, 6, 99, 104, 193
Dolvin, J. B. "Punch," 141, 142, 146, 148, 215, 224
Dorman, Robert, 7–8, 44, 45, 46, 154, 334n40, 361n113, 361n121
Dower, John W., 285, 374n71
Downs, Ed, 230
Du Bois, W. E. B.: and Commission on Interracial Cooperation (CIC), 6, 79–80, 81; on dependency of blacks, 62; influence of, on Lawrence, 307; as leader in southern race relations, 138; and Myrdal's *American Dilemma*, 11, 140, 193; on race relations and economic recovery of South, 175; on Raper's writings, 79, 80–81, 138; on urban migration of blacks, 40; on Woofterism, 80, 339n3
Durkheim, Emile, 49
Durr, Virginia, 168
Dust Bowl, 155, 160
Duval, Elsie West, 326–27
Dyer, Gus, 39
Dyer federal lynching bill, 73, 339n8

Early, Joel, 253
Eddy, Sherwood, 37, 150, 152–53, 354n17, 360n104
Education: of blacks, 61, 80, 84, 118, 124–25, 231, 245, 260–62, 361–62n127; and Commission on Interracial Cooperation (CIC), 59; and CWA teachers, 138; F. Raper's commitment to, 3, 19, 24, 26, 27–28, 33, 320; funding for, 59, 84; in Greene County, Ga., 124–25, 219, 224, 231, 254; higher, 277–78, 292, 319; and integration of schools, 231; in Japan, 286; Julia Raper's view of, 26–27; in Macon County, Ga., 124–25; in Mississippi, 84; in Pakistan, 303; and regionalism, 173; and teachers' salaries in South, 60; vocational, for blacks, 80
Edwards, V. A., 141, 142, 146–48
Egerton, John, 150, 165, 330n19, 332n8, 346n104
Egypt, 295, 296, 297
Elder, I. C., 225
Eleazer, Robert Burns, 34, 58–59, 70, 93, 94, 96, 101, 114–15, 211, 337n37, 351n74
Electricity, 11–12, 27
Elisofon, Eliot, 261–62
Ellis, Ann, 58–59, 161, 335n8
Embree, Edwin R., 59
Emory University, 65, 66, 232
Employment: of blacks, 69, 185–86; and wages, 60, 84, 183–86, 226–27

Enlightenment, 9, 57, 195
Environmental issues, 25–26, 132, 319, 320
Equality. *See* Race relations
Ethiopia, 157, 297
Ethridge, Mark, 358n68
Evans, Dr., 203
Evans, Walker, 11, 103–4, 183, 239, 240, 249–50, 366n6, 367n31
Evolution, 27–28
Exploitation, 132–33, 157–58, 181–82, 220

Farming. *See* Agriculture
Farm Security Administration (FSA): Alexander at, 5, 136, 161, 352nn85–86; and Bureau of Agricultural Economics (BAE), 216–26, 228–34, 273, 274, 282; critics of, 221; end of, 264–65; photography by, 103–4, 182–83, 238–49, 261, 264–65, 330n19, 346n102, 366n6; Raper's study of projects of, 191; role of, 5, 167; School Program of, 218; and Unified Farm Program (UFP), 217–26, 232–33, 250, 252, 254. *See also* Resettlement Administration (RA)
Faulkner, William, 6, 8, 98, 113, 249
Faust, Colonel, 205
Federal Emergency Relief Administration (FERA), 129, 137, 141
Fenno, Richard F., Jr., 371n29
FERA. *See* Federal Emergency Relief Administration (FERA)
Feudalism: in Japan, 284; medieval, 347n13; in South, 4, 174, 183
Films. *See* Movies
Fisk University, 39, 60, 71, 80, 94, 116, 336n16
Fleischauer, Carl, 239
Fleming, Walter, 39
Florida, 186, 187
Ford, Gerald, 317
Ford, John, 189
Ford Foundation, 302, 305
Foreman, Clark, 61, 137, 138, 167, 193, 357n68, 358n80
Formosa, 297
Fortune magazine, 247, 249
Franklin, Sam, 150, 151, 154
Frazier, E. Franklin, 61
Freud, Sigmund, 301, 333n33
Frontier, 7, 8, 48, 86, 181, 329n8, 360n110, 361n113
FSA. *See* Farm Security Administration (FSA)
Fugitives. *See* Nashville Fugitives

Gannett, Lewis, 99
George, Walter, 209
Georgia: barbers in, 186; lynchings in, 77–79, 90–91, 95; Raper's studies of New Deal in, 137–38, 141–48; Settlement Projects in, 138. *See also* Atlanta; Greene County, Ga.; Macon, Ga.; Macon County, Ga.
Georgia Citizen's Fact Finding Committee, 190–91
Georgia Tech, 63, 232
Gershwin, George, 6
Giddings, Franklin Henry, 41
Glenn, Giles, 29
Gone with the Wind, 191
Graham, Frank Porter, 8, 35–36, 39, 166, 171, 332n8
Grant, George, 90
Grant, J. L., 87
Grapes of Wrath, The, 12, 189, 240, 249, 261
Graves, Bibb, 168, 338n52
Greene County, Ga.: agriculture in, 69–70, 106, 107, 111, 112–13, 120–21, 219–20, 368n45; blacks' ownership of farms in, 347n14; Bureau of Agricultural Economics (BAE) program in, 212–13, 216–26, 228–34; changes in, during 1940s, 214–15, 218–23; commercial and governmental services in, 349nn45–46; compared with Macon County, 108, 111–13, 120–21; cotton culture in, 118–21; county fair in, 234, 244; disfranchisement in, 347n11; education in, 124–25, 219, 224, 231, 254; family makeup in, 126; Grand Jury investigation of Raper in, 229–33; history and description of, 106–8, 110, 111–13, 250–52, 368n41; jail in, 204–5, 242, 367n12; migration from, 107–8, 119–21, 217, 349n33; movie theater in Greensboro, 235–37; Myrdal in, 204–5; and New Deal, 113, 128–32, 219–20, 223, 254–57; nutrition in, 223–24; plantation economy in, 110–13, 121, 368n35; Populist movement in, 251; questions on, 118; race relations in, 108, 221, 222, 229–37, 252–53, 349n45; Raper family in, 213, 215–16, 218–19, 227–28, 257–60; Raper's articles on, in *Greensboro Herald-Journal*, 224–25; in Raper's dissertation, 118; Raper's fieldwork in, during 1927–1928, 118; Raper's fieldwork in, during 1941, 241–44, 259–60; Raper's updating data on, in 1934, 118; Unified Farm Program (UFP) in, 217–26, 232–33, 250, 252, 254

Greensboro, Ga. *See* Greene County, Ga.
Greensboro Herald-Journal, 224–25, 228–29, 247, 248, 250, 253, 257
Griffin, Herbert, 122
"Guide to Agriculture, U.S.A." (Raper and Raper), 274, 289

Hall, G. Stanley, 41
Hall, Jacqueline Dowd, 209, 316, 339n8, 356n43
Harris, Dave, 82
Harris, Joel Chandler, 141, 146, 147
Harris, Julian, 71, 93, 96
Harvard University, 27, 279, 317
Hayes, Wayland, 248
Haygood, Margaret, 179
Health services, 131, 254, 289
Henderson, Maud, 65
Hendrix, Jimi, 311, 377n5
Herskovitz, Melville, 193
Higher education. *See* Education; *and specific colleges and universities*
Highlander Folk School, 109, 360n104
History: cultural, 10; sociology versus, 351–52n82
Hobbs, S. H., 178
Hofstadter, Richard, 333n33
Holmes County, Miss., 150
Hoover, Herbert, 254
Hope, John, 60, 61, 63, 71, 93, 358n76
Hope, Lugenia Burns, 61
Huey, Belle, 229
Huntsville, Ala., 343n57
Hurston, Zora Neale, 346n104
Hus, John, 16

Ickes, Harold, 283
India, 277–78, 297
Individualism, 36, 48, 181–82, 329n8. *See also* Frontier
Industrialization, 183–85, 194, 277, 284, 306
Institute for Research in the Social Sciences. *See* University of North Carolina (UNC)
Integration, 81, 231
Intermarriage, 52, 230
Internationalism, 32, 134–36, 194, 369–70n1
Interracial Commission. *See* Commission on Interracial Cooperation (CIC)
Iran, 289, 293, 297–98, 311
Iraq, 289, 293, 295, 296, 298
Irwin, James, 77, 95

Israel, 295
"Is There a 'New South'?" (Raper), 306

Jackson, Walter, 159, 317, 361n111
Japan: Allied Occupation of, 279–86, 292, 374n72; and democracy, 282, 283–84, 286; education in, 286; feudalism in, 284; land reform in, 280–86, 289, 298, 374n72; and Manchuria, 157; Raper's work in, 279–86, 290, 374–75n7; societal introspection by, 374n71
Japanese Village in Transition, The (Raper), 281–83
Jarrell, Rev. C. C., 65
Jefferson, Thomas, 32, 223, 312
Jeffersonian agrarianism, 8–9, 11–14, 42, 122, 222, 223, 255, 277
Jeffersonian democracy, 102, 111, 195, 197
Johns, Mr., 142, 145
Johnson, Bob, 46
Johnson, Charles S.: *The Collapse of Cotton Tenancy* by, 136; at Commission on Interracial Cooperation (CIC), 6, 59, 60, 93; and Delta Cooperative Farms, 150, 152; and Myrdal's *American Dilemma*, 11, 140, 193; on race relations and economic recovery of South, 175; and Raper's writings, 80, 116–17, 211; and Southern Commission on the Study of Lynching, 71; and Southern Conference on Human Welfare (SCHW), 167, 169, 171; and tenancy crisis, 136
Johnson, George, 172
Johnson, Guy, 41, 59, 171, 191, 193, 211, 212, 227, 265
Johnson, James Weldon, 100
Johnson, Lyndon, 308
Jones, Alvin, 196
Jones, M. Ashby, 54
Jordan, 293, 295
Jung, Carl, 301, 333n33
Jury system, 186. *See also* Courts

Kajita, Masaru, 280
Kellogg, Paul, 179
Kennedy, Stetson, 346n104
Keppel, Frederick, 192
Kester, Howard, 150
Khan, Ahkter Hameed, 302, 304, 322, 376n54
King, Martin Luther, Jr., 308
King, R. H., 81
King, Richard, 329n8

King, William P., 92
Kirby, Jack, 347n7
Kirkland, Willie, 74
Knights of Columbus, 159
Krueger, E. T., 39
Ku Klux Klan, 14, 58, 139, 159, 163, 164, 191, 196, 203

Lamb, Mr. and Mrs. Harold, 246
Land prices, 19, 332n1
Land reform: in Iran, 297–98; in Japan, 280–86, 289, 298, 374n72
Land-use policy, 131–32
Lange, Dorothea, 103–4, 182–83, 226, 239, 240, 288, 316
Law enforcement: and lynchers, 74, 91, 156; "nigger" as term used by, 203, 363n31; and prevention of lynching, 203; and race relations, 198–99, 202–3; and Raper's "Race and Class Pressures," 195, 198–99, 207, 363n31; and Raper's research on Greene and Macon counties, Ga., 114; and Raper's research on lynchings, 74, 76, 91, 156, 338n52, 338n54, 342n49; and salary of sheriff, 84; and segregation in Birmingham, 166–67, 171
Lawrence, Charles, 306–7
League of Nations, 32, 157
Lebanon, 295, 296
Legal aid, 199
Legal system. *See* Courts
Lehman, J. B., 71
Let Us Now Praise Famous Men (Agee and Evans), 11, 249–50, 346n104, 367n31
Leuchtenburg, William, 352n83
Levine, Lawrence, 6
Liberalism in the South (Dabney), 100, 102, 104
Liberty League, 197
Libya, 289, 296
Life magazine, 9, 12, 104, 240, 247, 249, 261–62, 264
Lingold, Mr. and Mrs. Carl, 246
Lippmann, Walter, 1, 2, 44, 45, 94
Locke, Alain, 100, 193
Lomax, Alan, 12
Luce, Henry, 249
Luke, Roscoe, 74, 76, 338n54
Lynching: in Alabama, 115; and black community, 87, 95, 338n56, 339n2; Chadbourn on, 93; characteristics of lynchers, 89–90; characteristics of victims of, 88; Chivers's research on,

Lynching (*continued*)
with Raper, 74, 81, 88, 295, 338n50, 338n56; churches' responses to, 92; class implications of, 71; compared with charivari, 92–93, 343n56; and courts' lack of convictions for lynchers, 91–92, 340n13; crimes associated with, 88; and democracy, 86, 89; deterrence of, 85–86, 343n57; and federal antilynching legislation, 73, 95, 161, 208–9, 337n45, 339n8, 344n67, 364n51; and frontier ethos, 86–87; in Georgia, 74–75, 77–79, 90–91, 95; justifications for, 72, 90–91; law enforcement and lynchers, 74, 91, 156; media coverage of, 77, 83, 92–94, 98, 110, 338n51, 342–43n52, 344–45nn80–81; in Mississippi, 82–85; Myrdal on, 200; myths on, 72, 88; photographs of, 91; and plantation system, 89, 339n5, 341n36, 341n38; and rape, 88; Raper's and CIC publications on, 6, 73, 89, 93, 115, 161, 200, 340n26, 363n19; in Raper's "Race and Class Pressures," 200, 363n19; Raper's research and interviews on, 74–79, 87, 339n2; as rural crime, 86–89, 340–41n29, 341–42n39, 342n41; silence of community regarding, 74–77, 89, 94–95; statistics on, 70, 73, 88, 95, 110, 161, 338n53; Tuskegee records on, 73, 87; and whites' fear of blacks, 200; white townspeople as accomplices to, 89, 338n55, 342n45; women's involvement in prevention of, 72–73, 94, 356n44; Woofter on, 339n8. See also *Tragedy of Lynching, The* (Raper)
Lynd, Helen and Robert, 47, 239

MacArthur, Douglas, 281, 283
Macmillan, 240, 265
Macon, Ga., 77, 92, 97, 98, 202
Macon County, Ga.: agriculture in, 69–70, 111–13, 120–21; blacks' ownership of farms in, 122; commercial and governmental services in, 349nn45–46; as compared with Greene County, 108, 111–13, 120–21; cotton culture in, 118–21; Davidson on, 175; disfranchisement in, 347n11; education in, 124–25; family makeup in, 126; history and description of, 111–13; needs of blacks in, 349n41; and New Deal, 113, 128–32; questions on, 118; race relations in, 108, 349n45; in Raper's dissertation, 118; Raper's fieldwork in, during 1927–1928, 118; Raper's updating data on, in 1934, 118
Magasaysay, Ramon, 291
Magazines. See Media; *and specific magazines*

Manchuria, 157
Manhattan Project, 279–80
Marshall, Thurgood, 140
Mason, Lucy Randolph, 167, 170, 179–80
Mass media. See Media
Mays, B. E., 60
McCarthyism, 290
McGibony, Hamp, 204–5, 229, 235
McGill, Ralph, 291
McGloughlin, W. J., 96
Mclachlan, John, 196
McWhorter, Robert, 225
Meacham, William Shands, 248–49
Mead, Margaret, 6, 238, 239, 366n2
Mechanized agriculture, 149–50, 175–76, 187, 215, 274–79, 284–85, 306, 319, 353n2, 353n5, 372n40. See also Agriculture
Media: on civil rights movement, 2, 70, 79; Commission on Interracial Cooperation's (CIC's) use of, 34, 58–59, 70, 93, 114–15, 337n37; on Georgia's backwardness, 81–82; and immediacy, 10–11; on lynchings, 77, 79, 83, 92–94, 98, 110, 338n51, 342–43n52, 344–45nn80–81; and Raper's distrust of consumerism, 191; and Raper's *Tragedy of Lynching*, 79, 94, 97–101, 115; and rural farm families, 260; and sociology, 44, 307. See also Radio; Television; *and specific newspapers and magazines*
Methodism, 3, 17–19, 21–24, 31, 58, 59, 84, 92, 316, 318. See also Religion
Michigan State University (MSU), 302, 305, 306, 308
Middle East, 289, 293–99, 311. See also *specific countries*
Migration to urban areas: and Atlanta as home of rural migrants, 67–70, 107–8, 217, 349n33; by blacks, 1–2, 40, 52, 67–70, 79, 107–8, 217, 254, 273, 286, 349n33; Du Bois on, 40; from Greene County, Ga., 107–8, 119–21, 217, 349n33; and race relations, 52, 67–70; Raper on, 119–21, 254; Smithsonian exhibit on, 323–24
Mills, Walter, 98–99
Milton, George Fort, 70–71, 74, 93, 96, 337n48, 344n75
Minstrel show, 127–28, 157
Mississippi. See Bolivar County, Miss.; Coahoma, Miss.
Mississippi State Agricultural Extension Office, 272–73
Mitchell, George, 167

Mitchell, H. L., 6, 150, 156–58, 316
Modernity: and automobile, 25–26; and cooperative approach, 48; and democracy, 48, 51; questions of, 109; and race relations, 3–4, 73; and realism, 9–11; regionalists' attitude toward, 334n43; Singal on, 330n14; tools of, 10
Montezuma, Ga. See Macon County, Ga.
Montgomery, Ala., 206–7
Moore, John S., 232
Moravians, 3, 7, 16–19, 30–31, 320. See also Religion
Morehouse College, 60, 63, 71, 73, 81, 141, 307
Moton, Robert R., 37–38, 60, 61, 71, 93
Movies, 12, 44, 189, 191
Movie theater, 235–37
MSU. See Michigan State University (MSU)
Mumford, Lewis, 45
Music, 24, 54, 55, 65, 138–39, 159, 164, 216, 266–67, 300
Mutual Security Agency, 289–90, 297
Myrdal, Gunnar: arrest warrant for, 205–6; on black agency, 193–94; career of, 191; and communism, 210; and internationalism, 194; on lynching, 200; on race relations, 5, 11, 140, 191–95, 207, 210–11, 376n63; research approach of, 196–97, 363n22, 192; and Tuskegee Institute, 206; and Unified Farm Program (UFP), 218. See also *American Dilemma, An* (Myrdal)

NAACP (National Association for the Advancement of Colored People), 60, 96, 169, 364n48
Nashville Agrarians, 174, 175–77
Nashville Fugitives, 9, 40
Nation, 94, 97
Nationalist Chinese, 283, 290
National Recovery Act (NRA), 129
National Sharecroppers' Fund, 190, 315–16
National War Labor Board, 190
National Youth Administration, 5, 218, 229
Neely, Senator, 208
Negro in America, The, 140
Nelson, Bertha, 200–201
New Deal: and blacks, 129, 136–38, 231, 352n86; for farmers, 115, 129–31, 135–36, 156, 160–61, 164–65, 194, 220, 222–23, 255, 352n83; in Greene and Macon counties, Ga., 113, 128–32, 219–20, 223, 254–57; inequities in, 129, 136–38, 164–72, 222, 255, 352n86; opponents of, 116, 197, 221, 233; popular support for, 164; Raper's studies of impact of, 137–38, 154–55, 161, 191, 347n5, 352n86, 352n90, 363n37; and Raper's studies of Resettlement Administration (RA) projects, 154–55, 355n21; Raper's work with black researchers on, 141–48, 162–63, 177–79; and social science, 135–36; and Southern Conference on Human Welfare (SCHW), 165–66, 357n55; and tenancy, 130–31, 136. See also Roosevelt, Franklin D.; *and specific federal agencies*
New Left, 309
New Republic, 80, 94, 179, 306
Newspapers. See Media; *and specific newspapers*
New York Herald Tribune, 98, 99, 345n93
New York Times, 6, 96, 98, 189, 249, 257
Niebuhr, Reinhold, 150, 360n104
Niehoff, Richard, 305
"Nigger" as term, 201–3, 221, 230–33, 235–37, 363n31
90 Degrees in the Shade (Cason), 330n19, 346n104
Nixon, H. C., 167, 171, 330n19
Nixon, Richard, 66, 317
North Africa, 297, 311
North American Review, 176
North Georgia Review, 176
NRA. See National Recovery Act (NRA)

O'Brien, Michael, 334n43, 371–72n33
Ocilla, Ga., 77–79, 95
Odum, Howard: as Commission on Interracial Cooperation (CIC) director, 138, 162, 279, 339n7; disciples of, in sociology, 333n29; and frontier ethos of South, 7; and job offer for Raper at UNC, 171, 216; and Lippmann on South, 1; as mentor for Raper, 33–34; and Myrdal's *American Dilemma*, 193; Progressivism of, 3–34, 333n33; and Raper's activism, 171; and Raper's research on Macon and Greene counties, 69–70; and Raper's *Tenants of the Almighty*, 239; on Raper's *Tragedy of Lynching*, 96; and regionalism, 44–47, 154, 162, 173, 334n43; retirement of, 288; sociology as practiced by, 34, 44–47, 196, 333n29, 371–72n33; and Southern Commission on the Study of Lynching, 71; and Southern Conference on Human Welfare (SCHW), 165, 170, 171–72; at Southern Regional Council, 162, 172, 358n68; and Stryker, 239; and subsidy for publication of *Sharecroppers All*, 180, 359–60n101; at University of North Carolina, 35, 36, 41–46, 48, 54, 118, 156, 211, 216

398 INDEX

Office of Personnel: Orientation and Counseling Branch, 302
Office of War Information, 265
Oklahoma, 155, 263

Pacifism, 37, 134–35, 169, 209–10, 267
Page, Kirby, 37
Pakistan, 239, 297, 302–6
Park, James B., 242, 243
Park, Orville A., 81–82, 178–79
Park, Robert E., 40, 193, 345–46n100
Parrott, Alfred "Preacher," 243, 252–53, 262
Patterson, F. D., 150
Peace. *See* Pacifism
Percy, William Alexander, 346n104
Peterkin, Julia, 330n19
Philippines, 291, 297, 311
Philips, U. B., 110
Photography: of defense work, 244, 264; and Farm Security Administration photographs, 103–4, 182–83, 238–49, 261, 264–65, 330n19, 346n102, 366n6; in *Let Us Now Praise Famous Men*, 11, 249–50; of lynching, 91; newspicture, 367n19; in *90 Degrees in the Shade*, 330n19; in *Preface to Peasantry*, 245–46; in *Roll, Jordan, Roll*, 330n19; in *Sharecroppers All*, 10, 104, 182–83, 240; in *Tenants of the Almighty*, 10, 239, 240–49, 330n19
Plantation system: Davidson on, 176; and democracy, 108–9, 251; and economic structure of Bolivar County, Miss., 84–85; and feudalism, 183–84; and frontier ethos, 7, 48; in Greene County, Ga., 110–13, 121, 368n35; Kirby on, 347n7; and lynching, 89, 339n5, 341n36, 341n38; and race relations, 70, 108, 118; and segregation, 124
Police. *See* Law enforcement
Poll tax, 4, 162, 166, 168, 174, 184
Post, Marion, 183, 240
Post offices, 124, 349n46
Poverty: of blacks, 69, 118; in Greene County, Ga., 110; and New South, 306; and *Report on the Economic Conditions of the South*, 161, 166, 179
Powdermaker, Hortense, 193
Preface to Peasantry (Raper): on cotton culture, 118–21; C. S. Johnson's involvement in, 116–17; ethnographic detail in, 119; facts and statistics in, 118; and Highlander Folk School, 360n104; and Johnson's *Collapse of Cotton Tenancy*, 136; on land-use policy, 131–32; on migration to urban areas, 119–21; on New Deal, 128–32; photographs in, 245–46; publication of, 81, 115; questions in, 118, 128, 275; Raper's dissertation as blueprint for, 41; on remnants of master-slave regime, 121–28; reviews of, 6, 175–77, 179; sales of, 180; on segregation, 123–27; themes of, 7, 115, 117, 182, 183, 218, 224, 261, 329n7; and Wallace, 156; writing style and tone of, 7, 103, 116–17, 305, 329n7. *See also* Greene County, Ga.; Macon County, Ga.
Presbyterian Church, 54–55
Prior, Herb, 263
Prison chain gangs, 35, 46–47, 334n47
Progressivism: of Alexander, 33–34; of A. Raper, 3, 50; in Arcadia, 30–31; of F. Raper, 3, 19, 24–29, 33, 225, 320; goal of, 9; and Highlander Folk School, 360n104; and liberalism, 102; and limitations of market capitalism, 48; in North Carolina, 331n10; of Odum, 33–34, 333n33
Puerto Rico, 227, 228
Putnam County, Ga., 141–48

Quirino, Elpidio, 291

RA. *See* Resettlement Administration (RA)
"Race and Class Pressures" (Raper), 191, 195–201, 210–11, 216, 261, 363n19, 363n31, 364n58
Race relations: ambivalence of white southerners about, 30; and A. Raper's defense of dissertation, 49–50; A. Raper's interest in, as student, 36, 38–40, 62; A. Raper's *North American Review* article on, 176–77; A. Raper's use of titles with blacks, 231–33, 278; and attitudes about blacks' inferiority, 63, 123–24, 185, 199; and black women, 126, 186, 199–201; and clergy, 23, 59, 133, 335n8; and colonialism, 172–75; and commercial and governmental services for blacks and whites, 349nn45–46; and constitutionality, 358n76; Davidson on, 176; and Delta Cooperative Farms, 152–53; and democracy, 38–39, 71, 152–53, 158, 166, 339n8; and economic recovery of South, 174–75; and equality, 49–50, 52, 58, 185–88, 230–33, 291–92; and exploitation of blacks, 132–33, 157–58, 181–82; F. Raper's views of, 29; F. Roosevelt, 4–5; in Greene and Macon counties, Ga., 108, 221, 222, 229–37, 252–53, 349n45; and intermarriage, 52, 230; and law enforcement, 198–99, 202–3; and limitations of race and class lines generally, 4; and moder-

nity, 3–4, 73; and movie theater in Greensboro, 235–37; Myrdal on, 5, 11, 140, 191–95, 207, 210–11, 376n63; in 1950s and 1960s, 307–9; in North, 207–8, 355n32; and plantation system, 70, 108, 118; and religion, 23, 125, 166; and social vision, 64–65; and Southern Conference on Human Welfare (SCHW), 166–67; and technology and industrialization, 194, 277–78; and urban migration, 52, 67–70; and voting, 187; and World War II, 194, 234–35. See also *American Dilemma, An* (Myrdal); Blacks; Commission on Interracial Cooperation (CIC); Lynching; Segregation

Radio, 10, 27, 34, 44, 160, 174, 260, 337n37, 338n51, 372n40

Railroads, 162–63, 178, 227, 331n10

Rape, 88, 96

Raper, Arthur: and air travel, 373n49; barbering by, in college, 28, 34–35, 44, 201, 332n2; and Camp Sequoyah, 66–67; children of, 24, 66, 138–39, 164, 215–16, 228, 241, 257–60, 265–67, 300, 321; and conductor's game in Atlanta, 55–56; courtship of Martha Jarrell by, 65–66; death and funeral of, 154, 325–26; dreams of, 278–79; education of, as undergraduate at University of North Carolina, 8, 31–32, 36–39, 41, 65–66; education of, as youth, 33; education of, in doctoral program at University of North Carolina, 41–50, 53–54, 66, 118; education of, in master's program at Vanderbilt, 39–40, 53, 62, 106, 333n23, 337n35; family background of, 3, 15–22; and family finances, 227–28; files of, 316–17, 325; and financial resources for college education, 28, 34–35, 37, 332n2; health problems of, 203, 310, 321–22, 324–25; homes of, 66, 138, 215–16, 226, 257–60, 265–66; as Jeffersonian, 8–9, 11–14, 195; marriage of, 66, 232; mentors of, 33–34, 53, 211–12, 239, 364n58, 365n4, 376n54; and music, 24, 39, 138–39, 164, 216, 266–67, 300; and nature, 65–67, 164; optimism of, 318–19, 320; overview of contributions of and research by, 2–14; papers of, at University of North Carolina, 317; personality of, 63, 65–66, 242, 309; physical appearance of, 313; poetry by, 314–15; Progressivism of, 3, 50; on progress toward egalitarianism, 378n29; realism of, 9–11, 101–2, 348n24; and religion, 18–24, 54–55, 151, 228, 259, 315, 316, 318; retirement of, 12, 13–14, 310–25; on science and technology, 274–79, 319, 378n27; siblings of, 15, 20, 27; Slope Oaks farm of, 12, 13, 266, 288–89, 299–300, 310, 312–18, 321–25; and tractor accident, 321–22; youth of, 16–32
—career of: advantages and disadvantages of working for federal bureaucracy, 266, 287–88; audience for Raper's books, 133, 247, 250; Bureau of Agricultural Economics (BAE), 212–13, 216–26, 228–34, 265, 282; Commission on Interracial Cooperation (CIC), 4, 6, 54–77, 211–12, 232; Congressional testimony on antilynching bill, 208–9; Council on a Christian Social Order, 190, 351n70; editing of Raper's writings, 66, 265, 301, 321; Farm Security Administration (FSA) projects, 191; Federal Emergency Relief Agency (FERA) study, 137–38; Georgia Citizen's Fact Finding Committee, 190–91; Highlander Folk School, 360n104; interracial teams for research, 141–48, 162–63, 177–79, 196, 204–5, 295, 335n12, 367n12; interviewing skills, 35, 44, 75, 201–3; in Japan, 279–86, 292, 374–75n7; and Myrdal's *American Dilemma*, 5, 11, 140, 191, 193, 203–8, 363n19, 363n31, 364n58, 376n54; National Sharecroppers' Fund, 190, 315–16; National War Labor Board, 190; Office of Personnel, Orientation and Counseling Branch, 302; orientation for foreign-service personnel and foreign visitors to U.S., 288–89, 302; overview of, 3–14; Rural Trends Project, 265, 269–75, 371n27; security clearance for work in Third World, 292, 375n17; sociology as practiced by Raper, 10, 101, 102–3, 160, 245, 273, 282, 370n19; Southern Commission on the Study of Lynching, 71–79; Southern Conference on Human Welfare (SCHW), 165–72, 291, 356–57n55, 357–58n68, 358–59n80; speeches, 14, 51–52, 63, 64, 101–2, 132–33, 157–59, 163–64, 173, 174, 220–21, 275, 352–53n91; teaching positions, 4, 139–40, 163, 203, 216, 307, 308, 326–27, 351n73, 352–53n92; in Third World countries, 13, 287–306; Unified Farm Program (UFP), 217–26, 232–33, 250; University of North Carolina job offer, 171, 216; U.S. International Cooperation Administration (USICA), 289–306; Wage-Hour Division committee, 226–27; writing style and tone of writings, 79, 95–96, 105, 116–17, 182, 225, 305. See also Lynching; Race relations; *and specific titles of works*

Raper, Blanche, 65

Raper, Charles Franklin, 66, 138, 164, 257–58, 266–67, 321, 322

Raper, Cletus, 207
Raper, Frank: and automobile, 31; children of, 3, 15, 20, 21, 27; education supported by, 3, 19, 24, 26, 27–28, 33, 320; family background of, 17; farm of, 3, 15–16, 20, 25, 27, 332n1; marriage of, 16, 17; and race relations, 29, 225, 357n66; and religion, 17, 21; and road building, 24, 27
Raper, Harrison: and *Autobiography of Malcolm X*, 309; birth of, 138; childhood of, 164, 204, 241; and father's tractor accident, 322; and music, 24, 164, 266–67, 300, 321; and parents' deaths, 325, 326
Raper, Jarrell, 138, 266, 300, 321, 322, 326
Raper, John, 27, 279–80, 325, 373n53
Raper, Julia Crouse: children of, 15, 20, 21, 27, 138–39, 164; and education, 26–27, 37; family background of, 17; and finances, 24; marriage of, 16, 17; personality of, 24–25; and race relations, 30; and religion, 3, 16–19, 21, 320; and *Sharecroppers All*, 188
Raper, Kenneth, 28
Raper, Luther, 20
Raper, Margaret, 138, 215–16, 266, 321, 326
Raper, Martha Jarrell: on Arthur's personality, 309; and Arthur's teaching job at Agnes Scott College, 139, 159–60; back problems of, 300, 310, 321; children of, 24, 66, 138–39, 164, 215–16, 228, 241, 257–60, 265–67, 300, 321; courtship of, 65–66; and day-care center, 265–66; death of, 326; as editor of Arthur's writing, 66, 265, 301, 321; education of, 65; employment of, 139, 301; family background of, 232; and family finances, 227–28; in Greene County, Ga., 215–16, 218–19; and "Guide to Agriculture, U.S.A.," 274, 289; homes of, 66, 138, 215–16, 218–19, 226, 257–60, 265–66; on Julia Raper's views of blacks, 30; liberal views of, 66, 301, 320–21; on lynching research, 339n2; marriage of, 66, 232; and music, 65, 138–39, 159, 164, 216, 266–67, 300; personality and intelligence of, 66, 139; and religion, 316; and retirement, 12, 13, 310–25; Slope Oaks farm of, 12, 266, 288–89, 299–300, 310, 312–18, 321–25; in Third World countries, 300, 302, 304; on tractor accident, 322
Raper, William Davis, 16
Realism, 9–11, 101–2, 348n24
Reckless, Walter, 39
Reconstruction, 251, 287

Redding, Saunders, 346n104
Reed, John Shelton, 41
Reese, Bishop F. F., 63
Regionalism: decline in scholarly interest in, 288; Dorman on, 7–8, 44, 45, 46, 154, 334n40, 361n113; and education, 173; and modernity, 334n43; and Odum, 44–47, 154, 162, 173, 334n43; and Raper, 7, 8, 133–35, 173, 280; and Third World, 288
Reid, Ira De A.: and Commission on Interracial Cooperation (CIC), 60; Lawrence as student of, 307; and Myrdal's *American Dilemma*, 196; and race relations, 291; and *Sharecroppers All*, 177–79, 182, 184, 307, 329n8, 361n111; and *Tenants of the Almighty*, 239; and Unified Farm Program (UFP), 218; and U.S. Mutual Security Agency, 289–90
Religion: of blacks, 29–30, 127, 340n19; and community life, 18; and conservatism, 19; Jung on, 301; and ministers' responses to lynching, 92; and Mississippi churches, 84, 340n19; and Progressivism, 3; and race relations, 23, 125, 166; Raper's views of, 18–24, 54–55, 151, 228, 259, 315, 316, 318; and Sam Franklin, 151; and social division, 18–19, 23, 31, 48. *See also* Baptists; Methodism; Moravians; Presbyterian Church
Report on the Economic Conditions of the South, 161, 166, 179
Resettlement Administration (RA): Alexander at, 136, 137, 156, 161, 211, 352n85; establishment of, 156; Raper's study of impact of, 154–55, 355n21; Stryker at, 239. *See also* Farm Security Administration (FSA)
Rhodes, Lloyd, 229
Rice, James Edward, 330n19
Rice, T. B., 246, 348n18, 368n41
Riis, Jacob, 116, 246
Road systems, 19, 27, 126–27, 334n47
Rockefeller Foundation, 70
Roggioli, Renato, 333n33
Roosevelt, Eleanor, 6, 167, 169
Roosevelt, Franklin D.: and Farm Security Administration (FSA), 160–61; in 1936 election, 165; and popular support for New Deal, 164; portrait of, 246; and race relations, 4–5; and *Report on the Economic Conditions of the South*, 161, 166, 179; and special adviser on Negro affairs, 61. *See also* New Deal
Roosevelt, Theodore, 333n33

Rope and Faggot (White), 72, 344n67
Roper, John, 333n33
Rosenwald Fund, 59, 70, 211
Ross, Dorothy, 42, 43, 103
Ross, Edward, 43
Rosskam, Edwin, 104, 244–46, 248, 249, 265, 288
Rothstein, Arthur, 103–4, 239, 240
Rural Development in Action (Raper), 304–5
Rural Life in the United States (Raper and Taylor), 274–75
Rural Philippines, The (Raper), 291
Rural sociology. *See* Sociology
Rural Trends Project, 265, 269–75, 371n27
Russell, Richard, 209, 217
Rust, John and Mack, 150, 353n5

Schools. *See* Education
Schuler, Ed, 302
SCHW. *See* Southern Conference on Human Welfare (SCHW)
Scott, LeRoy, 85–86
Scottsboro Boys, 60, 96–97, 137, 168, 169–70, 344n75
Screven County, Ga., 85–86
Segregation: in Birmingham, 166–67, 169; and black researchers working with Raper, 141–48, 162–63, 178, 204–5, 338n50, 367n12; blacks' use of, for community and cultural independence, 62; and Commission on Interracial Cooperation (CIC), 123, 170; and democracy, 124; in Greene and Macon counties, Ga., 349n45; and Hope, 358n76; and plantation system, 124; *Preface to Peasantry* on, 123–27; of railroads, 162–63, 178; and Raper, 81, 123–27, 162–63, 178, 186, 242, 356n49; and Southern Conference on Human Welfare (SCHW), 166–67, 358n68. *See also* Blacks; Race relations
Settlement Projects, 138
Sharecroppers All (Raper): conclusion of, 188; cover of, 182; field research for, 177–80; as modernist jeremiad, 180–85; movie deal for, 12, 189; photographs in, 10, 104, 182–83, 240; portraits in, 103; publication of, 178, 180, 191, 261; Reid's contributions to, 177–79, 182, 184, 307, 329n8, 361n111; reviews of and readers' responses to, 178–79, 188–89, 355n34; subsidy for publication of, 180, 359–60n101; themes of, 7, 154, 174, 177, 180–88, 329n8, 362n131; writing style of, 182

Sharecroppers in non-farm enterprises, 178, 183–85, 362n131. *See also Sharecroppers All* (Raper); Tenancy
Shepperson, Gay, 141–42, 145
Sheriffs. *See* Law enforcement
Singal, Daniel, 36, 38, 88, 316, 330n14, 347n5
Slavery, 1, 49, 193–94, 252–53, 259. *See also* Plantation system
Slope Oaks farm, 12, 13, 266, 288–89, 299–300, 310, 312–18, 321–25
Smith, Lillian, 8, 14, 176, 189, 309, 346n104
Smith, Russell, 172
Smithsonian exhibit on migration, 323–24
Social change: conservatives' resistance to, 10; and crisis, 311–12; and Jefferson, 312; and realism, 9–10; Steiner on, 334n49. *See also* Modernity
Social science. *See* Sociology
Social vision, 64–65
Society for the Preservation of the White Race, 203
Sociology: and agency, 193–94, 196; case study in, 44, 47, 334n38; Chicago, 43–44, 103; comparative approach to research in, 271; and cultural history, 10; Davidson on, 175; history compared with, 351–52n82; and laws of life as seen by Raper, 56–58, 320; and mass media, 44, 307; Myrdal's approach to, 192, 363n22, 196–97; and Nashville Agrarians, 175–77; and New Deal, 135–36; Odum's approach to, 34, 44–47, 196, 333n29, 371–72n33; and personal diplomacy by Raper, 114; Progressive, 10; public interest in, 79; quantitative, 43, 264, 290; Raper's approach to, 10, 101, 102–3, 160, 245, 273, 282, 370n19; Raper's graduate work in, 41–50; and reform of American society, 104, 160, 194–95, 268, 287, 307–8; and regionalism, 44–47; rural, 6, 13, 109, 274–75, 279, 302–6; sampling in, 270; and social dynamics, 194; and social vision, 64–65; and statistics, 43, 103, 290
Sosna, Morton, 59, 168, 170, 335n12, 337n45, 339n8, 356n49
South. *See* Blacks; Plantation system; Race relations; Raper, Arthur; Regionalism; and *specific titles of Raper's works*
Southeast Asia, 289, 290, 297, 311. *See also specific countries*
Southern Association of Women for the Preservation of the White Race, 139

Southern Commission on the Study of Lynching, 70–79, 81, 93–94, 343n57, 343–44n61
Southern Conference on Human Welfare (SCHW), 5, 9, 165–72, 180–81, 291, 356–57n55, 358–59n80
Southern Regional Council, 162, 172, 339n7, 358n68. *See also* Commission on Interracial Cooperation (CIC)
Southern Renaissance, 45
Southern Tenant Farmers Union (STFU), 150–52, 155–57, 164, 180, 355n25
"South's Landless Farmers, The" (Raper), 164, 323
"South Strains toward Decency, The" (Raper), 176–77
Sparkman, John, 306
Spear, Robert, 37
Stange, Maren, 346n102
State Department, U.S., 284, 289, 293–94, 297, 299, 301–2, 310–11
Steelman, Roy, 59
Steichen, Edward, 104
Steinbeck, John, 5, 189, 249
Steiner, Jessie, 47–48, 196, 218, 334n49
Stevenson, Adlai, 306
Stone, Donald, 289
Stouffer, Samuel, 211
Stryker, Roy: and defense photographs, 244, 264; on documentary, 367n20; and Evans, 366n6; and FSA photographs, 239–40, 242–45, 248, 249, 261, 264, 265, 366n6, 367n19; on newspictures, 367n19; and Odum, 239; at Resettlement Administration (RA), 239; and role of Farm Security Administration (FSA), 5; and Steinbeck, 5
Suburbanization, 273, 372n36
Suez Canal Crisis, 298
Sullivan, Patricia, 166, 355n25, 357n68
Supreme Court, U.S., 140, 186, 210
Syria, 293, 295, 296

Taggert, Glenn, 289
Taiwan, 283, 287, 289, 290, 292, 295, 298, 300, 301, 311
Talmadge, Eugene, 115, 116, 203, 217, 220, 232, 335n5, 348n20, 348n22
Tate, Allen, 174
Taylor, Carl C.: and Bureau of Agricultural Economics (BAE), 216–17, 219–20, 274–75, 312; as mentor for Raper, 376n54; *Rural Life in the United States* by, 274–75; and Rural Trends Project, 265, 269–71, 275; and staff size at USDA, 288; and suburbanization, 372n36; and U.S. Mutual Security Agency, 289
Taylor, Paul, 226
Technology. *See* Mechanized agriculture
Telephone, 27
Television, 2, 12, 13, 79
Tenancy: and Bankhead-Jones Farm Tenant Bill, 135–37, 161, 167, 352n85, 354n10; and blacks' chronic debt, 122–23, 370–71n22; and cabin of sharecropper, 173, 323; and cash economy, 125–26, 215; and Commission on Interracial Cooperation (CIC), 164; and economics of sharecropping, 174–75; federal legislation on, 135–36; and field tools of tenant farmers, 360n108; and lynchings and white tenants, 341–42n39, 342n41; and New Deal programs, 130–31, 136; and "plow-up" of cotton crop, 350–51n63; and Raper's *Sharecroppers All*, 180–88; Raper's speech on, 163–64; and Smithsonian exhibit on migration, 323–24; and Southern Tenant Farmers Union (STFU), 150–52, 155–57, 164, 180, 355n25; and Unified Farm Program (UFP), 218–23. *See also* Agriculture; *Tenants of the Almighty* (Raper)
Tenants of the Almighty (Raper): appendices of, 248, 314; audience for, 247, 250; author's acknowledgments in, 239; captions for photographs in, 246–47; editing of, 265, 301; on gardens, 255, 325–26; history in, 250–52, 368n41; on migration to urban areas, 254; photographs in, 10, 239, 240–49, 330n19; portraits in, 103, 221; publication of, 240, 265; research for, 241–44; reviews of, 247, 248, 257; statistics in, 248, 314; themes of, 7, 240–41, 253–55, 277; writing style of, 225
Terrill, Thomas, 210
Third World: agriculture in, 291; balance between local, regional, and national initiatives in, 298–99; colonialism in, 294; and Comilla Rural Development Academy, 302–6, 312, 376n54; democracy in, 297–99; graft in, 297; interracial teams working with Raper in, 295; Martha Raper in, 300, 302, 304; military assistance and police training programs in, 293, 311; Raper's generalizations on, 296–97; Raper's security clearance for work in, 292, 375n17; Raper's work in, 13, 287–306; success-

Index 403

ful countries in, 297; and USICA, 289–306; U.S. officials' approach in, 280–81, 294–95; U.S. policy toward, 292–93, 311. *See also specific countries*
Thomas, Jesse O., 171
Thomas, Norman, 5
Thomas, William I., 43, 103, 334n38
Thompson, Rev. Nath, 163
Time magazine, 301
Tindall, George B., 41
Tobacco, 224
Tobacco production, 25, 33, 332n1
Tolnay, Stewart, 84, 91, 339n5, 341n36, 341nn38–39, 342n41, 342n45, 344–45n81
Tragedy of Lynching, The (Raper): case studies in, 10, 79–87, 89–90, 103; Chivers's work on, 74, 81, 88, 295, 338n50, 338n56; conclusion of, 102; Du Bois on, 79, 80–81; editing of, 96; Milton's introduction to, 337n48; 1968 edition of, 13, 308; organization of, 87; publication of, 73, 79, 81, 93–94, 113; publicity for, 93, 94, 96–97, 101, 115, 343n58; reviews of, 6, 80–81, 94, 97–100, 345n93; sale price of, 93; sales of, 100, 179–80, 345n93; significance of, 100–101; writing style and tone of, 79, 95–96, 105, 305
Treadway, Lane, 150
Truman, Harry, 280
Tugwell, Rexford, 136, 137, 156, 211, 239, 245, 347n5, 352n84
Turkey, 297, 299
Turner, Frederick Jackson, 32, 39, 86, 334n43
Tuscaloosa, Ala., 115, 202–3
Tuskegee Institute, 38, 60, 71, 73, 87, 139, 203, 205, 206
Twelve Million Black Voices (Wright), 5, 248–49, 330n19
"Two Years to Remember" (Raper), 257–60

UFP. *See* Unified Farm Program (UFP)
Ulmann, Doris, 330n19
UNC. *See* University of North Carolina (UNC); University of North Carolina (UNC) Press
Underwood, Marvin, 63
Unified Farm Program (UFP), 217–26, 232–33, 250, 252, 254
Unions, 5, 62, 150–52, 155–57, 164, 180, 290, 357n55
United Nations, 298
Universities. *See* Education; *and specific colleges and universities*

University of Chicago, 43–44, 103, 211
University of North Carolina (UNC): African American lecturers at, 37–38; Chase as president of, 41; establishment of, 34; F. Raper's children at, 27, 28; Graham as president of, 35–36; and Institute for Research in the Social Sciences, 2, 33, 41, 44, 104, 156, 180, 191, 216; job offer to Raper by, 171, 216; Odum at, 35, 36, 41–46, 48, 54, 118, 211; Raper's barbering at, 28, 34–35, 44, 201, 332n2; Raper's doctoral work at, 41–50, 53–54, 66, 118; Raper's papers at, 317; Raper's undergraduate education at, 8, 31–32, 36–39, 41, 65–66; School of Public Welfare at, 41; Southern Historical Collection of, 317
University of North Carolina (UNC) Press: and Chadbourn's *Lynching and the Law*, 93; and Couch's *Culture in the South*, 104–5; and Dabney's *Liberalism in the South*, 102, 104; publications of, generally, 2; and Raper's *Preface to Peasantry*, 81, 180; and Raper's *Sharecroppers All*, 178–80, 191, 261, 359–60n101; and Raper's *Tragedy of Lynching*, 73, 81, 96–97, 100, 101, 105, 179–80, 343n58, 345n93; significance of, 41, 105; subsidies from Odum to, 180. *See also* Couch, W. T.
Urban areas. *See* Migration to urban areas; *and specific cities*
Urban League, 60, 207
U.S. Agency for International Development (USAID), 289, 292, 302
USDA. *See* Department of Agriculture, U.S.
U.S. International Cooperation Administration (USICA), 289–306
U.S. Mutual Security Agency, 289–90, 297
USOM. *See* U.S. Overseas Mission (USOM)
U.S. Overseas Mission (USOM), 293, 298

Vachon, John, 183
Vance, Rupert, 41, 193
Vanderbilt University, 39–40, 52, 53, 62, 69, 106, 337n35
Van Norden, Langdon, 188
Van Nuys Anti-Lynching Bill, 208–9
Vidor, King, 6
Vietnam, 13, 289, 297, 317
Violence against blacks. *See* Lynching
Virginia Quarterly Review, 94
Voting: and blacks' rights, 368n43; and disfranchisement of blacks and poor whites, 1, 62,

Voting (*continued*)
  111, 162, 174, 184, 206–7, 347n11; eligibility for, 204; in Greene and Macon counties, Ga., 347n11; one-party system of, in South, 4, 184; and poll tax, 4, 162, 166, 168, 174, 184; and racial etiquette, 187; and Southern Conference on Human Welfare (SCHW), 168; and white primary, 4, 111, 162, 174, 184

Wade, John Donald, 63, 203
Wage-Hour Division, 226–27
Wages, 60, 84, 183–86, 226–27
Wallace, Henry, 136, 137, 156, 160–61, 217, 283, 359n80
War Department, U.S., 53
Ware, Carolyn, 10, 239
Warfare, 134, 267. *See also* Pacifism; World War I; World War II
Washington, Booker T., 38, 80
Washington Post, 13, 66, 267, 312, 318, 320–21, 362n132
Watergate, 13, 317
Watson, Tom, 251
Webb, Walter Prescott, 361n113
Welty, Eudora, 8
West, Nathaniel, 98
West, Wade, 204
Wheels within wheels, 8, 35, 280
White, Walter: and Ames, 209; and Commission on Interracial Cooperation (CIC), 60; on Communist Party, 97; and Myrdal's *American Dilemma*, 193, 207; and NAACP, 60, 364n48; and Raper's writings, 80, 98, 101, 188–89, 360n104; *Rope and Faggot* by, 72, 344n67; and Urban League, 207
White primary, 4, 111, 162, 174, 184
Whitfield, Stephen J., 210
Whitman, Walt, 313, 314
Whitten, Jamie L., 272–73, 371n29, 371n32
Wiebe, Robert, 4
Williams, Aubrey, 5
Williams, Clyde, 141, 142, 146–48
Williams, William Carlos, 103, 314, 315
Wilson, Woodrow, 31–32, 50, 333n33
Wolcott, Marion Post, 183, 240
Wood, Grant, 6
Woodward, C. Vann, 8, 11, 333n33
Woofter, T. J., Jr., 49–50, 80, 339n3, 339n8
Woolfolk, Ada, 68–69, 107, 217, 323
Works Progress Administration (WPA), 9, 222, 254, 353n4
World War I, 52, 134, 267
World War II, 194, 209–10, 234–35, 262–65, 267–69, 369–70n1
WPA. *See* Works Progress Administration (WPA)
Wright, Chuck, 296
Wright, Richard, 5, 248–49, 330n19, 346n104
Wyatt-Brown, Bertram, 343n56

YMCA and YWCA, 37, 39, 52, 53, 150
You Have Seen Their Faces (Caldwell and Bourke-White), 247, 346n104